Really you must forgive me, if I find it quite impossible
to express to you what I feel about your thought and generosity.
I have still to fathom the mystery, indeed, from beyond the
skies, some good angel has been inspiring your heart as well as
begin to thank you, and I must find out from you just who it is. I cannot
gift itself till I see you. Indeed I feel I cannot accept
not a dream, rather than the fulfillment of a vision, that

The moment I came in, I tried at once to reach you but
just ten minutes earlier. I shall watch for the first
that we each may have, to call upon you. I have found something
must not wait even for that to express something felt,
you. I shall, I fear, never be able to led you
deeply touched by any expression of friendship
I do see you, however, please believe that
to your generous heart, and which carries

surprised as I was
which I opened", I was
envelope attached to it, I read
ary's compliments".

fallen into my hands from the skies, for it is as if this
your mind and

perfect crystal ball in
amazed when on opening
words "with Mr A. H.

signed
George R.I

The Prime Minister of Canada prese
his humble duty to His Majesty the King.

It is expedient that a Proclama
should be issued in the name of His Maj
in Canada, declaring that a state of
German Reich has existed in Canada
September tenth.

The Prime Minister of
humbly submits to His Majesty
The King's Privy Council for
may approve the issuing of
His name.

The Prime Min

His Majesty's most fai

eep last night I read the chapter
elieve" on Psychical Research. It
The book was given me by dear Max
nd that placed it in mine last nigh
g that I am right in believing in the
lping me at this time. When men of t
lectual & scientific minds of William
think & speak & believe as they do abou
is the strongest reason why I should no
am entirely right in continuing to expl
believing in the "revelations" I have th
dreams, & in other ways. [.....] -

I could do very little - Thompson, the tail
the new Chinese silk suit, we had tea togeth
dinner.

After 7 went down and kissed little Anne
ay in her cot on her 6th birthday. Left a [195
andy beside her.

Joan most of William M. James' Essay on
guarded, but most convincing.
I read among

THE THIRD MAN

THE THIRD MAN

CHURCHILL, ROOSEVELT, MACKENZIE KING,
AND THE UNTOLD FRIENDSHIPS
THAT WON WWII

NEVILLE THOMPSON

SUTHERLAND
HOUSE
TORONTO, 2021

Sutherland House
416 Moore Ave., Suite 205
Toronto, ON M4G 1C9

First hardcover edition, May 2021

If you are interested in inviting one of our authors to a live event or media appearance, please contact publicity@sutherlandhousebooks.com and visit our website at sutherlandhousebooks.com for more information about our authors and their schedules.

Manufactured in Canada
Cover designed by Lena Yang
Book composed by Karl Hunt

Library and Archives Canada Cataloguing in Publication
Title: The third man : Churchill, Roosevelt, Mackenzie King, and the untold friendships that won WWII / Neville Thompson.
Names: Thompson, Neville, 1938- author.
Description: Includes bibliographical references and index.
Identifiers: Canadiana 20200259253 | ISBN 9781989555262 (hardcover)
Subjects: LCSH: King, William Lyon Mackenzie, 1874-1950. | LCSH: King, William Lyon Mackenzie, 1874-1950—Friends and associates. | LCSH: Churchill, Winston, 1874-1965. | LCSH: Roosevelt, Franklin D. (Franklin Delano), 1882-1945. | LCSH: Prime ministers—Canada—Biography. | CSH: Canada—Foreign relations—1918-1945. | LCSH: World War, 1939-1945—Diplomatic history.
Classification: LCC FC581.K5 T46 2020 | DDC 971.063/2092—dc23

ISBN 978-1-989555-26-2

For
Lynton (Red) Wilson
In friendship and for service to history

Contents

Epigraph

CHURCHILL HAS BEEN "RAISED UP" to meet the need of this day in the realm of war, to fight, with the power of the sword, the brute beasts that would devour their fellow men in their lust for power. Roosevelt, while far from being as great a man in his intellectual power, or military genius, is greater in his love for his fellow men and in his very sincere desire to improve their lot. Both men have great physical and moral courage but each is less great than he might have been had he been less personally ambitious to be great in the eyes of the world, less fond of and motivated in many ways by an inordinate desire for publicity. Churchill, I greatly fear, may not last out the war – because of drink . . . I pray it may not be so and that he may be spared to enjoy some of the fruits of victory, which he more than any other single man deserves . . . The President has overtaxed his strength in other ways. He has had a harder battle in many ways than Churchill. His fight for the people has made him many and bitter enemies. He has done too much, I fear for purely political reasons – the vast expenditures totally regardless of consequence, & which may leave the United States in an appalling condition some day He has used public office to ensure continuance of power, in some ways that can scarcely be justified – but I believe that he has been sincere in his determination to better the conditions of the masses. He is more human than Churchill, each desire to be at the top, Churchill would like to be the ruler of an Empire (Conservative) Roosevelt the head of a Commonwealth (democrat). I wonder if his ambition to figure too largely on a world stage may not be his undoing & the undoing of his strength & of his political power?

Mackenzie King
Diary, December 19, 1943

Acknowledgements

M Y FIRST AND MOST GRATEFUL THANKS must be to Kenneth Whyte, who edited the text so well. His skill in cutting, shaping and polishing is such that he is practically entitled to be the co-author. I also wish to thank Matthew Bucemi, the managing editor and associate publisher, for great help with many aspects of the manuscript and production. Neither they nor anyone else named here bears any responsibility for errors in the material or for the interpretation.

No author is "an Island, entire of it self" as John Donne generalized about humanity. Of the many who have aided and abetted along the way I should like to thank in particular my old friend Donald Smith, emeritus professor of history at the University of Calgary, who also provided the copy of an important letter from Roosevelt to King; Marian Soroka, an historian of Russia and nineteenth century diplomacy now living afar in Aquitaine and London, England; and, closer to home, Shauna Devine, an historian of medicine and the United States, who invited, indeed with a whim of iron insisted that I share her classroom lecture on President Roosevelt that was filmed for the C-span video library. I have greatly enjoyed and benefitted from discussing Mackenzie King, his international policies before the second world war and much else with the Hon. Roy MacLaren whose achievements go far beyond writing fine books on Canadian history. It will easily be seen that the view presented here differs from the one in his *Mackenzie King and the Dictators* (2019) but in Clio's house are many mansions. The fruitful interplay of interpretations results in a better understanding of the past.

At the University of Western Ontario I am grateful to the D. B. Weldon Library for providing a study carrel in what is now my intellectual home. Books furnish more than a room. As Samuel Johnson said, "A man will turn over half a library to write one book." Elizabeth Mantz, the history specialist, and all the librarians are a cheerful and ever-present help, I am also grateful to the members of the history department, present and past, including those now alas on a farther shore, who have for decades supplied collegial intellectual stimulus and camaraderie.

The book is dedicated to my friend and undergraduate classmate at McMaster University, Lynton (Red) Wilson in appreciation of his outstanding commitment and effective help to history, from research to popular dissemination. Following a stellar career in the public service and business, he co-founded (with Charles Bronfman) Historica Canada which encourages and supports the subject particularly in schools and on television. At McMaster, where he served as the chancellor from 2007-13, he established the L. R. Wilson Chair in Canadian History and the Wilson Institute for Canadian History housed in a new liberal arts building that he sponsored and rightly bears his name. I can only stand in awe and admiration of these and his other major and lasting contributions to history and much else in our alma mater and country.

To my wife Gail and our daughter Elizabeth, who put up with me in this and much else, my love as always.

INTRODUCTION

The Atlantic Triumvirate

THE PARTNERSHIP OF WINSTON CHURCHILL and Franklin Delano Roosevelt in the Second World War is one of the most momentous in history. Scarcely anything about the relationship of two of the towering figures of the twentieth century can fail to be of interest. They not only directed historic world events but in speeches and in conversations ennobled their aims in grand and memorable terms. They were two of the great orators of history and, until late in the war, when Roosevelt in particular was close to death, they competed, publicly and privately, with each other's eloquence. But this does not mean that they were entirely open in their exchanges with each other, and much less to the public.

Churchill and Roosevelt used their formidable rhetorical skills to disguise as well as to present their views. They were close allies but they differed significantly over the conduct of the war and the shape of the world to come. Churchill wanted to restore the past and for that, as he frequently acknowledged, and did not fail to realize, he desperately needed Roosevelt's help. In 1939, Britain had been confident, even after failing to secure an alliance with the USSR, that it could beat Germany. Subsequent events made it clear that the support of the British Commonwealth and Empire would not be sufficient for victory. Any major effort to turn the tide depended on the United States. Regulated by this reliance, Churchill was almost always careful to avoid confronting Roosevelt directly with his own military strategy and his ambition to enlist American power in shoring up Britain's declining global position.

Even before the United States formally became a belligerent, Roosevelt had his own distinct aim of building a new world order, and the material means to ensure that he prevailed in any dispute. But he had no desire to alienate the leader of the great power closest in outlook to the United States and applied his legendary joviality to avoid any appearance of disharmony. Like his practice of appointing people of different outlooks to similar offices and letting them fight it out, his apparent agreement with a diversity of opinions kept his options open and defused even the best-prepared resistance. Keeping control through confusion was Roosevelt's mode of operation. Soon after the United States entered the war, when he seemed gratifyingly receptive to Churchill's bold scheme of an Anglo-American alliance to control the world, Eleanor Roosevelt warned: "You know, Winston, when Franklin says 'yes, yes, yes', it doesn't mean he agrees with you. It means he is listening."[1]

What Churchill and Roosevelt really thought, and thought about each other, has been divined less from their written records than from those around them: for example, Roosevelt's close advisor, Harry Hopkins; Roosevelt's cousin, Daisy Suckly; Field Marshal Alan Brooke, the Chief of the Imperial General Staff; Sir Alexander Cadogan the permanent under-secretary at the foreign office; and many others high and low. But in all this investigation there is one critical source that has scarcely been touched: the diary of Mackenzie King, Churchill and Roosevelt's fellow head of government in the North Atlantic triangle (a term familiar primarily to Canadians) from 1921 to 1948, excepting the years 1930 to 1935.[2]

No other national leader was so intimate with both Churchill and Roosevelt. Indeed, King arguably knew them both better than they knew each other. No one else had such a privileged view of the evolution and workings of their relationship between the other two leaders. Few were so perceptive about them and none left so detailed an account of their circumstances, policy, and interactions. In addition to closely observing the two individuals, King, as the leader of a country vital to their interests, used his position to actively participate in the transfer of global hegemony from Britain to the United States, an outcome not entirely apparent until a decade or more after the end of the Second World War.[3]

---

1   Doris Kearns Goodwin, *No Ordinary Time: Franklin and Eleanor Roosevelt: The Home Front in World War II* (New York: Touchstone, [1994] 1995), 311.
2   This characterization for understanding relations between the three countries was devised by John Bartlet Brebner (1895–1957), a Canadian historian who spent most of his career at Columbia University: *North Atlantic Triangle: The Interplay of Canada, the United States and Great Britain* (New Haven, CT: Yale University Press, 1945).
3   Kori Schake, *Safe Passage: The Transition from British to American Hegemony* (Cambridge, MA: Harvard University Press, 2017), see, in particular, Chapter 11, 254–70.

This dialogue among the leaders, as recorded by King, provides a fascinating and important insight into the nature of democratic management at a time of great anxiety and tension. The three shared concerns about the political direction and control of their cabinets and legislatures. Each devoted much careful attention to his own speech–making and communications. Each studied and often critiqued the others' public performances. In dealing with each other, they were keenly aware of the interests of their own countries and the hazards involved in their necessary interactions. They recognized the need for other allies – notably de Gaulle and Stalin – but also the problems and even dangers of having to depend on those whose aims and outlook were very different from their own. King's record sheds light on these weighty matters while also detailing the interplay of personalities, particularly between himself, Churchill and Roosevelt, often in unguarded and confidential moments. It illuminates the tenor of the conversations and negotiations, the restraints under which they operated, their earnest desire for agreement, and the compromises by which policy was made. This was diplomacy on a highly personal level, reflecting the interests and outlooks of particular individuals. There were constant tensions between Churchill, Roosevelt, and King but their over-riding commitment to compatible ends enabled them to stick together to the finish, a major factor in the outcome of the war. Their personal friendship went far deeper than most political partnerships and was aided and secured by King's long acquaintance with both before the war. King was almost a member of both the Churchill and Roosevelt families, which gave him additional personal insight into these two great contemporaries.

* * *

Little known outside his own country or even, these days, within it, William Lyon Mackenzie King requires an introduction. Born in Berlin (now Kitchener), Ontario in 1874, he was son of a law professor and the grandson of William Lyon Mackenzie, leader of the failed Upper Canada Rebellion against British rule in 1837. He stands out among his predecessors and successors as Canadian prime minister for his educational attainments and worldliness. He graduated from his Master's degree from the University of Chicago, obtained his doctorate from Harvard, in addition to studying in London, making life-long friends in both countries. By his mid-thirties he had travelled extensively around the northern hemisphere. As prime minister he continued to travel a great deal, despite insisting that the best place for political leaders was in their own country. He was more at home in London, Washington, New York and other cities on both sides of the Atlantic than he was in most Canadian ones.

He had none of the intellectual range and commanding world view of Churchill and Roosevelt, but King was a remarkably successful politician, as his twenty-nine-year leadership of Canada's dominant Liberal party demonstrates. Like all politicians, he had supporters and detractors at home. He was not sufficiently pro-British for "Imperialists" in Canada. He was disparaged for his opposition to compulsory overseas military service; an imperial war council; a united British Commonwealth defence and foreign policy in war as well as peace; and for not demanding Canadian participation in the highest direction of the war. Most of these realities were not shortcomings for Churchill and Roosevelt, who refused to relinquish control of the war and valued the confidence in the dependable support of their most important western ally. But Canada, then as now, was a diverse and highly localized country: its francophone population, for instance, had little appetite for the imperial mission and represented an important part of King's electoral base. He demonstrated enormous skill in holding the country together in the war years, even if his methods were criticized as duplicitous.

With his long experience in world affairs, he was as well prepared to participate in discussions with Churchill and Roosevelt, as were most of those who surrounded them. He has been regarded as out of his depth and heavily dependent on civil servants in international matters. This was not how Churchill and Roosevelt and other outsiders saw him. As prime minister, he controlled all of Canada's external imperial and foreign matters. When the British Foreign Secretary, Anthony Eden came to Ottawa in 1943 for what was practically a three-day state visit, Oliver Harvey, the senior diplomat serving as his secretary, in his diary entry of April 2 1943, declared Mackenzie King "certainly a triton among minnows." He found him a person of "great charm, old-worldly, cultured," and judged that he was devoted to Roosevelt, Churchill, the king and queen and now, he hoped, Eden.[4]

It was a great advantage in his relations with Churchill and Roosevelt that King was by nature pacific and conciliatory, an agreeable companion and good listener who never itched to interrupt, to contradict those great talkers or vaunt himself. They spoke freely to him and took his discretion for granted. It must

4   John Harvey, ed. *The War Diaries of Oliver Harvey* (London: Collins, 1978), 242.

have been a reassurance as well as a source of amusement to Roosevelt when his press secretary told him that newspaper reporters complained: "William Lyon Mackenzie King / Never tells us a goddam thing."[5] Neither Roosevelt nor Churchill had any suspicion that King was watching them closely and recording their conversations in detail, their physical and mental conditions and their moods, as well as judgment of their opinions. If they had had any inkling, they would have been far more guarded and wary rather than seeking out his company.[6]

Different as Churchill and Roosevelt were from each other, it is on the face of it, hard to imagine anyone more unlike either of them than Mackenzie King. No one ever said of him, as Churchill did of Roosevelt, that meeting him "with all his buoyant sparkle, his iridescence" was "like opening a bottle of champagne."[7] No one wrote to King, as Roosevelt wrote to Churchill: "It is fun to be in the same decade with you."[8] On the contrary, King is customarily described as short, chubby, drab and unprepossessing. Physically he was more like Churchill than Churchill's brother (who was rumoured to have a different father). Both habitually wore the same kind of dark, three-piece suits with a pocket watch (King's with a much thinner chain), and homburg hats. Yet it was not build or dress that made King so different but personality and presentation. He had none of the grandstanding, highly masculine manner of Churchill and Roosevelt; none of

5   William D. Hassett, *Off the Record with F.D.R. 1942–1945* (New Brunswick: Rutgers University Press, 1958), 323; (Diary entry, 10 March 1945).

6   In addition to his extensive, open exchanges with Churchill and Roosevelt, King also heard about the two from a range of informants who similarly trusted his confidentiality. Among these were Arthur Purvis, a Canadian businessman who was in charge of British war purchases in the US, until his death in 1941; Field Marshal Sir John Dill, the chief British representative on the US-British joint chiefs of staff committee from early 1942 to his death in 1944; and Leighton McCarthy, Roosevelt's closest Canadian friend long before he became his country's emissary in Washington from 1941 to 1944. Not all the informants would have been happy to know that their frank opinions were being preserved for posterity.

7   Jon Meacham, *Franklin and Winston: An Intimate Portrait of an Epic Friendship* (New York: Random House, [2003] 2004), xii. Meacham cites as his source for this quotation, which appears in various forms, often with elaborations, box 10 of the Kate Halle papers, John F. Kennedy Presidential Library, Boston. Kate Halle (1904–97) was an American heiress to whom Churchill's nineteen-year-old son Randolph proposed in 1931. Though they did not marry, she remained a close friend of the whole family. Mary Soames ed., *Speaking for Themselves: The Personal Letters of Winston and Clementine Churchill* (Toronto: Stoddart, 1998), 352–3 and 654.

8   Roosevelt to Churchill, January 30, 1942. Warren F. Kimball ed., *Churchill and Roosevelt: The Complete Correspondence*. 3 vols. (Princeton: Princeton University Press, 1984), I, 337. This was in response to the sixty-seven-year-old Churchill's congratulations on Roosevelt's sixtieth birthday.

Roosevelt's dazzling smile or Churchill's grim determination; and none of their famous identifying symbols. His style was instead to deflect hostility by affecting a modesty at odds with his great political success – serving as a leader for twice as long as Churchill or Roosevelt. A non-smoker in an age when it was regarded as a reflection of character, he did not flaunt Churchill's big cigar, Roosevelt's cigarette in a long holder clenched in his teeth at a jaunty angle; not even the reassuring pipe of "Safety First" Stanley Baldwin on whom King tried to model himself. In contrast to the heavy drinking of Churchill and Roosevelt – another measure of manliness – he was a moderate drinker and was mostly abstemious throughout the war. King had none of Churchill's array of military costumes and "siren suits" (adult rompers) and would never have been photographed at his country house laying bricks in old clothes and a battered hat. Nor did he wear anything like Roosevelt's dramatic admiral's cloak (which was easier for him to manage than an overcoat) or his casual fedoras and panama straw hats. King stuck to Homburg hats and even in the country wore carefully pressed tweeds and a matching cap. He did not even drive a car as Roosevelt erratically did on his estate, despite his disability.

But King's greatest distinction was his failure as an orator. No great occasion was ever ennobled by one of his speeches. He had none of the rhetorical skill, the sensitivity to language, the gestures and ringing cadences of Roosevelt and Churchill, to say nothing of their distinct, resonant voices. In this and much else, however, it was Churchill and Roosevelt who were the great exceptions. Almost any politician measured against them would be found wanting. King was more like Baldwin and Calvin Coolidge, similarly conventional and reassuring leaders who likewise emerged from the upheaval following the First World War. What Walter Bagehot said of Lord Palmerston could, with far more truth be said of Mackenzie King: "[He] was not a common man, but a common man might have been cut out of him. He had in him all that a common man has, and something more."[9] No one would have said the same about Churchill or Roosevelt.

Mackenzie King also had far stronger religious feelings than the other two, but this was by no means publicly obvious at the time. Roosevelt, giving the reasonable assent of a reasonable person to the Episcopalian (Anglican) church, rarely went to services since his leg braces made it a major undertaking. Churchill,

---

9 Walter Bagehot, "Lord Palmerston" in *Biographical Studies*. Ed. Richard Holt Hutton (London: Longmans Green, 1881), 341.

a nominal member of the state Church of England, restricted himself to ceremonial occasions. A Scots Presbyterian on both sides of his family, King was also no regular attender, although St. Andrew's church was conveniently located across the street. Nor did he need to be. Apart from Protestant churches being congregations of the faithful rather than the necessary means to salvation, King was a mystic and spiritualist who received signs directly from God and messages from the departed. When this came to light after his death, it became the subject of high interest and low humour and has stuck, to a tiresome degree, as his main identifying characteristic in Canada. But neither Churchill nor Roosevelt, nor anyone else was surprised that he frequently appealed to religion and occasionally mentioned the spirit world. The British and American leaders never neglected God in their public appeals, Roosevelt most notably in the long prayer he composed and read out on the radio on D-Day. Churchill made similar, although shorter invocations, and never doubted that he was marked for great achievement by the Almighty in which he did not believe. All three took it for granted that (Protestant) Christianity was the highest form of civilization, readily agreeing in the middle of the war that it was vastly superior to passive Confucianism.[10] In the heyday of the occult, Churchill and Roosevelt were well aware of its widespread popularity and their regard for King would not have been lowered by knowing the extent of his involvement.

Late nineteenth century physics, by dissolving the certainties and solidities of matter, time and space, produced scientific support for a similar permeability between the quick and the dead. Sir Oliver Lodge (1851–1940), a (literally) towering physicist was a Christian spiritualist. In his popular writings and broadcasts over radio waves he had helped to invent, he confidently asserted that personality survived death and could communicate with the living. Among other leading proponents were Sir Alfred Russel Wallace, the co-discoverer with Charles Darwin of the theory of evolution; William James, the American pioneer of psychology; and the novelist Sir Arthur Conan Doyle.[11] The enormous death toll of the Great War (compounded by the Spanish flu pandemic beginning in 1918) multiplied the number of those who were convinced that they could connect with the suddenly removed. Air Marshal Sir Hugh Dowding (1882–1970), the commander in the Battle of Britain, believed that he conversed with his late wife; after retiring at

10 Diary, May 19, 1943.
11 Ruth Brandon, *The Spiritualists: The Passion for the Occult in the Nineteenth and Twentieth Centuries* (New York: Alfred A. Knopf, 1983).

the end of 1940 he published extensively on fairies, gnomes, and flying saucers, and no one thought the less of him.[12] King was decisively converted to spiritual- ism by the mid-1920s, perhaps by a conversation in London with Lodge.[13] But knowing that it provided a ready target for ridicule he prudently revealed little outside a sympathetic circle. There is no reason to think that the occult had any more noticeable effect on King than on any of the others mentioned here.[14] Signs and visions simply reinforced what he wanted to think and do, in the same way that for his great hero, the devout William Gladstone, the will of God coincided with the interests of the Liberal party.

While there is no evidence that Roosevelt ever had a mystical experience, Churchill did. In November 1947, he was in his studio at Chartwell, painting a copy of a portrait of his father, when suddenly the man himself materialized in an arm chair. Evidently inhabiting a district of the after-world that did not receive news of the terrestrial globe, Lord Randolph Churchill knew nothing about events since his death in 1895 or the career of his unpromising son. They discussed some aspects of the former; Lord Randolph characteristically expressed little interest in the latter. Then, as he struck a match to light his cigarette – per- haps the first in half a century – he vanished in the flash.[15] Mackenzie King was not so unusual after all.

Nor was he a lonely introvert, as often portrayed, despite self-pitying com- plaints about lack of companionship and not being married. He was certainly less gregarious than Churchill and Roosevelt, but he could hardly have been more so. He was also less eager for publicity and he carefully guarded his solitude. But it was a rare day that he did not have a social engagement and he enjoyed most of them. He had many friendships, notably with women. Both the earnest, energetic, and abstemious Eleanor Roosevelt and the reserved, neurasthenic and aristocratic Clementine Churchill appreciated his company and he theirs. For the last thirty years of his life his closest companion was Joan Patteson, who was five years his senior, and the wife of an Ottawa bank manager. Within what

12 David E. Fisher, *A Summer Bright and Terrible: Winston Churchill, Lord Dowding, Radar and the Impossible Triumph of the Battle of Britain* (Washington: Shoemaker & Hoard, 2005), 76–81 and 263–7.
13 Charles Stacey, *A Very Double Life: The Private World of Mackenzie King* (Toronto: Macmillan, 1976), 162–5.
14 A not very illuminating discussion by a psychologist is Paul Roazen, *Canada's King: An Essay in Political Psychology*. (Oakville, ON: Mosaic Press, 1998).
15 Churchill, Randolph (vols 1 and 2) and Martin Gilbert (vols 3–8), *Winston S. Churchill* (London: Heinemann, 1966–8), VIII, 364–72.

was practically a ménage à trois, the two enjoyed a sentimental, chaste relation-ship. The Pattesons were neighbours in town and King provided a cottage on his country estate. Joan Patteson was often his hostess and shared his spiritualism. At his houses and hers, they ate together, read together, sang hymns at the piano and communicated with the dead.[16] This was all the home life King needed. Even Joan Patteson's companionship he did not want all the time. He talked to his dogs, both when they were alive and dead. But it was above all into his diary that King poured his feelings and secrets as well as the record of events. It was this introspection, self-sufficiency, and compulsive chronicling, in addition to his political position, that made him the ideal eyewitness to Churchill and Roosevelt.

* * *

The three leaders shared many commonalities that eased their association. All were mother's sons, King most of all, during her life, which ended in 1917, and after her death. In the library at Laurier House was an oil painting of her, on an easel like an icon. She is represented as a saintly version of Whistler's mother, dressed in white, with John Morley's biography of Gladstone open in her lap. Churchill, Roosevelt, and other visitors needed no prompting to pay the obvious tribute. Churchill had a difficult relationship with his erratic politician father, who died when Winston was twenty. His equally self-absorbed mother "shone for me like the Evening Star. I loved her dearly – but at a distance." Continuing in widowhood as a high society *grande horizontale*, however, she applied herself to her ambitious elder son's career: "In my interest she left no wire unpulled, no stone unturned, no cutlet uncooked."[17] Roosevelt was the beloved only son of Sara Delano Roosevelt, whose husband was a widower, twenty-six years her senior (with a son from his first marriage). After he died in 1900, she concentrated her hopes on her eighteen-year-old heir. This was a great source of friction after he married his statuesque distant cousin Eleanor Roosevelt (niece of then-president Theodore Roosevelt) in 1905. His mother thought that he could have done far better than this relative who lacked a fortune but not radical views and

16 Stacey, *A Very Double Life*, 118–38 and 171–183 and elsewhere throughout the book. Stacey does not mention Eleanor Roosevelt or Clementine Churchill, but there is no reason he should, as these were not in any way romantic attachments.

17 Winston S. Churchill, *My Early Life: A Roving Commission* (London: Macmillan, [1930] 1942), 9 and 167.

unconventional friends. In 1918, Eleanor discovered that Franklin was having an affair with her former social secretary, the elegant Lucy Page Mercer. She agreed to a divorce, which would, at the very least have been a great impediment to the political hopes of the assistant secretary of the navy. Sara Roosevelt threatened, in that event, to disinherit her son. This preserved the marriage and Franklin's – and his mother's – ambitions, though it did nothing to improve relations between Sara and Eleanor. He promised never to see Lucy Mercer again but they remained in touch and, after she was widowed in the middle of the Second World War, she came back into his life.[18] A month before Roosevelt's death, Mackenzie King had dinner with them at the White House, with no idea about the relationship. He had no reason to suspect that the Roosevelts' marriage was other than happy.

Churchill, Roosevelt and King also shared the common upper-class culture of the English-speaking world. They were all self-conscious heirs to nineteenth-century liberalism. They were familiar with the same literary masterpieces, the same major historical events, and they operated in political and legal systems that stemmed from a recognizable English base. Churchill was unmistakably British but by the Second World War found it useful, when in the United States, to emphasize that his mother was American. Roosevelt, though of Dutch and French Huguenot ancestry, was an anglophile and, before his paralysis a frequent visitor to Britain, where Eleanor had gone to school. He even had a Canadian connection since his family's summer home was on Campobello Island, New Brunswick. King was proud of his Scottish ancestry and preferred the plain manner of North Britons and American plutocrats to the prescriptive status and affectation of the English aristocracy. But he was strongly attached to the whole of Britain, the Commonwealth (a term he disliked, probably because it implied a unity), and the Empire. So he was to the United States, although he worried about Canada losing its distinctiveness by assimilation to the United States. He had to tread a fine line in both his pro-American and pro-British opinions. Some within Canada were highly vocal in their support of their British lineage and correspondingly suspicious of the United States, while others, particularly in Quebec, were indifferent or hostile to the British and imperial connection. So, too, were many Americans. At Quebec City, in 1943, King warned Clementine Churchill that the East Coast anglophiles around Roosevelt did not represent

---

18 Joseph E. Persico, *Franklin and Lucy: President Roosevelt, Mrs Rutherfurd, and the Other Remarkable Women in his Life* (New York: Random House, 2008), 79–130.

the country and that her husband would have a more difficultly with a different kind of government.[19]

The three leaders also lived and worked in similar style. The British prime minister and American president's official residences were also their offices. Canada provided nothing of the kind but Mackenzie King managed the country mainly from the library on the top floor of his residence, Laurier House (willed to him by the widow of his predecessor, Sir Wilfrid Laurier), rather than his office in the parliament building or the one in the adjacent east block which contained the cabinet room and the department of external affairs. Each identified as an urbane countryman. Roosevelt's home was the family estate, Springwood, on the Hudson river at Hyde Park, ninety miles north of New York City, where he went as often as possible. For Churchill, it was the manor of Chartwell in Kent, an hour from London, which he bought in 1922, though as prime minister his retreat was the official country house of Chequers in Buckinghamshire. Mackenzie King, as a young civil servant in 1903, bought land and built a cottage at Kingsmere (named after an early settler), twelve miles from Ottawa in the Gatineau hills of Quebec. As he prospered over the next quarter century, he extended the property to almost six hundred acres of farmland and woods, houses and barns, which he improved and added an antique tone with picturesque stone ruins in the manner of an eighteenth-century British estate. Each of them was immediately at home at the others' similar properties, although Roosevelt never made it to Chartwell and, in 1943, had time only to drive through Kingsmere and pause to speak to the Pattesons.

At the 1943 Quebec conference, King had one of his secretaries learn the work habits of Churchill and Roosevelt and discovered that they were much the same as his own.[20] None was an early starter and all were late finishers. They were wakened about eight, with Churchill and Roosevelt generally having breakfast and working in bed for much of the morning. King got up, did some mild exercises until the middle of the war, had breakfast, read the Bible and "the little (daily devotional) books", and sometimes went back to bed before getting underway. Churchill and King always slept in the afternoon (and King frequently at other times). Roosevelt usually swam after tea (the latter being as fixed a part of his daily routine as it was for King) until his heart failure in 1944, after which

---

19 Diary, August 12, 1943.
20 Walter J. Turnbull, "Memorandum for the Prime Minister: Organization of Mr. Churchill's [President Roosevelt's] office and working practices," Diary, August 21, 1943.

he also slept at some point between lunch and dinner. All usually resumed work at night. A month before Pearl Harbor, Roosevelt told King that he could now only manage a couple of nights a week, but to the end of his life he kept talking over his ideas in the evening, which was an important part of his routine.[21] He and King generally went to bed about midnight, where the president read reports. Churchill, who was always at his best in the middle of the night, kept going to two or three a.m., often holding meetings to wear down opposition. Except when on holiday, travelling, ill, or exceptionally tired, this was their pattern every day of the week. Orderly Ottawa civil servants, far removed from the immediate pressures of war and crucial decision-making, complained about the disruption caused by King's selfish, bachelor habits, but Churchill's staff, and even Roosevelt's, would have found working for him a rest cure.

Mackenzie King's remarkable diary consists of 30,000 typewritten pages, about 7.5 million words, the equivalent of thirty-five volumes of this book. It begins in 1893, when he was a student at the University of Toronto, and continues to three days before his death in 1950. The entries were at first spasmodic, brief, and personal but as he rose in the world, particularly after becoming leader of the Liberal party in 1919 and prime minister in 1921, they became more regular and far more detailed. Until 1935, he wrote by hand. Thereafter, he customarily dictated, almost always to J. Edouard Handy, a twenty-five-year-old bilingual civil servant seconded from the elections office to be the prime minister's chief stenographer. Handy himself then typed the transcript. Sometimes dictation lagged by a few days, in which case King usually jotted down a few points to prompt his memory. To the very end of King's life, Handy was his good and faithful and closed-mouth servant. The married but uncomplaining Handy accompanied the prime minister on his travels and they often ate, shopped, and went to movies together.[22] In his will, King bequeathed him $10,000, probably about twice Handy's civil service salary. Until 1955, Handy was the first curator of Laurier House which King bequeathed to the country as a memorial to Sir Wilfrid Laurier, and even more to himself. The diary also remained in the house, where the handwritten parts were being transcribed. Handy was not an executor but he was influential in urging that it be preserved.[23] It was a near-run thing.

---

21 Diary, November 12, 1941.
22 No one later traced Handy for his reminiscences of King.
23 Christopher Dummitt, *Unbuttoned: A History of Mackenzie King's Secret Life* (Montreal: McGill-Queen's University Press, 2017).

King's diary is of course, like all similar ones, coloured by his self-centredness and perspective. But in many cases his is the only record. When there are others, it is usually King's that provides the greatest detail and the liveliest sense of personality. As the epigraph to this book indicates, even at the height of his admiration of Churchill and Roosevelt, when victory in the war was practically certain, he was far from entirely uncritical. At other times during these long associations, he was scathing, particularly of Churchill. It is this mixed perception that makes King's testimony particularly valuable. As Samuel Johnson, a pioneer of well-rounded biography – as well as being the subject of the best one ever written – pronounced: "If nothing but the bright side of characters should be shewn, we should sit down in despondency, and think it utterly impossible to imitate them in *anything*."[24]

The diary was a valuable aid to King, supplementing official documents and containing, to his own satisfaction, valuable evidence of his wisdom and consistency. In time, he also came to recognize that it would be the core of his memoirs or official biography. But there were dangers. Fully revealing such candid material close to the war, with few government documents open, so many leading figures still alive, and Churchill fighting for the supremacy of his version of events, would be certain to arouse great controversy and charges that King was abusing confidentiality and betraying his wartime allies. King, for instance, had a lot to say in his diary about Churchill's efforts to concentrate the Allies on the Mediterranean and the Balkans, and his resistance to American determination for a the risky, cross-channel D-Day landing. There is more on the matter of Roosevelt's health, particularly in the last year of his life, another sensitive issue for decades. And there was King's record of heady conversations in which Roosevelt and Churchill imagined running the world after the war, their fluctuating views of Stalin, de Gaulle, and much else. A great deal of material has surfaced in the seventy–five years since the war and King's diary is an invaluable part of it.

A memoir crafted by King from the diary might have resembled the short profile on him, published in 1944 by Emil Ludwig, the noted biographer of such figures as Napoleon, Jesus, Cleopatra and, in 1942, Stalin, who was treated sympathetically following the German invasion of the Soviet Union. Ludwig (originally Cohen) was a German exile from Nazism; he spent the war in the

---

24 Edmond Malone to James Boswell, March 15, 1782. James Boswell, *The Life of Samuel Johnson* (London: Oxford University Press, [1791], 1953), 1105.

United States as a Swiss citizen. When he visited Ottawa in 1943, Brooke Claxton, King's parliamentary assistant, enterprisingly suggested that he write something about the Canadian prime minister. King met Ludwig and had "seldom felt more elevated in my thoughts & feelings – as if I had been with a soul who saw into and understood mine."[25] He was convinced that a publication by Ludwig would be "widely read and long remembered. It will have its place in the reading of future generations."[26] To ensure this, King toiled laborious nights over Ludwig's draft in the early months of 1944 to achieve the right cloying tone. The result was dismissed by his opponents as a mere campaign biography (for the 1945 election); but it was as close as King ever came to an autobiography and represents how he wanted to be seen, not just as the ideal leader for Canada but also – his aspirations having been raised by Roosevelt and Churchill – as the moderator of world conflicts. The book informs the reader that his qualification for that role had been displayed in one of the great scenes in British parliamentary history, King's speech to the combined House of Lords and Commons in May 1944. Ludwig lent his name to this panegyric not for money but in the hope that Canada, which he judged a likelier prospect than the United States, would open its door to Jews who survived the German massacre. But even in a war against Nazism, when the horrors of the Holocaust were known to some extent, King was as hesitant as he (and Roosevelt) had been in peacetime to welcome the Jews. Until the service veterans were re–established, he said, "the country could not stand for much immigration." His fear was that if the government came out in favour of immigration, other parties would benefit by opposing any measures in the general election.[27]

Mackenzie King's diary has been widely used for Canadian domestic politics and also for imperial and foreign policy, but it has not previously been extensively employed to illuminate both Churchill and Roosevelt, their interactions with each other, and also with King. Apart from Nigel Hamilton's books, the diary has only occasionally been cited for Roosevelt, usually from the volumes edited by Pickersgill (discussed in the Appendix). On Churchill, the British historian David Dilks has published a collection of primary material, including passages from King's diary, with connecting narrative and commentary on Churchill's

25 Diary, August 26, 1943.
26 Diary, November 21, 1943, April 12 and June 27, 1944; Emil Ludwig, *Mackenzie King: A Portrait Sketch* (Toronto: Macmillan, 1944).
27 Diary, February 13, and June 11, 1944.

visits to Canada.[28] A kind of companion volume from the opposite perspective by a Canadian, Terry Reardon, on King and Churchill (with a significant amount on Roosevelt) consists mainly of passages from King's diary along with fine photographs. Unreservedly admiring of Churchill, to whom King is compared and generally found wanting, it does not have much context.[29] Both books, like Pickersgill's, might be said to be preliminary assemblies for a narrative and analysis, which this book seeks to provide.[30]

* * *

Mackenzie King took great pride in his efforts to bring the United Kingdom and the United States closer together both in war and peace. He was as conscious as Churchill that the United States was vitally necessary to victory in the Second World War and dismayed that it did not join the fight for freedom for more than two years after it began. He ensured that his strong commitment to the harmonization of the three Atlantic countries was commemorated in his official portrait that hangs outside Canada's House of Commons. The artist was his friend and contemporary, Frank Salisbury, a highly traditional British court painter who executed the official portrait of Roosevelt and did several of Churchill. King insisted on Salisbury charging his customary high fee, which he personally paid from a recent legacy. He posed for it in October 1945, when he was in London to confer about the still-secret Ottawa revelation of an international Soviet spy network. King is seated in a high-backed Jacobean chair, taking off his pince–nez glasses to gaze intently at the viewer. He holds a sheaf of papers which is no mere prop but carefully selected letters on the espionage matter signed by himself, British Prime Minister Clement Attlee, and US President Harry Truman. King was convinced that his transmission of this espionage information to the Americans and British was "the largest and most important world mission that any individual could participate in at the present time."[31] The only way that the message of being the

---

28 David Dilks, *The Great Dominion: Winston Churchill in Canada 1900–1954* (Toronto: Thomas Allen Publishers, 2005).

29 Terry Reardon, *Winston Churchill and Mackenzie King: So Similar, So Different* (Toronto: Dundurn, 2012).

30 Richard Toye, *Churchill's Empire: The World that Made Him and the World He Made* (London: Macmillan, 2010); using the Pickersgill volumes only: Peter Clarke, *The Last Thousand Days of the British Empire* (London: Allen Lane, 2007).

31 Diary, October 18, 1945.

vital link between the two countries could have been stronger would have been for the letters to have been to and from himself, Churchill, and Roosevelt at some critical point in the war.

At the very time that this portrait was being painted, a physical counterpoint of the belittling of King's role between Churchill and Roosevelt was nearing completion. In 1941, the Rainbow Bridge between Canada and the United States opened at Niagara Falls. A fifty-five-bell carillon on the Canadian side was ordered from Britain. Delayed by the war, it was ready by 1947. The largest bell, weighing ten tons, bore the name "Churchill," an excruciatingly bad poem, and the words: "To God's glory and in grateful memory of our nation's war leaders, Winston Spencer Churchill and Franklin Delano Roosevelt." When King heard of this, through the application for a waiver of import duty, he was incandescent. It was bad enough that Canadian war loan advertisements (privately sponsored) had featured Churchill and Roosevelt without mentioning King, and that on a day of national prayer and consecration they, but not he, had been specified in the prayers of some of the United Churches, Canada's largest Protestant denomination.[32] But it was intolerable that the same should be perpetuated forever on a public memorial authorized by the Ontario government. Furiously he told his cabinet that this insult included them. After much heat on all sides, "Churchill" and "Roosevelt" were removed entirely from the bell while the first part of the inscription remained as a tribute to Canada's unnamed leaders.[33] The impression nevertheless still endures that King was of no consequence to Churchill and Roosevelt, and not even as Canada's war leader.

Again, this was not how Churchill and Roosevelt and others saw it, although it is true that neither King nor any Canadian cabinet minister or military chief played a significant part in decisions about fighting or diplomacy. This was because Churchill, and Roosevelt even more so, refused participation from any other western ally. King might have argued on the basis of its huge contribution that Canada was a special case for inclusion. He might have threatened to be less cooperative and generous if this was denied.[34] But apart from his recognition that Canadian involvement would only mean sharing responsibility for decisions that would still be made overwhelmingly by the British and Americans, he sincerely believed that Churchill and Roosevelt and their huge professional

32 Diary, September 6, 1942.
33 Diary, May 1, 7, 9, 12, 29, June 11, 14, 16 and 18, 1947.
34 Canada's contribution to the war is summarized at the beginning of Chapter 13.

staffs (Britain had 9,000 military and civil representatives in Washington) were far better equipped than Canada to decide the issues of war and peace. His main insistence was that Canada be consulted whenever its forces or interests were involved. He optimistically claimed that Canada and other countries were included in matters which concerned them, although he was all too well aware that this practice was often observed in the breach.[35] In effect, then, King agreed with his detractors that Churchill and Roosevelt were Canada's true war leaders. But his co-operation and ready assistance was a contribution highly valued by the British and American leaders. King frequently received fulsome appreciation, publicly and privately, from Churchill. Roosevelt articulated his gratitude less frequently, probably because he recognised how much benefit the United States provided to Canada. All in all, King managed the situation shrewdly. If he had been more confrontational – like Charles de Gaulle, who had far less to offer – or the Australians, he would never have been taken so far into the confidence of Churchill and Roosevelt. By accepting the lesser role, he always had access when needed.

The three men met for the first time in the White House after Pearl Harbor, on Boxing Day, December 26, 1941. King knew both Churchill and Roosevelt far better than Churchill and Roosevelt did, who were practically together for only the second time. Given the previous relationship between King and the other two, they immediately launched into an easy discussion of an embarrassing incident close to the Canada's shore that concerned all three. To understand the well-grounded associations that King had nurtured, and how important they were in dealings with Churchill and Roosevelt, it is necessary to begin before the war. This provides important context for the relationships in the heat of battle in addition to being an interesting and illuminating story, from an unusual perspective, about Winston Churchill, Franklin Roosevelt, and Mackenzie King himself.

---

35 "War Direction and Military Organization," Diary, May 4, 1943.

CHAPTER ONE

King and the "Great Genius"

MACKENZIE KING AND WINSTON CHURCHILL first met in
Ottawa at Christmas 1900, in the dying days of the reign of Queen
Victoria. King, who had just turned twenty-four, was a fledgling
civil servant. Churchill, two weeks older, was already the well-known author of
dramatic newspaper accounts of wars in Cuba, India, Egypt and, most recently,
South Africa where, after being captured by the Boers, he made a heroic escape
from a prisoner of war camp. He had recycled his journalism into four books and
written a novel, *Savrola*, revealing his aspiration to be a man of destiny, leading
his country through great danger to triumph. Half a year earlier he had resigned
from the army, a career he had contrived to combine with journalism, to pursue
his true ambition, politics. In October 1900, he was elected to parliament for the
governing Conservatives. He continued to write since MPs were unpaid until
1911 (and then only at £500 a year with no expense allowance) and his scant
family means fell well short of the lifestyle to which he felt entitled.

Before parliament met in January 1901, Churchill lectured around Britain
and the US on the Boer War. He had been invited by the governor general of
Canada to spend Christmas in Ottawa before speaking there and in Montreal,
Toronto, and points west. Ottawa, the capital of the Dominion of Canada, was
a city of 60,000. It was a lumber town, with a pulp and paper industry emitting
sulphurous odours not inappropriate to parliament, which stood in neo-gothic
buildings on a cliff high above the factories. Canada as a whole, consisted of five
million people spread across 3,800 miles from the Atlantic to the Pacific. A colony
of the United Kingdom, it was the model for similar internally self-governing

British settlement colonies that would join it as dominions after 1907: Australia, New Zealand, South Africa, Newfoundland (which joined Canada in 1949), and southern Ireland in 1921.[1]

The capital's social life centred on Government House (now known as Rideau Hall), the governor general's baronial residence set in an eighty acre park in the middle of the city. As a peer, the governor general represented both the monarch and the British government. The incumbent in 1900 was the Earl of Minto, a military veteran whose elevated manner satisfied even the most fastidious local tastes. Like all who held the office until after the Second World War, he was happy to welcome people he knew, or knew of, bearing news from home. Churchill invariably stayed at Government House when in Ottawa so it could not have been the case, as recorded by Churchill's doctor forty years later, that King first met him in his hotel room. That Churchill was drinking champagne at eleven o'clock in the morning, another of the doctor's claims, is more plausible.[2]

Mackenzie King, a young civil servant and one of the best-educated people in the city, indeed the country, with a manner polished in Chicago, Boston, London, and continental Europe, was always welcome at Government House. For a time, he had even imagined himself in love with the Minto's second daughter, Lady Ruby. He paid close attention to who was staying with the governor general, although he came to resent the habit of the British elite using the official residence, and those of the lieutenant governors in each Canadian province, as free imperial boarding houses, despite the household costs including staff wages being paid by the governors.[3] This did nothing to diminish his eagerness to meet a celebrity such as Churchill. Perhaps King was taken to his bedroom but it is more likely that they met in a reception room.

The reason that Churchill may have been seeking solace in drink on that morning was that a fellow guest was the glamorous Pamela Plowden, with whom he had fallen in love, four years earlier in India, where her father was a civil administrator. She had apparently recently rejected his marriage proposal and been lured to the reliable Canadian Christmas weather by one of Lord

1 Robin W. Winks, *The Relevance of Canadian History: U.S. and Imperial Perspectives* (Toronto: Macmillan, 1979)–.

2 Lord Moran, *Churchill: Taken from the Diaries of Lord Moran: The Struggle for Survival 1940–1965* (Boston: Houghton Mifflin, 1966), 20; (Diary entry December 31, 1941).

3 In 1929 when Churchill and several family members again stayed at Government House, King grumbled that the imposition raised the issue of abolishing all such residences. Diary, August 12 and 17, 1929.

Minto's two aides-de-camp, a pair of Bertie Woosters who have been described as "jovial, frolicking school boys, but on a lark, who were brought out for their decorative and entertainment value rather than any practical talent." J. H. C. Graham, a Coldstream Guards lieutenant who preciously characterized himself as "a Scotchman by birth, an Englishman by occupation, a dilettante with a turn for writing inferior dialogue, a taste for literature, an ear for music, a retentive memory and a prodigious thirst," was evidently more appealing to Pamela Plowden than the intense and striving Churchill, who lacked an adequate and secure income.[4] Lord Minto, a friend of Churchill's mother, may have seen a matchmaking opportunity in the invitation to her son. In the same house as his beloved and a more favoured rival, the strain on Churchill must have been immense. After leaving Ottawa, he would tell his mother: "We had no painful discussions, but there is no doubt in my mind that she is the only woman I could ever live happily with." Lord Minto wrote to Lady Randolph that "everything seemed to me to be tolerably platonic,"[5] a state with which she was not overly familiar.[6]

Unfortunately, King in 1900 was not yet sufficiently addicted to his diary to record the meeting with Churchill. He did not even mention the latter's lecture at an Ottawa theatre on December 27. A local newspaper reported that the presentation was hampered by a lisp, and that Churchill made no pretence to oratory but spoke in short, pointed sentences laced with humour and sarcasm. "He simply tells the story of the war in a chatty, conversational style," at times "giving an impression of that amplitude of energy and determination without which he could never have won the reputation he did in South Africa . . . He has self–confidence and self-reliance, but more than that, he evidently has no low opinion of Mr. Churchill."[7] This would almost certainly have been King's opinion. Three years later, he did not dissent from this view, during a lunchtime discussion of Churchill's conceit and affectation with a couple of people who knew him.[8]

---

4   Carman Miller, *The Canadian Career of the Fourth Earl of Minto: The Education of a Viceroy* (Waterloo, ON: Wilfrid Laurier University Press, 1980), 57–8.
5   Randolph S. Churchill, *Winston S. Churchill*, Vol. I: 1874–1900 (London: Heinemann, 1966), 544–5.
6   The next summer Pamela Plowden conclusively declined Churchill and in 1902 married the earl of Lytton, who had no trouble sustaining an aristocratic lifestyle. She and Churchill remained friends to the end of his life, and in 1944 Mackenzie King recognized her at a reception in Downing street.
7   Dilks, *The Great Dominion*, 17–18.
8   Diary, October 31, 1904.

Churchill's defence of the war in South Africa was better received in Canada than in the United States, where many saw the Boer farmers fighting the British as analogous to the struggles of American revolutionaries. French-Canadian audiences in the bilingual cities of Montreal and Ottawa shared American hostility or indifference to the British imperial war but Canada's English-speaking majority was keen to fight for empire and had practically forced Sir Wilfrid Laurier's divided Liberal government to provide over seven thousand military volunteers. Mackenzie King, who had been in London in 1899 when the war started, thought it could have been avoided by negotiation; but once begun, and badly for the British, he believed that the imperial power must win.[9]

Still, King almost certainly shared the moral outrage of most British Liberals, particularly during the last two years, when the war became a guerrilla operation with the British destroying Boer refuges by burning farms and herding women and children into concentration camps. But he had to be discreet. His patron and family friend, William Mulock, the postmaster-general who had given King the job of editing the *Labour Gazette* and had already advanced him to deputy minister of labour (a department also headed by Mulock), was a far more imperial Liberal than King. At the conclusion of Churchill's lecture, in very British Toronto, Mulock thanked the speaker in fervent tones, assuring him of Canada's support for the war and looking forward to the day (which came in 1910) when a confederation of colonies in South Africa would join Australia and Canada to produce "three great outlying empires, composed of self–governing colonies, all recognising and paying allegiance to Great Britain, and all united to her by the common love for British institutions, freedom and justice."[10]

King never forgot his first encounter with the exotic Churchill, although he could scarcely have anticipated a fifty-year connection and their future closeness. For his part, Churchill did not recall meeting King in Ottawa until the Second World War improved his memory. He first dated their acquaintance to 1906, when the civil servant went on a mission to London, principally to see Churchill, whose views on empire and social policy were by then similar to his own. Churchill had risen far by 1906, and in a different direction than anyone expected. A thorn in the flesh of the Conservatives, as his father had been before him, he broke with the party in 1904 to join the Liberals over the Conservatives'

9 R. MacGregor Dawson, *William Lyon Mackenzie King: A Political Biography*, Vol. I: 1874–1923 (Toronto: University of Toronto Press, 1958), 89–90.

10 Dilks, *The Great Dominion*, 21.

threat to abandon more than four decades of free trade and introduce preferential tariffs in an effort to unite the empire. The Liberals won a huge majority in the 1906 election, pledging to maintain free trade and insisting that the empire was best held together by the powerful ties of heritage, common values, and sentiment. Churchill was appointed parliamentary under-secretary at the colonial office and, with the colonial secretary in the House of Lords, he had free rein in the Commons. Soon he was also trying to dominate the department. The new governor general of Canada, Earl Grey, an ardent empire tariff protectionist, told King that Churchill's selection was "a bad and dangerous appointment from an imperial point of view."[11] To King, it seemed that Churchill had seen the true light.

* * *

The purpose of Mackenzie King's visit to London in 1906, was to persuade the imperial government to rescue Canada from an acute social and political problem on its west coast by restricting Asian immigration. He was the ideal person for the mission: now the government's chief industrial arbitrator, he had a pleasing diplomatic manner and was familiar with London, where from 1899 to 1900 as a Harvard graduate student, he had investigated social conditions, attended classes at the new London School of Economics and Political Science, and met many leading social reformers. On this voyage to London, King prepared himself by reading Churchill's recent biography of his father.[12] A helpful personal connection was Churchill's parliamentary private secretary, Hamar Greenwood, a friend of King's since their student days at the University of Toronto. After leading a student protest and being warned that he had no future in the tightly knit Ontario legal profession, he went to London where he became a barrister. Elected an MP in 1905, his knowledge of Canada must have been an asset in the colonial office.[13]

Autumn was never a good time to see British ministers. Parliament was not in session and most of them were in the country. King had to be content with fellow civil servants. But Churchill was eagerly on duty. They must have had several

---

11 Diary, December 17, 1905.
12 Diary, September 23, 1906.
13 Roy MacLaren, *Empire and Ireland: The Transatlantic Career of the Canadian Imperialist Hamar Greenwood* (Montreal & Kingston: McGill–Queen's University Press, 2015), 7–45 and 50.

discussions but there is a record of only one, left by Evelyn Wrench (the passionately imperialist editor of Lord Northcliffe's *Overseas Daily Express*) of a luncheon at Churchill's house. Wrench was probably included because he had spent the summer in Canada. Another guest was John Burns, a self-educated engineer, a Liberal-Labour MP, and the president of the local government board which was similar to the Canadian department of labour. Also present was Churchill's new private secretary, the exquisite Edward Marsh who served his chief in every government office to 1929 and then continued in retirement as his literary assistant. Unfortunately, the only exchange that was noted was Burns asking Wrench why he wanted to increase emigration and spread London suburbs all over the empire.[14]

This was the first of Mackenzie King's many brief, but significant, political encounters with Churchill before the Second World War, all of them in Britain save for two in Canada. Despite Churchill's congeniality, King did not get much of what he wanted on the occasion. Even among Liberals, Churchill was conspicuous in insisting on the free movement of imperial subjects, particularly Indians, and he also did not want to antagonize Japan with which Britain had made a defence treaty in 1902. All that was conceded was an amendment to the merchant shipping act against fraudulent migration.

This did not close the matter and King made a second visit to London a year and a half later. In the interim, there had been riots against Asian immigration in Vancouver resulting in no loss of life but plenty of property.[15] Sent west to inquire and settle damage claims, King had concluded there was too much immigration and that it should be reduced at the source. President Theodore Roosevelt, dealing with similar sentiments on his own west coast, was of the same view but he was unwilling to get directly involved. Considering Canada well-placed to persuade the imperial government to press its Japanese ally to restrict emigration, he cleverly presented his west coast protests as a joint Canada-US problem, with the Japanese infiltrating his country from British Columbia. Alerted to Mackenzie King, Roosevelt flatteringly invited the civil servant three times to the White House. In his sabre-rattling way, he said that the British government needed to

---

14 Sir Evelyn Wrench, "Churchill and the Empire" in Eade ed., *Churchill by his Contemporaries*, 289.

15 Julie Gilmour, *Trouble on Main Street: Mackenzie King, Reason, Race and the 1907 Vancouver Riots* (Toronto: Allen Lane, 2014); more acerbically Avner Offer, *The First World War: An Agrarian Interpretation* (Oxford: Oxford University Press, 1991 [1989], 176–97; Dawson, *Mackenzie King*, 149–99. All these references include King's 1909 visit to the far east.

understand that Japanese expansion would lead to war with the United States. He also warned that if the Japanese got into the Canadian mountain passes, a hundred years of fighting would not get them out. Canadian Prime Minister Sir Wilfrid Laurier accepted the burden of conveying Roosevelt's message to London, although he was now more concerned about Indian immigrants, having already arranged directly with Japan to limit the numbers to Canada.

King thus returned to London to ask again for immigration controls on behalf of Canada and an American president. This time he dealt with senior cabinet ministers, an experience that appears to have spurred his international ambitions and, inevitably, his political designs. To continue his heady associations with great men, he needed to be in Canada's cabinet, or really, prime minister since that office, along with the governor general, handled external affairs. He was encouraged by Hamar Greenwood: "No one knows your abilities better than I do . . . [to] fight for the first position in Canada."[16]

King arrived in London in March 1908, in the middle of the parliamentary and social season. Liberal ministers objected strongly to restricting the movement of British subjects in Asia but King (who was a lawyer) dextrously urged scrutiny of the Indian emigration act, which revealed an overlooked provision forbidding Indians to leave for contract work in Canada. This was enforced. King passed along Roosevelt's ravings about war with Japan which were scorned by the Foreign Secretary, Sir Edward Grey and others. The president, who was coming to the end of his term, had by now lost interest in the issue and never inquired about the success of his overture.

Among the many political and social figures King interacted with in London was Churchill, who was soon to leave the colonial office. Again, he invited King to lunch at his house, and this time King recorded it. So that they could speak freely, the only other person present was Edward Marsh, before whom Churchill assured King that he could say anything. Churchill recalled the earlier exchange between Burns and Wrench, which King, marvelling at his memory, had forgotten. When Churchill was out of the room, Marsh asked King if their host was liked in Canada. King smoothly replied that "the people were following his career with interest each day." King admired Churchill's well-stocked bookshelves and his host said: "One could spend a year or more in a library and never miss the world and never be lonely." He pointed to a collection on Napoleon purchased

16 MacLaren, *Empire and Ireland*, 50.

from an American after the 1907 crash, saying that he was a great admirer of the emperor and read as much about him as he could.

In this confidential setting, Churchill was blunt about his personal feelings on immigration, revealing that he was much closer to Roosevelt than Grey. He sympathized with Canada's problem and claimed that if there was any difficulty between Japan and the United States, Britain would stand behind the Americans and let the 1902 Japanese alliance go. "He hated the Japanese," wrote King, "had never liked them, thought they were designing and crafty." But since neither country was prepared for conflict, he did not think there would be war. The Japanese would realize the strength of "the Great White Fleet" of sixteen warships Roosevelt had sent on a tour of the world. Turning to India, he said that he had told the minister, John Morley that there must be a system of passports to prevent people leaving for Canada. Pontificating in Napoleonic tones about "the movement of peoples and possibilities of war, etc.," he added what King regarded as a "rather characteristic" but "no less true" comment: "On large questions of this kind, I have a true instinct and seldom err."

King and Churchill agreed that the great issues of the day were not in international affairs but in social policy, and the Canadian did not dispute the assertion that Britain was "more democratic," meaning more responsive to social problems, than Australia or Canada. A few days later, on Henry Asquith becoming prime minister, Churchill was promoted to the cabinet as president of the board of trade and threw himself into improving the lot of the poor. Summing up their conversation, King wrote: "One cannot talk with him without being impressed at the nibbleness [sic] of his mind, his quickness of perception and his undoubted ability." He thought that Churchill had "lost a good deal of the egotism, at least so far as his manner is concerned, though one feels, that even yet it is Churchill rather than the movement with which he is identified that is the mainspring of his conduct."

When Churchill offered to do whatever he could for King, the latter expressed a desire to hear Churchill speak in parliament. Churchill arranged a place in the Distinguished Visitors' Gallery three nights' hence. King dined in Westminster with Bonar Law, a Conservative MP born in Canada who, in 1911 became leader of the party; however, Churchill did not speak in the debate on financial policy.[17] This was the last time they saw each other for fifteen years, although nine months

17   Diary, March 28 and 31, 1908 (microfilm [choose between "film" and "fiche"]).

later, at the end of 1908 King was in London briefly, to join the British delegation to an international commission at Shanghai attempting to stop the opium
trade. In the long interval, he closely followed Churchill's fortunes and events at
the heart of empire.

* * *

After throwing himself vigorously into social reform at the board of trade, then
as home secretary, and taking a prominent part in reducing the powers of the
House of Lords, Churchill's career changed abruptly in October 1911 when he
became First Lord of the Admiralty. He quit opposing high military expenditure
and now demanded funds for the latest warships to stay ahead of the growing
German fleet. After half a decade of convergence, a gulf was opening with King.

King himself entered parliament half a year after his trip to Britain, becoming
minister of labour until the government was defeated in 1911, over its support
for reciprocal free trade with the United States. His wounds were salved to some
degree by the wealthy British Liberal, social reformer, and imperialist Violet
Markham, who had come to Ottawa in 1906 to investigate Canadian social conditions. Theirs was an instant meeting of minds and she became one of the very
few who called him "Rex" (a pun on "King"). In 1911, she contributed to his
election expenses and after his defeat gave him £200 and then £300 a year for
the three years to help him continue to work on social causes. He also engaged
in journalism, gave speeches, and advised Sir Wilfrid Laurier, now leader of the
opposition. In August 1914, he was vaulted into affluence when the Rockefeller
Foundation hired him – ostensibly as a researcher but, in fact, as an industrial
conciliator at $12,000 a year – while allowing him to continue living in Ottawa
and engage in politics.[18]

On August 4, ten days before this arrangement was concluded, Britain went
to war with Germany. Canada and the rest of the empire were automatically
committed. After three months of fighting, King had an illuminating conversation in Ottawa with a sympathetic British Liberal MP, the aptly named Allan
Baker, a Quaker from Trenton, Ontario who had built a baking machinery business in London.[19] He said that radicals like himself had been powerless to prevent

18 Dawson, *Mackenzie King*, 224–34.
19 Elizabeth Balmer Baker and P. J. Baker, *J. Allen Baker, M.P.: A Memoir* (London: Swarthmore Press,
    1927). One of Baker's sons, the co-author of the biography was Philip Noel-Baker (he added

the government going to war. Churchill, the keenest minister, boasted that "this was his war, that he had forced England into it." King doubted that Churchill had such influence and thought that Sir Edward Grey would have averted the conflict if it had been possible "When, oh, when," King lamented, "will men learn that death and destruction are not the supreme ends of existence!"[20]

Winston Churchill, formed of very different clay from Baker and King, regarded war as a natural part of human nature, a noble test that brought out the best in individuals and societies. When a stalemate developed on the Western Front at the end of 1914, he boldly proposed attacking the enemy Ottoman Empire, forcing it out of the war, opening a far better supply route to Russia than the Arctic, and encouraging the Balkan states to join the Allies. This imaginative but ill-prepared plan foundered on far greater military resistance than expected and Churchill was the political casualty. When, in May 1915, Asquith formed a coalition with the Conservatives, they were adamant that Churchill must go, citing his failed Gallipoli operation as proof of his impulsiveness and incompetence. Demoted to nominal office, Churchill resigned at the end of the year and for a few months commanded troops at the front. But in July 1917, half a year after Asquith was pushed out of office by Lloyd George and the Conservatives, Churchill returned as minster of munitions. By 1921, he was colonial secretary and a year later he had a mighty clash with Mackenzie King, who was, by then, prime minister of Canada.

King, too, had been out of office and, like Churchill, his eventual elevation was a result of the war. After losing his seat in 1911, he failed to regain one in the 1917 election by opposing conscription for overseas military service, an issue that split his Liberal party primarily along language lines. French Canadians shared his objections; English Canadians, by and large, did not. He was fortunate to have been out of parliament in the divisive months that followed and at a party convention in the summer of 1919, following the resignation and death of Prime Minister Wilfrid Laurier, he was elected leader with strong support from Quebec. There was great scepticism that this neophyte would survive but within a couple of years he had succeeded in reintegrating the party. The Liberals won

his wife's surname), an Olympic athlete, Labour MP and cabinet minister, an activist for world disarmament and the 1959 Nobel Peace Prize laureate.

20 Diary, November 19 and 20, 1914. Lloyd George, to whom Baker had looked as leader of the radicals, when minister of munitions took over Baker's factories in 1916 for armaments production.

the 1921 election with a minority of one seat and King formed a government with the support of the new, agrarian Progressive Party. At least for now, he had achieved his ambition of becoming prime minister. He also had an appropriate house, bequeathed to him by Lady Laurier and renovated by Peter Larkin, the king of (Salada) tea, who went to Britain as high commissioner. It was a Victorian mansion closely resembling Franklin Roosevelt's home at Hyde Park.[21]

* * *

Imperial and international issues were at first of only marginal concern to King and his colleagues as they grappled with post-war economic and social problems. Then, on Saturday afternoon, September 16, 1922, as he was about to address his constituents outside Toronto, a newspaper reporter handed him the copy of a British colonial office request for troops to help enforce the peace settlement imposed on the Ottoman Empire a year earlier. The treaty stripped away all non-Turkish territory (about three-quarters of the total) and divided the heartland into spheres of influence for France, Italy and, most offensively, neighbouring hostile Greece. It also made the Straits from the Aegean to the Black Sea, including Constantinople, an international zone. The demeaning accord was accepted by the fainéant sultan but military nationalists under Mustapha Kemal, the Turkish victor in the Gallipoli campaign, rebelled and drove back the Greeks, who had undertaken to suppress the challenge. France and Italy came to terms with Kemal and British foreign secretary Lord Curzon wanted to do the same. But Lloyd George was determined to enforce the treaty by a show of strength that would pull together his fractious MPs and produce an electoral victory. He was strongly backed by Churchill, the colonial secretary, and his great friend Birkenhead, the Conservative Lord Chancellor. Twenty years later, the teetotal Hamar Greenwood, who had been the Chief Secretary for Ireland at the time, told King that all three were drunk.[22] Sober, the decision would have been the same.

Caught off guard, King could not comment but he was furious at the assumption that Canada and the other dominions (which received the same message) would simply comply as in 1914. The cable, which had been sent to the governor

---

21 Allan Levine, *King: William Lyon Mackenzie King: A Life Guided by the Hand of Destiny* (Vancouver: Douglas & McIntyre, 2011), 122–5.
22 Diary, May 19, 1944; MacLaren, *Empire and Ireland*, 257–9.

general, as was still the practice, at midnight on a Friday was decoded on Saturday and forwarded to King's office, with no one thinking to alert the prime minister earlier. That afternoon, Churchill issued a press release, approved by Lloyd George and Birkenhead, that was calculated to rouse British support for the ministry and put pressure on the dominion governments. Owing to the time difference it arrived in Canada in time for the afternoon newspapers. After returning overnight to Ottawa, King read the Friday cable which seemed "drafted designedly to play the imperial game, to test out centralization vs. autonomy as regards European wars."

King was not alone in regarding the matter as a cynical election manoeuvre and he had no intention of involving Canada in such a military operation.[23] When he protested about the cable being publicized before he could read it or consult his colleagues, Churchill plausibly replied that it had been directed primarily to Australia and New Zealand, which had taken a leading part at Gallipoli, but he felt the other dominions should be included in the circular as a matter of good form. He claimed that the threat to Kemal did not involve any probability of serious war, although he undermined that point by adding that anything Canada contributed to imperial solidarity would be a great help.[24]

King was not mollified: the situation was too much like the Balkans in 1914. He and his cabinet decided their government would not make any commitment. Churchill, perhaps alerted to other Canadians taking a more imperialist view, sent two further cables saying that the situation was deteriorating. But King firmly believed that refusing a commitment contributed to peace: "It is a serious business having matters in hand of a man like Churchill–the fate of an empire!"[25] When only New Zealand and tiny Newfoundland responded favourably, Curzon got his way. An armistice was produced and a new treaty in 1923 enabled Turkey to be an independent state.

The repercussions of Chanak were volcanic, not least for Churchill. A month later, a Conservative revolt led Lloyd George to resign and he was replaced by Bonar Law as head of a purely Conservative ministry. News of Lloyd George's

23 Diary, September 17, 1922.
24 Diary, September 19, 1922.
25 Diary, October 4, 1922; John Herd Thompson with Alan Seager, *Canada 1922–1939: Decades of Discontent* (Toronto: McClelland and Stewart, 1985), 44–6; C. P. Stacey, *Canada and the Age of Conflict: A History of Canadian External Policies*, II: *1921–1948: The Mackenzie King Era* (University of Toronto Press, 1981), 17–26; David Walder, *The Chanak Affair* (London: Hutchinson, 1969).

fall flashed across the Atlantic and Mackenzie King claimed some credit from his stand on Chanak. He thought Britain could only benefit from being rid of unscrupulous figures and he did not share the confidence of Churchill, who stuck by his chief, that Lloyd George was bound to return. King saw the fallen prime minister as "a betrayer of principles" and he had no more sympathy for Churchill who in international affairs seemed to be a Tory imperialist. When Churchill was ill (with appendicitis) during the ensuing election, King was sceptical: "I wd. not be surprised if he were on a spree. He has overshot the mark."[26]

All the prominent Lloyd George Liberals, save the man himself, were defeated in that election, among them Churchill and Sir Hamar Greenwood (a baronet since 1915). Bonar Law was diagnosed with throat cancer and died during the 1923 imperial conference. He was succeeded by the Conservative Stanley Baldwin, who had been a leader of the insurrection against Lloyd George. King attended Law's funeral and sent an official wreath for the first Canadian buried in Westminster Abbey. Baldwin assured King that Canada's attitude on Chanak had saved the situation: "It was pure madness and we were within an ace of a conflict." This was the beginning to a great relationship. On everything save tariffs, King admired Baldwin almost to the point of idolatry.[27]

* * *

The 1923 imperial conference was only the second time that Mackenzie King had been in Britain since 1909, the other being in the spring of 1919 when he gone to investigate industrial problems for the Rockefeller Foundation and Violet Markham had introduced him to the Conservative John Buchan, who a decade and a half later he would help to appoint as governor general.[28] In the autumn of 1923, King came in glory as prime minister of the leading dominion, highly regarded by the British Conservative government. Winston Churchill, by contrast, seemed a waning, if not a spent force, whose precarious situation was all the more reason to renew acquaintance with the Canadian prime minister and try to soothe hostility over Chanak.

In the leisurely six weeks of the conference, King also had plenty of opportunity to enjoy the garden of earthly delights: he stayed at the Ritz hotel, bought

26 Diary, October 19, 1922.
27 Diary, September 9, 1946.
28 Diary, May 28, 1919.

fine clothes, received customary membership in the British privy council, the freedom of the City of London, and an honorary degree from the University of Oxford. He attended a naval review at Spithead, receptions at Buckingham Palace, and endless social events.

Political meetings of the imperial conference were nominally presided over by Stanley Baldwin although it was Curzon, still foreign secretary, who presented the case for united foreign and defence policies to meet dangers in Europe and elsewhere. There was a delegation from India, implying that it was on the way to dominion status, and one from the new Irish Free State but both were excluded from confidential discussions on the technical ground that they did not have prime ministers. At the concurrent economic conference, preferential imperial tariffs were powerfully urged by Leopold Amery, the First Lord of the Admiralty who was married to Hamar Greenwood's sister. Mackenzie King strongly rejected both centralizing proposals.[29] He insisted that the dominions were equal partners with Britain with the same diplomatic standing. Each party would take responsibility for its own decisions, which the others would share only when it suited them. Canada would defend Britain and the other dominions, as they should Canada when in danger, but "we have no such interest in the Crown Colonies & Protectorates & their relations with other countries, nor with India."[30] This was silently approved by the Irish, who were ill at ease at their first imperial conference, and by Prime Minister Jan Smuts of South Africa, who wanted a strong imperial connection to protect his racially segregated country but was acutely aware that Afrikaners would not accept any automatic external commitments. On preferential tariffs, there was similarly no agreement whereupon Baldwin announced that he would introduce them for Britain, a measure that required an election.[31]

Winston Churchill had no part in the proceedings but was still a prominent public figure. He attended a Canada Club dinner in King's honour and was undoubtedly not cheered by King's sermon on diplomatic autonomy. The failure to agree on imperial tariffs caused him less grief since he regarded Baldwin's decision for Britain as suicidal. In this optimistic mood, he invited King to lunch.

29 Thompson, *Canada 1922–1939*, 46–8; Norman Hillmer, *O. D. Skelton: A Portrait of Canadian Ambition* (Toronto: University of Toronto Press, 2015), 96–111; Stacey, *Canada and the Age of Conflict*, II, 66–72.
30 Diary, September 7, 1923.
31 Diary, November 5, 1923 (microfilm edition).

Despite Chanak, the two met at Churchill's house as amiably as before the war. King was introduced to Clementine to whom Churchill had been married since September 1908. This was another instant friendship. The only other guests were Admiral Sir Roger Keyes and his wife, the former was present probably to discuss his leading part in the Dardanelles campaign, around which Churchill was composing the second volume of *The World Crisis*. The host pre-emptively broached the subject of Chanak, which he expected was on King's mind, in order to defend himself. He said that the cabinet (implying its entire membership) had discussed the situation and left him to draft the telegrams to the dominions. He repeated that he had really written to Australia and New Zealand and knew that Canada would have no concern in the issue, obviously forgetting that he had said he would be grateful for whatever Canada might contribute. When King said that Britain should not count on Canadian support of imperial wars, Churchill tactfully agreed: "this was something that each party must decide for itself according to its own conception of its interests." He defended the press statement by saying that he expected fighting to begin almost immediately, again not remembering that he told King that there was not much likelihood. When Clementine expressed surprise that the statement had been issued before British ministers were sure the dominion governments had been informed, Churchill sheepishly excused his haste by saying that it was the morning that their daughter Mary was born. The company urbanely laughed off the matter as an example of always blaming a woman for trouble. After lunch, the baby was produced and King declared that they would forever have an interest in each other.[32] Twenty years later, she would accompany her father to the 1943 Quebec conference.

On this happy note, King and Churchill parted in renewed friendship. Not that one assurance on Chanak, or anything else, was enough for King. In 1926 and again in 1932 he got Churchill to repeat his explanation.[33] And yet in his book on the aftermath of the war, published in 1929, Churchill defended his action, blaming the mishandling the situation on the irresolution of the late and now uncomplaining Lord Curzon. He insisted that the British government and the dominions, notably Australia and New Zealand, had prevented war and even claimed that his firmness was admired by the Turks and helped to strengthen relations.[34]

32 Diary, October 30, 1923 (microfilm edition).
33 Diary, October 18, 1926 and March 5, 1932.
34 Winston S. Churchill, *The Aftermath* (New York: Scribner's, 1929), 464

* * *

By the time Mackenzie King returned for the next imperial conference three years later, Churchill had undergone an astonishing political resurrection. Baldwin had lost the election of 1923 on the tariff issue, resulting in the first Labour Government, propped up by the Liberals. Subsequently renouncing protection, Baldwin won a huge majority in 1924. Some strongly anti–socialist former Liberals, including Churchill and Greenwood, were enlisted among his supporters and even Churchill, with his free-trade convictions, was appointed chancellor of the exchequer to assure the country that the government would abjure tariff protection. King was among those stunned. A year earlier, Baldwin had told him that Churchill and Birkenhead (now the secretary of state for India) were two of "'the three most dangerous men in the Empire', now he has taken them to his breast!"[35]

As chancellor, Churchill lived at 11 Downing Street, which shared an entrance with the prime minister's house. When the ministry had been in office for a year, the press baron Lord Beaverbrook, who detested Baldwin for abandoning imperial trade protection, told Mackenzie King that "Churchill is practically the government. He has got a complete strangle–hold on the younger reactionary [free trade] Tories, who used to move Baldwin about as they liked, and now keeps the Prime Minister in a padded room of his own." Before Baldwin went to the country at the weekend, he stopped at Churchill's bedside for the latest word.[36]

In his first budget given in 1925, Churchill demonstrated his Victorian orthodoxy by restoring the gold standard (making paper money redeemable for gold) and raising the exchange rate of the pound to the pre-war level of US\$4.86. This was based on impeccable professional advice as well as his own instincts but, while it increased confidence in the financial centre of London and reduced the cost of imports, it was a blow to exports by overvaluing the pound by as much as ten percent. Churchill soon saw the problem but could not publicly admit it.

A year later, the government ended the subsidies that had sustained the coal mines since the wartime boom, precipitating a lock-out in May 1926 when the miners refused a pay cut and a longer work day. This produced a nine-day national sympathy strike. Mackenzie King, taking a professional view from afar, correctly

35   Diary, November 7, 1924.
36   Beaverbrook to King, February 9, 1926. Martin Gilbert, *Winston S. Churchill*, vols. 3–8 (London: Heinemann, 1971–88), V, 144.

divined that it was Churchill who had influenced Baldwin to view the conflict as a political one, between labour and the state, rather than as an economic one between labour and capital in which government could act as umpire. King was sorry for Baldwin, George V, and others but "for Churchill I feel a scorn too great for words. He has been an evil genius in this." He feared troops and aeroplanes would be used against the workers and "some fool will make a mistake. Churchill may be shot, anything may happen & a revolution greater than England has ever known brought on."[37] In fact there was remarkably little violence and the general strike collapsed in the face of the government invoking emergency powers. Six months later, the miners were forced to accept the employers' terms.

Mackenzie King's political fortunes at this time were as turbulent as Churchill's and he, too, emerged triumphant. When King's administration was defeated in the House of Commons, the governor general decided to summon the leader of the opposition rather than accepting the prime minister's advice to call a general election (following one only six months earlier). The new prime minister was in turn voted down, after which the governor general reluctantly granted an election. There was much to be said, and it has been, on the both sides of the judgement of Viscount Byng of Vimy (at which battle he had led the Canadian troops) but the controversy was a godsend to King. He campaigned against improper conduct by a British-appointed governor general and demanded that this official in future be appointed on the advice of the Canadian government. Winning a huge majority, King went to London in October in a strong position to insist on dominion parity. He was followed a few days later by Lord Byng, who had finished his term. Byng was silent in public but expostulated in London to Leopold Amery, the secretary of state for the colonies and dominions, that King had "a great belief in himself and great ambition, and a general belief in God, [but] he has no political convictions or sincerities of any sort whatsoever and simply says what he thinks may pay at the moment."[38] The "King–Byng" dispute, like Chanak, was for Canada's prime minister another King Charles' head, to which he could never resist referring.[39]

37 Diary, May 3, 1926.
38 John Barnes and David Nicolson eds., *The Leo Amery Diaries*. Vol. I: *1896–1929*. (London: Hutchinson, 1980), 471. (Diary, October 15, 1926.)
39 In 1932, when in Ottawa, Churchill, who had effectively appointed Byng, was appealed to for an authoritative judgement and gratifyingly supported King. 'Memorandum by Lord Bessborough of a Conversation with W.S.C., March 6, 1932' and King, Diary, March 5, 1932. Dilks, *The Great Dominion*, 127–30.

* * *

At the 1926 conference, Winston Churchill briefly assured Mackenzie King that he had been in the right in his dispute with the governor general, while expressing relief that he had not attacked Byng personally or the British government during the election campaign. The occasion was a Canada Club dinner, presided over by Greenwood, in honour of Byng. King was at the head table, separated from Byng by the Prince of Wales with Churchill on his other side. This was his only meeting with Churchill during the conference, although the latter had hoped that they might meet again.

During the dinner, King carefully refrained from criticism when he and Churchill inevitably discussed the general strike. Churchill revealed that beneath his public belligerence he was sympathetic to the miners as well as concerned about weakening the industry. "Speaking very confidentially and very privately," he said, "the employers had been a damn selfish lot; that there was a stage [after the general strike] when, if they had been at all decent, all parties could have been brought together." Much of the problem, said Churchill, was owing to the fracture of the Liberal party. British Liberals had formerly included a good labour representation; now the workers were controlled by trade union leaders and many votes went to the Labour party. He himself was in favour of them being represented in the cabinet. All this confirmed for King the wisdom of the Canadian Liberal party holding the middle ground. When he asserted that the state should not have become involved, Churchill insisted that "it really was a revolution and that if a general strike had succeeded the Government itself could not have stood." He was proud that "not a shot had been fired and no one had been injured; that the British people had shown themselves at their best." He nevertheless championed the 1927 legislation banning general strikes and imposing other trade union restrictions that stayed in force until 1945 and the ascension of a Labour government.

Churchill also told King of his reception by the Conservative government and Stanley Baldwin, who would "back him up in anything he did." Baldwin had "taken him into the Cabinet without knowing him; no other man would have done this." When King inquired if Churchill still found time to read, he answered: "Not only reading but for the preparation of the third volume of my memoirs [*The World Crisis*]." He said that he dictated his books and speeches, going over the latter and then relying on memory and notes. King, who was a slave to correspondence, asked how he managed that. "It is all done for me by excellent men," said Churchill. "I seldom write a letter. A man at the head of a department should have a clean desk and have time to think. This was impossible if there was much correspondence to attend to."[40] Thinking was not the half of it. Churchill, even with a ministerial salary and an official residence, had overdue tax bills – a highly unusual situation for a finance minister – and was forced to keep at his lucrative writing to maintain his high standard of living.[41]

On the subject of the imperial conference, Churchill claimed a special interest, having been involved in the constitution of South Africa twenty years earlier, and the 1921 negotiations that brought Ireland dominion status. King was pleased by Churchill's judgment that it was Liberals who had done far more for the Empire than Conservatives. They were at one that self-government for South Africa was a great achievement, neither thinking of the acceptance of racial segregation. King gratified Churchill by saying that Britain's treatment of the dominions had been repaid by support for the First World War (although Boer opposition had to be suppressed). Churchill signalled his uneasiness about King's intentions at the conference by expressing the hope that the bonds of Empire would not be loosened. He did not expect anything from the meeting, optimistically anticipating that it would stick to helpful discussion.

After dinner, King heard Churchill speak for the first time in a quarter of a century, if indeed he had heard him in Ottawa, in 1900. He was the only true orator of the evening, the others, including King, being threats to digestion. Churchill's theme, like his conversation with King, was a warning against imperial separation. The empire was a non-partisan affair: in Victorian times, the "Conservatives nearly lost the Empire by trying to keep it and the Liberals kept it by trying to throw it away." He conceded that it was fine to discuss constitutional questions since the empire was always in flux and nothing was ever finally settled but it could get along well without writing things down. What made it stronger was "the unseen, unceasing heart–beat of a strong, powerful people," separated by immense distances but "united and associated for the purpose of mutual security and advancement; . . . most of all by the romance of history symbolized and sustained and enshrined in the imperial crown."[42]

40 Diary, October 18, 1926.
41 Lough, *No More Champagne*, 164–72.
42 Robert Rhodes James ed., *Winston S. Churchill: His Complete Speeches 1897–1963*, 8 vols. (New York: Chelsea House, 1974), 4103–4; Diary, October 18, 1926.

Mackenzie King, the next speaker, did not take issue with Churchill, insisting that he had no desire to destroy the Commonwealth but only wanted to increase the status of the dominions. The constitution of the empire would evolve like Britain's and those holding "the true view" had no difficulty reconciling "the aspirations of those who had a country of their own and those who had the aspirations and ideals of a great Empire like the British Empire."[43]

Churchill only rarely attended the conference but was chagrined that King got all the dominion freedom he wanted. King was further praised as a peacemaker between the Irish and South Africans who sought more concessions and the Australians and New Zealanders who wanted to keep close ties to Britain.[44] The conference's report defined dominions as "autonomous Communities within the British Empire, equal in status, in no way subordinate one to another in any aspect of their domestic or external affairs, though united by a common allegiance to the Crown, and freely associated as members of the British Commonwealth of Nations." Leopold Amery, who calculated that this freedom would keep the dominions firmly attached to Britain, later told King that at the beginning of proceedings only he and Balfour, the lord president of the council, favoured dominion equality. Churchill was furious at the outcome: "He liked to rule over people," said King.[45] As a cabinet minister, Churchill had to put the best public face on Balfour's wording but he did not like it, or its legal distillation five years later into the Statute of Westminster, which freed the dominion parliaments to legislate as they liked.

During the conference, King met with the expatriate Canadian Lord Beaverbrook (Max Aitken), who carefully preserved his personal as well as business links to his native land and frequently returned. The son of a New Brunswick Presbyterian minister, Aitken by the age of thirty was a millionaire from amalgamating companies. After antagonizing much of the business community by practices considered sharp even by the casual standards of the Gilded Age, he moved to London in 1910. Quickly, he became an imperial protectionist Conservative MP; a knight in 1911 – and by close connection to Bonar Law (also the son of a New Brunswick manse) who became the leader of the party that same year – a backroom political force. At the end of 1916, he helped to push out

---

43 "Canada and the Empire," *The Times*, October 19, 1926.
44 Hillmer, *O. D. Skelton*, 151–8; Stacey, *Canada and the Age of Conflict*, II, 83–9; H. Blair Neatby, *William Lyon Mackenzie King*, II, 177–94.
45 Diary, January 25, 1928.

Asquith as prime minister and install Lloyd George. His reward was a peerage and the appointment for a few contentious months as minister of information. Losing political influence when Bonar Law was succeeded by Stanley Baldwin in 1923, Beaverbrook was principally known as a newspaper proprietor, the popular *Daily* and *Sunday Express* and the *Evening Standard* serving as megaphones for his ideas on empire and much else. It would be hard to imagine anyone more different from Mackenzie King than this buccaneering Conservative. But Beaverbrook rarely missed an opportunity to cultivate a major figure. In addition to entertainment at his country house, Beaverbrook commissioned the stylish Sir William Orpen, whom he had employed for a series of portraits of Canadian war commanders, to paint the Canadian prime minister in his Oxford doctoral gown. King hung the picture with pride in Laurier House.

Laying on the flattery, Beaverbrook told King that he was in the strongest position of any dominion prime minister and in his own country would rank with Laurier and Canada's first prime minister, Sir John A. Macdonald. He praised King's recent electoral triumph over money and a hostile press. He said that a cabinet minister, whom King surmised to be Churchill, had bet Beaverbrook that Canada's Conservatives would win a majority. Pouring his customary poison about Baldwin into King's ear, Beaverbrook pronounced that Churchill and Birkenhead were the best members of the government, albeit dangerous in some respects. Churchill had "an exemplary private life" (something of which Beaverbrook, whose neglected wife died a year later, was never accused); high public ideals if erratic discernment; and good judgement on political matters. Beaverbrook acknowledged that cunning was the secret of his own success and said that Churchill possessed the same.[46]

* * *

In the late 1920s, Mackenzie King was in Europe only once, in the summer of 1928 to attend the League of Nations and have a holiday in France and Italy. In Rome, he was impressed by Mussolini and his fine Napoleonic head, although that shaven dome was completely empty of knowledge about Canada and dominion status. Like most of his kind, King judged that Mussolini had united his country, and he approved of Italy's banning of communists, beggars,

---

46 Diary, October 24, 1926.

and harlots.[47] In Paris, King added his signature to the Kellogg-Briand Pact, a noble statement banning war that was acceptable to him since it contained no provision for enforcement. In Geneva, he urged the League to study the example of the excellent relations between Canada and the United States, and to be an organization for conciliation, not for deterring aggression by threats, arms, or economic sanctions. More than imperial centralization, he feared that collective security through the League would require Canada to act against whatever country was declared an aggressor by a majority of its assorted member nations.[48]

After his speech, King returned to France for a weekend at Aix-les-Bains where Stanley Baldwin (who never attended the League) and his wife spent their summer holidays. The British prime minister was resting in preparation for the 1929 election which he was confident of winning. He expressed the highest regard for the "most companionable" Churchill. Corroborating from a different perspective what Beaverbrook had told King two years earlier, Baldwin said that Churchill dropped in every day for a talk, "walking up & down with a cigar & water." He read King a letter from Churchill, who was on holiday at Chartwell, "building a cottage and dictating a book: 200 bricks and 2,000 words a day." The latter, a financial necessity, was *The Aftermath*, a sequel to *The World Crisis*.[49]

Nine months later, the British Conservatives were surprisingly defeated in a quiet election. Labour won the most seats and formed a second minority government with the consent of the still fragmented Liberals. Churchill lost his office, salary, and house but had prudently insured himself with literary contracts and advances, most notably for a biography of his ancestor, the first Duke of Marlborough. In August 1929, he returned to North America after almost thirty years, again to make money and have a holiday. He came with the aura of the "golden chancellor" who had returned Britain to the gold standard and restored prosperity. For three months, he and his brother Jack, accompanied by their two sons, travelled in a railway car provided by Charles Schwab, the chairman of Bethlehem Steel, which had built ships for Britain during the war. The Canadian Pacific Railway contributed a stenographer and attached Churchill's car to its trains. Both Schwab and the CPR probably expected Churchill to return to office and had a lively sense of favours to come. On the trip, he gave speeches, sold

47 Diary, September 25, 1928.
48 Stacey, *Canada and Conflict*, II, 97–103; Neatby, *Mackenzie King*, II, 264–5.
49 Churchill to Baldwin, September 2, 1928. Gilbert, *Winston S. Churchill*, V, 301.

books, wrote up his impressions for publication, and speculated in the booming stock market.[50]

In Ottawa, the Churchill family group stayed at Government House with Governor General Lord Willingdon, an old friend and a fellow Liberal MP to 1910. Mackenzie King grumbled that he was "very little in sympathy with the whole social side of Govt. House life whether in Ottawa or elsewhere. Its patronizing attitude shrivels me completely." He also protested that his summer at Kingsmere was "eaten into right & left by people from the old country,"[51] but he did not want to miss any important visitor, and certainly not Churchill for whom he sped up improvements at his country estate. During dinner at Government House, King was charmed by the eighteen-year-old Randolph Churchill, "a fine looking young fellow & most intelligent & clever," who was always uncharacteristically well behaved with King.[52] The next day Churchill and his party lunched at Kingsmere. King fretted about the rain and slow table service. Churchill was also out of sorts and King got "little aid from my guests in the matter of conversation," probably owing to the absence of alcohol. The two friends walked around the damp estate and Churchill was so impressed by the dams that King was building that he did the same at Chartwell.[53]

Churchill was a star attraction at a Canadian Club luncheon at the Chateau Laurier hotel the next day: a colourful politician at the centre of empire for close to three decades, a renowned author, a famous orator and, above all, at a time when Canadian commodity prices were falling, an apparent master of financial policy. During the meal, he told Mackenzie King that it was income from his books that supported his political career. Elaborating what he had said in 1926 about dictating, he said that he revised the draft up to six times, then had it set in type for further alterations. In his address, he urged removing the restrictions on the British fleet imposed by the 1922 Washington naval treaty and extending empire trade, both of which indicated his aim of wresting the leadership of the Conservative party from Baldwin who was besieged by imperialists.[54] Opposed to both a naval race and imperial tariffs, King, in thanking Churchill, allowed in

50 Lough, *No More Champagne*, 177–95.
51 Diary, August 12 and 17, 1929.
52 Diary, August 13, 1929.
53 Diary, August 14, 1929.
54 Schake, *Safe Passage*, 235–53; Christopher M. Bell, *Churchill and Sea Power* (Oxford: Oxford University Press, 2013), 95–9; 112–140; Paul Addison, *Churchill: The Unexpected Hero* (Oxford: Oxford University Press, [2005] 2006), 126–30.

cool tones that he had "not said anything that will be taken exception to by any party in this country." He added a veiled warning that "if his addresses throughout the remainder of his tour in Canada are as carefully worded there will surely be only thanks to him for them."[55] He then took the visitors to the parliament buildings, where Churchill sat in the prime minister's place in the House of Commons and at the cabinet table, no doubt dreaming of soon doing the same in London. That night, King wrote that he had found Churchill "exceedingly pleasant & companionable. A fine mind, a nice nature." No longer complaining about losing leisure, he had "really much enjoyed his visit and society."[56]

When the two next met, in Ottawa in March 1932, the stock market had wiped out Churchill's speculation. The crisis had spread to the whole world economy and was now reaching its nadir. The political fortunes of King and Churchill were also in decline, although in retrospect this was probably a blessing. Baldwin's leadership of the Conservative party was saved by an all-party National government under Ramsay MacDonald, struck in August 1931 to deal with the financial situation. The coalition won an enormous majority in November. There could be no place in it for the rebellious Churchill, who had broken with Baldwin at the beginning of the year, and Churchill might not have wanted to be involved with a ministry that introduced tariff protection and started down the road to Indian self-government. In Canada, the political repercussions of the economic depression were not so dramatic but King's government was defeated in the 1930 election by the Conservatives under R. B. Bennett, who promised to use tariff policy to blast open markets for Canadian exports. King, a Victorian liberal who believed that the economy would cure itself without help from government, consoled himself on being absolved from having to deal with almost intractable economic problems.[57]

In December 1931, Churchill set off on another American lecture tour in aid of his personal finances, this time declaring the need for the English-speaking peoples to stand against communism. Scarcely had he begun, when he was knocked down by a taxi in New York, leaving him unable to resume his performances until the end of January. Towards the end of his labours, he was invited by Simpson's, a Toronto carriage-trade department store, to speak at Maple Leaf Gardens, a new hockey arena, for the handsome sum of $2,500 (twice his usual fee). In the

55 Dilks, *The Great Dominion*, 62–6; (newspaper report of the speech).
56 Diary, August 15, 1929.
57 Thompson, *Canada 1922–1939*, 201–5.

gathering economic gloom, only 6,000 of 14,000 tickets were sold but it was a rousing imperial event. The chair was Arthur Meighen, the once and future Canadian Conservative leader. The military band accompanying Churchill into the hall played "Rule Britannia." Here Churchill argued that the best guarantee of world peace was a strong British empire in partnership with the United States. He criticized the Statute of Westminster for trying to define dominion freedom in musty legal language but claimed that he did not fear that the dominions would seek independence. The forces of unity would "drown the discordant cries and yells of our internal foes and weaklings." Churchill, the leader of a rump of eighty Conservative MPs engaged in a relentless yet futile battle against limited self-government for India, pronounced that what the subcontinent needed was "firmness and fairness." The watchwords of the next summer's Ottawa imperial economic conference, he said, should be: "the British Empire first, and last, and all the time." He suppressed his disdain for the National government sufficiently to proclaim: "The Mother Country has revived! She is gathering her children around her and, hand in hand with Canada, will lead the Empire and the world out of the gloom and panic and depression into the sunlight of prosperity."[58]

Churchill then left for Ottawa to spend the weekend with yet another governor general, Lord Bessborough, a distant relative. Prime Minister Bennett held a luncheon in Churchill's honour in the parliamentary restaurant for MPs of all parties. Expecting more imperial tub–thumping, King forwent the pleasure of Churchill's speech, which expressed his confidence that Canada would take the right lead, as it had in the war: "Canada is once again on the Vimy Ridge, holding a strategic position in the British Empire, and ready to do her part in conquering the economic problems which beset us."[59]

It was unthinkable by this stage in their relations that King and Churchill would not meet. The next day, King was invited to lunch at Government House. After Churchill's loud beating of the imperial drum, he went in trepidation. To his surprise, the occasion turned out to be "quite the most pleasant and profitable" since Bessborough's arrival a year earlier. When the governor general left for a sporting event, King and Churchill continued talking until 4:30 in the afternoon. Churchill confided his real views, which were very different from those expressed in public and close to King's own. He said that he was glad to be out

58 Dilks, *The Great Dominion*, 121–4.
59 "A Vimy for Canada, So Churchill Says of Empire Policy," *Globe and Mail*, March 5, 1932. There is a slightly different newspaper report in Dilks, *The Great Dominion*, 126.

of the National government. "He had had a row with Baldwin," King told his diary," and he "could not stand Ramsay [MacDonald], never could." Churchill had even considered sitting on the opposition front bench with the Liberals. As a privy councillor, he asserted the right (which most did not) to speak from the front bench. When no one else claimed it, he spoke from the seat immediately below the gangway on the government side. This became practically his reserved place, from which for the next seven years he denounced almost every issue faced by the ministry of which he was a nominal supporter. When King suggested leading a real (free trade) Liberal party, since that was his instinct, Churchill, who had no interest in such a quixotic enterprise, said that "he had inclined more to the right as he grew older." He did not mention it, but his real aim was to take over the dominant Conservative party.

For his part, King told Churchill that the forthcoming economic conference in Ottawa to discuss tariffs was a great mistake. The fewer the imperial meetings, the better, in his opinion. He predicted that all efforts at centralizing would fail: "a decentralized Empire was the only form it could take." Churchill also doubted that there would be much economic accomplishment at the conference, although he thought the National government would go to almost any lengths for results. The two agreed that fixed tariffs would never work. King added that for Canada, flexible tariffs were the only system that would not face US objection. He also pointed out that Bennett's Conservatives could not allow British industries to compete with Canadian ones. If Bennett betrayed Canadian manufacturers, the manufacturers and his party would throw him out. When Churchill asked if King would participate in the Ottawa conference, King said that Bennett's government had to take full responsibility and, in any event, Bennett would not cooperate with anyone, even his own colleagues. Churchill, as usual, praised King "in an exceedingly nice way, saying that they were "old & close friends, that in Britain I was held in high regard by the best people of the country." When King complained of being misrepresented in Britain, probably over his opposition to imperial unity and centralized authority, Churchill insisted that he was "regarded as an Empire statesman & many looked to [him]."[60]

Churchill asked King to let him know when he next came to England, which he did a year and a half later. He was in Europe for a two-month holiday in the autumn of 1934 before the final session of parliament and the 1935 election.

60 Diary, March 5, 1932.

By this time, R. B. Bennett's administration, like most democratic governments in the depths of the economic depression, was deeply unpopular, and King was full of expectation that he would return as prime minister. The 1932 Ottawa imperial economic conference, as King and Churchill had foreseen, produced no great result. Close to three hundred delegates from Britain, the dominions, India and Rhodesia (regarded as proto-dominions) engaged in heady rhetoric about common interests but much hard bargaining for national advantage. Every government claimed significant achievement and economic imperialists insisted that the foundation had been laid for imperial integration. But while trade within the empire did increase somewhat following the dozen bilateral treaties on specific products, there was no overall agreement or a common tariff. Preferential tariffs in fact made it harder to negotiate lower duties with outside countries, as Bennett discovered in 1933 when he began talking about mutual reductions with the United States.[61] Churchill dismissed the conference as "Rottawa" and King was of the same opinion.[62]

During his 1934 holiday, King spent three weeks in London before going to France and Italy. He went to art galleries, shopped, and visited old friends such as Violet Markham and Hamar Greenwood, now a viscount and treasurer of the Conservative party. He was pleased to hear that Ramsay MacDonald, Stanley Baldwin, and Lloyd George, were all critical of the bullying manner of R. B. Bennett, who had recently visited London, and praise for himself as well as assurances that he would be prime minister again after the election. On his last day in Britain, a Sunday, he was driven to Chartwell for lunch by Randolph Churchill, "quite a handsome & most attractive young fellow," who had left Oxford without a degree to become a journalist and, like his father, a lavish spender well beyond his means. Winston Churchill took his visitor around the house and grounds, both of which King described as "beautiful, most artistic." He admired the streams and the ponds modelled on his own at Kingsmere, the sloping contours of the land, the contrasting colours of the trees and the stone wall and the brick cottage that Churchill had built himself.

Honest with his opinions, as usual, Churchill optimistically said that the National government, which had recently lost a by-election to Labour, was breaking up. He held that all coalitions were bad, an opinion he would reverse in his

---

61 Thompson, *Canada 1922–1939*, 219–21 and 279.
62 Neatby, *Mackenzie King*, II, 18–27; John Barnes and David Nicolson, *The Empire at Bay: The Leo Amery Diaries 1929–1945* (London: Hutchinson, 1988), 384. (Diary entry, July 19, 1934).

greatest days. Dreaming of a backbench revolt like 1922, he thought that the National ministry would be replaced by a Conservative one in which he clearly expected office, even to be prime minister. India was very much on his mind with the impending introduction of the Government of India bill. King had no difficulty seeing that this was a crucial moment for Churchill, though the legislation would pass with overwhelming majorities, even among Conservatives. Churchill thought that Baldwin yearned to be prime minister once more, although the Conservatives wanted to keep MacDonald until the election (no later than 1936) to preserve semblance of coalition. King already knew from MacDonald himself that he was suffering from glaucoma and mental decline and could not last more than another session. When King told Baldwin that he would soon have to take over, Baldwin, who was content to prop up the pliable MacDonald, "said he did not want it, but would wait."[63]

Apart from India, Churchill's great fear was Germany, which he judged was preparing for war in two to five years. "Says army in control in Germany," King wrote in his diary, "they can get all the food they need, all they want etc., & certain to be a powerful tyranny." Churchill did not regard Italy as a threat.

As he did with others, King raised with Churchill the issue of Canada's next governor general, which was imminent since Lady Bessborough's dislike of Canadian winters had convinced her husband to leave before his term ended in 1936. Not recognizing the full implications of the Statute of Westminster, Churchill thought the replacement should be a member of an old, wealthy family or one of George V's sons. This was contrary to the desire of Mackenzie King, who wanted a different kind of figure now that the appointment was on the advice of the Canadian government. He argued that a prince would create a "false aristocracy in Canada – & possible difficulty with the Crown." When he raised his long-standing preference for John Buchan, Churchill belittled the Baldwinite MP as "insignificant etc."[64] In a rare concurrence with Bennett, King got his way, though George V insisted on Buchan becoming a peer before rather than at the end of his term, which he did not live to see. This and much greater differences between King and Churchill did not mar their connection or lower King's estimation of his colourful contemporary. Half a year later, though Churchill was vociferously denouncing the Government of India bill, King read

63 Diary, October 14, 1934.
64 Diary, October 26, 1934.

an account of his leaving the admiralty in 1915 and pronounced him "a truly remarkable man, [a] great genius."[65]

After returning to office in 1935, Mackenzie King followed British foreign policy throughout the crises of the late 1930s which had great implications for Canada. At the same time, he was developing a more personal and confidential relationship with Franklin Roosevelt than any Canadian prime minister had ever enjoyed with an American president. Winston Churchill, who now seemed to King one of the main threats to the peace of Europe, also wanted to bring the United States and Britain into close harmony. But it was King who was in a position to bring it about.

65 Diary, March 9, 1935.

CHAPTER TWO

King and the Brave Neighbour

IN OCTOBER 1935, MACKENZIE KING once again became prime minister of Canada, this time with the biggest majority of any previous government. R. B. Bennett had been unpopular, like many leaders in the depths of the Great Depression. Earlier that year, he had suddenly announced an ill-thought-out programme modelled on Franklin Roosevelt's New Deal and the British social welfare system. King did not oppose the legislation (which was overruled by the judicial committee of the British privy council, then Canada's last court of appeal, as beyond the powers of the federal government) but he denounced Bennett as a dictator like those in Europe. King's solution, similar to Churchill's when he thought about such matters, was the Victorian liberal one of reducing tariffs and otherwise leaving the economy to heal itself. This, combined with fear of Bennett's threat to wealth, drew the support of business from its customary Conservative allegiance to the Liberals. The owner of the *Financial Post* and the popular *Maclean's* magazine warned in a widely advertised slogan that the blunt choice was "King or Chaos."[1]

On November 8, two weeks after being re-installed as prime minister, King was invited by Franklin Roosevelt to dine and sleep at the White House. Both wanted a trade agreement between their countries as quickly as possible: King

---

1   Floyd Chalmers, *A Gentleman of the Press* (Toronto: Doubleday Canada, 1969), 285–90; Thompson, *Canada 1922–1939*, 261–6 and 273–6.

to show his efficiency in fulfilling his election promise, Roosevelt to put it in place and sweep it under the rug before the 1936 presidential election. With the American economy seemingly recovering in 1934, Congress passed an act enabling the president to reduce tariffs by up to fifty percent with countries which reciprocated although some parts of the United States would inevitably suffer from increased imports. Negotiations had begun with Bennett and Roosevelt was eager to conclude them with the more sympathetic and less difficult King, who agreed on the benefits of lower import duties but was appalled at the heavy state intervention of the New Deal, which he considered bad economics and worse morality.

King and Roosevelt might well have met over a similar issue of trade six years earlier. In the summer of 1929, six months after being narrowly elected for a two-year term as governor of his native New York, Roosevelt was looking for some advantage in the 1930 election over the Republicans who supported the protectionist Smoot-Hawley bill then in Congress. Knowing the Canadian alarm at the legislation, he tried to engage King in talks on Canadian-US problems. King, well aware that his imperialist opponents would charge him with being too pro-American, declined to discuss such contentious issues with a state governor.[2] He was nevertheless well disposed to the reforming Roosevelt, judging that his re-election in 1930 with an increased majority might lead to him becoming president as voters everywhere turned against incumbents.

When Roosevelt became the Democratic candidate in 1932, King commented on one of his campaign broadcasts: "He gives the impression of strength & integrity & spiritual purpose & power."[3] Since Herbert Hoover was defending protection, King believed and hoped that Roosevelt would be elected, as he was, sweeping the country and the Democratic party did the same in Congress.[4] In the four months before the new president took office on March 4, (inaugurations thereafter moving to January) the US economy fell even further. Most banks closed in a financial panic. As King said, Roosevelt entered the presidency "at the darkest hour, & with fire & lightening about him." King could only hope that "it will end in a great improvement of conditions during his term of office."[5] Even Roosevelt's installation was providential: if an assassination attempt two weeks

2   Diary, July 3, 1929.
3   Diary, September 17, 1932.
4   Diary, November 4, 1932.
5   Diary, March 4, 1932.

earlier in Miami had succeeded, it would have been the vice-president elect, John Nance Garner who became president.

In his inaugural address to the crowd of 400,000 outside the capitol and tens of millions of radio listeners, Roosevelt declared: "the only thing we have to fear is fear itself – nameless unreasoning, unjustified terror which paralyzes needed efforts to convert retreat into advance." He denounced the banks, promised to bridge the gap between hunger and the glut of food, raised hopes but also fear of authoritarianism by saying that if Congress did not act, he would demand increased power to fight the economic and social emergency "as great as the power that would be given me if we were in fact invaded by a foreign foe." Mackenzie King, reading the address, overlooked the dictatorial threat and pronounced that Roosevelt was off to a good start. The speech strongly reminded him of his own in parliament a week earlier: "the ideas in the main the same. With a little more preparation and chiselling I might have got something equally good – not quite as good – but nearly so."[6] This was sheer delusion. King had droned on for two hours, four times as long as Roosevelt. His mouth was parched and he had found it difficult to utter his words, although he was relieved that he had managed to articulate that Christianity alone could save the world. Afterwards, he spent eight hours, until 4:30 a.m., chopping and changing the official Hansard record of the speech to make it reflect what he would like to have delivered.[7]

King had not expected Roosevelt's rhetoric to be followed by a frenzy of action. In the first hundred days of the administration, executive orders poured forth and legislation raced through Congress to regulate banks and securities exchanges, farm production, finance and home mortgages; to provide relief and public works for the desperate; to increase the security of workers and unions; and to repeal prohibition on alcoholic drink, which increased federal revenue at the expense of American and Canadian bootleggers (and the colluding Canadian government). Within a couple of months, King was regarding Roosevelt as "a bit of a bounder like Bennett – not to be trusted. I am beginning to think that he is & has become a little of a demagogue."[8] At a Liberal party conference in September 1933 to prepare for the next election, King flatly opposed a programme of government intervention in the spirit of the New Deal and even the more modest New Liberalism of Churchill and others in Britain before the First

6   Diary, March 6, 1933.
7   Diary, February 27, 1933.
8   Diary, May 7, 1933.

World War. Looking across the border he "dreaded the thought of what may come out of the U.S. experiment."[9]

That autumn in New York one of King's friends, Edward R. Hewitt, a rich automobile engine inventor, advised King in terms of doom to move his American securities from a Boston bank to Canada, wishing that he could transfer his own there and to Britain. Hewitt declared Roosevelt "'crazy', that he has gone mad, and that revolution is inevitable in the United States." He denounced the National Recovery Administration (NRA) which imposed maximum hours of work, minimum wages, banned child labour, encouraged collective bargaining and other horrors, as "frightful, certain to fail, an unwarranted interference with personal liberty and property." Hewitt thought Roosevelt was a dictator and was happy that King concurred that opinion was turning rapidly against the administration.[10] A few weeks later, King was heartened by the resignation of the treasury under-secretary, Dean Gooderham Acheson (whose mother was Canadian) in protest against currency inflation. King judged the president's reckless demagoguery as bad as the German Nazi leader's: "The action of his govt. & Hitler's etc. is equivalent to throwing overboard all intelligent direction of affairs, treating scientific knowledge with contempt, & handing over Govt. to the half-baked & half-educated. It may lead to anything."[11] But however much King disliked specific actions of the New Deal, particularly fixing wages and prices in response to what he considered a spurious claim of emergency, he believed that the general principles could have been taken directly from his own book, the comprehensive and infinitely flexible *Industry and Humanity* (1918) where, as he alone saw, they were expressed "as clearly as they can be stated."[12]

Winston Churchill was just as apprehensive as Mackenzie King about Roosevelt and greatly concerned about the effect on the US ability to support Britain internationally. In 1934 he wrote a careful article which began by praising Roosevelt as one of the greatest leaders of a country whose fortunes affected the whole world. He lauded his refusal to allow paralysis of the legs to deter him

9   Diary, September 5, 1933; Levine, *King*, 214–16.
10 Diary, October 29, 1933.
11 Diary, November 22, 1933.
12 Diary, November 24, 1933. The book, based on King's experience as an industrial conciliator and British New Liberalism before World War I, is a call to reduce class conflict by creating harmony between capital, management, workers and the community. Its high-minded but very general, even mystical terms could be used to justify almost any social reforms.

from public service and his "generous sympathy for the underdog, his intense desire for a nearer approach to social justice." Churchill was predictably pleased about the repeal of prohibition, which had been a considerable inconvenience during his visits. With the authority of a former chancellor of the exchequer, he also approved the expansion of financial credit. But he feared that the New Deal might destroy the country and its effectiveness in the world. He claimed to understand the anger of ordinary Americans against financiers but argued that capitalism must be given a fair chance, meaning leave the economy alone. Precipitously handing great power to trade unions and over-taxing the rich raised the spectre that business confidence would collapse, unemployment increase, and only public works would remain. Like King, Churchill pronounced Roosevelt a dictator "veiled by constitutional forms," though he hastened to add that comparing him to Hitler "is to insult not Roosevelt but civilization." He hoped that the American president would not be pushed aside by more radical forces and would succeed in providing a better life for people everywhere, eclipsing "both the lurid flames of German Nordic national self–assertion and the baleful unnatural lights which are diffused from Soviet Russia." The essay was republished unaltered in a collection of essays on Churchill's contemporaries in September 1937,[13] but during the war, the chapter on Roosevelt would tactfully be omitted.

Mackenzie King was saved from alignment with rock-ribbed Republicans by the defection from Roosevelt's ranks in November 1933 of Al Smith, a libertarian Democrat whose outlook was similar to King's. Smith had been Roosevelt's predecessor and supposed mentor as governor of New York. In 1928, Roosevelt had nominated Smith as the Democratic presidential candidate. But Smith became a critic of Roosevelt's activism in New York state, and in 1932, a rival for the presidential nomination. He came to terms with losing and campaigned for Roosevelt but soon broke with him and joined other opponents who charged the president with stifling individualism and antagonizing business interests when he should have been co–operating with them. King approved of Smith's denunciation of "all the mushy kind of thing the Administration is doing – acting on hunches – exchanging experience for experimentation – half baked professors etc. etc. It is a magnificent statement and I am wholly in sympathy with it, it may help to save the day for the U.S."[14]

13   Winston Churchill, "Roosevelt from Afar," *Great Contemporaries* (London: Thornton Butterworth, revised edition, [1937] 1938), 371–82.
14   Diary, November 25, 1933.

A couple of months later, King elaborated on his criticism of Roosevelt for "raising of prices artificially, thro inflation," particularly by paying farmers to take land out of production: "encouraging scarcity, or substituting scarcity for plenty as a part of government policy seems to me not only folly but blasphemy."[15] When the president's mother came to Ottawa for the wedding of the American minister's step-daughter, however, King did not miss the chance to meet "a woman of real character . . . a true and good nature." He smoothly praised the example and influence of her son outside of the United States.[16] But this did not indicate any real change of attitude. Anxious as King was to conclude a trade agreement in 1935, he disapproved of the president acting by executive order instead of risking Senate rejection of a treaty.

With these mixed feelings about Roosevelt, King set out by train from Ottawa on November 6, in high hopes of being able to announce a pact on November 11, the seventeenth anniversary of the end of the First World War. Hedging against failure, he announced merely that he was going to pay a personal call on the president. First he first met the secretary of state, Cordell Hull, who was if anything even more convinced than King that freer trade was the solution to most of the world's problems. It was an instantaneous meeting of souls and the beginning of a firm friendship. King pronounced Hull not only sound on economics but also on "the need to get back to higher standards in public and private life, if the world was not very seriously to retrograde." King pointed out the complementarity of Canada's primary and agricultural products and US manufactures and Hull pleasingly agreed that Roosevelt would also welcome an announcement on Armistice Day. During lunch at the Canadian legation, King repaid this welcome by instructing Hull and other US cabinet colleagues on the error of trying to regulate the economy artificially through the National Recovery Administration. He recommended instead a social system that "favoured self reliance rather than reliance on the State." His audience politely did not respond.

Roosevelt provided a car and a police escort for King, who dispensed with the latter. At the White House he treated King like a family guest. They first had tea with Eleanor Roosevelt, with whom King immediately established a firm relationship. Unfortunately, and very unusually, King recorded nothing about the Roosevelts' appearance, not even mentioning the wheelchair in which Franklin got around to chairs and couches. The president recalled their meeting

15 Diary, January 18, 1934.
16 Diary, February 10, 1934.

at Harvard in 1923, when he was on the board of overseers and King received an honorary doctorate; but King had no memory of Roosevelt on the occasion. The president also talked about his Canadian summer home at Campobello Island and of Lord Tweedsmuir, "a real friend of America" (whom he had met in New York in 1934), whose invitation to Canada he was eager to accept. After tea, King declined to join the president in his customary swim, preferring his own customary sleep. He was flattered to be shown by Eleanor to the Lincoln bedroom, which that president had used as an office and cabinet room and in which he signed the 1863 slave emancipation proclamation. She warned King not to be surprised if the Roosevelt's youngest son John, at home from Harvard and staying in the next room, turned up for a shower, which he did while the prime minister was dressing.

Dinner at the White House for a group of Canadians and Americans was an impressive occasion. King sat between Eleanor Roosevelt and John Gilbert Winant, a Republican friend of the president who had been a reforming governor of New Hampshire for an unprecedented three terms and was now head of the social security board; in 1941 he would become ambassador to Britain. King conversed happily with Eleanor about settlement houses, where in her New York youth she had taught dancing and physical exercise. Roosevelt in his toast to George V mentioned "having an old personal friend here," although they had only just met, "who comes from a neighbouring friendly country." King was almost overcome by this toast, made in the United States, a country lost by another King George (III) to an American George (Washington), and made in the presence of the grandson of the leader of another "revolution" for political freedom from Britain who was now prime minister of Canada. After dinner Eleanor Roosevelt took the other guests to see the new movie *Mutiny on the Bounty* while King and Hull went to the president's study to discuss the trade agreement. This time King noted that Roosevelt was helped onto the sofa by an attendant: "Both his lower limbs are between steel supports. He manages pretty well with a cane, but it is with the greatest difficulty that he gets up and down."

The president and the prime minister were well briefed on the trade plan which involved the United States importing more Canadian primary products in return for Canada granting "most favoured nation" tariffs (meaning no country lower) on American manufactures. Roosevelt mentioned his problem with agricultural interests – which meant almost half of the population, most of whom needed government aid – as well as the problem of the 1936 elections. King seized the opportunity to try to rescue the president from his policy mistakes. He said that the New Deal had fulfilled its expedient purpose in the 1932 election;

Roosevelt "would not be able indefinitely, either by legislation or use of the pub-lic treasury, to keep up wages and prices by artificial means;" and must now tell the people that "they would now have to find for themselves the means of maintaining the standards which he had raised." This King believed would be accomplished by increasing trade.

Roosevelt, like the cabinet ministers at lunch, did not reply to this advice but stuck to the main point, saying that he looked forward to announcing the trade agreement in his Armistice Day speech at Arlington National Cemetery. Showing North American leadership in the arts of peace through trade, he said, would be "a great stroke." King interposed that he always consulted his cabinet on these matters but he would hold a meeting that morning and confirm acceptance in time for the ceremony. After an hour, the president concluded the topic by airily saying: "The details can be worked out once the main decision has been made." The two then commiserated about the volume of their correspondence and the opposition of most of the press. Roosevelt said he received an average of four thousand letters a day and told King that radio (the use of which he had pioneered as governor of New York) was a powerful counterforce to newspapers. His request to King to help with relations with Britain fulfilled the Canadian prime minister's dreams.

After the movie, Eleanor Roosevelt came to tell her husband how much he would have enjoyed the naval drama. She also thought he should go to bed but added to King that he never took this advice. Three quarters of an hour later, Roosevelt wound up the conversation by saying that he would show King around the house in the morning. He always had breakfast in bed but King looked for-ward to sharing his with Eleanor. As they parted, Roosevelt told his now firm friend: "it was just great to be able to pick up the telephone and talk to each other in just a few minutes. We must do that whenever occasion arises. I will always be glad to hear from you."[17]

In the morning, Eleanor Roosevelt appeared in a riding habit since she and her son were going out on horseback. When King produced a picture of his mother, Eleanor needed no prompting to comment on her "lovely features and beautiful face." She was summoned to the telephone to talk to her mother-in-law who wanted to discuss going to Warm Springs, Georgia with her son. King overheard Eleanor call her "mummy" and could not detect any tension between them. When Eleanor returned to the table she guardedly told King that the

17 Diary, November 8, 1935.

president's mother "did not like people being around in numbers when she was with her son, she liked to have him to herself, which was natural, though impossible in his position." King understood perfectly. The two agreeably discussed social problems, peace, the danger of an arms race and the League of Nations, for which Eleanor had more enthusiasm than King. She said that she had seen the president before he went to sleep the night before and he had been much pleased with the after-dinner talk. Following Roosevelt's encouraging words, King observed that the trade agreement would enable a stronger Canada to have better relations with both the United States and Britain: "The best way for us to help England was to set up Canada."

On their tour of the White House, the president took particular pride in showing King the pool that had been built for him in the former servants' quarters between the west wing and the residence by a national fundraising campaign from schoolchildren.[18] As well as his daily swim, Roosevelt said he also had an alcohol rub and massage there before going to bed. They also went into the room where he met the press (twice a week), "mentioning that he did not like giving out written statements, but felt more at home speaking off the bat, as it were." What he meant was not firmly committing himself. King presented Roosevelt with a revised edition of *Industry and Humanity*, which he inscribed before leaving the house. The president suavely said he already knew the book and had the original publication. This King took to "imply that he and others of his staff had read it in connection with the N.R.A. policies," much as King disagreed with their implementation. As they parted, the president affably hoped that King would come again: "we are speaking the same language which makes it very pleasant to talk together."

While Canadian and US officials toiled on the wording of the agreement, King went to a large luncheon at the legation which included several members of the state department. Cordell Hull sat beside King and when he had to leave for a cabinet meeting his place was taken by Dean Acheson. Once again a prominent Washington lawyer, Acheson was probably included because he was almost Canadian, though in appearance he seemed more British (the birthplace of his father, who was an Episcopalian Bishop). The two pleasantly dissected the shortcomings of the NRA. King then went to Arlington National Cemetery

---

18 William Seale, *The White House: The History of an American Idea* (Washington: The American Institute of Architects Press, 1992), 218–20.

to lay wreaths on the memorial to Americans who had died serving in the Canadian army and the unknown soldier, made some social calls and returned to the legation to find two state department officials wanting to insert a clause in the agreement that the United States would not lose any tariff advantage by imperial preferences. King refused, insisting that "so far as the British Empire was concerned, it was for us to manage our affairs our way; we must, as against foreign nations, be regarded as one family, free to do as we pleased." Apart from his own strong feelings about the Commonwealth connection, he knew that conceding the American demand would enable his opponents to charge "that I had arranged matters so that, not only the Canadian tariff but that the British tariff was being made in Washington." As it was, "I was taking enough risk in coming over to negotiate at all."

That night there was a large dinner at the home of Hull's under-secretary, Roosevelt's rich and sociable friend William A. Phillips, who had been the first US minister to Canada (1927–1929). Among the guests were Woodrow Wilson's widow and Frances Perkins, the secretary of labour and only woman in the cabinet. At 10:30 a.m., the party broke up for King to go to Cordell Hull's apartment hotel to initial the draft trade agreement. Hull was annoyed that the treasury secretary, Henry Morgenthau Jr., objected to losing revenue by concessions on whisky imports just as US production was reviving following the end of prohibition. King and Hull initialled the document, subject to Morgenthau's agreement within thirty-six hours; by then, Roosevelt had persuaded Morgenthau to give way on Canadian whisky that had been aged for at least four years (before the repeal of prohibition) and the restart of US production. King left for Ottawa greatly pleased by the implicit understanding on trade and the personal attention from the president, the secretary of state, and many others.[19]

At home, the ministers of finance and trade and commerce were concerned about the whisky restriction but assured King that the cabinet would accept the arrangement, as it did the following morning, November 11, when King was informed of Morgenthau's capitulation.[20] He telephoned the president who was putting on his wing collar and top hat for the Arlington speech, in which he now could proclaim "another act cementing our historic friendship." Roosevelt said that his cabinet (whose members were advisory rather than having their own

19 Diary, November 9, 1935.
20 Diary, November 10, 1935.

political base as in the parliamentary system) had also agreed. He added: "'we will get through alright', meaning the threat to the Democratic party in the 1936 election." At the Canadian Armistice Day ceremony later in the morning, King told the governor general about the trade agreement and Tweedsmuir said that it was "what the world most needed, having a fine effect on conditions in Europe." King could not help gloating that R. B. Bennett, the leader of the opposition, looked "extremely tired and worn. I could not but feel that today's announcement would be a terrible blow to him." As he gazed over the crowd, he reflected on the benefits of the treaty for those "most in need of employment or of more adequate subsistence at less cost. I kept feeling that the agreement was a worthy memorial to the men whose lives had been sacrificed in the war, which it was hoped would mean better conditions in the world."[21]

Three days later, King was back in his railway car for another overnight journey to sign the final agreement before proceeding on a two-week holiday at Sea Island, Georgia with his under-secretary, O. D. Skelton. As the train left New York for Washington, he learned that Eleanor Roosevelt was in the parlour car and went to see her. She was knitting and had a bag of papers beside her, both of them to help deter interruptions. King felt a deepening respect for her earnestness and concern for ordinary people. She told King that the president was worried about opposition to the trade arrangement. At Union Station, Washington they parted since King was stopping first at the legation.

When he arrived at the White House, Roosevelt introduced King to the cabinet. Then about sixty reporters entered the room to witness King and Hull sign the three-year agreement. Roosevelt sat alongside while cabinet members and Canadian diplomats stood behind. A cable from the dominions secretary in London covered legal niceties from the sovereign (despite the Statute of Westminster) assigning plenipotentiary power to the Canadian prime minister. At the end of the brief ceremony, the three principal figures addressed the reporters.[22] King was proud that the matter had been arranged independently of the British government, though he did visit the ambassador, Sir Ronald Lindsay, to assure him that Canada had safeguarded the 1932 Ottawa agreements with Britain. Tartly he added: "we might have made a much better trade if they had not stood in the way." He also told Lindsay (whose present and late

---

21 Diary, November 11, 1935.
22 Diary, November 15, 1935.

wife were Americans and who had exceptionally good rapport with Roosevelt) what the president had said about Canada being an interpreter between the United States and Britain, and Lindsay agreeably concurred that that was the country's role.

King was just as aware of the risks of the trade agreement in Canada as Roosevelt was in the United States. He remembered all too well the Liberal party (and himself) coming to grief on a similar proposal in 1911. But this time the government was at the very beginning of its term, had promised a pact in the election, and the Conservatives had already started on it. Primary producers and consumers across the country saw the benefit while manufacturers complained, but the most that R. B. Bennett could charge was that King had been too hasty and that the concessions were greater than he would have made. The improvement in the Canadian economy, as King had foretold, did increase British investment and thus also benefitted that country.[23] In the United States there was great antagonism from the agricultural sector, despite the strict quotas on goods from Canada. In the 1936 election campaign, Republicans pledged to cancel the agreement but they were overwhelmingly defeated.

Mackenzie King was pleased that the trade agreement permitted him to establish a strong personal bond with Franklin Roosevelt. Although they met only over a few days, he was instantly on the same terms with the president as with Stanley Baldwin whom he had known for over a decade. He was, as he saw it, well placed to help bring Britain and the United States together. This rapport did not alter King's opinion of the New Deal, but it remarkably improved his opinion of Roosevelt. As he listened to the broadcast of the president's annual state of the union address to Congress at the beginning of 1936, he no longer regarded Roosevelt as a potential dictator but "a brave man . . . with his voice the nation will believe a sincere and a good man, determined to help his day and generation." His fear now was that the president would be assassinated since the hatred of the "monied interests and organized greed will be great." The mention of the trade agreement, as well as the announcement of a "good neighbour" policy towards Latin America, in Roosevelt's address led King to consider as evidence of "the New World redressing the balance of the Old." Once again,

---

23 John Herd Thompson and Stephen J. Randall, *Canada and the United States: Ambivalent Allies.* Fourth edition (Montreal: McGill-Queen's University Press, [1994] 2008), 137–8; Hillmer, *O. D. Skelton*, 228–33; Stacey, *Canada and Conflict*, II, 172–7; Richard N. Kottman, *Reciprocity and the North American Triangle 1932–1938* (Ithaca: Cornell University Press, 1968), 79–116.

he claimed that Roosevelt's pronouncement was practically identical to his own election campaign: "it was all Liberal doctrine."[24]

* * *

At the end of July 1936, Franklin Roosevelt made his promised visit to Canada, stopping for eight hours at the walled city of Quebec, on a rock high above the St. Lawrence river, on his way home by train from Campobello Island. The governor general's summer residence, the fortified citadel, stood beside the city wall. Begun under the French regime, it was completed by the British in its present form, as a stronghold against the Americans after the war of 1812. King arrived the day before Roosevelt and did not fail to insist to everyone (despite Tweedsmuir's invitation) that this first state visit by a US president was the result of his own initiative on the trade agreement. At 9:30 on a beautiful sunny morning, he and the governor general met the president's train with its huge security detail in the lower town. Roosevelt was brown from the sun but King thought tired, like one who had been through "a bit of brutal battering." Then Roosevelt's face broke into his famous smile "and the dark or sombre expression was lost in the radiant one." King was touched at how well Roosevelt managed to move around with the help of his twenty-eight-year-old son James: "I think the President is reaching people more thro' his infirmity, his strength of will, and with family scenes, than in any other way." Following a military display and the playing of the American national anthem, the motorcade travelled to the Chateau Frontenac hotel. At its entrance, Tweedsmuir, King, Roosevelt and others gave speeches that were broadcast across Canada, the United States, the British Empire and parts of Europe. Some spoke in French, the president getting a particularly warm reception for his remarks in that language (which he had been taught, along with German, by his governesses). His message was that different "races" living in harmony was a worthy memorial to those who had lost their lives in early Canadian conflicts. As King looked out at the people in their colourful summer dress, he was struck by the contrast with Europe where the Spanish Civil War had just begun: "the fear & hate there, & the confidence and good will here."

Before luncheon at the Citadelle, King, Roosevelt and the governor general talked privately for an hour. Tweedsmuir, a writer of history as well as fiction and

24 Diary, January 3, 1936.

well-versed in the classics as all well-educated Britons were at the time, thought that the world was facing a new dark age like that following the fall of the Roman empire in the west. He advised the president to invite the countries of the world to the United States "to discuss how we could save what we have of civilization." Roosevelt was all in favour but in light of American isolationism a meeting could not be held until after that year's election; even then it could not be in the United States but would best be held in the mid-Atlantic, perhaps the Azores. He was willing to invite Hitler, Mussolini, the British, the French and the Soviets, but not the Japanese whom he regarded as the real danger to the United States. This was the origin of the international conference he proposed, and Churchill claimed was a great missed opportunity, at the time of Anthony Eden's resignation in February in 1938. King, for his part, mused that in talking only about government leaders, Tweedsmuir and Roosevelt were thinking like dictators: "They are not the people, & the people won't be ruled by heads." His own contribution to the conversation was to alter the nature of the proposed summit meeting to a non-binding investigation into international problems by representatives of the various countries. He also thought that the initiative should come from others rather than the US president to avoid political difficulties. Roosevelt seemed well-disposed to these refinements. He also told Tweedsmuir that he and King had taken their political lives in their hands on the trade agreement but it was already working to the benefit of both countries.

Roosevelt told King and Tweedsmuir that he expected to win re-election in November. He cited as a particular menace the enormously popular Catholic "radio priest" Charles Coughlin, originally from Hamilton, Ontario. In 1932 Coughlin had been a solid supporter of Roosevelt and the New Deal, but now he was practically a fascist as well as an anti-Semite. Denouncing government favouritism to bankers, he demanded trade protection for labour and the nationalization of industry. He was curbed by the Vatican but not completely silenced until October 1939 when the government banned him from the air. King also knew from his wealthy American friends that monied interests were also powerfully opposed to the president and "spreading the most frightful lies about him." If Roosevelt was assassinated, it would mean class war, like Spain. King now conceded that the president's policies might have helped to prevent such a clash but still believed that he would have been more effective if his economic and social policies had not gone so far.

In the afternoon, the president showed himself to the public by driving with the governor general through crowd-lined streets. King walked with Marvin

McIntyre, one of Roosevelt's secretaries, on the Plains of Abraham where the British had defeated the French in 1759. They returned in a tourist caleche but to King's disappointment there was no photographer to record it. Perhaps prompted by King, McIntyre talked about the president's method of preparing speeches, saying that he got ideas from various people but put them together himself. King thought this very like his own method (in fact, his speeches were usually first drafted by others), although he characteristically grumbled that the president had "an infinitely better organization." He also recognized that Roosevelt was less compulsive about details than himself and had "an infinitely better capacity to delegate work & take off time from work completely." The president's visit concluded with tea, after which he urged King to come to see him again, perhaps at Hyde Park: "It was clear he was as friendly as he could possibly be."[25] Roosevelt retained a good impression of the Citadelle on that summer day and remembered it during the war as a good place for a confidential meeting.

Roosevelt, as he predicted, won the election of 1936, sweeping every state save the two that were most affected by the tariff deal, Maine and Vermont. The old adage, "As Maine goes, so goes the nation" was amended to, "As Maine goes, so goes Vermont." Convinced by their meeting that he knew Roosevelt's mind, Mackenzie King was soon invoking the president's authority to reinforce his own bid to end the League of Nations' sanctions against Italy and to effectively kill the League as a means of collective security.

* * *

After a year of noisy public preparation, Mussolini had launched an attack on Ethiopia (then known as Abyssinia) in 1935. In Britain, this stirred a moment of high enthusiasm for the League of Nations to stop aggression, albeit preferably by means short of war. Over eleven million voters participated in the Peace Ballot (really a public opinion poll) to impress this on the government. Baldwin, who had just replaced MacDonald as prime minister, adroitly appointed to the new post of the minister of League of Nations affairs the glamorous thirty-eight-year-old Anthony Eden who seemed to embody its ideals. The British Foreign Secretary, Sir Samuel Hoare, warned Italy at the League that Britain stood for collective security against aggression. France also threatened economic sanctions against

25 Diary, July 31, 1936.

Italy, and Canada, from some combination of R. B. Bennett's belligerence and eagerness to demonstrate that he was standing loyal to imperial Britain, had gone even further in calling for restrictions on Italy. King, on succeeding Bennett, regarded the Ethiopian situation as being like Chanak and saw no cause for Canada to risk being dragged into an obscure, far-away war.

Soon after the war began, Baldwin called an election with support for the League and sanctions as the main issue. The implication was that Britain would support Ethiopia. Conservatives, although disliking the international organization and seeing no reason to alienate Italy, particularly in fighting a primitive, slave-holding country like Ethiopia, had to acquiesce. Churchill, caught in the contradiction of wanting collective security against Germany and Italy, as well as hoping for office, could only argue for some compromise. After Baldwin was returned with a large majority, his Foreign Secretary, Sir Samuel Hoare, surprised his countrymen by making a deal with France to end the fighting by conceding most of Ethiopia to Italy and giving it economic hegemony over the rest. There was a great uproar in the British parliament, including from some of the ministry's backbenchers, over what appeared an enormous capitulation to Mussolini and a betrayal of Ethiopia. Baldwin was forced to repudiate the pact and replace Hoare with Eden, the very symbol of the League.[26] Mussolini proceeded with his conquest of Ethiopia. The League of Nations imposed sanctions which were ineffectual and only enhanced Mussolini's popularity at home. Hitler took advantage of this distraction to engage in what seemed the lesser larceny of seizing the Rhineland. As an association for resistance against aggression, the League was finished.

Mackenzie King was even more eager to retreat from the Ethiopian situation than were the British. He was greatly relieved at the end of League sanctions in the summer of 1936 and in September lectured that body against collective security and automatic commitments to action. He urged concentrating on negotiation and conciliation. In any event, Canadian obligations would be decided in Ottawa.[27] When asked at Geneva about the chances of the Americans joining the League, King claimed that if the provisions for sanctions were removed from its covenant, many in the United States would be more favourably disposed and Roosevelt might be persuaded to join after the forthcoming election. He

---

26 Thompson, *The Anti-Appeasers*, 66–101.
27 Thompson, *Canada 1922–1939*, 308–13; Hillmer, *O. D. Skelton*, 226–7, 234–6, 240–9; Stacey, *Canada and Conflict*, II, 179–90.

also disclosed the president's proposal of an international conference, adding his own caution against proceeding like an absolute ruler but pointing out that any American move would be a helpful beginning.[28] Anthony Eden questioned Roosevelt's sincerity, given his habit of appearing to agree with everyone. King, with his new intimate knowledge of the president, assured the British foreign secretary that Roosevelt wanted to preserve world peace and serve the people. Eden agreed with King that a conference would not accomplish anything unless matters were largely settled in advance but said he would certainly welcome American participation. When he suggested starting with the economy, King was quick to encourage a trade agreement between Britain and the United States, similar to the one with Canada.[29]

On his way home from the obsequies for the League and collective security, King stopped in London for two weeks. British ministers were as anxious as he to stay out of another war. But a more pressing problem was Edward VIII, who had succeeded his father in January and was shocking respectable society by rarely attending the state church the monarchy was obliged to defend. He also associated with workers far more than was considered suitable to his dignity and, worst of all, was having an affair with a married American woman who was about to divorce her second husband. This was not mentioned on BBC radio, a state-controlled organisation, and newspaper owners voluntarily excluded any mention of the affair beyond the simple statement of those attending royal social engagements. American publications were censored by British distributors. The US press and radio, on the other hand, were full of the news and fevered speculation that an American might become the British queen. These reports were closely followed in Canada where the moralism of Protestantism and Catholicism were on common ground. King fully shared the disapproval and the anxiety that Edward was bringing the monarchy into peril but he refused to be the cat's paw for British politicians in raising the matter with the king.

On October 21, King was seated beside Churchill at "an old Roman banquet" at the London house of the immensely rich gold and diamond "Randlord," Sir Abe (Abraham) Bailey, a protégé of Cecil Rhodes who now divided his political, business and cultural interests between Britain and South Africa. He had been a friend of Churchill's since the Boer war and was one of his financial benefactors.

28 Diary, September 24, 1936.
29 Diary, September 30, 1936.

For two years, from the end of 1932, Bailey's eldest son John had been married to the Churchills' eldest daughter, Diana, who was now the wife of Conservative MP Duncan Sandys. The guest of honour was the only slightly less wealthy Robert Bingham, a Kentucky newspaper owner who had been rewarded for supporting Roosevelt by appointment as ambassador to Britain in 1933. Like Churchill, Bingham was a believer in strong ties between the United States and Britain and an opponent of Nazism and fascism. He told King that Roosevelt had said that he had enjoyed their two days together the previous year "more than any he had for some little time."[30] At Bailey's house a flock of servants stood at the entrance and the dinner table was festooned with gold and silver serving dishes and similar ornaments. King noticed many people to whom he had paid attention in Canada and complained that they did not reciprocate, being "pretty much wrapped up in their own doings and concerns." They were content to regard Canada merely as "a sort of happy hunting ground . . . money, power and position is what most of them are after." A lot of those present were "able and brilliant men" but he considered that the occasion "represented as well, much of privilege, a great deal of complacency and self-satisfaction."

King described Churchill, as many did in the years before the Second World War, as being "rather heavy and fat in appearance," though his eyes "were very clear and his mind, very active." Working to build a wide-ranging domestic and international alliance for "Arms and the Covenant" (of the League of Nations), Churchill had even toned down his anti-communism in the hope of enlisting the Soviet Union. Though he was not concerned about Ethiopia and anxious not to alienate Italy, he was alarmed at the recent blow to the League and collective security that King had helped to deliver. Never, he told King, had Britain been "more contented and never in more danger." Inside of five years, he projected, "it was possible that she might be a vassal state of Germany." He wondered at Germany's spending on arms and concluded that "while she might have no real desire of aggression, she might be driven into war despite herself. All the time there was the tramp, tramp, tramp toward war." Like a great ship close to rocks, Germany "would swing from side to side and try to hold back but was driving onto the reef." Britain, meanwhile, was arming too slowly and was unprepared for the threat: "Her fortunes vis-a-vis Europe were lower than they had ever been. She was down, down, down relatively in the matter of her prestige. She was

---

30 Diary, October 28, 1936.

drifting terribly. It was all drift, drift, drift." The salvation of Britain was France. Churchill had seen the Maginot line, begun in 1930 and being hastily completed by France following the reoccupation of the Rhineland, and had no anxiety that that country would succumb, even with a socialist government supported by the communists.

When King asked Churchill's opinion about the civil war in Spain, he received no clear response. The latest in a seemingly endless series of revolts going back to 1808, it had begun in July with a nationalist military insurrection of monarchists and fascists against a popular-front republican government that included communists. Already it was becoming a proxy battlefield as Italy and Germany backed the nationalists and the Soviet Union the republicans. All of Churchill's instincts lay with the nationalists (who were monarchical) but he did not want to estrange the USSR. The best hope, he told King, was that the nationalists would win and be strong in their isolationist attitude against joining Germany. Britain and France should stay out and supply humanitarian aid. The conflict would rage into 1939 with both sides becoming more entrenched. By then, without changing his sympathies, Churchill considered that there was less to fear from the republicans than the friends of the victorious fascists. The nationalist dictator, Francisco Franco, would not join Britain in the war but nor did he become a real ally of Germany.

At the end of their conversation Churchill despairingly told King, who was similarly close to sixty-two, that he was "getting on in years but would not last long. It might not matter so much to him, he had done the best he could to save the situation but be believed it was coming."[31] King, in contrast, continued to be confident that international problems could be solved by diplomacy and conciliation – what was described at the time by the term "appeasement" – but the conversation with Churchill may have helped him to hedge his calculation about a possible European war.[32] He never questioned that Canada would defend Britain if it came to that, and Canada might even have to protect itself.[33]

Sailing home, King heard the news of Roosevelt's overwhelming re-election after a fierce campaign and over the opposition of most of the press and the plutocrats. The Democrat majorities in both Houses of Congress also increased. King was relieved that the Canadian trade agreement, as well as his connection

31 Diary, October 21, 1936.
32 There is a discussion of the varieties of appeasement and the term's fall from grace in Thompson, *The Anti-Appeasers*, 27–42.
33 Stacey, *Canada and Conflict*, II, 200–1.

to the White House, was secure. Dreading the possibility of a war between Nazi Germany and the communist USSR before the end of the decade, he considered Roosevelt to be in a good position to break down world trade barriers that would "go far towards preserving peace or at all events helping to maintain it among the democratic nations." Immediately he cabled congratulations to "my good friend and good neighbour" Roosevelt, to Cordell Hull and the US minister in Ottawa.[34]

In the spring of 1937, Mackenzie King and the governor general separately returned Roosevelt's official visit to Quebec. King went at the beginning of March as part of a two-week escape from parliament. Tweedsmuir followed more formally at the end of the month. He was the first governor general and first Briton to address Congress, which he did by delivering similar remarks in each chamber. King began his visit by discussing the gloomy situation and escalation of arms in Europe with Cordell Hull. The secretary of state believed that war was inevitable unless there was some improvement, a couple of times showing the strength of his feeling by exclaiming "Christ Almighty." When King asked about the prospect of the United States joining the League if sanctions were eliminated, Hull cautiously responded that it depended on a change in attitude on such matters as currency and disarmament but he conceded that it might be possible if the organization was given a different name and the way was prepared.

Hull also took advantage of King's British connection to convey what would happen if that country was dragged into war. A neutrality act at the beginning of 1937 closed gaps in 1935 and 1936 legislation in order to prevent the United States being drawn into the Spanish Civil War. American vessels were now forbidden to transport material to belligerents, although the president was authorized to allow sales to European countries on a "cash and carry" basis, meaning that they had to collect the material at US ports. Hull pointed out that the United States would not again get into loans and war debts but Britain's large merchant fleet and wealth (although not as great as Americans imagined) gave it an advantage in buying and transporting goods from the United States.

King had tea at the White House with Roosevelt and Sir Herbert Marler, the well-married Montreal lawyer who had recently been appointed minister to the United States after holding the same post in Japan. Also present were "Missy" (Marguerite) LeHand, the president's devoted secretary, and Jean du Pont, wife

34 Diary, November 4, 1936.

of the immensely rich industrialist and dependable Roosevelt hater Paul du Pont, whose daughter had recently married Franklin D. Roosevelt Jr. Conversation centred on the abdication of Edward VIII three months earlier. The president had an intimation that, after they married (as they did in June), the Duke of Windsor and Wallace Simpson might become his neighbours at Hyde Park since the home of their mutual friend and Sara Roosevelt's godson Herman Rogers was being extensively remodelled.[35] In fact, they continued to live in France.

King and Roosevelt had dinner alone but were joined for drinks beforehand by Jean du Pont and her daughter Ethel Roosevelt. The latter, who was recovering from a sudden appendix operation, King described as "a very slight, frail, fair-haired girl, quite pleasant in manner." The president insisted to King that the only alcohol he took was a cocktail before dinner, which was prescribed by his doctor: "With infantile paralysis, the feet became quite cold . . . the cocktail helped the circulation a little before the meal and . . . he really was taking it for that reason." King had orange juice, saying that he did not as a rule drink during the parliamentary session. Eleanor Roosevelt, perhaps to annoy her husband who enjoyed good food and could not easily get out, insisted on plain cooking in the White House, however, because she was away, the two dined better than usual on devilled crab, soup, pheasant, salad and pudding. They talked steadily for four hours – at least Roosevelt did – indicating how much even this early in their friendship the president confided in King, whose diary for the day runs to twenty typewritten pages.

The president insisted that he intended to follow the convention of not running for a third term in 1940, which may have been an indication that he was already thinking of breaking precedent. His main concern was to prevent war. The only major conflict in the world early in 1937 was the Spanish Civil War (the Japanese attack on China did not begin until July) but there were plenty of international tensions, grievances, demands from dictators, and threats of trouble on the horizon. The previous November, an Anti–Comintern pact had been signed by Germany, Italy and Japan, ostensibly directed against Soviet communism but really aimed to give a free hand for each signatory in their own sphere. Roosevelt feared that fighting in Europe would lead to a revolution in the United States. He also wanted the Pacific to be disarmed, with the significant exceptions of Hawaii,

---

35 Andrew Morton, *17 Carnations: The Royals, the Nazis and the Biggest Cover-Up in History* (New York: Grand Central Publishing, [2015], 2016), 115.

Singapore, and the islands close to Japan, his diplomats warning that any agreement with that country would be worthless.

Roosevelt talked at length about his trip to Buenos Aires by warship the previous December to the first conference of Latin American states that an American president had organized. His aim had been to secure the countries to the south of the United States against the threat from Europe. In his address, he hailed the peace of the entire hemisphere, including Canada, as an example to the world and promised that the United States would hereafter be a "good neighbour," consulting and working to ensure better relations rather than simply trying to impose its own will. Roosevelt said that he had had a wonderful reception and many countries that had hated the United States now showed true friendship. He even insisted that the leaders, most of them dictators, were in fact liberals similar to himself and King. Revolution, he patronizingly said, was regarded in those lesser countries as a natural part of constitutional proceedings: when people disliked what was happening they rebelled, then settled down again without much blood being shed. "The president laughed at their attitude which seems strange to us but which, he said, seems to work in their countries." Roosevelt and King nevertheless considered their democracies to be on a far higher plane, as evidenced by dictators fearing to leave their countries lest they be overthrown while truly democratic leaders were strengthened by useful foreign excursions.

Reiterating what Cordell Hull had said about US economic and trade relations with Britain if that country was at war, Roosevelt raised the anomalous position of Canada. In one sense, it would be involved in the conflict, but not in another, because of the distance from Europe. King said that his government had always stressed, and even Conservatives did not disagree, that rearmament was for the protection of Canada, not part of an imperial design, "excepting that the defence of Canada was part of Imperial Defence." He recognized the difficulty of Canada sending supplies to Britain that had originated in the neutral United States but thought that all the more reason for Canada to avoid being drawn into war by the League. Imperial relations needed to be such that Canada could "keep out of some of the wars . . . into which Britain may possibly be drawn." When King again raised the possibility of the United States joining the League of Nations if its principle was changed from collective security to peace and conciliation, Roosevelt was even more cautious than Hull. He would go no further than saying that it was acceptable for the United States to engage in social and economic questions and suggested that the name of the League be changed to the "Permanent Conference on Social and Economic Questions," which pleased King.

As at Quebec the previous summer, Roosevelt was fixed on the idea of a world conference to relieve international tensions. He had written to Mussolini, who replied in the way of dictators that it was difficult for him to get away at the moment. King doubted that such a meeting would achieve anything. The costs would be high, much planning would be required, and it would be difficult to secure attendance. He proposed instead a gathering at the League's headquarters of countries not in the organization – Germany, Italy, Japan, and Brazil – with League members being invited to send representatives. This hardly freedom-loving group King thought should tackle trade barriers, which he considered the main cause of the world's difficulties. Once these were reduced, disarmament would follow. Roosevelt gave the sense of being impressed and said he would reflect on the matter at Warm Springs. It was by now about 11:00 a.m. and Missy LeHand (who lived in the White House) arrived to ask King about breakfast, which he took as a signal to end the discussion. But the president was not so easily curtailed. He continued talking about the long-contemplated seaway on a deepened St. Lawrence river to the Great Lakes, which faced strong opposition from ports closer to tidewater and railways in both countries. Roosevelt also raised the issue of an American highway through British Columbia to Alaska, which would be useful in the event of war with Japan but was highly controversial in Canada. When he finally went to bed, he asked King to come to his room about 9:00 the next morning, while he had breakfast.[36]

After all this heady talk and rich food King found it difficult to sleep. Next morning, while breakfasting in his room, he worked on a proposal for the international conference until a servant came to take him to the president. Roosevelt was sitting in bed wearing a dark brown sweater. King read his paper and the president asked for a copy to study more closely. Full of emotion, King declared that he was willing to do whatever could further world peace, which was nothing less than "to realize, in human relations, the Christian purpose." The light in Roosevelt's face he recorded, "might have been expected in one who was a clergyman, a look of great refinement and of great peace." On Roosevelt's cheek, he discerned the stigmata of sensitivity, pain and internal suffering, without complaint or bitterness. A week later at Virginia Beach, he concluded that the two

36 Diary, March 5, 1937.

were like brothers and their agreement about the League and a world conference was "a fulfilling of the mission of Unseen powers."[37]

After leaving the White House, King was offered a different perspective on his new hero when he had dinner with Peter Gerry, a rich, conservative Democratic Rhode Island senator. Gerry, whose great-grandfather was a Founding Father and the pioneer of "gerrymandering" electoral boundaries, had been King's tutorial student at Harvard. He was incensed by Roosevelt's plan to "pack" the Supreme Court to stop it over-ruling New Deal legislation. Since there had been no vacancies during his presidency and six of the nine judges were over seventy, Roosevelt argued that Congress should give him the power to nominate a supplementary judge for each over that age. He had given a broadcast speech to a gala Democratic dinner celebrating the fourth anniversary of his inauguration that denounced the court for stopping democrat legislation that benefited workers, and called for a bench of judges who would not presume to be legislators. Democrats were more deeply divided on this than on any issue since Roosevelt had become president. Gerry said that there would be strong resistance in both branches of the legislature and, at very least, much bitterness and filibustering. Once again, listening to Gerry, King perceived that the wealthy were determined to preserve their fortunes. Now his sympathies were more with Roosevelt who was "quite sincere in his determination to equalize wealth and thereby opportunity." But even in his present mood King feared that the president had put himself too much into the hands of militant labour leaders who would use him for their own purposes: "if he wants to go much further later on, the way may be paved towards actual revolution such as is being witnessed in Spain rather than by betterment of conditions in a more permanent way through solidifying ground as it is gained."[38] In the event Congress refused the Supreme Court bill but Roosevelt's warning, the threat of dilution, and the strength of public opinion induced the court to retreat on rejecting legislation.

* * *

37   Diary, March 14, 1937.
38   Diary, March 6, 1937.

After his discussion with Roosevelt, King considered himself even better prepared to represent the American president to the British government when he went to the coronation and imperial conference in May 1937. On arrival, he found Winston Churchill more of an outcast than ever, owing to his attempt to prevent the abdication of Edward VIII. In early December, the British press dramatically broke its silence to announce that Edward wanted to marry Wallis Simpson. Baldwin was adamant that this was not acceptable but the press barons, Lord Beaverbrook and Lord Rothermere, rushed to the defence of the king in the hope of destroying the prime minister. Churchill's motives were more romantic, although he was far from uninterested in heading a government of "the king's friends" if sufficient support could be found in the commons. Mackenzie King told Lord Tweedsmuir that the alliance between Beaverbrook and Churchill was one of "wealth and power and intellect combined for power, for selfish ends." He correctly predicted that it would be defeated.[39] On December 8, perhaps the only time that he appeared in the House of Commons the worse for drink, Churchill pleaded for more time to settle the matter. Howled down, he stalked out accompanied only by Brendan Bracken, his "faithful cheela." His reputation was in ruins, along with his campaign for collective security. Baldwin's prestige, after being badly damaged by the Hoare-Laval agreement, soared to its highest level as he refused to budge on the royal marriage. On December 11, Edward VIII abdicated the throne in order to marry Wallis Simpson. He left immediately for France and was succeeded by his next, younger brother, hitherto the Duke of York, who became King George VI.

Churchill was well aware that Canada and the other dominions were solidly behind Baldwin on the abdication. But hoping that Mackenzie King would support his rearmament campaign, he wrote to justify his dissent. He said that he had been deeply distressed by what had happened and could not "help feeling that earlier and more skilful treatment would have prevented this catastrophe." All that should nevertheless now be put aside to concentrate on the perils he had told King about at Sir Abe Bailey's. "It is a comfort to me," he wrote, "that you are at your post in Canada, because I am sure the best will be done for all our difficult affairs."[40] King was not moved from his confidence in Baldwin, his ministers, and their policies. Churchill's warnings against Nazi Germany were widely discounted as overwrought in the relative calm of 1937.

---

39 Diary, December 6, 1936.
40 Churchill to King, December 14, 1936. Martin Gilbert, *Winston S. Churchill*, V, *Companion* (3 Parts, London: Heinemann, 1982), Part 3, 489–90.

At the coronation, Mackenzie King, not well disposed to what seemed a spent force, saw Churchill only a few times and never for a substantial conversation. But Churchill was still a prominent political figure who appeared as a matter of right at the coronation festivities. Despite Baldwin warning to King that he would find his old friend's appearance changed, at a state banquet at Buckingham palace two days before the coronation King found him looking "exceedingly well." King had been talking to Joachim von Ribbentrop, the German ambassador who had lived in Ottawa as a wine salesman before the war, when Churchill approached. Ribbentrop unsurprisingly spoke "in a reserved way," which King naively thought indicated "a sort of feeling that Churchill did not understand Germany." Churchill, of course, had fathomed Nazism and the fervent Ribbentrop, who became foreign minister the following year, all too well. Churchill was very friendly to King and anxious to have a good talk with him during his visit.[41] Unfortunately, it never happened. When they did meet at the royal review of the navy at Spithead, Churchill concentrated on pointing out the features of various ships.[42] For King, it was more pressing to convey Roosevelt's ideas on preventing war to British ministers than engage in conversation with the old adventurer.

At the same state banquet, King also talked to Neville Chamberlain who became prime minister after the coronation. He told Chamberlain about Roosevelt's anxiety for "some sort of united front between Britain and the States, given the rest of Europe." King presented this as "a common concerted action indicative of a desire for economic appeasement." He also mentioned what he thought was the president's inclination to join the League as well as his own suggestion of making personal contact with the dictators. His perception coloured by hope, King got the misleading impression that Chamberlain was even friendlier towards the United States than Baldwin. He could not resist congratulating himself on helping to bring the two countries closer together.[43]

At the opening of the imperial conference after the coronation, King boldly proclaimed that "enduring peace cannot be achieved without economic appeasement." He called on the English-speaking countries to show the way by lowering tariffs and expanding trade, claiming that a trade agreement between Britain and the United States would lead to the same with continental Europe. British and American cooperation would establish their solidarity and bring the latter

41 Diary, May 10, 1937.
42 Diary, May 20, 1937.
43 Diary, May 10, 1937.

out of isolation.[44] At the same time, King, as usual, opposed the British attempt at a unified imperial foreign and defence policy. But although he insisted that each dominion was free to make its own decisions, he gave private assurances that Canada would come to Britain's aid if it was in danger. In the comparative calm of 1937, this seemed no great risk.

After the conference, he went to Berlin to meet Hitler, as invited by Ribbentrop. He leapt at the opportunity to practise the sort of personal influence he had urged on Chamberlain. King was as impressed with the apparent sincerity and ami-ability of Hitler as Lloyd George had been the previous September. He genuinely believed that the Führer was primarily concerned with domestic problems and wanted peace. King also claimed that he warned Hitler that a threat to any part of the British Empire would bring the dominions together in defence. But his main impression as he left the German capital was that he had helped to bring the former enemies together.[45]

The day before King met Hitler, a weary sixty-nine-year-old Stanley Baldwin was succeeded as prime minister by an energetic, slightly younger Neville Chamberlain. Churchill insisted on his right to second Chamberlain's nomina-tion as party leader, because he was the senior Conservative privy councillor in the House of Commons. He was in hope of office. That hope was wasted since Chamberlain had no intention of allowing his patient diplomacy to be disrupted by a figure so insistently antagonistic to Hitler. King was never personally close to Chamberlain and never saw him again after 1937, but he was steadfastly confident that the British prime minister could avert war by appeasement.

To King's gratification, trade discussions between Britain and the United States began in the autumn of 1937. Canada was involved because it had tariff preferences with Britain on the very agricultural products on which the United States wanted duties lowered, in exchange for freer admission of British manu-factures. Also, the 1935 US-Canada agreement expired in 1938. By the time the protracted negotiations reached an end in 1938, Germany had annexed Austria and the Munich agreement had practically dismantled Czechoslovakia by surren-dering its German-speaking Sudetenland to the Third Reich. The proposal of an international peace conference that had so occupied Roosevelt, and Mackenzie King, was long dead.

44 Neatby, *Mackenzie King*, III, 217–19.
45 Stacey, *Canada and Conflict*, II, 202–13; Hillmer, *O. D. Skelton*, 267–75; Levine, *King*, 280–3.

The president was pushing an alternative plan by early 1938. This was conveyed to the British ambassador confidentially by Sumner Welles, who had had a major part in devising it. A wealthy and highly favoured relative of Roosevelt, Welles had been appointed as Cordell Hull's under-secretary in 1936 and was, in fact, Hull's rival for influence with the president. He told the ambassador that if Britain responded favourably within a week, the president would contact France, Germany and Italy – but significantly not the Soviet Union or Japan – about meeting to discuss arms reduction, the recognition of the laws of war and equal access to raw materials. Their agreement would then be put to a larger group of countries.

The ambassador, Sir Ronald Lindsay, transmitted this message to the British government with the advice to accept it swiftly and cordially. Foreign Secretary Anthony Eden, who was on holiday in the south of France, was well-disposed. The permanent under-secretary at the foreign office, Sir Alexander Cadogan, thought the idea was wild but did not want to discourage the Americans. Prime Minister Chamberlain thought Roosevelt's plan would interfere with his own imminent approach to Hitler and Mussolini and simply inflate their demands. He asked Roosevelt to delay and doubted, in any event, that anything practical would result.

Eden hurried home from France to argue with his prime minister: the dictators might dislike Roosevelt's initiative but still feel they had to disguise their feelings and be responsive to an agreement. After numerous exchanges with Roosevelt, Chamberlain on January 28, told the president that it would be difficult to proceed until he made his intentions more clear. Roosevelt had nothing very specific in mind and agreed to defer his plan, adding that he had no objection to British negotiations with Hitler and Mussolini. He was highly conscious of the hazard of becoming involved in Europe in a mid-term election year. America did not want war. Meddling overseas might encourage the very US isolationism he was trying to undermine.[46]

In retrospect, Chamberlain's discouragement of Roosevelt's initiative seemed one of the great missed opportunities of the late 1930s. Ten years later, Winston Churchill charged that it was the "first breath" of Anthony Eden's resignation three weeks later. He claimed that the president had been willing to take great

---

46 William R. Rock, *Chamberlain and Roosevelt: British Foreign Policy and the United States, 1937–1940* (Columbus: Ohio State University Press, 1988), 78–99; David Dilks ed., *The Diaries of Sir Alexander Cadogan 1938–1945* (New York: Putnam, 1972), 35–42.

political risks to stave off war by "the arrival of the United States in the circle of European hates and fears," while Chamberlain's inept rejection was "the loss of the last frail chance to save the world from tyranny otherwise than by war."[47] There was certainly a divergence between Eden and Chamberlain, but the main reason the foreign secretary left office on February 20, was disagreement over the prime minister's hope of appeasing Mussolini and prying him away from Hitler. Eden distrusted the Italian dictator far more than the Führer.

Three weeks later, Germany abruptly annexed Austria and the European situation became a relentless crisis. Churchill took the lead in warning the world against Germany's intentions. But Roosevelt, and King, saw him as the chief menace to Chamberlain's efforts to defuse European danger and preserve peace.

---

47 Winston S. Churchill, *The Second World War* (6 vols. Boston: Houghton Mifflin, 1948–53), I: *The Gathering Storm*, 251–4; David Reynolds, *In Command of History: Churchill Fighting and Writing the Second World War* (London: Allen Lane, 2004), 103.

CHAPTER THREE

A Visit in the Shadow of War

ACKENZIE KING, NEVILLE CHAMBERLAIN and Franklin Roosevelt observed Hitler's sudden invasion and annexation of his native Austria with the same fatalistic complacency as they had viewed his occupation of the Rhineland two years earlier. The treaty of Versailles forbad the union of the two states but there was no Austrian resistance. Hitler's troops were cheered as they marched through the streets of Vienna and the action was once more justified on the grounds of national self-determination of German people. Winston Churchill broke his comparative silence on foreign policy (as distinct from rearmament). In a powerful speech in parliament two days later, he demanded that any amalgamation must first be considered by the other European countries and the League of Nations and again called for a collective security grand alliance headed by Britain and France under the League as the last chance to prevent war. But only a few Conservative MPs who had hitherto been favourably disposed towards Germany's grievances were converted to fear for the balance of European power by this expansion of the giant power in the middle of the continent. Hitler's next target was clearly the Sudetenland, the German-speaking part of Czechoslovakia, now completely contiguous to the Reich.

As the pressure on Czechoslovakia became almost unbearable, Roosevelt made another brief visit to Canada on August 18, 1938. His mind was fixed on securing Canada for the safety of the United States in the same way that he had approached the Latin American republics through his "good neighbour" policy. The occasion was provided by the opening of the Ivy Lea bridge over the St. Lawrence river between Ontario and New York state and his acceptance of an honorary degree from Queen's University in nearby Kingston. Roosevelt did not trouble to give Mackenzie King any intimation of what he intended to say but simply assumed, correctly, that the prime minister would approve.

King met the president's train at Kingston at 10:00 a.m. The two congratulated each other on losing weight and Roosevelt claimed that he had reduced his eating by two-thirds. It was a beautiful sunny day and King did not have to stand in the shade of Governor General Tweedsmuir, who was on medical leave in Britain. With no representative of the monarch present, Roosevelt alone led the automobile cavalcade in his open car and greeted the crowds on the way to the football stadium. King uncomplainingly followed several cars behind.

In his speech, as King would later say, Roosevelt "dropped a bomb." Even Cordell Hull only learned about it from a wire report. Acknowledging that Canada was part of the "sisterhood of the British Empire," the president pledged that "the people of the United States will not stand idly by if domination of Canadian soil is threatened by any other Empire. We can assure each other that this hemisphere, at least, shall remain a strong citadel wherein civilization can flourish unimpaired." This was in effect an extension of the 1823 Monroe Doctrine warning European powers against interference with the newly independent former colonies of Spain and Portugal that in the nineteenth century had depended on the Royal Navy for enforcement. Roosevelt explained to King his concern that a hostile power might take over Canada and threaten the United States. In addition to the direct danger from Japan and Germany, he feared that the large number of Germans and Italians in Brazil might produce a revolution like the Spanish Civil War, which the fascists were now winning.

After lunch at the university, Roosevelt and King drove, together this time, to the bridge, where the president insisted on the prime minister sharing the ribbon-cutting ceremony before a crowd of 20,000 Canadians and Americans. In this speech, Roosevelt spoke of the span as an open door at which the guards would say "pass friend." Above all he urged the development of the river for ocean shipping and for the production of hydro-electric power. King added length if not eloquence or substance to the ritual. The two then returned to Roosevelt's train, where the president hoped that King would visit him soon at Hyde Park.[1]

---

1   Diary, August 18, 1939; "Famous Roosevelt Smile Sets Pace for Weather at Kingston Welcome" and "Whole Dominion Stirred by Promise of U.S. Assistance Against Invaders", *Globe and Mail*, August 19, 1938. (The newspaper printed the transcripts of Roosevelt and King's speeches.)

The appeal to make better use of the St. Lawrence river attracted much comment, particularly from those suspicious of American motives, but it was the pledge to defend Canada that required a prompt official response. Although caught off guard at Kingston, it was two days later, at a political picnic in his constituency, when King made the reciprocal promise that Roosevelt expected. He pledged that Canada would ensure that "enemy forces should not be able to pursue their way either by land, sea or air to the United States across Canadian territory." Fortifying the country's coasts was in any event the right thing to do. With great complacency King reflected: "at last we have got our defence programme in good shape. Good neighbours on one side; partners within the Empire on the other. Obligations to both in return for their assistance. Readiness to meet all joint emergencies."[2]

Mackenzie King's sense of safety in a menacing world was soon severely tested when the foundations of civilization shook. Hitler increased diplomatic pressure and encouraged agitation within Sudetenland so that it might join Germany. Neville Chamberlain regarded the claim as reasonable on the grounds of unifying German people and determined to settle the matter directly with Hitler in a more orderly fashion than the abrupt and unilateral annexations of the Rhineland and Austria. The Czechs did not have the power to deal alone with Germany. The French had no desire to be held to their commitment to defend the country and followed the British to whom they clung for their own defence. The USSR, which had a defence treaty with Czechoslovakia, was ignored, and no attention was paid to the importance of the industry, mining and defences of the Sudetenland that were crucial to the survival of precarious, multicultural and democratic Czechoslovakia but whose acquisition would now greatly increase Germany's economic power and military strength.

At the first meeting of Chamberlain and Hitler on September 15, the German leader seemed amenable to a well-worked out transfer of the Sudetenland, solemnly vowing that this was his last major territorial demand. But when Chamberlain flew back to Germany a week later, as he thought to conclude the matter, Hitler ratcheted up his terms and insisted under threat of war on occupying the Sudetenland by October 1, without a plebiscite. He now also demanded consideration of the claims of Slovaks, Poles and Hungarians to secede from Czechoslovakia. The Czechs and the French wanted to resist and the British

2 Diary, August 20, 1938; Hillmer, *O. D. Skelton*, 285–7; Stacey, *Canada and Conflict*, II, 224–8.

78

government was divided, with Lord Halifax advising refusal of the terms. War seemed inevitable. The Royal Navy was mobilized, trenches were dug in London in the expectation of bombing, gas masks were distributed to meet poison gas attacks, and preparations were made to evacuate children to the countryside.

King, who was suffering from sciatica, was not the only one almost reduced to nervous prostration at the prospect of another war like the one that had ended twenty years before. "How horrible, fantastic, incredible it is," Neville Chamberlain said in a broadcast that King heard after lunch on September 27, that Britain should be preparing for war "because of a quarrel in a far-away country between people of whom we know nothing." (The distance from London was about the same as to the top of Scotland where Chamberlain went to shoot and fish.) Chamberlain declared that he was a man of peace "to the depths of my soul," but "if I were convinced that any nation had made up its mind to dominate the world by fear of its force, I should feel that it must be resisted."

King found the statement "Deeply moving, very chivalrous." Having stood behind Chamberlain's effort to preserve peace, he accepted the responsibility to support Britain. The Canadian cabinet, at the end of an all-day meeting on American trade, accepted a press statement endorsing Chamberlain's address. This was made easier by King doubting that Britain would send an army to Europe or expect an expeditionary force from Canada. He anticipated that the dominion's role would amount to no more than "supplying munitions, air pilots, etc., and looking after our own defences." But he was adamant that it must be involved: to stay out of the conflict while the rest of the empire fought, just because the United States would not be engaged (Roosevelt was publicly calling for a new conference), would mean Canada would be "shamed in her own fame and the eyes of the world." If Britain was defeated in a world con-flict, which King foresaw also involving Italy and Japan, "the only future left for Canada would be absorption by the U.S., if we were to be saved from an enemy aggressor."[3]

The British parliament was recalled for September 28 to hear what was expected to be a declaration of war. In the packed house of commons, with the galleries full, Chamberlain delivered a long, detailed account of recent events. Before reaching his conclusion, he was handed a message saying that Hitler invited him to a four-power conference at Munich the following day, along with

3 Diary, September 27, 1938.

Mussolini and the French prime minister (but no Soviet official). Pausing to read it, he repeated it to the house and said that he would accept. The drama might have been deliberately contrived but the chamber erupted in cheers of relieved tension. Roosevelt cabled "Good man" and King felt the same.

King nevertheless insisted to Skelton, his isolationist under-secretary, that Canada would if necessary go to war, although the extent of its engagement would be decided by parliament. Apart from the fact that the monarch represented the whole British Empire and the enemy would therefore regard Canada as a belligerent, King felt as a matter of great principle that he could not "permit the fear of Force to dominate in the affairs of men and nations." This was in contrast to Skelton, and some others in the dominion, who saw no need for Canada to be concerned about European countries that were "purely selfish, looking after their own interests and the like." Skelton likewise saw no Commonwealth obligation to mutual defence.[4]

At the Munich conference the British and French prime ministers quickly accepted practically all of Hitler's demands, with the occupation of the Sudetenland being stretched over a few more face-saving days. The abandoned Czechs, who had no alternative, accepted a worthless guarantee that their rump state would be maintained. Poland and Hungary seized the territory they claimed from the dismembered Czecho-Slovakia (as it was now generally styled) and the Slovaks clamoured for independence. Chamberlain and Hitler signed an agreement that their two countries would never go to war against each other but settle their problems by consultation. Chamberlain waved the paper in triumph on his return to Britain, declaring "peace in our time." Mackenzie King fell to his knees, thanking God that peace had been preserved.[5] To Chamberlain he sent a cable that he also gave to the press:

> The heart of Canada is rejoicing tonight at the success which has crowned your unremitting efforts for peace . . . Your achievements in the past month alone will ensure you an abiding and illustrious place among the great conciliators whom the United Kingdom, the British Commonwealth of Nations and the whole world will continue to honour.

4   Diary, September 28, 1938.
5   Diary, September 29, 1938.

Roosevelt was similarly grateful but prudently increased warplane production, ostensibly for US defence but in fact to sell to the countries that would fight Germany if war came.[6] The release from terror was followed by a bitter four-day debate in the British parliament which produced divisions that lasted a generation. The hardest blows against the prime minister were struck by Winston Churchill, who on October 5, denounced the Munich agreement as "a total and unmitigated defeat." Presciently, he forecast that what was left of Czechoslovakia would soon be taken over by Nazi Germany. In hammer-blow phrases, he warned the western democracies: "Thou art weighed in the balance and found wanting." Nor was this the end: "This is only the first sip, the first foretaste of a bitter cup that will be proffered to us year by year unless by a supreme recovery of moral health and martial vigour, we arise again and take our stand for freedom as in the olden time." Many had guilty consciences about the price that had been paid for peace but took comfort in denouncing Churchill as an incorrigible warmonger. Even most of those MPs, including Anthony Eden, who now criticized Chamberlain's foreign policy, were careful to avoid associating with Churchill. But events soon increased his reputation. In early November, the Nazis unleashed their Kristallnacht ("night of broken glass") pogrom against the Jews, badly shaking the faith of many defenders of Munich in the value of Hitler's sincerity.

* * *

Ten days after this outrage, Mackenzie King went to Washington to sign the new three-year trade agreement that replaced the 1935 deal. He had hoped that Neville Chamberlain would be present to sign the British pact and meet Roosevelt but despite the Munich agreement, which had supposedly calmed Europe, the situation was far too uncertain for him to be absent for any length of time. King was not wrong to congratulate himself on the original trade accord and the new and improved ones that "all right minded people" would recognize as "a contribution to the cementing of Anglo-American friendships." But it took the faith that moves mountains to believe that lowering tariffs between the United States and Britain would serve as an example to reform the dictators. The arrangements

---

6   Frank Freidel, *Franklin D. Roosevelt: A Rendezvous with Destiny* (Boston: Little, Brown, 1990), 299–311; David Reynolds, *The Creation of the Anglo–American Alliance, 1937–41: A Study in Competitive Co-operation* (London: Europa Publications, 1981), 33–6; Hillmer, *O. D. Skelton*, 288–96; Stacey, *Canada and Conflict*, II, 213–19 (cable, 216).

did, however, provide a good basis for economic relations between the three countries when war began in less than a year.[7]

In Washington, King's train was met by Cordell Hull who pleasingly said that negotiations with Canada had been far easier than with Britain. He also spoke about the Kristallnacht atrocities and the Japanese war in China that had, by then, been going on for a year and a half. He was convinced that both Germany and Japan were aiming at bases in South America from which to attack the United States. For the signing ceremony at the White House, Roosevelt requested business suits. This to King demonstrated his democratic instinct, "even against matters of dress which serve as walls of separation between those less fortunate members of society who cannot afford some of the things that others wear, or feel uncomfortable when not similarly dressed." The venue was the White House ballroom, which could accommodate more reporters the room in 1935. Lincoln's cabinet table was used to sign what were in effect treaties. The British ambassador atoned to King for some of the hard feelings raised during the negotiations by saying: "We could never have had these Agreements but for you." A couple of days later an American official satisfyingly added that although the Canadians had bargained hard, every meeting with the British had been unpleasant. When King relayed this to the governor general, Tweedsmuir – whose great ambition was to be the British ambassador to the United States – responded that the Americans recognized that the British were more perfectly trained than Canadians in trade matters. King recorded his response to this annoying comment in his diary, noting that this was "typical of the English attitude."[8]

King was shocked at the physical change in Roosevelt in the three months since Kingston: not only was he much thinner, "there was a great weariness in his eyes, and I could see he was very fatigued." He thought it was the result of the recent elections which produced Republican gains in Congress (the Democrats still had large majorities) and state governorships. King agreed with the reaction to the New Deal, particularly since the economy had slumped in 1937, despite government management and increased spending. He approved of the reaction against the administration's forced "destruction of quantities of food and the limitations of production as a wrong policy and for the excessive expenditure of public money on relief" and was cheered by Roosevelt's retreat on some fronts,

7   Diary, November 16, 1938. Stacey, *Canada and Conflict*, II, 228–31; Neatby, *Mackenzie King*, III, 221, 273–4 and 283–7; Kottman, *Reciprocity in the North Atlantic*, 117–279.
8   Diary, November 19, 1938.

which demonstrated "evidence of some inherent conservative tendencies."[9] But overall he admired the president and was alarmed that his strength might not last to the end of his term in two years. He urged Roosevelt to rest and repeated the same to Eleanor Roosevelt the next morning. The president admitted he was tired but expected to rebound after a couple of weeks at Warm Springs (where he customarily spent Thanksgiving).

Roosevelt presided over the signing of the trade agreements by King, Hull, and Sir Ronald Lindsay. All made a few remarks for the benefit of the press and then adjourned to the Oval Office. Their first topic of discussion was the royal tour of North America the following spring. Roosevelt was particularly anxious to include a visit to Hyde Park and also to the World's Fair at New York. When they turned to the main issue, the Nazi outrages against the Jews, two others joined them: Sumner Welles and Myron Taylor, a friend of the president and former chairman of US Steel, who in July had led the US delegation at the thirty-two-nation conference at the French spa of Evian to discuss the problem of Jewish and gypsy refugees following the German incorporation of Austria. The gathering expressed much sympathy for the displaced populations but, at a time of high unemployment, few countries were willing to admit more immigrants. Roosevelt had denounced Kristallnacht and recalled the US ambassador. Germany had reciprocated, and diplomatic relations were reduced to chargé d'affairs. But a diplomatic protest and downgrading formal ties was a different matter from the repercussions of admitting refugees from Nazism. At the meeting in the White House, Roosevelt did express strong feelings about the inhuman treatment of the Jews and King was also outraged, although he had not even made a diplomatic protest, saying that he could not understand German stupidity in antagonizing the United States.

In an aside, the president said it was a technique of dictators to keep young people on the move with external adventures and repeated his conviction that Germany was seeking a base in South America for air attacks on the United States, and that Japan was working with Germany for the same purpose. The United States, he said, must be prepared for invasions on both coasts.

Returning to the refugees, Roosevelt insisted that domestic opposition prevented him from increasing the 1924 immigration quotas for countries, or from accepting the British offer to transfer their surplus allotment of 65,000 entrants

---

9   Diary, November 11, 1938.

to the United States to European Jews. What Roosevelt did permit, by what King described as a Machiavellian scheme, was to allow those already in the country with expired German or Austrian passports to remain. Among the 15,000 beneficiaries were Albert Einstein and Thomas Mann.

Thinking to find a solution somewhere else, Roosevelt said that the refugees could be sent to the colonies taken from Germany in 1919 (mainly governed by Britain on mandates from the League of Nations) rather than returning the territories to Germany, the latter having been a faint-hearted tactical demand by Hitler. The president mused that the displaced could be settled in South America (which did accept a considerable number) and in unpopulated lands that held promise of development. When Roosevelt returned to the subject later, Mackenzie King carefully avoided mentioning his own country. Piously he wrote in his diary that, "more than ever that we, in Canada, cannot afford to close our doors to people who are being persecuted in other parts of the world while countries like Britain and the United States [sic], on whose co-operation our existence depends, are doing what they are, and have more crowded areas." However much he believed in putting that fine principle into practice, he could not persuade the cabinet. Quebec and King's powerful provincial lieutenant Ernest Lapointe were particularly opposed. The Conservative leader, who was bidding for support in Quebec, elided the issue by resisting all immigration while unemployment was high. The federal government deftly passed the responsibility to the provinces by asking how many refugees they wanted. In the brief months before war, very few were admitted.[10] Nothing resulted from the discussion at the White House.

It was a measure of Roosevelt's weariness that instead of his usual swim, he, like King, slept before dinner. They dined with Missy LeHand, and were joined at the end by the president's former law partner, Major Harry Hooker. Afterwards, when Roosevelt and King were alone in the president's study, Roosevelt said that the British were thinking of sending as their next ambassador someone with an unpronounceable name, not all of which he could even remember. Not in a year's time, could such a figure get his personality across to Americans, thought the president. This was Sir Hughe Montgomery Knatchbull-Hugessen, the former ambassador to China, who was at home recovering from the Japanese air force shelling his car in Shanghai a year earlier. The president wanted a political

---

10 Levine, *King*, 286–91; Irving Abella and Harold Troper, *None is Too Many: Canada and the Jews in Europe 1933–1948* (Toronto: University of Toronto Press, [1983] 2012), 38–66; Stacey, *Canada and Conflict*, II, 197–8; Neatby, *Mackenzie King*, III, 304–5.

link, such as Walter Elliot, the minister of health, or Malcolm MacDonald, the colonial and dominions secretary and son of the late prime minister.

King put in a good word for the diplomat, a member a fine old family whose father had been an Anglican cleric. King had only recently appointed one of Knatchbull-Hugessen's relatives, Adrian Hugessen, as a senator for Quebec. Roosevelt allowed that King might be right but stuck to his objection to such a name. Evidently he did not know that the diplomat was familiarly known as "Snatch." King, despite his defence, thought that Roosevelt's attitude "illustrates splendidly what democracy at heart really feels about artificial barriers, and hyphenated names." Knatchbull-Hugessen, in the event, went to Turkey, where he achieved a certain kind of renown due to his butler selling copies of secret documents to the Germans. Sir Ronald Lindsay was kept at Washington for the royal visit but on the eve of war was replaced by the eleventh Marquess of Lothian, a convert from Catholicism to Christian Science and, more recently, from appeasement to opposition of Hitler. An impeccable aristocrat, he was a great admirer of the United States, which he had frequently visited, and a staunch advocate of unity between the two countries.

Discussing the set-back of the recent election, Roosevelt put the best face on it by saying that he was not sorry to lose so many reactionaries and indicted members of Congress. Looking ahead to 1940, he said that he would help his party secure the right nominee for president and participate in the campaign. The ever circumspect King observed that this would bring him no credit for success but blame for losses. Mulling over the possible Democratic presidential candidates, Roosevelt judged that Cordell Hull had the confidence of the public but doubted that he would be equal to the task or would like it (at the age of sixty-nine). In retrospect, it seems obvious that he was thinking that it would be necessary to sacrifice the unwelcome joys of retirement to the demands of duty, that stern daughter of the voice of God, and offering himself for a third term.

On rearmament, Roosevelt predicted that the US programme would astound the world. The priority was the air, in order to counter German and Japanese challenges in south America and the Pacific. He thought the British and French were too slow in production compared to the Germans since they stopped to include every latest refinement (which in fact proved a great advantage). With typical indirection, he considered that armaments could be funded in place of unemployment relief and public works since it would provide jobs as well as defence; and it was arms production for domestic use and international sale that did finally pull the United States out the economic depression. Roosevelt also talked about Canadian assembly plants just across the border to which Americans could conveniently sell components. The building of huge numbers of planes by the United States, Britain, and Canada would force the dictators to realize the futility of competing and agree to disarmament. If the United States had had more aircraft in production, Roosevelt considered that he would have been in a position to warn Hitler before Munich that, although an American expeditionary force to Europe was unlikely, American sentiment would favour supplying planes to Britain and France if they were attacked. But revealing the limits that existed to this diplomatic threat, Roosevelt recognized that, upon rearmament, he would "have to feed the information to the country by degrees so as to avoid startling Congress." King was in a similar situation, yet both could do much by emphasizing that defence was for domestic purposes.

Demonstrating that their attitudes on Munich had not changed substantially, despite Kristallnacht, Mackenzie King expressed his appreciation for Roosevelt's messages to Hitler beseeching peace during the Czechoslovakian crisis. He also assured the president that the British government deeply valued the intervention, although it is not clear how he knew this. Illustrating how quickly American public feeling changed, Roosevelt said that although Chamberlain had preserved the peace, he had become unpopular as a result of Germany's conduct (probably meaning Kristallnacht). "One sees from this," King or Roosevelt or both reflected, "the kind of winds and gusts and tempests that sweep the political seas." They then concluded their day, the president with a glass of beer, King, exceptionally, with whisky. In a thoroughly North American mood, the prime minister wrote that it was much easier to talk naturally with Roosevelt than with Tweedsmuir or Lindsay.[11]

King slept at the White House and had breakfast with Harry Hooker and Eleanor Roosevelt, who arrived by overnight train from a meeting to raise money for Jewish refugees. The table topic was communism. Hooker was opposed to its violence while Eleanor Roosevelt took the more benevolent view that it did not involve force but stressed "common interests, meaning particularly the interests of the masses as against privilege, etc." King, tending more towards Eleanor, said that communism in Canada was largely artificial, as evidenced by its tiny electoral support. The Catholic Church was strongly against communism as an atheistic movement and Canadian politicians took their cue, raising an agitation against

---

11   Diary, November 17, 1938. Freidel, *Franklin D. Roosevelt*, 299–304 (Munich), 308–12 (rearmament).

something that did not really exist. Wealthy mine owners and automobile manu-facturers similarly used the apparition to prevent the organization of labour. Eleanor Roosevelt said the same was true in the United States, with the additional factor of the Ku Klux Klan invoking the fear of communism to prevent poorly paid workers from unionizing. King himself was nevertheless apprehensive about the spread of subversive communism in conjunction with anti-Christian Nazism.

When he went to the president's bedroom to take his leave, Roosevelt, wearing his familiar matutinal brown sweater, looked better than the day before. He was much pleased by the press reception of the trade agreements. At the Canadian legation, King read a message from the British government thanking Canada for helping with the trade accord. Cordell Hull said the same at the celebratory luncheon. "One really could not help but feel," King wrote, "that one had been privileged to play a real part in bringing these three countries together at what, up to the present, is perhaps the most critical time in the history of the world." A real tribute was that both Hull and his wife, who rarely went out to dinner, came to one in King's honour at the legation. Among the other guests were the prime minister's old friend Julia Grant, styled princess Cantacuzène by her Russian mar-riage which ended in divorce in 1934. The grand-daughter of President Ulysses S. Grant, she was a fierce critic of Roosevelt. King had known her for forty years and rarely went to Washington without visiting her. This time he escorted her home and stayed to talk.[12] On his return to Canada, he reiterated that he had assisted at "one of the greatest achievements of the English-speaking world in this present distressing period of the world's history."[13]

As King listened to Roosevelt's State of the Union address to Congress two months later in January 1939, he rhapsodized that it was "the finest thing I have heard anywhere at any time, in the way of comprehensive constructiveness." He could only agree with Roosevelt's connection between religion and freedom, the warning about the vulnerability of the United States, the need to rearm for defence and to revise the neutrality legislation so that it did not bias aggres-sors. Above all, King was happy at the applause for the mention of government restraint. The president's call for an economically strong society he immediately recognized as another resonance with *Industry and Humanity* and again lamented his inability to deliver a message on radio as effectively as Roosevelt.[14]

12 Diary, November 18, 1938.
13 Diary, November 19, 1938.
14 Diary, January 4, 1939.

* * *

If King was becoming more American by his admiration of Roosevelt, the Royal Tour of 1939 restored his British disposition. The first visit of a reigning monarch to Canada – and the United States – was by the time it occurred not only a major social event but an important element in shaping public policy. At a critical moment, it strengthened Canadian ties to Britain and encouraged similar sentiments in the eastern, most international and anglophile parts of the United States.

By the spring of 1939, optimism about peace after the Munich settlement had given way to grim hope that war might be avoided by strong diplomacy backed by demonstrably increased military preparations. On March 15, Hitler sent troops into Prague on the pretext of bringing order to a chaotic frontier of his empire. The Czech lands became a "protectorate" of the Reich and the nominally independent Slovakia a satellite. This strike not only broke the Munich agreement but, for the first time, violated Hitler's alleged principle of national self-determination by annexing a non-German population. Neville Chamberlain limply regretted that the rump state of Czechoslovakia had "become disintegrated," which freed Britain from its guarantee. Two days later he was virtually compelled, above all by Lord Halifax, to announce that Britain would oppose any further German aggression by arms. A week later, Hitler nevertheless coerced Lithuania into surrendering Memel. He would next demand the neutral port of Danzig and the connected Polish corridor which divided east from west Prussia. Britain and France had guaranteed the independence of Poland, despite its having seized territory from Czechoslovakia after Munich. When Mussolini took possession of Albania on April 7 (Good Friday), similar guarantees were extended to Romania and Greece, and a mutual assistance agreement on the Mediterranean was made with Turkey.

Over strong objection from the opposition parties, the British government introduced military conscription. Along with France, it also made an overture to the pariah USSR for a pact to defend eastern Europe, confident that the Soviets would welcome increased security without insisting on any demands of their own. Lord Halifax even attended the previously dismissed League of Nations to affirm his country's commitment to collective security. Winston Churchill's stock rose and there was a great publicity campaign to take him into the government. But Chamberlain, apart from resistance to including his fiercest critic, feared that including such a bellicose figure would be taken as a sign that

Britain was abandoning diplomacy and accepting the inevitability of war. On March 20, three days after Chamberlain's declaration against German aggression, Mackenzie King reiterated to parliament what he had said in January: that Canada must stand by Britain in order to preserve its own freedom. Three days later, he elaborated to his anxious Liberal caucus that if Britain were attacked, Canadian ships, at very least, would be engaged. Relying solely on the United States for protection would mean paying "a price to that country much greater than we would have to pay any other for assistance," meaning that Canada would be subordinated. At the same time, he made it clear that he had no intention of giving Britain a blank cheque "to draft Canada into a war at any place and at any time." The dominion might be prepared to follow Chamberlain, who was dedicated to peace, but would not necessarily support a government containing Duff Cooper or Winston Churchill: "Ministers and issues changed. We could only deal with each as they arose."[15]

A month later Earl (Stanley) Baldwin and his wife stopped in Ottawa on their way to the University of Toronto where Baldwin was delivering a series of lectures on the English character. One of the couple flattered King by telling him that he was "a sort of institution which kept on going on and on," but warned against staying too long. Baldwin said that the pressure in Britain was terrible: "They were all getting to a nervous state of tension where they were preferring almost anything [to] the long continued uncertainty." Baldwin himself believed that war was coming, probably not immediately though it might happen suddenly. At a dinner in Baldwin's honour attended by members of all political parties, King spoke warmly of the Canadian people's attachment to Britain, which was "as jealous of the preservation of liberties and freedom as they were," and of an "increasing consciousness between all parts of the Empire, of freedom in each part being bound up with that of the whole."[16]

In Toronto, Baldwin belied his reputation for not standing up to dictators in the peroration of his last lecture. Declaring that he detested war and feared for civilization, he nevertheless insisted that if there was another great conflict Britain would not be found wanting:

15 Diary, March 23, 1939.
16 Diary, April 17, 1939.

In Luther's worlds 'we can do no other'. We were there when the Spanish galleons made for Plymouth: we were on those bloody fields in the Netherlands when Louis XIV aimed at the domination of Europe: we were on duty when Napoleon bestrode the world like a demi-god, and we answered the roll call, as you did, in August 1914. We can do no other. So help us, God.'[17]

* * *

Mackenzie King found some refuge from the international tension and dilemmas in preparing for the royal visit. No detail was too small for the prime minister, who considered himself the only right and proper person to arrange such matters. In his own mind, as well as Roosevelt's, he was also the appropriate "minister in attendance" to accompany the monarch to the United States and lobbied hard for it. The original intention had been to send Lord Halifax, giving him the opportunity to talk to the president, but the presence of both the British foreign secretary and the monarch would have aroused the suspicions of US isolationists. Halifax, in any event, did not lack occupation at home. The British concurred in Roosevelt's strong hint to appoint King and he was in turn delighted at this sign of dominion equality to Britain as well as his personal status as the link between the two heads of state.

From the moment that King George VI and the Queen Consort, Elizabeth Bowes-Lyon, stepped ashore at Quebec on May 17, until they re-embarked at Halifax on June 15, Mackenzie King never left their side. This had the not incidental purpose of reminding voters, with an election due within just over a year, of his attachment to the monarchy, to Britain, and to the empire. It was also a huge pleasure to travel with them to British Columbia and back, although he was always fretting that formalities were not correct enough. At least that other stickler for protocol, the governor general, largely disappeared from the scene as redundant when the monarch was in Canada (King found Tweedsmuir annoyingly presumptuous when he was present). In Ottawa, George VI gave royal assent to bills in parliament, received the new minister from the United States and, just in time for the Second World War, unveiled an impressive memorial to the first.

Returning from the west coast, the royal train on the night of June 7 crossed into the United States at Niagara Falls, where it was met by Cordell Hull and

---

17   Earl Baldwin, *The Falconer Lectures* (Toronto: University of Toronto Press, 1939), 39.

Sir Ronald Lindsay. Mackenzie King was sensitive to any lapses in observing his precedence as minister in attendance and prime minister of Canada, not, he constantly insisted in his diary, from any concern about personal dignity but for the prestige of the dominion he represented. At Washington, the president and his wife met the royal party at the train station. Roosevelt and King agreed that this was the day for which they had been living. The president told George VI that he and the prime minister were on a first name basis (though Roosevelt generally did not care to be addressed in that fashion by King or anyone else). The magnificent procession to the congressional building and the White House was described by King as "one of the finest scenes one could ever witness, and I imagine the finest witnessed in the Capital at any time," despite the sun making his open car like "the top of a stove." The royal couple stayed overnight at the White House, King at the Canadian legation. The minister, Sir Herbert Marler, was recovering from a heart attack, which soon caused him to resign but his socialite wife Beatrice, always a great favourite of King, accompanied him to the various celebrations.

The president's luncheon for the royal couple at the White House was a family event which included three of the Roosevelt's sons and their wives, Mackenzie King, Missy LeHand and a few others. The significant topic of conversation, far more tragic than acknowledged, was the German ship, the *St. Louis*, which had sailed from Hamburg carrying over nine hundred Jewish refugees. They had bought visas for Cuba but these were revoked before sailing and only a handful of passengers who bought more expensive ones were admitted to the country. Two days before the royal party arrived in Washington, the ship was compelled to leave Havana. Other Latin American countries refused entry and it was now sailing north in hopes that the refugees would be taken in by the United States or Canada. Roosevelt, fearing that his country would be flooded with immigrants, "explained the situation to the King," as he had the year before, collusively pointing out that Canada had a similar problem. King thought that this was far more a matter for the United States and Cuba than for Canada and took comfort in Hull's claim that there was fraudulence in the visas. During his absence from Ottawa, those acting on King's behalf refused to admit the ship, despite pleas from some prominent Canadians.[18] The *St. Louis* sailed back to Europe where the refugees were taken in by countries of western Europe. Only those admitted to

---

18 Black, *Franklin Delano Roosevelt*, 493–6; Abella and Troper, *None Is Too Many*, 63–4; Hillmer, *O. D. Skelton*, 312–13

Britain were spared Nazi barbarism, and even they were imprisoned as enemy aliens at the beginning of the war and, subsequently, many were sent to Canada where some eventually settled.

The desperate plight of the refugees did not disturb the pleasures in Washington. At lunch, King was far more concerned to counter Eleanor Roosevelt's wish to have the Queen Consort broadcast from Hyde Park as opposed to Canada at the end of the trip. At the garden party at the British embassy in the afternoon, he took great delight in presenting his old friends Peter Gerry and John D. Rockefeller Jr., their wives, and Julia Grant to the king and queen: "It was another case where the past had all come up to the moment of the present, and promises and desires more than fulfilled."

During speeches after dinner at the White House, King noticed the queen look pained as the president struggled to stand and remain upright by gripping the back of a chair. King thought that Roosevelt's remarks, without notes, were eloquent while his "countenance was radiant and his voice very sweet as he spoke." George VI read a response with scarcely a stammer (which had largely been corrected by an Australian speech pathologist). King thought he would never forget the sight of two men who had achieved greatness – albeit one of whom was an accidental, hereditary monarch – by overcoming infirmities. The moment also marked the fulfilment of a great dream of bringing the countries together: "seeing this mutual friendship declared between these two peoples and Canada referred to as a trusted friend."

At the concert afterwards, one of the performers was the African-American contralto Marian Anderson (misidentified in King's diary), who was famous in Europe but discriminated against in the United States. The Roosevelts championed her as a symbol of their opposition to racial segregation, despite the president's need for the political support of Southern Democrats. King congratulated her and praised her singing as being "like a medium interpreting voices from the other world, as beautiful a voice as I have ever heard."[19]

On the second day, Mackenzie King accompanied the king and queen to the Capitol where the monarch shook the hand of every senator and member of the house of representatives (only three were absent). The royals then travelled aboard the presidential yacht, flying their standard, to Mount Vernon, the home of George Washington. On the way, Cordell Hull revealed his imperfect

19   Diary, June 8, 1939.

understanding of constitutional monarchy by urging King to impress on George VI the importance of Britain joining the United States in promoting freer trade. He characterized Germany, Italy, and Japan as gangsters and pirates, conspiring to seize territory and make war. On the way back to Washington by car, the king laid wreaths at the Arlington National Cemetery on the grave of the unknown soldier and at the Canadian memorial. That night George VI held a dinner in honour of the president at the British embassy.[20]

After dinner, the royal party boarded an overnight train to New Jersey. Next morning, they crossed to the southern tip of Manhattan in a destroyer flying the royal standard. There they were met by the state governor, the mayor, and an unexpectedly large and excited crowd instead of protest that had been feared in the multicultural city. For security reasons, the motorcade avoided the downtown office canyons, travelling up the west side highway and through Central Park on the way to the World's Fair in Queens. All along the route, Mackenzie King witnessed people cheering and stretching out their hands. At the fair, he judged that there must have been a couple of million souls and he was surprised that the band played "Rule Britannia" and "Land of Hope and Glory." After lunch, at which there were no speeches, the group toured the pavilions of the countries of the British Empire. Mackenzie King was proud of the Canadian exhibits except for the art, which had "too much purely modernistic stuff" (particularly the Group of Seven). The procession then returned to Manhattan, again through packed streets, to a ceremony at Columbia University, founded by a charter from George II in 1754. Finally, the cavalcade, now an hour behind schedule, travelled the ninety miles to Hyde Park, to which the Roosevelts had gone directly by train from Washington. King was struck by the beauty of the recently completed southern section of the Taconic State Parkway, a National Recovery Administration public works project in which Roosevelt had taken a keen personal interest but of which King, in principle, should have disapproved.

Springwood was a modest manor house by British aristocratic standards yet the king and queen adapted to the cramped quarters. For Roosevelt and his mother, the weekend was a highlight of their lives. Two supplementary black servants were brought from the White House, leading the Hyde Park butler to go on holiday in protest. The imported staff were not familiar with the various levels on the main floor and dinner was marked by noises off. A "darky", as King called

---

20 Diary, June 9, 1939.

him, stumbled and dropped a tray of Limoges dishes recently presented by the French factory to Roosevelt in recognition of his efforts for peace. Later, a tray of drinks and crystal glasses fell in the same way. Both incidents were laughed off but, as King said, the damage must have been painful for the family.

After the ladies left, Roosevelt, George VI, and Mackenzie King spent two more hours, in the middle of the night at the end of a demanding day, on the serious business of the visit. The president knew that the monarch had no real power but he had influence with Neville Chamberlain and even more with Lord Halifax. Roosevelt wanted to impress the need for Britain and France to stop German expansion. He co-opted King by reiterating to the monarch that the two understood each other perfectly and communicated directly, bypassing obstructionist diplomats. For George VI, it was a heady experience to be included in such a confidential discussion. Emphasizing the sinister nature of Nazi Germany, the president indicated close secret intelligence relations between the United States and Britain by saying that the latter had provided the United States with information about a German submarine based off Brazil. He insisted that he would not tolerate European warships in the Americas or a repetition of the incident, in 1930, when a German battleship had visited New Orleans and been welcomed by the late, demagogic governor Huey "Kingfish" Long.

Roosevelt was confident, and King did not object, that if it came to war between Britain and Germany, Canada would still be able to help American naval patrols by allowing them to refuel and refit at Halifax. This, of course, overlooked how US isolationists might react to such an involvement with a belligerent. The president emphasized the part that Canada played between the United States and Britain and again urged King to build aeroplane assembly plants as quickly as possible. Notwithstanding its neutrality act, which the president hoped (in vain) would soon be repealed, the United States could covertly supply plane engine components and wings, claiming that they were not necessarily destined for warplanes. Roosevelt gave the impression that he would do everything short of going to war. The king repaid this frankness by saying that he had told the British government that Germans, including his own relatives, had been spying on the country for some time. He added that his father, after the First World War, would never shake the hand of a German ambassador.

None of this meant that any of them considered war inevitable. Even while thinking about what was needed, if worse came to worst, George VI and Mackenzie King were confident that Chamberlain would find a way to avoid a military conflict. Roosevelt almost certainly agreed. The monarch revealed his fear of Britain provoking or impulsively starting hostilities by making the astonishing statement for a constitutional monarch to a foreign head of state, even in a private conversation: "he would never wish to appoint Churchill to any office unless it was absolutely necessary in time of war." King, who at this point regarded Churchill as "one of the most dangerous men I have ever known," was relieved to hear it. It did not occur to him that resisting the advice of a prime minister was the very issue on which he had clashed with Lord Byng in 1926 and harped on ever since. When they finally went to bed, King (who was in the connecting room) encouraged George VI's sense of being at the centre of events by saying that, however tiring, the journey "was helping to save the world."[21]

Sunday was more relaxed, although the president did not relent in his diplomatic campaign. The party attended the small Episcopalian St. James's Church at Hyde Park where Roosevelt, like his father before him, was a warden. As they drove together, the president again repeated to the monarch that King was the official interpreter between the two heads of state. The standard morning service, which included the Church of England's state prayers for the king and the royal family, was conducted by a bishop, assisted by the rector and the clergyman from Campobello Island. King found the sermon on social reform too long and annoying and both Roosevelt and George VI agreed that it was "a bit off the mark." The casual picnic lunch at Top Cottage, the wheelchair accessible stone house that Roosevelt was building for his retirement, was attended by servants, friends, clergy, and politicians. A great novelty for the king and queen was hot dogs. Afterwards there was Indigenous American entertainment. The visitors then went down the slope to visit Val-Kill, formerly a handicraft workshop sponsored by Eleanor Roosevelt from 1927 to 1938, to supplement the income of local farmers, which she was converting into her own cottage. King declined the invitation to swim with the president and the sovereign, choosing instead his usual sleep. He later reproached himself, as historians might, for missing the political discussions at the pool, on the drive around the estate, and in the library that Roosevelt was building beside the main house for his archives.

Since the royal party was leaving immediately after dinner, Roosevelt used the meal as a final opportunity to emphasize the German threat. He said that he had received further messages about German submarine bases near Trinidad

---

21 Diary, June 10, 1939.

as well as Chamberlain's apprehension that something would happen about the beginning of August. Yet the tone at the table was far from morose. There was so much hilarity that, as the ladies left, they paused in the doorway to watch the men laughing almost to tears. At the end of the occasion, the president expressed his pride and pleasure at having the king and queen as guests in his home and country and the monarch, in turn, invited the Roosevelts to reciprocate the visit. As they went to the train station, the president suavely deflected the invitation by claiming that going to Britain would mean having also to visit France and pointing to his physical difficulties. His real fear was giving the dangerous impression that he was committing the United States to Europe. The king inspected a guard of honour, the crowd of over a thousand sang "Auld Lang Syne." As the train steamed away, Roosevelt called to the royal couple on the observation deck: "Good luck to you! All the luck in the world." King thanked Providence that all had gone so well.[22]

Back in Canada, King emphasized again, as Roosevelt had expected, that the president was prepared to do everything except go to war to help Britain. "What a fine fellow he is!" said the king, adding what was by now far from absent from Roosevelt's own mind, that he should continue as president unless someone similar could be found. The monarch showed Mackenzie King a notebook in which he had recorded the conversations with Roosevelt, including the one at Hyde Park that King had missed and other presidential remarks that King had forgotten to record. Roosevelt had said that he was trying to educate his country about the consequences of Germany winning a war and the British and French navies being wiped from the sea: "They [Americans] would lose entirely their export markets and if they were given a chance to import into those countries, it would be wholly on the terms of the Dictators themselves." The king apparently kept the notebook by him throughout the war.[23] He repeated to Mackenzie King his anxiety about Churchill succeeding Chamberlain and thought that it would not be well received by Roosevelt and the Americans. Even in the confidence of his diary, King did not feel that he could write what George VI would do to avoid

22 Diary, June 11, 1939; Sarah Bradford, *King George VI* (London: Weidenfeld & Nicolson, 1989), 281–9; Blanche Wiesen Cook, *Eleanor Roosevelt* (3 vols., New York: Viking, 1993, 2000 and 2016), III, 71–8; David Reynolds, "The President and the King: The Diplomacy of the Royal Visit of 1939," *From World War to Cold War: Churchill, Roosevelt and the International History of the 1940s* (Oxford: Oxford University Press, 2006), 137–47.
23 Bradford, *King George VI*, 296.

Churchill, although he agreed with it, considering such an appointment to be "inviting disaster, simply challenging Germany."[24]

King's farewell to George VI and the Queen Consort at Halifax was marred only by what he regarded as attempts by the Tweedsmuirs to outshine him. He told the royal couple that only they could have "helped to unite Canada and different parts of the Empire and to consolidate a continent in friendly feeling." Believing that assertion of the solidarity of the Atlantic triangle was sufficient to deter Germany from war, he asked them to take back the greetings of Canada to Neville Chamberlain and his wife and to assure them that they were constantly in the thoughts of the dominion. After their ship had sailed, King told a British reporter who had covered the journey that the monarch and the president were agreed that the way to preserve peace was through reconciliation and adjusting differences. The sceptical journalist, who considered war inevitable and probably imminent, predicted that King "would probably have a responsibility greater than any I have ever known which would turn my hair white."[25]

* * *

The journalist's prediction seemed to come true two weeks later, when Mackenzie King's happy Dominion Day at Kingsmere was destroyed by a secret letter from the British high commissioner in Ottawa. London reported that Hitler's demand for Danzig had created a very delicate situation and developments might occur "at very short notice." King did not object to the Baltic port being restored to Germany, although the loss of it and the corridor would destroy Poland as effectively as detaching the Sudetenland had Czechoslovakia. Nor did he believe that there would be war to prevent it. He was nevertheless convinced that the British government, pushed by Winston Churchill, Labour and the Liberals, had made commitments along with France to protect Poland from which retreat would be next to impossible. The only hope of peace lay in keeping Churchill, Eden and Duff Cooper out of the government. Without them, there might still be "much long and continued discord & uncertainty–but civilization saved." With them, "war seems to me inevitable." Joan Patteson had almost ruined his digestion when she arrived at lunch to repeat what turned out to be only a radio rumour

24 Diary, June 12, 1939.
25 Diary, June 15, 1939.

that Chamberlain was taking in Churchill and Eden: "I said if that be true and it is done there will be war without doubt & London will be bombed with(in) 24 hours." Fretting about Canada's position, he declared: "We would not like to stand behind Churchill–or Russia. It is all a terrible muddle."[26]

The alarm passed but at the end of July, Mackenzie King's peace of mind was again unsettled by the arrival of Violet Markham whose assessment of the British government was diametrically the opposite of his and Tweedsmuir's. She thought anything the Chamberlain ministry had done right was the result of pressure from the Liberals and Labour. Even worse, she thought highly of Churchill and wanted him in the government. King did not want to quarrel with her but expressed his conviction that Churchill in the cabinet would mean war. Violet Markham further compounded King's discomfort by demonstrating more concern over unemployment in Canada than he was. Her pleasure in this visit to Canada must in turn have been marred by King's complaints about the unwarranted pomposity of her friend, the governor general, and his slights to the prime minister.[27]

Danzig continued to be the focus of anxiety but there was a general expectation that some agreement between the Soviet Union, Britain, and France would stop Germany from seizing it by military force. Then, on August 21, came the dumbfounding announcement of a ten-year treaty of non-aggression between the USSR and Germany, which was signed two days later. The threat to Germany from the east vanished. Even though the territorial terms of the treaty were secret, it needed no great insight to recognize that the two dictatorships would divide the lands that lay between them. Britain and France had been outbid by refusing to surrender to Stalin the countries they had guaranteed against Hitler. They had not even been able to persuade Poland and Romania to allow passage of Soviet troops, which those countries were not wrong to fear would not leave.[28]

The British government did not relent in its guarantee to Poland. It appealed to Germany to submit its claims to arbitration, upon which King had pinned his hopes. In company with Roosevelt and many other leaders, he sent entreaties for a peaceful settlement to Hitler, Mussolini, and the president of Poland. He even

26 Diary, July 1, 1939.
27 Diary, July 30, 1939.
28 Bruce G. Strang, "John Bull in Search of a Suitable Russia: British Foreign Policy and the Failure of the Anglo-French-Soviet Alliance Negotiations, 1939," *Canadian Journal of History*, 41, no. 1 (2006), 47–84. The article is based on material contained in Russian archives.

urged Neville Chamberlain to have the king and queen issue a call for peace on behalf of women and children. The British prime minister, probably fearing that this would weaken his government's stand, tactfully declined.[29] King dreamed that he might himself "be brought in somewhere to help effect justice between nations." His recommendation would have been to surrender Danzig and the corridor, which had previously been a part of Germany: "a way should be found to return it, securing Poland in other ways." He considered the main obstacle to a reasonable settlement to be British stubbornness about not losing face. No call came for King's mediation but he took comfort that Chamberlain and Halifax were at the helm and prayed that Churchill and his like would not get in the way. He expected the Labour and Liberal parties to be less aggressive than their rhetoric when it came to the real risk of war and to "lie down at the canon's [sic] mouth as they did at the time of Munich a year ago."[30] In this, he was totally wrong.

Even when German troops invaded Poland on September 1, King continued to yearn for war to be avoided. Yet on that day he did not hesitate to tell the antipathetic Skelton that if Britain fought, Canada would stand with the country that embodied "the defence of freedom, not her own freedom only, but the freedom of mankind." He thought no dominion could do otherwise, although Ireland remained adamantly neutral and South Africa was touch and go. Britain and France did not declare war for two more days but King, in expectation, recalled parliament for September 7 to endorse his government's decision. Discussing the formalities with the governor general, who like the prime minister, still clung to the hope of peace; King said that he was proud that he could "bring Canada to the aid of Britain as a united country and with a unanimous Cabinet." Tweedsmuir responded that at the time of Munich (when he had been in Britain), he had assured Chamberlain that this would be the case. King, he said, had achieved many things but "this would remain as the greatest so far."

What shocked the prime minister was that Roosevelt did not make a similar declaration of solidarity with Britain. King could not admit to himself, even in his diary, that he had been far too optimistic in his interpretation of what the president had indicated about Atlantic unity during the royal visit. There was, in fact, nothing that Roosevelt could have said that would have persuaded Congress to declare war. Any sign that he was even thinking that the United States might at

29 Levine, *King*, 297–300; James Eayrs, *In Defence of Canada*, II: *Appeasement and Rearmament* (Toronto: University of Toronto Press, 1965), 79–80.
30 Diary, August 28, 1939.

some point be involved would have destroyed his authority as president and any chance of a third term. Instead, Roosevelt told the press that the country ought to be able to stay out of the conflict. Canadian cabinet ministers were understandably puzzled about how a neutral United States could honour its pledge to defend Canada if it were to fight.[31]

When Britain and France declared war on Sunday, September 3, after Hitler gave no reply to the ultimatum to remove German troops from Poland, Canada was immediately involved to a significant extent, although its formal declaration followed a week later. On the first night that the Allies were in arms, King listened to Roosevelt's fireside chat affirming that the United States would stand clear of what King deemed to be "this great issue, which affects the destiny of mankind." He was filled with shame at the "mere words, words" used by Roosevelt to assure Americans that their country would remain aloof "in the name of peace when everything on which peace is based is threatened." King was not wrong to think that American engagement at the beginning might have helped to save the lives of millions. But he totally misjudged the country he claimed to understand when he wrote that it would "not stand for what Roosevelt has said," that there was enough spirit among Americans to "cause a demand for participation in the interests of humanity, justice and life, and all that is dearest and [in?] the hearts of men."[32]

31 Diary, September 1, 1939; Hillmer, *O. D. Skelton*, 314–19.
32 Diary, September 3, 1939.

CHAPTER FOUR

A Dangerous Pilot

THE WAY THE WAR BEGAN helped reconcile King to the abstention of Roosevelt and the United States: there was no immediate threat to Britain and France as the German *blitzkrieg* was concentrated on Poland. Nor did the Allies take any initiative, claiming that there was nothing they could do to help the country they had guaranteed to protect, not wanting to attack Germany for fear of retaliation before they were better prepared. This delay in any sort of fighting that would involve Canada was a great relief to King, who hoped the war would be short and not need a great army. It might be possible for Canada to restrict its contribution largely to money and supplies, the navy and the air force, sparing it the bitter discord over army conscription that had occurred scarcely twenty years ago.

It is odd that King did not comment in his diary on Churchill immediately becoming First Lord of the Admiralty and a member of Chamberlain's nine-man war cabinet. He evidently accepted that Churchill was well-suited to war, now that it had begun. But he stuck to the conviction that taking him into the government earlier would have brought hostilities sooner.[1] The Royal Navy, now under Churchill's leadership, was of particular concern to Canada as the sword and buckler of its trade and sea defence. This became tragically obvious as Churchill entered office. A German submarine sank the British liner *Athenia*, west of Ireland en route to Montreal. Of the 1,100 passengers – including 150 refugees and

---

1   Diary, October 5, 1939.

300 American citizens – more than 100 died. This resurrected the spectre of unrestricted U-boat activity as in the later stages of the First World War. This did begin three months later but, at the outset, Hitler feared that violating the 1936 agreement against attacking civilian ships not carrying contraband, or at very least ensuring the safety of those aboard, would bring the United States into the war. Germany continued to insist, to the very end of the war, that the sinking of the *Athenia* was the work of Winston Churchill to draw neutral countries to Britain.[2]

Churchill did hope the sinking would draw the United States into war. His wish was shared by King who lamented the loss of life but thought "it might be the best thing that could have happened . . . I could not help but feel that this would bring home to Americans the need for their intervention and that it was a terrible rebuke to Roosevelt."[3] The United States, however, was not so easily provoked, particularly with the Germans obfuscating the responsibility.

King's attitude towards the United States improved significantly two days after Britain went to war, when the president and Hull together telephoned for clarification of Canada's status before issuing the list of belligerent countries to which Americans were forbidden to sell arms. King confirmed that although the armed forces were mobilized, the final decision on war had not yet been made by parliament. This technical neutrality was an advantage in allowing American armaments to be rushed across the border for almost a week. In the telephone call, Roosevelt expressed his regret "about the way matters had developed" but asked King to keep in touch and said that he himself would be "right there, right on the job, and would be watching things." King was considerably mollified by this "friendly gesture to indicate sympathy and readiness to co-operate in so far as might be possible."[4]

The biggest obstacle to the latter was the 1937 neutrality law that Roosevelt had not so far been able to persuade Congress to repeal. With Europe at war and the United States and its interests in some danger, more legislators were now willing to accept his lead. He called Congress into a special session in late September, telling a joint meeting of both houses that repealing the arms embargo would help to keep the United States out of the war and preserve its trade. On November 4,

2 Jonathan Dimbleby, *The Battle of the Atlantic: How the Allies Won the War* (London: Viking, 2015), 2–5, 8–9 and 14–16.
3 Diary, September 4, 1939.
4 Diary, September 5, 1939.

a new act permitted belligerents to purchase goods, including munitions, for cash provided that they collected the material in US ports, since American ships were still forbidden to go to countries at war. This benign neutrality, as Roosevelt and Hull had already told King, worked to the benefit of Britain and France which had the money and the ships and were far less affected by blockade than Germany. The president even allowed them to buy American ships to carry the purchases.[5]

Despite the telephone call from Washington, King worked some oblique criticism of the United States into his speech presenting the case for war to parliament three days later. On the principle that the length of the speech should match the gravity of the occasion, he spoke for four hours (with a two-hour intermission for dinner and other necessary restoratives). He claimed that Germany's real object was not Poland but the British Empire, in which Canada with its great mineral and agricultural wealth was the most desirable part. This was a reflection of his and Roosevelt's anxieties about attacks on north American and their mutual assurances of defence in August 1938. Indirectly censuring the United States, as well as his own under-secretary and others who saw no reason for involvement in this war, King warned European countries against the temptation of neutrality. If Britain and France were defeated, no other state would last long and, if Europe fell, North America would be the next target. Neutrality would turn out to be "a mere myth. There will be no freedom on this continent; there will be no liberty. Life will not be worth living. It is for us on this continent to do our part to save its privileged position by helping others."[6] At the end of his speech, seeking to inspire the palpably fading MPs, he read all fourteen verses of the American anti-slavery poem "The Present Crisis" by James Russell Lowell. King was followed by his Quebec lieutenant, Ernest Lapointe, who made the crucial, solemn promise that there would be no military conscription for overseas service. With little dissent, parliament voted for the government's recommendation to go to war.

At the time of King's veiled reproach, Roosevelt was already working on changing his country's neutrality legislation. King never knew that the president was also opening a direct line of communication with the British government

5   Nicholas Wapshott, *The Sphinx: Franklin Roosevelt, the Isolationists, and the Road to World War II* (New York: W. W. Norton, 2015), 140–8; Reynolds, *The Creation of the Anglo-American Alliance 1937–41*, 65–6.
6   *Canada, House of Commons Debates*, September 9, 1939, 18–41.

to circumvent his isolationist, appeasing, and now defeatist Ambassador Joseph P. Kennedy (father of the future president). A potential Democratic presidential candidate in 1940, Kennedy had been sent by Roosevelt to Britain in 1937 to get him out of the way. The choice of correspondent was Winston Churchill, which was on the face of it surprising. The only time they had met was at a grand dinner in London in July 1918, where the US assistant secretary of the navy was an important guest but considered that he had been snubbed (perhaps inadvertently) by the brash minister of munitions. In 1939, he told Kennedy, who was always looking for evidence to denigrate Churchill, that he had "acted like a stinker."[7] Churchill himself had forgotten the occasion until his memory was improved by the Second World War. He subsequently recorded in his memoirs that in 1918 he had been struck by Roosevelt's "magnificent presence in all his youth and strength. There had been no opportunity for anything but salutations."[8]

Roosevelt would also have known Churchill's criticism of the New Deal and certainly heard nothing good about him from George VI and Mackenzie King. Nevertheless, he recognized from Churchill's many articles in American magazines that he was militarily the most knowledgeable of the war cabinet, the most pro-American, and an exceptional writer. He was also in charge of the navy, in which Roosevelt always had a particular interest and which was sure to play an important part in the conflict. In the letter inviting a correspondence, he claimed to have enjoyed Churchill's massive biography of the Duke of Marlborough (that ran to six volumes in the American edition, four in the British one, and a million words in either case). He may also have sensed that if the war turned out like the last, Churchill might be the man of destiny as Lloyd George had been. Roosevelt sent his overture on September 11 but for some reason it did not arrive until October 3, five days after the fall of Poland. Churchill was ecstatic at the chance of influencing the leader of a country so important to Britain's success. Quickly, he got the approval of Chamberlain and Halifax to write to the American president. In the next seven months, the code-named "Naval Person" sent nine messages to Roosevelt about the war at sea, a prelude to thousands that he as prime minister, or "Former Naval Person," exchanged with the president.

Just a few hours after Churchill's first letter, the president himself telephoned him to say that the Germans were warning that a US ship on its way from Ireland

---

7   Meacham, *Franklin and Winston*, 3–5.
8   Churchill, *The Second World War*, I: *The Gathering Storm*, 440.

would be sunk in circumstances similar to the *Athenia*, meaning that they again intended to fix the blame on Churchill. The First Lord of the Admiralty replied that the vessel was too far from Europe to be sunk by a U-boat; it could only be destroyed by a time-bomb hidden aboard in Ireland, by the Germans, who would claim credit for warning Americans in time to save the crew. A search revealed no bomb and the ship safely reached its destination. In this helpful, trusting, and informal way, the epochal relationship between Churchill and Roosevelt began.[9]

The president's telephone call may have been encouraged by Churchill's first broadcast of the war a few days earlier. Now that he was a cabinet minister, the proscription against him throughout the 1930s by the BBC, the sole radio service in Britain, was removed. It was no onerous requirement for Churchill, the head of the only branch of the armed services that was actually engaged, to report on the activities of the Royal Navy and much else to the public. King's opinion soared as he listened to the broadcast on Sunday, October 1. Poland had just fallen to Germany and the USSR, which had joined the attack to claim its territory under the Nazi-Soviet pact in mid-September. Churchill praised the Poles' resistance and confidently predicted that they would rise again "like a rock." He even put an optimistic interpretation on the Soviet aggression, saying that it drew a line against further German expansion. The USSR might be a "riddle wrapped in a mystery inside an enigma" but anxiety about its own safety gave it a community of interest with Britain and France. At sea, despite dismaying shipping losses, Churchill claimed that Britain's command would enable it to "bring the immense resources of Canada into play as a decisive air factor." He expected the war to last three years though it might end sooner; all depended on how long Hitler "and his group of wicked men, whose hands are stained with blood and soiled with corruption, can keep their grip upon the docile, unhappy German people." Britain would in any event go on to the end, "convinced that we are the defenders of civilization and freedom."[10] King immediately cabled his old acquaintance: "Your broadcast magnificent – as perfect in its appeal to the New World as to the Old."[11]

Churchill knew nothing of King's scorn for him before the war and undoubtedly regarded this as a sign of the Canadian prime minister's solid support for

9 Gilbert, *Winston S. Churchill*, VI, 53–5.
10 James, *Churchill: Complete Speeches*, 6160–4.
11 Diary, October 1, 1939.

his view of the war. Admiring Churchill's oratory, however, was not the same as accepting his judgement about the fundamental issues of war and peace. Throughout the "phoney war" of the next half year, during which there was no large-scale military action by Britain or France, King combined praise for Churchill's speeches with private criticism of his opposition to a negotiated peace. King had no strong feelings about the preservation of Poland and much dread about the spread of Soviet communism. He continued to believe that more conciliatory diplomacy might have produced a compromise to avoid war. Now a combination of the USSR, Germany and Japan might overwhelm Europe: "It is the worst situation that could possibly be conceived. God knows what may come of it." In the conventional fashion of most appeasers, he blamed the situation on those who had sought vengeance rather than justice after the last war, clung to the letter of the Versailles treaty, built up armaments, and refused to play fair with Germany when it was weak. He thought British foreign policy would have been much better managed under the Liberals and principally blamed Lloyd George and Churchill for the political fragmentation, although he condemned the rump of independent Liberals as well as the Labour party for pushing the National Government to war and precipitously guaranteeing Poland "before it knew who its allies would be, and on whom it could count." The pledge was another example of British arrogance and conviction that "no power can be superior to themselves; that England must win and cannot possibly ever lose. That other nations must bow to its will." But he had to admit that most of the guilt for war lay with the "deceit, lying, treachery etc. of the Germans and their evident determination on aggression from the outset."[12]

* * *

Mackenzie King was not the only one who saw the fall of Poland as an opportunity to end the conflict. Five days after Churchill's speech, Hitler tried to lure Britain and France into accepting the result by telling the Reichstag that there was no need for further hostilities. Now that he had achieved his supposed last demand, he proposed a conference be held and that Germany, Italy, the USSR, Britain and France be invited to agree on peace while warning of the consequences if Churchill and his bellicose associates prevailed. Even

12 Diary, September 15, 1939.

before this seductive bid, Lloyd George, who at the beginning had seemed as resolute as in the last war, was urging the government not to reject negotiations out of hand. Denounced in parliament, he was provided with a newspaper platform by Lord Beaverbrook who likewise saw no reason to fight for Poland. The like-minded ambassador, Joseph Kennedy, appealed to Roosevelt as "a combination of the Holy Ghost and Jack Dempsey" to intervene and save democracy by reconciling the opponents. The president, as usual, simply ignored him.[13] Two days after Hitler's speech, King, with the governor general at the Presbyterian church they both attended for a national day of prayer, passed the time making notes for a message to the kings of Italy and Belgium to investigate the situation. He had no high hopes but thought "almost anything which will save civilization is worth attempting." If Germany did not cooperate, he thought, it would draw in neutral powers, including the United States, to the Allies' cause.[14]

The British war cabinet was also very concerned about neutrals, including Italy, which even Winston Churchill hoped to attract, or at the very least to not alienate. It spent close to a week crafting a careful response to Hitler. On October 12, Chamberlain announced in parliament that Britain and France would not recognize Germany's conquests or rely on Hitler's word after years of broken promises. Any negotiations must be preceded by amends for the "wanton acts of aggression" against Poland and "grievous crimes against humanity." In the hope of encouraging an uprising against Hitler, he said that the obstacle to agreement was not the German people, who longed for peace to pursue their culture and material prosperity, but the government which had to demonstrate that it wanted to end the war.[15] King and Tweedsmuir, reading an advance copy of the statement, had no difficulty in detecting the vocabulary and cadences of Winston Churchill. King feared that he would resist peace overtures and had too much power and desire to fight to the end: "Probably sees himself already as War Prime Minister of Great Britain with a name which would rival that of his illustrious ancestor Marlborough." Within a week, King wrongly forecast, people would be

---

13 Michael Beschloss, *Kennedy and Roosevelt: The Uneasy Alliance* (New York: W. W. Norton, 1980), 193–7; Anne Chisholm and Michael Davie, *Lord Beaverbrook: A Life* (New York: Knopf, 1993), 370–1.
14 Diary, October 6, 1939.
15 Christopher Hill, *Cabinet Decisions on Foreign Policy: The British Experience October 1938–June 1941* (Cambridge: Cambridge University Press, 1991), 100–45 and appendix 3: Chamberlain's statement.

questioning "a blank refusal of what the world will construe as peace overtures and the failure . . . on Britain's part to make a definite proposal of her own."[16]

There was no pressure from the Germans on Hitler, who was livid at the British attempt to turn his population against him. London and Paris braced for merciless air attacks though none came. But two days after Chamberlain's speech a German U-boat managed something that had never been accomplished in the first war, breaking into the naval base of Scapa Flow in northern Scotland. The battleship *Royal Oak* was sunk and 800 of its 1,400-man crew drowned. Further south, warships near Edinburgh were also bombed. Churchill escaped condemnation only because he had been at the admiralty for just a month.[17] In mid-December, the humiliation was avenged by the destruction of the "pocket battleship" (a heavily armed cruiser) *Admiral Graf Spee* which had been wreaking havoc on merchant ships.[18]

Winston Churchill used this heartening news, which helped to counterbalance shipping losses, to give another inspiring broadcast. This time Mackenzie King was angry that he included disclosure of the arrival the day before of the advance guard of the first Canadian division, "taking the gilt off the gingerbread" after Canada had agreed to the admiralty's request to hold back the news until all the troops were safely landed. It was clear to King that Churchill was "trying to monopolize the stage for the Admiralty" and emphasize British convoys rather than Canada's contribution: "Very wrong in every way." King also sensed drink in Churchill's voice: "I shall be surprised if he carries through to the end of the war. It is amazing what some men who drink are able to stand."[19]

The Canadian division, which had been announced as available on September 19, consisted entirely of volunteers for overseas service. Commanded by General Andrew McNaughton, it had fully mobilized by early February 1940. Fortunately, it was not required for battle since it still needed a great deal of training.[20] Britain's war continued to be a naval one and Churchill was amply justified in the agreeable duty of representing the government on radio. A month later, following a speech that contained no element annoying to Canada, King sent another cable

16 Diary, October 11, 1939; Stacey, *Canada and the Age of Conflict*, II, 276–7; Eayrs, *In Defence of Canada*, II, 154–7.

17 Dimbleby, *The Battle of the Atlantic*, 34–7.

18 *Ibid.*, 45–51.

19 Diary, December 18, 1939.

20 David J. Bercuson, *Our Finest Hour: Canada Fights the Second World War* (Toronto: HarperCollins, 2015), 23–9.

of praise, having been moved again by "the effectiveness of the language and the imagery and its moral tone, particularly its interpretation of the significance of the war and its appeal to the moral sense of mankind."[21]

King continued to be distressed that the United States persisted in neutrality rather than adding its strength to speed victory. When, at the end of November, a new battle began after Finland, unlike Estonia, Latvia and Lithuania, refused to submit to the USSR, King was glad that Roosevelt at least condemned the Soviets. (Finland was the sole European country that had repaid its First World War debts to the United States.) He recognized the difficulties preventing Roosevelt from joining the war but warned an American visitor: "before very long if freedom was not to perish from the earth . . . all neutral countries loving freedom would have to rise to preserve it."[22] Churchill was keen to help Finland, despite having implied that the Soviet Union might eventually fight Germany. With the Baltic frozen, an expeditionary force would have to pass through non-aligned Norway and Sweden, which had the additional huge benefit of enabling it to seize the high-grade Swedish iron mines which supplied Germany. But by the time Britain decided to violate their neutrality, Finland had capitulated, on March 12.[23]

Two weeks later, King's hand in dealing with the war, and everything else, was strengthened by winning the general election of March 26 by an even larger majority than in 1935: 117 seat-majority over every other party. Churchill was quick off the mark to congratulate his assumed loyal ally. Next day, he cabled his satisfaction that King was more secure than ever in his command of the most vital dominion and the conduit to the United States. "I am very glad we shall be able to continue to work for the common cause," he wrote, ending with fondest regards from himself and his wife and unusually signing himself "Winston."[24]

In the next six weeks, the fortunes of war and Churchill's own were dramatically transformed, ironically by a disaster for which he was primarily responsible. After finally getting the British and French governments to agree to a smaller violation of Norwegian neutrality, the Royal Navy began to lay mines around the northern port of Narvik, through which the Swedish iron ore was shipped to Germany in the winter. That very day Hitler began a military operation that

21 Diary, January 27, 1940.
22 Diary, December 1, 1939.
23 Max Hastings, *All Hell Let Loose: The World at War 1939–45* (London: HarperPress, 2011), 30–8.
24 Churchill to King, March 27, 1940. Martin Gilbert ed. *The Churchill War Papers.* 3 vols. (London: Heinemann, 1993–2000), I, 922.

quickly overran neutral Denmark without resistance, seized Oslo and took over Norway's ports along seven hundred miles of coastline. Although the Royal Navy put up a good fight in Norway, destroying large numbers of German warships, the Allied troop landings and the contest for the airfields failed.[25] The fiasco precipitated a wide-ranging parliamentary drama that brought down the British government and forced a new one just as a far more perilous situation developed.

* * *

The campaign in Norway was just getting underway as King, obviously not unduly concerned, set off for a three-week vacation in Virginia. When his train reached New York, a state department official came aboard to say that the president would like to see him at Warm Springs, Georgia or Washington if the president needed to return to the capital. King happily agreed to whatever suited Roosevelt.[26] (A month later, when circumstances were totally different, King deluded himself into thinking that he had intended all along to confer with the president and praised "the wisdom of my so–called holiday to the United States." He sanctimoniously wrote: "Imagine being condemned by the public for going there, when the whole purpose was to help the British to keep the bond of friendship strong between England and the U.S., and Canada and the U.S., in this crisis.")[27]

For his part, Roosevelt may have wanted to discuss the war with King but he was in no great hurry. Not until ten days after the prime minister arrived in Virginia was he bidden to Warm Springs, taking with him the trusty Edouard Handy. To pre-empt criticism of meeting the leader of a belligerent country in the United States, the president issued a press statement saying that the visit was of no political significance and that there was no discussion of policy. King likewise claimed that he was making a purely social call.

Warm Springs was the place that Roosevelt loved best next only to Hyde Park. He had first gone to the run-down winter resort, seventy miles south of Atlanta,

25 Nicholas Shakespeare, *Six Minutes in May: How Churchill Unexpectedly Became Prime Minister* (London: Harvill Secker, 2017), 1–153; Bell, *Churchill and Sea Power*, 184–94; John Kiszely, *Anatomy of a Campaign: The British Fiasco in Norway, 1940* (Cambridge: Cambridge University Press, 2017).
26 Diary, April 13, 1940.
27 Diary, May 24, 1940.

in 1924, hoping that the hot mineral pool would enable him to walk again. In 1926, he bought the thousand-acre property with an inn and fifteen cottages for $200,000, about two thirds of his personal fortune. The next year (when he received a substantial inheritance from his half-brother James "Rosy" Roosevelt, whose first wife had been an Astor), he turned it into the charitable Georgia Warm Springs Foundation, a year-round treatment centre for polio victims. Eventually it had a hospital, a therapy building, a theatre, a chapel and much else. In 1938, the foundation was extended to become the National Foundation for Infantile Paralysis, popularly known as the March of Dimes. Every one of his stays at Warm Springs, particularly when he was president, encouraged and comforted Roosevelt. His simple cottage was called "The Little White House" and he made a point of celebrating Thanksgiving with his fellow "polios." Eleanor Roosevelt, disliking the terrible poverty and segregation (the only blacks were servants), rarely attended.[28]

Mackenzie King was accommodated in a cottage close to Roosevelt's. The president said that he had been looking forward to their time together as a holiday and from the time King arrived, at mid-day, to his departure the following afternoon, the two spent most of their waking hours together, eating, going for drives, swimming, lying in the sun, and talking. They were, as usual, easy in each other's company. Roosevelt shared confidential papers with King and insisted that he remain in the room during telephone calls with Washington. The president had lost ten pounds since the royal visit and was in better form than King expected: not "haggard or worn looking," though his eyes seemed tired and he was "quite nervous at times and also showed real fatigue." This demonstrated both the benefit of Warm Springs but also the lingering effects of a collapse at a dinner in February, which his doctor, admiral Ross McIntire, an ear, nose, and throat specialist who was better at optimism and cover-up than at diagnosis, identified as a slight heart attack. All spring, Roosevelt had felt unwell and unable to work at his usual pace.[29]

Their conversation naturally focused on the war. Roosevelt was primed by a report from Sumner Welles, whom he had dispatched in February to report on

---

28 Theo Lippmann Jr., *The Squire of Warm Springs: F. D. R. in Georgia 1924–1945* (Chicago: Playboy Press, 1977); David Oskinsky, *Polio: An American Story* (New York: Oxford University Press, 2005), 36–9.

29 Kathryn Smith, *The Gatekeeper: Missy LeHand, FDR, and the Untold Story of the Partnership that Defined a Presidency* (New York: Touchstone, 2016), 220–1.

conditions in Rome, Berlin, Paris and London; Moscow was omitted because of the ongoing conflict with Finland. The British feared that he had been sent to try to find a peace settlement accepting Germany's conquests while American isolationists were suspicious that the mission was a step in Roosevelt's supposed effort to draw the United States into the war. Insofar as Welles had any policy intention, it was to deter Hitler from further aggression until the Allies were better prepared. Scarcely was he back home than the Scandinavian offensive began.

Welles had found the Italians ambiguous, the Germans rude and bellicose, and the French dispirited. His best reception was in Britain, particularly from Churchill who talked to – or at – him for a long time. Roosevelt told King that Churchill "drank a lot of whisky and made a speech of an hour's length to Welles. At the end of the hour's talking he had become sober."[30] There was no hint from the president that he was corresponding with Churchill but King judged that he was getting about the same information as Canada from Britain. It was easy to see that the president and his advisers were strongly on the side of the Allies, although there was no sign of any intention to intervene.

On the campaign in Norway, where the Anglo-French military force had just landed, Roosevelt was not impressed. He thought the Allies were not acting fast enough, had not sent enough troops, and that Britain should be conscripting more. As with Canada in September, he was delaying recognizing Norway as a combatant for a few more days in order for it to keep buying US arms. This, in fact, made little difference since the country's resistance was crushed the next week. The president correctly predicted that Mussolini would join Hitler and invade Greece and that Hitler lacked the patience to resist triggering an enormous ground war in the west. He expected the Germans would destroy British coastal towns, although perhaps not London, and that the Allies should do the same against German cities except Berlin. Both he and Missy LeHand (who lived in the Little White House) judged that if Germany began to win, the increased danger to the United States would harden American opinion against it. If Germany managed to gain a base in South America, Mexico would be particularly vulnerable. Roosevelt also worried about bombing and gas attacks along the inadequately defended US and Canadian Atlantic coasts. Apart from

30   Michael Fullilove, *Rendezvous with Destiny: How Franklin D. Roosevelt and Five Extraordinary Men Took America into the War and into the World* (New York: Penguin, 2013), 26–62.

improving communications between the two countries, he offered to sell Canada and Newfoundland material from the First World War, including binoculars and mines, at nominal cost.

Canada's particular concern was Greenland, a dependency of Denmark which was now occupied by Germany. The Aluminum Company of Canada wanted protection for its cryolite mines, a mineral necessary to the production of aluminum, which was needed to build aeroplanes. Roosevelt also wanted to keep the island out of German hands but, not wanting to become involved in the war, advised Canada to avoid provocation by not doing "anything in particular." King, who never itched for adventure, called off the preparations for a military force intended to occupy Greenland for the duration of the war. A year later, when the United States was still neutral, the issue was resolved by the American government, under cover of consent from the former Danish ambassador, stepping in to safeguard the island, where it built an air force base.[31]

When King and Roosevelt discussed the strength of Britain and France, the vital bulwark for the security for North America, the president indicated that he was already thinking about what soon became an agreement to exchange US destroyers for foreign bases if the Allies became hard pressed. Meanwhile, he complained that the British were not buying much from the United States. When King said it was because they lacked dollars, the president, who shared the general American belief that Britain was a very rich country, thought this exaggerated. He judged that the real reason was the British desire to hang on to their investments in the western hemisphere, for example, South American street railways. The British government, he said, could commandeer private assets if it wished. Soon it would be compelled to do so, and sell the investments to Americans at distress prices.

Addressing the approaching presidential election, Roosevelt again claimed that he did not propose to run for a third term, although he would not rule it out. He tepidly endorsed Cordell Hull as his successor but immediately backed off that position by saying that Hull's interests were mainly trade and foreign affairs, and that he would be sixty-nine (eleven years older than Roosevelt). When King said that the president would do himself an injustice to run if he felt physically unequal to another term, Roosevelt revealed the toll taken by his recent illness by admitting that he was mentally tired. It was impossible to rest in office. What

31 Stacey, *Canada and Conflict*, II, 308–9; Eayrs, *In Defence of Canada*, II, 167–72.

he would like was a year off. Apparently anticipating retirement, he said that he was looking forward to working on his memoirs, with his great confidant Harry Hopkins organizing the material. He also mused about being an international "moderator," reconciling different world views and bringing peace, a theme he would return to many times in the next four years. Missy LeHand, hoping for an even closer relationship with her beloved chief, privately wanted him not to run again.

As King left Warm Springs, Roosevelt said that he might be back in the capital when King stopped there in a few days and looked forward to seeing him there.[32] Three days later, King was surprised that among those meeting his train in Washington was Cordell Hull. The secretary of state was worried about Norway, where the Allies were already beginning to withdraw, and also that Mussolini would soon join Hitler and perhaps bring in Spain. It was this anxiety that brought Roosevelt back to Washington. King went to the White House, again innocuously insisting that it was a purely personal visit. The president said that he was jittery about Europe and had not been able to enjoy his rest. That morning he had sent a verbal message to Mussolini, saying that he did not think that Germany could win the war and warning that, if Italy entered, it would mean fighting in Africa and Asia as well as Europe. "I am trying in this way," he told King, "to let him see that we intend to see that Germany and Italy do not conquer." King added, and Roosevelt thought Mussolini would see, that if Italy did go to war there would be a moral embargo which ensured that Italy got nothing from the United States. Roosevelt wanted King and the dominions to put a burr in Britain's tail since it was slow about everything. The only people who saw the magnitude of the problems ahead were Chamberlain and Churchill, thought the president, and "Churchill was tight most of the time." King could not help moralizing about the disgracefulness of Churchill being in that state when he saw Welles. He thought it another indication of the arrogance and superiority that made the British so many enemies.

The conversations at Warm Springs and Washington gave King good reason to think that he was as well briefed as anyone could be about the attitude of the American president and government. He was convinced that his presence and what he regarded as his assistance in the United States had been guided by Providence: "No man ever received a more wholehearted or brotherly welcome

---

32 Diary, April 23–4, 1940.

than I did from everyone in connection with the Administration with whom I came in contact. It is not short of a miracle that, in the matter of timing, the visit should have come at the very hours and minutes that it has."[33]

* * *

Ten days after King returned to Ottawa, on May 7 and 8, the British House of Commons debated the Norway campaign. This quickly widened into an emotional inquest into the whole conduct of the war and responsibility for it. Even many Conservatives turned against Chamberlain. Leopold Amery, who had opposed him since the Austrian Anschluss, voiced the feeling of many backbenchers when he pronounced the terrible words of Oliver Cromwell to the Long Parliament: "You have sat too long here for any good you have been doing. Depart, I say, and let us have done with you. In the name of God, go!" Churchill, the minister primarily responsible for the Norway operation, reaped the benefit of his long criticism of the government's diplomacy and rearmament programme before the war. When he intervened in Lloyd George's condemnation of the government to insist on his share of the responsibility, his former colleague warned against allowing himself to "be converted into an air-raid shelter to keep the splinters from hitting his colleagues." At the end of the debate, Churchill made as strong a defence of the Norway disaster and the ministry as anyone could. But by this point it made no difference. The house divided in an uproar: thirty-three government MPs voted with the opposition; sixty-five abstained or did not attend; and thirty voted for the administration with the promise that it would be reconstructed. The government's customary majority of over two hundred fell to eighty-one, a clear moral defeat for Chamberlain.

The next day Chamberlain accepted that there would have to be a new, truly national war coalition including the Labour and Liberal parties which refused to serve under him. The choice was between Halifax and Churchill, both of whom were acceptable to the opposition. Late in the afternoon the prime minister and the chief whip met with both. Chamberlain favoured the foreign secretary, despite his being a member of the house of lords. Churchill claimed that he remained silent but two years later Malcolm MacDonald, Chamberlain's colonial secretary and the only person who ever gave such an account, told King that Churchill

33 Diary, April 27–9, 1940.

struck the cabinet table and said that only he could save the country.[34] In either case Halifax disclaimed the post by saying that he felt sick to his stomach at the thought of the responsibility and that it would be Churchill who ran the war.

Chamberlain did not resign immediately, and it seemed that he might manage to cling to power. But at first light of the next morning, May 10, Germany began its invasion of neutral Holland and Belgium. Chamberlain believed it his duty to stay during this emergency. But Sir Kingsley Wood, the hitherto impeccably loyal chancellor of the exchequer, led the cabinet in telling him that he must go. By evening, with the Germans moving rapidly, Churchill was appointed prime minister, without enthusiasm, by George VI.[35]

Came the hour, came the man, it soon appeared. But it might easily not have happened at all. Two years earlier Churchill had been on the verge of having to leave politics because he was almost bankrupt. He was saved by Sir Henry Strakosch, a financier originally from Austria, who gave him a loan of £18,000, which was covered by a bequest on Strakosch's death (in 1943) of £20,000.[36]

Politically, too, Churchill was initially on insecure ground as he constructed an all-party government. Chamberlain was still the leader of the Conservative party and Churchill had no real alternative to keeping him in the war cabinet, now reduced to five, which he did as lord president of the council. For similar reasons, Lord Halifax remained foreign secretary and a member of the war cabinet. They were joined by the Labour leader, Clement Attlee and his deputy Arthur Greenwood, both occupying nominal offices. The Liberal leader, Churchill's old friend Sir Archibald Sinclair, was the secretary of state for air throughout the war but was never in the war cabinet. Churchill himself also assumed the new title of minister of defence, making him a kind of civilian commander of all the armed forces, like the American president, or Smuts of South Africa. There was great disquiet about his recklessness among many Conservative politicians, senior civil servants, and the leaders of the armed forces, and no certainty that he would last. On Monday, May 13, after he had put together the main elements of his government while the military conflict raged on the continent, he appeared in

34 Diary, August 1, 1943.
35 Shakespeare, *Six Minutes in May*, 259–411; Jonathan Schneer, *Ministers at War: Winston Churchill and His War Cabinet* (New York: Basic Books, 2014), 3–43; Neville Thompson, *Canada and the End of the Imperial Dream: Beverley Baxter's Reports from London through War and Peace, 1936–1960* (Toronto: Oxford University Press, 2013), 136–42. Shakespeare usefully remarks on the contradictions in the accounts of these few days, how much is uncertain and how much unknown.
36 Lough, *No More Champagne*, 261–5, 288 and 303–15.

the house of commons for the first time as prime minister. He asked for approval of his ministry and warned in grim terms that might have come from his novel, *Savrola*, that he had nothing to offer but "blood, toil, tears and sweat." But it was the deposed Chamberlain who got the bigger cheer from the Conservatives.[37]

Across the Atlantic there was similarly no great beating of shields for the new British prime minister. King dutifully sent a cable assuring him of Canada's wholehearted support in "the war effort of the Commonwealth and wishing him vision and endurance to guide public affairs in this most critical of times." But his heart remained with Chamberlain whose doleful voice on the radio announcing his resignation he found "full of anguish but it was the expression of a truly noble and good man." King sent a telegram of consolation, expressing pride at having been at Chamberlain's side throughout his premiership."[38] Reading the report of the Norway debate the next day, he reflected on how wise Chamberlain had been and "how reckless the nation in their condemnation of him, not having the knowledge he had." King thought it would have been far safer to keep Chamberlain: "I have far more confidence in his judgement and guidance than that of Churchill." If the debate had been delayed until the German invasion of the Low Countries, King thought Chamberlain's position would have been secure, though the desire to get rid of him might have been even more fierce.

On his very first night as prime minister, Churchill telephoned Roosevelt at 3 a.m. (10 p.m. in Washington). There is no record of what they said but Churchill evidently made no very favourable impression.[39] Two days later, the president, still showing the influence of Sumner Welles's report, half-heartedly told his cabinet that he "supposed Churchill was the best man that England had, even if he was drunk half of the time."[40]

Roosevelt's hesitations about Churchill were evident in his response to the new prime minister's urgent plea five days after taking office. As the Germans poured into the Low Countries, he tried to jolt the president into firm support by warning that "the voice and force of the United States may count for nothing if they are withheld too long. You may have a completely subjugated, Nazified Europe established with astonishing swiftness, and the weight may be more than we can bear."

37 Harold Nicolson, *Diaries and Letters 1939–45*, ed. Nigel Nicolson (London: Collins, 1967), 85. (Diary, May 13, 1940.)
38 Diary, May 10, 1940.
39 Goodwin, *No Ordinary Time*, 38.
40 Meacham, *Franklin and Winston*, 47.

Since Germany was clearly the aggressor, he pressed Roosevelt to proclaim non-belligerency status for the United States, permitting it to provide everything short of armed forces. Churchill's list of what was needed was daunting: old destroyers, new aircraft, military equipment, ammunition, steel and other materials. He also wanted the United States to keep quiet "that Japanese dog," to dispatch a naval squadron to preserve Ireland's neutrality, and to give an assurance that when Britain could no longer pay in dollars, "you will give us the stuff all the same."

This would have been a breathtaking set of requirements even if the United States had been a fully mobilized ally. Munitions production was at a low level and the presidential election was only six months away. Roosevelt had to be careful about anything his critics could construe as evidence that he was manipulating the country into war. He was not even convinced that the situation was as serious as Churchill represented. Even if it was, Roosevelt was not yet convinced that the old adventurer was the best person to handle it. He assured Churchill that he was happy to continue their private correspondence but rejected all the requests. Some matters needed congressional approval, he said, and this was not the best moment. (Churchill never fully grasped the American division of power.) It would also take considerable time to produce the material, and much of it was needed for the defence of the United States. Roosevelt ended his bleak response with a cheery flourish: "The best of luck to you."[41]

The total rejection of his high expectations was a blow to Churchill but he could not afford to show disappointment or give up on the leader of the country whose help, at very least, he considered necessary to defeat Germany, perhaps even to protect Britain itself before long. In his continuing campaign of persuasion, he was fortified by a stock of references to the common heritage of the two countries that was fresh in his mind from the recent draft of a history of the English-speaking peoples (albeit almost exclusively focused on Britain and the US; the dominions were scarcely mentioned). The book was not published, in four volumes, until after his retirement in 1955, but the events and analogies of two millennia were from the very beginning of the war an ever-present aid for messages and speeches.[42]

41 Churchill to Roosevelt, May 15; Roosevelt to Churchill, May 16, 1940. Warren F. Kimball., *Churchill and Roosevelt*, I, 37–9.

42 Peter Clarke, *Mr. Churchill's Profession: The Statesman as Author and the Book that Defined the "Special Relationship"* (London: Bloomsbury Press, 2012; Jonathan Rose, *The Literary Churchill: Author, Reader, Actor* (New Haven: Yale University Press, 2014), 296–7.

* * *

Whatever Roosevelt might have thought, the military situation for the Allies in western Europe was rapidly deteriorating. The German assault on the Low Countries, which had been expected to be from the north as in the First World War, came instead, from the south, through the wooded hills of the Ardennes that had been regarded as impassable by heavy vehicles. In a sickle-like movement the Germans trapped the Allied force that had advanced into Belgium, driving it north towards the Channel while their own army invaded France. On May 15, the day that Churchill wrote to Roosevelt, the Netherlands surrendered and the French, demoralized as Welles had reported, feared a repetition of the slaughter of the Great War.

In his first broadcast as prime minister, on May 19, Churchill concealed his anxieties about the French and put the bravest face on events. He emphasized that only a small part of France had been invaded and insisted that both that country and Britain, sustained by "their kith and kin in the great Dominions and the Empires which rest beneath their shield," would not relent in the fight against Nazi tyranny. It being Trinity Sunday, he exhorted Britons in the words of the stern seventeenth-century Puritans to: "Arm yourselves, and be ye men of valour, and be in readiness for the conflict." King listened to this stirring account of the great battle on the continent and his confidence in Churchill leadership soared. He sent a cable to the British leader and ensured that it would be published by reading it in the Canadian parliament the next day. He told Churchill that Canadians had followed the speech with "feelings deeply stirred, and with profound admiration and pride" and pledged his country to muster its strength for a "full contribution to the triumph of right which must and will prevail."[43]

King put this into practice by immediately dispatching Canada's three best destroyers. Canada's coastal defences were left bare but King hoped the ships would help to tip the balance against Germany. In his diary, he testified that Canada owed Britain "such freedom as we have. It is right we should strike with her the last blow for the preservation of freedom." Even Skelton was converted, along with many other isolationists, to what King claimed had all along been his own conviction: "that the real place to defend our land is from across the seas."[44]

---

43 Diary, May 19–20, 1940. *Canada, House of Commons Debates*, 1940, I, 65. (May 20, 1940)
44 Diary, May 19–20, 1940. *Canada, House of Commons Debates*, 1940, I, 65. (May 20, 1940)

Soaring as Churchill's rhetoric was, it could not slow the German momentum nor hearten the French and the Belgians, or even his own colleagues. The French government appealed to Mussolini to find a settlement, and the British war cabinet was itself divided on coming to terms with Germany. Ahead was what a few weeks earlier had been almost unthinkable: no French army or Allied base against Germany in continental Europe. Joseph Kennedy urged Britain and France to negotiate a compromise while they still had something to offer and exhorted Roosevelt to apply US neutrality to the same purpose.[45] Again the president did not respond to his ambassador. He also had a lively sense that the Allies might be defeated but his message to Britain disguised it. And instead of Kennedy as his intermediary, Roosevelt turned to his friend Mackenzie King, who had a better outlook and relationship with the British government. This was the role King had eagerly sought.

On May 24, Roosevelt asked King to send a trusted confidant to discuss a matter that was too sensitive for paper or the telephone. The president did say that it concerned the Royal Navy, and King must have thought that Roosevelt had found a way to reinforce it. The prime minister drafted Hugh Keenleyside, a senior external affairs officer who had just returned from a futile quest to get American planes for the Commonwealth air training program that had recently begun in Canada. The United States, the president had told him, had scarcely enough for its own needs.[46] Keenleyside's new mission was clandestine. To ensure confidentiality, Roosevelt and Hull were artfully disguised as "Mr. Roberts" and "Mr. Hughes," Churchill as "Mr. Clark" and King as "Mr. Kirk."

The president and secretary of state told Keenleyside that they feared France would soon capitulate and Britain would not be able to withstand German air bombing. They expected Germany to offer preservation to Britain in return for its navy and the colonies which, apart from those in the Americas, they thought would be shared with Italy and Japan. Adding the British and French fleets to Germany's would make it far more powerful than the US Navy and North America would not be able to counter an attack from the sea. To prevent this, Roosevelt wanted King to lead the dominions in a strong stand against Britain making any such "soft peace." If it did come to defeat, Britain should move the king to Bermuda, which would be more acceptable to Americans than having

45 John Lukacs, *Five Days in London: May 1940* (New Haven, CT: Yale University Press, 1999) is a detailed examination of the discussions from May 24 to 28.
46 Bercuson, *Our Finest Hour*, 37–9; Cook, *The Necessary War*, 161–7.

a monarch in Canada, and disperse the fleet to the empire. In that case, the president promised that the ships would be admitted to US ports for repairs. The combined British and American navies would be able to form a blockade from Greenland to Africa that Roosevelt was confident would bring about the defeat Germany, even if it took a couple of years.[47]

As he listened to Keenleyside's report over lunch, King's heart sank. This was no offer of help to Britain but simply a plan to save the United States by appealing to the self-interest of the dominions. He refused to be Roosevelt's cat's paw, writing that he "would rather die than do aught to save ourselves or any part of this continent at the expense of Britain." The next day he telephoned Cordell Hull who claimed that the purpose of the discussion had not been to make any immediate communication with Churchill – the exact opposite of what Keenleyside had understood – but merely to prepare the dominions. The prime minister sent Keenleyside back to clarify the matter and tell the president to approach Churchill himself; if that was not feasible, King would be the go-between.[48] Roosevelt, who was being careful not to make a direct and formal commitment to Britain, grasped at King's offer. He even improved his terms by saying that if the Royal Navy was saved, the ships could be outfitted and provisioned in American ports and the United States would help to strengthen British naval bases around the world.[49] How even he thought he would be able to manage it in a neutral and isolationist country is a good question.

King glumly recognized that this proposal was as good as he was going to get. He composed a careful cable to Churchill which he thought "may well be the most significant of any message that has, thus far, crossed the ocean since the beginning of this war."[50] Making it perfectly clear that it was Roosevelt's view he was conveying, he said that the United States could not give immediate belligerent aid but if Britain and France held out for a few months, then assistance could probably be provided. Churchill must have interpreted this as meaning the presidential election that was coming in November and that Roosevelt would be a candidate. If France left the war and Britain was devastated by German bombing,

47 Memorandum from Counsellor Keenleyside] to Prime Minister, May 26, 1940. *Documents on Canadian External Relations* [DCER], VIII, Part II, 67–71.
48 Diary, May 26, 1940.
49 Memorandum from Counsellor [Keenleyside] to Prime Minister, May 29, 1940. DCER, VIII, Part II, 74–8.
50 Diary, May 30, 1940.

King expressed the president's view that the Royal Navy must not be traded for better peace terms. As much as could be managed of the fighting fleet and the merchant marine should be dispersed to the dominions and colonies and the rest destroyed. In return, King said that Roosevelt promised to open US ports – as far as possible under international law (a highly significant qualification) – to assist in fortifying such bases as Halifax, Singapore and Simonstown in South Africa, and to join Britain in a naval blockade of Europe. If German retaliation was vicious, for example by starving Britain to force the return of the navy, the president was confident that American opinion would demand action. Food ships would be sent under naval escort and any interference would be considered a cause for war.[51]

For Churchill, this small ray of contingent hope in the event of real disaster was only a slight improvement on Roosevelt's flat refusal of help two weeks earlier. As clearly as King, he saw that the main concern was American security. No great reliance could be placed on promises which might be difficult to fulfil. But if the worst did happen, the offer did provide a chance that the struggle against Nazism might continue and eventually be won, a matter that seemed in the balance at that moment. Belgium had just capitulated and Chamberlain had urged the divided war cabinet at least to consider German peace terms. The day before King's letter arrived, Churchill had beaten this down by appealing to the full cabinet and getting its enthusiastic endorsement to continue fighting. The army, pinned against the Channel at Dunkirk and considered practically lost, was now being evacuated by sea more successfully than anyone had dared hope. Over ninety percent of the troops, 338,000 in all, were extricated in a few days, despite heavy aerial bombardment, because the German army was, fortunately, concentrating on the main front in France. Two-thirds of the rescued soldiers were British (the rest being mainly French and Belgian), ensuring that there would be an army in Britain, where there were now only two Canadian divisions, to meet any invasion attempt. The "miracle of Dunkirk," particularly the part played by small boats ordered out to supplement the Royal Navy, caught public imagination and raised morale.[52]

In this relatively heartening situation, Churchill felt no urgent need to reply to King's message. On June 4, the last day of the Dunkirk operation, he made a defiant parliamentary speech. He expressed gratitude for the almighty deliverance

---

51 Prime Minister to Prime Minister of Great Britain, May 29, 1940. DCER, VIII, Part II, 80–4.
52 Hastings, *All Hell Let Loose*, 64–7.

but warned against euphoric complacency by pointing out that "wars are not won by evacuations." He was emphatic that, despite reverses, Britain and France would fight to victory. He qualified this by adding that, if necessary, Britain would carry on alone: "we shall fight on the beaches, we shall fight on the landing grounds, we shall fight in the fields and in the streets, we shall fight in the hills, we shall never surrender." Drawing on what King had relayed, he ended with the declaration that even if Britain was substantially conquered and starving, the struggle would be pursued by the empire and the fleet across the seas until "in God's good time" the new world of the United States "with all its power and might, steps forth to the rescue and liberation of the old."[53]

Churchill did not repeat the speech on the radio but a BBC announcer read excerpts. Mackenzie King and his civil servants were overjoyed that the peroration reflected their handiwork.[54] But instead of praise, the next day brought a sharp retort from Churchill designed to be forwarded to Roosevelt. He pointed out to King, in case he had missed it: "We must be careful not to let the Americans view too complacently [the] prospect of a British collapse, out of which they would get the British Fleet and guardianship of the British Empire, minus Great Britain." Seeking to increase his own bid for US intervention, he pointed out that transferring the fleet in extremity to an ally would be the natural step but if the United States remained neutral and Britain was overpowered, he threatened that no one could tell what a pro-German administration might do. He agreed that Roosevelt was Britain's best friend but so far there had been no practical help, not even a "worthy contribution in destroyers or planes, or a visit of a squadron of their Fleet to the southern Irish ports." He urged King: "Any pressure you can apply in this direction would be invaluable." Obviating any censure of the Canadian prime minister, he added his gratitude for sending the destroyers, which were now in service.[55]

Mackenzie King added his own lengthy exegesis and sent Keenleyside with the message to Washington. Assuming that his offer had been accepted, Roosevelt opened the meeting by saying that he had been "thrilled and delighted" by Churchill's "wonderful speech." His mood fell as Keenleyside read the communiqué to him and Cordell Hull. King said that while Churchill was a great fighter

53 James, *Churchill: Complete Speeches*, 6260–8.
54 Diary, June 4, 1940.
55 Dominions Secretary to Secretary of State for External Affairs, June 5, 1940. DCER, VIII, Part II, 87–8.

who would never surrender, he was also a scrupulous constitutionalist who, if opinion turned against him, would give way to a government that would negotiate with Germany. King claimed that that this was no bargaining bluff – which it was, whether he realized it or not – "but solely to make the position absolutely clear to Mr. R." As Churchill had implored, King through Keenleyside added his own opinion that "it would be impossible to over-estimate what effect on the entire progress of the war, any additional assistance which the United States could give in any shape or form would be certain to have."

This was not what Roosevelt had expected to hear but he quickly assembled his thoughts. If Churchill's telegram expressed his real attitude, he replied, it was "alarming and distressing" and inconsistent with his bold speech. No stranger to saying one thing publicly and another privately, it was clear to him that Churchill was playing his best, perhaps his only card, to get immediate help from the United States. A couple of days later, Churchill increased the pressure by having the British ambassador tell the president directly that a minister under the fascist leader Sir Oswald Mosley (who had been jailed under emergency powers), or someone of the kind (he was too tactful to mention the more likely Halifax or even Chamberlain) would be able to obtain better surrender terms in exchange for the navy. In that case, the United States might also fall: "If we go down, Hitler has a very good chance of conquering the world."[56]

In his conversation with Keenleyside, Roosevelt tried to pin Churchill down to his public pronouncement. He claimed that a traitorous government could only be imposed by German bayonets. A true British one might capitulate but it would not have to give up the navy. The British should at least match the "guts" of the Germans who had sunk their fleet when it was interned at Scapa Flow in 1918. "Surely the British would not do less! The British Fleet at the bottom of the ocean would be better for the world than the British Fleet converted into a German Fleet." Roosevelt and Hull brushed aside pettifogging quibbles about constitutional niceties by observing that there was nothing to prevent the escape of the navy. If it was impossible to set up an "Imperial Council" to coordinate the empire's actions – something even King might have accepted in an emergency – the dominions and colonies could at least use the warships to defend themselves. The president insisted that Churchill stick to his speech, "a 'marvellous' performance worthy of the best traditions of British history." He denied the unworthy

---

56 Churchill to Lord Lothian, June 9, 1940. Gilbert, *The Churchill War Papers*, II, 270–1.

interpretation that rescuing the fleet was "an American Plan." It was one "to save the Empire" and restore British liberties. An enlarged German navy, acting in conjunction with Japan, would make it impossible for the United States, except in the Americas, to protect the British Empire. Roosevelt raised his own bid by saying that if his offer was rejected, the chief victims would be the people of Britain and the empire: "And they will have to share in the responsibility for the destruction of our type of civilization."[57]

Mackenzie King did not hurry to translate this hard retort into tactful terms for Churchill, partly because his minister of national defence and one of his closest colleagues, Norman Rogers, died in a plane crash. On that same day, June 10, Italy joined Germany in the war, attacking the south of France and threatening Britain's position in the Mediterranean and the Suez Canal, the shortest sea route to the empire in the east. The French government fled Paris before the German army, moving west to Tours where Churchill, in what proved to be his last mission to keep the fragmented ministry in the war, promised Britain's complete support. In a bold move, without concern for constitutional niceties or any consultation, he proposed a union of the two countries and their empires, which would at very least provide a basis for continuing the fight from French colonies in north Africa if the metropolis surrendered. Mackenzie King, himself overseeing a country of which about one-third was francophone, was enthusiastic about this proposed union, excitedly telling parliament that "the resources of the whole of the North American continent will be thrown into the struggle for liberty at the side of the European democracies ere this continent will see democracy itself trodden under the iron heel of Nazism."[58] This was exactly what Churchill and those French leaders who wanted to persist in the war wanted to hear but King had no authority to speak for the United States. No wonder the American minister "coloured up" when he and King discussed the speech, defensively maintaining that there were many things that could be done short of war and that the president was doing all he could.[59] King sent an encouraging cable to the French government but it was of no consequence. With no chance of an American rescue, the French rejected amalgamation on the grounds that it would mean dominion status at best. On June 16, Marshal Henri-Philippe Pétain, the eighty-four-year-old hero

---

57 Memorandum from Counsellor [Keenleyside] to Prime Minister, June 8 (?) and Memorandum by Prime Minister, June 6 (?) 1940. DCER, VIII, Part II, 95–7 and 89–93.
58 *Canada, House of Commons Debates, 1940*, I, 78–9. (June 14, 1940.)
59 Diary, June 14, 1940.

of the First World War, who despaired of his country in another such carnage, became prime minister and opened negotiations with Germany.

That day, Churchill sent another message to King. He had not yet received Roosevelt's response to the one ten days earlier but he was highly conscious that Canada was now Britain's principal support. Perhaps thinking that the threat of a collaborationist British ministry had given Roosevelt and even King pause about sending vital aid, he altered his tone to insist that Britain would not fall. The message was a preview of the speech he gave in parliament (and this time also broadcast) two days later. In the cable to King, he expressed the hope that those French leaders who refused to yield to Germany would carry on the war from north Africa but "whatever they do, Hitler will have to break us in this island or lose the war." He saw no reason why Britain could not meet the challenge alone. Indicating that King should share the information with Roosevelt, he confidently reviewed the strength of the three armed services without even hinting about the additional advantages of having broken the German military radio codes and the radar stations that detected incoming German planes.

Starting with the Royal Navy, Churchill admitted that it would never be able to prevent small raids of up to 10,000 marauders but he did not see how it could fail to stop a real invasion of 80–100,000 and the subsequent reinforcements. He also conceded that the RAF had suffered great losses in France and at Dunkirk but told King that he had hardened his heart and "managed to husband our air fighter strength in spite of poignant appeals from France to throw it improvidently into the great land battle which it could not have turned decisively." (In fact, the decision had been forced on him by a dramatic confrontation in the war cabinet, where Air Marshal Sir Hugh Dowding, commander-in-chief of RAF Fighter Command, argued the necessity of not losing the means of Britain's own defences.[60]) As a result, the RAF was as strong as ever (thanks in part to Lord Beaverbrook, now the minister of aircraft production). The only limiting factor was lack of pilots. Churchill optimistically claimed that British fighter planes had inflicted losses of at least two to one in the battle over France and three or four to one at Dunkirk. Over Britain they would do even better despite the larger German numbers: "All their shot down machines will be total losses, many of ours and their pilots will fight again." The Germans would soon realize the

---

60 Fisher, *A Summer Bright and Terrible*, 117–24.

danger of daylight raids and restrict themselves to less accurate night ones, while Britain would continue to bomb their air bases and industry. He hoped that the British would endure the assault as well as the Germans since "it will on both sides be on an unprecedented scale." Churchill pointed out that since the Dunkirk evacuation there were more soldiers in Britain to resist an invasion than there had ever been during the last war. These were now being rearmed, "at any rate good enough for home defence," and Churchill was sure that they could destroy any landings, which would in turn deter other attempts. While "no one can predict or guarantee the course of a life and death struggle of this character," he assured King that "we shall certainly enter upon it in a good heart." He also believed, or at least fervently hoped, that "the spectacle of fierce struggle and carnage in our island" would bring the United States into the war. But if the worst did happen, he now declared that the fleet could in fact be sent overseas to protect the empire and continue the fight, "in conjunction with the United States, until the Hitler regime breaks under the strain." He assured King that he would let him know at every stage how Canada could help and was confident that "you will do all in human power as we for our part are entirely resolved to do."[61]

Two days later in the speech to the House of Commons and broadcast on the radio, tactfully omitting mention that June 18 was the anniversary of the Battle of Waterloo as Pétain's government negotiated with the Germans, Churchill adamantly asserted that Britain would face the struggle with Germany whatever it brought. This time he made no mention of any possibility of defeat or what might follow. He praised by name each of the dominion prime ministers and thanked them as well as the United States for their help and concluded: "Let us therefore brace ourselves to our duties and so bear ourselves that, if the British Empire and its Commonwealth last for a thousand years, men will still say, 'This was their finest hour.'" It was also encouraging that on the same day, General Charles de Gaulle, who had served briefly as France's under-secretary for war, broadcast from London his defiance of the Pétain government and called on his fellow French citizens to carry on resistance to it and the Germans.

In the day between Churchill's telegram and his speech, Mackenzie King finally composed his now superfluous account of Roosevelt's reaction to Churchill's message. He advised Churchill to clarify that the proposal to move

---

61 Dominions Secretary to High Commissioner of Great Britain, June 16, 1940; and Churchill to King, June 24, 1940. Churchill, *The Second World War*, II: *The Finest Hour*, 227. The cable is also in DCER, VIII, Part II, 99.

the fleet to safety was not for any bargaining purposes with the United States, but rather because the prospect of France surrendering its navy made it urgent for the British to have a contingency plan. He also pointed out the necessity, without specifying what would prompt it, for the United States to be prepared to defend Iceland, Greenland, Newfoundland and British colonies in the West Indies, "to prevent the Germans gaining a foothold in these areas." Canada, he regretted, was not in a position to do much since it had sent its destroyers and aircraft to Britain.[62]

On June 22, Pétain's government signed an armistice with Germany, ceding occupation of the north and west of France, including its naval bases on the Atlantic as well as the Channel. When Mackenzie King was told this the next morning, he could not bring himself to say that Britain might be beaten but he gloomily thought it "difficult to see how she will be able to hold out against the concentration of forces that will take place around the British Isles."[63] The southern third of France was nominally independent but was, in fact, a collaborationist state under the authoritarian rule of Pétain, and whose capital was the small spa city of Vichy. Pétain severed diplomatic relations with Britain but not with Canada. The French minister, René Ristelhueber remained in Ottawa representing the new regime but his Canadian counterpart, Georges Vanier, left France for the high commission in London. There Vanier's former first secretary, Pierre Dupuy, became the chargé d'affaires to Vichy, visiting the French government there three times between November 1940 and September 1941. After the first trip, he told Churchill that Pétain (who was probably hedging his bet) hoped for a British victory and agreed to maintain contact, although he needed to appear hostile to Britain to avoid provoking Germany into occupying all of France. At that beleaguered moment, Churchill grasped at any hint that Vichy France might be pried away from the enemy. He praised Dupuy's "magnificent work" to King and hoped the envoy would soon go back to Vichy: "The Canadian channel is invaluable, and indeed at the moment our only line."[64]

---

62 Secretary of State for External Affairs to Dominions Secretary, June 17, 1940. DCER, VIII, Part II, 98–9.
63 Diary, June 23, 1940.
64 Olivier Courteaux, *Canada between Vichy and Free France* (Toronto: University of Toronto Press, 2013), 40–2 and 56–69; Churchill to King, December 29, 1940; Conversation between Churchill and Dupuy, December 21, 1940. Gilbert, *The Churchill War Papers*, II, 1272–3 and 1303.

By the end of June 1940, Britain stood alone against Nazi Germany, supported by the dominions, India and the empire and able to buy and transport supplies from the United States. But despite Winston Churchill's confidence, it was debatable if he or anyone could save Britain from defeat, much less lead it to victory. And if the British barrier went, Canada and the United States and the rest of the world would be vulnerable to the same threat.

CHAPTER FIVE

Who Weathered the Storm

THE FALL OF FRANCE and uncertainty about the survival of Britain spurred Canada and the United States to secure their own defences. On the day that Churchill delivered his "finest hour" speech, Mackenzie King introduced what was enacted three days later as the National Resources Mobilization Act. Like its British counterpart a month earlier, it gave the government sweeping powers over the population and its property. Everyone between the ages of sixteen and forty-five was compelled to register, with single men between twenty-one and forty-five being identified for military service. The first conscripts, aged twenty-one to twenty-four, were selected in October.[1] Just ten days after Hitler launched his attack on western Europe, Canada announced that its second army division (also volunteers to serve outside the country) would be sent to join the first in Britain. These troops arrived between August and September, during the air battle over Britain.[2]

In the United States, there was far more dispute over the Selective Service Training bill that was introduced in both Houses of Congress on June 20. America's first peace-time draft, it provided for men between the ages of twenty-one and thirty-six to be chosen by lottery for military duty in America or its possessions. On the same day, Roosevelt moved to make his military policy more bipartisan and to undermine the Republicans on the eve of their presidential nominating

---

1   Bercuson, *Our Finest Hour*, 206–7; J. L. Granatstein, *Canada's War: The Politics of the Mackenzie Government 1939–1945* (Toronto: Oxford University Press, 1975), 99–103.
2   Bercuson, *Our Finest Hour*, 42–3.

convention by appointing two of that party's senior figures to armed services posts in his cabinet. The new war secretary was the wealthy seventy-seven-year old Henry Stimson, who had held the position in Howard Taft's administration from 1911 to 1913 and been Herbert Hoover's secretary of state from 1929 to 1933. The navy went to Frank Knox (whose parents were Canadian), a sixty-five-year old newspaper publisher and the 1936 Republican vice-presidential candidate. The reconstruction of the cabinet also intimated that the president was aiming to stay in office for more than half a year.

Still, the fate of the selective service bill hung to a large extent on the Republican nominee for president, who would be chosen at the convention a week later. The surprising choice, on the sixth ballot, was Wendell Willkie, a large, handsome New York utilities lawyer, an internationalist and, until recently, a Democrat who had accepted most of the New Deal except the Tennessee Valley Authority, which by providing cheaper power, had forced him to sell his own company to it in 1939. Two months after the convention, when he was ritually notified of his nomination at a grand ceremony in his Indiana home town, he endorsed selective service. The bill passed, although most Republicans continued to vote against it until it was finally enacted in mid-September.[3]

The fate of Britain, meanwhile, depended to a great extent on Winston Churchill, and how much he could be relied upon to stand fast, and even how physically fit he was for the great task. King was heartened by Churchill's rhetoric but concerned about his drinking. He worried to the American minister to Canada that he might suffer a stroke and be replaced by his government in a panic.[4] However, a strong indication of Churchill's will, and what he might do about the Royal Navy if Britain was defeated, came just ten days after France left the war. The French government refused Churchill's appeal to send its fleet to British ports before making terms with Germany. Instead, it accepted internment of the disarmed warships in French ports under German and Italian control. This was the most fatal term of capitulation for Churchill, who did not trust the Germans not to use the ships. He could do nothing about those in France but he was determined that the Germans should not have those outside. The ones in Britain and at Alexandria in Egypt submitted to the British demand for surrender. The commander of the force at Mers-el-Kébir in Algeria, however, refused.

3   Goodwin, *No Ordinary Time*, 139–42 and 149; Freidel, *Franklin D. Roosevelt*, 347–8.
4   Confidential communications with Prime Minister Churchill and President Roosevelt; Diary, June 27, 1940.

The British opened fire. Some ships escaped to France but two battleships and a cruiser were sunk and 1,300 sailors were killed.[5] This reconciled many in France to the peace with Germany; but the violent act of necessity also clearly showed that Churchill would do anything, even against a recent ally, to stop the enemy. American confidence in him markedly increased and King began to see him as the indispensable leader.

Peace of mind, however, remained elusive for King. He was completely unsettled, two days after Mers-el-Kébir, when his friend Sir Campbell Stuart brought inside information about the war to Laurier House. The rich expatriate from Montreal and director of *The Times* newspaper was once again, as at the end of the First World War, Britain's director of propaganda in enemy countries. Badly shaken by Mers-el-Kébir, Stuart told King that it was a signal to repent. He said people like himself had been too much in love with pleasure and position but he, at least, was now turning from those false gods to Christian principles and concern for the less fortunate. He told King that Churchill was drinking heavily, half a bottle of brandy a day, and was surrounded by the worst kind of upper-class people. Stuart hinted darkly at corruption in Lord Beaverbrook's air production contracts. He had a similarly low opinion of Duff Cooper, the minister of information. He thought that Chamberlain had made poor appointments and should go. Baldwin, he pronounced, had been weak and never amounted to much. Far more disquieting to King was that Stuart claimed many Conservatives were willing to make a deal with Hitler to preserve their possessions, and some high-placed people were in Germany's pay. He was by no means sure that Britain could withstand Germany and thought that salvation lay in a union between Canada and the United States (where he was also well-connected). From now on, the centre of the British Empire would be Canada, with King having more influence with Roosevelt than anyone in the world. After this apocalyptic outburst, King had to seek solace in poetry before falling into fitful sleep.[6]

Roosevelt's information about Churchill and the state of British morale, resources, and Churchill was no better than King's since his ambassador continued to be contemptuous of the prime minister and desirous of negotiating with Hitler. To get a clearer assessment, Roosevelt sent Colonel William "Wild Bill" Donovan to London; he was a former classmate from Columbia University

5   Hastings, *All Hell Let Loose*, 80–1; Bell, *Churchill and Sea Power*, 197.
6   Diary, July 5, 1940.

Law School, a First World War hero, and soon to be the head of foreign intelligence operations. Donovan ostensibly travelled on behalf of his friend and fellow Republican Frank Knox. He was in Britain for close to three weeks from mid-July. The Battle of Britain, the large-scale attack by the German air force, had just begun after Churchill, "not being on speaking terms with Hitler," had scornfully refused his latest truce offer. Carefully avoiding Joseph Kennedy, Donovan was greeted as the harbinger of greater American help, if not engagement in the war. He was impressed by the British determination, the means to fight, and by Winston Churchill, although there is unfortunately no record of their conversation. On his return to the United States, he had no hesitation in telling the president that Britain and its leader were well worth strong backing.[7]

Roosevelt was by this time the Democratic presidential candidate for a third term. Until the very last moment he had insisted that he would not run again and made ostentatious preparations to retire to Hyde Park. But he also believed that he alone could guide the country through its perils, and he loved the job. Nor did the Democrats have anyone else who could beat the highly appealing Willkie. A draft of Roosevelt was coordinated by his confidant Harry Hopkins, the secretary of commerce. On the first day of the convention in Chicago, the keynote speaker, talking well after midnight, read a statement from the president saying that he had no wish to be a candidate again. This was not exactly a refusal. As the delegates considered what it meant, a loud, deep voice, like the voice of God, boomed through the stiflingly hot hall: "We want Roosevelt." It was the city's commissioner of sewers speaking into the public address system from the basement. Thereafter, particularly by those who detested Roosevelt, this became known as "the voice from the sewers." The cry was taken up the delegates and the band struck up "Happy Days Are Here Again," Roosevelt's campaign theme song since 1932. For an hour, it was pandemonium. But the fix was in; the decision was made. Next day Roosevelt was overwhelmingly selected. Modestly, the president announced by radio from the White House that he could not refuse the summons. But he would only accept if the convention chose as his running mate the secretary of agriculture, Henry Wallace, another recent Republican convert (as well as a mystic, similar to Mackenzie King). Wallace was a man of radical views, popular among rural isolationists but a source of alarm to

7   Fullilove, *Rendezvous with Destiny*, 63–102.

many who feared that Roosevelt might become incapacitated or die.[8] From Ottawa, King sent his congratulations to the president. He was also concerned about the physical demands of a third term but thought it was a great opportunity. Presciently, King expected Roosevelt to become a war president, although re-election would depend on keeping the United States out of the fighting.[9]

* * *

After discussing impressions of Britain with Donovan at Hyde Park in mid-August, Roosevelt continued on a tour of military bases. When the American minister in Ottawa reported that prominent Canadians were pleading for defence cooperation with the United States, the president told a press conference on August 16 that his administration was discussing acquiring naval and air bases from Britain for the protection of the western hemisphere, and was engaged in separate talks with Canada on mutual security.[10] This was the first King had heard of it. To add some verisimilitude to what he had said, Roosevelt telephoned to invite King to a meeting the next day at the military base of Ogdensburg, New York, thirty miles south of Ottawa. King, fortunately, had no more pressing concerns than the condition of the Pattesons' elderly dog and the secret entrusted to him of the hiding place of the Scottish Coronation Stone, removed from Westminster Abbey, to ensure that it did not fall into German hands.[11]

After a haircut the next day, Saturday, August 17, King optimistically collected a list of material the department of national defence hoped to obtain from the United States and informed the governor general of his mission. The new governor general, was the Earl of Athlone who had succeeded Tweedsmuir, following his sudden death in January of that year. Athlone set off by car at 5 p.m. with the American minister, J. Pierrepont Moffat. Crossing the St. Lawrence river by ferry, they arrived at a military camp of 94,000 National Guardsmen, which was decorated for the presidential visit. The river was patrolled by an armed boat and Roosevelt's train was heavily guarded. King observed that the train had been

---

8   Goodwin, *No Ordinary Time*, 124–36; David L. Roll, *The Hopkins Touch: Harry Hopkins and the Forging of the Alliance to Defeat Hitler* (New York: Oxford University Press, 2013), 62–6.
9   Diary, July 19, 1940.
10 Hillmer, *O. D. Skelton*, 326; Stacey, *Canada and the Age of Conflict*, II, 311
11 Diary, August 16, 1940.

moved to a quieter setting. The real reason was that there were two large gas tanks near the original siding.[12]

Roosevelt and Stimson, his secretary of war, were in the railway car drinking lemonade after spending five hours in intense heat reviewing troops whose physical condition and equipment were far from impressive. King pronounced the patrician Stimson the "highest product of the best culture of the New World." The president was happy and well, although he complained about the trouble he was having with Congress (presumably over the military draft bill). King was astonished at dinner to see him eat a steak eight times the size that he or Stimson could have managed. During the meal, the text of Willkie's acceptance speech arrived in relays on the teleprinter. Both Roosevelt and Stimson were relieved by his endorsement of selective service and aid to Britain for the defence of freedom. When King asked the president about his own election chances, he said they were very good unless Britain made peace, in which case there would be the cry that a businessman was needed for reconstruction. King thought there was no likelihood of such an agreement, astonishingly adding: "desirable as that might be from some points of view."

Two weeks earlier, the king of Sweden had proposed a peace conference that was rejected by Britain and the dominions. Roosevelt had no idea until King told him. King himself may not have been aware that Churchill told Halifax that he would consider the overture only if Germany restored all the territory it had taken, including Czechoslovakia and France. Churchill had also declared "the intrusion of the ignominious King of Sweden as a peace-maker, after his desertion of Finland and Norway, and while he is absolutely in the German grip, though not without its encouraging aspects," to be "singularly distasteful."[13] Stimson was confident that the RAF would beat the Germans in the ongoing Battle of Britain. Throughout the visit, King made a point of relaying the thanks of Churchill for all that the United States was supplying.

Serious discussion got underway after dinner. It could not, as King said, have been pleasanter or freer. Having already agreed on the principle of the joint defence of North America, talk focused on the plan, which Donovan had encouraged, to provide Britain with fifty First World War destroyers in return for Churchill's promise to save the Royal Navy and to grant military bases in

---

12 Goodwin, *No Ordinary Time*, 145.
13 Minute of August 3, 1940. Gilbert, *Winston S. Churchill*, VI, 694–5.

the Americas to the United States. Churchill did not hesitate over the fleet but was not the only one who bridled at surrendering imperial jurisdiction. King, however, advised the president to ignore such trifling objections: "there were always some fools who liked to hear themselves talk in these ways." Yet, closer to home, King insisted that arrangements about Newfoundland must involve Canada which had military stations there and was concerned about the island's sovereignty. In fact, King's air minister was on his way to Newfoundland at the moment to negotiate Canadian command of the colony's armed forces.[14] King also said that Canada, while willing to consider arrangements with the United States, had no desire to sell or lease any of its own territory.

Roosevelt observed that the important point was to get American troops to Canada as soon as possible in the event of invasion. He thought 30,000 troops could be moved into Nova Scotia within three hours. Similarly, if the United States was engaged in a war in Latin America, Canadian soldiers could be rushed by railway to Portland, Maine. He disclaimed any interest in British colonies beyond having bases, saying the West Indies would simply be a source of trouble for the United States. He said that he had already sharply told the British ambassador that he did not understand the hesitation: if the United States was at war and needed the islands, it would simply seize them. It was far better, he had argued, to have a friendly agreement in advance.

Roosevelt told King that American alarm over its own defence after the fall of France was so great that he had almost despaired of being able to meet British needs. Even now, two months later, he needed to demonstrate that he had made a good bargain for the destroyers. He also wanted to avoid congressional approval which would take months. A week earlier, Dean Acheson along with other leading lawyers had published their professional opinion in *The New York Times* that, although the law prohibited sale of material necessary for the protection of the United States, the president could dispose of obsolete ships by executive order. Fortified with this authority, he said that only technicalities of the transfer remained. He asked King to have Churchill send crews to Halifax and other Canadian ports to collect the ships, which presumably no Americans objected sailing to a belligerent.

The next morning, King accompanied Roosevelt and Stimson to inspect 150 planes. (Germany was then attacking Britain daily with as many as 1,800.)[15] The

14 Stacey, *Canada and the Age of Conflict*, II, 360–1.
15 Freidel, *Franklin D. Roosevelt*, 350.

president got a great reception and at the field church service King was pleased by the reference to visitors from Canada. Back in the train, he produced the list of Canada's military requirements. Roosevelt and Stimson promised to see what they could do but, as was painfully obvious at Ogdensburg, the United States itself was short of equipment. Then, in pencil, the president drafted a brief statement announcing the establishment of a joint US-Canada defence commission. At King's request this was changed to "board," to avoid the necessity of making official appointments. King also questioned that it would be "permanent" but acquiesced when Roosevelt said the body was intended for more than just present circumstances. The announcement by the two heads of government was then typed and mimeographed for the press, with release being delayed until 9 p.m. In this casual way, without signatures or consultation with either cabinet (which was highly unusual for King), came into being a permanent joint board of defence to advise the governments of both countries (it still exists). With a civilian chairman from each country and an equal number of representatives, it gave the appearance of parity to Canada, and for the same reasons, it was why the first meeting was held in Ottawa ten days later. Stimson pronounced the agreement "a good day's work" and King concurred. Canada now had the security to risk more for Britain. The measure also drew the United States deeper into the war, while drawing Canada more into its orbit.[16]

At 1 p.m., King and Moffat set off for Ottawa. King reflected that he and Roosevelt had as usual got along so well because they had so many things in common: in addition to strong religious beliefs and a great reverence for their mothers, "we each felt that the important things of life are very simple and that all that is needed is good-will and sincere intent to effect any great end." Even the meeting place was auspicious since Ogdensburg and Prescott on the Canadian side had been important sites in the war of 1812 and in the 1837 rebellion when King's grandfathers had been on opposing sides: "No one will make me believe that this is mere chance or coincidence. It is part of a definite plan, illustrative of eternal laws of justice." Everything, King thought, confirmed that the purpose of his life was to bring Canada, the United States and Britain together.[17]

16 Thompson and Randall, *Canada and the United States*, 143–5; Granatstein, *Canada's War*, 128–132; Stacey, *Canada and Conflict*, II, 311–14; Kearns, *No Ordinary Time*, 142–9; Kimball, *The Juggler*, 56–61; Freidel, *Franklin D. Roosevelt*, 350–2.
17 Diary, August 17 and 18, 1940.

From Ottawa, King cabled Churchill, assuring him that Roosevelt and Stimson were anxious to provide all possible assistance and that the destroyers should be ready for crews within a week. He added that the United States would supply a quarter of a million rifles (it could not spare ammunition), twenty new torpedo boats (which the president would disingenuously declare were too small for his own country's use), ten flying boats (ostensibly to be tested in war conditions), and 150 to 200 planes that had been ordered by Sweden when it seemed it might be attacked by Germany. He emphasized that Roosevelt had to insist that he was acting in the defence of the United States and to justify the destroyers by acquiring the military bases. He also reminded Churchill, as he had Roosevelt, that Canada was involved in Newfoundland. And he recommended giving another assurance about the fate of the Royal Navy. He reported that Roosevelt was in good spirits and, far more important: "I am convinced that outside the British Commonwealth, you have no truer friends or stronger allies than are to be found in the President and Secretary Stimson."[18]

King's under-secretary, the cabinet, and Canadian newspapers were enthusiastic about the joint defence board. But King's old opponent, Senator Arthur Meighan, the once and (briefly) future Conservative leader, was furious that the same prime minister who had refused to participate in joint imperial defence for fear that it would drag Canada into war now eagerly embraced a permanent commitment to the United States. "Really," he wrote, "I lost my breakfast when I read the account this morning and gazed on the disgusting picture of those potentates posing like monkeys in the very middle of the blackest crisis of this Empire."[19]

Two days after the Ogdensburg conference, Winston Churchill delivered a buoyant account of the war over Britain in parliament that was notable for his tribute to the RAF fighter pilots: "Never in the field of human conflict was so much owed by so many to so few." At the end, claiming that the United States was becoming more involved in the struggle to preserve the freedom it shared with the British Commonwealth, he announced that the government had decided some months ago, "spontaneously and without being asked," that it was in their joint interests for Britain to lease sites to the United States for its air and naval

---

18   Secretary of State for External Affairs to Dominions Secretary, August 18, 1940. DCER, VIII, Part II, 135–8.
19   Granatstein, *Canada's War*, 129–30; Hillmer, *O. D. Skelton*, 326–7; Stacey, *Canada and Conflict*, II, 311–12.

defence against Germany. "In all this line of thought," he added, "we found ourselves in very close harmony with the Government of Canada." Britain was prepared to grant the ninety-nine year leases, certain that they would benefit Canada, Newfoundland, and other colonies in which they were located. He insisted that there was no question of transferring sovereignty or indeed anything contrary to the interests of the colonies (which were not consulted). The arrangement was simply an indication of the mixing up of the British Empire and the United States, a process he regarded with favour and could not stop even if he wanted: "Like the mighty Mississippi, it just keeps rolling along. Let it roll. Let it roll on full flood, inexorable, irresistible, benignant, to broader lands and better days."[20] There was no mention of any bargain for US aid. The implication was that Britain, even in extremity, was generously helping American security.

Mackenzie King's conviction that he had been a great help received a nasty blow a couple of days later when an imperious cable arrived from Churchill. Disclosing his true suspicion that Roosevelt and the Americans were taking advantage of Britain's distress to try to split the Commonwealth and take over as much of the empire as it could, he told King: "It would be better to do without the destroyers sorely as we need them than to get into a haggling match between the experts as to what we ought to give in return for munitions . . . Each should give all he can without invidious comparisons." As for Canada turning from Britain and the empire to seek security with the United States, he sharply observed: "Supposing Mr. Hitler cannot invade us and his Air Force begins to blench under the strain all these transactions will be judged in a different mood to that prevailing while the issue still hangs in the balance."[21]

King was stunned, particularly at this imputation of isolation as his motive for the permanent defence board. A few days later, when the board met for the first time and Canada agreed to US bases in Newfoundland, he told the British High Commissioner, Sir Gerald Campbell, that Churchill's message showed a lack of appreciation for anything that did not suit the current British mood: when things were going badly they made urgent appeals to the United States and wanted King's help; when it looked as though the RAF would enable them to win, they were less interested in American cooperation. The embarrassed Campbell tried

---

20 James, *Churchill: Complete Speeches*, 6275–7. (August 20, 1940.)
21 Prime Minister of Great Britain to Prime Minister, August 22, 1940. DCER, VIII. Part II, 142.

to temper King's wrath by saying that he was glad that Churchill had at least not sent such a message to the Americans.[22]

Two and a half weeks later, on September 7, King received a very different message from Churchill. By then, the Germans had switched from bombing airfields to bombing London in the hope of breaking morale and the population demanding an end to the war. The strategy saved Britain but devastated vast areas of the capital, particularly the poor, crowded areas in the east end docklands. It also signalled what lay ahead for other cities. Across the Channel, the Germans assembled troops and landing craft for invasion. Churchill was one of the very few who did not believe that it could succeed but in a broadcast he called for heroic resistance if it did happen. Defeating such an incursion would be a triumph, "not only for ourselves but for all; a victory won not only for our own time but for the long and better days that are to come."[23]

King, despite his sore feelings over Churchill's reaction to the Ogdensburg agreement, could not help being deeply moved and sent a congratulatory message (which he shared with Canadian newspapers). Churchill lost no time in replying. Invasion or not, he could not afford to antagonize the Canadian prime minister. After the intervention of Sir Gerald Campbell, he was anxious to expunge his earlier bad temper. He told King that he was "touched by the personal kindness of your telegram, and all our people are cheered and fortified to feel that Canada is with the Mother Country heart and soul." He did not mention the squadron of the Royal Canadian Air Force (as well as Canadians serving in the RAF), which suffered heavy losses,[24] but he was thankful for the two Canadian army divisions that were helping to guard Britain. Most pleasing of all was Churchill's gratitude "for all you have done for the Common Cause and especially in promoting a harmony of sentiment throughout the New World. This deep understanding will be a dominant factor in the rescue of Europe from a relapse into the Dark Ages." King thought that Churchill had made amends "in magnificent fashion." The cable gave him "more pleasure than almost anything that has happened to me at any time." He released it to the press as all the shield he needed against Conservative denigration of Ogdensburg.[25]

22 Diary, August 26, 1940.
23 James, *Churchill: Complete Speeches*, 6275–7. (September 11, 1940.)
24 Bercuson, *Our Finest Hour*, 47–8.
25 Diary, September 13, 1940; Churchill to King, September 12, 1940, Gilbert, *The Churchill War Papers*, II, 804; Granatstein, *Canada's War*, 130–1.

Two days later, the great battle over London that had been raging for a week reached a climax on Sunday, September 15, later commemorated as Battle of Britain Day. The RAF sent up almost all its reserves but the gamble paid off. After heavy losses, Hitler decided to abandon defeating Britain for the present and turned instead to eastern Europe, the locus of his real territorial ambitions. Only Churchill and a tiny number of others had any intimation of this. Britain still seemed a besieged island as London and other cities were bombed by night raids through the winter. German destruction of shipping resulted in further rationing and a shortage of everything as those exempted from the armed services struggled amid bombing, deprivation, and exhaustion to produce civilian and military necessities of war. Another invasion attempt was expected as days lengthened in 1941. King, while relieved at the success of the great air battle in September, feared that France, Spain, the Soviet Union, and other countries would soon join Germany. Britain could only be saved in combination with the United States, "and in this no force will have been greater than that which the Liberals of Canada have exerted for years past."[26]

At the beginning of September, Britain and the United States signed the agreement which exchanged the fifty destroyers for the ninety-nine year leases on bases from British Guiana through the Caribbean to Bermuda and Newfoundland (the last two were notionally not part of the deal but granted on the basis of friendship). Roosevelt announced that acquiring these outposts was the most important event in United States defence since the Louisiana purchase from Napoleon in 1803. Willkie did not disagree but charged that the president with undermining congressional authority by acting through an executive order. He was not alone in this objection, but general opinion was that the United States had got the better deal.[27] The value of the ships, apart from the welcome provisions with which they were generously filled, was initially mainly symbolic: many needed extensive refitting, and few could be put into service before the end of the year. Six destroyers were allocated to the Royal Canadian Navy and after extensive modification renamed after rivers on the American border.[28] The transfer of the warships, the military draft act, and Roosevelt's extension of the American-patrolled neutrality zone to two hundred miles off the US coast in August all increased isolationist suspicions that the president was manoeuvring the country into war. Winston

26   Diary, September 16, 1940.
27   Goodwin, *No Ordinary Time*, 147–9.
28   Bercuson, *Our Finest Hour*, 45–6.

Churchill hoped this was true but privately continued to doubt that it would happen and remained apprehensive that the Americans were taking advantage of Britain.[29]

* * *

Whether Roosevelt really was aiming to bring the United States into the war or strengthening Britain and his own country in order to prevent it (something on which he probably had no fixed idea), he had to compete with Willkie through-out the election campaign in assuring Americans that they would not be sent to fight in a foreign war. The two candidates were not far apart in foreign policy but both Winston Churchill and Mackenzie King were relieved when the familiar quantity was re-elected by a convincing majority on November 5 and that the Democrats maintained majorities in both Houses of Congress. Churchill sent his congratulations: "I prayed for your success and . . . am truly thankful for it. That does not mean," he tactfully added, "that I seek or wish for anything more than the full and free play of your mind upon the world issues now at stake in which our two nations have to discharge their respective duties."[30] His uneasiness was not lessened when Roosevelt did not reply. King was more optimistic, thinking that American assistance in the next presidential term would ensure the defeat of Germany and Italy. He telephoned the president at Hyde Park at 10 a.m. the morning after the election and was told that he was sleeping, which was not surprising since he had followed the results until the middle of the night. Early in the afternoon Roosevelt called back and King told him how delighted he and everyone else in Canada was. The president said he would rest for a few days (in fact, he returned to Washington the next day) and hoped that King would visit soon.[31]

Four days later, on November 9, Churchill was able to make a new start on his own administration when Neville Chamberlain died of cancer. His illness had already forced him to resign from the war cabinet and the leadership of the party, in which he was succeeded by Churchill, but even in death he commanded great loyalty and respect among Conservatives. On November 12, Churchill carefully

29 Warren F. Kimball, *Forged in War: Roosevelt, Churchill, and the Second World War* (New York: William Morrow, 1997), 56–61; Reynolds, *The Creation of the Anglo-American Alliance 1937–41*, 113–32; *Meacham, Franklin and Winston*, 70–3.
30 Former Naval Person to President, November 6, 1940. Kimball, *Churchill and Roosevelt*, I, 81.
31 Diary, November 6, 1940.

paid him one of his finest tributes in the House of Commons (then meeting in Church House rather than in the more obvious bombing target of Westminster palace). In Ottawa, King ordered the flag on the parliament building lowered to half-mast in tribute.[32]

A month after Chamberlain, Lord Lothian, the ambassador to the United States, died of kidney failure for which, as a Christian Scientist, he had refused treatment. His replacement in this most crucial embassy called for an impressive figure. Churchill first thought of the seventy-seven-year-old Lloyd George, perhaps to remove him as a potential Pétain for those who wanted to make peace with Germany. For that reason, Roosevelt was not enthusiastic to have him in Washington.[33] Lloyd George in any event refused. Churchill, encouraged by that fertile intriguer Lord Beaverbrook, then settled on Lord Halifax, another principal contender as the rallying-point of opposition to his own leadership. Halifax, and even more strongly his wife, protested this exile but Churchill would brook no rejection of what he presented as a glittering prize. To soothe Halifax's feelings and enhance his credentials, he was allowed to continue as a nominal member of the war cabinet.[34] The lofty – in every sense – aristocrat was never as intimate with Roosevelt as his predecessors, Lindsay and Lothian, but they got along well and Halifax was an effective and impressively experienced figure. Anthony Eden was promoted to foreign secretary from the war office and soon designated by Churchill to be his political heir. But, like Roosevelt and Mackenzie King, Churchill kept the major elements of foreign policy and, above all, the relationship with Roosevelt, to himself.

In March 1941, Britain also got a new American ambassador. The election safely over, Roosevelt no longer needed to keep Joseph Kennedy in his post. At the beginning of December, Kennedy saved the president much trouble by grimly predicting the end of democracy in Britain and the United States and resigning. The new envoy was John Gilbert ("Gil") Winant, Roosevelt's old Republican friend and, since the beginning of 1939 the head of the League of Nations' International Labour Office, which he moved from Geneva to McGill University in Montreal in August 1940. Winant was an unflinching champion of Britain and quickly became one of Churchill's intimates. He was even more intimate with

32 Diary, November 10, 1940.
33 Richard Toye, *Lloyd George & Churchill: Rivals for Greatness* (London: Macmillan, 2007), 375–8.
34 Andrew Roberts, *'The Holy Fox': The Life of Lord Halifax* (London: Phoenix Giant, [1991] 1997), 272–8.

the prime minister's red-haired actress daughter Sarah, who was still technically married to the comic actor Vic Oliver. Churchill apparently regarded this and another similar Anglo-American relationship within his family with the urbanity as he did his ambitious Restoration ancestors' affairs with royalty.

The way in which the two new diplomats were received was a measure of their stature and the importance of the connection between the two countries. Halifax's warship was allowed to enter neutral American waters and Roosevelt met it aboard the presidential yacht. After a welcoming luncheon on his boat, he took Halifax and his wife in his own car to the British embassy. Mackenzie King thought the gesture "a very bold and splendid mark of friendship on the part of the U.S. and Britain at this moment."[35] Winant flew to Britain where his plane was met by the Duke of Kent, the king's brother, who took him by train to Windsor. At the station, George VI greeted the ambassador and escorted him to the castle.[36]

These changes affected Mackenzie King's world. Since Halifax had only briefly visited the United States once and had no natural affinity for Americans, Sir Gerald Campbell, the high commissioner to Canada, who had previously been a highly successful consul general in New York, was moved to Washington. Campbell himself had been considered as the ambassador but ran afoul of Churchill by expressing "heat and prejudice" against Lord Beaverbrook on the matter of air training in Canada. Churchill was so outraged by Campbell's disrespect for his close colleague that he considered dismissing him from the diplomatic service altogether.[37] His reassignment as minister in the Washington embassy was important, but no professional promotion.

Replacing Campbell in the most vital dominion also required a noteworthy person. Again it provided Churchill with an opportunity to shed another unwanted colleague. On January 28, just hours before his under-secretary O. D. Skelton died of a heart attack at the wheel of his car, King received a message from Churchill inquiring about the acceptability of Malcolm MacDonald, the minister of health and leader of the tiny National Labour party (formed by Ramsay MacDonald and those who followed him into the 1931 National

35 Diary, January 24, 1941.
36 Roger Daniels, *Franklin D. Roosevelt: The War Years, 1939–1945* (Urbana: University of Illinois Press, 2016), 162.
37 Churchill to Lord Cranborne (Secretary of State for the Dominions), October 13, 1940. Gilbert, *The Churchill War Papers*, II, 941.

government). Churchill detested the son as much as the father, whom he had once described in parliament as "the boneless wonder." He had trenchantly denounced the younger MacDonald's appeasement of Ireland when, as dominions secretary in 1938, he was the minister responsible for surrendering the three naval bases reserved to Britain by the 1921 treaty. Failing to get them back by negotiation, Churchill kept threatening to seize them by force, although he never did. King for his part was delighted. He had been a friend of his father and had known Malcolm at least since 1924 and had had a good relationship with him when he was the dominions' secretary. King regarded the thirty-nine-year-old bachelor as a kind of nephew and was one of very few he called by his first name. Innocently, he asked if Churchill could spare "so valuable a man."[38] But, as in the case of Halifax, Churchill steeled himself to the loss. MacDonald took some persuading but Churchill appealed to his sense of duty and King's alleged disappointment if he refused. MacDonald was allowed to continue as a member of parliament and his standing meant that he had Churchill's ear. It was a cause of no dismay to Labour leaders that his departure was effectively the end of his party, which disbanded in 1945.[39]

* * *

Just before these diplomatic rearrangements, Mackenzie King was appealed to by Henry Morgenthau, the US treasury secretary, on a crucial matter of goods for Britain. The negotiator for British war procurement had hitherto been Arthur Purvis whom King knew well. After the First World War, when he had been in charge of purchasing American explosives for Britain, Purvis became a prominent industrialist (at age twenty-nine) in Montreal. He was a governor of McGill University (despite having left school at thirteen) and, in 1936, King appointed him as chairman of a commission which successfully recommended unemployment insurance for Canadians in 1940. Two months into the Second World War, Purvis became the director of British purchasing in the United States. By the summer of 1940, he was working closely with Roosevelt and Morgenthau.

38 Diary, January 28, 1941.
39 Clyde Sanger, *Malcolm MacDonald: Bringing an End to Empire* (Montreal: McGill-Queen's University Press, 1995), 201–4; Malcolm J, MacDonald, "King: The View from London" (which is mainly about his time in Ottawa) in John English and J. O. Stubbs eds., *Mackenzie King: Widening the Debate* (Toronto: Macmillan, 1978), 40–54.

When he was recalled to Britain for policy discussions, he was replaced by Sir Walter Layton, the former editor of *The Economist* who was now working for the ministry of supply. Morgenthau told King on the telephone that Layton was likeable enough but fussy and not someone with whom he could do business. With the intense air and sea war consuming military material at a rapid rate, and much being sunk in transit, Britain was hard-pressed to pay for purchases and American industry not producing enough. Purvis' skill in identifying the most urgent requirements was desperately needed.

King promptly cabled Churchill and was able to assure Morgenthau that Purvis would be returned. Churchill was grateful for the intervention, telling King that Purvis would have been given a knighthood except for the 1919 resolution of the Canadian House of Commons that the monarch refrain from granting titles to Canadian residents.[40] Purvis was instead appointed a British privy council-lor. A. J. P. Taylor, who would have got the judgement from Lord Beaverbrook, described Purvis as "a negotiator of genius" who "stood in the first rank of British makers of victory."[41]

Among those who kept King well informed about Churchill and the British situation was Air Marshal Sir Hugh Dowding, the first guest of 1941 at Laurier House, on New Year's Day. King expressed his gratitude to Dowding "for having helped to save us all" in the Battle of Britain. Dowding had made meticulous preparations for the air defence of the island and told King that he was glad when France fell since it wanted everything and would have left Britain exposed. Relived of his post as head of Fighter Command (after being extended three times since 1939) on the ground that a different leader was needed to combat German night raiders, he had stopped in Ottawa while on a purchasing mission to the United States for Lord Beaverbrook's air ministry. One of the few air mar-shals who esteemed the newspaper magnate, he told King that the service did not share his view but Britain would have been defeated without Beaverbrook's "well nigh miraculous" production of aircraft. He did not expect a short war since Britain could not take the offensive until it was superior on land as well as in the air and at sea. An infantry attack would be madness and there was no point returning to the continent until Britain had enough tanks, which meant 1942 at the earliest.

---

40   Churchill to King, December 7 and 12, 1940. Gilbert, *The Churchill War Papers*, II, 1185 and 1222; Diary, December 5 and 11, 1940.
41   A. J. P. Taylor, *English History 1914–1945* (Oxford: Clarendon Press, 1965), vii and 496.

When King asked the most pressing question after Britain's survival and the chances of winning, Dowding was confident of the final result, although the country would suffer great losses and its urban areas might be practically obliterated. His own house had been bombed but he told King that he regretted only the destruction of buildings with ancient associations and traditions since those things were spiritual. Possessions otherwise did not matter. He claimed that people were realizing that eternal realities were worth more than all that was lost. No wonder King thought "One could not find a pleasanter type of man, or a finer type of man. One felt the strength that was behind as one talked to him." (He would have been even more impressed if he had known of Dowding's spiritualism.) To help Dowding in the United States, King contributed his own judgments of Roosevelt, Hull, and Morgenthau and asked Dowding to use his name. After a few months, however, Dowding was recalled for contradicting British policy by telling Americans that there was no need for bombers, which were useless without fighter escorts and might be outmoded by the time they were put into action. He had recommended concentrating on tank production instead.[42]

Three weeks after Dowding came Sir Walter Citrine, the general secretary of the Trades Union Congress (the coordinating body of British unions) since 1926 and president of the International Federation of Trade Unions for almost as long. A great believer in cooperation between labour and capital, and that unions did more than the Labour party for the improvement of workers. At a government dinner in his honour, Citrine said that some of Britain's best planes had been destroyed by the Germans and, for a time, production had been reduced by thirty percent. Black as the situation was in Britain, he thought it no better in Germany where he believed the British bombing offensive was going well. He doubted that the United States could be very effective before the end of 1941 since it was so far behind in production and labour relations were much more tense than in Britain. Citrine was as loud as Dowding in praise of Beaverbrook, telling King over tea that until Churchill's ministry, plane manufacturing had been hampered by business rivalries. Beaverbrook had intervened using "rough methods" and stopped at nothing to spur production.[43]

---

42 Diary, January 1, 1941; Richard Hough and Denis Richards, *The Battle of Britain: The Greatest Air Battle of World War II* (New York: W. W. Norton, [1989], 1990), 319–25, 332–3; Vincent Orange, "Dowding, Hugh Caswell Tremenheere, first Baron Dowding (1882–1970)", ODNB.

43 Diary, January 21, 1941.

Following Citrine, J. L. Ralston, King's minister of defence, returned to Ottawa from a two-month absence overseas. He had had a good reception from Churchill, who sent his warm greetings to King. Ralston thought conditions in Britain far worse than Canadians realized. He would not say that he was "anglicized, but filled with more admiration for the people of England than ever, and feeling that everything possible should be done to help win." He also reported that the Germans were making detailed arrangements for invasion and had twice as many troops for the purpose as Britain had for defence. Ralston was nevertheless impressed by the island's preparations: barbed wire on the beaches and tank obstructions in the streets. Britain would not attempt a landing in Europe in 1941, and none at all until Hitler's empire began to disintegrate, although it would continue striking at various places. Ralston was awed that the British (really Churchill) had risked sending an army to the Mediterranean to defend the Suez Canal and Greece. So far, those campaigns were going well. Ralston felt more Canadian soldiers were needed in Britain.[44] Soon he was advocating overseas conscription for the purpose.

On the same day, C. D. Howe, King's minister of munitions and supply, landed in the United States from Britain aboard Lord Halifax's destroyer. (His outward passage had been memorable: his ship was sunk off Iceland. He and other survivors were rescued by a merchantman but one of the three businessmen accompanying him drowned.)[45] Howe's account to King was far more pessimistic than Ralston's, but King thought it more reliable and he thus made a more detailed record of it. He said that those in the best position to judge had strong doubts that Britain could win, although it might not lose. If it did eventually succeed, it would take at least five years (not far off the mark). Howe thought the German army was five times the size of the British, the air force even more powerful, while the Royal Navy was trying to do what in the First World War had taken four navies and almost three times as many ships. Germany's expected spring invasion would fall mainly on south-east England, which was defended by the two Canadian divisions which, Churchill told Howe, were the best trained and best equipped in the country. Everyone praised Canada's contribution, without which Howe was convinced Britain would not have survived.

44 Diary, January 24, 1941.
45 Robert Bothwell and William Kilbourn. *C. D. Howe: A Biography* (Toronto: McClelland and Stewart, 1979), 9–12.

Howe had no praise for the British administration, which he believed to be inferior to the Canadian cabinet and much less informed. Churchill was everything, Beaverbrook was unpopular for his methods but so powerful and close to Churchill that nobody dare criticize him. Sir Archibald Sinclair scarcely understood his air ministry. Howe did have praise for Sir Edward Duncan, the relatively unflamboyant minister of supply, an industrialist who had earned King's high regard while serving on three Canadian royal commissions. Duncan, however, thought it would be better for Britain to fight without the Americans, who would claim credit. Churchill, whose view was opposite, praised King's help with the United States and agreed that it was better not to have an imperial war council but for dominion prime ministers to manage their own countries.

Howe thought that it would be a waste of time for King to go to London since the British government (namely, Churchill) would do what it wanted. King's conclusion from this report was that there was much to fear and little to cheer about Britain's circumstances, save the spirit of the people and "a certain genius for war." If Japan entered, the situation would become truly desperate. What would Canada do without the United States and Britain without Canada? "It would, I fear, be the end of the British Empire."[46]

Ten days later, Arthur Purvis, at dinner at Laurier House with King and Howe, made some frank comments that would have given Churchill pause about making him the privy councillor. He emphasized the great dislike of Beaverbrook, who wanted to control everything, and the criticism of Churchill for bringing this intimate into the government. Purvis thought it might even result in the end of Churchill's career, who also made many mistakes from excessive drinking, including voicing his anger over certain elements of Roosevelt's policy. He hoped that the two would not be in charge of the peace. King got the clear impression that the government was divided, and that Churchill was practically a parliamentary dictator. No one could tell the outcome of that spring's expected big fight with Germany but Purvis judged the greatest menace to be submarines. The Germans had to fly too high for accurate bombing; for the same reason they could not use poison gas. He was confident that the RAF could keep the enemy at bay, though there was no possibility of Britain returning to the continent for at least a year. In the meantime, the British government might collapse over Beaverbrook. Purvis, whose job was to get what material necessities for war he could from the United

---

46 Diary, January 24, 1941; Bothwell and Kilbourn, *C. D. Howe*, 142–3.

States, said that although Britain was practically bankrupt, its leaders failed to understand or appreciate the Americans: "but for Canada and our interpretation, the two countries would be wide apart."

At the moment, the British government was aggrieved over the requirements to qualify for "lend-lease," a program slowly working its way through Congress. Largely to meet Britain's inability to pay, Roosevelt after the presidential election had proposed "lending and leasing" materials that were vital to any country whose defence was essential to that of the United States. Whatever was provided, he airily assured his fellow citizens, could be returned in some form later, like a neighbour borrowing a hose in a fire. Many in the United States shared the belief, expressed by Roosevelt to King the previous spring, that Britain was still a rich country, although temporarily cash-short. Thus the lend-lease bill sent to Congress at the beginning of January required Britain to demonstrate its desperate necessity by first liquidating whatever financial resources it had for cash purchases, whether private dollar holdings in the United Kingdom (including those in Canada), or British gold reserves in South Africa for safekeeping. In a situation in which all the cards should be on the table, Purvis charged that British authorities were undervaluing and failing to disclose the full extent of the country's assets.[47]

After two months in Congress, lend-lease was enacted on March 11, with the final terms still to be settled. Later in the year, Winston Churchill, recognizing that it was essential to Britain's survival, publicly extolled the measure as "the most unsordid act in the whole of recorded history." Privately, he was furious at the asset stripping and knew that there were even more demands being made as detailed negotiations continued. Britain in time would have to agree to concentrate on war production, which drastically harmed its exports, and also had to accept the principle of free trade and the end of imperial preferences, while the Americans said nothing about their own tariffs. By the end of the process, Churchill was almost choleric but prudently forbore sending the expostulatory cable he drafted. He never confronted Roosevelt on the issue. This has been described by one historian as "one of the great suppressed crises of the war."[48] No one could have predicted (although Roosevelt would not have been surprised) however, that Britain's financial obligations under lend-lease were largely cancelled in 1946.

47 Diary, February 3, 1941.
48 Clarke, *The Last Thousand Days of the British Empire*, 10–55 and 24–6.

Mackenzie King recognized that necessity was forcing Britain to be practically a beggar. But as he watched the process, he was critical that Americans were shirking their responsibility to freedom. Listening to Roosevelt say in a fireside chat at the end of 1940 that supporting Britain against Nazism meant protecting the United States, he thought that the president had probably gone as far as he could. It was not good enough, however: "It lacks chivalry. The people are escaping something that they ought to share and bear in part if they hope to preserve their own souls. . . To accumulate wealth while others die to preserve freedom is not the way that gains blessings for one's own."[49]

King was far more approving of Roosevelt's State of the Union address to Congress, which followed the lend-lease request. The president proclaimed that the United States was "the arsenal of democracy," and called for a staggering amount of rearmament and staked out an American claim to world leadership after the war, even if it was not a belligerent. All humanity declared Roosevelt should adhere to "Four Freedoms": of speech, of worship, from want and from fear. King hailed the speech as an open challenge to Hitler and optimistically considered "the U.S. is now in the war."[50]

At the beginning of the lend-lease bill's tortuous passage through Congress, Roosevelt sent another personal agent to investigate the condition of Britain and its prime minister, to determine what material it most needed, and to judge if it could defeat Germany with American aid. This inquiry was all the more necessary since it was the interval in which the two countries did not have ambassadors. The president dispatched his closest confidant and a resident of the White House, Harry Hopkins. Churchill was well aware of the intimacy and scarcely let Hopkins out of his sight, from the moment he arrived by air on January 9, until he left a month later. He took the frail visitor everywhere, to see both the bombing devastation and Britain's defences. Hopkins met every important person but had no difficulty in discerning that Churchill was the driving force. "Jesus Christ!" he pronounced, "What a man!" At a reception in Glasgow he went far beyond his authority in responding to a speech by the prime minister calling for US aid by quoting the biblical Book of Ruth: "Wither thou goest I will go; and where thou lodgest, I will lodge: thy people shall be my people and thy God my God." Then he added: "Even to the end." Churchill was in tears, although Hopkins had

49 Diary, December 29, 1940.
50 Diary, January 6, 1941.

raised hopes that could not be fulfilled. His conduct in Britain also did nothing to lessen the fears of American isolationists. On his return, he told Roosevelt that Churchill was a rock and that Britain would survive though it needed more material than Americans realized.[51]

As Hopkins' mission came to an end, another representative, in a way, of the US president arrived for ten days. This was Wendell Willkie, the defeated Republican candidate, who on January 12, announced that he supported lend-lease and was going to Britain to see the situation for himself. Seizing this bipartisan opportunity, Roosevelt skilfully invited Willkie to the White House and gave the impression that he was also going to Britain on behalf of the administration. In his own hand, the president wrote a letter of introduction to Churchill and from memory a verse of Henry Wadsworth Longfellow's "The Building of the Ship":

> Sail on, O Ship of State!
> Sail on, O Union, strong and great!
> Humanity with all its fears,
> With all the hopes of future years,
> Is hanging breathless on thy fate!

Willkie was received as enthusiastically as Hopkins and was equally impressed by Britain and Churchill. Recalled to the United States to address the Senate foreign relations committee on the lend-lease bill (which had already passed the house of representatives), he told a room of twelve hundred people that he unreservedly endorsed the measure. When challenged about his criticism of Roosevelt during the election campaign, he said: "He was elected President. He's *my* President now." Impressive as his testimony was, it probably did not change any Republican votes.[52]

Once lend-lease had begun, Winston Churchill, in a broadcast to the United States to "Give us the tools and we'll finish the job," read the verse Roosevelt had sent with Willkie and replied by quoting Arthur Hugh Clough's "Say Not the Struggle Naught Availeth":

51 Fullilove, *Rendezvous with Destiny*, 112–52; Roll, *The Hopkins Touch*, 78–98.
52 Fullilove, Rendezvous with Destiny, 153–97.

And not by eastern windows only,
When daylight comes, comes in the light,
In front the sun climbs slow, how slowly,
But westward, look, the land is bright.

King listened to the speech but surprisingly did not mention the poems. He praised the address as an exceptionally fine one at a dark hour but thought that Churchill went too far in encouraging American cooperation since it was a matter on which that country was divided.[53]

King made his own assessment of Willkie two weeks after the enactment of lend-lease, when the Republican came to Toronto in late March for a day-long war bond appeal. He resented that Willkie got almost as much rapture as the king and queen, and the high praise for lend-lease when Canada was contributing far more in money and blood. But he found Willkie and his wife as glamorous as movie stars and judged that he would have a good chance in the 1944 presidential election: "He is making himself a great man by being a good loser and coming out strongly in support of the administration." King thought he went much too far following his after-dinner speech by jumping on the table and waving at the audience. But King was happy to receive a cheque for £5,000 collected from Americans to purchase a Spitfire fighter.[54]

The administrator of lend-lease was Harry Hopkins, who directed the huge operation from his bedroom in the White House. He persuaded Roosevelt to send as his own personal lend-lease representative to the British his immensely wealthy friend, Averell Harriman. The deliberately informal terms of Harriman's appointment avoided the necessity of Senate approval. There was plenty of friction with Ambassador Winant, a situation the president always enjoyed. Harriman, like Winant, was a firm supporter of Britain who was quickly absorbed into Churchill's inner circle. Like Winant, he became a kind of family member by his affair with Pamela (Digby), the wife since 1939 of Randolph Churchill, who was now in the army in the Middle East.[55]

As soon as lend-lease was passed, Lord Beaverbrook, always keen to preserve his Canadian links and perhaps sensing that critical tales were being carried across the Atlantic, sent a timely cable praising King as "the leader whose

---

53 Diary, April 27, 1941.
54 Diary, March 24, 1940; *Globe and Mail*, March 25, 1940.
55 Fullilove, *Rendezvous with Destiny*, 207–11 and 214–30.

initiative is responsible for such an immense improvement in our conditions."
King kept this testimonial close by to ward off Conservative accusations of being
too accommodating to the US and not supportive enough of Britain. He read it
and one from Churchill in alerting the Liberal caucus that if anything happened
to Britain, "Canada might become the part of the Empire from which the battle
for its preservation would have to be fought."[56]

* * *

There was plenty of reason for alarm about Britain in the spring of 1941, not
least of which was the expectation of the German invasion. The air bombardment of the island, which had lessened during the winter, intensified again in the
middle of March. There were great raids on London, other industrial cities and
western ports as far north as Glasgow and Belfast, which were centres of shipbuilding as well as entry points for military and food supplies. The climax came
on May 10, the anniversary of Churchill becoming prime minister. In the most
damaging attack of the war on the capital, the House of Commons was among
the many buildings destroyed. It seemed certain that the bombing was the prelude
to a landing. (Churchill, however, knew from secret intelligence that it was a feint
for Germany's preparation to attack the Soviet Union.) German submarines were
hoping to starve Britain into submission and cargo vessels were being lost faster
than they could be replaced.

Still, even in the black month of April, only 16 of the 307 ships in convoys and
11 unescorted ones were sunk.[57] Replacing the ships was difficult, partly owing to
Churchill's insistence on concentration on the air force but also from the shortage
of skilled labour after little ship-building for twenty years. Nor – despite what
Citrine had told King about industrial relations in Britain – was the temper of
the workers improved by Churchill appointing Sir James Lithgow as controller
of merchant shipbuilding and repair. Lithgow was an industrial magnate who
had profited from the shipbuilding industry by consolidation and was loathed by
the trade unions.[58] Overseas, the situation was also bleak as Britain had suffered
defeats in the Mediterranean when Germans forces took over from the Italians.
The British troops sent to fortify Greece were repulsed, those in Libya were driven

56 Diary, March 15 and April 2, 1941.
57 Hastings, *All Hell Let Loose*, 274–5.
58 Dimbleby, *The Battle of the Atlantic*, 117–32.

back into Egypt, and the Suez Canal was in jeopardy. The lively possibility that Britain might be overpowered and North America exposed to German attack finally motivated King to accept Franklin Roosevelt's repeated invitations to visit. King was beset by a range of economic problems that threatened to become far worse with lend-lease. He thought it best to deal with these in a personal meeting.

Canada's imports from the United States for war production were generating a huge Canadian trade deficit with that country. At the same time, Britain, after selling its gold and dollar investments, could no longer afford to buy from Canada. Lend-lease would give the British relief on their American purchases and likely lead to a drastic curtailment of British procurement in Canada. These developments put Canada in an economic bind, one in which Americans had a stake by virtue of the high level of exports to Canada and their many business investments there.

The Canadian government, having observed the British experience, declined lend-lease. It did not want to make the necessary trade and economic concessions to the United States. Nor would it agree to sell gold and US securities as the program required. King also refused to sell French gold that had been sent to Canada for safekeeping, even though it could be argued that it was being used to help liberate that country. As Canadian, British, and American officials wrestled with these complicated issues, a meeting of the heads of government seemed the best way to cut the Gordian knot.

The occasion for consultation Roosevelt was another spring holiday for Mackenzie King at Virginia Beach during the Easter parliamentary recess in mid-April. He expected to join the president again at Warm Springs. On his way south, he stopped for a day at Washington, having tea at the White House with the president, Missy LeHand, and Eleanor Roosevelt. Roosevelt looked very tired: "his face was rather narrower than it was, and he looks a bit older and more like a man who is being driven."

Roosevelt told King confidentially that he was in close touch with Churchill and worried that Britain did not have enough men or material to get through the expected dangers of the summer. He was encouraged that the Germans forces pouring into Greece and Yugoslavia were so far being held in check. He did not expect victory but thought that the fighting should be kept going as long as possible to delay German expansion. His main concern was the Atlantic, which he considered the real battlefront. A week earlier, he had extended the US security zone eastward to a line from Greenland to the Azores, 2,600 miles from the North American shore, telling King that he need no longer worry about German designs on Labrador. US navy and air force patrols in the sector informed the British about enemy vessels so that convoys could be saved. The conversation, which lasted an hour, was not the time for King to raise the trade issue since the president was tired and unprepared. Roosevelt thought he would not go to Warm Springs which was suffering from a measles epidemic. King instead would stop at Washington on his way home from the coast. Roosevelt's despondency was hardly dispelled for King by Julia Grant, who added her fear that the spectre of communist revolution was stalking the United States.[59]

The following night, the new Canadian minister to the United States, Leighton McCarthy, agreed with King's assessment of Roosevelt and thought he might not last long if he did not get some rest.[60] This was spoken with great authority since McCarthy was a close friend of the president as an investor and neighbour of the president at Warm Springs. (McCarthy's son John suffered from polio.) There is no evidence that Roosevelt had suggested his appointment to Washington but he was certainly pleased by it. During the fatal illness of the previous minister, Loring Christie (a professional diplomat), King judged that no better person could be found than McCarthy, a wealthy lawyer and company director who accepted the post as a public service without salary. Canadian civil servants were not impressed: one of the legation staff described the seventy-one-year-old McCarthy as "a nice chap, but too ignorant & too old to learn . . . A six hour day in a four day week is about all he can manage . . . the whole thing is rather grotesque."[61] Lester Pearson, his second-in-command and eventual successor, was more diplomatic, observing that McCarthy curiously combined admiration for Roosevelt as the greater of all statesmen with a devotion to the British Empire that amounted to "an almost colonial attitude" by the Canadian towards Great Britain.[62] King privately agreed that McCarthy's best days were over and advised him to leave most of the work to professionals and concentrate on personal contacts. For the next four years, Canada had better diplomatic access to Roosevelt than any other country.[63] The same day that King talked to McCarthy, he called on Cordell Hull who was more optimistic than the president about the war, believing that

59 Diary, April 16, 1941.
60 Diary, April 17, 1941.
61 J. L. Granatstein, *The Ottawa Men: The Civil Service Mandarins 1935–1957* (Toronto: Oxford University Press, 1982), 124.
62 John English, *Shadow of Heaven: The Life of Lester Pearson*, I (Toronto: Lester & Orpen Dennys, 1989), 253. (Pearson diary entry, January 7, 1943.)
63 Diary, February 14 and March 5, 1941.

Germany could be defeated by the naval blockade since it must be short of oil and fats (but which, in fact, it got from the USSR and Romania, which Germany had occupied in October). King also visited the treasury, disingenuously telling reporters that he was going to congratulate Henry Morgenthau on his twenty-fifth wedding anniversary. In fact, he went to discuss the trade deficit, which King suggested could be solved by bartering goods. Morgenthau's far more heartening solution was for Americans to purchase military requirements from Canada for cash. This proposal was further improved when he added that American industry, racing to increase production, was prepared to place large orders. On that highly advantageous ground for Canada, the matter was resolved before King left the United States.

King had lunch at the house of Sir Gerald Campbell, who had arrived at the British embassy from Ottawa. Also present were Lord Halifax and the film star Douglas Fairbanks Jr., a great champion of Britain and soon to be a celebrity US Navy officer. King was astonished when Halifax said that if France had not collapsed when it did, Britain would have been defeated, although he had heard the same from Dowding three months earlier. King, in turn, surprised the British ambassador by rejecting Fairbanks' prediction that the United States would be in the war within a couple of months. No one, thought King, should depend on it fighting Germany, or Japan, which might soon join the war against Britain. Roosevelt could only go so far against neutralist feeling. This did not mean that King approved of the American attitude: he asked the highly religious Halifax what fate awaited a country that was increasing its wealth but was not prepared to shed blood in the great cause of freedom.

* * *

As King was leaving Washington for the overnight journey to Virginia Beach, he received news of Yugoslavia's surrender to Germany and heavy fighting in Greece.[64] The next morning, he decided that the Balkan situation and the bombing of London required him to abandon the holiday and return to Ottawa. After a day at the coast, he travelled overnight to New York, inquiring about seeing Roosevelt at Hyde Park. This was better than another meeting in the capital and appearing to influence Americans on the war. The president immediately invited

---

64 Diary, April 17, 1941.

King to tea and dinner the next day (Sunday) before he returned to Washington that night. King stayed as usual at the Harvard Club and spent Saturday seeing a play.[65] Next morning at breakfast, he was briefed for two hours on a draft agreement of the trade issue by Clifford Clark, his deputy minister of finance, and E. P. Taylor, the brewery tycoon and one of the "dollar a year" men (their salaries were continued by their companies) who joined C. D. Howe's ministry of munitions and supply for the war.

When King's train arrived at Hyde Park, he was met by Roosevelt's press officer. The president greeted him at the door of Springwood along with his wife, one of their sons, and Missy LeHand. Although King did not comment on it, Roosevelt was clearly in far better spirits than he had been four days earlier. For resting and changing, he gave the prime minister the bedroom that had been occupied by George VI, "the King's room in a double sense," as he said. At 4 p.m. the president drove King around the estate in his erratic style and showed him the recently completed library for his papers and memorabilia. He said he was having a hard time with American defeatism, which had increased with the Balkan disasters, but he admired Britain's honourable defence of Greece which had delayed Hitler's advance and provided time to strengthen Britain and the Atlantic: "the battles that will affect the future of the world."

At Top Cottage, the two sat in the sun in shirt sleeves, reminisced about their past together and agreed that the friendship had created a valuable bond for Canada and also Britain. Before Harry Hopkins arrived, Roosevelt wanted to discuss hemispheric defence and the way in which it was helping Britain. Having American convoys would be an act of war, to say nothing of incensing isolationists, so the president was using ship and aircraft patrols to make large circuits around the convoys from Halifax to Britain in the security zone the United States now claimed across the Atlantic. When enemy ships were spotted, the British were alerted, the convoys scattered, and warships attacked the raiders. These patrols were justified on the ground that US coastal defences were not sufficient to prevent sudden, unannounced German attacks. Roosevelt said that he intended to establish a base at Shelburne, Nova Scotia to protect US troops and planes on their way to Newfoundland and King did not object. (The proposal was never realized.)

When King inquired about Canada acquiring PBY Catalina amphibious planes for Labrador, Roosevelt said he was already sending a dozen to protect

---

65 Diary, April 18 and 19, 1941.

Newfoundland and Labrador. King also wanted anti-aircraft guns for Halifax but the president said these were the hardest thing to obtain. Canada had moved six of them inland to northeast Quebec to defend the smelter for aluminum that was crucial for aircraft production in Canada and the United States. Roosevelt considered that there was no risk so far inland and advised returning them to the coast. Speaking in general terms, he pronounced the US defence of North America an extension of the "good neighbour" policy towards Latin America. King did not demur, although he regarded Canada as having a totally different relationship to the United States than the southern republics. Characteristically, Roosevelt said that he did not intend to make any great public announcement about any of this but to "let it out by degrees."

In greatest confidence, Roosevelt told King that he was in constant touch with Churchill. (King did not even dictate the name to his secretary, Handy, but filled in the blank in his diary by hand.) The president had decided that the two should meet. King privately thought the risk (presumably mainly to Roosevelt) greater than any benefit since they were already in such close contact. The president had considered a variety of places, Bermuda, Iceland and Greenland, but since all were far from the United States and dangerous, he had settled on Newfoundland. At this moment, Hopkins arrived and Roosevelt revealed the intention to him for the first time. As a cover, if he could get away in mid-May or later, the president proposed a visit to Ottawa, a trip down the St. Lawrence inspecting defences, after which he would drop the press and head to Newfoundland. All, of course, depended on Churchill being able to leave Britain. Hopkins thought the plan excellent. King, without even hinting that he should be included, was enthusiastic about having Roosevelt in Ottawa.

The three were taken by a chauffeur for a cold drink at the nearby house of "Polly" (Laura) Delano (so called because as a child she would drink only Apollinaire water), the president's unmarried cousin who was devoted to him and, not surprisingly, disliked Eleanor. On the way the president turned to the war materials issue. They discussed the idea of Canada producing goods for the United States to buy and send to Britain under lend-lease. Roosevelt thought that might be going a bit far. King helpfully pointed out that the goods might just as easily be destined for Latin America or China. Hopkins corroboratively added that once things were assembled, it was hard to tell where the components had been made. They also discussed exactly what it was that Canada could best provide to the United States: aluminum, ships, gun barrels, explosives, small arms, and clothing. When King said that he had a suitable statement on the matter with him, Roosevelt, without even looking at it, said that was "first rate." Morgenthau was at his own nearby estate and any refinements could easily be settled with him. In this casual manner, the whole principle of US war purchases from Canada was decided.

Dinner at Springwood included Eleanor and Sarah Roosevelt (who died four months later) and Missy LeHand. The president made the astonishing revelation that John L. Lewis, the powerful head of the United Mine Workers of America since 1920 and of the giant amalgamated Congress of Industrial Organizations (CIO) since 1938, had proposed himself to Roosevelt in 1940 as the vice-presidential candidate. The president could not possibly be so close to trade unions, nor did he want such a forceful vice-president. When he rejected the offer, the former champion of the New Deal turned against him, supported Willkie, and denounced Roosevelt as a dictator who would take the country to war; but union members did not follow him in their votes. It was Lewis' anger, Roosevelt said, that accounted for the recent labour unrest and strikes. Prefiguring his refusal to allow any halt to defence, two months later ending a strike at a California bomber aircraft factory by executive order enforced by 2,500 troops, the president declared that one good thing, which King's great antagonist, the Liberal premier of Ontario, Mitchell Hepburn had done was to fight the CIO.

After dinner, Roosevelt in his study went over the draft agreement on American purchases from Canada that King had brought. He made a few changes and telephoned Morgenthau, who approved each sentence as King read them to him. Then the president called in his press secretary and a stenographer to make copies of the final text. When King asked if they should initial one of them, Roosevelt said there was no need. Taking a pencil he wrote on the original typescript: "Done by Mackenzie and F.D.R. at Hyde Park on a grand Sunday, April 20, 1941" and handed it to King. The six-paragraph statement had no heading but immediately became known as the Hyde Park Declaration. At the train station, Roosevelt distributed copies to reporters. As they rushed to the telephones, King was thankful that he was not required to make a comment. After the president's train had steamed away, he sank to his knees in his own railcar and thanked God for what He had vouchsafed throughout the day. Overlooking the great preparations by his staff, King believed that he and the president had been inspired to solve the difficult matter with no need for advisers and no assumption that "only those in specialized positions have brains and judgment." Never, he thought, was there stronger evidence of divine guidance: "It surely was the Lord's work on the Lord's day."[66]

The Hyde Park Agreement committed the two countries to speed up defence by coordinating their efforts and providing each other with what they could best supply. US components for Canadian military items that were supplied to Britain were charged to the lend-lease account, and therefore free to Canada. This and the increased American purchases from the country eliminated Canada's trade deficit with the United States. When lend-lease was extended to the Soviet Union (with no reciprocal concessions or expectation of repayment) later in 1941, and after the United States became a belligerent in December, Canada developed a huge trade surplus that lasted until early 1944 when the United States stopped purchasing war material from it. The Hyde Park Agreement was a huge benefit to American rearmament and brought great prosperity to Canada. This, in turn, enabled the dominion to continue donating, free of obligation, billions of dollars in purchase credits to Britain.[67] King received endless praise for this contribution to the war effort from Churchill and others. Lord Beaverbrook, who never had any difficulty recognizing a profitable business deal, congratulated King on the agreement four months later and assured him that Canadian Conservatives also supported it.[68]

Beaverbrook, despite his unremitting suspicions of American business, expressed no fear about Canada's further integration into the American economy, but King remained aware of the risk of US domination. The best way to retain independence, he continued to believe, was to preserve the British Commonwealth as much as possible, particularly since "Canada in time, and sooner than we expected perhaps, would become its centre." It was far better to have "two peoples and two governments on this continent understanding each other and reciprocating in their relations as an example to the world, than to have anything like continental union."[69]

For Winston Churchill, even before he had any inkling of the extent of the indirect benefit to Britain, the Hyde Park Agreement was a beacon of hope in a

66 Diary, April 20, 1941.
67 Robert A. Wardhaugh, *Behind the Scenes: The Life and Work of William Clifford Clark* (Toronto: University of Toronto Press, 2010), 199–208; Granatstein, Canada's War, 132–45; R. D. Cuff and J. L. Granatstein, *Canadian-American Relations in Wartime: From the Great War to the Cold War* (Toronto: Hakkert, 1975), 69–92; Thompson and Randall, *Canada and the United States*, 157–60.
68 Diary, August 24, 1941.
69 Diary, April 23, 1941.

dark world. The next day he had to order the evacuation of Greece, thwarted in his hope of a noble last stand to the death at Thermopylae as in the days when the ancient Greeks had faced the Persians. There were also defeats in north Africa. At home, heavy bombing continued, with the anticipation of a German landing to follow. After less than a year as prime minister, the bloom was off Churchill's reputation. He was attacked for autocratic control and charges of rash judgment rose again. There were even mutterings about the necessity of a compromise peace. Salvation at that moment lay in increased material help from the indus-trial powerhouse of North America. Churchill was ecstatic in congratulations to King for taking this initiative in the common cause: "Like yourself, I have always attached the highest importance to dovetailing Canada's war effort in production and finance with the efforts of the United States to aid us both." In apprecia-tion he sent a photograph of himself inscribed "to my old and valued friend."[70] Soon King was also giving political aid and comfort to the hard-pressed British prime minister.

* * *

Three weeks after the Hyde Park Agreement, Robert Menzies, Prime Minister of Australia for the past two years, came to see Mackenzie King from the United States, where he had stopped on his way home after two months in London. His aim was to impress the Canadian prime minister with his energy, enterprise, and leadership qualities and enlist King in his scheme against the seemingly vulner-able Churchill. King instead regarded Menzies as an improved version of R. B. Bennett (who had retired to England and was just about to be elevated to the House of Lords): "a fine looking fellow, splendid presence, great vigour, and has a wonderful gift for speaking. He has endless confidence in himself and does not mind putting himself very much in the limelight . . . [He] is thinking pretty much of Menzies most of the time." During his day in Ottawa, Menzies gave a forceful speech to the Canadian Club and another to the House of Commons in which he forcefully declared: "So long as the Dominions stand, Great Britain shall not fall." He attended a meeting of the war cabinet and a government dinner in his honour (afterwards showing slides of his travels, which included Singapore and the middle east).[71] As King said, he "took this city more or less by storm."

70 Diary, April 27, 1941; Churchill to King, April 25, 1941. Gilbert, *The Churchill War Papers*, III, 544.
71 "A Great Empire Leader," *Globe and Mail*, May 8, 1941

Despite his public resolve, Menzies was by no means confident that Britain could survive unless it got far more support from the United States. Like many of the British political elite, before as well as during the war, he feared that a long conflict with Germany would mean the end of the empire and Britain as a world power. His main purpose in going to Britain was to demand the strengthening of Singapore in order to protect Australia from a possible attack from Japan and to get aircraft and shipbuilding contracts for his country. He had found no joy in either. Churchill would not divert armed forces from the Mediterranean to the far east and Britain could get planes and ships more easily from North America, which was both closer and more industrialized.

The acclaim for Menzies's powerful speeches in Britain and his tours of bombed areas fired his ambition to be a leading figure at the centre of empire. Like all visiting dominion prime ministers, he was invited to the war cabinet and impressed some ministers by daring to confront Churchill over the reverses in the Mediterranean where Australians were fighting. It was obvious, and not to King alone, that Menzies yearned far more to be a member of the British government than prime minister of Australia. To critics of Churchill's high-handedness, relentlessness and impulsiveness, Menzies seemed a better leader, perhaps one who would end the hopeless conflict by a compromise peace. When he left for home, there was a great clamour for his early return from the newspapers of Lord Beaverbrook and Lord Kemsley as well as *The Times*, all of which had defended the appeasement of Germany (as had Menzies). Beaverbrook, Menzies' greatest champion, resigned as minister of aircraft production at the beginning of May. This was announced as being for health reasons (he did suffer from asthma) but the more likely reason was that he dreamed of becoming the kingmaker if Churchill fell, perhaps hopeful of a peace settlement, or simply coppering every bet since he continued as a member of the war cabinet as the undefined minister of state. At the end of June, the improved prospects of war had the same effect on his health and he became the minister of supply.

Churchill was well aware that Menzies intended to establish himself in London as a permanent challenger, not least from the confidential report of a well-lubricated dinner Menzies held for Australian journalists that the censor forwarded to Downing street.[72] An imperial war conference was the means which Menzies saw to force himself into the British war directorate; perhaps,

---

72   Day, *Menzies & Churchill at War*, 159–60 and 176–9.

he dreamed, being accepted as the representative of all the dominions. There was plenty of pressure within Britain for an imperial council in order to limit Churchill, but the prime minister had no intention of allowing it. While claiming to be in favour a Commonwealth meeting, he worked hard to prevent one. He did the same about Menzies's return to London. Knowing King's opposition to a meeting, Churchill recognized him as his strongest ally.

When Menzies told King that Churchill had asked him to discuss an imperial conference, the Canadian prime minister had no difficulty sensing what was afoot. In the Canadian war cabinet Menzies said that "there was no British Cabinet, no war Cabinet – that Churchill was the whole show, and that those who were around him were 'yes men', and nothing else." Meetings were held only about once a week, all discussion was arranged in advance, and no one other than Churchill dared say anything. Nor were there meetings of the full cabinet for the general business of the country. The only person really doing things was Beaverbrook, who had given up attending the war cabinet. Lloyd George (bitterly jealous of Churchill) was critical of the government and agreed with Menzies that the dominion viewpoint was needed, particularly when it differed from Britain's.

It was clear to King that Menzies' reason for wanting an imperial war cabinet was "a lack of any confidence in the British cabinet as constituted. He believed that Churchill was capable of mistakes." When King raised the question of something happening to Churchill, Menzies said that the British refused to discuss it, though it might occur any night. He modestly refrained from speculating who might be the best successor. King told Menzies that a Commonwealth meeting would be mere "responsibility without power." As soon as the dominion prime ministers left, the British would do as they wanted. Any meeting on strategy, he continued, would require the attendance of the professional armed services heads, the dominion prime ministers and their military cabinet members, all of whom were needed at home. King thought it far better for individual ministers to go to London and take up matters with their counterparts. When Menzies was sceptical of this piecemeal approach, Howe and Ralston insisted that they had accomplished a great deal on their trips to Britain. King added that there was an ample exchange of information between Britain and the dominions. Menzies tactfully retreated, conceding that no two members of the Commonwealth were the same but all should want more consultation.[73]

73 Diary, May 7, 1941.

Just as King thought might be the case, Menzies discovered that he had lost ground by being away from Australia for so long. This event was thereafter frequently invoked by King to verify his conviction that a leader should mainly stay at home. In August, Menzies was forced out as prime minister. His hope for a role in British politics was blocked by Churchill.[74] The fall of Menzies caused no grief to the British or Canadian prime minister. On the eve thereof, Churchill said to King in Britain: "he loathes his own people. He wants to be in England. You cannot hope to be Prime Minister of a people you don't like."[75]

A week after Menzies came again Sir Campbell Stuart, a director of *The Times* newspaper that had been so inspired by Menzies. Stuart confirmed that Menzies wanted to be the British prime minister, adding that some were prepared to accept him. Stuart judged that there was no one in Churchill's circle who was up to the job. Given his present left-wing outlook (like *The Times* during the war), he believed if anything happened to Churchill, the prime minister would be Ernest Bevin (despite the Conservatives having an overwhelming majority in parliament). Stuart showed his agreement with Menzies by saying that the British government was very weak, that Churchill took risks and erred in judgment, and that his main strengths were writing and speaking. Stuart was far more despairing of victory than Menzies had appeared to be in Canada and doubted that the British realized that Germany could probably not be defeated.[76] If Stuart expected to shake King's confidence in Churchill and win him over to Menzies and an imperial conference, he failed utterly.

To thwart Menzies and the British conspirators, Churchill disingenuously proposed an imperial conference lasting a month or six weeks in July or August, knowing perfectly well that this was unacceptable to King, who dismissed it as a mere matter of appearance.[77] When Churchill then suggested a shorter meeting, King similarly regarded it as a response to pressure on Churchill and again rejected it as an empty spectacle entailing great risk for the dominion leaders to leave their countries.[78] King himself went to Britain in August for three weeks but this was a purely individual visit, prompted by a great change in the war. While he was there, Jan Smuts sent a cable to Churchill praising King's "outspoken

---

74 Day, *Menzies & Churchill*, 228–30.
75 Diary, August 24, 1941.
76 Diary, May 15, 1941; Day, *Menzies & Churchill*, 179.
77 Diary, May 12, 1941; Churchill to King, May 11, 1941. Gilbert, *The Churchill War Papers*, III, 650.
78 Diary, June 12, 1941; Churchill to King, June 11, 1941; Gilbert, *The Churchill War Papers*, III, 795.

condemnation" of agitation for an imperial cabinet. "It seems to me unwise with vast dangers looming in Africa and Pacific to collect all our Prime Ministers in London," wrote Smuts. "Our Commonwealth system by its decentralization is well situated for waging world war, and diffuse leadership in all parts is a blessing rather than a handicap. I agree with him [King] that our system of communication leaves little to be desired."[79] Churchill never forgot his gratitude for being freed from Menzies and an imperial conference by King. In their very last conversation, in 1948, he again repeated his thanks.[80]

* * *

The first major transformation in the balance of the war came not, as Menzies and King feared, from a Japanese attack on the British Empire but from the massive German assault on the Soviet Union in the summer of 1941. This was an astonishing event for the whole world, save for a very few like Winston Churchill who knew from decrypts of intercepted messages that Germany was concentrating military force on the eastern border of the Reich. At first light on Sunday, June 22, three million soldiers supported by the Luftwaffe advanced into the USSR along an 1,800-mile front. Hitler was as confident of an easy victory as Napoleon had been on the same day in 1812. Stalin was taken by surprise, having refused to be lured into making preparations against friendly Germany by the suspect warnings from Churchill and even his own spies. Following Stalin's great purge and execution of army leaders in 1937-8 and the poor Soviet performance in the war against Finland, the USSR seemed unlikely to survive for more than a few months. Hitler would then be well provided with oil, grain, and other resources, and be able to return his attention to Britain. Churchill and his military advisers agreed with this grim forecast, but the new front at least provided a respite from the threat of invasion and bombing (although it did nothing for the danger at sea). The respite offered a chance to increase Britain's military strength and perhaps even reverse its defeats in the Mediterranean. Churchill was also safe, politically, for the moment. The Soviet Union was not the source of salvation he hoped for but it was nevertheless welcome. At the end of the first day of the German operation, without consulting anyone, he gave a broadcast

79 Diary, August 24, 1941.
80 Diary, October 29, 1948.

enthusiastically greeting the new ally – not merely an associate against a common enemy – while frankly admitting that he had been hostile to Bolshevism since the 1917 Russian revolution. He also promised aid for the new front, which he would be hard-pressed to provide and deliver.

Mackenzie King, in no more than tepid agreement with the general ideals of communism, pronounced Churchill's speech, he did so many others, "one of the greatest he has delivered." King was as astonished as anyone by the turn of events but hailed it the most fortunate since the fall of France. He expected communist agitation to decline and sympathizers to support the war (as they instantly did) rather than hating Britain and the United States. He also considered that Britain's chances of winning had improved and believed that Hitler had spelled his own doom. In the meantime, there would be "horrible misery and suffering and chaos to millions of innocent people in the Asiatic world, and possibly the spread of the war to India etc."[81] In general he was right but for a very long six months there was no certainty that the Soviets would avoid capitulation.

81 Diary, June 22, 1941.

CHAPTER SIX

Fighting for Roosevelt

G ERMANY'S SWIFT AND WELL-PREPARED attack on a seemingly friendly power required Roosevelt to rethink his European strategy for defending the United States. In Washington, where it was still the previous evening, he and Harry Hopkins studied the first reports of the new war to the accompaniment of another drama in the White House. Missy LeHand, Roosevelt's devoted secretary and frequent hostess for twenty years, was being carried out on a stretcher. Only forty-three, she had suffered a minor stroke three weeks earlier and been confined to her apartment on the top floor. Now she had had a major stroke and was taken by ambulance to hospital. On release, she convalesced at Warm Springs and the White House but it was clear that she would never recover and resume her job. She went home to her family in Massachusetts and died three years later. Roosevelt, whose own vulnerability made him ill at ease with invalids, rarely visited or even communicated with her, although he paid her medical expenses and made provision for her in his will if he died first. Grace Tully, Missy LeHand's assistant, was promoted to chief secretary but she never had the same part in Roosevelt's life or made the same almost flirtatious impression on visitors such as Mackenzie King.[1]

Roosevelt was thankful for the reduction of German air and land threats to Britain but unsure what to do about helping the USSR. Stimson, Knox, and the armed services chiefs prophesied that the Soviet army would not last and many

---

1 Smith, *The Gatekeeper*, 242–71; Goodwin, *No Ordinary Time*, 241–6;

politicians rejoiced at the hope of the mutual destruction of communism and Nazism. Roosevelt was sceptical about Soviet weakness and he was encouraged by his long-time friend and supporter, the immensely rich Joseph Davies, to think Stalin could withstand the invasion. Now an assistant to Cordell Hull, who was ill, Davies from 1936 to 1938 had been ambassador to the USSR, where he had absurdly justified Stalin's dictatorship and purges. Now showing better judgement, he told the president that the Soviets had great armament resources safely beyond the Urals. Three weeks after the German attack, Roosevelt sent Hopkins to London to discuss extending lend-lease to the Soviet Union and to arrange a meeting between himself and Churchill, as he had discussed with King in April.[2]

Churchill was immensely heartened by the emissary's visit. Hopkins showed him a map Roosevelt had torn out of *National Geographic* magazine and indicated in pencil the zone, only two hundred miles from Scotland, within which the US Navy would guard convoys that included ships flying American or Icelandic flags. This freed many British war ships for the dangerous supply route to the Soviet Union over the top of Norway to Murmansk. Since the Soviet ambassador in London lacked Stalin's authority to specify the needs of the USSR, Hopkins next got Roosevelt's permission to go to Moscow, towards which the Germans were now rapidly advancing. After two discussions with Stalin, Hopkins was convinced that the USSR would never back down, and that it was worth risking US aid, which would be lost in the event of surrender. Stalin expressed a new-found morality about Hitler's attack, effectively disclaiming that the Nazi-Soviet pact was in any way responsible for the war. He also had a far longer list of requirements than the United States could immediately supply. With these assurances, the ailing Hopkins flew to Scotland and sailed with Churchill to the conference with Roosevelt.[3]

Mackenzie King hailed Hopkins's "remarkable" mission to Stalin, which he thought guaranteed Britain's ultimate triumph, even if, as he thought inevitable, Japan joined the war. A week earlier he had discussed the new prospect with two cabinet ministers, both dedicated drinkers, who had just returned from Britain. Ian Mackenzie, the minister of pensions and national health, and C. G. "Chubby" Power, the air minister, reported that the German campaign in the USSR had saved the day for British, who were amazed at the Soviet resistance

2   Roll, *The Hopkins Touch*, 108–15.
3   Roll, *The Hopkins Touch*, 108–36; Fullilove, *Rendezvous with Destiny*, 251–315.

even in retreat. If the Soviets held out for another couple of months, it was possible that the German population would rise up against the Nazis. They reported that British rationing was becoming more restrictive, despite American lend-lease supplies, owing to shipping losses. Neither of them was eager to see the United States in the war since it would reduce the aid available to Britain. They brought back high praise for Canada's war effort and its troops, which were the best equipped in the country and restive for action. Lord Beaverbrook had pronounced that there was no need for Canadian overseas conscription since more soldiers were not required. They reiterated that an imperial conference was unnecessary, although Churchill would be happy to see the Canadian prime minister.[4] King was considering a mid-August visit, with no idea that Churchill and Roosevelt would be meeting at that time.

* * *

Ten days later, on August 5, King heard on the radio that an important person was leaving Britain. Since Churchill was absent from parliament that day (he had sailed the day before) and Roosevelt had two days earlier left for a "fishing trip" to New England (where he secretly transferred to a warship), it was not difficult for King to surmise that they would gather in Newfoundland.[5] The next day, Malcolm MacDonald brought a circular from Churchill informing the dominion prime ministers of the meeting. "I hope," he wrote, "you will approve of this action, which may be productive of important benefits and can hardly be harmful."[6] Roosevelt said nothing to King, but neither did he to his wife or his mother.

Meeting Churchill, prime minister of a belligerent country, was a political risk for Roosevelt, bound to give more ammunition to isolationists. As he later said, it was not possible for him to bring King.[7] If he had used the deception of a state visit to Ottawa, King would probably have been assuaged. Left out, he angrily wrote in his diary that it was totally unnecessary for the British and American

4 Diary, July 25, 1941.
5 Diary, August 5, 1941.
6 Churchill to Dominion Prime Ministers, August 6, 1941. Gilbert, *The Churchill War Papers*, III, 1035.
7 Theodore A. Wilson, *The First Summit: Roosevelt and Churchill at Placentia Bay 1941* (Boston: Houghton Mifflin, 1969), 19.

leaders to leave their countries at great hazard, particularly for Churchill. Everything could have been settled by cables and meetings of officials: "To me, it is the apotheosis of the craze for publicity and show. At bottom it is a matter of vanity."[8] The next day he protested on the telephone to the luckless MacDonald that his colleagues, officials and the public would regard it as extraordinary to hold such a conference without him. He understood Churchill's practical inability to invite all the dominions and Roosevelt's desire to avoid trouble with the British Commonwealth and Latin American countries for exclusion, but there should have been a Canadian at the meeting. In this mood, King concluded that Canada should be "a nation wholly on her own vis a vis both Britain and the United States. That we can never expect to have any recognition of the Empire in any other way." He remembered Hitler, of all people, telling him that "countries only sought out others when they thought them so strong that they would hit back unless recognized."[9]

The dramatic meeting of the two towering figures took place from August 9 to 12 at Placentia Bay, on the south shore of Newfoundland. They conferred aboard their respective destroyers which were surrounded by a flotilla of battleships and planes patrolling for German vessels. After so much correspondence, they had a good sense of each other and immediately established a warm personal relationship.

Churchill had optimistically brought a huge retinue of military and civil officials to coordinate the activities of the two countries but the US service chiefs were totally unprepared for any such discussion, having not been told where they were going until they boarded the president's ship. Their concern was still the defence of the United States. Roosevelt, sympathetic and affable as he was, had no intention of creating a formal link with Britain. This was a blow to the British but the limits on what the president could do was starkly demonstrated at the end of the conference when the House of Representatives by a single vote extended the service of the 1940 military draftees by eighteen months, narrowly preserving the army that had been created. Even this was achieved only by the speaker refusing to allow members, as was permitted under house rules, to change their vote after the initial tally. To control what was revealed about the conference, Roosevelt had carefully excluded the press and was not pleased

8   Diary, August 6, 1941.
9   Diary, August 7, 1941.

that Churchill disregarded his request and brought journalists, photographers, newsreel cameramen and the author of popular travel books to record what he expected to be a pivotal event in world history. All were banned from US ships and from interviewing Americans.[10]

Roosevelt's confidence in Churchill as a war lord if anything increased through the meeting, but there was still an underlying tension, with Churchill standing for the restoration of the past and Roosevelt looking to build a better future. The president's priority was to get Churchill's commitment to the ideals of the four freedoms that he had announced to Congress in January, and with which he hoped to shape the post-war world. This was far from the top of Churchill's priorities but he could not afford to discourage or disappoint the president in any way. Recognizing his lack of enthusiasm, Roosevelt shrewdly asked him to prepare the first draft of a statement.

Churchill passed the job to Sir Alexander Cadogan, the permanent under-secretary at the foreign office. Over breakfast, Cadogan compiled a list of Anglo-American liberal principles that according with the four freedoms and the fourteen points of Roosevelt's hero Woodrow Wilson. The British cabinet, chaired by Clement Attlee, reviewed the draft and gratified the president by added a commitment to better economic conditions and increased social welfare. Churchill disliked most of the document but hoped that it would be merely an anodyne statement. He was most concerned that national self-determination should not have any practical application to India and the colonies.

Pushed by Lord Beaverbrook, who arrived by air on the last day of the conference (and was lucky not to have travelled with Arthur Purvis, whose plane crashed, killing him), Churchill strenuously objected to the commitment to freer trade, saying that it would destroy the empire. Harry Hopkins preserved cordiality by a phrase exempting existing arrangements but a pledge to trade liberalization, justified by the Atlantic agreement, was nevertheless extracted from the British in the final terms of lend-lease half a year later. Just after the conference, Roosevelt told King on the telephone that Churchill had "gone up in the air" about interfering with the 1932 Ottawa agreements.[11] King remembered

10 Wilson, *The First Summit*, 85–6. The travel writer and former Beaverbrook journalist H. V. Morton, who was present, produced *Atlantic Meeting: An Account of Mr. Churchill's Voyage in the H.M.S. Prince of Wales, in August 1941, and the conference with President Roosevelt which resulted in the Atlantic Charter* (London: Methuen, 1943).

11 Diary, August 17, 1941.

well the old free-trader's deprecation of "Rottawa," and a week later at Chequers pursued Roosevelt's comment. Churchill defended himself by saying that he was now the Conservative leader: he was still unsympathetic to protection, but it was his duty to stand up for the party's policy.[12]

The joint declaration by Roosevelt and Churchill had no title (or signatures) but quickly became known as the Atlantic Charter. It was endorsed by many countries, including Canada and the USSR, and became an important basis for lend-lease conditions and, later, the creation of the United Nations, world trade and monetary agreements, and post-war decolonization. On his return to Britain, Churchill claimed that it amounted to an assurance that the United States would join the war, although he privately feared that might never happen. His apprehension was not diminished by Roosevelt pre-empting isolationist criticism by telling reporters that he and Churchill had merely had an exchange of views; that the agreement was of no practical consequences and did not bring the United States any closer to war.[13] This dampened the enthusiasm Churchill had felt during the conference after Hopkins had indicated to the war cabinet in London that the United States would eventually join the war and gave a broadcast saying that Roosevelt stood with Churchill against Hitler.

When Malcolm MacDonald brought the news of the conference to King, he complained again about Canada being ignored and the dominions not having the same opportunity as the British cabinet to review the declaration. It was another example of "the way in which the British lost their friends, wanting them in foul weather and ignoring them in fair. So long as they got their own way that was all they wanted." All the same, he congratulated himself for having rejected the meeting of the dominion prime ministers which would have meant Churchill forgoing or at least postponing the conference with Roosevelt.[14]

* * *

12 Diary, August 24, 1941.
13 Hamilton, *The Mantle of Command*, 3–40; Meacham, *Franklin and Winston*, 101–24; Fullilove, *Rendezvous with Destiny*, 323–30; Roll, *The Hopkins Touch*, 137–47; Chisholm and Davie, *Lord Beaverbrook*, 404.
14 Diary, August 12, 1941.

The day after Churchill and Roosevelt sailed from Newfoundland, Mackenzie King received a telephone call from Lord Beaverbrook, who stopped in his beloved New Brunswick on his way to Washington to urge speed on war production. He asked King to delay his journey so that Churchill would be in Britain to greet him, adding that the British prime minister had set aside the latter part of the following week for him. Beaverbrook even offered his own plane to take King to Britain. Despite the opinions of his under-secretary and Malcolm MacDonald, who detested Beaverbrook and doubted that he spoke for Churchill, King decided not to arrive before Churchill. Beaverbrook also urged him to visit Roosevelt first: "You have done more than anyone else in bringing him along to where he is with United States and I cannot think of any greater service you could render than being as much at his side as possible." King declined since it would look as though he was getting his information about the Atlantic Conference from the Americans rather than the British. But he was grateful that the power behind the throne was making arrangements with Churchill's office: "That is the role that he, above all others, likes to play and has played very effectively."[15]

Two days before leaving, King did make a brief and largely inconsequential telephone call to Roosevelt. He said nothing about being omitted from the Atlantic Conference but congratulated the president on it. Perhaps to spare King's feelings, Roosevelt said it had been a very simple affair, a real holiday. Despite the disagreement over freedom of trade, he merely said that the two sides had managed to sort out some supply tangles. He wished King had been there but offered no explanation why he had not been invited. To raise his spirits Roosevelt said he wished that he was going with him to Britain.[16]

On August 19, King left Montreal in a B-64 bomber, the first time he had ever flown. The plane was fitted out with a cabin for the prime minister containing a bunk, a couple of reclining chairs and a heater. He still needed to sleep in his clothes and a cap. The half dozen officials who accompanied him, including the trusty keeper of the diary, Edouard Handy, passed the night following the fuelling stop at Newfoundland in chairs, wearing thick, hooded coats in the unheated part of the plane. King had no fear of flying and was delighted to see the ground from such a height, observing the majestic banks of clouds and watching the sun rise in a golden path from Britain. He felt that he was rising to a higher spiritual

15 Diary, August 13, 1941.
16 Diary, August 17, 1941.

plane and coming closer to God and the souls of those who had gone before: "The vision went much beyond what David could have seen when he spoke of the stars and of God being mindful of man." As the plane flew over Robert Burns' Ayrshire, King sang "Flow gently, sweet Afton, among thy green braes." At 8.30 a.m. "Scotch time," as King said, the plane landed at Prestwick.

He was met by the Canadian High Commissioner, Vincent Massey, a Scottish Fusiliers guard of honour and a Highland military band. After breakfast at the air force mess, King and Massey drove north to Glasgow. This was the first time that King had been to Britain since the coronation four years earlier and he noticed the careworn appearance of women on the streets. In his suite in the very hotel from which he had left to visit Hitler in 1937, King received welcoming messages from the monarch, the Dominions Secretary, Lord Cranborne, and Winston Churchill, who extended a thousand welcomes and invited him to the war cabinet the next day and to Chequers for the weekend. The lord provost (mayor) of Glasgow assured him that everyone liked the extraordinarily well-behaved Canadian troops, only one or two of whom had apparently drunk a little too much.[17]

At night, King and Massey left the blacked-out city by train for London. There, he was greeted by General Andrew McNaughton, Lord Cranborne, and Sir Archibald Sinclair, among others. Although he saw much bomb damage, it was far less than he expected (the east end would have been a very different matter). It was a Thursday but seemed like Sunday with so few people on the streets and not many vehicles owing to severe gasoline rationing. His hotel, as always thereafter, was the Dorchester. Built a decade earlier of reinforced cement, it was considered to be almost bomb-proof. It was a wartime home for the wealthy, including the Masseys, with a luxurious shelter in the basement. King's suite, looking west over Hyde Park, had a bedroom, a large drawing room, an office, and a lobby. He had breakfast with Peter Fraser, the new Labour prime minister of New Zealand, who had delayed returning home in order to meet his Canadian counterpart. King thought the former labourer, who had left Scotland at the age of twenty-six, "a sound, sensible man," probably because he agreed with King on everything. Fraser also thought an imperial conference unnecessary but if there was one, Ottawa was preferable to London. They were in accord that the best place for dominion leaders was in their own countries, that communications

17 Diary, August 20, 1941.

within the Commonwealth were excellent, and that no one other than the prime minister should represent the dominion in the British war cabinet. Fraser said that he liked Menzies but disagreed that Churchill was a dictator. At the many meetings of the war cabinet he had attended, there was always a full and free expression of opinion.

On his way to Downing street, King noticed the anti-aircraft barrage balloon overhead. He stopped at Buckingham Palace to deliver letters from Lord Athlone and was surprised that damage to the building had been repaired so quickly. Westminster Hall was also being restored after suffering minimal damage. At Number 10, Churchill, who had arrived the day before, came to the door to greet King and said how much it meant to have him there. Amid the strains of war, he was not so bloated as the last time King had seen him. He was astonished that Churchill "looked as fresh as could be, and really more youthful than I have ever seen him on different occasions. He said the trip at sea had done him great good." After such a long acquaintance, they immediately resumed personal relations.

In the cabinet room, Churchill introduced the ministers as they arrived. There was no urgent business for the war cabinet and nothing at all from the Atlantic Conference. The whole session had the appearance of a performance to impress the Canadian prime minister. Churchill had a cigar in his mouth but did not smoke much of it. He began by praising King and the far greater part that Canada was playing in the present war than in the last, particularly in finance. The unity of Canada (so far) this time he attributed to King's leadership and long experience. He also spoke of King's friendship with Roosevelt and his work in bringing the English-speaking peoples together. In response, King said that he was in Britain to see how Canada could be more effective. He said the country was "of one mind in its determination to be in the war at the side of Britain till the end with all the resources, human and material, that we could effectively employ." Compared to Britain, the Canadian government had no troubles and he affirmed that relations between the two had never been better.

As business proceeded, King found, contrary to what he had heard in particular from Menzies, that the ministers were all well-prepared and the discussion admirable. Churchill predicted fewer but more damaging German air raids: "Little blitzes at considerable intervals of time." He observed that losses were considerably reduced at sea: "Said they always published the worst and kept the best a secret lest the people got over-optimistic." He warned against a premature invasion of Europe, with the risk that Britain would have to evacuate again, suffering great losses and giving the enemy a chance to build up its power. The chiefs of staffs' presentations suggested that the best hope of the Soviets was that they could keep fighting while continuing to retreat. Churchill thought that if they were defeated they would blame it on lack of British aid, but it was not easy to get supplies to that country: "geography was very stubborn in her dictation." The USSR, in any event, was to blame for refusing earlier assistance and not preparing against Germany. King was impressed by the magisterial manner in which Churchill summed up topics, "in graphic phrases and a wonderful command of language and knowledge of history which he uses freely, and an ability to keep looking ahead[,] making decisions in the light of the long run rather than the short one." Talking before lunch in the reinforced basement of the house, King and Churchill agreed for their own reasons that an imperial war cabinet was impractical. It was difficult to get the four dominion prime ministers together and one could certainly not speak for all. With relief on both sides, King observed that they were "closer in our views than we imagined. He said he was sure of that." There were ten others at lunch, including Jack Churchill (who spent the war in the house), who recalled the visit to Kingsmere in 1929, and Clementine and Pamela Churchill. King declined drink, which he had given up for the war, telling Churchill, perhaps pointedly, that he felt less tired without it. He was astonished at the quantity and variety of liquor that Churchill consumed, noticing that his face became much less intellectual, "though it was clear that his brain became very stimulated and he talked very freely and most interestingly." Clementine told King that her husband was not a natural orator, meaning a spontaneous one like Lloyd George, but had to devote great care to his speeches. Peter Fraser, who had been at Chequers when the Germans invaded the USSR, had told King the same thing that morning, that Churchill had spent all day on his radio broadcast: "sometimes thoughts came with a rush; everything seemed to come at once but usually it was a trickle."

At the luncheon, Churchill did not mention the Atlantic Conference but did express his admiration for Roosevelt, the way he had overcome his infirmity, and his great courage. Probably further to gratify King, he said without prompting that there was no need for conscription in Canada: "That this was not a war of men but a war of specialized machines." Later at the hotel, King was careful to tell his Navy Minister, Angus Macdonald, who was leaving for Canada, to relay Churchill's opinion to the cabinet.

After the ladies left the table, King, probably thinking to return Churchill's compliments, reminded him of his 1936 prediction at Abe Bailey's that Germany would conquer Britain unless there was a war to stop its rapid rearmament. When he added the, what he expected to be the agreeable observation that the League of Nations had been a mere façade, Churchill said that he had liked its ideals of opposing aggression but it required an armed force ("Arms and the Covenant"). King also produced what was for him the novel argument that it was the coalition National Government that had prevented the Conservatives from fighting for rearmament, something for which he had no enthusiasm at the time. Churchill agreed, blaming Baldwin for pacifying left and right in order to live a quiet life, like "a toad basking in the sun." King did not break the mood of the occasion by defending the figure he had so admired. (Nor, to avoid the appearance of being critical of Churchill, did he visit Baldwin, then or later.)

Churchill only partially agreed with King that Chamberlain had not received enough credit as an early champion of rearmament, saying that after Munich he was so convinced that peace was secure that he had turned the other way. Like Baldwin, he had also gone too far in pacifism and appeasement. King defended his own stance, saying that Canada would never have gone to war as a united country at the time of Munich, although he claimed that he was prepared to do so. He made the important point that the interval before the war began convinced many that the issue was aggression; but Churchill insisted that it would have been easier to stop Germany before it acquired the Sudetenland and increased its armaments. The war, as he ever afterwards reiterated, in his speeches and writings, could easily have been prevented two or three years earlier: "the people to blame for this war are the British themselves."

As he accompanied King to the door, Churchill said that the Canadian troops were possibly getting restive about not being in action but insisted that they were needed for Britain's defence. They would, he said, have plenty of fighting before the war was over. Earlier in the day, King had told McNaughton that he was prepared for them to serve anywhere, so long as the Canadian government was consulted on the place. King pulled out the preface to a collection of his war speeches that was about to be published and Churchill must have been pleased that the title was *Canada at Britain's Side*. He amiably invited King to drop into the house and the cabinet at any time. That night, as he dictated this account for his diary, King looked into the blackout and saw cars with pin-prick headlights and reflections in the sky of the searchlights of the anti-aircraft batteries in Hyde Park.[18]

---

18 Diary, August 21 and first paragraph of 22, 1941.

* * *

Next day, at a luncheon in his honour at the Savoy Hotel, King sat between Churchill and Clement Attlee. The British prime minister made a point of explaining that he would have liked to have had King at the Atlantic Conference but wanted it to be a tête-à-tête to get to know Roosevelt. There was no mention of the US president's problem with the attendance of the Canadian prime minister. King tactfully said that he perfectly understood and recognized the embarrassment that his presence alone would have been to the rest of the empire; but he could not forebear adding that he was the first person to whom Roosevelt had confided his intention of the meeting. Churchill emphasized the necessity of keeping in close touch with Roosevelt. Without the United States, the war could not be won. He said that he would rather have an American declaration of war and give up aid than have involvement delayed and the help continued. King gave it as his judgement that Roosevelt, Hull, and Stimson were all eager to be engaged. The problem was Congress, which reflected the desire of the country. He thought no one should count on the United States coming in quickly. Churchill asked Lord Cranborne to give King a full report of the Atlantic meeting and told the whole table that there was no one who knew the president like King, and how pleased he was that he was present in Britain immediately after the conference with Roosevelt.

When King inquired about Stalin, Churchill declared him "a great man. He was a medieval tyrant but he was quick on decisions. Had a very clear mind. Was very powerful." But he repeated that the Soviet Union had only itself to blame if it was defeated. If it had gone to war at the same time as Britain and France, the war would have been won by now. Instead, the Soviets had been convinced by Munich that Britain would not fight and were not willing to be a sacrifice. Churchill said he had given Stalin a warning a month before the German attack but it had evidently been dismissed. Without revealing that he had secret intelligence, Churchill claimed that he had seen in a flash from the Germans' easy march through Yugoslavia that their next target would be the USSR.

Churchill also talked about Rudolph Hess, Hitler's deputy and confidant, who had flown alone to Scotland on May 10 with a peace proposal, either on behalf of the Führer or on his own initiative, just as Germany was preparing to attack the Soviet Union. Churchill considered the mission "like a schoolboy's performance in mentality." All the Nazi leaders were like schoolboys, thinking that they were using the military machine while it was probably using them. Churchill judged that Hess had become less important, more unbalanced and paranoid as Hitler drew closer to the army. He was now being held in a heavily guarded house near London and, in great confidence, Churchill said that he had recently tried to commit suicide (by jumping off a balcony). He managed only to break a leg, which Churchill thought had brought him back, somewhat, to his senses. At the end of the war, he intended to ask Roosevelt for an electric chair under lend-lease since the gallows were too good for Hess and the other gangsters.

Once more, King raised the unfeasibility of an imperial conference during the war. When there was a storm at sea, all the captains did not usually go aboard one ship, even the flagship. Churchill added: "you have already got war cabinets–five of them. You have got a continuing conference between the lot, what more do you want." The other ministers nodded approval and several voiced their endorsement. King told them that his most important object was to keep Canada united.

In proposing King's health at the end of the luncheon, Churchill said that they had been friends for thirty-five years, which he joked was before most of those present had been born. They had not, as he carefully phrased it, always seen eye to eye but the friendship had grown. Again he added praise for Canada's war contribution and the prime minister's skill in preserving unity. King responded by saying that such a tribute from Churchill and his colleagues was one of the proudest moments in his life. The only thought of the Canadian cabinet from the beginning had been how it could help the British leader and government which were carrying the great burden of the war. Hailing the example of Churchill's courage and leadership, he said that if the war did cross the Atlantic, Canada would fight to the utmost of its strength and resources. Churchill was visibly moved and asked King to give a broadcast in Britain. In briefer conversation with the less loquacious Attlee, King spoke of the importance of maintaining British parliamentary institutions, including elections, in wartime. Attlee said that a general election in Britain was impossible, even if anyone wanted one. In his own east London constituency, so many people had been bombed out, killed, or were in the armed services that the voters could not be collected for a poll. With halls and churches destroyed, there was not even a place for meetings.[19]

19 Diary, August 22, 1941.

* * *

The following day, before going to Chequers, King had a dispiriting visit to the Canadian army camp at Aldershot, south west of London, which was having a sports Saturday. He was always uncomfortable in a military setting and it did not help that it was raining. His car was late. Lunch was delayed. McNaughton said that most of the troops were homesick. King was not inspired as he addressed the 5,000 soldiers. There was some booing mixed with the cheers and one soldier loudly asked when they were going home. Whether the jeers were related to the weather, his lateness, the frustration at not fighting, the desire to go home, or, as King suspected, "Tory tactics," they were disconcerting. Much was made of them in Canadian newspapers hostile to him.

After a sleep at his hotel, King went by car to the prime minister's country residence. On the way, he noticed barbed wire and fallen trees on wheels to be put across the roads in case of invasion. The house itself was guarded by two hundred soldiers. Churchill was in a "siren suit", working on a broadcast report on the Atlantic Conference for the following day. From time to time, he came into the hall from his study on the floor above and at 8:30 p.m. he called from the gallery: "Now children dinner is ready." Among the ten at table were Mary who, at twenty-two, was the Churchill's youngest daughter, whom King had last seen as a baby and who was now an anti-aircraft gunner; General Sir Hastings Ismay, the deputy secretary to the war cabinet and Churchill's closest military aide; and Lord and Lady Cranborne (the last a particular favourite of the prime minister). King again noticed that Churchill did not stint on wine, which quickened his intelligence and facility of expression: "He really is a big boy at heart, untiring in energy and interest."

King was struck by Churchill's "great tenderness and gentleness and lovableness in his own home and with his own family." He reiterated that there was no need for Canadian conscription and that he was opposed to sending the troops in Britain to the heat of the Mediterranean (as though Canadians never experienced such): "This is the place to save." But he did hint that they might be used in raids on temperate Norway to "roll the map down from the top," revealing his ever-strong feeling about peripheral campaigns. He said that there could be no attack against the continent until 1943, when he expected popular uprisings against the Germans. Three days later, McNaughton told King that he agreed about winning the war from the north down and thought forays into Norway would help the spirit of the soldiers and prepare them for a winter war. Churchill's Norwegian rhapsody, however, came to grief on resistance from the army chiefs and the awkward fact that it was beyond the range of British fighter planes.[20]

Turning to Japan, which had invaded French Indochina in July, prompting the United States to cut off oil exports to the aggressor and increase its military strength in the Pacific, Churchill was confident that Japan would not dare attack American or British possessions. If it went to war against the United States, it would have to fight Britain as well. If it also took on the Soviet Union, there would be nothing left of it, after the troops it had already lost in China. The next day, Churchill told King that he had hardly been able to sleep for thinking about how to warn Japan in his broadcast. He showed King as soon as it arrived the copy of a message Roosevelt had sent to the Japanese. King thought it should have been more forceful, although he understood that there would be as much difficulty in getting Congress to agree to a war against Japan as Germany. Britain would have to do most of the fighting, at least initially.

When Churchill asserted that he was a Tory, King retorted that he was rather Liberal-minded. Churchill agreed but said that he must have his authority obeyed, although he was no despot: "I hate autocracy." He was "a servant of the people. There can be no prouder privilege than to be a servant of Parliament. If Parliament says I must do a thing, then I must obey, do the will of Parliament." Having a coalition and almost every MP supporting his ministry was a help; but Churchill, an old rebel, was acutely conscious of not taking their confidence for granted. King said it was good that he had not been in government before the war, which would have made him many political enemies. He thought that there was a destiny to Churchill's life that chose him for the present moment. Churchill, as he later did in his war memoirs, agreed: "It looks like it in a way, as though it were meant." Once the war was over, he insisted that he would retire: "There is nothing that anyone could give me or that I could wish for. They cannot take away what I have done."

After dinner, the company watched a newsreel of the Atlantic Conference. King was shocked that Roosevelt looked like a man at the end of his life. This was followed by a German film of their atrocities in the USSR, which was designed to strike terror into the Soviet population. Everyone agreed that it should be shown in the United States, followed by the one of the Atlantic meeting, to induce Americans into the war. After King went to bed, Churchill went back

---

20 Hastings, *Finest Years*, 207–8.

to work on his speech. At 1:30 a.m., King heard a gramophone with Churchill singing along.[21] In the morning, he sent the text to King, who made a few amendments, notably removing a provocative remark about Ireland that would offend Irish-Americans.

On Sunday afternoon came Roosevelt's son Elliott, a US Army Air Force officer working on establishing bases at Baffin Island, Greenland, and Labrador and who (with his younger brother Franklin Jr.) had been at the Atlantic Conference. Lord Beaverbrook arrived from a transatlantic flight so harrowing that he advised King to return by ship. At 8:30 p.m., the guests gathered in the library to listen to Churchill's broadcast on the radio and which he delivered from his study. Clementine Churchill said that he limited them to increase their effect, and because they took so much preparation. In the speech, he reported on meeting the American president "somewhere in the Atlantic," warned Japan to cease its aggression, condemned the German barbarity in the USSR, praised Soviet resistance, and informed Hitler that he would share the fate of Napoleon. King was most affected by the account of the church service on deck at the Atlantic Conference, with hundreds of Britons and Americans singing familiar hymns that were part of their common heritage. Among them were, "O God, Our Help in Ages Past," based on Psalm 90, in which, as Churchill said, "the brief, precarious span of human life is contrasted with the immutability of Him to Whom a thousand ages are but yesterday, and as a watch in the night."[22]

At dinner afterwards, Churchill told the company that he had been overcome at the service: "He pretended it was the cold he had, but really found it impossible to keep back the tears." For King, this was evidence that Churchill was deeply religious: "It would be strange if it were not, with his love of truth, love and justice, and his profound hatred of cruelty, barbarity and wrong." He said that his text of his broadcast had been typed in separate sentences for ease of reading, and the pages attached by string so that they could be readily turned. He had coughed a few times and Clementine said that he would get letters about it, including cures. In Churchill's euphoric mood, and well-lubricated by dinner, he turned on the radio for music and danced up and down. Seizing the stone-sober King, the two waltzed arm-in-arm while everyone laughed hysterically.[23]

21 Diary, August 23, 1941.
22 James, *Churchill: Complete Speeches*, 6472–8.
23 Diary, August 24, 1941.

* * *

By the time he returned to London on Monday morning, King was exhausted. He curtailed his activities, attended some war cabinet meetings, contacted friends, and twice visited Canadian army bases. When McNaughton told him that he would be expected to address the troops, King felt "what was like a dart pass through my bowels." But all went better than the trip to Aldershot. There was no jeering and his impromptu remarks to four groups of 3,000 were cheered. The soldiers seemed in fine form but King perceived that many "were young men who had hardly had much in life of its necessities and but very few of its comforts." As he thought of them facing the possibility of death, he could not express his feelings: "I cannot talk the jargon of war. There is no use attempting . . . Offering their lives is infinitely greater than anything I myself am called upon to do, except to suffer perpetually from a Tory mob."[24] The following weekend, he spent with the royal family at Balmoral castle in the Scottish Highlands, reminiscing about the 1939 tour. The happy occasion was marred by the moderator of the state Church of Scotland appearing at dinner kitted out in full court dress of knee breeches and a lace ruff, and next morning preaching in a lace-trimmed gown and sporting a large ring. Over this otherwise enjoyable interlude for King hung the ordeal of his speech at the Lord Mayor of London's luncheon that would be broadcast to Britain and Canada.[25]

In fact, the speech at the Guildhall luncheon was one of his best. It contained everything that Churchill could want, although neither he nor any other British minister saw it in advance. King praised the valour of Londoners and all Britons, pointed to the soldiers, materiel and food that Canadians, "one of the least military peoples on earth," were providing, and declared that Canada would share Britain's burdens to the end. Addressing Churchill directly, he returned his compliment at the war cabinet by saying that although they had not always seen eye-to-eye, they had enjoyed an unbroken friendship for over a third of a century (meaning since Ottawa in 1900). He expressed all of Canada's admiration for Churchill's leadership: "By the power of your eloquence, by the energy of your conduct, and by the genius of your leadership, you have galvanized a great people into heroic action, rarely equaled and never excelled in the history

---

24 Diary, August 26, 1941.
25 Diary, August 30 and 31, 1941.

of warfare." King praised Churchill's pronouncement in the broadcast from Chequers that Britain would stand with the United States in the far east and boldly added, knowing Americans would be listening: "A similar declaration on the part of the United States, as respects Nazi Germany, would, I believe, serve to shorten this perilous conflict. At the same time, it would constitute a realistic recognition that Britain is the one obstacle in the way of a Nazi attack upon the New World."

Churchill followed with extemporaneous thanks, which he rarely gave, but on this occasion he had no option. He expressed his gratitude that King had stated in terms more pointed than a British minister could, "that overpowering sense we have that the time is short, that the struggle is dire, and that all free men of the world must stand together in one line if humanity is to be spared a deepening and darkening and widening tragedy."[26] Violet Markham and other who were present added their praise; and next day *The Times* printed the speech along with a highly approving editorial.

After the luncheon King went with Herbert Morrison the (Labour) home secretary, Violet Markham and others to see the bomb damage to historic buildings in the City and to houses and workplaces in the east end. He visited an Underground station used as an air raid shelter by the poor and "could imagine nothing worse than having to spend any time with the numbers of people there."[27] The next morning, his last in London, he went to Dover with Jack Churchill, General Sir Bernard Montgomery, the military commander of the south-east, and other officers to inspect the defences against invasion. Churchill and his wife had intended to go but he was prevented by a message from Stalin threatening that the USSR might not be able to continue fighting without more equipment from Britain and a greater effort to deflect Germans to the Middle East. Montgomery spoke highly of McNaughton but thought most of the Canadian officers too old for battle. He considered that forty (he was himself fifty-four) was the right age for the present war. Soon the First World War veterans were being replaced.

In the afternoon, King went to Downing street to take leave of Churchill who was sitting in the garden with Anthony Eden, undoubtedly talking about the Soviet Union. Churchill was sorry that none of the guns at Dover, which

---

26 W. L. Mackenzie King, *Canada and the Fight for Freedom* (Toronto: Macmillan, 1944), 1–12; Gilbert, *The Churchill War Papers*, III, 1155–7.
27 Diary, September 4, 1941.

could hit the coast of France thirty miles away, had been fired for King's ben-efit. He showed King a cable from Sir Stafford Cripps, the ambassador to the USSR, endorsing Stalin's plea, and his own draft reply regretting that Britain could not possibly increase its efforts in the Middle East but promising help in some other direction. He was prepared to send large quantities of supplies to the Soviets, hoping they would be matched by the Americans, but to supply the entire amount if necessary. (A couple of weeks later, Harriman and Beaverbrook went to Moscow to promise on behalf of Britain and the United States a billion-dollars' worth of aid by the following summer.) Again Churchill said that the Soviets had only themselves to blame if they were defeated.

Even though there was really no good news at the moment, Churchill thought that the worst of the war was over. It might last another couple of years, or something might cause a sudden ending. He said that the British and Americans would have to come closer together in order to help control the world. He called on science for an analogy, saying that protoplasm existed only for union: "The English-speaking democracies must inevitably come more and more into one great organization." He and King, he said, were helping to lay the foundation for the new order: "We will not see it in our lifetime, but it will surely come." At the door, Churchill reiterated the helpfulness of King's visit and said that any messages marked "Winch" were personal, to be decoded by King's secretary and not put into the official files.[28] Although they probably did not expect to see each other for a couple of years, or the end of the war, they did actually meet in greatly altered circumstances in less than four months' time.

King was in high spirits when he left Britain: his Mansion House speech had been a huge success; he had renewed his personal relationship with Churchill, seen and heard about the war situation as well as anyone could; and, gained an understanding of the members and the proceedings of the British war cabinet. Above all, he carried home the valuable assurance that Canadian military con-scription was unnecessary. King's admiration of Churchill as a war leader had soared as a result of the visit. And Churchill was as firmly committed to him as he to Churchill. Shortly after King left, the Canadian Conservative leader, Richard Hanson, and some of his colleagues arrived and were sorely disappointed not to find any ammunition in Britain. Churchill attentively invited them to Chequers but as "Chubby" Power and Malcolm MacDonald reported on their own return

28 Diary, September 5, 1941.

from Britain, he made it plain that he saw eye-to-eye on practically everything with King, who was one of his oldest friends. He had nothing but praise for Canada's war effort and must have galled his visitors by insisting that there was no need for conscription. Other British ministers provided no more comfort. Arthur Greenwood, a (Labour) member without portfolio of the war cabinet, sharply pointed out that Wendell Willkie had come to Britain to help Roosevelt, not to talk against him.[29]

* * *

After returning to Canada, Mackenzie King continued to worry about the war in the Soviet Union and what its capitulation would mean for Britain, whose smallness and vulnerability to simultaneous attacks by air, sea, and land had struck him on his visit. Unless the United States intervened, "there would be no saving of the peoples who are in a position to reconstruct the world." He implored the American Minister to Canada, J. Pierrepont Moffat, to impress on Roosevelt the British cabinet's belief that it could not win without US intervention. Equally fearful of what might happen were Japan to declare war on the United States, King considered Roosevelt's best option would not be immediate involvement but a strong declaration that Germany could not win and the United States would ensure that it did not. King also asked Moffat to tell the president, whose mother had just died, that he would be happy to see him at any time, suggesting that Hyde Park would be better than Washington.[30]

At the beginning of November, King went to Hyde Park for a weekend. This time he was not dissembling in announcing it as a personal visit since the two discussed nothing of importance. King blamed himself more than the wet weather for the dispiriting occasion, for being there too long (he arrived on the Saturday morning), and for Roosevelt also having to entertain crown princess Juliana of the Netherlands and her two young daughters, whom King brought from Ottawa where they were spending their wartime exile. (Eleanor Roosevelt admired the rabbit-fur lining of the children's coats, only to learn that it was ermine.) But it was Roosevelt's exhaustion, compounded by the death of his mother that was responsible for the unusual lack of animation. He seemed to King much older

29 Diary, October 15 and 16, 1941.
30 Diary, October 10, 1941.

than only three months before: "[a] thinner, at times haggard look. Heavy under eyes. Sighing breaths as though very tired now and then." He repeated himself a lot and said that he could now usually work only one or two nights a week. He could be in Washington only so much and he therefore tried to get to Hyde Park as much as possible. He told King that the seemingly spontaneous fireside broadcasts took him and a team about a week to prepare. Roosevelt nevertheless drove the party around the estate and after lunch at Eleanor's cottage, along with Hopkins, Henry Morgenthau and his wife and daughter, and several male and female politics students, spent an hour with the students around the fire discussing post-war reconstruction. He voiced the opinion that (like Churchill) he favoured the United States and Britain joining together to keep world peace. Eleanor told King that this weekend was the first relaxation her husband had had for a long time. She thought it would do him good and help clear his mind, but during the whole two days, Roosevelt had nothing significant to say. King, who was tired himself, thought that a drink would have helped him at least: "I wd. have given anything for just one glass of wine or sherry as a cocktail, but I held out." All night, he wrestled with the temptation to get up and have one.

As he left on Sunday night, he was convinced that the weekend had been a total failure. But ten days later, Roosevelt, perhaps sensing King's unease at his own dejection and unsociability, sent a cheery message saying that it was a "grand and glorious thing" that Canada and the United States had the team of "Mackenzie and Roosevelt" (an indication of how the president saw himself in relation to others) at the helm in days like these. King proudly showed this missive around, modestly adding that probably both countries could get along without their particular leaders but not neglecting to add that their personal association brought benefits to Canada and the United States.[31]

* * *

A month and a half later, King, Roosevelt and Churchill met together for the first time. The world had turned upside down and the United States had been plunged into war. This was not the result of the Battle of the Atlantic or of any event in Europe, where the Soviets were holding out better than anyone had dared to hope, or North Africa which was no worse than a stalemate but, rather,

---

31 Diary, November 12, 1941.

as King had feared, from Japan, which had suddenly struck directly at the United States as well as the British Empire.

The Japanese air attack on the American naval base at Pearl Harbor, Hawaii on Sunday morning, December 7, was less of a surprise to King than to the American and British leaders. King's long-standing fear that Japan would act with its Anti-Comintern partners, Germany and Italy, increased after the military party seized power in Tokyo in mid-October. He thought that Britain and the United States should have been more forceful in deterring Japan. His great nightmare, like Churchill's, was that it would attack British colonies alone, forcing Britain into another war, on the far side of the world with, at best, material help from the United States. By the middle of November, King expected fighting by the end of the month.[32] On the last day of the month, returning from the funeral of his Quebec lieutenant Ernest Lapointe, he was met by dispatches indicating that a Japanese attack was about to begin. It was a false alarm, although the Japanese armada was already secretly sailing to battle stations. King warned Churchill, whose sixty-seventh birthday it was, against fighting Japan without assurance of American support. To his immense relief, his message crossed a circular from Churchill to the dominion prime ministers stating that as long as Japan stayed away from British territory it would have to be appeased until the United States declared war. After exaggerating for a year and a half how close the American government was to military involvement, Churchill was now compelled to admit that the prospect was extremely unlikely.[33]

Churchill and Roosevelt had expected some Japanese offensive beyond French Indochina following the Japanese neutrality treaty with the Soviet Union in April, most likely against the Dutch East Indies. Both seriously underestimated Japanese military strength and skill, and were sure that they had done enough to deter threats to their own countries' possessions. A week before Pearl Harbor, Churchill was privately confident that the Japanese would not risk Anglo-American retaliation: if that resulted, the "wops of the Far East" would "fold up like the Italians."[34] At the beginning of 1941, it seemed that Roosevelt had crippled Japan's military

---

32 Diary, November 17, 1941.

33 Diary, November 30 and December 1, 1941; Churchill to Dominion Prime Ministers, November 30 and War Cabinet: Confidential Annex, December 1, 1941. Gilbert, *The Churchill War Papers*, III, 1538–9.

34 John Ramsden, *Man of the Century: Winston Churchill and his Legend since 1945* (London: HarperCollins, 2002), 206. The remark was recorded but not published by the admiring American journalist John Gunther.

capacity by freezing its assets in the United States and forbidding sales of scrap iron, steel and oil. Britain, similarly, froze Japanese holdings and strengthened the defences of Hong Kong and Singapore, although not enough to assure Australia and New Zealand. In October, Canada responded to Britain's request by sending two infantry battalions to Hong Kong that were not trained for combat but suitable for the expected garrison duty. At the same time, Churchill sent a traditional warning to Japan by dispatching to Singapore two new destroyers, *Prince of Wales* (on which he had sailed to the Atlantic Conference) and *Repulse*. They arrived on December 2, but lacked air cover since the aircraft carrier had been forced to stop for repairs. These threats by Churchill and Roosevelt had no effect. The Japanese were well aware that Britain was compelled to concentrate on its own defence and had suffered nothing but defeats in Europe and the Mediterranean, while American rearmament was at such an early stage that this was the best moment to strike.[35]

When the first report of the Japanese attack on Pearl Harbor – and the US Philippines, Guam, Wake and Midway Islands, as well as the British colonies of Malaya and Hong Kong and the Dutch East Indies – reached Ottawa at 3:30 p.m., King was on his way to bed for his customary afternoon nap. Since it was no more than a rumour, his rest was untroubled for an hour until his under-secretary telephoned to confirm the news on the authority of Roosevelt via Lord Halifax. King immediately summoned the cabinet and called the leaders of other political parties who were scattered around the country. All agreed to an immediate declaration of war against Japan. Since this was an extension of the 1939 decision to defend Britain against aggression, King saw no need to consult parliament (which was not in session) but issued an order in council. Mistakenly believing that the Japanese were acting in concert with Germany and Italy, King told his cabinet colleagues that Providence "had certainly been on our side in that the attack by Japan was on the U.S. in the first instance." In addition to aggression against British territory as the reason for Canada to go to war, he added assault against the United States to the order in council. King was proud that this was entirely a Canadian decision, taken without any direction from Britain. Since it was announced on the 11 p.m. news, Canada became the first country to declare war on Japan, though the formal proclamation was not signed by George VI until the next day, when Britain and the U.S. declared the same. King thought that

35 Daniels, *Franklin D. Roosevelt*, 214–25.

this "most crucial moment in all the world's history" would in the end shorten the war.[36]

News of Pearl Harbor had arrived in Washington at 1:30 p.m. while Roosevelt and Hopkins were having lunch at the president's desk. Hopkins thought that Pearl Harbor must be a mistake for the Philippines, but the president immediately recognized the reality of a daring strike against the main US base in the Pacific, 4,000 miles from Japan. The station was totally unprepared. Even the Japanese planes, which were sighted on radar, were thought to be American reinforcements. The devastation of the bombing was horrendous: two of the eight battleships in port were destroyed, several cruisers and smaller vessels were sunk or badly damaged, 188 aircraft on the ground were wrecked and 159 damaged, 2,400 sailors, soldiers and civilians were killed and 1,200 were wounded. Bad as this was, it could have been far worse: half the fleet, including aircraft carriers, was safely at sea and fuel tanks which might have exploded were not hit. Within a year, six of the battleships were back in service.[37]

As news of the devastation poured in, Roosevelt remained preternaturally calm, as he usually did in a crisis, making decisions, issuing orders, and dictating a brief speech to deliver to Congress the next day. That night, the decision for war was approved by cabinet and congressional leaders. After being divided on the European war, the country was practically united by this direct attack on America. Roosevelt, in cadences of memorable outrage – "a day that will live in infamy" – called on Congress to recognize that a state of war had existed from the moment of Japan's assault. Within an hour, the measure passed both Houses, with only one pacifist congresswoman dissenting, as she had in 1917. Mackenzie King listened to Roosevelt's address on the radio and hailed it as a great triumph, although he still thought that the United States had failed in its moral duty by not going to war sooner: "They have waited much too long in trying to keep out."[38]

In Britain, it was evening when the Japanese bombardment began. Churchill was at dinner at Chequers with Gil Winant and Averell Harriman, sunk in despair that the United States would ever join the war. Suddenly, on the news at 9 p.m., came the first announcement of Pearl Harbor. As soon as it was officially confirmed, Churchill's spirits soared. He told his guests that Britain would go to

---

36 Diary, December 7, 1941.
37 Black, *Franklin Delano Roosevelt*, 683–9.
38 Diary, December 8, 1941.

war against Japan at once. Winant telephoned the president and put Churchill on the line. "It is quite true," said Roosevelt: "They have attacked us at Pearl Harbor. We are all in the same boat now." Responded Churchill: "This certainly simplifies things. God be with you."[39]

Listening to Churchill's broadcast declaration of war the next day, Mackenzie King recalled the difficulty he had had at Chequers in August in trying to convince Churchill that Japan was sure to go to war against Britain. As usual, he marvelled at Churchill's ability "to seize the right words and to express them under such a day as this has been." But he thought Churchill sounded "terribly tired, indeed he has seen the vision of what Japan coming into the war really means. Much more appalling, I think, than he ever conceived."[40] King had no sense of Churchill's great joy, catastrophic as the immediate situation was. Three days after Pearl Harbor came the terrible disaster of the Japanese air force sinking the two British warships that had been sent to Singapore to try to defend Malaya. King was stunned: "It seemed to me to sweep away the last hope of the British being able to protect effectively any of their possessions in the Orient, and that it threatens the existence of Australia and will lead to the Japanese Empire expanding very much to the south."[41] The following day, he grimly reflected that no one could say that the British Empire would survive the war, and the consequences that would result for Canada: "[A]s one who loved the Empire, and felt strongly about belonging to it as against belonging to the [United] States, we had to be careful to see that our moves did not lead the people in the latter direction instead of the former now that a hemisphere war was on."[42]

The United States, of course, was only at war with Japan. Churchill dreaded that this would leave Roosevelt concentrating on the Pacific and reducing lend-lease aid to Europe. But the president wanted to keep the focus on Europe. In his fireside broadcast after Pearl Harbor, on December 9, Roosevelt did his best to link the Japanese strike to Germany and Italy. King considered the speech rather thin, designed primarily to prevent Americans from panicking when they learned the full extent of the losses at Hawaii. Like Churchill he feared that Europe would be "blotted out" as the United States dealt with Japan. Gloomily, he thought the

39 Meacham, *Franklin and Winston*, 130.
40 Diary, December 8, 1941.
41 Diary, December 10, 1941.
42 Diary, December 11, 1941.

Vichy government might join against Britain and transfer the neutralized French navy to Germany.[43]

Two days later, Hitler provided a merciful deliverance. Germany was stalled in the Soviet Union but with the United States locked into war with Japan and seemingly unable to engage militarily in Europe, he dreamed of a truly global victory by the alliance of Germany, Italy and Japan. On December 11, he declared war on the United States, quickly followed by Mussolini. He then delivered a vituperative speech to the Reichstag condemning Roosevelt, the New Deal, the Atlantic Charter, and the Jews who he claimed were behind the president, while praising the Japanese action. It was, as Mackenzie King wrote, Hitler, not the Americans, who had to be thanked for the United States joining the European war.[44] The isolationists were silenced and Roosevelt sent a message to Congress asking for recognition of a state of war between the United States and Germany, forestalling any legislative debate about priority of effort between the Atlantic and the Pacific. Ten days later, he made it clear to the cabinet armed service ministers, Harry Hopkins and the military chiefs of staff, that Germany was the main enemy.[45] This was exactly what Churchill, who arrived in Washington the next day, wanted to hear.

* * *

Churchill began clamouring to discuss the war directly with Roosevelt immediately after Pearl Harbor. Conscious that he was no longer the single greatest hope of the free world but had to share the role with the American president, he wanted to assert his seniority in experience and to argue for Europe before the United States became overwhelmingly committed to the Pacific. Roosevelt sought time for events to develop and to think out the situation for himself before debating strategy with the formidable Churchill. He urged postponing the visit for a few weeks and pointed to the hazards of an Atlantic crossing. But Churchill was not to be deterred. On December 10, Roosevelt agreed to his arrival as soon as possible. Just two days later, Churchill set off by warship, accompanied by the armed service chiefs of staff, Lord Beaverbrook and Averell Harriman. By now his task was easier since the United States had been plunged into war with Germany in the intervening day. At sea (which he did not reveal), he cabled

43 Diary, December 9 and 10, 1941.
44 Diary, December 11, 1941.
45 Hamilton, *The Mantle of Command*, 87–95; Roll, *The Hopkins Touch*, 168.

Mackenzie King in confidence that he was planning to be in Washington for a week from about December 22 and hoped also to see him.[46] This meant King meeting him in Washington. King said nothing about Churchill's trip but word was leaking in US circles. C. D. Howe told the war cabinet on December 19 that he had heard from Washington that Churchill was on his way.[47]

The rough, ten-day voyage gave both Churchill and Roosevelt time to prepare what each would impress on the other. Churchill worked on a series of strategy papers designed to give the British the initiative in discussions on the joint effort with the Americans. The most important point was to continue main attention on Europe and the Battle of the Atlantic, restricting the war against Japan to naval operations. Once Churchill's ship was out of range of German radio interception, the documents were transmitted to Lord Halifax for Roosevelt who instructed his advisers to prepare their own plans.[48] Mackenzie King and Malcolm MacDonald, when they had tea together on December 22, had none of this information but they did not need it to know that the real problems of war were just beginning. King correctly saw that the Americans, with their overwhelming capacity if not present means, would want to take things into their own hands. MacDonald could not disagree but doubted that the "very much prima donna" Churchill would ever give up control of the war from London, though some compromise might be arranged.

At 5:25 that afternoon (King for once failed to note that the hands of the clock were together), Roosevelt telephoned. "Hello Mackenzie," he began in his cheery manner, announcing that a "certain person" would be arriving in Washington in a couple of hours. (The president had also just told his wife and the staff who had to rush to accommodate this unexpected Christmas guest.) With no indication of being prompted by Churchill, he said that he wanted King in Washington and would let him know when as soon as possible, possibly on the evening of Christmas Day. King was thankful that the other two would not be meeting again without him, preventing the opposition from ridiculing his claim to be a link between them. The president told King that there were going to be important discussions about war policy and revealed his determination that the supreme council would be in Washington, adding "there will probably

46 Martin, *The Churchill War Papers*, III, 1638.
47 Diary, December 19, 1941.
48 David Bercuson and Holger Herwig, *One Christmas in Washington: The Secret Meeting between Roosevelt and Churchill that Changed the World* (Toronto: McArthur and Company, 2005), 112–16.

be quite a time over this." King was allowed to bring with him the three service ministers plus the minister for munitions and supply and the under-secretary for external affairs, but he saw clearly that Canada would have real difficulty gaining recognition even for the part it was playing on its own coasts, let alone in broader policy.[49] Churchill, and even more Roosevelt, had no intention of diluting their leadership and complicating discussion by adding other allies. The Soviet Union was a different case since it was practically conducting a separate war. But if King would not influence strategy, he did have the confidence of Roosevelt and Churchill, both of whom valued his opinion and wanted his support.

On Christmas Eve, the US minister to Canada notified King that the president would like him to arrive at the White House in time for lunch on the twenty-sixth. MacDonald, at the same time, reported that Churchill would come to Ottawa. On that same day in Hong Kong, Canadians along with troops from other parts of the British world were at the end of a hopeless week-long battle to save the port from the Japanese. Churchill exhorted the commander to fight on heroically to the very last but on Christmas Day he capitulated to overwhelming force. Among the killed were 290 of 1,975 Canadian soldiers. Another 268 died or were murdered in prisoner of war camps, where the Japanese treated with brutal contempt those who chose surrender.[50] But what was chiefly exercising Roosevelt and Churchill when King joined them was not Hong Kong, the war in the Pacific, the Atlantic, Europe, or North Africa but a "comic opera" victory close to the Canadian coast two days earlier.

Temporary Brigadier-General Charles de Gaulle, who left for London on the eve of Pétain's capitulation, was recognized by the British as leader of the Free French, and allowed to retain command of the armed forces (other exiled governments put their armies under the British). But Churchill refused to acknowledge that de Gaulle was the legitimate authority of France, resulting in volcanic disputes between the two similar temperaments. (The United States, which continued diplomatic relations with Pétain's government after joining the war, took the same attitude.) Grateful as Churchill was to de Gaulle, he continued to hope that Pétain could be detached from Germany, and that a more consequential leader might yet defect from Vichy. Most of the French soldiers who had been rescued at Dunkirk chose repatriation over serving with de Gaulle.

49 Diary, December 22, 1941.
50 Nathan M. Greenfield, *The Damned: The Canadians at the Battle of Hong Kong and the POW Experience, 1941–1945* (Toronto: HarperCollins, 2010).

His force consisted of 3,000 servicemen and two hundred vessels. But he was able to carry with him the colonies in equatorial Africa, providing a secure air corridor from the Atlantic to Egypt and Sudan as the Mediterranean became extremely dangerous.

In September, 1940, at the height of the Battle of Britain, de Gaulle failed in a mission, assisted by the Royal Navy, to capture the prized port of Dakar in Senegal at the furthest extension of Africa into the Atlantic, from the colonial Vichy government. But by November 1941, he was receiving US lend-lease aid to secure the vital African territory he did control. After Pearl Harbor, he saw an opportunity to impress both Churchill and the new American ally. He ordered Admiral Emile Henri Muselier, who had recently attempted a coup against de Gaulle, to seize the tiny French fishing islands of Saint Pierre and Miquelon off the south coast of Newfoundland, where a powerful radio transmitter was broadcasting Vichy propaganda and helping the German navy search for Allied ships. Muselier took the three Free French corvettes and the submarine that were with the Royal Navy at Halifax, plus a reporter from *The New York Times*, and sailed to the islands. In half an hour, on Christmas Eve morning, he took over the government and silenced the transmitter. The next day, the change in authority was endorsed by ninety-eight percent of the voters in a plebiscite.[51]

This bold strike was a welcome contrast to the grim news from the far east. It was hailed by the American, Canadian, and British press. Churchill, who was in Washington, signalled his approval. Mackenzie King, who had consistently refused to take the islands by force, was shocked. In addition to the sensitive issue of Vichy (with which Canada still had diplomatic relations), he was well aware that the Americans regarded the whole hemisphere as their own domain. In his diary, he condemned the take-over as "an arbitrary action contrary to the agreement of all parties concerned and certainly without prior knowledge or consent in any sense of the United States Government." On Christmas Day, Hull demanded that Canada, which he thought must have been complicit, eject the interlopers. King, who was on his way to Washington, refused to do anything until the matter was decided by Roosevelt and Churchill.[52]

---

51 Douglas Boyd, *De Gaulle: The Man Who Defied Six Presidents* (Stroud: The History Press, 2013), 71–83; Simon Berthon, *Allies at War: Churchill, Roosevelt, and De Gaulle* (New York: Carroll & Graf, 2001), 135–60.
52 Diary, December 24 and 25, 1941; Boyd, *De Gaulle*, 105–9; Courteaux, *Canada between Vichy and Free France, 1940–1945*, 116–39; Bercuson and Herwig, *One Christmas in Washington*, 145–7; Stacey, *Canada and the Age of Conflict*, II, 302–6.

When he arrived in Washington, King heard from Lord Halifax that de Gaulle had gone too far and that Churchill, adjusting to Roosevelt's position, was prepared to pull him up. At the state department, Hull told King that anything upsetting American relations with Vichy would be serious. The United States feared above all that Pétain would turn over the French fleet to the Germans. And if de Gaulle were allowed to get away with his action, the Latin American states would feel that they could not trust US assurances that it would not allow outside interference. Since the main issue was the radio transmitter, Hull, whom King saw first in Washington, proposed to King that Churchill remove the Free French and restore the Vichy administration, ludicrously suggesting that an international commission supervise the radio. King pointed out that the governor was pro-Axis and his wife German. He added that Canada was pleased by de Gaulle's achievement and that, whatever happened, the Allies could not appear to be letting down the Free French, a point which he undertook to impress on Churchill. On this note, the two walked next door to the White House for tea and King's first meeting with both Roosevelt and Churchill.

CHAPTER SEVEN

New World vs. Old World

M ACKENZIE KING'S TRAIN WAS three hours late and he missed lunch with Churchill and Roosevelt on December 26. This time he was not invited to stay at the White House, which was crowded with regular residents, Churchill and some of his attendants, and other Christmas guests, including the glamorous princess Martha of Norway, a great favourite of the president. Her husband, Crown Prince Olav, had been brought from London as a Christmas present. To Roosevelt's great pleasure, Martha had established herself just outside of Washington after having been discouraged from doing so in her native (and neutral) Sweden, which did not want to antagonize Hitler.

Churchill was nevertheless the star guest. Although he was stimulating company and Roosevelt's White House was never the most orderly place, Churchill was by any standard an exceptionally demanding and disruptive force for the wheelchaired president and everyone else. What Roosevelt's press secretary wrote about a later visit applied to them all: Churchill was "a trying guest – drinks like a fish and smokes like a chimney, irregular routine, works nights, sleeps days, turns the clock upside down."[1] Once he had tested several and decided on a satisfactory bed, additional rooms had to be found for his valet, his secretary, his aide, commander C. R. "Tommy" Thompson, and two Scotland Yard bodyguards. Other members of his entourage were in and out of the house at all hours.

---

1 Hassett, *Off the Record with F.D.R.*, 169 (diary entry, May 27, 1943); Eleanor Roosevelt, "Churchill As A Guest" in Eade, ed. *Churchill by His Contemporaries*, 227–32.

Churchill also required accommodation for his travelling map room and staff office, where he followed the course of the war. Roosevelt, who had a lifelong fascination with maps and postage stamps, soon adopted the same practice. The following Christmas, General George Marshall gave him a fifty-inch globe that from his chair he could tilt in any direction and see parts of the world from any perspective.[2]

Lodged at the Mayflower Hotel as a guest of the president, King stopped first at the State Department and arrived in this White House melee with Hull. Since King knew both Churchill and Roosevelt, the three were immediately at ease. Also present was Freeman Matthews, a career US diplomat who had been first secretary in the embassy to France and was now being transferred as counsellor to London. He joined Churchill in a scotch and soda while the rest had tea, King and Hull sitting on either side of the president on a sofa in the oval study. Talk began with the topic of Churchill's speech at mid-day to a joint meeting of Congress in the relatively smaller senate chamber, presumably because most legislators were out of town. He was only the second Briton (after Lord Tweedsmuir) to receive such an invitation. In the train, King had heard part of the inspirational address, the theme of which was what Churchill later called the special relationship between Britain and the United States and their joint effort in what was now a world war on an unprecedented scale. The thunderous applause left no doubt that Churchill had already established himself as a heroic war leader for the United States as well as his own country, although there was an uncomfortable silence when he insisted that the war could easily have been avoided if the two countries had stuck together after the one twenty years earlier.[3] At tea, Churchill said he had been delighted by the whole proceeding.

After this pleasantry, discussion turned to the hope of attracting to the Allied side important French leaders. A lively prospect seemed General Maxime Weygand, a defeatist and collaborationist at the fall of France but a waverer who, at Hitler's insistence, had been dismissed in November as delegate-general of the French north African colonies for opposing the granting of bases to the Germans. Both Churchill and Roosevelt had been working on him for some time

---

2   Alan K. Henrikson, "FDR and the 'World-Wide Arena,'" in David B. Woolner, Warren F. Kimball and David Reynolds eds., *FDR's World: War, Peace, and Legacies* (New York: Palgrave Macmillan, 2008), 35–61.

3   James, *Winston S. Churchill: His Complete Speeches*, 6536–41.

and Weygand opportunistically encouraged their expectations.[4] Now they were considering in what position they would accept him if he brought the armed forces to the Allies. They similarly wanted Pétain to stop what they considered his wobbling and join them in order to save France.

Nothing came of any of this but a serious impediment to the delicate process seemed to be the sudden seizure of the tiny French islands of Saint Pierre and Miquelon, off the coast of Newfoundland, two days earlier by the forces of the Free French leader general Charles de Gaulle, the nemesis of Weygand and Pétain, who wanted recognition as leader of all the French outside the control of Germany. Roosevelt and Hull were further enraged by an incursion into the American sphere of influence. Despite a hasty plebiscite on Christmas Day that overwhelmingly supported the transfer, the president thought that the Vichy governor should be restored, and the Free French forces removed. In regard to supervision of the powerful radio transmitter that had been a great aid to the German ships, Canada should appoint what would have been a totally unworkable supervisory commission consisting of one member each from Vichy, the Free French and Canada. King pointed out that the governor was strongly proGerman and defended the way in which de Gaulle had solved the radio problem.

Churchill, in a tight spot, said there must be some compromise but felt that he had to side with Roosevelt. He went so far as to admit that he had at one point supported de Gaulle's action, but claimed that he then turned against it since the United States was opposed. Now he was prepared to take de Gaulle "by the back of the neck and tell him that he had gone too far and bring him to his senses. He had on more than one occasion behaved in a troublesome way." Despite this, Churchill the next day sent a supportive cable telling de Gaulle that his abrupt move had "raised a storm which might have been serious if I had not been on the spot to speak to the President." But "I pleaded your case strongly to our friends in the United States . . . I am always doing my best in all our interests."[5]

Though Roosevelt and Hull remained confident that they could find a solution, there was none. The islands remained in the hands of the Free French, although the incident did nothing to improve the American leaders' opinion of the arrogance and presumption of de Gaulle. The issue rumbled on for weeks until it was simply abandoned. There was no general discussion of the war at the

4 Berthon, *Allies at War*, 100–4 and 145–7.
5 Churchill to de Gaulle, December 29, 1941. Gilbert, *Churchill War Papers*, III, 1705.

White House but Leighton McCarthy afterwards told King that Churchill had indicated at a separate conference of dominion diplomats that the conflict in the far east would be purely defensive, meaning a long struggle and the temporary loss of British and US possessions. Churchill had added that he would keep a careful eye on Singapore and gave assurances that Australia would be protected. New Zealand was said to be outside the danger zone.[6] This was a clear sign that Europe would continue to have priority, not so much a result of Churchill's persuasion but because it was what Roosevelt wanted, despite domestic pressure to direct his country's main effort against their Japanese enemies.

The next afternoon, accompanied by McCarthy and the three Canadian service ministers, King attended another meeting between Churchill and representatives of the Commonwealth and India at the White House. Lord Halifax was present and so was Roosevelt, to show solidarity and probably to observe relations between the British leader and the dominions. It was clear to King that the gathering was a mere matter of form, that the two crucial leaders were filling time until the military chiefs worked out plans. It was just as obvious that Churchill and Roosevelt were keeping decisions to themselves and not looking for advice. This did not trouble King who was convinced of their suitability to direct the war. When he asked if Canada could provide more or different help, which McCarthy narrowed down to the question of men or production, Churchill, while not mentioning conscription or suggesting any reduction in material help, said: "I need all the men I can get, and of men you can let me have, let me have them." The widening of the war and the prospect of troops from the British world being eventually (it took over two years) outnumbered by Americans had altered Churchill's perspective that this was primarily a war of machines.

As he looked at Roosevelt and Churchill, King thought they were tired, and Churchill flabby as well: "I could not help thinking of what a terrible thing it is that the fate of the world should rest so largely in the hands of two men to either of whom anything might happen at any moment."[7] There was far more reason for anxiety than he knew. The night before, scant hours after their tea together, Churchill had suffered a slight heart attack in wrenching open a bedroom window. Even before this, his pulse had been racing. The next morning, he asked his doctor, Charles Wilson (Sir Charles from the beginning of 1942, Lord Moran

6   Diary, December 26, 1941.
7   Diary, December 27, 1941.

by 1943) about the pain. Wilson recognized that it was angina but told Churchill only that his circulation was a bit sluggish and not to over exert himself. At the time, the treatment for angina was six weeks' bed rest, which would have meant telling Churchill, and the whole world, that he was an invalid with an uncertain future. Letting him carry on meant risking serious illness or even death, which would be blamed on the doctor. But Wilson decided immediately that it was more important for Churchill to manage the war, although he dreaded the trip to Ottawa with its cold weather.[8]

* * *

The next afternoon, Sunday, December 28, King went to the White House to accompany Churchill and his doctor to the train. He had learned practically nothing on this Washington visit, but he tactfully assured Roosevelt of his gratitude. Roosevelt, perhaps uneasy at having neglected the Canadian prime minister, said he was sorry that that they had not seen more of each other. Again King thought Roosevelt looked "considerably older and more fatigued." This was hardly surprising given the strains of war and close to an intense week of late nights, smoking, drinking and relentless talk with Churchill, whose three-day absence was a welcome relief to the president. King perceived nothing unusual about Churchill but Dr. Wilson noted that in the car that he seemed short of breath, complained of lack of air and opened the window.[9] The time of Churchill's departure was secret but he greeted the few people on the streets and at the station with his familiar V-for-Victory sign. Of the secret servicemen surrounding the car he said: "What good were they? If a man took a shot they could only follow him up."

In conversation with King on the way to the station, Churchill implied that he was the senior partner in the transatlantic alliance, saying that he was glad that he had come to Washington to give the president helpful suggestions and to strengthen him in his task. He maintained that they were at one in everything, although he already recognized that Roosevelt had his own strong views. The night before, Churchill had accepted what would be called A Declaration by the United Nations. This was an extension of the Atlantic Charter, wherein the

---

8   Moran, *Churchill*, 13, 17 and 18 (diary entries December 24 and 27, 1941).
9   Moran, *Churchill*, 19 (diary entry, December 19, 1941).

twenty-six allied countries pledged to fight a total war and not to make separate peace. When McCarthy brought the first draft from Lord Halifax that morning, King worried that "total war" might mean conscription but McCarthy had assured him, "It was held that it did not." King made some amendments to the wording and Churchill agreed that they were improvements but showed his indifference to what he considered another anodyne statement of ideals by saying that Roosevelt and the Americans should have whatever they pleased.

A year later, the president told Mackenzie King that he and Churchill had worked late into the night to find the best term to describe the countries fighting the Axis powers. In bed, Roosevelt kept turning over various phrases containing "united" until he hit on "united nations." He could hardly wait for morning to tell Churchill. Before breakfast, he had his valet wheel him into Churchill's room. Churchill called him in but said that he was in the bath. In Roosevelt's telling, there was no mention that of the mythic tale that Churchill was nude, which Churchill afterwards denied. Nor did Roosevelt add Harry Hopkins' embellishment that Churchill declared: "The prime minister of Great Britain has nothing to conceal from the president of the United States." If he had said anything of the kind, it would have become one of Roosevelt's favourite stories. Churchill was almost certainly wrapped in a towel. The president said: "Winston [pointing at him] I have it: the United Nations." Churchill immediately accepted and, as King said, the term was "properly baptized at the same time." Roosevelt was proud of the expression, comparing it to the Victorian historian J. R. Seeley's phrase "the expansion of England." He revealed more than he realized when he told King: "This was the expansion of the U.S. The U.S. had grown into the United Nations, etc.,"[10] though he meant values and ideals rather than territory.)

It gave Churchill great pleasure to tell King in the car, and the other dominion prime ministers by cable, that he had that very morning succeeded "beyond expectations" on the Pacific war. At Roosevelt's suggestion, the supreme commander of the whole area would be General Sir Archibald Wavell, the commander-in-chief of the army in India. While Churchill presented this as a great British triumph, it was really a clever move by the Americans to get their own way. Churchill and the British military staff opposed an overall commander for each sector of the war but the forceful general George C. Marshall, the US Army Chief-of-Staff,

---

10 Diary, December 5, 1942; Roll, *The Hopkins Touch*, 173–4.

impressed his preference on Roosevelt.[11] Appointing Wavell was a graceful way to secure Churchill's agreement.

* * *

Roosevelt provided his train for the journey to Ottawa. Churchill occupied the president's car, the Ferdinand Magellan (which was soon armoured), and King his own, which was attached. After both had slept, Churchill, his doctor, and air marshal Sir Charles Portal, the RAF chief of staff, came to King's carriage to talk about the Ottawa speech. Churchill agreed to King's suggestions of a passage in French, to saying something about Hong Kong, and also mentioning the Canadian forces in Britain. At 8 p.m., Churchill returned with Portal for dinner with King and the three Canadian service ministers. King later went to Churchill's car to discuss what he described as "my problem," the pressure in Canada for overseas conscription and a national government to enact it.

King told Churchill that he feared conscription would split the Canada, as it had in the first war. Despite what he had said in Washington about needing more troops, Churchill reminded King that in Britain he had told the Canadian Conservatives, whose bitterness he had sensed, that he could not ask for conscription and that in any event shipping was more important. At the same time, he pointed out that industrial demands would make manpower scarce for Britain. American troops would relieve the situation, Churchill said, but he would be grateful for any Canadian help. King mentioned that Canada intended to give Britain a gift of a billion dollars' worth of credits. Unaware of Churchill's heart condition, he thought him too tired to absorb the information. It was, wrote King, "the right thing to do, though an amazingly generous thing for so young a country. Certainly Britain is receiving a reward for what she has done to ensure freedom. Never were the results of responsible government made more evident."[12]

At ten a.m. on December 29, the train reached Ottawa, forty-one years almost to the day since Churchill had first been in the city and met Mackenzie King. It was also the twentieth anniversary of the formation of King's first government. The morning newspapers had been allowed to announce the arrival and there

11 Hamilton, *The Mantle of Command*, 139–40; Andrew Roberts, *Masters and Commanders: How Roosevelt, Churchill, Marshall and Alanbrooke Won the War in the West* (London: Allen Lane, 2008), 67–8.
12 Diary, December 16 and 28, 1941; Wardhaugh, *Behind the Scenes*, 220, 225–6 and 235–6; Granatstein, *Canada's War*, 186–95.

was a vast congregation to welcome the hero many Canadians regarded as practically one of their own. King quickly introduced the dignitaries in the cold station and put Churchill into a car to Government House, noting: "He thoroughly enjoys meeting the crowds and adopting characteristic poses with cigar in mouth, hat on end of cane, making the sign 'V' with his 2 fingers, and generally stirring up enthusiasm like a 10-year old."

Later that morning, Churchill attended the war cabinet. Churchill talked about his friendship with Roosevelt, praised Harry Hopkins, and said that coming to Washington had enabled him to get better results than in any other way. He flatteringly said that Mackenzie King had been involved in the United Nations Declaration when the, as yet uncirculated document, was read to the group. When Churchill was pointedly asked, as King had done, if total war meant conscription, he said that it was up to each country to decide the form of its commitment; but he probably considered that he was helping King by commenting that Australia, South Africa, and Northern Ireland, the only part of the United Kingdom exempt from compulsory military service, would insist that it not be required.

About the two battleships that had been sent to Singapore and sunk, Churchill was defensive, insisting that it had been the right move. It was the "ill fortunes of war" that had taken them beyond aircraft protection. He tried to diminish the effect of the well-publicized defeat by saying that the public did not yet know the extent of the American losses at Pearl Harbor, which were far worse than revealed. In order to guard against a Japanese attack, he urged Canada to secure its west coast. Shortly thereafter, Japanese-Canadians, 22,000 in all, were forcibly relocated to the interior from the coast of British Columbia and their property confiscated without compensation. Similar action was taken against 120,000 Japanese-Americans in California.[13] In both cases, fears of Japanese raids, invasion attempts, and fifth columnists were grounded in the attitude towards Asian immigration since the beginning of the century.

In the meeting, Churchill, in effect, told the war cabinet to trust him to manage Canada's interests with the Americans. At the moment, he was furious that the Prime Minister of Australia, John Curtin, had complained to Roosevelt that the troops destined for Singapore were inadequate and had announced in a newspaper article that Australia looked to leadership from the United States, "free

13 Bercuson, *Our Finest Hour* (sic), 179; Daniels, *Franklin D. Roosevelt*, 250–6.

from any pangs as to our traditional links with the United Kingdom."[14] Churchill assured the war ministers that Canada was entitled to some representation in decision making but hoped they would "take a large view of the relationships of the large countries, to avoid anything in the way of antagonisms." In this he was expressing not only his own desire but Roosevelt's even stronger one.

Churchill treated the group to one of his sweeping surveys of the war, emphasized the part that luck had played in the successes. Hitler's invasion of the USSR was a case of "some Cherub above watching over and directing affairs." How different, he said, if Hitler had made a bargain with the Soviets and gone through Turkey to the oil fields of the middle east. Later in the day, he added that he had literally danced at the news of Pearl Harbor, great as the initial losses were. Things were "3 times better with Japan fighting America" and bringing her into the war than the situation would have been if Japan had not struck. The Japanese might capture Malaya and other colonies but he was confident that Singapore could hold out for six to eight months, during which more ships would be provided for its protection. He even claimed that the Battle of the Atlantic was going better, although the Germans were sinking ships off the US coast (where cities were not yet blacked out). He qualified this by saying that submarines were still a major menace and that there was a great need for merchant vessels and warships. Britain, he insisted, was well fortified against invasion, and he looked forward to 1943 when the Allies would be able to "roll tanks off ships at different points in Europe in countries held by the Germans, getting rifles into the hands of the [resistance] people themselves, making it impossible for Germany to defend the countries she has now overrun." He also judged that the Soviet Union would manage to hold on and inflict huge damage on the Germans. Churchill's predictions were hopes but his assurance must have stoked the confidence of Canadian ministers in his leadership.

Lunch at the Chateau Laurier included the full cabinet, the chiefs of staff, and diplomatic representatives. Mackenzie King toasted Churchill in fulsome terms. Churchill, in response, commended Canada's part in the war and said that his friendship with King that was so long that it must seem that they had been adolescents together. Later in the day, the cabinet passed an order in council appointing Churchill to the Canadian privy council. He was sworn in before dinner at Government House. When there was some discussion as to whether or

14 Barnes and Nicholson, *The Empire at Bay*, 723.

not the monarch's consent was required, it was Churchill who pointed out that Canada, under the statute of Westminster, had full jurisdiction. In a rare flash of wit, Mackenzie King told Lord Athlone that with this appointment he was coming to have a strong government.

King noticed with approval that before dinner, as at lunch, Churchill had only tomato juice rather than sherry or cocktails. King took this as a sign that he was watching his health, which may have been true at that moment, although he was probably already fortified in case there was no alcohol at the meals. Churchill, in any event, detested cocktails, getting rid of Roosevelt's lethal martinis when he could. King did not record much of Churchill's table talk. He did say that the two political figures he missed most were Lord Birkenhead and Lord Balfour: "The former, habits very bad but brilliant intellectually. The latter, almost ascetic in life, spiritually minded; a lofty character." Primed by the Conservatives, whom he had met earlier in the day, he tried to urge King towards conscription and a national government, while saying that he would never press him. King pointed out that it was Arthur Meighen, the (briefly) new again Conservative leader who was making conscription a political issue. King also suspected that financial interests wanted to gain control of policy through a national government.[15]

* * *

The next afternoon was the public highlight of Churchill's visit, his speech in parliament, just four days after the one to the US Congress. King greeted him at the entrance to the building with a guard of honour. Side by side, the two prime ministers walked into the House of Commons, which was full of as many MPs and senators as could be assembled, along with judges, diplomats (including the Vichy minister) and other dignitaries. For the first time in the chamber, there were radio microphones, a film camera, which required bright lights, and press photographers with flash bulb cameras. When King asked on Churchill's behalf if the floodlights had to be on all the time, he was told they did. Churchill spoke from the head of the clerks' table, on which he had asked for a box for his notes, as in the British house. Although it was not a meeting of parliament, Churchill addressed the speaker, who sat behind him, on this occasion unrobed, in his

---

15 Diary, December 29, 1941. Some of the material for this date is at the beginning of the entry for December 30.

elevated chair. King was delighted that his introduction was greeted by loud applause and the banging of desk lids (the custom at that time), "particularly so paid in the presence of Churchill, and . . . heard over the radio in all parts of the world. It would leave no doubt as to the feeling toward myself." He carefully recorded that the ovation for Churchill was no greater than the one for himself and that Churchill's tribute to him as an old friend and prime minister for fifteen of the past twenty years "helped to bring that fact anew to the public mind."

Churchill was well aware that the broadcast and that the newsreel would draw attention all over Canada, the United States, Britain and the free world. He said to King, "what a job it was to prepare a speech, this one in particular." King thought it less effective than the one to Congress and, for reasons only Dr. Wilson knew, saw "evidences of fatigue in its delivery and, in part, its matter was less clear-cut than some of his addresses." But it was, even by Churchill's high standard, a fine oration and a memorable experience for those who attended. A newspaper reporter rhapsodized that their hearts underwent "a strange, indefinable transformation." When they emerged "they weren't quite the same people." They had heard "the waves beating on the coasts of England, listened to the guns of British ships, felt the scorching heat of the African deserts, heard the roar of Spitfires in the skies. They had listened to Churchill. They had heard the voice of England."[16]

In characteristic fashion, Churchill ranged widely. He naturally praised Canada's magnificent war contribution, and lauded the country's imperial tie and the drawing together of the old world and the new. He extolled the sacrifice at Hong Kong, which he asserted had slowed the Japanese advance. He devoted particular attention to attracting the support of French-Canadians for the war and away from admiration of Pétain's Vichy regime by dwelling on the fight as one to liberate France and spoke a few sentences in the language. Contrasting the demoralized French government's refusal to continue the fight to the firm British resolve, he said: "When I warned them that Britain would fight on whatever they did, their generals told the Prime Minister and his divided cabinet, 'In three weeks, England will have her neck wrung like a chicken.' Some chicken! Some neck!" This unexpected swoop from high rhetoric to the demotic produced huge applause and banging of desks. Churchill lauded de Gaulle and the Free French

---

16 *Ottawa Morning Citizen*, December 31, 1941 in Dilkes, *The Great Dominion*, 219, which includes other accounts.

who, he claimed, were "held in increasing respect by nine Frenchmen out of ten throughout the once happy, smiling land of France." This public support and implicit endorsement of capturing Saint Pierre and Miquelon contradicted what he had said at the White House and so enraged Cordell Hull.[17]

At the end of the speech, the speaker called for the national anthem, "God Save the King," followed by three loud cheers for Churchill. As King shook his hand there was a final round of applause which King interpreted as being for both: "I felt that the atmosphere had wonderfully cleared, and that his visit had served to put the facts in their right place." They went to the speaker's apartment for tea, Churchill having a scotch and soda, after which he alone spent half an hour with some Conservatives. King then escorted him to an off-the-record conference for newspaper editors and publishers and the retiring Conservative leader. Churchill was in fine entertaining form but said nothing of substance. On the way to the newspaper conference, he told King that the Conservatives complained that they should be in the war picture. Once again he urged a coalition, saying that from his own experience in Neville Chamberlain's cabinet people were very different in office than in opposition. Probably what he intended was to strengthen King's hand even further by adding Conservative support but King, with his huge majority, was adamant about not including those who had been elected (during the war, he might have added) to oppose him.

After meeting the press leaders, Churchill was tired from the events of the day and ready for a refreshing sleep. He was far from pleased that King had arranged a photography session with a local practitioner, Yousuf Karsh. Churchill complained that plenty of pictures had been taken already but he curtly agreed to just one more. Karsh had been in the gallery of the House of Commons observing Churchill and had a good sense of the impression he wanted to capture. When Churchill grumpily refused to remove his cigar, Karsh snatched it from his mouth, snapped the shutter and made his reputation. The glowering picture that emerged became the most famous representation of the defiant war leader. But it was not that simple. The raw print showed Churchill all too realistically, as King had described him three days earlier. Only with shading and special paper in the darkroom was the portrait transformed, as Karsh's biographer says, from "an unpromising negative of a tired, overweight, sick and slightly annoyed man into a photograph of a heroic figure who had just told the world, 'If anybody

17 Diary, January 8, 1942.

likes to play rough, we can play rough too.'" It became "a visual analogue of the Augustan language so familiar in Winston Churchill's speeches."

Instead of being angry, Churchill was amused at Karsh's boldness and the photographer quickly captured that expression, too. In this sunny mood, Churchill allowed the photographer four more of pictures of him and King, one showing Churchill lighting a new cigar to replace the snatched one that was pocketed by Karsh's assistant. A week later, when King saw the prints, he thought the soon-to-be-celebrated one could not be better. The photos of himself he judged not so good and he was shocked that Karsh sent one of him laughing to Canada's *Saturday Night* magazine: "I do not like that kind of expression in relation to the war."[18] The scowling Churchill was also printed with excerpts of his Ottawa speech in the magazine, "like facing pages of a book, classical and heroic in the way that they complemented each other."[19] The widely reproduced photograph became an important artifact in winning the war as well as fixing Churchill's image. Karsh became an internationally fashionable photographer; everyone wanted their portraits taken by him. But neither Churchill nor his wife warmed to the famous picture. They told King two and a half years later that his expression around the mouth was really more playful.[20] Churchill never used this photograph in his war memoirs.

King was particularly pleased that Churchill and three of his entourage came to dinner that night at Laurier House with the Canadian war cabinet. People stood in the snow to watch the great man arrive and leave. Dr. Charles Wilson, who knew King as his patient when in London, came early and recorded that he found King agitated about Churchill, saying that he was "rather put off by a strain of violence" in him. Wilson, claiming to sense that this was more than a passing mood for King, defended his patient, saying that Churchill's bellicosity was nothing more than lack of restraint. (The doctor's diary was so much rewritten and shaped by books that appeared in the twenty years after the war that this is not necessarily an exact report. The same is true of the passage of Wilson's comment that Churchill took King for granted.[21] Churchill, at times, did take

18 Diary, January 7, 1942.
19 Maria Tippett, *Portrait in Light and Shadow: The Life of Yousuf Karsh* (Toronto: Anansi, 2007), 139–51. All Karsh's photographs are reproduced in Reardon, *Winston Churchill and Mackenzie King*, frontispiece and 182–3.
20 Diary, May 6, 1944.
21 Moran, *Churchill*, 20–1.

King's acquiescence for granted but he also spent much effort cultivating him, which Wilson could not know because he was rarely at their meetings.)

At Laurier House, King served alcohol in honour of his guest but again noticed that Churchill did not have a cocktail. Relaxed after his speech and with none in the offing, Churchill told many stories which King unfortunately did not record. He did note that Churchill's vision of the liberation of Europe lay, as he had indicated in the prediction of tank landings to the war cabinet, not in one or more massive landings but in peripheral operations all the way from Norway to Greece, with the local populations being supplied with arms. By now, Churchill had fully grasped the importance of Canada's billion-dollar gift and asked "how we could possibly do it; what we had done in a financial way was very great. He spoke really with amazement at what was contemplated." He also reverted to his opinion that the war was one of expensive machinery and strategy rather than men. When King toasted the health of the latest Canadian privy councillor, Churchill hoped that his would not be the fate of two other British members, Lord Baldwin and the equally unpopular Duke of Windsor.

After dinner, conversation continued in the library on the third floor, where the group was joined by Billy Bishop, the First World War flying ace, who had hoped that Churchill would stop at his house on the way back to the governor general's residence. Churchill must have come close to giving his doctor heart palpitations by bounding up the first flight of stairs. Not as fit as he tried to demonstrate, he walked slowly the rest of the way. Like every visitor, he had to admire the painting of King's mother, "a lovely face, a lovely face." King showed him an 1837 poster offering a reward of £1,000 for the capture of his grandfather, William Lyon Mackenzie, and Churchill ruefully said that the Boers had only offered £25 for him. [22]

* * *

The next morning, Churchill's final day, there was a half-hour press conference at Government House which he asked King to attend. At the outset, reporters presented Churchill with a sealskin hat which he wore to much comment throughout the day, and also to the amusement of Stalin and Roosevelt at the 1943 Tehran conference. He gave the journalists a good sense of his personality and his verbal

---

22 Diary, December 30, 1940

skill while revealing nothing. Saint Pierre and Miquelon he dismissed as "a very minor matter." Asked if Singapore could hang on, he categorically asserted that it could, despite having told King the previous evening that he was anxious about the matter. As for an imperial conference, he presented King's argument that it was "difficult for the Prime Ministers of the Dominions to leave their own Dominions, where they have . . . Parliaments to lead." There were, he pointed out, individual visits, such as King's in August, and an immense flow of dispatches. There was great applause when he answered the question of conscription by saying: "I do not interfere in matters of this kind in the Dominions. You have to settle your own problems." Asked about peace feelers from the Axis powers he cleverly said: "We have had none at all, but then I really think they must be hard pressed for materials of all kinds, and would not want to waste paper and ink."[23]

Before leaving, Churchill made a final effort to persuade King to form a coalition with the Conservatives. King characterized the conversation as "very nice" but did not conceal his hostility to the Conservatives, particularly Arthur Meighen who, an Ottawa paper that morning maintained, had been excluded from meeting Churchill. In fact, Meighen was confined at home in Toronto with influenza; King also tartly noted that it had not kept him from the Albany Club, a Conservative bastion. King was pleased by Churchill's characterization of Meighen in the words of Shakespeare's *Julius Caesar.* "Yon Cassius hath a lean and hungry look."

Churchill did not reveal that he had received from Meighen an admiring letter saying that what Canada needed was not praise for past performance but "a ringing challenge to the manhood of this nation," meaning a call for con-scription or at least more overseas volunteers. Any such declaration by Churchill would have helped Meighen in the forthcoming by-election that he hoped would return him to parliament. When Churchill did not touch the subject in his speech, Meighen fumed that he was as bad as other Britons in simply accepting whatever King offered. With no inkling that Churchill was privately trying to advance his party's aim of a coalition, Meighen considered publicly denouncing him.[24]

At 3 p.m., King saw Churchill off on his overnight New Year's Eve journey to Washington. The time had been kept secret but there was still a multitude which

23 Dilks, *The Great Dominion*, 220–2. This transcription is from Churchill's official papers (PREM 4/71/2). The press reports follow in Dilks.
24 Roger Graham, *Arthur Meighen: A Biography*. 3 volumes. (Toronto: Clarke Irwin, 1960–65), III, 136–8.

Churchill walked through pronouncing "God bless you all" in episcopal fashion. In the railway car, he said to King: "You can count on me. You can count on me," and King repeated the same. As the train steamed away, Churchill came onto the observation deck to give the V-for-Victory sign and King from the platform responded with the same.

The two-day visit was a triumph for Winston Churchill and for Mackenzie King. It would have been strenuous for anyone, but it was remarkable even for someone of Churchill's vitality after an angina attack and a demanding week in Washington. As King wrote, Churchill was "deeply touched by the evident feeling of the people toward him and the complete unanimity of that feeling." He had been "wonderfully kind, sympathetic and understanding" and quick to grasp the Canadian political situation. Churchill, who if he had stuck to his original plan would now have been going back to Britain, told King that he expected to return by ship from Halifax and invited him to meet again there. But King thought the voyage would be safer if there was no indication leaked of where and when he was leaving. Looking back that night on the eventful week, the eventful month, and the eventful 1941, King declared Churchill's visit to "a wonderful close to a wonderful year."[25]

* * *

After dinner on New Year's Day, Roosevelt, Churchill and the Soviet and Chinese ambassadors signed the Declaration of the United Nations on behalf of the leading powers. The president later styled them the "four policemen" that would enforce the peace of the world after the war. The signatures of the representatives of twenty-two further countries, including Canada and the other three overseas dominions, European governments in exile, and Latin American countries, were added the next day. Churchill strongly objected to India signing, despite having been represented at the 1919 peace conference and being a member of the League of Nations, however anomalously, since it was in no sense self-governing. "It was something sort of unthinkable to him," Roosevelt told King a year later. But the president insisted on India's inclusion for the importance to other countries, not least the United States.[26]

25 Diary, December 31, 1941.
26 Diary, December 5, 1942.

By the New Year, Churchill was exhausted, suffering the effects of angina, and painfully realizing from his discussions with Roosevelt, and those between the two countries' military professionals which were lasting far longer than he had expected, that he and his country were regarded not as equals but as junior partners in the transatlantic coalition. He left the White House in low spirits on January 5, for five days of sun and warmth in Florida, hoping to recover his physical and mental vigour. This second absence allowed Roosevelt to concentrate on his first wartime State of the Union address to Congress the first day that Churchill was away. On the telephone a couple of days later, the president told Mackenzie King, who expected that Churchill was by now on his way back to Britain, that they were both having a real rest. He said that he had slept for two days.[27]

The president's speech to Congress warned enemies of the United States of the massive resources that would be mobilized against them. In the current year alone, Roosevelt called for the production of 60,000 aircraft, 45,000 tanks, 20,000 anti-aircraft guns and 6,000,000 tons of merchant shipping. In 1943, when industry would be fully mobilized, he wanted far more. These staggering figures, far beyond what business leaders thought could be met, probably originated with Lord Beaverbrook who suggested that the president multiply the projected Canadian figures for planes and tanks by fifteen.[28] (The population ratio was 12:1.) King, listening on the radio, was impressed by these huge numbers although his own country was proportionately committed to producing almost the same. He noted that there was not much applause when Roosevelt cited his relationship with Churchill, nor at the announcement that troops would be sent to Britain, concluding that the new ally was still not very popular in the United States. In contrast to the enthusiasm for production targets, the president's budget request for fifty-six billion dollars was greeted with dead silence.[29] War and production were one thing, paying for them another.

In the four days that Churchill was back in the White House, business was quickly wrapped up between him and Roosevelt. The main item, as the president had indicated to Congress and to King before Churchill even crossed the Atlantic, was a combined committee of the chiefs of staff of both countries with headquarters in Washington and British representation, asserting American lead

---

27 Diary, January 8, 1941.
28 Roll, *The Hopkins Touch*, 175.
29 Diary, January 6, 1941.

in the war.[30] Churchill had no choice but to accept. To help make it palatable in Britain, the arrangement was in the first instance established only for a month.

Among the military officers Churchill had brought with him was Field Marshal Sir John Dill, whom he had appointed chief of the Imperial General Staff on becoming prime minister. Recently developing impatience with "Dilly–Dally," Churchill had let his term lapse on Christmas Day, Dill's sixtieth birthday. Afterwards, probably prompted by Roosevelt who was urged by General Marshall's high opinion of Dill, Churchill left him in Washington as his personal representative. After a couple of weeks in this nebulous post, Churchill clarified that Dill was the head of both the British army staff in Washington and the British section of the joint chiefs of staff committee. Soon Dill was directing a staff of three thousand, one third of the British agents in Washington (one thousand of whom were in the embassy). When this casual appointment turned out to be brilliant, Churchill claimed that he had made a careful choice. In the combined Anglo-American military machinery, Dill was, in the words of his biographer, "the fulcrum." He spoke with Churchill's authority to the American military leaders, with whom he had an outstanding relationship. Like Harry Hopkins he was another buffer between Churchill and Roosevelt.[31]

In their last days together, Roosevelt and Churchill reaffirmed that Germany was the primary enemy. US troops and bombers were sent to Britain and the hard-pressed Soviets were bolstered with supplies, hazardous as delivery was. It seemed a triumph for Churchill that the president agreed to an American landing in French north Africa by the end of 1942 to trap the Germans between the British to the east instead of the direct assault on northern Europe which Marshall and Stimson wanted as soon as possible. Churchill argued that an ill-prepared landing would risk failure or a stalemate as in the previous war. Roosevelt's agreement was another case of Churchill's desire concurring with the president's calculation. He did not want American conscripts facing hardened German professionals in any large-scale conflict way until they had some battlefield experience. The Mediterranean was the ideal place to get it.[32]

30 Hamilton, *The Mantle of Command*, 140–3. (quotation, 11)
31 Alex Danchev, *Very Special Relationship: Field-Marshal Sir John Dill and the Anglo-American Alliance 1941–44* (London: Brassey's Defence Publishers, 1986), 10–33.
32 Hamilton, *The Mantle of Command*, 102–8

* * *

On January 17, Mackenzie King was relieved to hear that Churchill had arrived safely in Britain by plane.[33] His physical safety was one thing, however, and his political safety another. Despite returning home as the statesman who had cemented relations with an indispensable ally, Churchill was met on his return by a barrage of criticism for the shocking losses in the Pacific and lack of progress in north Africa. Despite having a coalition government, the virtues of which he had extolled to King, he was criticized even by his own MPs for concentrating excessive power in his own hands. Much ostensible solicitude was expressed that he was overtaxing himself after a year and a half in which Britain had been fighting for its life. It seemed time for a different leader to lead the country to victory, as in the earlier war. It did not help that Churchill was suffering from a bad cold, the lingering effects of angina, and a gloomy sense of what had really transpired in Washington.

Mackenzie King followed Winston Churchill's political troubles with professional and personal interest. When, after ten days, there was no decrease in grumbling about the war and his leadership, Churchill decided to challenge his detractors in a three–day parliamentary debate and a vote of confidence. On the very eve, he deftly neutralized the most obvious candidate to replace him. This was the left-wing Sir Stafford Cripps, the ambassador to the Soviet Union (and still an MP), who had just returned to Britain with tremendous public acclaim for having seemed to bring the USSR into the war. When Churchill offered him a cabinet post, Cripps hesitated but was thus muzzled during the debate, after which he refused.

In his opening speech, Churchill did not disguise the discouraging news from the Pacific and Mediterranean and insured himself by warning that there would be more ahead. He hailed his North American trip as a great success, citing the close relationship with Roosevelt, the joint direction of the war, and claimed by implication some of the credit for Canada's increased contribution, including the billion-dollar gift which had just been announced. Mackenzie King read the speech and agreed with most British MPs that Churchill had put on a fine performance, demonstrating yet again that he was by far the best person to command the situation. The British Empire might be close to destruction, "However with

33 Diary, January 17, 1942.

him, I think that there is light to be seen beyond the clouds." King also appreciated the acknowledgment of the billion-dollar donation.[34]

By the end of the debate, Churchill gave in to those opposed to his concentration of power by agreeing to a minister of war production, although he himself still continued as minister of defence. To no great surprise, the person soon appointed to the new ministry was Lord Beaverbrook. Churchill by a combination of boldness and deft manoeuvring, sailed to victory in parliament by 464 votes to 1.

Two weeks later came another great British humiliation as the Germans defied the Royal Navy blockade of the Channel. On February 12, the German battlecruisers, *Scharnhorst* and *Gneisenau*, the heavy cruiser *Prinz Eugen*, six destroyers and fourteen torpedo boats, under heavy air cover, broke out of the French port of Brest and sailed to Germany in preparation to defend Norway, where Hitler was convinced the Allies would land. This was a blow to the government and a shock to the public, although the triumph was not as great as it seemed. The two battlecruisers were damaged and most of the German fleet was still under blockade. King, however, was not the only one who considered this a tremendous addition to Churchill's burdens and wondered how long he would be able to carry them.[35]

Far worse came only three days later – when Singapore capitulated to the Japanese. Churchill in Ottawa had confided to King his doubt that it could be held, but he wanted it to resist to the end. He ordered a heroic last stand: "Commanders and senior officers should die with their troops. The honour of the British Empire and the British Army is at stake." But soldiers were already deserting and officers would not sacrifice themselves. As at Hong Kong, the commander on February 15, surrendered the force of over a hundred thousand Britons, Australians, and Indians to an opposing force half the size. These prisoners were as brutally treated. When the "Gibraltar of the Far East" fell, so did Britain's reputation for invulnerability. It was covered up but 40,000 of the 45,000 Indian troops joined the Japanese forces.[36] Japan was then moving rapidly through Burma to the gates of India, where the Indian elite was demanding freedom from Britain.

---

34 Diary, January 27, 1942.

35 Diary, February 13, 1942; Dimbleby, *The Battle of the Atlantic*, 273–6.

36 Hamilton, *The Mantle of Command*, 201–6; Hastings, *All Hell Let Loose*, 211–14; Christopher Bayly and Tim Harper, *Forgotten Armies: The Fall of British Asia* (Cambridge, MA: Harvard University Press, 2005), 137–44.

Furious at the surrender of Singapore, Churchill that very night gave a preemptive broadcast designed to placate the United States, his critics, and the bewildered public. He blamed the defeat on the sinking of the US fleet at Pearl Harbor, which exposed the British base to the Japanese. He also pleaded the demands of war elsewhere, particularly in north Africa and the USSR. Looking on the bright side, Churchill cheeringly hailed the final victory that would result from the British alliance with the United States and the advance of the Soviet army. King thought it significant that he made no mention of the German warships in the Channel. The speech was "a manly endeavour to brace the country against the most desperate situation with which it has been faced since the fall of France; to brace the free world against the most appalling situation with which it has been faced." But he was annoyed that Churchill addressed Britain's kin in the United States without mentioning Canada.

That same evening, King was pleased by Roosevelt's reference in a fireside chat to "my old friend" Mackenzie King whose presence at the Washington meeting in December was cited. Charitably granting that Churchill's attention was fixed on Asia, King nevertheless grumbled: "Is it to be wondered at that some people sometimes think that Canada counts for little in the eyes of Britain except where she can be used to some purpose [?]"[37]

The Singapore disaster prompted the resignation of Lord Beaverbrook, just two weeks after he had become minister of wartime production, again officially on grounds of health. Now under the spell of Stalin, Beaverbrook and his newspapers began a great campaign for "A Second Front Now." His unaccustomed main allies were left-wing admirers of the Soviet Union. He also had considerable American support. It did not escape Beaverbrook's attention that Churchill was exposed. Beaverbrook, moreover, was in a good position to know the true state of Churchill's health. In the shuffle following Beaverbrook's departure, Churchill convinced Sir Stafford Cripps to join the war cabinet as lord privy seal and leader of the House of Commons. King was among those who saw him as Churchill's successor and welcomed the prospect of Beatrice Webb's nephew as prime minister: "He represents a new school of thought which is concerned with the well-being of the people, and not with privilege."[38]

While Churchill struggled with dissenters inside and outside government, King himself faced a similar situation over conscription. The Canadian army

37 Diary, February 15, 1942.
38 Diary, March 3, 1942.

had so far scarcely been engaged in battle save for Hong Kong. Nor was there any shortage of volunteers for overseas service. But war in the Pacific and popular expectation of the early invasion of Europe indicated that more troops would soon be needed. Conservatives clamoured for compulsion, and most English-language newspapers demanded it. In cabinet, the adamant anti-conscriptionist Ernest Lapointe was dead and J. L. Ralston, the minister of national defence, pressed for it.

Two and a half weeks before Meighen's by-election, King took command, announcing in the speech from the throne at the opening of parliament that there would be a national plebiscite on releasing the government from its pledge against overseas conscription. The poll on April twenty-seven produced sixty-three per-cent in favour and thirty-seven percent opposed. This did nothing to resolve the division since seventy-two percent in Quebec voted against. Meighen, moreover, lost his by-election to the CCF which was opposed to conscription. Long and emotional debates in parliament on amending the mobilization act lasted until the middle of July. One minister resigned and both Ralston and King, at various points, threatened the same. After the conscription legislation was enacted, King, pinning his hope on Churchill's equivocal statements about the war being one of machines and on early victory, pronounced that his policy was "not necessarily conscription but conscription if necessary."[39]

Three weeks after the plebiscite, King received an extraordinary sugges-tion from Roosevelt to solve the disagreement between French-Canadians and pro-British Canadians. The president had been thinking about the matter dur-ing a three-day weekend at Hyde Park. He admitted to King that the proposal "may sound to you a bit amateurish" but considered that it might "have some merit in these days of national planning." Reflecting on the large numbers of French-Canadians who had gone to work in New England in the late nineteenth century who at first had kept to themselves but were now assimilated into "the original Anglo-Saxon stock," Roosevelt wondered if some joint planning, "per-haps unwritten planning which need not even be public policy," would produce even greater integration. He recommended providing greater opportunities for French-Canadians throughout both countries as well as encouraging others to mingle more with them in their own centres. The president saw this as part of a large, post-war American issue. He had put the National Resources Planning

39 Granatstein, *Canada's War*, 208–43.

Commission to work on a strategy to encourage "the distribution of certain other nationalities in our large congested centers. There ought not be such a concentration of Italians and of Jews, and even of Germans as we have today in New York City."[40] This was not a matter that King wanted to touch, during the conscription debate or at any other time. Nor, in fact, did the United States.

* * *

In the far east, Churchill's main fear after the fall of Singapore was the fate of India. Rangoon, the capital of Burma fell on March 7. The Burma road from India, which supplied China, was closed at the end of the month. And by the beginning of April, the Japanese fleet was devastating British war and merchant ships in the Indian Ocean.[41] If the Soviet Union capitulated, Germany might join Japan in the attack on India. The anti-imperialist Roosevelt, whose views Churchill could not ignore, was convinced that India would fight effectively only if it was granted independence. King, who had anticipated Indian self-government as long ago as 1908, similarly believed that it should be an autonomous dominion like Canada (although this was not the conventional view among the professionals in his department of external affairs).[42] In Britain, many politicians were of King's opinion, among them Sir Stafford Cripps, who had established good relationships with Mohandas Gandhi and Jawaharlal Nehru in the 1930s. In the war cabinet with no departmental duties in the war cabinet, Cripps concentrated on the issue.

Churchill resisted the pressure to move on India as long as he could. At the beginning of March, he told Roosevelt that the cabinet was considering dominion status after the war, including the right to leave the Commonwealth, but reiterated his warnings about abandoning the Hindus the Muslims, the Untouchables, and the many princely states, which were governed by treaties with Britain.[43] He sent a circular to the dominions claiming that following the war there would be a constitutional assembly, with each Indian province having the right to decide

---

40 Roosevelt to King, May 18, 1942. Library and Archives Canada, MG26, Series J1, vol. 332, file pages 284204–5. I am very grateful to Emeritus Professor Donald Smith, University of Calgary, for providing a copy of this letter.

41 Bell, *Churchill and Sea Power*, 283–4.

42 H. S. Ferns, *Reading from Left to Right: One Man's Political History* (Toronto: University of Toronto Press, 1983), 165–7.

43 Churchill to Roosevelt, March 2 and 4, 1942. Kimball, *Churchill and Roosevelt*, I, 373–5.

on joining a new political structure. This implied a separate Muslim Pakistan and even princely states. King urged Churchill to lose no time in making the offer public.[44]

In the threatening military situation, Churchill could not hold off for long. On March 11, Roosevelt in a "Purely Personal" message, recommended to Churchill that India be granted immediately a temporary dominion government to manage the public services and prepare for a permanent constitution after the war. This he said would be like the American states as they moved from independence to the new federal constitution of 1789. Just as the early Americans had made their way to their final form of government, this would give the Indians trial and error experience. He also thought this would help the Indians to forget their past hard feelings and become more loyal to the British Empire.[45] In his war memoirs, after Roosevelt was dead, Churchill scorned the historical analogy as being "of high interest because it illustrates the difficulties of comparing situations in various countries and scenes where almost every material fact is totally different, and the danger of trying to apply any superficial resemblances which may be noticed to the conduct of war."[46] But the day after the cable, he announced that Cripps was going to India to negotiate a settlement.

Sir Stafford was not given any freedom to bargain.[47] His instructions were those Churchill had circulated to the dominion leaders, with the addition of British control of India's defences until the end of the war. If the Indian leaders agreed, Churchill could claim the credit. If not, Cripps would bear the blame and his reputation would sink. King thought it would be helpful for each dominion to declare its willingness to accept India as an equal after the war. The sympathetic Leopold Amery sent "warm appreciation of your generous initiative, which I am sure will bear useful fruit" but asked King to stay his hand for the moment. Churchill signalled that he did not expect the envoy to succeed by telling King that "the grim issues which Cripps is valiantly trying to settle" were not simply between the British government and India but "between the different sects

---

44 Churchill to King, March 2; King to Churchill, March 6 (2 cables); Churchill to King, March 8, 1942. DCER, IX, 987–9

45 Roosevelt to Churchill, March 10; same to same (stronger) draft, February 25, 1942. Kimball, *Churchill and Roosevelt*, I, 400–4.

46 Churchill, *The Second World War*, II, 214.

47 Peter Clarke, *The Cripps Version: The Life of Sir Stafford Cripps 1889–1952* (London: Penguin Books, [2002] 2003, 292–322; Yasim Khan, *The Raj at War: A People's History of India's Second World War* (London: The Bodley Head, 2015), 132–5; Hamilton, *The Mantle of Command*, 241–53.

or nations in India itself." Staking out the high ground whatever happened, he added sternly: "We had resigned ourselves to fighting our utmost to defend India in order if successful to be turned out."[48]

After Cripps had been in India for a week, King had a gloomy discussion of his mission and other imperial matters with the like-minded Malcolm MacDonald. The high commissioner had plenty of experience of Churchill's opposition to Indian self-government and feared that Britain might lose the entire empire in the far east. He judged that the Pacific colonies would be taken over by the United States, Canada, Australia, and New Zealand, with the United States as the dominant power. Neither he nor King considered any of the colonies ready for self-government.

MacDonald said that on his forthcoming trip to Britain he would raise the ongoing issue of Commonwealth representation on various policy making groups. A month earlier, Churchill had made a symbolic gesture of including them in the war cabinet by appointing Clement Attlee as both dominions secretary and deputy prime minister (the first time this term had been used). Similarly, Richard Casey, hitherto the Australian minister to the United States, was sent as minister resident to the Middle East with a seat in the war cabinet. The real motive, MacDonald confided to King, was to get Casey, who was pressing his country's vulnerability in London, off Churchill's back, although Churchill could hail it as proof of Commonwealth involvement at the highest level of the war.[49]

In early April, the forceful Australian secretary of state for external affairs, Dr. Herbert Evatt arrived in Ottawa. He came from Washington where he urged more American military aid for his country. Churchill was furious as what he saw as the undermining of the empire and Britain's standing with the United States Evatt protested to King that Britain was over-insured compared to other parts of the empire and complained of everything being left to Churchill and Roosevelt. The dominions should have more participation. The British were indifferent to anything that did not suit their purposes and stream-rolled everything else. But this did not mean that Evatt was seeking an imperial war cabinet. What he wanted was Canada to send troops to Australia. King evasively said that the country's war effort was fitted into Britain's, to which almost everything was sent.

48 King to Churchill, March 15; King to Soong, March 16; King to Lachlan Currie, March 16; Amery to King, March 17; Churchill to King, March 18, 1942. DCER, IX, 991–2.
49 David Day, *The Great Betrayal: Britain, Australia & the Onset of the Pacific War 1939–1942* (North Ryde, New South Wales: Angus & Robertson, 1988), 292–5; Diary, March 21, 1942.

Roosevelt had asked Evatt to invite King, and bring him by force if necessary, to a meeting of the new Pacific War Council made up of countries at war with Japan.[50] Roosevelt was looking for a reliable ally in dealing with the two Pacific dominions and a like-minded confidant to talk about India. King accepted, considering the meeting important not only for himself but for Britain and the empire: "there is a tendency to recognize only Churchill and the President, and to crowd both Canada and myself off the map." He feared that unless Britain was careful, the United States would become the star "around which self-governing nations of the Empire will find their orbit instead of the U.K. This will include Ireland among their number and Scotland as well." But much as he and Evatt complained about the concentration of power in London, they agreed that Churchill, despite criticism, was the best bet as war leader: "he was the man who would save Britain in this situation and needed all the co-operation we could give him."[51]

At that very moment, on April 10, came news that the All Indian Congress rejected self-government after the war and demanded an immediate transfer of power. Gandhi dismissed the British offer as a post-dated cheque, which some journalist improved by adding "on a failing bank." King rightly suspected that Cripps had not had a free hand and that many wanted him to fail so that he would not overshadow Churchill. He feared that Britain and India would come to blows, with the sub-continent joining Japan and helping to link it to Germany. It would be "a miracle if the British Empire is saved at all, or if the U.S. is able to gain control of the Pacific and Britain and the U.S. regain many of their possessions."[52]

Roosevelt was similarly alarmed at the breakdown of negotiations, urging Churchill to keep Cripps at his task by authorizing minor concessions. Once again, he recommended an "articles of confederation" government until the end of the war. Churchill was so stung by this intervention in what he regarded as a purely British matter that he threatened to resign if that would preserve good relations with the United States.[53] A rupture was prevented by Harry Hopkins, who was in London.[54] But Churchill would not be moved to any compromise and

50 Diary, April 8, 1942.
51 Diary, April 9, 1942.
52 Diary, April 10–12, 1942.
53 Roosevelt to Churchill, April 11; Churchill to Roosevelt, April 12, 1942 (two cables, the first not sent). Kimball, *Churchill and Roosevelt*, I, 446–9.
54 Hamilton, *The Mantle of Command*, 244–53.

Cripps was recalled. A real crisis in India was averted, and the military threat to Australia relieved, by American bombing of Tokyo and the US navy's victory at the Battle of Midway in early June. With Germany now being pushed back by the Soviets, there was also no chance that it could attack India. This deferred but certainly did not end the tension over self-government in India.[55]

* * *

On the late winter night of April 14, King set off from Ottawa and met spring on the way. At the White House the next afternoon, Roosevelt joked about being in shirt sleeves. The Pacific Council met for two and a half hours in the cabinet room. A perfect example of form without substance, the organization of Allies in the Pacific had been established and was chaired by the president "as a body to talk, not act," leaving the Americans in full control.[56] Not wanting to be constrained by any detailed record, Roosevelt instructed Captain John McCrea, his naval aide, not to take notes but to write a memorandum afterwards. The only detailed account is in King's diary.

Discussion ranged far beyond the council's ostensible concern, although Roosevelt was careful not to reveal much specific information since an excessive amount was already reaching the press. He did say that Pétain was going to appoint the pro-Nazi Pierre Laval as prime minister which indicated even closer collaboration with Germany. He spoke about the loss of two British warships in the Indian Ocean caused by ignoring American advice not to let them get beyond land-based air cover. He also mentioned the Alaska highway which was being built with Canadian agreement from Dawson Creek, British Columbia to Fairbanks, Alaska by the US Corps of Engineers assisted by Canadian contractors, to protect against a Japanese landing. Above all, the president was anxious to relieve the military pressure on the USSR by opening a second front. The week before, he had sent Harry Hopkins and General George Marshall to persuade Churchill to a large-scale European landing in 1943 and a smaller one in 1942. King contributed his readiness to have Canadian soldiers in Britain serve anywhere, adding that many regretted they were not yet fighting. Roosevelt commented that the same was true of US units in the United Kingdom, although they

---

55 Hamilton, *The Mantle of Command*, 254–64, in which the account of the visit is based largely on King's diary.
56 Kimball, *Forged in War*, 134.

had scarcely arrived. But no dominion was enthusiastic about an early landing in continental Europe. King shared Churchill's anxiety, observing that it would be as difficult to land troops in Germany as Germans in Britain. Evatt agreed on avoiding another Dunkirk.

After dinner at the White House, Roosevelt in the Oval Office, asked King what he thought of the Pacific Council. Not being on oath, King said that it met a real need and the discussion was informative and helpful. The next day King, who was staying at the White House, recalled that the president had said "they had the worse case of jitters in Britain that he thought they had ever had," which King thought was caused by the threatened invasion of a divided India. Roosevelt was convinced that his "articles of confederation" proposal would have been acceptable to Cripps and the Indians but it had been blocked by Churchill. He believed that all the parts of India could come together and that it would be a great mistake to allow any part to separate, which might lead to a civil war like the American one (and, which in a way, it did in 1947). He pronounced that India's future would have to be settled by the United States and China. At that moment, he also considered all the foreign possessions, save North Guinea and possibly Borneo, could manage self-government.

Roosevelt's main concern was the Hopkins-Marshall mission, which he told King was too secret for the Pacific Council. The president was now convinced by Marshall's argument that an early offensive in western Europe was imperative and that 300,000 troops (about one-third of the eventual D-Day force) could be landed. Still fearing a Soviet defeat, he thought it would be better for the operation to occur before that dread event. If the Soviets did persevere, the landing would be a great help. He was pleased to have just received Churchill's agreement, although it turned out to be no more than a facile acquiescence in principle, soon followed by objections. King reiterated his warning that "if armies got across to Europe and were massacred there, there would be no saving Britain [from] the armies that would cross over to occupy the island." He added that General Andrew McNaughton was of the opinion that the Germans would attempt an invasion of Britain in August or later. Roosevelt retreated only to the extent of saying that he would carefully consider the timing of the landing, but even keeping up agitation for it would keep the Germans on the alert and draw forces from the USSR.[57]

57 Diary, April 15, 1942.

King slept better than Roosevelt, who said the next morning that before going to bed he had had a couple of cables from Churchill which were "the most depressing of anything I have read." Churchill relayed that the Japanese were assembling a powerful fleet to take Ceylon and Calcutta and preparing for a landing in troubled India where anything could happen. He pleaded desperately for two US battleships to replace the ones that had been sunk. Roosevelt refused, not wanting to reduce the American naval build-up in the Pacific, which two months later, would produce victory at Midway Island. He had already agreed to send planes.

Later, at lunch, King noticed the clutter of political memorabilia in the Oval Office in the west wing, demonstrating that Roosevelt enjoyed "nothing more than political campaigning and its associations. The game of politics is a great stimulus to him. He is a good fellow among the men of his own party and keeps them attached to himself and has as many personal contacts as possible."

Roosevelt and King issued a press release so that King would have something to show for the visit. This did not mention what they had actually discussed but announced that considerable progress had been made in pooling war supplies and that an air-training conference would be held in Ottawa.[58] King hoped that the president himself would come to Ottawa, preferably in June, as a counterpart to Churchill's visit in December. Roosevelt replied that he would try, but it was hard to get away. He could no longer work more than two nights a week and went to Hyde Park whenever possible. King understood that his absences from the White House were disguised by leaving the presidential flag flying for part of the time. Roosevelt said that he was trying to acquire an old inn or some such building at Hyde Park to house officials. When King asked if Leighton McCarthy had mentioned being too old for the job of Canadian minister, Roosevelt threw up his hands at the prospect of losing this old friend, saying: "Oh, on no account let him go. He has just been down to Warm Springs and had a little holiday. I have no doubt he finds the grind here considerable but persuade him to stay."[59]

After leaving the White House, King spent another day and a half in Washington, seeing the reliably anti-Roosevelt, communist-fearing Julia Grant, attending a dinner in his honour at the Canadian legation, which was joined by three US cabinet ministers and various diplomats, and a dinner at the Chinese

58 Roosevelt to Churchill, April 17, 1942. Kimball, *Churchill and Roosevelt*, I, 457.
59 Diary, April 16, 1942.

226

embassy with T. V. Soong, whom he liked and admired. He stopped in New York to shop and visit a spiritualist. On the way to Ottawa he read about the first American bombing raid of Tokyo and the appointment of Laval as French Prime Minister.[60]

King reported to the cabinet on his Washington discussions, his colleagues shuddering when he told them: "There is no escaping that this was as anxious a time as Britain has ever experienced and the world had ever known."[61] A few days later, Sir Dudley Pound, the first sea lord sent by Churchill in the vain hope of persuading Roosevelt to provide ships for the Indian Ocean, stopped in Ottawa and assuaged some of King's fear by assuring him that there would be no European landing until at least autumn, since the British insisted on more preparation. Pound also told King the other side of the story he had heard from Roosevelt about India: Churchill, after receiving "some very hot wires" from the president, told Hopkins that Roosevelt did not know much about Britain.[62]

* * *

Two months later, King met with Roosevelt and Churchill in Washington. He had an intimation of Churchill's visit when he was summoned out of a conscription debate in the House of Commons on June 11, by a telephone call from Roosevelt. The president said that Queen Wilhelmina of the Netherlands was coming from London to spend two months in the United States, stopping in Ottawa to collect her daughter and heir, Princess Juliana, and her children. Roosevelt loved being the equal of crowned heads and being able to help them, particularly when an attractive young woman such as Juliana was involved. He told King that he had found the family a house at Stockbridge, Massachusetts (seventy-five miles from Hyde Park), affecting to complain that their request "was pretty much the limit in the way of imposition." Since the house was not ready, he asked King to detain them in Ottawa. At the end, he gave a clear indication of the next visitor by saying that King should be prepared to come to Washington on short notice.[63]

A week later, Churchill arrived by plane in the US capital. King sent a cable of welcome and, with a lively sense of the value of Churchill's support during

60 Diary, April 18, 1942.
61 Diary, April 20, 1942.
62 Diary, April 24, 1942.
63 Diary, June 11, 1942.

the conscription controversy, invited him to Canada. Malcolm MacDonald told King that Churchill would probably be in Washington for only a few days, and that his purpose was to defer a second front. The Americans, said MacDonald, did not realize the power of Germany and what was required to fight them. He engaged to tell Halifax that Churchill should visit Ottawa. King, knowing that he would be invited to Washington, with prim disingenuousness said that he would not think of suggesting it himself.[64]

To persuade Roosevelt that a huge force and careful preparation were necessary for a successful attack on the continent, which would in any event not draw many Germans from the Soviet front to the already large number in western Europe, Churchill had sent to Washington Lord Louis Mountbatten, the glamorous but reckless vice-admiral whom he had recently appointed commander of combined operations against Europe.[65] His argument would be countered by another visitor, Vyacheslav Molotov, the Soviet foreign minister, who arrived to secure Roosevelt's agreement to "the urgent tasks of creating a second front in Europe in 1942."[66]

The president was at Hyde Park when Churchill arrived in Washington on the Thursday. Churchill flew there and was met at the airport by the president who drove his own car back to Springwood.[67] This was Churchill's first visit to the estate; one very similar to Chartwell. Harry Hopkins was also present. The three discussed the secret research on atomic weapons (code named "Tube Alloys"), reaching oral agreement on an equal British-US partnership on the project, which was still at the laboratory stage. At least, that was what Churchill wrote after the other two were dead. But if it was the case, no American scientist was informed and the whole matter, as it moved to extremely expensive industrial application, would have to be reviewed again. The understanding at Hyde Park may simply have been an indication that Roosevelt was trying to put Churchill in an agreeable mood without committing himself.[68] Churchill presented the well-rehearsed case for concentrating on north Africa and continuing to bomb Germany rather than risking a premature and potentially disastrous invasion of

---

64 Diary, June 19, 1942.
65 Diary, June 11, 1942.
66 Daniels, *Franklin D. Roosevelt*, 271–2.
67 Hamilton, *The Mantle of Command*, 293–321; Meacham, *Franklin and Winston*, 181–7; Rollins, *The Hopkins Touch*, 200–7.
68 Kevin Ruane, *Churchill and the Bomb in War and Cold War* (London: Bloomsbury Academic, 2016), 42–5.

Mackenzie King, aged 67, in his library at Laurier House, 1942.

"Pass, friend": Roosevelt and King cutting the ribbon opening the bridge over the St. Lawrence river between Canada and the U.S., August 1938.

Royal visitors after church at Hyde Park, June 1939: (l-r) Queen Elizabeth, George VI, Roosevelt, son James, mother Sara, wife Eleanor and Mackenzie King.

Churchill and King, Ottawa, December 1941, after Karsh had taken his famous photographs of Churchill.

Churchill addressing the Canadian parliament, December 1941. King is in the first seat of the front row to Churchill's right.

The 1943 Quebec conference: King, Roosevelt and Churchill with the British-US chiefs of staff behind. In the background are the flags of the United States, Canada and Britain.

Quebec conference, August 1943. Roosevelt greeting Anthony Eden, who had just arrived by sea plane from Britain. Princess Alice and Churchill also seated. The Earl of Athlone is behind Eden. King is standing, along with Sir Alexander Cadogan and Brendan Bracken, both of whom had come with Eden.

King introduces Roosevelt (on the arm of Rear Admiral Wilson Brown) to the crowd in front of the Peace Tower, Canadian parliament building, August 1943. Governor-General Lord Athlone stands to the left.

King addressing the British parliament, May 1944. On the platform behind are (l-r) Lord Cranborne, Lord Chancellor Simon (obscured), Churchill, Clifton Brown (Speaker of the House of Commons) and Clement Attlee. Among those in the front row are Sir John Anderson, Anthony Eden, Jan Smuts and Vincent and Alice Massey

Inspecting D-Day preparations, May 1944: (l-r) King, Churchill, Peter Fraser (New Zealand), General Dwight Eisenhower, Sir Godfrey Huggins (Southern Rhodesia) and Jan Smuts.

On the terrace of the Citadelle at the 1944 Quebec conference (l-r): Clementine Churchill, Lord Athlone, Roosevelt, Princess Alice, Churchill, Eleanor Roosevelt and King. In the background is the tower of the Chateau Frontenac, which housed the military and civilian staffs.

Friends at last: Roosevelt welcomes de Gaulle to the White House, July 1944. In the background are Cordell Hull and Anna (Roosevelt) Boettiger.

King greeting the arrival of Fedor Gusev (daughter on the right), the first Soviet envoy to Canada October 1942. Gusev almost certainly organized the spy ring centred on Ottawa.

King, Edouard Handy, his trusted stenographer and keeper of the diary, and one of King's three successive Irish terriers, all named Pat.

The burial of Roosevelt, Hyde Park, April 1945. Eleanor Roosevelt is in the centre left, closest to the coffin.

France. This conversation was adjourned to Washington where the two returned by train on the Saturday night.

On Sunday morning, General Marshall came to the White House with the shattering news that Tobruk, the Libyan port that the British and Commonwealth forces had managed to hold against the Germans while other troops were being pushed back into Egypt, had surrendered. Over 30,000 men and more than 1,000 tanks fell to general Erwin Rommel's force of half the size. For Churchill, this was worse than Singapore, which it could be argued was impossible to protect. The Suez Canal, the only secure surface route to north Africa was now in jeopardy.

Roosevelt immediately asked what he could do to help. Churchill requested as many as possible of the new M-4 Sherman tanks with swivelling turrets. Within days, three hundred of these plus a hundred self-propelled guns were on the way in fast transport ships around Africa through the Suez Canal. This was a pivotal decision for the Europe theatre. The loss of the tanks made a second front in the north that was pressed by Marshall and Stimson for 1942 highly improbable. But for Roosevelt, Tobruk was not only a warning but an opportunity. He could now ignore his military advisers and insist that inexperienced American soldiers develop their combat skills in north Africa, which was where he had promised Churchill to concentrate at the beginning of the year.[69] This firm commitment was a huge relief to Churchill, who was under the impression that it had been his personal mission, which had convinced Roosevelt.[70]

* * *

Two days after Tobruk, Mackenzie King received the expected telephone call from Roosevelt with Churchill at his side, both urging him to attend the Pacific War Council a couple of days hence. King was invited to spend the night at the White House but owing to the conscription debate he could only spare a few hours in Washington. To ensure that he was on time, he left Ottawa by train that midnight and passed the following day in New York. He and Edouard Handy saw *Mrs. Miniver*, a Hollywood movie designed to raise American sympathy for Britain. Depicting the fortitude of a middle-class village family during the Battle of Britain, King thought it wonderful. The male lead was the Canadian Walter Pidgeon, playing opposite Greer Garson. Four months later, King and Pidgeon

---

69 Hamilton, *The Mantle of Command*, 318–21 and 327–9.
70 Barnes and Nicolson, *The Empire at Bay*, 820; diary, July 16, 1942.

were photographed together in Ottawa for victory loan publicity, King finding the actor an "extremely pleasant, attractive and able – a very fine character."[71]

When King arrived in Washington at 11 a.m., he and Leighton McCarthy went straight to the White House. Before the Pacific Council was a meeting between Churchill and dominion representatives. Before proceedings began, Sir John Dill told King about the seriousness of Tobruk and the difficulty of fighting in the desert. Two Australian divisions were leaving to defend their own country and Dill gave the impression that it might be impossible to save the Suez Canal. Churchill strove to counter Australian anxieties by saying that he would rather lose Suez than sacrifice their country.

Churchill asked King to sit beside him at the dominions gathering and King was surprised to find him "remarkably fresh, almost like a cherub, scarcely a line in his face, and completely rested, though up to one or two the night before." King, of course, knew nothing about Roosevelt's concurrence in delaying the second front and concentrating on the Mediterranean. In his report to the group, Churchill did not disguise his devastation at the surrender of Tobruk. The next worry was the nominally independent and indifferent Egypt, which the British continued to regard as a colony, and the defence of the Suez Canal. Churchill claimed that the Germans would find fighting without water very arduous and was confident that they would be stopped before Suez. He emphasized the importance of keeping the British army well supplied but, perhaps for security reasons, said nothing about the US tanks and guns. He also predicted that the USSR would hold the Germans, although it would be a bitter fight (three days later a huge German offensive began in the south). If the Soviets persisted until autumn, he was sure the Allies would win the war.

In the far east, Churchill pointed to the good news that the Japanese fleet had been compelled to withdraw from the Indian ocean by American victories in the Pacific. He insisted that India was better protected than ever. He asserted that Britain had made the best offer it could of self-government and repeated that India was not a country but a very diverse continent in which Muslims could not be abandoned to the mercy of the more numerous Hindus. Churchill further claimed that the situations of Australia and New Zealand had improved, speculating that Japan might move north, attacking Siberia if the USSR suffered a major defeat by the Germans. The east, with its vast spaces and limited resources,

71 Diary, October 22, 1942.

was like a man in bed with a small blanket covering one part, then another, and risking pneumonia.

Pausing dramatically, Churchill then said that the situation was far better than it had been when France fell and the USSR and the United States were still outside the war. Now, he hailed "the heroism of the Russians and the magnificent work which the Americans were doing on their production, etc." But there was an even greater ally than the Soviet Union or the United States. Again halting for effect, he pronounced that it was air power, revealing his continuing belief in a war principally undertaken by machines. British and American production would continue to increase, and the enemies would not be able to keep up. He pointed to the massive raids on Cologne and Essen and indicated that there would be many more. The object was military targets, although he conceded that sometimes the airmen missed. No ship could stand against dive bombers (something he had only recently realized) and pilots were volunteering for the perilous task. Confident that air raids would wear down the Germans (although they had not the British, who were presumably made of sterner stuff) he pronounced that nothing "by God" would induce him to attack Europe without sufficient strength and the certainty of winning. In the meantime, there should be commando raids and, as Roosevelt had said to King, the impression maintained of an early landing to keep the "Hun" away from the USSR Barring serious Soviet defeats, there could be no second front before 1943. King did not hesitate to add his endorsement.

Following this pep talk, the group moved to the Pacific Council in the cabinet room. On the way, Churchill took King's arm and told him confidentially that he was leaving that afternoon. King, in turn, unburdened himself of his anxiety about the conscription debate and the fear that his majority of 180 seats might fall to 30. Churchill, who was facing parliamentary criticism of his own, sympathized. Roosevelt, of course, presided at the council. First they all went to the portico for photographs. Churchill said that he did not know how to look, particularly after Tobruk: "If one were smiling, the public would think they were taking things too lightly. On the other if we looked too serious, they thought there was a crisis." Roosevelt invited King to stand between him and Churchill. The next day, the *Ottawa Citizen* published the picture of Roosevelt and Churchill with King (and others) cropped out. King kept the clipping as evidence of what he had to endure from some of the press.[72]

---

72 Diary, June 26, 1942.

At the meeting, Churchill was on Roosevelt's right, King on his left. It was another public relations event. The point, as King wrote, was "to have it over with as quickly as possible, simply to have enough said to give the gathering a significance in the eyes of the public, but to avoid too much in way of questions." The president observed that the Pacific situation was much improved by the naval victories, although there was still a problem of supply routes to China. He asked King if British Columbians had been alarmed by the recent Japanese coastal raid. Five days earlier a Japanese submarine had fired on a Vancouver Island lighthouse (to no effect). King thought they had, adding that they were in good company: the day after, a military base in Oregon had been shelled by a submarine, also ineffectually.

At lunch, the group was joined by Cordell Hull, Sumner Welles and Harry Hopkins, Churchill and King again sitting on either side of Roosevelt. Hopkins, on King's other side, reassured him that there would be no second front in 1942. King had expected a discussion of India at the Pacific Council and told Lord Halifax that he did not think that Churchill realized the state of affairs. The former viceroy said that he was working on his own plans and promised to send them to King. Roosevelt said he would like to go to Montreal to accept an honorary degree offered by McGill University and then have a couple of days at Georgian Bay where Leighton McCarthy had a cottage, but he did not see how he could get away.

Churchill, provoked by a disparaging resolution tabled that day in the House of Commons by the chairman of the Conservative foreign affairs committee, defiantly said that the critics of Tobruk would be sorry. He would never give up his position of minister of defence. He would bait the malcontents into a vote on their resolution. Parliamentary government, he said, was not just debate but decisions. A vote would fix responsibility and show what support he had.

After lunch Churchill and Roosevelt hurried away for a last conversation before Churchill flew home. King left for Ottawa that afternoon.[73] He was far too preoccupied with the conscription debate to follow the British parliamentary drama closely, although he was impressed by Churchill's forceful handling of opponents. Things had come to a head when Sir John Wardlaw-Milne charged that Churchill had too much power and recommended a strong, separate minister capable of controlling the armed services. When he proposed the Duke of

73 Diary, June 25, 1942.

Gloucester, the king's obscure, heavy-drinking brother, as head of the army, the House of Commons collapsed in a fit of laughter and Churchill broke into a great grin. He knew he was perfectly safe. He suffered some hard blows during the two-day debate but won by 475 votes to 25.[74] Inspired by Churchill's example, King took a strong line in the final speech of the drawn-out conscription debate, a few days later. He told the cabinet that if he did not have a majority, he would resign and would advise the governor general against an election, meaning a new Liberal leader or perhaps a coalition with the Conservatives. Practically quoting what Churchill had said in Washington, King told his ministers: "I did not think members of the Opposition or anyone in the House should be allowed to get away with mere discussion but should be obliged to vote, and by their vote let the country see where they were standing." He won the division to release the government from its 1939 guarantee by 158 votes to 54.[75]

* * *

Three weeks later, King had an opportunity to repay Churchill's friendship when Randolph Churchill telephoned to say that he was flying to Ottawa that day to see him. He was now an army captain and an MP, thanks to the political truce whereby the incumbent party was not challenged by the other two members of the coalition. Busy as King was at the end of the parliamentary session, he had to make time for this visitor. They talked in his office, sat together in the gallery of the House of Commons and had dinner at Laurier House before Randolph flew away. King enjoyed the occasion and found his guest "greatly improved. Had, indeed a nice manner, though still a little aggressive. . . He is a real young man [he was 31] of the world, but with genuine ability." King did not record any mention by Randolph of his son, Winston, born in October 1940, or his wife Pamela, with whom he accused his parents of colluding in her affair with Averell Harriman, if not actually dangling her before him.[76]

A couple of weeks later, Winston Churchill was on his way to Stalin with the unwelcome news that there would be no front in northern Europe in 1942, softened by information of the approaching American landing in north Africa.

74 Thompson, *Canada and the End of the Imperial Dream*, 194–6; Schneer, *Ministers at War*, 144–7.
75 Diary, July 7, 1942; Granatstein, *Canada's War*, 239.
76 Sonia Purnell, *Clementine: The Life of Mrs. Winston Churchill* (New York: Viking, 2015), 277–8; Diary, July 27, 1942.

King thought he would be needed in London for a meeting of dominion prime ministers. He grumbled that it would prevent him from catching up on work before parliament resumed in the autumn but felt obliged to go. Five days later, however, plans for the meeting fell apart, which was a mercy for the British.[77] The very next day came the Dieppe raid, the worst tragedy of the war for Canada. If King had gone to Britain, Churchill and others would have had to justify the disaster to him personally.

* * *

The first King heard of the Dieppe expedition was on the 8 a.m. radio news on August 19. By then, the operation was over and those lucky enough to survive were escaping back to Britain. The attack was larger than the customary hit-and-run strike to hearten the French in the occupied zone and keep the Germans on edge about an invasion. It was also designed to give the Allied troops experience for the eventual full-scale cross-channel landing.[78] Such attacks were the sphere of highly trained marine commandos.

When General Henry Crerar, temporarily in charge of the Canadian troops in Britain while McNaughton was on leave, heard that a major operation was in preparation, he petitioned general Bernard Montgomery, the head of south-east command, to include Canadians, some of whom had been training in Britain for two and half years. Fighting would raise morale and provide valuable battlefield practice. Soon Canadians made up most of the force that was prepared and trained. In early July, however, Montgomery called off the raid owing to weather, the tides, and the Germans learning what was afoot. When he was transferred to the Middle East, he warned against continuing the operation but it was revived by Lord Louis Mountbatten, the director of combined operations, who was eager to restore confidence in the military after the humiliation of Tobruk. Churchill approved the original decision and knew that it was revived since he

77 Diary, August 18, 1942.
78 Sixty years later, it would be argued, without direct evidence, that the action was the cover for a special commando unit directed by Ian Fleming, the future author of the James Bond novels, to capture German code books. David O'Keefe, *One Day in August: The Untold Story Behind Canada's Tragedy at Dieppe* (Toronto: Alfred A. Knopf Canada, 2013); Andrew Lownie, *The Mountbattens* (London: Blink, 2019, 137–47); Bercuson, *Our Finest Hour*, 85–7 and 91–105; Cook, *The Necessary War*, 253–85; Hastings, *Finest Years*, 332–3; Roberts, *Masters and Commanders*, 272–4.

told Stalin that there would be a serious raid to give the impression of invasion in mid-August, weather permitting.

Of the 6,000-strong force finally assembled, close to 5,000 were Canadians. General Kenneth Stuart, the commander in chief of the Canadian army, assured King's war cabinet that the soldiers were well-equipped and had been thoroughly trained on the Isle of Wight to seize a town on a height of land.[79] True as that may have been, the operation lacked the support of other services that Mountbatten needed. His position carried high rank in all three services but not the power to command them. The Royal Navy would not risk warships and the RAF refused to deploy heavy bombers against the guns on the cliffs, which would have killed many civilians. Mountbatten nevertheless proceeded with the expedition, 250 vessels carrying the troops and 60 tanks, protected by 800 aircraft fighters from bases in Britain.

During the night crossing, the convoy was detected by the Germans. Dieppe was also well-prepared for attack. The landing craft were bombed from the air, the tanks could scarcely gain traction on the shingle beach, and gunfire from the heights devastated the soldiers before they landed. After a desperate effort lasting five hours, a disorderly retreat began.[80] Only 2,210 Canadians made it back to Britain; 907 had been killed and 1,946 captured. The RAF and RCAF lost 99 planes, the largest number on any day of the war, and the Royal Navy suffered 550 casualties. King was impressed to learn that the army chaplain, the Rev. John Weir Foote, had conducted services during the passage, counselling the soldiers in the words of the Epistle to the Ephesians to "'put on the whole armour of God.' The latter is the only spirit in which this war can be won, towards justification of the killing of men in battle."[81] The chaplain volunteered to go into captivity with the prisoners, for which he received the Victoria Cross.

Despite the huge price in men and equipment, which was not immediately known, the operation was initially depicted as a triumph. Mountbatten assured Churchill in Cairo that the Germans were badly shaken and the soldiers who returned to Britain were in high spirits. The latter was echoed by the Canadian

---

79 Diary, August 19, 1942.
80 Four years later, when he unveiled a memorial to Canadians killed there, Mackenzie King could not believe that such a place had been chosen for a landing: "It was sending men to certain death without a ghost of a chance." King thought that those who were responsible should have been cashiered. Diary, August 18, 1946.
81 Diary, August 19, 1942.

General Harry Letson, who interviewed the wounded and pronounced that they had no complaints and were ready to fight again. He also believed, as many did, that the Germans had suffered great air losses.[82] But the long list of casualties took the gloss off the heartening reports. Churchill, initially preoccupied with Stalin and the war in the Middle East, was soon troubled by what seemed foolhardiness. But it did his favourite's career no harm. Next year, Mountbatten was appointed supreme commander in south-east Asia. When Churchill reached Dieppe in his war memoirs, he was told that for secrecy reasons very little had been written down. The memories of those involved had also faded a great deal in the following half decade. In the end, he simply published the self-serving account Mountbatten provided.[83] Lucky he was that King never challenged him on the subject.

At the time, King suspected that the main reason for Dieppe was the need for Canadian troops to do something. He judged that it would have been better to keep the specially trained force for the decisive moment but deferred to professional opinion that it might work out for the best in the long run.[84] A month later, he read with scepticism the official report maintaining that the heavy losses were justified by the information gathered for a real invasion. The enemies, he wrote, "are able effectively to represent the whole episode as a gain for themselves between the numbers taken prisoners and those who have been killed. It is a very serious blow to the Canadian forces."[85]

Dieppe's real success was the result of its failure. Until D-Day in June 1944, it remained an awful warning, often invoked especially by Churchill, against an untimely second front. Roosevelt told King that the Canadian experience at Dieppe "made clear how terribly dangerous the whole business of invasion across the Channel was."[86]

* * *

82 Diary, August 26, 1942.
83 Reynolds, *In Command of History*, 345–8.
84 Diary, August 21, 1942.
85 Diary, September 19, 1942.
86 Diary, December 6, 1942.

A more immediate consequence of Dieppe was controversy over shackling prisoners of war, a matter that absorbed enormous attention and strained relations between King and Churchill.[87] A British order instructing the invaders to bind the hands of their captives to prevent them from destroying documents was inadvertently carried ashore and fell into the hands of the Germans. The British denied the directive but two months later used binding in a commando raid on the German-occupied channel island of Sark. The German government retaliated by directing almost 1,400 prisoners of war to have their hands manacled (it was not known that this was only half-heartedly applied by the camp commanders). Winston Churchill, in a state of high tension as the crucial clash in north Africa approached, insisted that temporary binding on the battlefield was very different from shackling prisoners and persuaded the war cabinet to retaliate. Canada was not involved in the decision, although most of the Dieppe prisoners were Canadians and the vast majority of German captives were held at camps in Canada. The British government decided to manacle 200 prisoners and asked Canada to shackle 2,000. Ralston, who was in London, and Massey were appalled and suggested some settlement between the two sides. King, protesting lack of consultation or any attempt at mediation, cabled that the Canadian government doubted the wisdom of shackling; it would nevertheless handcuff 1,100 prisoners to avoid a breach with Britain which had already announced its action.[88]

The Germans, in turn, declared that they would shackle three times as many prisoners as Britain, 4,128 in all. The British then asked Canada to manacle 3,888. Churchill appealed personally to King: "Earnestly hope that you will stand by us in this anxious business in which we both had much at stake. Am sure it will be of short duration."[89] But King would not budge in his resistance. The war cabinet refused further manacling until Switzerland, the protecting power for Canadian interests in Europe, and the Red Cross were appealed to for intercession. King told Churchill: "we see nothing whatever to be gained in competition in reprisals in which the dice are obviously loaded against United States."[90] The members of the British war cabinet evidently agreed since Malcolm MacDonald

---

87 Jonathan F. Vance, *Objects of Concern: Canadian Prisoners of War Through the Twentieth Century* (Vancouver: UBC Press, 1994), 134–9. The same author deals with the subject more extensively in "Men in Manacles: The Shackling of Prisoners of War, 1942–3," *Journal of Military History* 59 no. 3 (July 1995): 483–504.

88 King to Attlee, October 9, 1942. DCER, IX, 475–6.

89 Attlee to King and Churchill to King, October 10, 1942. DCER, IX, 482–3.

90 King to Churchill, October 11, 1942. DCER, IX, 486.

reported that there were four meetings on the subject, at which they felt compelled to subordinate their judgment to Churchill's dominance.[91] As Roosevelt commented a month later: "Winston was inclined at times to take things a little too quickly in hand himself."[92]

Finally, after victory in north Africa, Churchill changed his mind. He took the opportunity to recover the Canadian prime minister's valuable support, telephoning to tell King that the issue was being settled in accordance with his wishes: next day, he was going to announce the end of shackling. King agreed to the same, rejecting the advice of his under-secretary for a separate, immediate declaration to show Canada's independence. King believed that this "would be bad before the enemy and might create a serious feeling in Churchill's own mind."[93]

* * *

Another aggravation to Churchill as the decisive battle in north Africa loomed was supplied by Wendell Willkie, hitherto regarded as one of Britain's greatest American friends. In late August, he embarked on a seven-week goodwill tour of the world, including the Middle East, the Soviet Union, and China. Unofficially, he was travelling on behalf of Roosevelt who provided a military airplane and was happy to see him out of the United States for most of the mid-term election campaign. Willkie bore the Roosevelt-ian message of freedom and international cooperation as the foundation of world peace. An important element for Willkie, and Roosevelt, in creating "One World" (the title of Willkie's subsequent book which sold two million copies) was ending the British Empire. On his return to the United States, Willkie asserted in a widely-heard broadcast "that there is no more place for imperialism . . . in the society of nations."

Nothing could have infuriated Churchill more. Nor were his suspicions about American intentions allayed by Roosevelt at a press conference the next day saying that Willkie was merely making the point that the Atlantic Charter applied to "all humanity." Churchill later told Charles Taussig, the president of the American Molasses Company and Roosevelt's adviser on colonial matters, that Willkie knew little about the empire and had seen only airports in the few parts

91 Diary, October 21 and November 7, 1942.
92 Diary, December 4, 1942.
93 Diary, December 7 and 10, 1942.

he had visited. Defiantly, he threatened: "I am not going to accept less favourable terms from that other German Willkie than I could get from Hitler." [94]

Mackenzie King found Willkie's broadcast, apart from his grating voice, too partisan, too disparaging of Roosevelt a week before the US congressional elections, and too critical of Britain and its policies in India and elsewhere. [95] He and Malcolm MacDonald agreed ten days later that the speech had made the difficult Indian situation even more embarrassing. That night, King telephoned Roosevelt on the second anniversary of his 1940 re-election. With no idea that the president had encouraged Willkie's global venture, he said that the broadcast had been in bad taste and not well received in Ottawa. Roosevelt, who was offended by Willkie's presumption in his highly publicized statements around the world, said: "I could have torn Willkie limb from limb if I had wished to say anything." He added collusively: "you and I play the same sort of game, and I thought it just as well to let him say what he likes." He pronounced the just-concluded 1942 congressional election results not bad, though the Democrats had lost ten Senate seats and forty-seven in the House of Representatives while retaining a majority in both houses.

Roosevelt ended the conversation by inviting King to Washington for a couple of days, suggesting a month hence. [96] There was by then much to talk about. The situation in north Africa had been transformed. The Soviets were beginning to push the Germans back. The US naval victories in the Pacific continued. The tide had turned. In addition to the next phase of military operations, Roosevelt, as he almost certainly intended to signal through Willkie, was increasingly concerned to settle the future of the world before the fighting ended. In this, there seemed to be an important role for Mackenzie King.

94   Wm. Roger Louis, *Imperialism at Bay: The United States and the Decolonization of the British Empire, 1941–1945* (New York: Oxford University Press, 1978), 198–9 and note 3; Lewis, *The Improbable Wendell Willkie*, 225–70.
95   Diary, October 26, 1942.
96   Diary, November 6, 1942.

CHAPTER EIGHT

The Future of the World

T HE GREAT TURNING POINT in the interconnected fortunes of Churchill and the Mediterranean war was the unqualified triumph at Alamein, four months after the loss of Tobruk. Brendan Bracken, a month before the battle, told Churchill's doctor: "If we are beaten in this battle, it's the end of Winston." The government would have to be reconstructed and he would never agree to continue as prime minister without his plenitude of powers.[1] After the victory, Churchill was back on top of the world and for the rest of the war there was no significant challenge to his leadership.

The British advance began on October 23, raging back and forth for twelve days until November 4 when Rommel's army was in full retreat.[2] The British were helped by American tanks and self-propelled guns and information about the German movements from Enigma decrypts. They used artful deception and had a preponderance of numbers in an army that included Australians, New Zealanders, South Africans, and others. Only a few Canadians were present for training purposes. Ralston had reiterated to Churchill the willingness to have the troops in Britain go wherever they were needed but Churchill decreed that they be kept in the country. At the right time, which he did not expect before the autumn of 1943 at the earliest, they would be used "as a sort of hammer which is to strike a blow at the centre of Europe."[3]

1   Moran, *Churchill*, 83; (Diary, September 30, 1942).
2   Hastings, *Finest Years*, 337–9.
3   Diary, October 21, 1942.

What secured the win at Alamein was Operation Torch, the Anglo-American landings, to the surprise of the Germans, in the French colonies of Morocco and Algeria. The 100,000 troops were transported directly from the United Kingdom and the United States in over a hundred ships covered by air power.[4] The United States hoped that the invaders would be welcomed as liberators by the Vichy authorities who, in fact, resisted with varying degrees of enthusiasm. They scuttled the fleet to prevent it falling into Allied hands and did not oppose German reinforcements that were flown into Tunisia. After a few days, however, Admiral François Darlan, Pétain's deputy and chief of the armed services who was by chance in Algiers visiting his son who had polio, accepted a ceasefire, changed sides, and ordered the armed forces to do the same in return for his recognition as head of the French government in the region. Expedient as it may have been to accept a particularly odious collaborator who in 1940 had reneged on his promise to deliver the French fleet to Britain, the Free French were outraged and soon Darlan was assassinated. Hitler demanded that Pétain declare war on the invaders of French territory. When Pétain refused, German troops occupied Vichy France, although the French managed to destroy much of the fleet at Toulon. Diplomatic relations ended between the United States and the Vichy government, and Canada followed suit.

With success in north Africa practically guaranteed, although it took another five months of hard fighting to drive out the Germans, Winston Churchill was able to say at the annual Lord Mayor of London's banquet on November 10: "This is not the end. It is not even the beginning of the end. But it is, perhaps, the end of the beginning." Even though Torch and perhaps Alamein could not have been achieved without the United States, Churchill believed that he was now in a strong position to defend the British Empire. Countering Willkie, and more importantly, by implication, Roosevelt, he declared: "We mean to hold our own. I have not become the King's First Minister in order to preside over the liquidation of the British Empire . . . Here we are, and here we stand, a veritable rock of salvation in this drifting world."[5]

4 Hamilton, *The Mantle of Command*, 421–37.
5 James, *Churchill: His Complete Speeches*, 6692–5; Louis, *Imperialism at Bay*, 199–204. It is significant that Churchill made no reference to this speech in Vol. IV of his war memoirs, *The Hinge of Fate* (1950), published first, as all were, in the United States after India, Pakistan, Ceylon and Burma had become independent.

Mackenzie King, listening by radio, had no objection to the defence of empire and thought the whole address "exceedingly eloquent. I could imagine no finer action [in north Africa] for a great oration, and Churchill was certainly equal to it." King did regret that the dominions were brought in only as an afterthought.[6] A month later, when Roosevelt at the White House said that Churchill had done great harm by opposing the end of empire, King defended him, adding that it gave Churchill "a great internal kick to say certain of these things." The president did not change his mind, as Churchill was soon painfully aware. On this occasion, not wanting to disrupt the happy relationship with his Canadian neighbour, the president laughed off the matter.[7]

* * *

The Pilgrims Society, at which Mackenzie King gave an after dinner speech on "the defence of our common liberties" on December 2, was a well-connected transatlantic organization for the promotion of close relations between Britain and the United States. It was founded in 1902 when Cecil Rhodes and Lady Randolph Churchill were among those dreaming of reuniting the two countries. Among the prominent members in Britain were King's friends Hamar Greenwood and Sir Campbell Stuart. For King's speech, Leighton McCarthy and Lord Halifax came from Washington. In his half-hour address, King reviewed Canada's contribution to the war for freedom and looked forward to a world in which "Equality, Brotherly Love, Co–operation [were] Keys to Prosperity," as the none-too-friendly *Globe and Mail* put it.[8] Next day, at a show at Radio City Music Hall, where King and the President of Ecuador were acknowledged with great applause, Harry Hooker, the president's former law partner and friend, said the president loved him and that their talks were a joy to him.[9]

King had been asked on behalf of the president to go straight to the White House when he arrived by overnight train. Just before 10 a.m., Roosevelt asked King to come to his bedroom, where he was sitting in bed, wearing a grey sweater, smoking, and reading the newspapers. King thought "even at that hour of the morning, he seemed a bit tired and breath a bit short, but on the whole he was

6 Diary, November 10, 1942.
7 Diary, December 5, 1942.
8 "Base Future on Human Rights: King," *Globe and Mail*, December 3, 1942.
9 Diary, December 3, 1942.

looking better than I had expected to see him." He congratulated Roosevelt on Torch and asked about Darlan's change of side. The president said he considered Darlan "a scoundrel who was looking after himself" but, citing a Romanian proverb about walking across a bridge with the devil so long as he could be thrown off at the end, he said: "in time of war every means had to be taken to meet the situation." They discussed the difficulties of a cross-channel European invasion, the option of landing in Norway, which Roosevelt had discussed with Stalin, who was opposed, and the president's preference for attacking the Germans through southern Europe, the best "soft place," he said, using a term associated with Churchill.

Roosevelt had intended to take Mackenzie King for the weekend to the newly acquired presidential retreat seventy-five miles away in the hills of Maryland but the weather was too cold and his rudimentary cottage had no heat. The former children's camp, designated Shangri-La by Roosevelt (and later renamed Camp David by president Eisenhower), had been built by the Civilian Conservation Corps in the 1930s and adapted for the use of the president, particularly in summer, whenever he could not go to Hyde Park. Escaping Washington's summer heat and humidity along the coast aboard his yacht was no longer considered safe.[10] Instead, the president said they would have dinner with princess Martha of Norway's at Pook's Hill, in suburban Washington. The only others would be Harry Hopkins and his (third) wife, the glamorous Louise (formerly Macy), former editor of the Paris edition of *Harper's Bazaar*. They had married in the White House with Roosevelt as best man at the end of July, and Louise and her maid had moved into the presidential boarding house.

King was also invited by Roosevelt to lunch but he had already accepted to join Cordell Hull, which the president pronounced "first rate." The two later met alone for tea, at which, as the president poured, King noticed that his hand was "very, very shaky. He looked rather tired but brightened up as we began to talk." Roosevelt said that he was having trouble with the Australians and New Zealanders, particularly Walter Nash, the New Zealand representative who asked embarrassing questions at the Pacific Council and informed the press. Roosevelt confided that his technique in dealing with awkward questions was to stall by telling a story; by the end people had forgotten or lost interest in what they had asked. This was of no practical use to King, who was no raconteur and (like

10 Goodwin, *No Ordinary Time*, 385–6; Hamilton, *The Mantle of Command*, 373–4.

Churchill in Britain) rarely held a press conference. When King hoped there might be a meeting of allied countries to get food and clothing to prisoners of war in Japanese camps, the president said it was hopeless. The Japanese would listen to nothing.

The group going to dinner assembled just before 7 p.m. King met Louise Hopkins and was delighted that her husband was "a perfectly different man than when I had last seen him. He has picked up wonderfully in health." In the car, Louise Hopkins sat between the president and the prime minister, her husband on the jump seat. King raised the subject of so many valuable French ships having being sunk at Toulon and Roosevelt said "unfortunately they are not." The French had destroyed about two-thirds of the fleet but the Germans had managed to seize a large battleship, three cruisers, some destroyers and other vessels.

King had previously met Princess Martha at the White House and in Ottawa, along with her official staff who were also at the dinner. (The Norwegian army and air force trained at "Little Norway" on Toronto Island, and in Muskoka.). Roosevelt had telephoned ahead to say that King would not drink but, moved by the occasion or by princess Martha, he had a glass of light Norwegian wine. The princess herself had cooked an omelette as part of the dinner, which King pronounced delicious. Afterward, Hopkins told King that it was important to decide on the European military campaign for 1943 to get supplies to the right place. He thought the focus would be an attack from Britain but King knew that Roosevelt had decided on the Mediterranean. Hopkins agreed with King that it was possible that there would be terrible anarchy once the Germans were driven back.[11]

Next day King and Roosevelt had lunch in the president's study, which lasted about two hours, the president expressing his appreciation of being able to talk in this quiet way. Once more he revealed his racist contempt for the Japanese, saying that they were descended from a beautiful Chinese princess who had drifted in a boat to the islands and mated with apes. He declared that a sudden, unannounced strike such as Pearl Harbor was as natural to them as first declaring war would be to a western country. Turning to self-government for Asian colonies after the war, he thought they might best begin, like the Americans, with municipal government, then move up to the national level and complete independence. He reiterated that an "articles of confederation" transition would work well for the large and complex India. He disagreed with Churchill's proclamation,

11 Diary, December 4, 1942.

a month earlier, about not liquidating the British Empire, but in a good-natured way, saying that Churchill was "a sort of puck." Even after he had been up late at night in the White House, he was "a sort of cherub in appearance." Roosevelt did not know how he could stay up to 3 a.m. and next day be "looking as fresh as could be." As for British islands with lend-lease bases passing to the Americans, a subject that worried Churchill, Roosevelt said "there were some things that he would like to acquire, and the one thing that he did not wish to acquire was a headache." The West Indian colonies would simply increase the US black problem. Newfoundland was a bankrupt concern and he had "no desire to acquire any bankruptcy estates." King reminded the president that he had said that Canada should have the island and he repeated that that was his view: "You might be able to make something of Newfoundland." Roosevelt thought it seemed well suited for raising sheep.

They expected to continue their discussion at tea but the president was prevented by a meeting. Dinner was again in Roosevelt's Oval Office, with Harry and Louise Hopkins, at a small round table which, as King said, was best for intimate conversation. The president thought that colonies in the far east should be administered in the transition to sovereignty by trustees of the allied countries. He claimed the Philippines, until the Japanese conquest, were being prepared for independence (which would be granted in 1946). Roosevelt knew that Churchill would not be interested in such a scheme and the president only hoped that he did not want more territory for Britain. When the two had discussed the colonial issue, Churchill had said that "he would not have to do with these matters. That when the war was over, he would be through with public life."

The main topic of conversation was the report on British social services by the Liberal, Sir William Beveridge. It had been published to great anticipation just five days earlier and copies sold wildly. His sweeping proposals to eliminate poverty, provide more equal opportunities and an insurance scheme to provide a minimum of medical care and social security "from cradle to grave" stirred great enthusiasm in Britain and in the United States and Canada. "You and I should take that up strongly," Roosevelt told King. The president considered insurance not only good politics but the right kind of reform for the United States, which would never stand for socialism. King inferred that Roosevelt was already thinking about a fourth term in 1944 on a platform of having won the war and now proposing social reconstruction. Canada, he complacently informed the president, between the federal and provincial governments already had most of the Beveridge programme. When King pointed out that his infinitely interpretable

Industry and Humanity went well beyond Beveridge, Roosevelt tactfully promised to look it up.

Whatever King had written in his book, and whatever welfare system existed, the expectations of Canada's population were raised further by Beveridge. The research director of the Canadian government committee on post-war reconstruction, Leonard Marsh, a socialist academic from Britain and student of Beveridge's at the London School of Economics, quickly devised a social security proposal in time for the opening of parliament at the end of January 1943. Implementation, apart from an immediate increase in old age pensions, was deferred until after the war, as it was in Britain (apart from education in 1944 and family allowances in 1945).[12] In May, Beveridge testified to the Canadian committee and King thoughtfully gave him a copy of *Industry and Humanity*.[13]

After dinner at the White House, there were documentary films in the hall. One was on Roosevelt's career and King marvelled at all that he had done and the way he had stood up for ordinary people in his speeches. King thought this ended the evening, but the president had an important matter he wanted to discuss. The two returned to his study, where they were briefly joined by Hopkins. Roosevelt ordered "horse's necks" (ginger ale with lemon rind), asking King to join him on the couch on the side of his good, right ear. The subject was the president's vision for the post-war world, which he thought might be far closer than it would be. King considered it significant that the discussion began with the hands of the clock together at 10 to 10 and ended at 5 to 11.

Roosevelt's started by saying that his aim for the world was the four freedoms he had announced to Congress in January 1941 and which had been elaborated in the Atlantic Charter. Nothing much he said could be done about two of them. People had to work out freedom of religion for themselves. The state, he thought, could not impose anything, ignoring that it could at least legislate against intolerance. Freedom of speech would also take care of itself, although at lunch he had said that something should be done to restrict untrue and exaggerated press reports. Freedom from want the president saw as dependent on freedom from fear, which could only be guaranteed by preventing countries from arming against each other.

---

12 Dennis Guest, *The Emergence of Social Security in Canada.* Second edition. (Vancouver: UBC Press, 1985 [1980], 105–11; Granatstein, *Canada's War,* 254–62.
13 Diary, May 24–5, 1943.

Roosevelt insisted, like General Ulysses Grant in the American Civil War, that the Allies must demand unconditional surrender, not negotiate peace with Germany and Japan. Germany should not be deprived of territory or development but become again a federation of states in order to divide power. It would also be denied the right to produce arms. This would be enforced by the great powers, the United States, Britain, the Soviet Union, and China –"four policemen" who would command an international air force paid for by all countries, at a great savings in national armaments. To monitor Germany, there would be a commission of inspectors: one from Canada, one from South America and one from China. If it discovered war production, "the Germans were to be told that unless that stopped within a week's time, certain of their cities would be bombed." If they persisted, the country's borders would be sealed, with no trains, goods, or people allowed in or out. (Recording this later, King thought the president might have put sealing the borders before bombing.) King interjected that a peace settlement should require elected institutions: "if the people's representatives had had a vote on war, war would never have taken place." But Roosevelt considered plebiscites, with a two-thirds majority, a better means of taking public opinion on important issues. For King, this proved the wisdom of Canada's conscription referendum.

The crucial element in any such arrangement was the agreement of Stalin. Churchill would certainly concur in Britain and the United States controlling the world, and China, the US client, could be taken for granted. In response to a question from King, Roosevelt professed confidence in Stalin: foreign minister Molotov he thought "an Imperialist but he believed that Stalin was less and less on those lines." But the president revealed his hesitation about the Soviet Union by adding that "it was clear that the U.S., Britain, China could not defeat Russia . . . The thing to do was to get them all working on the same lines."

Very confidentially – "for God's sake, don't give me away" – Roosevelt then revealed that he wanted to arrange a meeting for this purpose with Stalin and Churchill. He doubted that the other two would see eye to eye on some post-war issues but he was sure he could resolve their differences. The matter was urgent since Germany might "crumple up at any moment." There were many reports of food shortages and discontent over lives lost on the Soviet front. To avoid the problems of the victors at the end of the First World War, it was imperative to have plans ready in advance. The place that the three leaders would meet had to be secret but Roosevelt judged that Alaska would be best. Apart from the latter issue, what King was listening to was a rehearsal of elements of Roosevelt's

State of the Union address upcoming on January 7, as well as what he intended to propose to Churchill and Stalin. At the end of the conversation, King inquired about the next military target after north Africa. The president evasively said that at least ten places were being considered in detail. There might be some combination. It was very difficult to get the military chiefs to agree but something had to be decided soon, if only to get the material organized.

There was much for Mackenzie King to think about as he made notes on the conversation in his room while Roosevelt, in his, went through a basket of papers before sleeping. One thing stood out clearly in King's mind: he had anticipated everything about the post–war world and the Beveridge report a quarter of a century earlier in *Industry and Humanity*. "I believe the book could, at this moment, be made the basis of the whole social programme. Also matters of arbitration and the like. How I wish I had more of youth and less of the fatigue of years on my side. I must try to get in shape for this post-war work. That has been my real purpose in life."[14]

Next day, King had Sunday lunch with Roosevelt and Eleanor, who had just returned from New York, the Hopkins, and about ten others, including Lord and Lady Halifax. The talk was entirely social. Eleanor Roosevelt, sitting next to King, told him about her recent flight to Britain, where she spent three weeks on behalf of the president inspecting American bases and observing conditions. It had been practically a state visit – her train was met by the king and queen – and she had stayed at Buckingham Palace, at Chequers with the Churchills, and in Ambassador Winant's suite in the Dorchester Hotel. Having been a student in London, the city and country were familiar places. She was immensely popular, clearly sympathetic to the plight of the poor and the grievances of the servicemen. Privately she clashed with Churchill, about whom she had mixed feelings, over Franco and the Spanish Civil War.[15] Her experiences, she said, would keep her busy writing and speaking for some time. She had many invitations from Canada for the Aid to Russia fund and hoped to come to Ottawa, where her niece had recently had a baby. She did not get to the capital but a month later King was at her side as she spoke at a Russian relief rally at the Montreal Forum hockey arena.[16] As the other guests left, King said that he must also say goodbye. Both the president and his wife were disappointed, having thought that he was

14 Diary, December 5, 1942; Hamilton, *Commander in Chief*, 23–32.
15 Cook, *Eleanor Roosevelt*, III, 439–50; Goodwin, *No Ordinary Time*, 379–84.
16 Diary, January 19, 1943.

staying until the following night. Eleanor said that the president enjoyed talking with King and that she had invited the Morgenthaus to dinner. But despite the temptation, King insisted that he had taken up enough of her husband's time and had work to do in Ottawa.

Before King left, Harry Hopkins came to his room to say that Roosevelt would be sure to keep in close touch and that King could be a great help with post-war problems. The president really needed someone to talk to, by telephone if necessary: "That he and I understood each other so well, that I could not fail to see him frequently." As King and Roosevelt parted, the president expressed his own appreciation of their conversations. Elaborating on King's earlier question about the Mediterranean, he said that he had asked the military chiefs in Washington and London that afternoon what they were considering next. His own inclination, matching Churchill's desire, was to "let the fighting continue in Africa indefinitely. We can wear down the Germans there by a process of attrition." This was reinforced by Dieppe which, he said, demonstrated how difficult an invasion of the continent would be. It was wise, he added, to keep the strong Canadian force in Britain to ensure that the Germans maintained a heavy concentration in western Europe.

At the train station, Cordell Hull came to see Mackenzie King off and Leighton McCarthy travelled with him as far as New York, complaining that the Canadian military representatives in Washington were spending a lot of money without doing much good. Nor did he think the British diplomatic mission in Washington very good. Halifax "clicked" neither with the president nor Hull. For this reason, McCarthy urged King to keep in touch with the president: "It prevented him getting off the track at times, in pressing some things too far and in helping to avoid others working in an antagonistic way."[17]

Despite King's excellent relationship with Roosevelt, and his preference for the president's style over the self-conscious superiority of the British, he did not relent in his conviction that the best defence of Canada's identity and independence was its association with Britain and the Commonwealth. During a war cabinet discussion of the Alaska highway a few weeks later, he was much concerned that the United States would try to control Canada and draw it out of the orbit of the British world into its own:" I am strongly opposed to anything of the kind. I want to see Canada develop as a nation to be, in time, as our

---

17 Diary, December 6, 1942.

country certainly will, the greatest of nations of the British Commonwealth.[18] As he heard Big Ben on the BBC's New Year's Eve broadcast, he was confident in Britain as "the citadel of freedom." He also hoped, on the basis of what Roosevelt had told him, that the war in Europe would end in 1943.[19]

* * *

Listening to the president's State of the Union address a week later, there were no surprises for King. Roosevelt expressed his optimism about the war in 1943, pointed to the enormous increase in American war production and the armed services in the past year, and promised "cradle to grave" security against economic hazards. King thought the speech "A model in itself" and could only complain: "What I would give to have just a few men around me who would be continuously devoting their time to preparation of State papers of the kind. However I have one or two good men and we shall probably get through in our lesser way, I pray satisfactorily."[20]

He was also not surprised, ten days later, by a confidential message from Malcolm MacDonald saying that Churchill and Roosevelt were meeting in a secret location. He doubted that in winter it was Alaska or any similar place and wondered if Stalin was also there.[21] Stalin, in fact, had told the other two that he could not leave his country. The Soviets were launching great military offensives at Stalingrad, to which they had been clinging, street by street, house by house, since August. In his paranoid way, Stalin had no intention of providing an opportunity for his deposition. The place that the western leaders met was Casablanca, on the coast of French Morocco recently liberated by the Torch operation, though as usual, nothing was revealed until after the event. Eleanor Roosevelt told King in Montreal the day after MacDonald's communication that she had seen her husband off by train at Washington but had no idea where the conference was being held.[22] A couple of days later, King was told the location and received a summary of the decisions but it was another month before he had a detailed and informed account. The initial news that the meeting had

---

18 Diary, December 30, 1942.
19 Diary, December 31, 1942.
20 Diary, January 7, 1943; Daniels, *Franklin D. Roosevelt*, 305–7.
21 Diary, January 18, 1943.
22 Diary, January 19, 1943.

occurred at all struck him as sufficiently impressive: "Churchill and Roosevelt flying continents and oceans to meet on territory won back from the enemy was as dramatic as anything that has taken place in history."[23] Both arrived by air, Roosevelt flying, for the first time as president, from Miami via Trinidad, Brazil and the British colony of Gambia (a "pestiferous hole" that confirmed his opinion of colonialism).

The main business of the ten-day session was the next stage of the war against Germany and Italy. But even without Stalin's attendance, Roosevelt wanted to get Churchill's agreement to his plans for the post-war world well before the fighting ended.[24] The mood was more relaxed than it would have been if Stalin had been there pressing for a second front in the north. Tension was much higher among the military professionals: the US army chief arguing for an early invasion of France; the head of the American navy demanding priority for the war against Japan; and the British pressing for Sicily as a base to invade mainland Italy or the Balkans. Since Roosevelt, as he had said to King, favoured the Mediterranean, he and Churchill easily made the decision on Sicily, with a well-hedged commitment to invade France in 1943 if resources permitted. There was also a firm pledge to the Pacific as a secondary consideration to Europe. Churchill made a commitment to recapture Burma to demonstrate that Britain was not leaving the colonies to be liberated by the Americans. At the press conference closing the conference (the reporting of which was delayed), Roosevelt announced that the enemies must surrender unconditionally, citing the example of Ulysses Grant, as he had told King. This came as a surprise to Churchill but he accepted the principle, which helped to reassure Stalin that his allies were not intending a separate peace.

That the French were finally united in a fight for liberation seemed to be demonstrated at Casablanca. The awkwardness of democracies supporting the French fascist Darlan had disappeared with his assassination on December 24 and Mackenzie King was far from alone in thinking this best for the Allied cause.[25] General Henri Giraud, captured by the Germans in May 1940, had escaped from a German prisoner of war camp and returned to Vichy France, which refused to surrender him to the Nazis. He was rescued by Americans before the Torch operation and, although he made no great impression on Roosevelt, was recognized by

---

23 Diary, January 26, 1943.
24 Hamilton, *Commander in Chief*, 3–15; 63–129; Daniels, *Franklin D. Roosevelt*, 308–13; Hastings, *Finest Hour*, 352–62; Roberts, *Masters and Commanders*, 244–63; Roll, *The Hopkins Touch*, 244–63.
25 Diary, December 24, 1942.

the president and Churchill as Darlan's successor. De Gaulle saw this as another American insult. At Roosevelt's insistence, de Gaulle was practically compelled by Churchill to meet with Giraud at Casablanca, where the president met him for the first time. De Gaulle and Giraud were photographed stiffly shaking hands as co-presidents of the French Committee of National Liberation with Roosevelt and Churchill in the background, but there was no love lost between them and no acceptance of the committee as the government of France.[26]

A few days earlier, at a dinner in honour of Sultan Ben Jussuf (later Mohamed V) of Morocco, Roosevelt had added to Churchill's distress about the lack of alcohol (he left briefly, ostensibly to take a message, and returned in a better mood) by expatiating on the dream of a world without empires. He also spoke of the greater prosperity and improved social conditions he had expressed to Mackenzie King and to Congress. The sultan was inspired to agitate for Moroccan independence, although this was not achieved until 1956. Churchill was appalled at this dangerous rhapsody on the end of empire, particularly in such susceptible company. Nor was he any happier that the president had embraced the spirit of the Beveridge report. Two months later, however, Churchill had to bow to domestic pressure and deliver a broadcast looking forward to a world of full employment, enhanced social services, and peace preserved by the United Nations. The declaration, he hoped, was sufficient until the post-war world arrived. King, who was in no greater hurry on social reform, was impressed by the address.[27]

* * *

King was no more aware of the military decisions of the Casablanca conference than anyone else. At the beginning of March, General Kenneth Stuart returned from Britain with news about the European war plans that King considered so confidential that he recorded them in a separate memorandum for insertion in his diary. Stuart said that there would be a pincer movement, with one attack launched from north Africa in August, the other from Britain against Cherbourg on the Atlantic coast of France in September, for which the Canadian army in Britain was training in Scotland. King was glad that only 5,000 more Canadian troops were needed, which would not require conscription, but knowing what he

26 Berthon, *Allies at War*, 233–50; Boyd, *De Gaulle*, 124–31.
27 Diary, March 21, 1943.

did, he was more sceptical than Stuart and also his minister of defence that there would, in fact, be a risky invasion from the north in 1943.[28]

A couple of weeks later, Sir Percy Noble, the Royal Navy's representative on the combined chiefs of staff committee in Washington, told the Canadian war cabinet that plans had changed since Casablanca. Great shipping losses on the Atlantic, owing to the lack of long-range air protection against submarines, was slowing the assembly of troops in Britain. Supplies were short in the Mediterranean and the Allies were not making much headway in Tunisia. (In February, raw American troops had been badly mauled by German reinforcements at the Battle of the Kasserine Pass). Noble pointed to Germany's strength – the ease with which it could move forces from east to west in Europe – and guessed that there would be no invasion until 1944.[29] Two weeks later, Anthony Eden stated the same, more authoritatively, on a stop in Ottawa on his way home from a mission to Roosevelt conveying Churchill's offer to go to Moscow to soothe Stalin. The Soviet leader was incensed at the lack of a second front and insufficient lend-lease material owing to shipping losses, the needs of the north African campaign, and the level of US production. The fear was that Stalin would use the Soviet triumphs in ending the terrible seventeen-month siege of Leningrad and the German capitulation after six months' hand-to-hand fighting in Stalingrad to negotiate favourable peace terms with Hitler. The president did not reveal to Eden that he was trying to arrange his own direct, bilateral meeting with Stalin.

Eden told King that Roosevelt was well despite an infection picked up in Casablanca. Churchill, however, had been seriously ill with pneumonia after the conference. King was reassured by Eden's report there would be no invasion of northern Europe in 1943, and his agreement that a premature attempt would be suicidal. Eden's reasons were essentially the same as Noble's, although there was always the possibility that Germany would collapse. The next military move would be through Italy, Eden expected, which he said Roosevelt supported. When Ralston raised the familiar point about Canadian troops needing fighting experience, Eden repeated that it was best for them to remain together for the final blow in Europe.[30] He must have been pleased that King gave him the same treatment as Churchill: dinner at Laurier House, an address to a joint meeting of parliament,

28 Diary, March 4 and "Most Secret & Confidential: Private Memo. Re. 1943 Plans," begun March 17, 1943.
29 Diary, March 17, 1943.
30 Diary, March 30 and 31, 1943.

and photographs by Yousuf Karsh. Churchill cabled his appreciation, saying of Eden: "He is a great help and standby to me, and so are you my old friend." Soon the prime ministers themselves would meet again in Washington.

* * *

King learned of Churchill's arrival on the day itself, May 11. He immediately sent a cable of welcome and another invitation to Ottawa.[31] The next day Churchill replied, saying that he had suggested to Roosevelt a meeting of the Pacific Council for King to attend and that he was anxious to discuss other topics with him.[32] Roosevelt followed with the information that the council would meet on May 20, asking King to come to the White House for a talk the afternoon before.[33]

The purpose of this trip by Churchill was to discuss war plans for the rest of the year, particularly since progress in north Africa, as Noble and Eden had told King, had been slower than expected at Casablanca. With victory now clearly in sight, Churchill was anxious to meet with Roosevelt to settle the next step.[34] He and a large staff crossed on the *Queen Mary*, prepared to make a strong case for the Mediterranean. Below decks were 5,000 German and Italian prisoners of war from north Africa on their way to camps in Canada. Among those the prime minister brought was Lord Beaverbrook, now out of office but whose company he could never resist. He may also have hoped to end Beaverbrook's public campaign for a second front by demonstrating that the Americans supported a Mediterranean strategy. If so, he failed.

By the time King arrived in Washington at midday, May 18, Churchill and his party had been there a week. The day after they had landed, the enemy in north Africa surrendered, with 230,000 troops falling to the Allies. The way was open to Sicily but there was great division between the British and the Americans over what to do next. The Americans insisted that forces be transferred to Britain as soon as possible to prepare for a cross-channel invasion. Churchill and the British wanted to preserve the Mediterranean front, defeating Italy and taking

31 Diary, May 11, 1943.
32 Diary, May 12, 1943.
33 Diary, May 14, 1943.
34 Daniels, *Franklin D. Roosevelt*, 328–30; Roberts, *Masters and Commanders*, 356–75; Hamilton, *Commander in Chief*, 201–58; Roll, *The Hopkins Touch*, 265–78.

the pressure off the Soviet Union (and perhaps pre-empting its westward expansion) by attacking the Germans from the south. They also hoped that Turkey could be attracted from neutrality (which Churchill had already tried unsuccessfully). Above all, they continued to fear that the United States would direct its main effort to Japan.

On the first weekend, while the British and American officials had a social, cooling-off interlude at colonial Williamsburg, Roosevelt took Churchill, Hopkins, Beaverbrook and a few others to Shangri-La. Churchill stuck to his Mediterranean argument and became so angry at Beaverbrook's insistence on a cross-channel invasion that he accused him of disloyalty. Beaverbrook stormed off but remained in America for two months agitating for his cause.[35] It was into this smouldering atmosphere, although never being entirely aware of it, that Mackenzie King joined the other leaders.

At 6 p.m. on May 19, King went to the White House to see Churchill, who was in bed wearing a black and white silk nightgown (he always wore silk next to his skin), with a glass of scotch to hand. Showing the strain of the negotiations, the weekend, and the preparation of an address to Congress the next day, he seemed "very frail. He has lost the florid colouring and his face was quite white. Looked soft and flabby." Obviously having forgotten King's abstemiousness, Churchill asked if he would like something to drink or smoke. He said that he had not finished his speech and would be having a sleep before dinner, which King took as a hint not to stay more than an hour. To enlist King on his side against the Americans, Churchill outlined his plan for the next stage of the European war, which he insisted simply followed from what had been decided at Casablanca. He disingenuously claimed that he and Roosevelt were "very much of the same view though he admitted that there were differences of emphasis on the parts of the chiefs of staff of Britain and the United States."

Churchill thought that the first thing to do was to get Italy out of the war, which he expected would be fairly easy. He told King that "he would not treat them too badly if they gave up, particularly if they were to yield up their fleet," which could be used against Japan. Europe could then be invaded from Sicily and Sardinia, "either on through the Balkans or possibly through France depending on how matters developed," gaining "footholds all along the way." If the Soviets simultaneously mounted a strong offensive, the western powers would work

---

35 Roll, *The Hopkins Touch*, 274.

towards joining up with them. He told King that he still had hopes for Turkey but was not putting pressure on it. He said that one of the Canadian divisions in Britain would take part in the southern attack.

Rehearsing his case against an early cross-channel landing, Churchill said that "he did not want to see the beaches of Europe covered with slain bodies of Canadians and Americans. There might be many Dieppes in one day." There were only eighteen army divisions in Britain of which only one was American. If the United States did not provide many more (as it intended to do from the Mediterranean), he did not see how an offensive could be mounted. Unless Germany showed signs of crumbling before the end of summer, it was safer to wait until winter for a better chance of success. In the meantime, he was confident of the effect of bombing Germany, and Stalin recognized that north Africa had drawn Germans from the eastern front. King was relieved that there would be no ill-prepared assault from Britain but asked if the Americans were likely to make much difficulty. Churchill indicated that it was only the US service chiefs who were pressing for northern Europe. But however close he and Roosevelt were, they "could not settle all these things at once. They had to run along for a time." In the end, the American military leaders would accept the decision of their commander in chief.

Churchill then asked King if he knew about "a certain something which was very far reaching." This was King's guarded way of referring in his diary to nuclear research and the race for atomic weapons, which Germany had by now abandoned in favour of developing high-powered rockets. When King, who had forgotten, said he knew nothing about the matter, Churchill said he should be told but to keep the information entirely to himself. He proposed that King be briefed the next morning by Lord Cherwell (the recently ennobled Frederick Lindemann), professor of physics at the University of Oxford, Churchill's long-standing adviser on statistical and scientific matters and a cabinet member holding the nominal office of paymaster general. Churchill's grievance was that British scientists had done most of the basic research and shared it with the United States but, despite his oral agreement with Roosevelt at Hyde Park about an equal partnership a year earlier, the Americans with their huge resources "had it in mind themselves [alone]. It was something that ought to be agreed upon together." His concern was not just a possible atomic bomb but also peacetime commercial uses. Canada was important in this, not only for its own significant research but as a source of scarce uranium and heavy water.

King left with a draft of what Churchill had so far prepared of his speech to Congress. Reading it in an adjoining room, his major objection was, as in other addresses, that "we" referred only to British and American forces. He told Churchill's secretary that Canada and the other dominions and India would be hurt. Churchill should remember that he was speaking very near Canada (where the broadcast would be heard) and that "our people would be sensitive to having no reference made to that part. After all the air force had been doing a good deal of bombing over Germany and had helped materially in the African campaign."[36]

* * *

Mackenzie King moved into the White House the next morning for an overnight stay. At eleven, he went to see "the prof." A rich, teetotal vegetarian, Lord Cherwell made King's lifestyle seem positively sybaritic. He was also notoriously frugal with praise but spoke highly of Canada's physics research as well its military production and supply to Britain. With statistical authority he said it was still far higher than that of the United States. Despite his professional opinion that working on a nuclear bomb was an expensive dead end, he loyally explained the need to speed up the effort by pooling British and American knowledge. At this point, King recalled having been told about the research almost a year earlier by Malcolm MacDonald and a couple of British scientists. Cherwell repeated Churchill's complaint about American unwillingness to share their knowledge and added that they had made exclusive contracts for all of Canada's uranium and heavy water. (When Churchill himself had protested this, Howe responded that there was no better alternative but by the end of 1942, the practical problem had been solved by moving Cambridge University's atomic team to Montreal to work with Canadian scientists.[37]) Cherwell said that the lack of cooperation was the result of the US army taking over the programme: "They are as difficult about it in their relation with Britain as Stalin had been in telling of what was being done in Russia." Cherwell did not perhaps know that the Americans were suspicious that secrets were not safe with the British. Over the next couple of days, Churchill assured King that matters were becoming more satisfactory, but

---

36 Diary, May 18, 1943.
37 Bothwell and Kilbourn, *C. D. Howe*, 168–9; (Diary entry, June 15, 1942).

they did not markedly improve for another three months when another nuclear agreement was reached at Hyde Park.

King left Cherwell at noon to join those who were leaving the White House for the Capitol. Among them were the Duke and Duchess of Windsor on their latest escape from the boredom of the Bahamas. They were staying at the embassy, to the displeasure of the Anglo-Catholic Lord Halifax, who had strongly disapproved of divorce and the abdication. The duke importuned Churchill, to no effect, for a better post. He immediately greeted King, who noted that the former monarch had lost none of his old charm. Then entered Churchill theatrically announcing that he felt a bit like Sydney Carlton (the hero of Charles Dickens' *A Tale of Two Cities*) just before his execution. King, however, thought him "more refreshed. Like his old self." He was impatient to leave and invited King to drive with him. On the way, he flashed his V-for-Victory sign to the bystanders. He told King it was a good thing that he had come to Washington since the military chiefs could never have worked out things themselves, meaning getting the Americans to agree to the Mediterranean strategy. He also said that it was "quite a venture" to give a second address to Congress. His first welcome, a year and a half earlier, had been good but he was not sure that it could be repeated. King did his best to allay Churchill's tension by praising the text that he had read.

This time, Churchill spoke not in the Senate but in the far larger House of Representatives to a much bigger audience. He also gave a far longer address on the joint war that had had now been going on for almost a year and a half. On his arrival, he was greeted by Sol Bloom, the long-serving New York congressman, Roosevelt loyalist and chairman of the house foreign relations committee, who invited King to the luncheon for Churchill that he was holding along with Tom Connally, the chairman of the senate committee. From the executive box in the gallery, King had a fine view of Churchill at the rostrum. Among the others seated with him were the Windsors, Princess Martha, and the financier Bernard Baruch. King was pleased by Churchill's acknowledgement of him and the reference he had prompted to Canada's war contribution, "so massive and so invaluable," which was greeted with thunderous applause. Carefully addressing American concerns about Japan, considered by many the primary enemy, Churchill said that after victory in Europe, Britain would also direct its efforts to Japan until its cities were reduced to ash heaps. But the war against Germany must take precedence since its defeat would ensure Japan's, while the reverse was not the case. The western Allies must take the pressure off the Soviet Union. By comparing the victory in north Africa to Stalingrad, he implied that the Mediterranean was the place to do it. He even held out the hope that bombing alone might destroy Germany and Italy, albeit warning against over-confidence.[38] He left to huge cheers and must have been certain that he had convinced Congress that he was the man who knew how to win the war.

The luncheon was for about two dozen, King sitting between Lord Halifax and Lord Cherwell. He heard Churchill, playing to American sensibilities, censure de Gaulle's ingratitude and extreme vanity, saying that he had "raised him as a pup and now de Gaulle was prepared to bite the hand that fed him." He praised the choice of general Dwight Eisenhower as supreme commander in north Africa and helped push the opinion of congressional leaders in his own direction by saying that "the plan" was to invade Europe from the Mediterranean.

After the meal, the group was joined by the members of the foreign relations committees of both houses. Churchill confidently invited them to "try to knock him off his perch" with questions. But first he elaborated what he had said in his speech and at lunch. He emphasized the importance of taking Italy out the of the war and not dealing too harshly with it so long as it surrendered the fleet. Clearing the Mediterranean, he argued, would provide a foothold onto the continent and make contact with the far east (through the Suez Canal) much easier. Allied forces pressing up through the Balkans would provide great relief to the Soviet Union and might induce some Germans satellites to change sides. He did not disguise his opposition to a premature attack from the north where he asserted heavy bombing of Germany would continue. When the question of poison gas was raised, he said that Britain could do more damage to Germany than Germany could to Britain and that he would not hesitate to use it if the Germans did anything of the kind. Reaffirming his commitment to defeating Japan, he pointed out that there were already more American forces in the Pacific than in the Atlantic and European area.

Mackenzie King thought it indiscreet of Churchill to express the hope that the United States would send representatives of both parties and Houses of Congress to a peace conference, implying that Woodrow Wilson had made a great mistake in keeping matters in his and his party's hands. King also regarded it as tactless to hint that the conference would be in Europe. When this was recounted to Roosevelt that evening, the president "put his hands to his face and shook his head a bit as much as to say he wished that part had been left alone."

---

38 James, *Churchill: Complete Speeches*, 6775–84.

As he told King, "he did not know that there would be any peace conference. As far as he was concerned, there would be total surrender." What he had in mind were small conferences for particular issues, but no overall one like 1919. For King, this was a "division of view which is certain to come as the war approaches its termination. However, these are the kind of difficulties that work out through events determining results."

One congressman asked Churchill if it would be a help or harm to have a Senate resolution on keeping the boundaries of the USSR as they were (probably meaning before the Nazi-Soviet pact). Churchill hoped that there would be no such declaration. Keeping his options open on an issue that was already contentious, and would become far more so, he cautiously said, "we must realize Stalin's difficulties for the present." After the war the states of central Europe should form "something in the nature of a Danubian confederation," a kind of more federal Austro-Hungarian Empire. Germany, itself, he thought should be divided, with Prussia becoming a separate state forbidden to arm, a modification of Roosevelt's musing to Mackenzie King. The legislators must, like King, have considered this flow of ideas "as interesting an hour as I have had at any time." Churchill must also have been confident of making a strong effect, although the person he really had to convince was the president. Roosevelt had listened to the congressional speech on the radio and when his visitors returned to the White House, the first time King had seen the president on this occasion, congratulated both on the good hand that they had from the audience.

Before the pre-dinner cocktails, King had a short conversation alone with Roosevelt who said that an agreement with Churchill was practically in final shape. This obviously meant something different from what Churchill had been saying since the president wanted to emphasize "the building up of the forces in Britain so as to be certain of an attack from the North in the spring of 1944." There was not much discussion of business at dinner and if there was tension between the two leaders, it was not obvious to King. When Roosevelt said that the Canadian troops in Britain were anxious for action, Churchill responded in Miltonic terms that they also serve who only stand and wait and insisted that a division would soon be fighting in the Mediterranean.

After dinner, a Sherlock Holmes spy movie set in the present war was screened. Churchill then went to his room but Roosevelt called him back for further talk. In the meantime, he confided to King that he was still trying to arrange a meeting alone with Stalin and thought Alaska the best place. At that moment in Moscow, Joseph Davies, the former ambassador who stood high in Stalin's esteem, was delivering the president's invitation. Roosevelt confessed his trepidation about telling Churchill he was not included but King assured him that it was natural for the two to meet separately, as Churchill and Stalin had in Moscow, and that it would be a good preparation for a conference of the three.

When Churchill returned, the president talked mainly about the fear of a general strike (there had already been sporadic local ones) by the badly paid and worse treated coal miners, which would have a serious effect on war production. He brightened at one point and exclaimed that the solution was before his eyes: "Here is Mackenzie King. He has settled a large number of strikes. I am prepared to leave the whole matter to his arbitration." When King said that he could not consider it, the president said he was only joking but King thought "he had put this forward to see whether I would be prepared to consider the matter." Earlier in the evening, King had advised the president to side with the workers and emphasize the need to win the war. Eleanor Roosevelt was urging the same. The president managed to keep the mines operating by the government temporarily taking them over as an emergency matter. He also succeeded in raising the wages, but at a bitter social and political cost.[39]

Vital as American industrial relations were, this was not a topic close to Churchill's heart. He left again at midnight while Roosevelt and King talked on for another hour. The president once more raised the issue of an authority to keep world peace. In addition to a supreme council of the victorious United Nations, he now believed there should be a moderator (rather than a committee as he had thought earlier) to supervise the terms, particularly disarmament, that were imposed on the defeated countries. The moderator would alert the council to any need for action. The problem, said Roosevelt, was to find the right individual. Smuts would be ideal but was too old at seventy-three. The president thought that he himself might do it, but for some reason that King could not remember, doubted it: "It may have had reference to his being required for further services in the office he is now holding [a fourth term in 1944]. It may have been a feeler to see how I would regard it." The post of international arbitrator backed by the peace-loving countries of the world could not fail to appeal to all of King's instincts.

The theme continued next day at lunch. Surveying the problem of governing the world, the only people Roosevelt and Churchill could see as an international

---

39 Goodwin, *No Ordinary Time*, 440–4; Daniels, *Franklin D. Roosevelt*, 325–7.

moderator other than themselves, who had more important jobs, were Smuts, Harry Hopkins (also at the luncheon), and Mackenzie King. This was early thinking about what became the far more active secretary-general of the United Nations Organization than the merely administrative secretary of the League of Nations. Roosevelt simply assumed that the American president would in effect appoint the official, and that the whole institution, like the wartime coalition, would be led the United States.[40]

When Roosevelt raised his proposal of King as the global mediator – "Mackenzie would be accepted by the entire world" – Churchill immediately agreed. The three claimed that they had more experience in government than anyone in the whole world (forgetting, at least, Stalin), and King had been in office the longest of all. In a spirit of helpfulness, he refreshed the others' memory of the details. Roosevelt pointed out that he and King had a long connection going back to Harvard, but Churchill outdid him by saying that his association with King had begun in 1900. There could not, he said, be too much friendship between the British Empire and the United States, and Mackenzie King was clearly the person to help it.

King's complaints of exhaustion and the demands of office evaporated as visions of being a world statesman danced in his head. He wrote in his excitement:

> It was obvious from the importance of experience in world government affairs . . . Churchill's emphasis on my having a place of confidence in the minds of the British people equal to what I have in the Americans, and to my standing out as the greatest Imperialist of the day in light of Canada's war effort being what it has been, etc., it is quite plain that there is something there which time will disclose.[41]

Of course, all depended on Stalin falling in with Roosevelt's post-war plans and this, for the president, was a high priority. Churchill was acquiescent and Chiang Kai-shek's participation with China being recognized as a great power could be taken for granted. Nor were Roosevelt and Churchill wrong to think that King would have worked to ensure that the United Nations Organization reflected the values and interests of their countries.

40 Mark Mazower, *Governing the World: The History of an Idea* (New York: Penguin, 2012), 191–213.
41 Diary, May 19, 1943.

In addition to the heady discussion of Mackenzie King being the front line enforcer of world peace, the luncheon marked a turning point in Canada's international diplomatic status. Roosevelt observed that every Latin American republic had elevated its Washington legation to an embassy and wondered why Canada did not do the same. It is hard to think that he did not have in mind raising the personal standing of his friend Leighton McCarthy. King said that he had not favoured an embassy "out of sense of proportion." (The 1818 congress of Aix-la-Chapelle established the convention that only major powers exchanged ambassadors; representatives of other countries were of lesser rank). When King asked Churchill's opinion and what he thought the view would be in Britain, he promptly said that he was in favour, "that Canada should be as strong in every way as she could be." Churchill did not know the opinion of the foreign office but agreed with King that it was Canada's decision.

Thus prompted and encouraged, King on November 11, raised McCarthy to ambassador, the first Canadian to hold that rank. The United States simultaneously did the same for its minister to Canada. King hoped that on that Remembrance Day, "Canada's fighting men would feel that the government was seeking to identify service and sacrifice of those who fought in the last war with the full recognition of Canada's status as a nation – indeed a world power which they, above all others, had helped to gain." He was proud that Canada was the first dominion to appoint an ambassador and have "equality of status with the U.K. – but not of stature."[42] In another month, the Canadian ministers to Mexico, China and Brazil were likewise promoted. After the war, practically every diplomatic representative of every country became an ambassador, save within the Commonwealth where they continue to be high commissioners.

Roosevelt also wanted reliable Canada to join the Pan-American Union (later the Organization of American States). Just after Pearl Harbor, King had expressed to the Brazilian government his willingness to belong but the United States had vetoed membership.[43] Now he deflected joining the US-dominated organization by saying that it was "a matter of time and season." He observed that the US state department might still regard Canada as representing British influence, while in other countries (mainly Canada) there might be "a false impression . . . as seeming to represent a closer association with North America

42 Diary, November 1, 1943.
43 Stacey, *Canada and Conflict*, II, 393.

than with the British Empire." Churchill might have been expected to agree with the latter but in the White House he was more eager to encourage the former. He urged King to accept, saying that Canada could indeed help represent Britain to the United States by speaking up "quite strongly about Canada and her exceptional position in interpreting the two countries to each other." Churchill went further, propounding a world governed by a regional council each for Europe, Asia and the Americas (Africa presumably being subsumed under the European colonial powers), with an overall world council of final appeal, which would fit Roosevelt's scheme. He thought the US president should be on all three councils, and perhaps Britain, too. In this arrangement, Canada might represent Britain as well as itself on the Americas council. Roosevelt drew back (for good domestic reasons) from the United States being so involved in a European body but Churchill insisted that it was necessary in order to control continental countries and prevent another war. Passionately, he declared: "I am saying this in the presence of Canada's Prime Minister, deliberately to you, Mr. President. I beg of you not to keep aloof from the European situation." When Roosevelt tried to evade the issue by saying that what Europe needed was a mediator like the Presbyterian church, Churchill snapped that far better would be "a very firm hand to prevent them doing anything."

After this elating lunch, King was invited by Churchill to his room to urge the importance of the conference of dominion prime ministers he was trying to organize. As an attraction, he held out the enticement of a luxurious voyage aboard the *Queen Mary*. Accommodating a prime minister in appropriate style only involved displacing four hundred troops or prisoners of war. "What is that compared to the importance of having you in Britain? Of course, there are risks, but there are always risks. Today, they can manage the ships very skilfully." It was not the peril of the Atlantic that concerned King. A far greater danger was all the dominion prime ministers being away from their countries in wartime. He reminded Churchill of the terrible example of Menzies and said that going to Britain would open him to Canadian accusations of becoming an imperial centralist. Churchill said that King was a great imperialist, meaning a mediator between Britain and the other dominions as well as the United States. He added praise of King's unification of his country and mobilized its outstanding war effort: "what Canada has done under your direction has not been surpassed, and you will be identified for all time with that part." King could not help being affected by this flattery, particularly after a lunch of the same, but while assuring Churchill that he only wanted to help, he would not give a firm commitment.

At 6 p.m., Churchill and the British service chiefs met with representatives of the Commonwealth and India in the White House state dining room. J. L. Ralston and the Canadian service chiefs came from Ottawa. Norman Robertson, Lord Halifax and Malcolm MacDonald were also present. Churchill began by observing that it was a "remarkably historical event" to hold such an assembly in "the very centre of the White House really as guests of the President, talking confidentially of the plans of the war; past achievements and future activities; also relations between the Americans and ourselves." The symbolism could just as easily have been presented as evidence of American predominance. There was nothing new for King as Churchill repeated what he had said in the past day and a half but it must have been instructive to the other Canadians to hear his insistence on the Mediterranean, on defeating Italy and using its navy against Japan. Even in attacking Europe from the south he emphasized that there was no great hurry. Each step should be carefully secured. He did not think there was much chance of Germany suddenly collapsing: the populace might become demoralized by bombing but it was the army that had to be defeated. The USSR above all had to be supported. China, he bluntly said, "in a way was a liability at present. We had to carry her in a basket, as it were, while Russia was doing most of the fighting." He closed with an emotional appeal for close relations with the United States and for the empire and Commonwealth to be "united as one in maintaining its position in the world, and the future place it would hold in the world."

King offered thanks on behalf of the group and reiterated that his government was confident in leaving strategy to Churchill and Roosevelt and their military advisers, and willing for its forces to serve wherever "they could be most helpful in winning the war. That we were quite prepared to have them fight as one great army. We were equally prepared to have the forces divided up." Churchill, for his part, repeated the importance of Canadian troops in protecting Britain and gave assurances that Canada would be consulted before there was any deployment.

After all the stimulation at the White House, it was relaxing for Mackenzie King to have a quiet dinner with Cordell Hull and his wife at their hotel. Hull had agreed on the wisdom of concentrating on the Mediterranean. He expected the USSR would be doing the main fighting that year, and would win, but he worried about what it portended for the future. It was thinking only of its own interests and had not "learned how to live in a company of nations." The same was true of Japan. Both, he said, would have to be educated to it. King afterward spent a quiet night in his railway carriage. Next morning, he recorded: "Glad to have the sense of freedom which my own car afforded. Also the rest from being away from other people."[44]

* * *

The following day, Friday, May 20 was King's last in Washington. In the morning, he discussed atomic matters at the Canadian legation with Malcolm MacDonald (and was very discreet in his diary). At 12:30 in the afternoon, he went to see Roosevelt. Despite the pressure of business, the president looked "very fresh and cool." He wanted to discuss his proposed meeting with Stalin. After going over much of what he had said before, including his unease about telling Churchill, he told King in great secrecy that he proposed, as a feint, first going to Ottawa. He and King would then inspect the Alaska highway and Roosevelt would slip away to meet Stalin while King returned to Ottawa by a different route. King was excited at this, particularly the idea of the president giving a speech outside the parliament building that would draw people from all over the country. Roosevelt said that if Stalin could not meet him, he might come to Ottawa anyway. Afterwards they could both go on his revenue cutter through the Great Lakes to Georgian Bay (McCarthy's summer home) for a week's fishing. This was also agreeable to King. When Roosevelt inquired about the fishing, King being no angler, said that he would have to look into it. When King asked about the strategy discussions and the next stage of the war, the president circumspectly replied that he thought everything was in good shape. He would have the draft agreement with the British that afternoon and take it to Shangri-La for the weekend to review it carefully: "It was a matter of emphasis and arrangement."

King then went to Churchill's room to say goodbye. After his bath and shave, still in his underwear and slippers, he called for King: "He really was quite a picture but looked like a boy – cheeks quite pink and very fresh." Churchill went over what he had said before, urged King to attend the meeting in London, and reiterating that he would entrust Canada with Britain's interests in a north American council. King said that this needed careful thought, "my own feeling [being] that it would not do for Canada to assume to act for Britain." Churchill repeated that Canadian troops would soon be in action in the Mediterranean and there would be no invasion from Britain in 1943: "I tell you that." He confided

44 Diary, May 20, 1943.

that he was leaving Washington the following Wednesday and going directly to Africa, which seemed to confirm that it would remain the centre of operations. Then, anointing himself with aftershave lotion, Churchill went to have lunch with Roosevelt.

Before taking the overnight train to New York, King was the guest of honour at dinner at the Canadian legation. Also present was Sumner Welles, the under-secretary of state, who talked to King almost until midnight about the plan he was drawing up for Roosevelt (without Cordell Hull's knowledge) for a council by which the four great victorious powers would run the world. King did not disclose that he had already heard about this from the president. Welles may have gone on at such length because Roosevelt had indicated the role he had in mind for the Canadian prime minister, or at least the importance of his support for the scheme.

Roosevelt did go to Shangri-La alone for the weekend, largely to recuperate from the demands of Churchill's company before their final two days of nego-tiation. When Churchill left, the president went to Hyde Park and slept for four days.[45] Mackenzie King yearned for a week at the seaside. Instead, he settled for a couple of days in New York, enjoying the somnolence of the Harvard Club, shopping for sheets, and going to Noël Coward's popular *Blithe Spirit*, whose spiri-tualism he not surprisingly found full of significance. He also attended Richard Rodgers and Oscar Hammerstein's new musical *Oklahoma!* with Beatrix Robb, his friend of a decade and a half. On the Sunday, he took his secretary, Walter Turnbull, and Edouard Handy by subway to Coney Island where they strolled the boardwalk and lunched at the best hotel. King was entranced by the scene: "the contrast of peoples and garbs . . . Different money making booths, people basking on the beaches, some even in boats."[46]

* * *

During Churchill's last two days in Washington, he and Roosevelt worked out a compromise on the European war for the next twelve months. Sicily would be invaded immediately but once the island was secure, the bulk of the battle-hardened troops would be transferred to Britain for the continental invasion

45 Goodwin, *No Ordinary Time*, 439.
46 Diary May 22 and 23, 1943.

scheduled for May 1, 1944. The forces left in the Mediterranean would try to defeat the forces on mainland Italy and draw German troops away from the Soviet front. Churchill was highly displeased and did not relent in insisting that it was better to attack from the south than the north. He hoped to demonstrate this by what actually happened in Sicily and the Italian peninsula. From Washington, he went straight, as he had told King, to north Africa to confer with Eisenhower who was directing the Sicilian campaign. With him, he took General George Marshall whom he hoped to convert from the conviction that everything should be put into the invasion in the north. Roosevelt, for his part, trusted his army chief to counter any diversion from what had been agreed in Washington.

Once Churchill was back in Britain, Roosevelt felt obliged to tell him that he was trying to arrange a meeting with Stalin, lest he learn this from someone else. The most likely person was Lord Beaverbrook, who could never resist provoking a conflict. Instead of communicating the information directly, the president assigned the thankless task to Averell Harriman, who got to bear the first brunt of anger. When Churchill protested his exclusion to Roosevelt, the president boldly lied that the proposal was Stalin's and that the meeting was designed as a prelude to a conference of all three. But Roosevelt did not want to alienate his most valuable ally in war and shaping the peace. To assuage Churchill, he proposed that they, and perhaps also Stalin, should gather in August in Quebec City.[47]

The president had happy memories of his 1937 summer visit to the city and knew that the walled citadel was perfect for a conference. The weather was also far better at that time of year than steamy Washington or even Hyde Park. (Many wealthy Americans, including Mackenzie King's friends, Julia Grant and Beatrix Robb, summered ninety miles east on the St. Lawrence river at Murray Bay, now La Malbaie.) It was an easy overnight rail journey from Hyde Park. And since Canada was a member of the British Commonwealth and the Citadelle, technically a royal palace, Churchill could be represented as being the senior leader. For that reason, and to further mollify the British prime minister, Roosevelt suggested that Churchill make the overture to King, who Roosevelt was sure would be happy to make the arrangements. Not until the end of the conference did King learn that that the proposal originated with the president and not with Churchill. But for King, no matter whosoever's

47 Roll, *The Hopkins Touch*, 275–8.

suggestion it was, it would be a great event. Bringing both great western leaders to Quebec would demonstrate the importance of the country and himself to the war and make that province, tepid towards the conflict, seem involved in the major decisions.

CHAPTER NINE

On the Rampart of Quebec

W INSTON CHURCHILL'S TELEGRAM Of July 19 to Mackenzie King requesting the meeting at Quebec did not arrive at the highest point in their relationship. Ten days earlier, on the night of July 9, the First Canadian Division was among the 160,000 troops that were landed in Sicily by over 2,000 landing craft guarded by warships. This was the largest amphibious operation in history so far and the Canadian army's first engagement in a major battle.[1] King naturally expected acknowledgement of Canada but the supreme commander, General Dwight Eisenhower, did not mention the Canadians, not wanting the Germans to know how many had been removed from Britain. Two days before the operation, King was furious to learn that the communiqués would refer to the landing only as an Anglo-American one. When the British refused to deviate from the Americans and include Canadians in their announcement, King telephoned Harry Hopkins, who was dining with Roosevelt. The two Americans discussed the matter with Lester Pearson, the acting Canadian minister in the absence of Leighton McCarthy. The president agreed to name Canada in his own message and said that King should as well.

Already tense about the impending event, King fumed that there could be no better example of the difference between the British and Americans, as Canadians were "within a day of risking their lives off the shores of Sicily in an engagement with the enemy in the waters of the Mediterranean." No wonder

---

1 Bercuson, *Our Finest Hour*, 267–90; Cook, *The Necessary War*, 331–75.

Canadians "were antagonized at the English, and were beginning to be more friendly with the Americans?"[2] Of course if Roosevelt had informed Eisenhower of the change and the British had followed suit, the bad feelings would have been avoided entirely. King might also have contacted Churchill, whom he thought might be close to the scene of the attack.

The morning after the landing began, King gave a broadcast saying that Canadian troops were at the centre of the action. Washington also mentioned Canadians but not London or Eisenhower's headquarters. A few days later, when King was goaded in parliament about the lack of information, including the name of the Canadian commander in Sicily (General Guy Simmons), he defended himself by saying that he had been able to reveal as much as he did only as a result of the telephone call to Roosevelt, whom he praised for playing "as fairly and squarely as he did." He knew that the great applause and the newspaper reports would make displeasing reading in Britain but "it was necessary to save worse situations later."[3]

Politicians at Westminster picked up the matter and three days later an embarrassed Malcolm MacDonald arrived at Kingsmere with a telegram from Churchill asking for suggestions to reply to a parliamentary question about the lack of recognition for Canadian troops and adding that King's observations were unacceptable. Churchill often used this peremptory tone with his own ministers but it was not the way to ensure King's cooperation. Angrily, King told MacDonald that if the British prime minister made any difficulty for him and there was an uproar in Canada, he would fight an election on the issue.[4] When they continued the discussion the next day, King's temper was no cooler while MacDonald's face was "the colour of a red Indian." At length, the high commissioner slunk off to compose a draft of what Churchill might say in parliament, Norman Robertson reviewed it and the two took it to King who was eventually persuaded that sending it prime minister to prime minister would carry more authority.[5]

The next day in Parliament, Churchill delivered a convoluted answer about wording and timing of the invasion announcement and claimed that after an agreeable exchange of cables between him and King, "the misunderstanding

2 Diary, July 8, 1943.
3 Diary, July 15, 1943 (includes Hansard record of statement in House of Commons).
4 Diary, July 18, 1943.
5 Diary, July 19, 1943.

for which no one is to blame, can now be regarded as cleared away." When the radical Labour MP Aneurin Bevan asked why the communiqué had not simply said "allied" forces and left it to war correspondents to specify particular units, the prime minister said that it was exactly the word "allied" to which the Canadian government objected.[6] This was not the case and King did not consider Churchill's statement a fair one: "Indeed it makes the issue quite other than the one which in fact it is." But "with war on, it is perhaps better as well to let the matter lie where it is."[7] Of course, King could not leave such a matter alone. As soon as Churchill arrived at Quebec, King tackled him on it. After listening without comment, Churchill said that whenever King was deeply concerned about a matter "not to hesitate to ring him up, if need be; say I was worried over a situation and he would do all he could to that end." Partly to ensure that King was in the right frame of mind before the conference began, Churchill assured him that the Canadians "had done well in Sicily. Remarked upon them being the hinge, with the Americans to one side, and the British on the other."[8]

* * *

It was while he, MacDonald, and Robertson were discussing the telegram to Churchill that King brought up the request for a meeting at Quebec. Robertson thought that the position of the Canadian prime minister would have to be carefully considered. Although it was not necessary for the Canadian chiefs of staff to meet with their British and US counterparts, "the people of Canada" would expect King to be "in full conference with both Churchill and Roosevelt." Eager to overcome the present disharmony, MacDonald went well beyond his function as the British government's representative to agree. King saw their point but even in his present irritation, he was not going to risk missing so great an opportunity. Refusing the Canadian site would "occasion real disappointment on the part of both Churchill and the President, and resentment as well by Churchill." Demanding to be included in the talks was also "more than could be expected of them. They would wish to take the position that jointly they have supreme direction of the war. I have conceded them that position." King would in any event be the host and present throughout, making the conference practically one

6   172 H.C. Deb. 5s, cols. 689-90 (July 20, 1943).
7   Diary, July 20, 1943; Dilks, *The Great Dominion*, 239–43.
8   Diary, August 10, 1943.

of the three, "without having the question raised too acutely or defended too sharply."[9] He did not object to MacDonald pressing the status of the Canadian prime minister on Churchill and did not neglect to have Robertson ensure that such a message was sent. Whatever the circumstance, being with Churchill and Roosevelt at the Citadelle would be "a memorable and marvellous event in Canadian history as well as in the history of the entire war. It would, too, I believe, greatly please French-Canadians."[10]

MacDonald conveyed King's expectation of being the host at Quebec, despite recognizing that there would be talks that were confined to the two and their staff and that he could not be an equal partner without awkwardness about the other dominions. But he emphasized that "it would be extremely embarrassing politically to the Government here if the Canadian Prime Minister seemed to be less than a fairly full partner in a meeting in Canada and would cause undesirable comment from general point of view in Quebec and everywhere in Canada." Once that was clarified, MacDonald assured Churchill that the conference would "of course delight everyone here and do much solid good." After the recent contretemps, Churchill lost no time in confirming the position of King, saw no difficulty in him attending all plenary sessions over which he and Roosevelt presided, and the Canadian military service heads being included in plenary (the word underlined in both cases) meetings of the combined chiefs of staff. This would not preclude private conferences between Churchill and Roosevelt and the combined chiefs, "whenever the nature of the discussion renders this desirable." If King approved, Churchill said he would submit the arrangement to the president. King was delighted by this "buoyant and cheerful response."[11]

It was Roosevelt who put his foot down. He told Churchill that including the Canadian military staff would produce the same demand from China, Brazil, and Mexico (tiny as the war contribution of the last two was) and probably other dominions and allied countries. "We have," he told Churchill, "until now succeeded preventing the deterioration of our Combined Chiefs of Staff in Washington into a debating society by refusing membership to representatives of the other Allied Nations." Rather than admit Canada, he would prefer to hold the meeting somewhere else, perhaps Bermuda. Churchill had little choice but

---

9   Diary, July 19, 1943.
10   Diary, July 20, 1943.
11   Diary, July 23, 1943. MacDonald to Dominions Secretary, 20 July, Churchill to MacDonald, July 23, 1943. DCER, IX, 253–4.

to acquiesce, telling the president that he understood his position. To King he explained that "very little business can be done when large numbers are present," but there was nothing to prevent the British and Canadians conferring together. Roosevelt also sugared the pill by asking Leighton McCarthy to go to Ottawa to explain the situation to "one of my oldest personal friends," as he described King to Churchill.

King expressed no disappointment at Roosevelt's decision, even pointing out that he had never suggested that the Canadian military professionals meet with the combined chiefs of staff. That proposal was entirely Churchill's, "evidently feeling he wished to meet our wishes as far as possible. I said that there would be no difficulty on that score." He assured Churchill that while expecting consultation when Canadian forces were involved, he would not permit at Quebec "any situation to arise which would be a source of embarrassment to other United Nations who will not be represented."[12] He also recognized that use of the Citadelle would require formal permission from the monarch; that Churchill would in a sense be on British soil; and that for Canadians it would effectively be as if they were going to London. This pettifoggery to smooth the path for Churchill and Roosevelt was a contrast to King's usual emphasis on the sovereign as the Canadian head of state, acting on the advice of Canadian ministers. He recognized that it increased his task in maintaining "with care and due deference our own position as a country in no way subordinate to Britain–in any aspect of its domestic or external affairs. A very difficult position for me."[13]

With only a couple of weeks before Churchill arrived and three before the conference began, preparations had to be made in a hurry and in secrecy. The costs were born by the Canadian government and King did not spare himself overseeing the arrangements. The governor general supplied servants, silverware, and even transferred some of his private stock of wine from Government House to the Citadelle (his official summer residence). King himself, wanting some separation from Churchill and Roosevelt, did not stay in the main building but displaced the military commander of the Citadelle.[14] British and American staffs were housed on alternate floors of the nearby Chateau Frontenac. Emptying it,

12 Diary, July 24, 1943; Roosevelt to Churchill, July 24, Churchill to Roosevelt, July 25, 1943. Kimball, *Churchill & Roosevelt*, II, 344–5; Churchill to King and King to Churchill, 25 July, 1943. DCER, IX, 254–5.
13 Diary, August 4, 1943.
14 Diary, August 9, 1943.

save for an old lady and her maid, was impossible to conceal from the public. The press was taken into confidence, and rumours that the hotel was being taken over as a military hospital or accommodation for the recently deposed Mussolini (who should have been so lucky) were to some extent suppressed.[15] Even after Churchill arrived, unheralded, at Halifax aboard the *Queen Mary* on August 9, he asked King to announce only that he was a guest of the Canadian government and would later be meeting President Roosevelt, without mentioning the place.[16] The president himself had only just returned to Washington from a week's fishing in Georgian Bay. The trip had, as usual, been kept secret until after the event. The ruse before meeting Stalin had turned out to be unnecessary since the Soviet leader had still not agreed to a date to meet in Alaska, or anywhere else. Half way through Roosevelt's fishing holiday, Harry Hopkins had joined him in case Stalin did suddenly decide to meet and the president had to fly directly from Canada. As Roosevelt's train steamed back to Washington, Stalin sent word that he could not leave the command of the war in the USSR.[17] There would thus be no previous consultation with Stalin before the discussions with Churchill.

* * *

The first phase of Churchill's visit was entirely Canadian. On the afternoon of August 10, Mackenzie King, the lieutenant general, the premier of the province and various other officials went to meet Churchill's train at the last station before Quebec City. Accompanying Churchill was his wife, who had not visited Canada, or the United States since the early 1930s, when her husband had been struck by a taxi in New York. (Churchill insisted on paying her fare, £76,[18] about £3000 today.) Also with them was their youngest daughter, the twenty-year-old Mary, an officer in the Auxiliary Territorial Service (ATS) who was seconded for the trip as her father's aide-de-camp. Although Churchill's arrival in Canada had not yet been reported, a crowd was attracted by RCMP officers and others in uniform and the civilian notables. As Churchill descended from the train, King thought that he looked well, but heavier than he had been in Washington. Churchill admitted that he had gained three or four pounds, which King judged to be more

---

15 Diary, August 3, 1943; Dilks, *The Great Dominion*, 264.
16 Diary, August 1, 1943.
17 Hamilton, *Commander in Chief*, 289–90.
18 Dilks, *The Great Dominion*, 300.

like six or eight. Scrutinizing him later in the day, he thought Churchill had aged in the three months, though his mind was as active as ever: "Lower part of his face has got to be quite heavy. In fact his whole face is pretty flabby. Eyes seem to be a bit smaller and further back in his head."

After greeting the dignitaries, Churchill pleased the public and himself by walking along the crowd to great applause. He and King drove into the city across the bridge, which Churchill recalled had collapsed in 1907. He remarked on the beautiful scenery and the expanse of the river. Driving along the Plains of Abraham, where the battle for supremacy in North America had been fought in 1759, and the 1828 monument stood to the victorious General James Wolfe (and the French commander Louis-Joseph de Montcalm, who was also killed), Churchill reminded King that he had shown him Wolfe's statue of Wolfe in his native Westerham, the town adjacent to Chartwell.

As they motored along, Churchill said that he hoped that King would not want him to hurry away. He would like to stay about a month, keeping in touch with Roosevelt from the Citadelle and going back and forth to the United States as necessary. In between, he flatteringly said, "you and I would carry on the war from this side." Churchill looked forward to the two of them driving through the streets of Montreal and Toronto, even going again to Lake Louise in Alberta, which he thought would please his wife and daughter. The advantage of being nearby in Canada, Churchill told King, was that "much more can be done by allowing time for things to develop. I can do more with the President by not pressing him too hard at once. He is a fine fellow. Very strong in his views but he comes around." This heady prospect for King was not fulfilled. Churchill did stay for a month but scarcely travelled in Canada and enjoyed (along with King) only the adulation of the crowds in Quebec. There was, in fact, no need for the meeting in Quebec at all, the direction of the war having been settled in Washington in May. But Churchill had not brought two hundred and fifty military and civilian staff merely to arrange the details of moving resources from the Mediterranean to prepare for the invasion from Britain. As King immediately grasped, he and his advisers were going to make a last-ditch effort to persuade the Americans that the Mediterranean was the best and safest base from which to launch an attack.

The success in Sicily seemed a strong argument for it. After deceiving the enemy into thinking that they were aiming at Greece, the Allies had scarcely been opposed by the Italians. The Germans put up a stronger fight but in the intervening month most of the island was occupied and remaining resistance was crumbling. Bombing Naples and Rome ten days after the landings had led the fascist government to try to save the country, and prompted the king to dismiss Mussolini, who was subsequently arrested. His successor, Marshal Pietro Badoglio appeared to stand with the Germans but secretly bargained with the Allies. Churchill told King that he did not trust Badoglio: "a man who is ready to betray another is apt to betray you." But with the Italian situation so fluid, he repeated that he was not inclined to insist on unconditional surrender: "What they must do is yield, and when they yield, they will be given such reasonable terms as those who have them yield, are prepared to give. They will not get back their empire but they will have their own country to live in." Much would depend on what Germany did if Italy left the war, but Churchill was entranced by the great opportunities in the Mediterranean.

In this optimistic mood, Churchill said that the enemies were beaten, although the end would take some time. Anything could happen. Victory in Europe, depending on what happened in Germany, might take as little as six months, a year, or perhaps two. Then there would be Japan. Two or three times during the drive, Churchill said that great events in the war were going to be settled in Canada: "That this was a crucial time, and great decisions had to be made here." He regretted that Stalin would not be present but added that he was "very ill-mannered and very stubborn," meaning that he would oppose the Mediterranean bid. Churchill told King that he and the British military leaders had been surprised at Stalin's strength: "perfectly amazing." In an indication of how he intended to persuade Roosevelt, he pronounced that it was "better not to have too much in the way of pressure . . . and that much was done in informal talks." He hoped also that his staff would have a holiday, like his own impending trip to Niagara Falls on the way to Hyde Park before the conference formally began.

A great reader of newspapers, Churchill knew that the Liberals had the day before lost four by-elections (two to the CCF, one to the Labour-Progressives, and one to the Quebec anti-war Bloc Populaire) and hoped King was not too troubled. This scarcely affected the government's huge majority and King stoically said that he had expected it since wage and price controls made it difficult to compete with left-wing promises, and the government had been neglecting domestic political organization to concentrate on the war. Churchill had faced a similar challenge for the past year from the new Common Wealth Party which called for implementation of the Beveridge report but so far it had elected only one MP, against a Conservative, and Churchill dismissed it as a mere irritation. Obviously having no intention of retiring at the end of the war, he told King that he intended to win the election afterwards and that in his experience, "by-elections don't mean anything when you place a really large issue before the public." Next day, in a striking metaphor, he compared a by-election to "a fire started on ice. That it blazed up very much at the beginning but did not necessarily . . . spread over the whole, but went out after a while." This had not been his judgement in the 1930s when he had engaged in by-elections to embarrass his own party leaders.

Waiting for Churchill at the Citadelle to discuss "Tube Alloys" was Sir John Anderson, the lord president of the council. Two days earlier in Ottawa, Anderson had talked to King as a member of the inner circle on the matter. Continuing British resentment about Americans taking advantage of the cooperation on nuclear research was one of the most important, and highly secret topics for Churchill's meeting with Roosevelt. Anderson was the ideal person to prepare the ground. An outstanding administrator of modest manner, he had previously been a senior civil servant, governor of Bengal, and a non-party government MP. Now he was directing Britain's wartime economy. In the cabinet, only Lord Cherwell understood nuclear physics better than Anderson, who had spent a postgraduate year at the University of Leipzig working on the chemical properties of uranium. But at least as important as his scientific knowledge in dealing with the United States was his diplomatic skill.[19] On the way to the Citadelle, King told Churchill that Anderson seemed pleased with the agreement he had worked out with the Americans. Churchill repeated what he had said in May, that it was "too important a matter to let others get ahead of the rest of us on it. There had been some effort he thought on the part of the Americans to get ahead of the British."

Anderson had told King that in working out a pact he thought Churchill and Roosevelt would sign, he had insisted that the British were concerned with the war and not the seemingly distant commercial applications. (Conceding the sharing of commercial applications to the discretion of the US president was to cause much trouble later.) Anderson added that both Germany and the USSR were engaged in nuclear research and that he expected the Soviets to succeed first, "which would be a terrific thing for that country." Twice the British had destroyed a critical German heavy water plant near Oslo. The war might be over before a bomb was produced but whichever country possessed it would have absolute

19 Ruane, *Churchill and the Bomb in War and Cold War*, 31–2.

control of the world. If one was developed before the fighting was over, Anderson told King, it would guarantee immediate victory, "so powerful was the destruction this discovery was capable of effecting." He said that the Americans were secretly spending millions on research and wanted to go alone, partly because they had the means but also because "there still persisted the old myth that where they worked anything jointly with the British, the British got ahead."[20] (There was no mention of American security concerns.) On the first evening in Quebec, Churchill showed King a draft of Anderson's agreement that he was taking to Roosevelt at Hyde Park and obtained King's assent to his Minister, C. D. Howe, being a member of the three-country policy coordinating committee.

That night at a family dinner and afterwards, King and Churchill conversed for three hours. Churchill was anxious to clear up any ill-feeling over the Sicily announcement, or anything else, before Roosevelt arrived. The most important matter, said Churchill, was preserving the president's confidence and understanding: "he really is the one friend we have, and we must keep in as close touch as we can with him." King raised "Canada's problem," which was to have the country feel that "we were really having a voice in all matters pertaining to the war." The parliamentary opposition, the cabinet, and department of external affairs were all pressing for places on the Anglo-American joint chiefs of staff committee and the like, suggesting that King was letting Canada's position go by default and that the nation would have no voice in the peace. Churchill made a great show of sympathy but had no solution. Apart from not wanting any dilution of his own war authority, he knew as well as King that Roosevelt would not accept any additions to the decision-making bodies. Churchill tried to compensate for the exclusion by praising Canada's air force, which he said was doing forty percent of the Atlantic patrolling and had been doing much of it even before the United States entered the war. When King mentioned that he was marking the twenty-fifth year of his political leadership, Churchill seized the hint to announce to his wife that there was "no man who had better judgment of the peoples on this continent than I had," and heaped on flattery about his and Roosevelt's confidence in King's opinions.

As soon as Churchill arrived at dinner, he handed King a telegram from Stalin, similar to the one to Roosevelt, expressing congratulations on the Sicilian operation and proposing an early meeting of the three. General Ismay thought that

20 Diary, August 8, 1943.

they had better get busy arranging it. With the Soviets decisively pushing back the Germans after the gigantic tank battle at Kursk a month earlier, Stalin was riding high. Churchill told King that he admired the Soviet achievement but Stalin was "very indifferent and was rude." Churchill had stopped writing him for a time because some of his communications had gone unanswered. The prime minister hoped his silence would let convince Stalin "to fall in line." The Soviet leader was "very selfish, thinking of himself and Russia. Not as appreciative as he should be."

Churchill also talked about the seemingly intractable issue of Charles de Gaulle and the French Committee of National Liberation headed by him and General Henri Giraud, which claimed to be the legitimate government of France. Mackenzie King, who had hosted a government dinner in Giraud's honour the previous month and who was always sympathetic to de Gaulle, was keen to recognize the new authority. So was Churchill, who welcomed King as an ally in the argument with Roosevelt. But the president and Cordell Hull continued to resist the presumption of the self-selected generals that they would govern France after the war, also because they considered Giraud ineffective and de Gaulle arrogant. Churchill said that he "thoroughly disliked de Gaulle, though he thought he had many manly qualities." He was "one of those Frenchmen who hated Britain and might even be prepared to join with the Germans in attacking Britain some time. His ambition to control France was very great." Prompted by her husband, Clementine Churchill told King that de Gaulle had made many maladroit remarks in their house, for example, saying that if the British had sunk the French ships at Toulon, instead of their being scuttled, "we would probably have shot you." Churchill claimed that de Gaulle's reason for sending Giraud to North America was to increase his own power on the Committee of National Liberation. But despite all this, Churchill thought it would be splendid to persuade Roosevelt and announce recognition of the French authority from Quebec.[21] This was done only in a very limited way.

* * *

Next morning King and Churchill went to the Chateau Frontenac to meet with the Canadian war cabinet. Everyone knew that Churchill was in the city and there were cheering crowds along the short rue St. Louis. The gathering lasted from

---

21 Diary, August 10, 1943.

11:30 a.m. to 2:00 p.m. and was described as a joint session of the British and Canadian war cabinets, even if the only members of the former were Churchill and Anderson who sat on either side of King. As in Washington, the purpose for Canadian ministers was to hear and question Churchill. For Churchill, it was an opportunity to address any concerns and make sure the Canadians supported him before the Americans arrived. The issues were largely those that he and King had discussed the day before, with a couple of new ones. Ralston said that since a cross-channel invasion was not imminent, more Canadian troops should be used in the Mediterranean. Much as Churchill's heart must have warmed to this seeming endorsement of his strategy, he circumspectly replied that this depended on the outcome of the deliberations of the joint chiefs of staff, but which, in reality, meant himself and Roosevelt. King again emphasized that Canada recognized the direction of the war by Churchill and the president but wanted the country to share as much as possible in the fight which it joined two years before the United States. He also raised the sore point of actions being taken without consulting Canada. Churchill returned a reassuring answer, observing that there would be a meeting that afternoon of the British and Canadian chiefs of staff and others would be held as necessary.

At the end, Churchill was asked about the Soviet Union. He gave an impassioned statement about its military performance but pointed out that at the beginning of the war it had been prepared to "leave Britain to be swallowed up by Germany." (In parentheses King commented: "There was the other side that Britain would have allowed Russia to be swallowed up by Germany.") Churchill judged, or at least hoped, that the USSR was now more anxious to rebuild its country than to spread communism. But in what King regarded as a magnificent statement, he made a powerful case for preventing Soviet domination through what he (alone among the Canadians) knew was Roosevelt's plan for a new organization to preserve the peace:

> We must not forget that she was very advanced in her scientific developments and industries and would soon become all powerful. That her doctrines were certain to be powerful enough to more than control the rest of the world unless, in the interval, some new system of world control were instituted which would prevent anything of the kind on the part of any country.[22]

22 Extracts of the minutes, though not the section on the USSR, are in Dilks, *The Great Dominion*, 257-61.

There was no discussion about a second front from Britain but Churchill afterwards indicated to King the stand he was going to take with the president. Objecting that secretary of state for war Henry Stimson believed that an invasion of France was the only way the war could be won and that Sicily was a waste of time, he remarked that the Americans "did not appreciate how long these operations took and how difficult it was to get supplies etc." When King asked about Beaverbrook's dogged campaign for a second front, Churchill said that he was grieving at not being in the government but he really did believe in what he was endorsing: "I do not mind his doing it. It is just as well to have someone advocating it." At some point, King recalled the next day, Churchill elaborated on his caution over a second front. Undoubtedly referring to the Dardanelles, he said he was much changed from having "made many mistakes in the first war. He was making fewer mistakes in this war because of those he had made earlier. He had learned a great deal. Above all he had learned to consider very carefully many matters and to be cautious." King could only approve. He also noticed that Churchill drew many of his similes from family relationships and nature, "from wild animals, tame animals and the like, the cat and the mouse business; growling; and when one gets one's back up it is hard to get it down."

Among those who were waiting for King and Churchill at lunch after the war cabinet meeting were Lord Moran, a young nuclear scientist travelling under a pseudonym, and Churchill's new protégé, the twenty-five-year-old "dambuster" hero, wing commander Guy Gibson, V.C., who had been a shipboard companion for Mary Churchill. King found him to be "a fine young boy." Gibson was introduced to Roosevelt at Quebec, before leaving for a lecture tour of Canada and the United States. The next year he became the prospective Conservative candidate to succeed the Canadian baking and grocery magnate Garfield Weston in the British parliament but died in August, when his plane crashed in Holland.[23]

In the afternoon, after a brief call with the lieutenant governor at his residence, King and Churchill went to the legislature to meet Premier Adelard Godbout and his cabinet. On the way, King suggested that Churchill say a few words in French. King opened proceedings by testifying to the helpfulness of the provincial Liberal government to the federal one and, since Churchill had expressed an interest in fishing, suggested that ministers let him know the best places. Churchill spoke slowly in French, saying afterwards to King that he probably mixed up the

---

23 David Gunby, "Gibson, Guy Penrose (1918-1944)," ODNB.

genders and tenses but regarded the French language as "a beautiful medium for expression." Aware of the attitude of most French-Canadians to the war he concentrated on France but did not mention de Gaulle in a place where Pétain was more admired. He spoke of seeing a free France restored to its place in the world and made a veiled allusion to the possible recognition of the Committee of National Liberation by speaking of "the historic significance of the meeting here, and what it might mean to the world to have decisions made in this old city that would help to relieve the situation in France."

Soon afterwards, Churchill left by train on his circuitous journey by way of Niagara Falls to Hyde Park. The president of the Canadian Pacific Railway (who provided the train and who also owned the Chateau Frontenac) and his brother were at the station. Mary Churchill accompanied her father but not her mother, to the great disappointment of Churchill who had hoped she would help in charming the president, whom she had not yet met. Clementine had been exhausted (not an unusual condition for her) before leaving Britain and the voyage that she had hoped would revive her left her even more drained.[24] King told Churchill that it was best for her to rest before the real conference began and promised to keep a "paternal" or "fraternal" eye on her. Churchill was happy to leave her in King's care: "She is very fond of you. Likes you very much, and will appreciate having a chance to talk to you."[25]

* * *

In the four days that Churchill was away King was as good as his word. On the first afternoon, he and Clementine Churchill spent almost two hours together at tea. She told King that apart from weekends, this was her first rest since the war began. (Her main cause was chairing the Aid to Russia Fund to provide clothing and medical supplies.) King, of all the peculiar topics, talked about his visit to Hitler and the problem of postwar civil aviation which was a source of friction with the United States which, with its huge advantage in planes, wanted a world-wide "open skies" policy. He told her that most Americans who dealt with her husband Roosevelt – Winant, Harriman and Hopkins – belonged to a particular group, mainly New England and Dutch, which was friendly to Britain but not

24 Purnell, *Clementine*, 309–10.
25 Diary, August 11, 1943.

representative of the majority of Americans, "who if the President were once defeated, might take a very different attitude." He warned about the strength of private US business interests and associated himself with the British by saying that "we" should be careful to preserve the closest friendly relations with the US but not be "over-trusting in anything." Clementine recounted a number of interesting things about her husband. His patience, generally, had increased since the 1930s, when he learned in writing the biography of Marlborough that it had been one of the duke's great qualities.[26]

The next day, after dinner with Louis St. Laurent, the minister of justice and an MP for Quebec City, King and Clementine Churchill went to the Chateau Frontenac where the Canadian government provided a sumptuous buffet for four or five hundred people on the eve of the conference between the British and American chiefs of staff. The Canadian chiefs and civilian aides were also included. King thought the feast too lavish for wartime. He and Clementine received the guests and shared a light supper with some of the leading dignitaries. That night King was elated to receive confirmation that Roosevelt would make his long-promised visit to Ottawa immediately after the Quebec conference.[27]

King and Clementine Churchill held a tea the following afternoon at the Château for the one hundred and fifty reporters who were covering the conference but not allowed near it. They went to a theatre that evening to see a Canadian army show that had toured camps and towns across the country since the spring. Tactfully, they shared their box with two Britons, General Sir Alan Brooke and Field Marshal Sir John Dill, and two Americans, General George Marshall and Admiral Ernest King. Brooke declared that it was the first thing of the kind he had seen in four years and Clementine "fairly screamed with laughter." Crowds gathered to see her, and their car was mobbed as she and King left the theatre. During the show Brooke told King about several near shaves during the war, particularly Dunkirk, when he said it was Churchill's courage that had saved the day, and Tobruk when it seemed the enemy would control the Mediterranean and cut off Britain's oil supplies. Brooke said that he could not work late at night and by 1 or 2 a.m. could no longer argue against Churchill, which was the prime minister's intention. After such a night, Brooke said that he was not able to do much the next morning.[28]

26 Diary, August 12, 1943.
27 Diary, August 13, 1943.
28 Diary, August 14, 1943; *Globe and Mail*, August 16, 1943.

As well as looking after Clementine Churchill, Mackenzie King was also busy with preparations for the main conference. He had some ambivalent assistance. Colonel Henry Willis-O'Connor, the governor general's aide-de-camp, acted as though he and not King was in charge at the Citadelle. Norman Robertson and Arnold Heeney, the cabinet secretary, took it upon themselves to pay formal calls on the Catholic cardinal and the Anglican bishop and King had sharply to remind them that this was the function of cabinet ministers, and particularly the prime minister, not bureaucrats. ("I think Heeney has lost his head a bit.")[29] "Chubby" Power, the air minister and one of the city's MPs, after promising King to abstain from drink during the conference, went on a bender and was hurried out of town.[30] A few days later, when Churchill and Roosevelt were present, he was back, crawling drunkenly around the Chateau without his trousers. When he finally left, he took three bottles of the hotel's scarce supply of whiskey. To get him off the stage, King enlisted the lieutenant governor, who feared that Power would sign supply contracts without knowing what he was doing.[31]

* * *

Winston and Mary Churchill returned on Sunday morning, August 15. In the two days at Hyde Park they had enjoyed the novelty of hot dogs and watermelon as well as swimming. The stifling heat and humidity were another matter; one night Churchill left the house and sat on the lawn overlooking the Hudson river until dawn. The visit was no mere social prelude to the conference at Quebec. Churchill had tried to convince the president, apart from his military chiefs, to make Italy the priority and defer the cross-channel second front but Roosevelt would have none of it. But in return for Churchill's reaffirmation of their agreement in May about a second front in 1944, the president accepted the co-operative agreement on atomic research that had been worked out by Sir John Anderson. To ensure that the decision about the second front was carried through, General George Marshall was appointed as commander. This was a stunning blow to Brooke who, despite his scepticism, had already been promised

29 Diary, August 13 and 13, 1943.
30 Diary, August 14, 1943.
31 Diary, August 19, 1943.

the post. Not sparing Brooke's feelings, Churchill brusquely conveyed the news as soon as he was back at Quebec.[32]

The main decisions had thus been made at Hyde Park before the conference at Quebec even began. This did not prevent Churchill continuing a rear-guard action for the Mediterranean and against an operation from Britain. The atomic agreement was formally signed at Quebec, committing the two countries to pool their knowledge but not to share it with any other country without both agreeing. A Control Policy Committee (including C. D. Howe as Canada's representative) was established in Washington to oversee the development of a nuclear bomb. Although work was concentrated in Los Alamos, New Mexico, some of it was carried out at Chalk River, Ontario, and many British scientists soon came to work at both locations. Roosevelt and Churchill also pledged never to use atomic weapon against each other or a third party without joint consent.[33]

Mackenzie King met Churchill's train from Hyde Park and thought he looked remarkably fresh. At the Citadelle they talked for an hour, Churchill saying that he had had a good time but was glad to be back in the refreshing air of Quebec, where he now talked of staying for a couple of months. He reported on the atomic agreement and told King that it was important not to let the Soviets gain the lead. (Denying information to any other country without joint concurrence was, in effect, directed against the USSR.) On Stalin's proposal of a meeting of the three, he said that he and the president had decided to "send the 'blighter' an invitation to try to have him meet us. If he does not accept, we can't help it." De Gaulle was still a difficult problem, but Churchill had appealed to Roosevelt to treat the general with generosity.

In great confidence, Churchill told King, asking him not even to tell his cabinet for a day or two, that the Canadian troops in Sicily, which were now resting, would within four days be landing in Italy "at the front in a very conspicuous role." (In fact, the landing did not take place for another couple of weeks.) King, particularly with Churchill now intending to stay so long, aimed to improve the shining hour in Ottawa by having the British prime minister in the capital at the same time as Roosevelt but Churchill said that he had already been, and the

32 Alanbrook, *War Diaries 1939–1945*. Ed. Alex Danchev and Daniel Todman. (Berkeley: University of California Press, 2001), 441. (diary entry, August 15, 1943); Hamilton, *Commander in Chief*, 313–5; Meacham, *Franklin and Winston*, 232–3; Goodwin, *No Ordinary Time*, 456–7.
33 Ruane, *Churchill and the Bomb*, 62–6; Roll, *The Hopkins Touch*, 292–4; Sanger *Malcolm MacDonald*, 245–7.

president should go alone. He also told King that Roosevelt was concerned about keeping the time of his arrival at Quebec a secret and having no ceremony at the railway station. Hoping to keep the president for a couple of weeks, Churchill emphasized the importance of providing good fishing, even if it meant stocking the lakes.[34] When they did go fishing, Roosevelt, who prided himself on his skill, caught none while Churchill caught one.

King and Churchill talked again for three and a half hours the next day, at lunch with the Churchill ladies and afterwards alone. Churchill was much concerned about the restrictions on Canadian whiskey exports to Britain (distilleries were concentrating on industrial alcohol). King said that he was not drinking during the war and preserved his health and judgement by rest. Clementine Churchill commented that he looked remarkably well but her husband said that he felt the same without self-denial. King gracefully conceded that everything depended on the habits of youth, and for Churchill to stop drinking now would probably kill him.

On a more substantial level, Churchill showed King a dispatch stating that the Italian government was making peace overtures through the British ambassador in Spain. The general who had been sent to Madrid reported that the Italians hated the Germans and were ready to rise and fight with the British, and warned that if the British did not come to the rescue, the fascists might try to recover their influence. Churchill was emphatic that the Italians must surrender their navy and pledge to fight the Germans in order to keep their arms. This heady prospect of an easy victory increased his resolve to persist in arguing for the Italian front. He told King (incorrectly) that Canadians were probably already on their way to spearhead a landing, and King thought it would be magnificent if they disembarked just as Italy surrendered. Once again reviewing the voluntary engagement of the overseas dominions in the war, King insisted to Churchill that in Canada, "Liberals were just as much for being a part of the British Empire or Commonwealth–whatever it was called–as the Conservatives, though the latter sought to monopolize the loyalty cry and to have it appear that the others were opposed."[35]

* * *

34 Diary, August 15, 1943.
35 Diary, August 16, 1943.

Roosevelt's train was scheduled to arrive at 6 p.m. the following evening, Tuesday, August 17. That morning the governor general and his wife arrived to welcome the president and hold a dinner to mark the opening of the conference. They intended to return to Ottawa overnight but were persuaded by Churchill to remain for official photographs the next day. King and Churchill drove in an open car to meet the president's train and got a fine reception along the way, with Churchill remarking how easy it would be for someone to fire a shot from the bushes. King asked if he wanted protection. Churchill said that he "liked to be on his own. In London, he walked through the streets by himself" (with a detective). At the station, Lord Athlone, the lieutenant governor, and the premier joined the two prime ministers as they went to Roosevelt's railway car. King thought the president looked very well, and Roosevelt said how much he had enjoyed the fishing trip to Georgian Bay. He was hoisted out of the train (an elevator had not yet been installed) and into his automobile which he shared with the governor general. King and Churchill followed behind Roosevelt's security guard.

At the Citadelle, Roosevelt told King that he would come to Ottawa the following Wednesday. He had originally intended Monday but Churchill persuaded him to stay at Quebec another day. At dinner, despite the objection of his security detail, he said that King might publicize the visit a few days in advance. Organizing Ottawa events from Quebec became a major occupation for King. Roosevelt said that he would go from Ottawa to Hyde Park, to the great disappointment of Churchill who had hoped that he would return to Quebec for another week. Churchill instead followed the president to the United States.

After the president and governor general had greeted some of the military chiefs and a few others, Churchill and Roosevelt turned to the Italian peace proposal, which they considered genuine. The capture of Sicily was completed that same day. "Quadrant," as the conference was codenamed, had now formally begun.[36] The governor general's opening dinner was small, including Harry Hopkins, Averell Harriman, Lord Leathers (the British minister of war transport) and a military representative from each of the three countries. Jollity was increased by it being the birthday of both Harry Hopkins and the president's son and aide, Franklin D. Roosevelt Jr.[37]

36 Daniels, *Franklin D. Roosevelt*, 349–53; Hamilton, *Commander in Chief*, 319–50; Roberts, *Masters and Commanders*, 391–408; Roll, *The Hopkins Touch*, 287–97.
37 Diary, August 17, 1943.

The Churchills' luncheon the next day in honour of the Athlones was also convivial as well as politically insignificant. King had an earnest discussion with Sir John Dill about "forces from Beyond that were working with us and guarding us." Afterwards photographs were taken on the terrace of the principals in various configurations. King was proud that the Canadian flag in the background was at the same height as the British and American ones. While the session was underway a seaplane, which had left Britain the day before, landed on the river below. Aboard were Anthony Eden, his Under-secretary Sir Alexander Cadogan, and Brendan Bracken, the minister of information. They were immediately whisked up to the Citadelle and more photographs were taken to include them.

Mackenzie King held a dinner that evening in honour of Churchill and Roosevelt at which there was also little political discussion. In the toasts, both King and Churchill spoke about the importance of drawing Britain and the empire and the United States closer together and the role of Canada and King in bringing this about. Churchill praised King's contribution as "a service to civilization itself." Not surprisingly, the Canadian prime minister left the dinner with "a feeling of something very sacred and very beautiful." His emotions were more mixed about the films he had arranged to be shown afterwards. The first, on the Group of Seven and A. Y. Jackson, he thought was as embarrassing as the paintings at the 1939 World's Fair had been: "I felt really ashamed of the exhibition being announced as Canadian art, a lot of beautiful natural views were destroyed and distorted in the painting." The second film, a Walt Disney production on South America, he found more acceptable.

After the party broke up at midnight, King, Roosevelt and Churchill continued talking for some time, the latter two fuelled by scotch and soda. Roosevelt said that with King having sworn off alcohol for the duration, "won't there be a celebration when the war is won."[38] Their conversation was mainly about the chances of the war coming to an end. Churchill, while enthusiastic about the capitulation of Italy, was not as optimistic as King that it and the bombing of Germany alone would finish the European fighting in 1943. The western Allies, he said ominously, had not yet confronted the powerful German army. This was another warning about the difficulty of cross-channel invasions.

* * *

38 Diary, August 18, 1943.

King received a note from Clementine Churchill in the morning inviting him to talk about the visit she and Mary intended to make to Ottawa after the conference. (In fact, they did not). This agreeable tête-à-tête was interrupted by Minister Brendan Bracken whom "Clemmie," as he addressed her, considered as bad an influence on her husband as Lord Beaverbrook. Bracken annoyed her further by never going out of his way to deny that he was Churchill's illegitimate son. Practically self-educated and a compulsive talker, he held forth at length on Francis Parkman, the nineteenth-century American historian of the British and French in North America. "Like so many Englishmen," wrote King, "he monopolized the conversation as if he knew more of Canada than I did myself and should be regarded as an authority." The night before Roosevelt, evidently with less resentment, had told King that Bracken knew more about the US than most of its citizens. In 1951, he put his interests to good use by founding the popular magazine *History Today*. Bracken was also at the luncheon that day, along with Eden, many of the chiefs of staff and most of the provincial cabinet at Spencer Wood, the residence of the lieutenant governor. Since Roosevelt was not present, Churchill could without embarrassment toast the monarch's representative as having marched with him in the Boer war, although Major-General Sir Eugène Fiset had in fact been a military surgeon.[39]

Two days later, Mackenzie King's opinion of Brendan Bracken underwent a marked improvement when he came to lunch and stayed talking, fuelled by half a dozen scotches, for two hours. His main purpose, obviously on behalf of Churchill, was to recruit King to try to overcome the antipathy of Cordell Hull (who had arrived the day before) to de Gaulle and recognition of the French National Committee. But he also imparted much other fascinating information. King hugely enjoyed the conversation, if that is the right word, since Bracken "talks so much on every subject that one can really say nothing. I allowed him to sail out and I am sure that gave him the most satisfaction."

Bracken said that it was he who handled Churchill's royal patronage, including peerages. King thus learned how his former political opponent, R. B. Bennett, a friend of Bracken (through Lord Beaverbrook), got his rank in the peerage. He had originally been slated for a barony but when Buckingham Palace sent word that he should be an earl, as in the case of a former British prime minister, Bracken said that was going too far: "He was after all getting his title as one

39 Diary, August 19, 1943.

who was intended to be in the House of Lords; not as a Canadian but as a person who had come to reside in England and whose citizenship was there." The compromise was the rank of viscount, between baron and earl. Speaking of the other Canadian viscount, King's friend Hamar Greenwood, Bracken said that the Conservatives realized too late that they had made a mistake in appointing a teetotaler as party treasurer: "They found as soon as he came to collect funds, they all fell off from the liquor interests, and he had, therefore, to make way for someone else."

Having secured the attention of his Canadian counterpart in patronage matters, Bracken urged the case for a senatorship or something of the kind for Leonard Brockington. After a year as a mellow-toned Canadian radio correspondent in London and adviser to Bracken's ministry of information on commonwealth affairs, Brockington wanted to return to his family in Ottawa. Originally from Wales, he had been the city solicitor for Calgary, a member of R. B. Bennett's law firm, chairman of the Canadian Broadcasting Corporation, and from the beginning of the war to 1942, King's publicity manager. The prime minister was not a little jealous of Brockington's oratory, although he pruned the flourishes from the speeches Brockington produced for him. He had no intention of providing him with a platform in the Senate or anywhere else. Brockington soon joined an Ottawa law practice. King was happier that Bracken intended to tell George McCullagh, the publisher and owner of the Toronto *Globe and Mail*, one of the conservative papers most critical of King, that his stance was driving people to the CCF. No longer grumbling about Bracken's garrulity and assumption of superiority, King now thought that he perceived "the Conservative party was fading out in Canada." Bracken also pronounced that the CCF, by loading up on grievances against the government, was similar to the Common Wealth party in Britain, which he was confident would be quashed in time, not appreciating that its beneficiary would be the Labour party.

This agreeable monologue ended only because Cordell Hull was waiting to go with King to tea with the lieutenant governor. King tackled the secretary of state on de Gaulle and the French National Committee but Hull was as mistrustful as ever. He said that de Gaulle aimed at far greater power than the United States wanted him to have. He also suspected that the close relations between de Gaulle and Britain mean that France would grant its neighbour trade preferences. Despite all the money the United States had given de Gaulle, Hull complained that he had used much of it to attack Americans: "He spoke of him as a man who could not be trusted. He was one thing to one, and another to another."

King turned down the invitation to a quiet dinner with Churchill, Roosevelt and a few others that night in order to prepare for a broadcast at 10 p.m. The subject was the engagement of almost 500 Canadians in the army, navy and air force in a total US force of 34,000 sent to liberate Kiska, one of the Aleutian islands off Alaska which had fallen to the Japanese in June, 1942. The islands had not, as expected, become stepping stones for the Japanese to North America, a fear that had led to the building of the Alaska highway. Recovering the Aleutians was a matter of pride to Americans. The heavy assault met no resistance since the Japanese had evacuated two weeks earlier but they had left booby-traps which killed four and injured some others. "Friendly" fire in dense fog increased the casualties to twenty-eight dead and fifty injured.[40] Although there was no real action to report, King considered it important to tell the country about this operation of Canadians fighting alongside the Americans.

When he returned to the Citadelle at 11 p.m., he found Roosevelt, Churchill and Eden in the sun room drinking whiskey. All were in slippers, Roosevelt wearing a smoking jacket, Churchill a siren suit, and Eden a casual jacket. Cordell Hull had gone to bed. Sensing some tension, King made to leave after a few minutes but Churchill said, "no, we want you here." What they were discussing, as they had been at dinner, were plans for government of the world. Roosevelt wanted the Quebec conference to issue a declaration, similar to the Atlantic Charter, proclaiming the principles of world order. The proposal was the one that had been mooted earlier between himself, Churchill and King: regional councils for Europe, the Americas, and Asia with a "supreme council" of the Big Four (the United States, Britain, the USSR and China). By this time, Roosevelt obviously intended to run for a fourth term as president in 1944 and wanted a scheme to preserve the peace in his platform in good time. Churchill argued that it would be better to wait and see how matters developed but since the president was Britain's best friend, he would tell the British cabinet that it must support whatever he wanted. He protested again, however, against China being accepted as a great power, despite Roosevelt's insistence that it was needed as a buffer between the Soviet Union and the United States. King was at one with the president that there was now a new, youthful China that must not be underrated.

---

40 Bercuson, *Our Finest Hour*, 82–3; Galen Roger Perras, *Stepping Stones to Nowhere: The Aleutian Islands, Alaska and American Military Strategy, 1867–1945* (Vancouver: UBC Press, 2003), 136–57.

This time King warned, as he had not earlier, that the dominions and the other united nations would oppose such supremacy by the great powers. Lesser countries, the dominions in particular, would concede much to Churchill and Roosevelt but "We would not agree to the government of the world by the four most powerful powers–it was contrary to conception for which this war was being fought." Siding with Churchill, he suggested "letting the evolution of the 'final order' follow naturally from control at the outset by the powers that did the conquering of the enemy . . . but not to arrange anything too final in advance." Roosevelt said that he was anxious to get the United States into an international organization for peace but doubted that it could be managed if it was once again in Europe. To make a clean break from the League of Nations – which continued a shadowy existence in Princeton, New Jersey – he suggested spreading sections of the new organization among various countries, with Geneva being maintained only for the International Labour Office (which was now relocated to Montreal). Churchill, observing that it was the "Nations" that had had failed the League, fell in with this arrangement.

On this occasion, there was no mention of King, or anyone else, as the universal moderator. The discussion was another stage in the evolution of the United Nations Organization and its Security Council. The discursive conversation also extended to another attempt to get Roosevelt to recognize the French National Committee, and there was much general reminiscing. "Isn't it fine," said the president as King walked beside him out of the room at 2 a.m., "that we can all talk so freely, concealing nothing."[41]

* * *

On the second last day of the conference, Mackenzie King and Winston Churchill had the great pleasure of driving together in an open car at noon through the streets of Quebec. Roosevelt, who was wary of his physical condition being commented on by foreign reporters who did not share the convention of American journalists of saying nothing, did not leave the Citadelle between coming and going to his train. At times, Churchill sat up on the back of the car seat. It was like a victory parade and those in front of the city hall seemed "like a vast throng hailing a deliverer." But King had some unwelcome news for Churchill on this

41 Diary, August 21, 1943.

excursion. Thinking that the increased Labor majority in the Australian election two days earlier was bound to help the CCF, he decided that he could not go to London in the autumn but needed to stay in Canada to keep the country behind the Liberals. Churchill said he would do all he could to help: as soon as the president left, he was going to a fishing lodge and would work on a broadcast emphasizing Canada's contribution to the war.[42]

The week-long summit effectively concluded with a press conference at midday Tuesday, August 24. This was King's suggestion to Brendan Bracken since the reporters were getting restless at the lack of news. King was invited to preside, with Churchill and Roosevelt on either side and Eden, Bracken and Hopkins behind. King allowed four minutes for photographs at the beginning and at the end praised the journalists, who had not received a scrap of information, for their coverage. They did not learn anything on this occasion either but they did get to see and hear the leaders and their solemn assurances that the necessarily secret decisions had been made without controversy. At Roosevelt's suggestion King called first on Churchill, who complained of the short notice. He began by feeling his way, as he often gave the appearance of doing, even in great orations, but ended by giving "quite a speech." He talked of the value of conferences between himself and the president and between the large staffs that were necessary for such a huge collaborative war effort and claimed, without fear of contradiction, that all of them had scarcely had a free minute. He talked mainly about Britain, the United States and the Soviet Union until King whispered a reminder to mention China. (T. V. Soong had arrived the day before and had been left to King to entertain.)

Roosevelt, in his remarks, emphasized the importance of industry and civilian support for the fighting services, and the intensifying operations against Japan. He made particular reference to Canada and its forces, which he said to King afterwards he thought important since Churchill had not said anything about it. The reporters were not allowed questions and the session ended with King expressing the honour to Canada of the meeting being held in the historic city of Quebec.[43]

Except for the nuclear pact, which he already knew about, King had no more idea of what had been decided at Quebec than the reporters, although he was told much the next day in Ottawa by Roosevelt and by Churchill later in Quebec. The most important military conclusion, after impassioned arguments

---

42   Diary, August 23, 1943.
43   Diary, August 24; *Globe and Mail*, August 25, 1943.

– despite what Churchill and Roosevelt said publicly – between the British and the Americans, was to reiterate, yet again, that highest priority in Europe was preparation for the second front from Britain in May 1944. Veteran units would be moved there from the Mediterranean starting in November. At the same time, there would be an attack in the south of France. More immediately, mainland Italy would be invaded in the hope of an quick victory.

* * *

Immediately after lunch with the Churchills, Roosevelt and Eden, Mackenzie King left for Ottawa to make smooth the path for the arrival of the American president the next day. The first visit of a US president in office to the Canadian capital would under any circumstances have been a major ceremonial event. In the middle of the war, and following the conference at Quebec, it was an even greater one. The governor general greeted Roosevelt's train at 11:30 a.m. and the two went in the president's open car to Parliament Hill. They passed slowly by the guard of honour and as they reached the peace tower at the centre of the building the band played "The Star Spangled Banner." The customary noon gun was fired and the carillon in the tower played "O Canada." Only those inside the base of the tower could see that Roosevelt was helped out of the car and to the stand where he stood in his leg braces behind a lectern and was framed by the arch. There were microphones to amplify the sound to the crowd and broadcast the speech to the country and the whole free world. Seated facing the president were cabinet ministers, MPs, senators, diplomats and other dignitaries. Behind them on the lawn were about 40,000 people in bright summer clothes.

Mackenzie King gave the introduction, including a few sentences in French on which he had been coached by Edouard Handy. He then stood behind and to one side of Roosevelt and witnessed the physical effort it took to deliver the address. The president's arms shook, and he had to hold on to the stand and a chair. He kept his place in the text, which was in a three-ring binder, by running his little finger along the lines. He praised King and Churchill and asserted that major decisions had been made at Quebec in a friendly, family-like atmosphere. Although these could not be revealed, they would appear in events. Roosevelt's main message was a version of the declaration he had wanted to make at the end of the conference and intended as part of his election platform for 1944: the need for all the united nations to pull together for absolute victory and afterwards to reject isolationism and continue to work together to safeguard peace and build a world based on the principles of the Four Freedoms and the Atlantic Charter.[44] This inspirational declaration was greeted with loud applause. At the end, he was thanked by the speaker of the House of Commons (in English) and the Senate (in French). King thought that both were dignified but too long.

Roosevelt and Lord Athlone drove away slowly along the crowd, King and Princess Alice following, to his great disappointment, in a closed rather than the open car he had expected: "I would have given very much to have driven in an open car with H.R.H. in order to have shared with her the sight of the people, recognizing that the P.M. also had an important place in the procession." At the First World War memorial, the motorcade stopped and a wreath was laid on behalf of the president while the band played the hymn "Abide with Me." There were cheers all along the streets to Government House for a luncheon attended by the cabinet and a few others. Lord Athlone, as Chancellor of the University of London, conferred an honorary degree on the president and Yousuf Karsh, now himself a celebrity, took photographs.

King and Roosevelt set out in the president's car after lunch on a tour of the city and out to Kingsmere. Rain had not diminished the number of spectators but the top had to be put up for most of the way. Being an hour behind schedule, they drove quickly. The staff of the US legation was gathered outside to meet the president. Beyond the city, and out of the public eye, the car broke down and the president had to be carried to a similar one that was travelling in reserve. At Kingsmere there was only time to drive through the grounds and stop to greet Joan and Godfroy Patteson and King's dog. As they drove along Roosevelt admitted that he did intend to run for re-election in 1944 and for that reason wanted the war to end as soon as possible. He said that he would not campaign around the country, only speak on the radio, and that not very often.

The president assured King that the Quebec conference had been harmonious, the best he had known with Churchill. They had agreed on the attack on France from Britain, and Roosevelt hoped to get a million soldiers across the Atlantic by the end of the year. On the last evening they had received a cable from Stalin replying to their invitation for a meeting. He was deeply suspicious that he was not being informed about the Italian peace negotiations (which was not true) and the whole tone was "most disconcerting; very rude and wholly uncalled for." Stalin implied that he had better things to do than attend a conference and

---

44 *Globe and Mail*, August 26, 1943; Hamilton, *Commander in Chief*, 335–40.

would arrange one himself. In the meantime, he wanted representatives of the three countries to meet in Sicily. Churchill had been furious and wanted to send a sharp answer but Roosevelt persuaded him to stay his hand. To gain time, the president had a secretary tell Stalin that he had left Quebec and would receive the message at Hyde Park in a day or two. He said the most charitable explanation was that the Soviets were with you one day, the next against. A more serious interpretation was that Stalin was working up a list of terms to which the western Allies would never agree as an excuse to make a separate peace with Germany. Roosevelt talked at length about the importance of China as a buffer against the Soviet Union: "Felt unless the Chinese were friendly with us, there was no telling what might develop in Asia itself."

Reflecting later, in tranquillity, on the conversation, King was awed by Roosevelt's profound grasp of the world situation, which he thought based on an understanding of history and places, much like Churchill's. The difference was that Churchill "still remains a monarchist and a Conservative. Roosevelt is clearly for the people and they know it. Churchill is for his country and its institutions. A great empire but less belief in the abilities of people to govern themselves." The president said that Churchill had not expected John Curtin's Labor party to win re-election in the Australian election, which King thought reflected what Churchill and some of those around him desired for Britain. King had already expressed his concern about the possible repercussion in Canada and thought the shock would help Churchill to see "how important it was that we should watch the whole democratic trend on this continent."

At the end of the drive, there was tea at Laurier House and whisky for those who wanted it, with the governor general, Leighton McCarthy, and members of Roosevelt's staff, including Grace Tully. The president was carried in the back door to his wheelchair. While he was in the washroom, King looked into the dining room and was appalled to see the table set with a cloth for a meal rather than placemats. After tea, he took Roosevelt in the elevator to the library on the top floor. Among the items on display was, peculiarly enough, the photograph signed by Hitler. The president, not surprisingly, reacted with "a shudder." Since his train had been intended to leave an hour earlier, the president and the governor general hurried to the station, Roosevelt first shaking hands with the Laurier House servants.[45]

45 Diary, August 25, 1943.

* * *

Five days after Roosevelt's visit to Ottawa, King, the war cabinet and the chiefs of staff returned to Quebec for a purely Canadian denouement with Churchill. The meeting had been postponed for a couple of days so that the Churchills could prolong their holiday at the fishing camp of the pulp and paper manufacturer Colonel Frank W. Clarke at Lac-des-Neiges about forty-five miles north of the city. Churchill did not neglect to send King some of the trout he caught. By this time, the American military leaders and most of the British had left. Since there was no head of state present, King stayed in the governor general's quarters in the Citadelle.

Churchill arrived at 11 a.m., and was still working on the radio address he was giving at 1 p.m. He told King later that he had toiled at it for about six hours over the past few days, and the night before he been dealing with dispatches until 4 a.m. When King remarked that the broadcasts were distinctly his own, Churchill said, "yes, I have to do that myself. I have others 'vet,' check what I have written but find I have to do it practically all myself." He said that he dictated because he did not have the patience to write, but that meant having to know what he was going to say from the beginning, or as King put it, getting the plow to move. As he did so many times, Churchill talked about the strain of speeches. Having one in the offing, he said, was like having a vulture watching over him. He had not been able to enjoy the fishing until the last day when the text was well underway. Both agreed that there was no moment of freedom like that following a broadcast.

While Churchill addressed the world from a room in the Citadelle, King and the Canadian war cabinet and some British military and civilian staff listened by radio in the sun room. "Here at the gateway of Canada," Churchill began, "in mighty lands which have never known the totalitarian tyrannies of Hitler and Mussolini, the spirit of freedom has found an abiding home." His main theme was to mollify Stalin after his ill-tempered messages. However angry Churchill and Roosevelt had been, the Soviet leader was still essential to winning the war in Europe and the plans for world peace. Churchill paid high tribute to the USSR and said that he and the president would continue their efforts to meet Stalin. With no fear of contradiction since the proceedings were secret, he boldly claimed that it would have been embarrassing to invite Stalin to Quebec since a large part of the discussion concerned Japan, against which the Soviet Union was still neutral. He assured his listeners that there would be a second front but only when there was a good chance of success: the lives of soldiers would not be expended merely for political considerations. At the same time, he indicated that a strong effort would be continued in the Mediterranean by exulting in the fall of Mussolini, the success in North Africa and Sicily, and mentioning a third front. He also spoke of the importance of the continued bombing of Germany. And in the heart of French Canada he declared that France would rise again. As promised, he lauded Canada's great war effort and King as the experienced statesman who had led a united country into war.[46] When King affected to protest that this was too much, Churchill replied: "not at all, not at all. I don't know how we could have done without you. Your services have meant everything."

Once the speech was over, Churchill looked "fresh and rested and very relieved." King, having heard Roosevelt's version, asked Churchill at lunch for his account of what had happened over the exchanges with Stalin. Circumspectly, Churchill claimed that the message he and the president had sent had not been properly translated, and that Stalin had probably read it too quickly. Contrary to what Roosevelt had told King, Churchill said it was the president who was furious at Stalin's response. Stalin had then evidently re-read the cable and replied in a better tone, proposing a meeting in Sicily of the foreign ministers of the three countries (which did not happen). When King asked if he thought that Stalin would make peace with Hitler, Churchill was more emphatic than Roosevelt that he would not: "They had come to hate each other with an animal hate." Later, he added that if Stalin kept winning, the Germans might open their borders to the western Allies rather than be conquered by the Soviets. He also said that, whatever the Americans wanted, there would be no cross-channel operation before the spring. By then, things might be quite different in Germany. No one could tell. It was like betting on a horse race. He reiterated that he expected great things in Italy. He thought that, within two months, Italian forces, including freed prisoners of war, would be fighting with the Allies while civilians would be destroying rail lines and making things difficult for the Germans. He again told King, in great confidence, asking him not to tell his war cabinet, that very soon, perhaps even as they spoke, three divisions, one Canadian, one American and one British, would cross the Straits of Messina from Sicily to the mainland while another force landed further north. As an inducement to overcome King's

46 James Churchill: *Collected Speeches*, 6816–22.

refusal to attend the projected meeting of dominion prime ministers, Churchill recommended going by way Italy. "It would be a great thing for you to address your soldiers in Rome," he said, revealing how swiftly he dreamed the campaign would go. Rome did not in fact fall for another eight months.

The assault from Sicily two days later got off to a good start. Allied troops landing on September 3, were welcomed rather than resisted by the Italians. On the same day, Badoglio's government agreed to an armistice and five days later Italy surrendered. This was announced as being unconditional, although as Sir John Dill told Mackenzie King five months later, it was nothing of the kind.[47] Badoglio and the royal family fled to allied protection in the south. Most of the fleet (some of which was bombed by the Germans) sailed under guard of the Royal Navy to Malta. The allied disembarkation at Salerno, south of Naples, on September 9, however, faced strong German resistance.[48] Three weeks later, the troops managed to take Naples but further advance was stopped by Hitler's occupying forces. Mussolini was rescued from captivity and set up as the puppet ruler in the north. The government in the liberated south declared war on Germany in mid-October. In the north, the Germans disarmed Italian forces, even putting them in prisoner-of-war camps, while the civilian population was treated like a conquered enemy. A German defensive line from sea to sea through the Apennine mountains north of Naples confined the Allies for the winter. Thereafter, contrary to Churchill's high anticipation, it was a brutal fight north until the very end of the war in Germany itself.

Before all this began, Churchill at Quebec was full of confidence in his assessment of the "soft underbelly" of Europe. He repeated to Mackenzie King that although he had made many mistakes in the past, they were becoming fewer. The loss of life in Italy, he forecast, would be lower than in Sicily. This authoritative optimism led King to agree with the minister of defence and the army chief of staff, both of whom had been pressing for it, that a second or even third Canadian division could be sent to Italy from Britain rather than reserving it for the invasion of France. The more who served in the south, he thought, "the fewer there are likely to be who are involved in the crossing of the Channel, which as Churchill says, will be a very rough business." Over British objections, the Fifth Canadian Armoured Division went to Italy beginning in November, along with a corps

---

47   Diary, January 29, 1944.
48   Hastings, *All Hell Let Loose*, 451–6; Bercuson, *Our Finest Hour*, 295–300.

headquarters, but it lacked adequate equipment for effective engagement until well into 1944. And fighting in the mountainous terrain turned out to be no less perilous than in France.[49]

At lunch after his broadcast, King noticed that Churchill took in a great quantity of scotch, brandy and port. As well as talking about the war, he drifted into the electoral success of British radicals outside the established parties. He thought the discontent sprang from "a great movement among the working classes in which they felt that there was plenty of the world's goods. That science and Nature working together could provide all that was needed for men to have a fair living. That what was required was more just distribution." While not embracing Roosevelt's Ottawa vision of greater prosperity after the war, Churchill at that moment was prepared to admit that the people were justified in their belief, adding that "great care would have to be exercised as to the way in which this could be brought about. He was sure that there would be a more equitable distribution as time went on."

A year and a half later, as the war in Europe was ending, Churchill reverted to the conviction that the best way to increase affluence for all was the traditional liberal prescription of reducing taxes and state control. To what must have been King's discomfort, Churchill expressed dislike of Cordell Hull and his rigid views, saying that if he had not come to North America there would have been no recognition of the French National Liberation Committee. He obviously blamed Hull's presence for his own failure to get Roosevelt to move beyond acknowledging the committee's authority over French overseas territories that accepted it, while the British recognized that it also directed the war effort. The slight US change was something but what Churchill did not know was that the Americans were still looking for an alternative to de Gaulle.[50]

Having had so much to drink after a short night, it is not surprising that Churchill was "rather heavy" at the afternoon meeting with the Canadian war cabinet. Along with him came General Hastings Ismay, Sir Alexander Cadogan and Admiral Sir Dudley Pound, who had suffered a stroke and would soon resign as First Sea Lord. Churchill did not mention the imminent attack on Italy and otherwise mainly repeated what he had already said to King. He also read out the anodyne and unrevealing report on the conference that was being circulated to

49 Bercuson, *Our Finest Hour*, 302-6.
50 Boyd, *De Gaulle*, 146–7; Berthon, *Allies at War*, 287–9.

the dominions. King took the occasion to warn about command of the world by the Big Four powers. This, he elaborated did not reflect any criticism of Churchill and Roosevelt, but they would not be forever at the head of affairs and "any post-war order would have to take into account the persons who might take their places, and that each nation would want its say and that the Dominions would wish their individuality respected." In the evening, King saw the Churchills off to Washington. As the train started, King called for three cheers and Churchill called from the observation platform, "God Bless You All."[51] A few days later Churchill telephoned to say that he would like to return to Quebec to keep in touch with events in North America, meaning Roosevelt. But to the great relief of King, who felt that he would have to be in attendance, Churchill changed his mind and went straight back to Britain.[52]

* * *

The two weeks in the United States marked the last of the many and varied scenes of the conference centred on Quebec. The Churchills spent ten days in the White House, with the prime minister and the president having much to talk about far into the night: the landings and progress of the fighting in Italy, but above all trying to arrange a meeting with Stalin.

On September 6, Labour Day, Churchill went to Harvard University to accept an honorary degree. Two years earlier, as chancellor of Bristol University, he had awarded one *in absentia* to president James B. Conant, a physical chemist and chairman of the National Defense Research Committee overseeing research for an atomic bomb. The Boston visit was not marred by any indication that Conant opposed sharing nuclear information with the British. Drawing on the theme of his yet unpublished *History of the English Speaking Peoples*, Churchill called for a closer union of Britain and the United States as the basis for post-war security. He wanted a common citizenship among the British Commonwealth and empire and the US, based on a common heritage. This was not well received in the American press but such a (voluntary) association fitted King's outlook perfectly.[53] Listening to Churchill's speech on the radio he pronounced it "the greatest of all his utterances." He sent a cable saying: "It will ring down through the centuries

51 Diary, August 31, 1943.
52 Diary, September 3 and 4, 1943.
53 Clarke, *Mr. Churchill's Profession*, 266.

as an ever-present inspiration to the English-speaking peoples from these tremendous times to cherish their common heritage and to realize its highest possibilities
in the service of mankind." King thought it fitting for the declaration to be made
at a university (founded in 1639) that had been British almost as long as it had
been American. Characteristically, he regretted that Churchill neglected to men
tion that he and Roosevelt were Harvard graduates. Once again he bemoaned
his own lack of literature and history, of training, and of satisfactory staff for
such a speech. Liquor might have been the great blot on Churchill's life, but King
conceded: "The question that many will debate is whether stimulants have helped
or hindered his career."[54]

Clementine and Mary Churchill saw a great deal of the president at the
White House (Eleanor was on a six-week tour of military bases in the Pacific),
as they had at Quebec. They recognized his charm but were more impervious
to it than Churchill who needed American support. The decorous Clementine
was particularly wary of Roosevelt, whose geniality must have resembled all too
much that of Lord Beaverbrook and Brendan Bracken, and she considered it
presumptuous for him at the start to address her as "Clemmie." Mary Churchill,
not yet twenty-one but accustomed to the company of leading public figures,
perceptively described his contradictions: "To me he seems at once idealistic–
cynical–warm-hearted & generous–worldly-wise–naïve–courageous–tough–
thoughtful–charming–tedious–vain–sophisticated–civilized." She admired him
and his achievements and appreciated his kindness, but while making her laugh,
he also bored her.[55]

After living in close proximity for over a week, Roosevelt escaped the heat
of Washington and Churchill's demanding presence for Hyde Park. He told the
prime minister to treat the White House as his own for the remaining day until the
Churchills stopped at Hyde Park on their train journey to a destroyer at Halifax.
Churchill took full advantage, holding a meeting of the joint chiefs of staff committee at the White House to increase the number of troops being landed in
Italy. Then he and his wife and daughter and attendants travelled overnight to
Hyde Park. After lunch at Top Cottage, Churchill lay on his back in the sun and
commended God on his wisdom in making the sky blue and the trees green: "It
wouldn't have been so good the other way round." At dinner in Springwood,

---

54 Diary, September 6, 1943; James, *Churchill: Complete Speeches*.
55 Mary Soames, *A Daughter's Tale: The Memoirs of Winston Churchill's Youngest Child* (New York: Random House, 2011), 252–3; Purnell, *Clementine*, 310–11.

Roosevelt toasted Churchill and his wife on their thirty-fifth wedding anniversary. Afterwards he drove the family himself to the train.[56] The denouement at Hyde Park was the final end of the Quebec conference, as the overture there had been its real beginning.

---

56 Soames, *A Daughter's Tale*, 254; Meacham, *Franklin and Winston*, 239–41.

CHAPTER TEN

Churchill on the Brink of D-Day

FOR TWO MONTHS FOLLOWING the Quebec conference, Mackenzie King lived in a mixed state of anticipation and dread about going to London, with a side trip suggested by Churchill to see the Canadian troops in Italy. It would be a great expedition but he knew that Churchill and his ministers would press again, appealing to the necessities of war and preparations for peace, to weld the Commonwealth together under British leadership. King had no intention of undoing his work of the past twenty years, particularly since the decentralized and voluntary association was working well in the joint war effort. The British intention seemed clearly indicated in a broadcast to America on November 20, by Lord Halifax, who was not only the ambassador to the United States, but a nominal member of the war cabinet. King was incensed that he spoke only of British and US armies fighting side by side in Italy and their bombers flying together over Europe at a time when a second Canadian division was landing in Italy and the Royal Canadian Air Force was prominent in the raids against Germany. The dominions were lumped together in a grudging reference to "our Empire and Commonwealth," implying subordination even of the self-governing countries.

King thought that Canada needed to make clear, yet again, that it was fighting as an equal nation. A clash in London had been postponed until the spring, ostensibly because the prime ministers of Australia and New Zealand could not attend sooner. The new time suited King better since it would free him from the part of the parliamentary session and provide international prominence closer to the election, scheduled for 1945. He also hoped that the war in Europe would end by the summer of 1944, as a result of the invasion that would be launched from Britain.[1] This did not happen but the spring meeting enabled King to observe Churchill's state of mind and the preparations for D-Day.

The real reason for delaying the Commonwealth conference was that Stalin finally accepted to meet Churchill and Roosevelt at the end of November. He would go no further from the USSR than Tehran. Roosevelt's main purpose was to establish a personal relationship with Stalin, to give him a guarantee of the second front in the spring of 1944, to ensure that the Soviets kept the German army heavily engaged in the east, to get agreement that the USSR would enter the war against Japan after the defeat of Germany, and to enlist the Soviet leader in the four-power scheme to maintain peace after the war.[2] Three days after the president secretly left by warship, Leighton McCarthy told King on the telephone that he had been "as keen as a boy to get away. That he had set his mind on this trip to meet Stalin and could hardly think of anything else." King expected Churchill would be less eager, "hoping for a chance for John Bull to come in pretty much on his own, not being too keen to have the ultimate victory shared with Uncle Joe. In a way, it is a race between the three looking to posterity and fame."[3]

On the way, and as a cover for the meeting at Tehran, Roosevelt, and Churchill met at Cairo for five days with the Chinese leader, Chiang Kai-shek and his strong, glamorous wife, who was also a fluent English speaker, and sister of T. V. Soong. The president pledged firm support to China against Japan, although not everything was delivered as quickly as Chiang expected. Roosevelt also wanted to affirm and impress on Churchill China's standing as a great power and one of the four post-war "policemen." Churchill acquiesced unenthusiastically, failing to raise his esteem for the country or its leader. His principal hope, once again, before meeting Stalin, was to convince Roosevelt to maintain military strength in the Mediterranean and build on the opportunities created by the invasion of Italy rather than the risky assault across the Channel. Roosevelt was well aware of this and carefully avoided being alone with Churchill.[4]

1   Diary, November 8, 1943.
2   Nigel Hamilton, *War and Peace: FDR's Final Odyssey D-Day to Yalta, 1943–1945* (Boston: Houghton Mifflin Harcourt, 2019), 97–136; Daniels, *Franklin D. Roosevelt*, 367–74; Roberts, *Masters and Commanders*, 420–54; Warren F. Kimball, *Forged in War*, 232–56; Rollins, *The Hopkins Touch*, 299–330; Meacham, *Franklin and Winston*, 245–66.
3   Diary, November 15 and 16, 1943.
4   Hamilton, *War and Peace*, 85–93.

In Tehran from November 27 to December 1, Roosevelt turned his famous charm on Stalin, who flattered the president by taking every chance to side with him against Churchill, giving a sense that the United States and the USSR were closer than Britain and the United States. Churchill had no choice but to accept Roosevelt's affirmation of the timing of the second front, particularly after Stalin questioned the prime minister's commitment following his eloquent disquisition on the Mediterranean. When Stalin insisted on further confirmation by being told the name of the commander, Roosevelt, who now wanted to keep general George Marshall in Washington, hastily decided on the highly favoured general Dwight Eisenhower, the supreme commander in the Mediterranean. Roosevelt and Churchill also promised Stalin a landing in the south of France concurrent with a major Soviet offensive against Germany. Stalin agreed to fight Japan after Germany's defeat and gratifyingly accepted Roosevelt's plan for post-war collective security.

As Churchill witnessed decisions being made between the American and the Soviet leaders, he reportedly said later to Lady Violet Bonham-Carter, Asquith's daughter: "I realized at Tehran for the first time what a small nation we are. There I sat with the great Russian bear on one side of me, with paws outstretched, and on the other the great American buffalo, and between the two sat the poor little English donkey who was the only one, the only one of the three, who knew the right way home."[5] Whether or not he did know the best way home, it was painfully obvious that in order to maintain Britain's standing with the United States and the Soviet Union, he had to ensure dominion solidarity.

After the Tehran conference, Mackenzie King was on a ten-day holiday, mainly at Williamsburg, Virginia, hoping to meet Roosevelt when he returned to the United States. Unfortunately, they did not overlap. King had instead to be content with dinner with Cordell Hull. The Tehran meeting had just been announced (five days after the event) and King, probably reflecting Hull's opinion, wrote that it was, "everything considered, very discreet and wise. No attempt to appeal to German people over the heads of their leaders but evidence of strong cohesion and cooperation between Great Powers both for the remainder of the war and for years of peace." Hull talked mainly about the recent preparatory conference of foreign ministers in Moscow, the first time in his life that he had

5 John W. Wheeler-Bennett ed., *Action This Day: Working with Churchill* (London: Macmillan, 1968), 96 and note 1. The remark did not surface until 1967, two years after Churchill's death, though he said something similar in 1945 to President Eduard Beneš of Czechoslovakia.

flown. Like Roosevelt, he had "tried to foster conviction of confidence between Russia and himself." He, too, had found the Soviets at cross purposes with the British. Stalin, as he did with Roosevelt, made a point of cultivating Hull, who told King that he was "quite interesting and agreeable to talk with. Said he had quite a sense of humour. Would let himself go on informal occasions."[6]

Churchill traveled to Morocco after Tehran, where it was announced in mid-December that he was seriously ill with pneumonia. This was far more dangerous than the bout he had had suffered after the Casablanca conference at the beginning of the year. He also had heart fibrillation (which was not publicly disclosed). Fearing the worst, Clementine Churchill flew to Marrakesh, where her husband spent a month recovering, at first scarcely able to get out of bed. King worried, on the one hand, that Churchill's condition would give the Germans fresh impetus to fight, knowing that he would be out of command for some time, and, if he died, it would be a blow to the Allies' morale. On the other hand, King thought it might induce the Germans to surrender more quickly, calculating that they could get better terms than those that were acceptable to Churchill: "The fight is one essentially between his will and purpose and that of Hitler."[7] King did not know that Roosevelt and Stalin wanted a harder peace with Germany.

On December 17, King's birthday, he was pleased to learn that Canadian churches would offer special prayers for Churchill the following Sunday. He told the press that no one was more needed in the world: "I said he had a lion's strength. I believed that strength, which meant everything to him in the past, would stand him in good stead in the present."[8] Five days later, he received a personal message from Churchill, thanking him for the message on his illness he had sent to Attlee. Churchill considered it a manifestation of their long friendship. He told King that he hoped he was through the worst of the ailment and claimed that "I have at no time relinquished my part in the direction of affairs." But he needed rest, "as a half-timer at some sunny place up here before returning to the fogs and flu of London."[9]

* * *

6 Diary, December 6, 1943.
7 Diary, December 16, 1943.
8 Diary, December 17, 1943.
9 Diary, December 22, 1943.

An indication of the British government's idea of the role of the dominions seemed to be articulated by Lord Halifax in a speech made on January 24, 1944, marking the centenary of the Toronto Board of Trade. King was deeply immersed in crafting the government's legislative programme for what was expected to be the final session before the end of the war in Europe and his next election and declined the invitation to attend. When he emerged from a cabinet meeting on the appointed day, one of his secretaries, Jack Pickersgill, told him that Halifax was going to give a "perfectly terrible speech" in Toronto that night, one that "seemed to go to frightful lengths in the opposite direction to all that we had been working for." Pickersgill wondered if it could be stopped but King saw no need to try. The thousand-strong event, in any event, had all the appearance of a Tory feast. The Conservative leader, John Bracken, was loudly cheered and the Progressive Conservative premier of Ontario, George Drew (no friend of King) gave the fulsome thanks to Lord Halifax. King could not find the broadcast on the radio and fell into an untroubled sleep that night.[10] He was jolted into high alert by a newspaper report the next morning. Halifax had told his audience that Britain's standing as a superpower with the United States, the USSR and China depended on the Commonwealth. Although the Statute of Westminster had given dominions control over their own external policy, what was needed was agreement on foreign policy, defence, economics, colonial issues, and communications, which would benefit and increase the international position of all. "Not Great Britain only," he intoned, "the British Commonwealth and Empire, must be the fourth power upon which, under Providence, the peace of the world will henceforth depend."[11]

King was "simply dumbfounded. It seemed such a complete bolt out of the blue, like a conspiracy on the part of the imperialists to win their own victory in the middle of the war." British Tories, he fumed, had learned nothing since the days of Lord North and the American revolution. He burst out to the governor general, who could not understand King's perturbation, that "if Hitler himself wanted to divide the Empire – get one part against the other, he could not have chosen a more effective way, or a better instrument." If not for the war, King expostulated, he would fight an election on the matter. One of King's

---

10 Diary, January 24, 1944.
11 *Globe and Mail*, January 25, 1944; Adam Chapnick, "Testing the Bonds of Commonwealth with Viscount Halifax: Canada in the Post-War International System," *International History Review* 31, no. 1 (March 2009); Roberts, *The Holy Fox*, 294; Stacey, *Canada and the Age of Conflict*, II, 364–5.

cabinet ministers pointed out that Halifax provided as good an opportunity for the Liberals as Lord Byng in 1926.

Particularly incensed that he had not been consulted in advance on a major speech by a prominent outside public figure in Canada – although he had done nothing of the kind before his own speech in London in 1941, nor had he expected it of Churchill and Roosevelt in Canada – he telephoned Leighton McCarthy to ask if there had been any discussion in Washington. With King in such a rage, no one in the embassy was eager to admit having seen or even heard of the speech before delivery. Pickersgill, however, could only have got his information from there. McCarthy claimed that he had not been involved in any way and read the text only as Halifax was speaking. Later he called back, his aging memory refreshed by the realization that King might eventually discover the extent of his responsibility, admitting at least that he had on behalf of friends in Toronto urged Halifax to accept the invitation. When the British ambassador asked what he should speak about, McCarthy, a far stronger imperialist than King, claimed that he had merely suggested "unity."[12]

The kind of unity Halifax had in mind and elaborated in Toronto was no mystery for a great proponent of the imperial connection like McCarthy. His speech, along Churchillian lines, called for a commonwealth bloc in a world of regional councils. The prime minister of Australia, with the support of his New Zealand counterpart, and Smuts of South Africa had recently said something similar. But in these cases, the hope had been for British support for their sub-imperial territorial ambitions. Canada, with the United States next door, had no such aspirations, save in the case of Newfoundland, which Roosevelt favoured it acquiring.[13]

To soothe King, there was the usual diplomatic backing and filling by down-playing Halifax's speech. Malcolm MacDonald, returning from Britain with the gloomy news that the European war was not expected to end until autumn and the more welcome assurance that he had advised Lord Cranborne, once again the dominions secretary, not to raise constitutional issues at the conference of prime ministers, said that if he had been in Ottawa, Halifax would have sent his text of his address and MacDonald would have pointed out the problems. He gave King a message from Halifax regretting any embarrassment and saying that he

12 Diary, January 25, 1944.
13 John Darwin, *The Empire Project: The Rise and Fall of the British World–System, 1830–1970* (Cambridge: Cambridge University Press, 2009), 516–22.

CHURCHILL ON THE BRINK OF D-DAY

was not aware that the speech would cause distress. Lester Pearson, McCarthy's second-in-command, without acknowledging any prior familiarity with the text but revealing the extent of his own belief in the British Commonwealth, told King that "by the change of a few paragraphs, the speech would have been made quite all right."[14]

Churchill must have been annoyed that Halifax had blurted out what he himself hoped to achieve by subtler means. A week after the speech, on February 1, he mollified King by saying in parliament that Halifax had not spoken with the authority of the British government. The day before, King had similarly told the Canadian House of Commons that the ambassador was only voicing his personal opinion, as a philosopher as well as a statesman. But he did add that Canada could not accept Halifax and Smuts' idea of a balance of power and inevitable rivalry between the great powers after the war. What was needed was cooperation between the major states and all like-minded countries to preserve the peace. A couple of days later, he decided with satisfaction that this declaration against imperial centralizers and the domination of the world by associations controlled by a few strong states was (yet again) one of the most significant speeches of his life.[15]

* * *

This was the vigilant mood in which Mackenzie King approached a meeting of dominion prime ministers at the end of April. He even tried to get the meeting moved to Canada, holding out the prospect to Churchill that it would be convenient for him to see Roosevelt. But with D-Day in the offing, Churchill said he could not leave Britain.[16] A week before King left for London, Churchill sought to put him in the right mood by inviting him to address a joint meeting of parliament. All the Commonwealth leaders were provided with a major event, but none at this level. Smuts, who had given the same kind of speech a year and a half earlier, would receive the freedom of Birmingham, and Curtin and Fraser the same from the City of London. King's distinction was, to some extent, reciprocation for Churchill's speech to the Canadian parliament but it was also a recognition of his pivotal role among the dominion prime ministers. For three weeks, King had been working on some speech he knew he would be expected to

---

14 Diary, February 8, 1944.
15 Diary, February 2, 1944.
16 Diary, February 29 and March 8, 1944.

give in Britain and welcomed this "very high honour, though the very thought of not being prepared and the fear of what I have prepared being not really suited to the occasion, made me feel very depressed through the afternoon. It was like adding a very heavy load to a weary body."[17] It was not, however, one he had any intention of shirking.

On April 26, King took off across the Atlantic in an American B-24 Liberator bomber with a US crew. This was distinctly more comfortable than the trip two and a half years earlier, the cabin being like a Pullman railway car, with pull-down beds. Leaving at 11 a.m., it stopped at Stephenville, Newfoundland and Prestwick, arriving in London the next afternoon. Vincent Massey took King to the Dorchester hotel where, in his own suite, he held a grand dinner in the hope of being included in the conference. The effort backfired, and King made a jaundiced observation that London society had not changed during the war: there was still the same luxurious food, the same quantity of wine and the same banal conversation.[18] Far more in harmony with the sacrifices of ordinary people and the armed services was his rich friend Violet Markham, who lived in a relatively modest house in Bloomsbury, made her own breakfast, did social work every day, and saved her food rations to give a dinner party of sausage rolls for thirty or forty people once a month. During bombing raids, she went next door to play cards with Vernon Bartlett, the journalist and an MP for the Common Wealth party.[19]

King's first visitor the next morning was Lord Cranborne, eager to discover the Canadian prime minister's state of mind. King expressed his desire to be helpful but made clear his opposition to centralism, saying that it would be a mistake to define relations within the Commonwealth too closely or institutionalize them in any way. When he asked about the precise meaning of the much–used conjunction "commonwealth and empire," Cranborne said that it had been coined by Churchill and generally adopted. He personally distinguished between the "commonwealth", referring to the five self-governing countries (neutral Ireland was not included), of which Britain was one, while "empire" signified the colonies and India. King pointed out that since Britain was the head of the latter it counted twice, and Cranborne could not disagree.

Next to call was King's old friend Viscount (Hamar) Greenwood. Pleasingly, he said that Churchill, who may have sent or at least briefed him, was impressed by

17 April 1 and 20, 1944.
18 Diary, April 26 and 27, 1944.
19 Diary, May 15, 1944.

King's close friendship with Roosevelt and was, along with others, a great booster of King and not of Lord (R. B.) Bennett. A businessman himself, Greenwood was amazed at the war production of his native country. Finally, came Sir Alan Lascelles, the king's private secretary, who warned King that he would find many people exhausted by the war. Churchill, in particular, since his illness following Tehran now inclined him to be garrulous and impatient. Touching on the conference, Lascelles said it was difficult to get Americans to understand the nature of the dominions and even some Britons were puzzled about the Statute of Westminster. Confidentially, he revealed that the great question at the palace was finding the right husband for the eighteen-year-old crown princess, Elizabeth. The depredations of the past thirty years had depleted the pool of royal candidates.

In mid-afternoon, Mackenzie King went to 10 Downing Street. Churchill came to the door wearing a siren suit with a white neckerchief. King thought this an unprepossessing outfit and Churchill's neck thinner. Taking King by the hand, Churchill led him to the cabinet room at the back of the house where Edward Stettinius, the US under-secretary of state since September, was waiting with others to have photographs taken. When the session was over, the two prime ministers sat side by side at the cabinet table. As Lascelles had warned, Churchill seemed profoundly weary, soft, flabby, and stooped. King thought his real spring had gone:

> his eyes seemed to get quite weary and to continuously fill with water. His nose seems to have enlarged a bit; to have lost its shape in a way, to be a little more contracted towards the centre. His hand seems steady enough but I felt I was talking to a man who would find it hard just to have to do anything for very long, and whose judgment, except for the great background, knowledge and experience he has, would hardly serve him well.

Churchill seemed not much better than King's old patron, Sir William Mulock, now a hundred-and-one, "whose mind, at times is keen enough, but who one feels is thinking of other things while one is talking." King had the sense that any great strain might suddenly kill Churchill: "He is no longer the man he was at Quebec. I should indeed be surprised if he is spared to preside at a peace conference. Even to see the day of the Armistice. It gives me a feeling of deep sadness, compassion and concern."

No agenda for the conference had been announced and only now did Churchill give King a preview of what was intended. Disarmingly, he said that the discussions would be informal, interspersed with social events. But Churchill and the British government were not devoting so much time and effort amid the preoccupations and anxieties of D-Day merely to inform and entertain the dominion leaders. Churchill said that the meeting would not settle the future of the world but would make great decisions. The aim was the one articulated by Lord Halifax in Toronto: to ensure that Britain in close association with the Commonwealth and empire remained a great power like the United States and the Soviet Union. To encourage such unity, the British would demonstrate to the dominion prime ministers their competence in handling military and diplomatic matters for the whole organization. Churchill told King that the two most important elements he wanted from the meeting were annual conferences of prime ministers, usually in London but occasionally elsewhere, and a standing defence committee.

King did not mar this agreeable occasion by objections, but he was well aware of what to expect. Evasively, he agreed with the need to meet from time to time but hoped that there would be no fixed arrangement since it was difficult for prime ministers to leave their countries. On the military committee, he remained silent until more was disclosed. He did ask about the expression "commonwealth and empire" and Churchill, in contrast to Cranborne, said that he used the terms interchangeably, as in the seventeenth-century civil war, when Royalists described the country as an empire and parliamentarians as a commonwealth. Churchill himself favoured "British empire" but considered it identical to "the commonwealth," confirming that he regarded the colonies, the dominions, and India as part of one unit. So, in a way did King, although he made a clear distinction between autonomous dominions, which freely belonged to the Commonwealth, and colonies which had no choice in being part of the empire.

With so many Canadian troops involved in the impending invasion, Churchill told King that he was entitled to know the time and place of D-Day. But he asked King not to tell his colleagues any more than that he had the information. Churchill thought that the landing would be easy enough, but it would take hard fighting and heavy losses for two weeks to secure it. On a map, he pointed to Italy and the Soviet Union from where other attacks would be made. The combined assault would make Germany "like a bear out in the snow. The heat would be taken out of his body till he has nothing left but a little warmth in his heart," he said, pointing to his own troubled organ. He did not expect the European war to end in 1944 unless the Germans gave up. He also appreciated King saying that one of the most important things he had done was to hold off the invasion for a couple of years, and hoped he would keep repeating it. Many people, said Churchill, thought he was impetuous. Others believed that the second front should have been launched sooner but he was convinced that "we would all have been slaughtered if it had. It would have been terrible." When King asked about Stalin, Churchill said he was confident about the promised Soviet offensive but revealed that there was deep disagreement over the amount of Poland that the USSR demanded. The argument had become so strong that he had stopped corresponding with Stalin altogether: he had "turned one cheek and then the other; and turned another cheek and then the other, until, he said, there were no more cheeks to turn."

King told Churchill that he was in a different situation from the other three dominion leaders who were in strong positions after recent elections while he faced one within a year. Churchill, whose country had not voted since 1935, thought it unwise to call one in 1944: "You cannot be having an election all the time." He judged that King would be able to "put it all over" John Bracken, the leader of the renamed Progressive Conservative party, by his speech to the British parliament. Churchill said that he would preside at it, unless the eighty-one-year-old Lloyd George, the longest serving MP, wanted to do so, as he had for Smuts. In that case, Churchill would give the thanks. He did not ask to see the text, or even inquire what King would speak about but hoped that King would mention the "Old Country" people, who needed all the cheering up they could get. Again revealing his instinctive imperialism, he asked if King objected to the term "mother country," saying that he did not himself care for "sister nations." King pointed out that Britain was not the mother country of French Canadians, who made up a third of the population; nor did the expression mean much to the third and later generations of emigrants from the United Kingdom. The conversation came to an end with the arrival of Peter Fraser of New Zealand for his appointment. Churchill walked King to the door and warned that there might be a "toot" – an air raid – that night. He expected it would not be serious since the Germans were saving their resources for the allied invasion.[20]

* * *

20 Diary, April 28, 1944.

The conference of prime ministers formally opened three days later, on Monday, May 1, at noon at 10 Downing Street. In addition to the four dominion prime ministers were two Indian representatives and Sir Godfrey Huggins, prime minister of what was considered to be the proto-dominion of Southern Rhodesia. Before the session, King warned Cranborne that he could not agree to annual meetings: in 1945 he expected to be preoccupied with a general election and if he was defeated did not think that his successor would want to begin with an imperial conference. Cranborne said that Curtin, who had earlier seemed keen on closer relations, was of the same opinion.

King was astonished that Churchill, who presided at the session, had recovered so much energy over the weekend. He began by saying that it was important at that crucial stage of the war to demonstrate that the solidarity of the Commonwealth was as great as that of the Union of Soviet Socialists Republics, even then not the happiest analogy. He also expressed the desire for annual conferences. King, who was the first to respond, said that he did not wish to begin with objections. He assured Churchill, in terms repeated by others, that "all he had expressed found an echo in our hearts." After five years of cooperation he would discover that the dominions were closer than ever at his side. At that point, photographs were taken.

Afterwards Churchill, six of his colleagues and the cabinet secretary met with the four dominion prime ministers only to set the order of business for the next two weeks. Churchill proposed beginning that afternoon with a review of the war situation in Europe, then moving to reconstruction and finally the war against Japan but at Fraser's request he readily agreed to discuss Japan after Europe. Disclosing his apprehension about the cross-channel attack, he said that victory was certain but it would not be a matter for rejoicing: "There were little homes, little cottages through America and elsewhere as well as in this country that would realize many lives had been lost; must necessarily be lost, and this would bring great sorrow with it." Nothing of the kind could have been attempted in the past two years with any assurance of success. He predicted that the European war would last at least until the end of 1944. Once the ports were secured, ships would be freed to be used against Japan, which he did not expect to hold out much longer than Germany.

Since they would be discussing important military and diplomatic matters, Curtin and Fraser wanted to have their military and civilian advisers at the meetings. Churchill objected, ostensibly because he wanted to keep the group as small as possible and was not going to reveal to anyone other than the prime ministers the date of invasion. More likely, he did not want any disagreement with the professionals. He looked for an opinion to King, who suggested two kinds of meetings: one with staffs, the other of prime ministers only for very confidential information. At length, Churchill concurred. In his diary, King recorded his agreement with Curtin and Fraser. It was impossible for four dominion prime ministers to battle alone against half a dozen well-prepared British ministers with advisers to hand. He also intended to make it clear, even then, that he could not himself bind Canada: "matters of contribution to the war would have to depend on the decisions of our War Committee."

At 5:30 p.m., the prime ministers returned to the map room at 10 Downing Street for a confidential briefing on the European war. This was not only for information but also, like all the presentations, to impress on dominion leaders the skill and wide framework within which the British were handling the situation for the whole empire and Commonwealth. Churchill spoke for an hour, essentially expanding on what he had already related to King: the success in the Battle of the Atlantic, clearing the Mediterranean, invading Italy, bombing Germany, and the Soviet advance. At the end, he described the plan for D-Day and other assaults, which King did not feel he could record in his diary. He did note that Churchill considered initial success to be crucial. Once bridgeheads were established, the hard battle would begin. The Germans had more army divisions than the Allies but would have to fight on several fronts, while the invaders were vastly superior in the air and at sea. Churchill held out no hope of easy victory and King's heart sank at the prospect of the great loss of life. Churchill also mentioned the expected German (V-1) rocket attacks on Britain but optimistically said that the RAF had already destroyed seventy percent of the missiles and would soon destroy the rest.

There was a dinner that evening at Buckingham Palace in honour of the dominion prime ministers. Mackenzie King sat between the queen and princess Elizabeth, who was attending her first official banquet since coming of age (eighteen) a month earlier. Prompted by her mother, she had an easy time with King on one side and Jan Smuts on the other, who told her that South Africa was a much better country than Canada, which was covered with snow in winter. King noticed that George VI had practically mastered his stutter but seemed older and more nervous than in 1941. The Duke of Kent having died in a plane crash in 1942, the king spoke of the Duke of Gloucester (who was present) as his only brother, meaning that he had disavowed the Duke of Windsor.[21]

21 Diary, May 1, 1944

Next day, the military discussion continued in the map room. Churchill was present but left it to the service chiefs to elaborate the themes he had presented at the opening of the conference. Mackenzie King was accompanied by Norman Robertson, General Kenneth Stuart, and Air Marshal Lloyd S. Breadner, the former air chief of staff and now commander in chief of the RCAF overseas. Between the morning and afternoon sessions, Lord Cranborne held a luncheon in King's honour at the Savoy Hotel. King again warned the British ministers in attendance against a new organization for the Commonwealth: "To leave well enough alone, not to create some façade that would only raise suspicion as to commitments." He also reiterated his disagreement with annual meetings, citing the instructive caution of Robert Menzies who had lost his position. All the decisions about the Canada's involvement in the war had been made in Canada and King thought that it would be useful for the Commonwealth if the same could be said post-war. The smooth Lord Chancellor, Viscount (formerly Sir John) Simon agreed, observing that there had been consultation with the dominions but no conference at the time of Edward VIII's abdication, when Simon had been home secretary.

As they drove away from the hotel, Vincent Massey made a bid to attend the conference but King found a ready excuse in citing Churchill's desire to keep the number small. When Massey persisted, King became annoyed at his impertinence: "He cannot avoid putting himself to the fore in everything," sniffed one who never thought of thinking of himself at all. Both Masseys were thereafter markedly cool towards King. Even after his speech to parliament, it was only with difficulty that a reluctant compliment was pried out of the high commissioner.[22]

The next day, the presentation on the European war concluded and the one on the Pacific began, interspersed for King by a private, inconsequential luncheon with the king and queen at the palace. At the end of the D-Day discussion, Smuts gave an assessment and thought that victory would come by the end of the year. Churchill was far less optimistic, saying that if the invaders got the worst of it, "we will just have to dig in and continue the war for another two," or even modify the demand for unconditional surrender. Smuts supported Churchill's argument that much could be achieved from the sidelines, particularly in Italy and the Balkans. Churchill interjected that there were advantages to joining up with the USSR in south-eastern Europe, suggesting that one was to keep the

---

22 Diary, May 2, 1944.

Soviets as far east as possible. But King got the clear sense that the Americans insisted on playing down the Mediterranean.

When the conference turned to the Pacific, King was astonished at the loud complaints of British neglect by Curtin and Fraser: "They speak out from the shoulder quite emphatically." Constantly they interrupted and insisted that the United States was doing more than the British recognized. Curtin pointed to Australia's limited manpower (its population was just over seven million, less than two-thirds that of Canada) and said that if it was also expected to produce supplies, it would have to reduce its armed forces. When after the meeting, General Stuart suggested sending a token Canadian force to the far east, King said that, like Australia and New Zealand, before making any such commitment, he wanted to know how many men were needed at home to produce food and armaments, and he certainly did not want to raise the prospect of conscription. King admired Churchill's self-control during the onslaught from Curtin and Fraser. He promised to send a powerful fleet against Japan. King, whose orientation, like Churchill's, was more towards Europe, thought it better to concentrate on that war: "If it fails, Heaven knows what the consequences will be." After the meeting, Churchill privately expressed his hope that King would stay for "the big event" (D-Day). King said that he could not be absent from parliament for more than a month.[23]

* * *

After three days of military discussion, the conference turned to foreign policy. Anthony Eden gave an impressive world survey, scarcely looking at his notes. By the end, King thought he looked distinctly tired, despite a recent holiday. It seemed, as Lascelles had said, that the British ministers were exhausted, the most notable exception being the astonishingly buoyant Churchill. Sir Archibald Sinclair, the air minister, seemed to King "almost lifeless in appearance, but I recall that he has always had a sallow look." Ernest Bevin, the minister of labour, looked "pretty heavy and worn," as did A. V. Alexander, the First Lord of the Admiralty. Leopold Amery, the secretary of state for India, was "wizened and like a man who had been much crushed. Has lost much of his assertiveness." This was not surprising since his unstable elder son John (who was one-quarter Jewish, though he may not have known it) was championing the Nazis in broadcasts from

23 Diary, May 3, 1944.

Berlin. Lord Beaverbrook, who, in the previous September had been induced by Churchill to abandon his second front campaign since a date had been set for it, was back in government (not the war cabinet) as lord privy seal. He, thought King, "looks like a gnome. There is nothing attractive in his appearance."

Eden's extensive presentation on the Soviet Union produced a long discussion about its power after the war and the danger of communism spreading in Europe and Asia. King perceived that the British leaders were concerned but both Eden and Churchill expressed optimism that the Soviet Union was becoming a conventional country. Eden illustrated this by saying that ballet performances were becoming events more for the elite than the workers, like capitalist countries. He and Churchill also found comfort in the Comintern (the international arm of the party) being in the grip of Stalin, who could switch it on and off as he liked. Churchill exhibited his broadmindedness by saying that he had no hesitation in supporting whatever faction was most likely to defeat the enemy. In Yugoslavia, for example, he backed the communist Tito rather than the monarchists. About China, where the division between Chiang Kai-shek's nationalists and the communists was worse than ever, the two Pacific dominion prime ministers were at odds. Fraser opposed British dismissiveness of China and endorsed Roosevelt's assessment of its importance while Curtin was emphatic about Britain clinging to vital bases such as Hong Kong and Singapore and making no concessions in the far east. Churchill commented that his policy was to ask for nothing and expect that Britain would have to renounce nothing. All the same, he ruefully conceded that undesirable decisions would have to be made to preserve harmony among the Allies (meaning the United States) in the peace settlement.

When Curtin, during the meeting, asked King what he thought of each dominion having a representative in the British foreign office to acquire information, the Canadian prime minister quickly pointed out that, as could be seen from the present gathering, the British would always dominate by a proportion of eight to one. He thought it far better for the dominions to have their own diplomats, and judged that Curtin and Fraser were also "beginning to see pretty clearly the dangers of having matters settled in London." Despite their strong criticisms, they nevertheless expressed their confidence in British policy and King did the same, believing that the present harmony resulted from constant communication with the dominions, not centralization in London. In his diary, King added that he disagreed with those in his own department of external affairs who urged "too emphatically an isolationist or autonomous position in Intra-Imperial relations." Canada, with its extensive and vulnerable territory, needed both the United States and the Commonwealth for protection. The British had a "disposition to defend their liberties as no others" but the best way for Canada to support the Commonwealth was "to avoid the centralization and to strengthen all we can the good-will between all the parts and extend that policy to other nations of the world."

At the end of the day's session, Churchill got to the heart of the purpose of the conference by making an impassioned appeal for the dominions to support British foreign policy whose aim was to prevent another world war. Collective security would require an international organization with force behind it (similar to his pre-war "Arms and the Covenant" campaign). This, he said, would not be easy to create, implying that it required the solidarity of Britain with the dominions. He did not disguise that he regarded China as no addition to the task, but he accepted American insistence on admitting it as a great power. Both Churchill and Eden took the occasion to praise King as an important link to the United States.

Later in the afternoon there was a reception for several hundred people at Number 10. Among them were Lady Lytton (formerly Pamela Plowden) and her husband, who had been in Ottawa in 1900 when King first met Churchill. King was happy to circulate among so many old friends and acquaintances, although his enjoyment was eroded somewhat by the sourness of Vincent and Alice Massey.[24]

At the final meeting of the week on Friday morning, Churchill asked King to open the discussion. This he did by touching on various aspects of foreign policy. Smuts followed with an impressive survey of Europe, emphasizing the risk presented by the Soviet Union and the spread of communism. Fraser and Curtin again interrupted, speaking out against Toryism and saying that the best preventative against communism was showing people that they were getting their share of the world's plenty. Smuts predicted that France, although largely undamaged, would take a long time to recover from the war. Denmark, Norway, and Sweden, he declared, were more substantial countries. He must have pleased Churchill by insisting that Britain would remain the centre of world leadership, "despite what Mackenzie King thinks to his part of the world." Smuts nevertheless afterward remarked to King on the similarity of their opinions and predicted that Churchill would soon be on their backs about "Imperial unity and damn nonsense of the kind."

24 Diary, May 4, 1944.

Churchill's summing up on the day struck King as that of a real liberal, envisaging a post-war world in terms that they had shared with at Quebec. Churchill emphasized the empire and Commonwealth "keeping together in friendly cooperation, fitting ourselves into the larger framework of free nations, and above all having a fraternal association with the U.S. perpetuated at all costs, and finally a world order that would compel all nations to maintain order." Churchill said that each country would contribute to an international military force, which might act as a barrier to the Soviet expansion he feared. He did not hide the fact that he regarded the USSR as barbaric but "cannot bring himself to believe" that it would be aggressive. China he again dismissed as corrupt and ravaged between communists and nationalists.[25]

* * *

Mackenzie King went by car to Chequers for the weekend on Saturday afternoon. He saw the bombing damage in the city but found the countryside "a beautiful and smiling land, birds singing, sheep grazing – nothing to disturb the peace and beauty of rural England." Among the others in the house party were Sir Godfrey Huggins, Sir Alan Brooke and his wife, Lord Cherwell, representatives of both factions in Yugoslavia, and the MP-diplomat-soldier Fitzroy Maclean whose team included the distinctly odd couple of Randolph Churchill and author Evelyn Waugh. At dinner, Churchill voiced his anxiety about the USSR controlling too much of Europe. He also praised the conference of prime ministers and the whole empire in rising to support the war. When he asked how this could be accounted for, King said that it was the product of "British freedom and the British sense of justice." Churchill suggested that King include this in his speech to parliament, which might coincide with a major battle in Italy. (In fact, the great offensive against Monte Casino, which opened the way to Rome, and in which Canadians played a leading part, began the night following King's address.) He encouraged King to speak for an hour and dropped further hints about topics he might incorporate by saying: "we all look to you as the link with America. That fraternal association must be kept up . . . You alone could have done it."[26] But he never asked to see the text or to be told what it contained.

25 Diary, May 5, 1944.
26 Diary, May 6, 1944.

As he so often did, Churchill rehearsed his next pronouncement at lunch on Sunday. This one was to the dominion prime ministers reinforcing what he had already said about the post-war organization of the world that he and Roosevelt were devising. He outlined the plan for a world court, regional councils for Europe, Asia and the Americas, and an overall general assembly. Foreshadowing what he would famously announce at Zurich in 1946, he hoped for a united states of Europe that would help to restore the smaller countries and keep the USSR at bay, although he expected the Soviet Union to be a member. He reiterated the hope that Canada would represent Britain on the Americas council.

King did not hesitate to voice his reservations about this grand scheme, wanting assurance that the great powers would only take over the world for the transition to peace. Churchill hedged by saying that the structure was designed to preserve peace and that there would be plenty of opportunity for all countries to make regulations in the general assembly. King also objected, again, to Canada representing Britain in the Americas council, saying that there were "no differences so unfortunate as family differences. That I felt Canada would not want to take on that responsibility." Churchill smoothed this over by saying that Britain was entitled to its own representation by virtue of the colonies of the West Indies. Imperial preferences, about which he had had no enthusiasm since the 1932 agreements, he now defended again, as he had earlier in Ottawa for their value as "a loose girdle round the person of the Empire so to speak." As King noted, he "clings to that vision of Empire very strongly."

Over dinner, Churchill and Brooke reminisced about Britain's close shave after the fall of France. Churchill said that if he (not mentioning Dowding by name) had not held back the fifteen air divisions, nothing would have stood between Britain and defeat. Brooke, who had been a field commander, added that if Sir John Dill, then chief of the imperial staff, had not telephoned to say that the French government had capitulated, the Canadian forces that were arriving in France would have been annihilated. Looking gloomily ahead to the cross-channel invasion, Churchill reiterated that he was not one of those who thought the war might be over by November 1944, or even November 1945. Earlier in the day he had shown King a message to Roosevelt urging caution in the air assault covering the landings to keep down the number of French people who would be killed. The military authorities calculated that these would amount to 70,000, but Churchill pleaded for no more than 10,000. Brooke told King that the Americans believed that planes could destroy the enemy ahead of the army. Churchill expected real fighting on the ground. That afternoon Lord Cherwell, clinging to his faith in bombing Germany and reflecting Churchill's view about where the war effort should have been, said that if the Americans had agreed to a greater military campaign in the south, the air raids from Britain would have brought the Germans to surrender before the D-Day landing.[27]

* * *

The conference of prime ministers resumed on the Tuesday to discuss the post-war world. Churchill presented the set-piece he had rehearsed at Chequers, vigorously endorsing a united states of Europe and regional councils for the world. Eden, for his part, emphasized the central international organization. King sided with Eden and opposed beginning with local councils which he thought raised the risk of North America, in particular, retreating into isolation: "To keep the world as united as possible the emphasis must be on the central organization." He repeated the importance of recognizing small states and indicated that Britain should represent itself only, not also the dominions, on the world organization. It should have been obvious by this point that the conference would not produce a united Commonwealth policy but Churchill continued to live in hope of a reasonable show of harmony, for which Mackenzie King was the key.

King was treated with great consideration that evening at a dinner in Downing Street for the prime ministers, some of their advisers, and the British chiefs of staff. He was seated between Churchill and Eden. Beforehand, Churchill showed him where a bomb had fallen in the garden and recalled another occasion when the servants were narrowly missed. He pleased King by saying grace – "For what we are about to receive we thank God" – strengthening King's conviction that he was a person of deep religious feeling, even if it took an imperial form. The prime ministers each made a few impromptu remarks, Smuts standing out with an inspiring paean of praise to the empire, which he qualified afterwards by saying to King: "all this business of Empire, unity etc. was a thing of the past. That it did not belong to this particular time."[28]

Curtin and Fraser received the freedom of the City of London the following morning. Mackenzie King (who was already a freeman) was surprised to encounter his old opponent Viscount (R. B.) Bennett at the ceremony: "Just why

27 Diary, May 7, 1944.
28 Diary, May 9, 1944.

he should have been there, I don't know, except as a former Prime Minister of Canada and a Freeman of the City of London," which was surely enough. The two shook hands and exchanged perfunctory greetings. King, not knowing that Bennett had diabetes and was probably already suffering from the heart condition that would kill him three years later, thought his face was that "of a man who must be suffering a great deal in his own mind. Had a sort of cut to pieces appearance, much as I have seen him when he has been very much over-wrought in Parliament. He looks considerably older." King judged Curtin's speech, made without notes, to be excellent while Fraser's showed lack of preparation.

At the luncheon afterwards in Downing Street, King struck a happy note by observing that it was the fourth anniversary of the formation of Churchill's government. He congratulated Churchill and allowed himself a small drink. At the afternoon conference session, Lord Beaverbrook presented an empire scheme for post-war civil aviation and Lord Leathers did the same for shipping. King made it plain that Canada, while it did favour an association of companies in various parts of the empire, would not be bound by any restrictive imperial plan.[29]

* * *

Thursday, May 11 was a momentous day for Mackenzie King, marking both a clear confrontation with Winston Churchill and also his speech to parliament. To the morning meeting, he brought Norman Robertson and a document setting out Canada's position on which Robertson and a junior official, John Holmes, had worked until almost two in the morning. No one was anxious to open the discussion. Churchill and Eden seemed hesitant and even in doubt about what was to be considered. Eventually Curtin and Fraser said they had written statements on their countries' position on the proposed world organization and King said he had the same. Someone suggested that King begin, which he did.

Reading from his paper, King stated that the United Kingdom was entitled to be a member of the great power council but only in its own right and not on behalf of the entire empire and Commonwealth. Canada accepted the war leadership of Churchill and Roosevelt on the basis of regular consultation, but in peacetime it insisted on its own distinct "right of representation, if not as one of the big 3 or 4, at least as one of the medium powers that would be brought into the world organization in our individual position." This was no more than Canada had had in the League of Nations but it was a fatal blow to Churchill's hopes of one imperial voice. He asked King for a copy of the document to circulate within the British government, saying with restraint that there were "parts of it that ran counter to his views." Perhaps he hoped that close scrutiny would reveal some way to reconcile it with his own conception of the Commonwealth. Curtin and Fraser's statements were similar to King's but what particularly dismayed Churchill and pleased King was the insistence of Smuts on "the necessity of each part of the Commonwealth maintaining its own identity but being represented in its own right, the danger of anyone speaking with a single voice for the Empire and Commonwealth."

The tone of the meeting was polite but, as King said, this was hardest battle of the conference, "because it required very straight and direct talking to and differing from Churchill on the things he feels most deeply about . . . [T]he British Empire and Commonwealth is a religion to him." Churchill could not say much in direct response to this solid front by the dominions. He did his rhetorical best, making a heartfelt appeal for collective security that indicated the need for the whole Commonwealth to stand with Britain. He did not conceal that his main concern was Europe, giving the impression that the Americas and Asian councils were simply for international balance (or to please Roosevelt). "He spoke very eloquently of the necessity of Europe saving itself, saying quite frankly that he did not want the polar bear coming down from the white snows of the steppes of Russia to the white cliffs of Dover." This he feared would happen if the USSR was not brought into a union with the other European countries, warning the Commonwealth prime ministers that the Soviet Union was a great scientific (meaning atomic) as well as military power. Also, in order to avoid renewed aggression, "though it might be terrible to say it," he wanted Germany inside a European union within five years. None of this moved the dominion leaders to alter their stand.

* * *

Compared to his insistence on dominion autonomy in the morning, Mackenzie King's speech to parliament in the afternoon was relatively insignificant. It was nevertheless an important public and symbolic event, the first time that a Canadian prime minister had ever received such an honour. In carefully measured terms that he had been working on for a month, and until midnight the night before, he openly broadcast what he had said privately a few hours earlier to the prime ministers' conference.

At the entrance to the Palace of Westminster was a small ceremonial guard of honour comprised of Home Guard veterans of the First World War. King spoke to each one. He was then taken to the prime minister's room, which he had last seen in the first days of Neville Chamberlain's administration. He was told that the 778 members of both Houses of Parliament would be attending (plus the dominion prime ministers, other notables, and even King's valet, John Nicol, who had been pleased to receive a ticket). Given King's fixation on numbers, he wondered why it could not have been 777, which had an auspicious spiritual significance.

Churchill himself arrived shortly before 3 p.m., showing no sign of ill will regarding their fundamental difference that morning. They walked to the grandiose royal gallery with its huge murals of the battles of Waterloo and Trafalgar, and up the central aisle of chairs, the lords on one side, the commons on the other, accompanied by the lord chancellor (who presided over the house of lords), the speaker of the House of Commons, the Deputy Prime Minister (Clement Attlee) and Dominions Secretary Lord Cranborne. Churchill presided, Lloyd George, who was eighty-one and in frail health (he died within a year), having presumably declined. In his introduction, Churchill praised King's long political experience, his part in Canada's magnificent contribution to the war and his role in the "fraternal association" between the United States and the Commonwealth and empire. The address, which King entitled "The Glory and the Dream," was no flower of oratory but its central message was clear enough, particularly to policy makers. "It required a lot of courage if I say so myself," in such a setting he wrote, "to hold firmly to the line I felt would be right and not to be influenced by all there has been in way of pretence and hospitality."

After paying tribute to Churchill, the royal family, the "heroic endurance" of the British people, and reviewing Canada's war effort, of which half the supplies to Britain were a free gift, he got down to the central message. Saying that he was not attempting to distinguish the Commonwealth from the empire, he hailed the entire association as one of free nations by quoting from a 1907 speech by "one whose fame to-day is not surpassed in any part of the world, if indeed, it has been equalled at any time in the world's history," the then-young Liberal Colonial Under-secretary Winston Churchill. Churchill had long forgotten the speech and afterwards asked King for the reference. Only then did King learn with some chagrin that what an assistant had supplied was one of Churchill's attacks on the specific policy of imperial preference. He felt that using the quote was like "going into a man's house, accepting his hospitality and, as it were, helping to destroy the things that were most precious to him."

Implicitly rejecting a more formal imperial union, King told his audience and the world that the war had produced "close consultation, close co-operation, and effective co-ordination of policies," without needing any "visible War Cabinet or Council." Rapid communications made possible a "conference of Cabinets which deals, from day to day and, not infrequently from hour to hour, with policies of common concern." Decisions could thus be made "after mature consideration by all members of the Cabinet of each country, with a full responsibility to their respective parliaments." This, he claimed, was far superior to meetings of prime ministers cut off from their political base. Improvements were always possible, but he warned against limiting the freedom of the dominions and trying to make the Commonwealth appear to be a bloc in world politics: "Let us beware lest in changing the form we lose the substance; or, for appearance's sake, sacrifice reality." The greatest possible cooperation should not mean exclusiveness, and nor was it just great powers that were needed to defend liberty:

> When peace comes it is our highest hope that the peoples of the British Commonwealth and the United States will continue to march at each other's side, united more closely than ever. But we equally hope that they will march in a larger company, in which all the nations united to-day in defence of freedom will remain united in the service of mankind.

The free association of the British Empire and Commonwealth he proclaimed was a model for the reorganization of the world.[30]

There was much cheering throughout the speech and at the end a vote of thanks moved by the lord chancellor and seconded by the speaker of the House of Commons. King and Churchill, joined by Clementine Churchill and Smuts, then walked back down the aisle. Churchill told King that with most of his old friends gone, Smuts was one of the few who had been through the First World War with whom he could talk over old associations. He praised King's speech as "very good, very good indeed," although King realized that he could not have been pleased by it. In fact, sitting behind King and by now increasingly deaf, he

30 King, *Canada and the Fight for Freedom*, 310–26.

could not even hear it, as he admitted the next day when he repeated his approbation after reading the newspaper transcript. On their way back to his room, Churchill showed King the ruined House of Commons, saying that it made him sad, that he did not like the House of Lords (where the Commons continued meeting until 1950). He also said that at the end of the war he intended to lead the National Government in a general election. If that was not possible – if the Labour party refused to continue participation – he would head the Conservatives with some of the best men from other parties, such as Ernest Bevin, whom he was sure he could secure. King thought it would be a mistake for Churchill to stay in politics but tactfully kept silent.

Later in the day, Lord and Lady Cranborne held a reception for King. Among his many old friends and fellow Canadians was George McCullagh, the publisher of the highly critical, conservative Toronto *Globe and Mail*, who promised that it would have nothing but commendation of his speech. The reality fell somewhat short as the editorial took issue with King's opposition to strong imperial union; *The Times*, however, thought his emphasis on voluntary association "a fine and helpful contribution to the philosophy of the Commonwealth and Empire and to the thought of all free peoples."[31] At a small dinner held for King by Anthony Eden, the American Ambassador, Gil Winant, who shared Roosevelt's view about post-war organization, said that he had cabled a report of the speech to the president and thought it would be most helpful to the United States.[32]

* * *

The only item left on the agenda of the prime ministers' conference was to devise a final communiqué, which might provide another opportunity to articulate some basis for future imperial unity in foreign, defence, and perhaps even trade and aviation policy. Before that occurred, Mackenzie King inspected the D-Day preparations in the company of Winston Churchill. At midday on the day after the speech to parliament, following a desultory discussion about post-war demobilization and emigration which neither Churchill nor Smuts troubled to attend, King set off by train with them. Churchill said at lunch that "one of these days he intended to deliver an old-fashioned Gladstonian mid-Victorian speech which

31 Commonwealth and World, *The Times*, May 12, 1941
32 Diary, May 11, 1944.

would be explosive, but which was against the theories about vast expenditures etc." Both King and Smuts encouraged Churchill's stand against statism and public expenditure in peacetime. When he did deliver such a broadside, in the general election campaign a year later, it did nothing to halt the Labour landslide, and probably increased it. King, whatever his personal view, was more prudent about accommodating social welfare in his own election platform.

Churchill, who always liked to show himself to the people, sent word ahead of the train and invited King to share the acclaim as it passed through military camps, towns, and villages. At Hastings, Churchill treated King to a lecture on the 1066 victory of William the Conqueror and, as a bonus, the Duke of Marlborough's continental campaigns. At the military bases, the three prime ministers saw demonstrations of grass fires to cover troop advances, mat bridges for vehicles to cross swamps, clearances of road obstructions, and a sports day. All this inspired Churchill to recall his own involvement in wars on three continents in his early twenties. He waxed lyrical about "the love of adventure of youth, and how it seemed to surmount all fears and to cause men to be prepared for anything." King was more restrained in his appreciation of the romance of war, suffering, and death. At a display of the dangers of booby traps, which included Canadians serving in the British army, he saw on the faces of the young men that these lessons could mean the difference between life and death.

At Ascot, the group was joined by Peter Fraser, who had been in Edinburgh to accept the freedom of the city. General Eisenhower also came for dinner and talk that lasted until midnight. The commander increased King's confidence in the invasion, about which he and even more Churchill still had misgivings. Eisenhower wished that he had more troops to make landings at additional points and Churchill hastened to say that this had been his concern all along. Fatalistically he added: "we must go on now." Neither was sure how high the casualties would be but agreed that the initial slaughter would be terrible. Eisenhower spoke of rockets that would be fired from ships as the troops landed. They discussed poison gas, which Eisenhower opposed using unless it would shorten the war, "say get it through by July." Churchill was in favour since he thought it would save lives. Eisenhower, saying that he did not trust the Huns, was taking gas masks. King's dismayed impression of the conversation was that the war might last well into 1945, and even end in a stalemate.[33]

33 Diary, May 12, 1944

Next morning, the four prime ministers sailed through the 5,000-vessel invasion fleet, from Portsmouth to Southampton, an admiral providing Mackenzie King with a professional commentary. Churchill made another bid to get King to stay in Britain for D-Day by saying that he could show him much more of the preparations. There was much talk about de Gaulle, who was in Tunisia and wanted to know the plans for the invasion of France. Roosevelt, who was still holding him at arm's length, did not object to Churchill inviting him to Britain, so long as he was not involved in the D-Day decisions or anything else of importance. But since de Gaulle wanted to send cables and travel back and forth from Britain to Tunisia, where no information was secure, he was not brought to Britain until two days before the operation began.

Reaching London by train on the Saturday afternoon, Churchill continued to Chequers, while King passed a cultural interlude in the capital. That night he invited to dinner, at the Dorchester, the spiritualist literary biographer Catherine Maclean, whom he had not previously met, in the hope that she would write a biography of his grandfather William Lyon Mackenzie. Being of modest means and living on rations, she was impressed by the roses presented to her and the lavish meal, at which even King drank. (She did start the biography at the end of King's life but died before completing the manuscript, which may have been destroyed.)[34] On Sunday, King went to Hampstead to visit and attend church with his dear friends for the past seven years, the artist Frank Salisbury and his wife Maude. Salisbury showed King a painting in progress, of Churchill receiving the freedom of London in 1943. Clementine Churchill objected to their three daughters being eclipsed by the Archbishop of Canterbury and the lord chancellor, but after discussing it with her husband she assented.[35]

* * *

By Monday, Mackenzie King was in good form to discuss the statement that would be issued from the conference of prime ministers. The cabinet secretary, Edward Bridges (the son, King was careful to note, of the late poet laureate and hymn writer Robert Bridges), had prepared a draft while King was on the

---

34 Stacey, *A Very Double Life*, 217. Stacey gives no source but may well have received the information from the publisher, John Gray, of Macmillan in Canada, who also happened to be his own publisher; Diary, May 13, 1944.

35 Diary, May 14, 1944.

military excursion. On his return, he suspiciously asked Norman Robertson if it contained any mention of a common policy. Robertson said that he had already caught that and warned Bridges to change it to the plural. Churchill approved the communication and left Attlee to chair the discussion since he was going with the king, the chiefs of staff, and Smuts to Eisenhower's headquarters for a final review of the D-Day plans. He had, however, instructed Bridges to show the draft to King before the session began. He observed that it should refer to the countries rather than the prime ministers. He also objected that it did not include any expression of gratitude to the armed services or mention China, although it did mention the United States and the Soviet Union. Bridges suavely assured King that his comments were helpful but in fact no changes were made before the document was considered.

Attlee opened the meeting by asking King what he thought of the statement. Surprisingly, he said that he was pleased. Brendan Bracken, the minister of information, however, objected that it was too lukewarm, vague, and general. His desire for a more assertive proclamation on the eve of D-Day was endorsed by Curtin and Fraser. Another British minister, probably hoping for an endorsement of imperial solidarity, said that Germany wanted to make it appear that Britain and the dominions were divided. At this point, King raised the comments he had made to Bridges about including the armed services and China. Curtin objected as China was not doing much and someone else made a slighting comment but King insisted that Churchill's disregard of China in a radio broadcast had provoked much hostility in the United States: "if they did not want to revive that feeling, they might bring in something about the long resistance of China. After all, China had been in this war for 7 years."

The gathering was quickly becoming a confrontation with Mackenzie King, whose closest ally, Smuts, was absent. Discussion became even more heated over the passage that the conference was agreed on future intentions in the war against Germany and Japan. King pointed out that it had been stated in that very room that even Britain had not determined its role in the defeat of Japan: "That none of us had discussed the future plans. They were not settled at all." Discord was still sharper over foreign policy. Eden wanted to restore the singular imperial "policy" in place of the plural that Robertson had secured, while King insisted, in opposition to Curtin and Fraser: "In our discussions it was settled that our policies would converge. There was no agreement about there being one foreign policy." This, in any event, was bound up with trade and commerce, on which Churchill had told the conference the British cabinet was divided: "How could we say that we were all agreed on all aspects of foreign policy [when] as a matter of fact we were not agreed on that aspect of foreign relations." King held his ground and the foreign policy matter was abandoned. At the end, it was decided to send the alterations, plural policies, including China and omitting Japan for Churchill to incorporate with his literary polish.

Nothing seemed to remain but the formality of approving the finished communiqué the next day when suddenly Lord Cranborne produced a long paper on imperial defence. King could hardly believe it: "Everything they had been trying for years was jammed into this statement," including a joint board of Britain and the dominions. This "really amounted to high pressure of the worst kind in trying to shove this kind of thing through at the last moment." When Attlee asked for King's reaction, he hoped that he succeeded in conveying that it was "a bit of underhand work," while gracefully saying that the statement would be interesting for the various governments to consider. But he refused to give any opinion or undertaking: before making any commitment, the dominion prime ministers should wait to see the result of the war. With much satisfaction, he recorded in his diary that he had fought the good fight and held the situation for Canada throughout the conference: "Where would we have been if [R.B.] Bennett had been in office at this time? What annoys me is the social devices and other attentions paid with a view of getting some things done, to influence one's mind even against one's better judgment." But he did not leave the room in anger, pausing with characteristic courtesy to thank Sir Eric Machtig, Cranborne's under-secretary, who must have had something to do with the defence paper, for his help.[36]

The final session next day was a full-dress occasion, presided over by Churchill and including the British cabinet, the chiefs of staff, numerous senior civil servants and the dominion high commissioners. The night before, King had asked Robertson to prepare a statement of Canada's position as the basis for his remarks. An hour and a half before the assembly opened, Robertson handed King a brusque account of the points he had gained at the conference. King did not think this would help parting on a note of goodwill and wished that he had stayed to work on the statement the previous night rather than visiting Violet Markham: "There was scarcely a cordial note in the whole of it. . . There was no reference to Mr. Churchill's own part in the proceedings. Nothing gracious

36 Diary, May 15, 1944.

or kind in reference to the proceedings generally." While King raced against the clock to prepare something more appropriate, Robertson kept up a chorus that plain language was better than rhetorical embellishment. Finally, King reminded the head of the Canadian diplomatic establishment that it was necessary to show "some warmth and real appreciation of what was best." Continuing to work on softening the tenor of the paper in the cabinet room, he missed some of the opening discussion.

King approved the communiqué as revised by Churchill and opposed the attempt by Curtin and Fraser, and some British ministers to inject more imperial unity. But when Churchill suggested that he and the dominion prime ministers sign it on behalf of their governments, King objected that none of his cabinet colleagues had received a copy or knew its contents. Churchill muttered about "these matters which keep cropping up" but did not persist. King thought Churchill spoke "feelingly, briefly and well" in his final remarks. His own contribution, given his difficult brief, he considered so unsatisfactory that he almost lost his voice. The mortification was all the greater since Curtin spoke well without notes, Fraser read a substantial statement, and Smuts delivered some very fine comments.

There was no ceremonial farewell as the conference ended. The participants simply drifted away. King was affronted that there was "not a works of thanks for what we had done or a kindly expression of goodbye." Sir John Anderson tried to detain him to discuss more Canadian financial aid but King, who had been alerted by Robertson, deflected the matter by saying that he would have to take it up with the minister of finance. Canada's extraordinary generosity was not checked but King was offended that Anderson seemed to assume that Canada had an obligation: "Just because British expenditures had expanded and we had gone on helping in different ways, now it had become a sort of duty to meet a request of the kind." When he got back to Ottawa, he voiced to Malcolm MacDonald his grievances about Anderson wanting more money, Sir Archibald Sinclair requesting more airmen, and Cranborne raising imperial defence at the very wrong moment. King knew MacDonald would carry his comments to British ministers on his forthcoming trip to London: "I said just enough to let him see that I felt no resentment or antagonism, but that there was need for a greater appreciation of what we had done and less in the way of pressure."[37]

37 Diary, May 22, 1944.

A lofty public statement in Churchillian cadences emerged from the meeting of dominion prime ministers three weeks before D-Day. It declared that the Commonwealth was united, "not in any formal bond, but in the hidden springs from which human nature flows. We rejoice in our historical loyalties, and proclaim our sense of kinship to one another. Our system of free association has enabled us, each and all, to claim a full share of the common burden." The world was told that, "although spread across the globe, we have stood together through the stresses of two world wars, and have been welded the stronger thereby. We believe that when victory is won and peace returns, this same association, this inherent unity of purpose, will make us able to do further for mankind."[38]

It is unlikely that Churchill took any paternal pride in these sonorous but nebulous phrases which artfully masked the failure of the conference to achieve any of his aspirations. There was no permanent organization; no imperial defence committee; not even a commitment to regular meetings of the prime ministers. In his six-volume memoir of the war, Churchill did not trouble to mention the gathering and Martin Gilbert's authoritative, official biography only lightly touches on it. The imperial protectionist, Leopold Amery dismissed the communiqué as "a number of moral sentiments of an unexceptional character." He thought the meeting had been "very successful and useful" but "nothing much of a positive and constructive character could have been expected."[39] It simply reaffirmed the status quo. The pressure of war had pushed the dominions closer to Britain and to each other but the dream of a united empire did not come to pass, although the hope lingered after the war. Largely because of King's efforts, there was no rolling back of the Statute of Westminster that year. The conference was as much his as the one in 1926 had been.

However disappointed, Churchill was prepared for the outcome, and the situation was no worse at the end of the meeting than at the beginning. The dominions were committed as firmly as ever to the war effort. Afterwards, when he was confident that he would still be Britain's leader, Churchill trusted that his skill and experience would find some way to persuade the dominions to continue working closely with Britain. While he might have hoped that King would at this point be more favourable to imperial integration, he bore him no ill-will and continued to value him as a friend and ally, not only in continuing Canada's

---

38 "Pledge to the Oppressed," *The Times*, May 18, 1944.
39 Barnes and Nicholson, *The Empire at Bay*, 984; Diary entry, May 16, 1944.

unstinting support of the war but as an important link with Roosevelt. After the conference, he provided his own train for King to visit Canadian forces north of London. For a day, King occupied Churchill's railway car, ate meals prepared by Churchill's cook, and slept in Churchill's bed, while dreaming different dreams.

* * *

There was nothing on King's military tour that could be construed as hostility. On the first day, he met a couple of hundred RCAF airmen and was greatly affected by the thought that so many young men from all parts of Canada would soon be dead: "It makes all the rest, conference proceedings and the like, pale into a sort of outer darkness, as placing the emphasis wholly on the wrong place."[40] Reviewing troops and taking the salute as 20,000 soldiers marched past, he marvelled at Canada's achievement. He was greatly relieved that General Harry Crerar, who had replaced McNaughton in December as commander of the Canadian invasion force, considered that there would be no need of conscription to replace the losses before the victory that he expected by the end of the year. Crerar also agreed with King that it was a mistake for the Americans to insist on the cross-channel landing rather than sticking to the Mediterranean.[41]

King lunched with General Sir Bernard Montgomery, the commander of the operation's ground forces. With his religious nature and austere habits (no smoking, no drinking, in bed by nine) Montgomery was a man after King's own heart. King detected none of Montgomery's enormous egotism but "an almost boyish light-heartedness of manner which was evidence of a free and kind nature, and of one who is sure of himself and whose convictions are founded in a sound belief." Montgomery said that his two principles were to win battles and to save lives. He extolled the Canadian army but was still apprehensive that the officers lacked experience for the landing. King, who was also concerned about saving lives, said that if for military reasons it was better for the troops to be under British command, the Canadian government would not object. Montgomery, like Eisenhower and Churchill, expected a great slaughter in the first two weeks, as well as heavy German bombing of London and other parts of Britain, but he was confident that the war would end by November.

40 Diary, May 16, 1944.
41 Diary, May 17, 1944.

On Friday, May 10, three days after the end of the conference, King went to Downing Street to bid farewell to Churchill. The British prime minister expressed his gratitude to King for help at what he claimed had been a successful and harmonious meeting of minds. King cannot have believed that these were his real opinions but Churchill had no wish to estrange this valuable partner, from whom he now requested the favour of arranging another conference in Canada with Roosevelt. This, said Churchill, depended on "whether the President's health would permit his moving about." He did not elaborate but this was a clear indication that the British prime minister knew of Roosevelt's physical deterioration since they had last met at Tehran. The president had cancelled their intended conference in Bermuda in early April, ostensibly because he was suffering from "grippe," and there was no chance that he would be in Britain for D-Day.

Six weeks earlier, on March 28, Roosevelt had in fact been diagnosed with congestive heart failure at Bethesda Naval Hospital. His blood pressure was twice what would be acceptable a few decades later. Thereafter, he was attended by a physician in the new specialty of cardiology. He was told to reduce his working hours to four a day, to stop swimming, to restrict his drinking, and cut back to six (from thirty, unfiltered) cigarettes a day. He was prescribed digitalis which strengthened his heart but could not cure the condition. He began to sleep more, including in the afternoon like Churchill and King. He was also losing his hearing. In April, he went to Bernard Baruch's estate in South Carolina for four weeks' rest. By the time he returned to Washington on May 7, he had been functioning at a low level for two months. Never again did he recover his vigour. This was carefully concealed and Roosevelt worked at putting up a good front.[42]

Churchill desperately wanted Roosevelt, the best hope of support for Britain, to run for a fourth term as president in November. He hoped they could discuss in person the last phase of the war and Churchill's priorities for the organization of the peace. He may not have realized the full seriousness of Roosevelt's condition. Mackenzie King had not seen the president since before his illness and had no knowledge beyond the public medical assurance that he was in good health for a man of sixty-two. Even the president himself may not have appreciated

---

42 Joseph Lelyveld, *His Final Battle: The Last Months of Franklin Roosevelt* (New York: Alfred A. Knopf, 2016), 72–124.

his deterioration. He denied that he was physically weak and insisted that he was functioning well mentally. Nevertheless, if the president could not come to Britain, Churchill told King that Quebec was a good alternative: a pleasant, commodious and private place, an easy railway journey for Roosevelt and far removed from the pressures of Washington. Asked if the Citadelle would be available again, King leaped at the chance. The United States was not the only North American country approaching an election. He told Churchill that "anything we could do in any way we would be glad to arrange." With this happy possibility in mind, he went on his way.

King's parting from the Greenwoods and the Salisburys was equally pleasing. From the Masseys, rather less so. The high commissioner's final luncheon, with Eden and King, was pleasant enough but on a rare visit to Canada House, King was shocked to discover his portrait hanging askew beside a back door. His first impulse was to take it back to Canada but he restrained himself by merely drawing it to the attention of the punctilious high commissioner. King then intended to please Alice Massey by going to the nearby Beaver Club ("Mother Massey's Hash House"), funded by wealthy Canadians and operated by the YMCA for privates and non-commissioned officers. Suddenly she arrived to announce that he was too late.[43] When King thanked them for their kindness at the Dorchester the next morning, she snapped that "it was nothing but part of the job." King concluded that she was even worse than her husband: "the ambitions of both have no bounds. They have won such a place for themselves in London that they cannot think of anyone else having a position of higher authority."

King left in the same Liberator that had brought him to Britain. Half an hour after takeoff, a fuel leak forced it to land.[44] The second attempt, via the circuitous route of Prestwick, the Azores, and Newfoundland was uneventful. The day after his arrival in Ottawa, the House of Commons greeted him with great applause. He made a brief statement that the conference had represented the complete unity of the Commonwealth, conveyed the gratitude of Britain for the support of Canada and the other dominions, and said that he had never been so proud to be a Canadian and a citizen of the British Commonwealth. Canadian Conservatives took the opportunity of the parliamentary debate on estimates for the department of external affairs to criticize his refusal of an imperial war

43   Diary, May 19, 1944.
44   Diary, May 20, 1944.

council, a centralized secretariat, and a single voice for the empire.[45] King was assisted through this ordeal by his secret and sustaining knowledge that he might soon be involved in another, far greater world occasion if Churchill and Roosevelt decided to return to Quebec.

---

45 Diary, August 4, 1944.

CHAPTER ELEVEN

The Return to Quebec

A LTHOUGH HE HAD HEARD nothing about a possible meeting at Quebec for three months, Mackenzie King was not surprised when in the middle of August both the governor general's secretary and the deputy British high commissioner suddenly told him that Churchill and Roosevelt would like to use the Citadelle a month hence. King quickly agreed, rightly considering early autumn, with its cool temperature and red leaves, a fine time in that beautiful city: "Besides nothing could be more interesting than the questions which will be discussed and to be so completely on the inside in relation to all of them would mean a great deal." With a federal election looming in 1945, following the defeat of Liberal governments in Ontario, Saskatchewan, and Quebec, "the close relationship of Churchill, the President, and myself cannot fail to help me politically."[1]

Again, King had no idea that Quebec was not the first choice to meet, particularly after what Churchill had said in London in May. The two western leaders wanted another conference with Stalin and proposed holding it aboard warships off the coast of Scotland. Once more, the Soviet leader insisted that he could not leave his country. Churchill was disappointed that Roosevelt had not come for the D-Day landing but still hoped to attract him to home ground to ensure that Britain and the empire would have a leading role in defeating Japan and recovering British colonies in the far east. The prime minister also

---

1 Diary, August 12, 1944.

wanted to signify Britain's standing in the post-war world as well as demon-strate the need for continued American financial support during the transition to peace. Without the presence of Stalin, however, Roosevelt, who had accepted the (unopposed) Democratic nomination for president on July 20, could not afford to allow Republicans to charge that he was under British influence. He proposed a meeting aboard ships at Bermuda but Churchill pointed out that it was hot and humid in September. He recommended the more temperate Quebec, for which he already had Mackenzie King's concurrence. Roosevelt readily agreed and set September 10 or 11 for his arrival.[2]

A Canadian under-secretary returning from London told King that this sec-ond Quebec meeting would last about a week and be similar in form to that of 1943, although only about half the number would attend.[3] As at the ear-lier conference, King was not included in the official sessions between Churchill and Roosevelt or with the Anglo-American joint chiefs of staff. But Churchill again had a session with the Canadian war cabinet and military chiefs and King, by virtue of friendship, was seamlessly incorporated into the frank and wide-ranging discussions at meals and informal gatherings between the British and American leaders.

* * *

By the time the Quebec conference was settled, D-Day, the invasion of France, had been underway for over two months. On Tuesday, June 6 there was a loud knocking on his bedroom door at 4:30 a.m. and one of the RCMP officers on duty at Laurier House entered to announce: "Mr. King the invasion has begun. Mr. Robertson wants you on the phone." Alerted that something was afoot, Norman Robertson had stayed awake but did not call the prime minister until the operation was officially confirmed. King appreciated the consideration but grum-bled that he should have been forewarned. In their last talk in London, Churchill had indicated that the attack (which was postponed for two days because of weather) might be in late June and that he would let King know a day or two in advance. King's service ministers were also caught off-guard and only the navy minister was in Ottawa.

2 Roosevelt to Churchill, August 8, Churchill to Roosevelt, August 10, Roosevelt to Churchill, August 11, 1944. Kimball, *Churchill and Roosevelt*, III, 266–7, 270–1 and 272.
3 Diary, August 18, 1944.

By the time King was awake, it was late morning in Europe and Eisenhower had publicly announced the landing, this time mentioning Canadians as well as the British and Americans. The Germans had been deceived into thinking that the attack would be across the narrowest part of the Channel against the Pas de Calais, or even in Norway. Instead, it was over the beaches of Normandy in the west of France. During the night, 24,000 paratroopers were dropped and on the first day 150,000 troops landed, the Canadians on the easterly, Juno beach. The initial casualties were far less than expected – only about 4,500 (and almost as many French civilians) – and by the end of the day King was sharing the general relief that all had gone so well. He thought it a good omen for the early defeat of Germany that two days earlier Rome had fallen to general Alexander's forces which also included Canadians.

The Italian capital was of more symbolic than military significance and heavy fighting still lay ahead in the north. But in parliament at noon on D-Day, Winston Churchill began with an account of this seeming vindication of his Mediterranean strategy before revealing the successful beginning of the invasion of France. Roosevelt was wakened with the news at 3 a.m. and at 10 a.m. broadcast a prayer he had composed in Episcopalian cadences. It ended:

> Lead us to the saving of our country, and with our sister Nations into a world unity that will spell a sure peace, a peace invulnerable to the schemings of unworthy men. And a peace that will let all of men live in freedom, reaping the just rewards of their honest toil. Thy will be done, Almighty God. Amen.[4]

After dinner at Laurier House, King and Leighton McCarthy listened to the rebroadcast, which King pronounced "very noble and well done though perhaps the prayer itself was a little longer than was needed . . . but it was the right thing to do."[5]

A million soldiers, vehicles, and supplies, were poured into northern France over the next three weeks and the bridgeheads were joined in a continuous front.[6] But despite the simultaneous offensive by the Soviets, the Italian front, and in August the relatively inconsequential landing on the French Riviera, progress was

---

4   Daniels, *Franklin D. Roosevelt*, 401–2.
5   Diary, June 6, 1945.
6   Hastings, *All Hell Let Loose*, 532–46; Roberts, *Masters and Commanders*, 487–90; Bercuson, *Our Finest Hour*, 341–69; Cook, *Fight to the Finish*, 118–66.

agonizingly slow. The Germans put up strong resistance, helped by the hedgerows on mounds of earth around small fields that were almost as effective for defence as the mountains of Italy. A week after the invasion, the Germans also unleashed their small, pilotless V-1 rockets upon London that fell to earth when their fuel was exhausted, detonating 1,000 lb bombs. A hundred a day were launched from bases in northern France. About half were shot down but the devastation and the effect of those that got through on the war-weary, hungry population was similar to the blitz of 1940–1941. A month later Mackenzie King feared that Hitler would, in desperation, add chemical weapons and even more powerful explosives.[7] The former did not happen, but the latter appeared in September in the form of V-2 supersonic rockets that carried a ton of explosives. These could not be stopped, although as the Allies advanced the launching pads were forced further back into Germany. Only when the last bases were captured, just before the German surrender, did the attacks finally end.

Mackenzie King did not pay great attention to military events after D-Day, leaving them to the service ministers and military officials. But he was always glad to hear predictions on good authority that the war would soon be over, both for its own sake and to keep the threat of overseas conscription at bay. Malcolm MacDonald returned from London ten days after the landing with the expectation that fighting would end by October or November.[8] At the beginning of August, General Stuart returned with an even firmer assurance of early victory and the confidence that there were plenty of Canadian troop reserves for the duration.[9] In between, General Charles de Gaulle arrived in Ottawa with the same optimism.

The invasion of France raised the simmering issue of de Gaulle to boiling point. Some French authority needed to be recognized by the invaders to encourage the cooperation of the population, including resistance fighters. The obvious person was de Gaulle, now the president of the provisional government, as he had just renamed the Committee of National Liberation. He had insisted on his forces being included in the liberation of their country. Eisenhower, the supreme commander, was impressed and Churchill was highly sympathetic, despite their differences, but he could not part course from Roosevelt who still detested de Gaulle's autocracy and refused to go beyond limited acceptance without evidence that the French people agreed.

7   Diary, July 6, 1944.
8   Diary, June 15, 1944.
9   Diary, August 3, 1944.

When de Gaulle was brought to Britain from Algiers two days before D-Day, he was furious at not having been included in the planning and at Eisenhower's preparing to call on the French to accept his military administration in liberated areas until elections could be held. De Gaulle threatened to withdraw his liaison officers from the expedition and refused to make a broadcast calling on the French to cooperate with the allied invaders. In the nick of time, he relented on both but would not disclose the text of his D-Day broadcast, which was pre-recorded so that it could be suppressed if he criticized Britain or the United States. The under-secretary at the foreign office commented that Churchill, Roosevelt, and de Gaulle all behaved like "a girls' school," estimating that forty of the seventy-two critical hours spanning the landing had been occupied by "all the Higher Ups wrangling about purely imaginary and manufactured grievances against de Gaulle!" But on D-Day itself, Roosevelt extended an olive branch by telling de Gaulle that he would be happy to see him in Washington around the end of the month. A week after the landings began, de Gaulle was allowed to go to the liberated area, where he was enthusiastically received and hailed by the American press. He established a capital at Bayeux and was, in practice, accepted as head of the French government [10]

At the beginning of July, Roosevelt sent a plane to bring de Gaulle to the United States. He received him, in French, at the entrance to the White House. For five days, from July 6, de Gaulle was treated almost as a head of state, although he was always carefully referred to as "general." At an official banquet, the president toasted him as "our friend." This adroit change of attitude was seconded by Cordell Hull, who had previously been one of those most opposed to recognition. In this cordial atmosphere, de Gaulle held his tongue while Roosevelt described his plan for the four great powers – not including France – to police the world. After de Gaulle left, Roosevelt caught Churchill off-guard by announcing at a press conference that he accepted de Gaulle as the de facto civil authority in liberated France, with final military power still in Eisenhower's hands. In the United States, this was vastly overshadowed by Roosevelt's declaration on the same occasion that he would accept the Democratic nomination for president. By this time, it would have been a great surprise if he had not. The two statements were not unconnected: accepting de Gaulle enabled

---

10 Berthon, *Allies at War*, 298–314; Boyd, *De Gaulle*, 158–63; Dilks, *The Diaries of Sir Alexander Cadogan*, 634–5; Diary entries, June 5–7, 1944).

Roosevelt to bury the embarrassment of having for so long recognized the collaborationist Pétain.[11]

On the day of Roosevelt's announcement, July 11, de Gaulle arrived in Ottawa for an overnight stay. After the great gains in Washington and fine receptions in New York and Montreal, he was in top form. King had long admired him but could not recognize him as the French leader in advance of Churchill and Roosevelt. As earlier, he experienced none of de Gaulle's arrogance and was struck again by his modesty and agreeableness as well as his command of English. He was treated like a real head of state, staying at Government House, giving a broadcast address from the arch of the Peace Tower at the front of the parliament building like Roosevelt, and being honoured by a government dinner. In his speech on parliament hill, de Gaulle spoke in English and French, hailed the common cause of Canada and France, praised Canadian forces in France and Italy, and thanked the country for training Free French aviators. At the end, there were cries from the crowd of "Vive de Gaulle."[12] (Some of those present must have remembered the occasion, when, twenty-three years later then-President de Gaulle of France on an official visit to Canada cried from the balcony of the Montreal city hall "Vive le Quebec libre!" and was practically forced to leave by prime minister Lester Pearson who sharply observed that Canadians, who had fought for the freedom of France, did not need to be liberated.)

In his benign mood, de Gaulle told Mackenzie King that he had enjoyed his talks with Roosevelt and Cordell Hull who he thought, correctly, now realized their great mistake in continuing to recognize the Vichy regime rather than himself as the government of France. He said that the more Americans dealt with Vichy and attacked him, the more they rallied true Frenchmen to himself and helped make him the acknowledged head of the French nation. All that, he now loftily pronounced, was in the past: "The main thing was friendship for France, He was satisfied to allow everything to be subordinated to that." What he meant was that France should be accepted as one of the world's great powers. King did not take such an exalted view of France, or, for that matter, his own country. He continued to think that the four countries directing the war on behalf of the United Nations should be allowed to prolong their control during the transition to

11 Boyd, *De Gaulle*, 161–71; Berthon, *Allies at War*, 298–320; Daniels, *Franklin D. Roosevelt*, 410–11; Black, *Franklin Delano Roosevelt*, 936–43; 957–62.
12 "De Gaulle Says France to Regain Authority," *Globe and Mail*, July 12, 1944; Courteaux, *Canada between Vichy and Free France*, 183–8.

peace, after which all states should share in international administration.[13] Within half a year, however, France was recognized as one of the – now five – great powers, receiving a permanent seat on the Security Council of the United Nations.

Although de Gaulle never knew it, he had a good ally in King at the 1944 Quebec conference where this matter was discussed. King was not as convinced of France's grandeur as were his minister of justice, Louis St. Laurent, and Norman Robertson, both of whom were present at the Ottawa discussion with the "provisional president." St. Laurent, abetted by Robertson, even wanted to send a Bastille Day (July 14) message to France saying that it should be a member of the grand world council dealing with the war and the aftermath. King overruled it by saying that it would "certainly be misunderstood by Churchill and Roosevelt" and look as though Canada was supporting France's case to be one of the Big Five before it was even free.[14]

* * *

Before the Quebec meeting, Mackenzie King was concerned, with good reason, about the health of Churchill and Roosevelt. Just before sailing for Halifax aboard the *Queen Mary*, Churchill cabled to say that he was looking forward to seeing King but confided in great secrecy that he had had "a touch of his old complaint." His confidence that "barring accidents, [he] felt he would be able to keep his engagements" did nothing to put King's mind at ease. If Churchill was indicating bronchitis, King thought it might not be so bad; pneumonia would be far more serious. It was the latter, from which Churchill been had suffering since his three-week visit to the Italian front.[15] It was a mild bout but enough to make the voyage uncomfortable, particularly when the ship sailed through the humid heat of the Gulf Stream.

Roosevelt signified that something was amiss by fussing over the accommodation at Quebec and the size of the international press contingent, despite knowing that the arrangements would be the same as the year before and that reporters would not be allowed into the Citadelle and the Chateau Frontenac, which would again be occupied by the military and civilian staffs.[16] King had

13 Diary, July 11, 1944.
14 Diary, July 12, 1944.
15 Moran, *Churchill*, 189 (diary entry, September 8, 1944); Diary, September 3, 1944.
16 Diary, September 3, 1944.

not – which was highly unusual – seen the president for a whole year and, apart from what Churchill had implied in London, had no real knowledge of his condition. To the public, Roosevelt seemed to have made a good recovery from the vaguely described indispositions earlier in the year and to have been in good form to accept, and to actively engineer, his re-nomination for president. He had manoeuvred the radical Henry Wallace off and the safer senator, Harry Truman, onto the vice-presidential ticket to reassure party leaders should anything happening to him.

From mid-July to mid-August, Roosevelt went on a tour of American bases on the US west coast and throughout the Pacific, which included policy discussions with the military commanders. This appeared to confirm that he was in fighting form for a fourth term. In fact, he rested for most of the trip. The highly publicized strategy conference at Hawaii lasted a mere two and a half hours. A couple of alarming episodes were carefully concealed. On the outward journey, Roosevelt collapsed in his railway car at the naval base of San Diego just before attending a military exercise and only hours before broadcasting acceptance of his nomination by the Democratic convention at Chicago. When he returned to the United States, he stood upright, for the first time since his heart trouble in the spring, to deliver a broadcast on an unsteady warship to a crowd of 10,000 navy yard workers. His leg braces no longer fitted, due to weight loss, and during the rambling half-hour speech, he suffered from angina but managed to keep clinging to the lectern until the end, when he was carried below. At Quebec, a month later, his blood pressure was still as high as 240/130.[17] Clearly, what he again feared was that foreign correspondents would report on his appearance. With the Republican candidate, Thomas Dewey, being twenty years younger, Roosevelt did not need any corroboration that he and his team were old and exhausted.

When Churchill and his wife had been at sea for two days, he cabled King to say that they would land at Halifax on September 10, and reach Quebec by train the following morning, with Roosevelt and his wife arriving later in the day.[18] That, at least, was the plan. No sooner had King installed himself in the commander's house at the Citadelle, did he learn that Roosevelt had advanced his train to 9 a.m., ostensibly to welcome Churchill an hour later.[19] More likely,

17 Lelyveld, *His Final Battle*, 173–212; Ferrell, *The Dying President*, 78–85.
18 Diary, September 7, 1944.
19 Diary, September 10, 1944.

he wanted to prepare King for the change in his condition in privacy. The next morning, he sent word that he would like to see King before Churchill arrived.

King complied and was shocked at how much Roosevelt had shrunk in the past year. He thought the president must have lost thirty pounds (it was about twenty, but almost entirely from the upper body). King wrote that he was "very much thinner in body and also is much thinner in his face. He looks distinctly older and worn." Roosevelt nevertheless cheerily insisted that he was better for the Pacific excursion and at dinner that night bitterly complained that his opponents abused him as a "senile old man." King tried to find out about Roosevelt's health from his naval aide, Vice-Admiral Wilson Brown, who said that the gaunt appearance was due to deliberate weight loss. He nevertheless added the disturbing comment that the president's doctor, Vice-Admiral Ross McIntire (the main figure in the cover-up) was very concerned. Brown told King that part of the problem was that Roosevelt did not get enough exercise and sun, but insisted that he had benefitted from the Pacific trip, where there was no shortage of the latter.

Roosevelt had nothing in particular to discuss in the train with King, who considered it a presumptuous breach of protocol for the president to arrive in a dominion before the British prime minister. Roosevelt was "rather assuming that he was in his own country." They conversed about their respective forthcoming elections, King saying that there was a greater possibility of the Canadian Liberals being defeated than Roosevelt. But the president was pessimistic about his own chances. The Democrats could not get people to register and vote and at lunch he said that several states were preventing absent soldiers, who were favourable to him, from the polling. When King said that he was considering compulsory voting and a transferable ballot (neither idea went anywhere), Eleanor Roosevelt thought that requiring the vote would be very helpful. In the United States, the result would have been that it would have enfranchised the black community in the southern states.

When the Churchills' train arrived, King left Roosevelt to greet them. He said how well they looked, and in comparison to the president, this was no exaggeration. Churchill insisted that he was much better. On the drive to the Citadelle, he told King that he had had a patch on his lungs and spent most of the voyage in bed but at Halifax his spirits had been raised by the crowd which he had led in song. That evening, Clementine Churchill confided to King that she was very anxious about her husband, who had been seriously ill at sea. She thought he must stop flying since the rapid changes of temperature (planes were then not well heated) increased the danger of pneumonia. But Churchill showed no sign of lacking vitality. At lunch he downed scotch and brandy and seemed to King "as fresh as a baby." It was "a delight to listen to him talk. He does so in such a distinguished way, not affected but genuine." Revelling in his own energy, Churchill was seriously concerned about the frailty of Roosevelt, on which so much that concerned Britain rested. After a few days of his company, Clementine Churchill wrote to her daughter Mary that "with all his genius" he could not function around the clock like her husband. Perceptively she judged: "I should not think that his mind was pinpointed on the war for more than four hours a day, which is not really enough when one is a supreme war lord."[20]

By the time that King and the Churchills joined the Roosevelts at the railway station, the president had been moved via the recently installed elevator in the *Ferdinand Magellan* to his open automobile. He wanted King to drive with him at the head of the procession, but the prime minister correctly deferred to the governor general. Churchill and King followed in the third car, after the wives of the heads of state, in what Churchill was disappointed to find was a closed car. When King raised the most pressing question, if the European war would end that year, Churchill replied that the military authorities believed so, but he still did not. He praised the Canadian troops that he had seen fighting exceedingly well in France, regretted the casualties, and repeated his appreciation for all Canada was doing, particularly the latest instalment of financial aid for Britain. King assured him that "we were anxious to do everything that can be done. That as far as I was aware, we had left nothing undone which we could have done." Churchill pleasingly offered the opinion that the electoral prospects of the Canadian Liberals had improved. Nor could he see that Roosevelt could fail to win re-election: "Said that it would be ingratitude itself." It must have seemed almost inconceivable that he would himself be defeated within a year.

At lunch with the Churchills, the Roosevelts, and Governor General Athlone and his wife, King learned, without knowing the content, that a message had arrived which was very satisfying to the British and American leadership. It was from Stalin, finally agreeing to help the desperate uprising in Warsaw against the Germans that had been going on for over a month. The Poles wanted to liberate their capital before the arrival of the Soviet army, which had halted across the Vistula river since Stalin wanted non-communist resistance destroyed before Soviet forces entered the city. Churchill was eager to help the Poles by airlifting

---

20 Clementine to Mary Churchill, September 18, 1944. Gilbert, *Winston S. Churchill*, VII, 969.

supplies, after which the planes needed to land and refuel at Soviet bases, but Stalin refused. Believing that the revolt was hopeless and a dispute with Stalin would imperil negotiations for air bases in Siberia against Japan, Roosevelt hesitated for two weeks to send a joint demand with Churchill. Two days before the British and American leaders arrived at Quebec, Stalin had agreed to open Soviet airfields and promised to aid the insurrection. This seemed a hopeful sign of cooperation, not only on Warsaw but for the rest of the war and the organization of the peace. But Stalin well knew that it was far too late for anything but the most powerful assistance for the Poles. On October 2, the Germans deported the population of Warsaw and destroyed the city before retreating. This opened the way for the Soviets to impose a communist government in January.[21]

Despite Stalin's message of ostensible cooperation, Churchill said at Quebec that some communications from the Soviet leader had been very rude, one so insolent that he told the Soviet ambassador he could not accept anything of that kind from anyone. In October 1943, Stalin responded to Churchill's promise to do his best to send winter convoys to Murmansk by claiming that they were an obligation and the prime minister's letter was a kind of threat. Churchill suppressed his anger sufficiently to summon the Soviet ambassador and hand back the offending letter with the precise diplomatic term that he regarded it as "nul et non avenu" (never having happened).[22] Despite all this, at dinner the first night at Quebec he said of Stalin that "there was something about him that he really liked." This may have been designed, in part, to please Roosevelt.

Churchill must have expected the same response from the president when he criticized de Gaulle, who had refused to meet him at Algiers when he had stopped on his way to Italy. But his account of de Gaulle's truculence was interrupted by Roosevelt who said that he and de Gaulle were now friends. Churchill suddenly realized that there had been far more to de Gaulle's reception at Washington and acceptance of his civilian authority than he had appreciated. King and Princess Alice also spoke up for the French leader and the favourable impression he had made in Ottawa. Next day, King noticed that Churchill had made the appropriate adjustment.

When Churchill observed that Roosevelt was now the head of the strongest military power in the world, the president said that he found that hard to grasp.

---

21 Black, *Franklin Delano Roosevelt*, 983–6; Kimball, *Forged in War*, 273–4.
22 Dilks, *The Diaries of Sir Alexander Cadogan*, 567–9; diary entry, October 18, 1943.

He disingenuously claimed that he did not like being in such a position and did not feel that he was. He asked if King considered himself to be the leader of a strong military country and the Canadian prime minister, despite the huge production and military effort of the past five years, more plausibly than Roosevelt said that "it did not enter into my feelings." But after laying the groundwork by praising the strength of the United States, Churchill came to his real point, which was the need for continued American aid for Britain to re-establish its economy after the war. He made the case that if Britain had not fought as it had at the beginning, the United States (and Canada, too) would have had to struggle for its existence: "If Hitler had got into Britain and some quisling govt. had given them possession of the British navy, along with what they had of the French fleet, nothing would have saved this continent . . . with Japan ready to strike." Roosevelt could not disagree and had recognized this at the time.

Conversation at dinner was more circumscribed by the presence of Cardinal Jean-Marie-Rodrigue Villeneuve, the Anglican Bishop Philip Carrington, and the newly elected provincial premier Maurice Duplessis. The conservative and Quebec nationalist Duplessis was no friend of Mackenzie King but he was much gratified that he would bring Churchill to meet his cabinet. At the end of the meal, King saw more evidence of Roosevelt's decline when he had to be reminded by Churchill to propose a toast to George VI, which he did in a rambling manner: "There was [in his toast] the closest friendship with everyone – the same for the King, the same for the Athlones, the same for Churchill, etc. Rather a lack of discrimination. I felt as the President spoke more than ever he had lost his old hearty self and his laugh."[23]

* * *

The second day at Quebec was another informal preliminary to the two official meetings between Churchill and Roosevelt and the joint chiefs of staff committee. It was the Churchills' thirty-sixth wedding anniversary, which Clementine had forgotten until her husband brought her a bowl of roses. At midday, just after the encouraging news that Canadian troops had captured the French port of Le Havre, there was the customary photography session in brilliant sunshine on the terrace of the Citadelle with the Roosevelts, the Churchills, the Athlones,

23 Diary, September 11, 1944.

and King in a variety of groupings. At lunch, King, despite having been his own minister of external affairs for a total of close to twenty years, was acutely aware of being "woefully ignorant of questions on which I should be best informed, when associating with the President and Mr. Churchill." He learned that the USSR had promised to join the war against Japan once Germany was defeated. And he witnessed Churchill putting up a strong defence of British rule in India, which was the main focus of American anti-colonialism. He insisted that no country had witnessed "less loss of life by steel and lead between two peoples," as though, even if it had been true, that was sufficient reason to deny India self-government. Pre-empting the sensitive issue of the recent famine in Bengal, in which three million died of starvation and disease and which he was personally accused of being reluctant to relieve, he insisted that it was owing at least in part to hoarding for speculation, and implied that the population was too large for its food production by pointing to early marriages. (He might have bolstered his defence by adding that Burma, the customary source of food in shortages, was occupied by the Japanese who refused exports to India.) King had no difficulty in recognizing that Churchill was "making clear in the presence of the President and Mrs. Roosevelt that there were two sides to the story of conditions there." The famine continues to be a highly charged matter in which Churchill never appears in a good light.[24]

An argument about India was forestalled by Churchill saying that he and Roosevelt "agreed if the President left his Indians alone, he would leave the President's Chinese alone." When the conversation segued to the blacks in Africa, Churchill seized the opportunity to invoke the prestige of Smuts, who like King stood high in American esteem for favouring self-government for India. He pointedly remarked that Smuts refused to discuss the racial situation in South Africa: "he just would cut it off from the rest of his Liberal views." As everyone undoubtedly appreciated, particularly Eleanor Roosevelt who was always urging

---

24 A severe indictment is Madhusree Mukerjee, *Churchill's Secret War: The British Empire and the Ravaging of India During World War II* (New York: Basic Books, 2010), 81–238 and 265–75. Arthur Herman, *Gandhi and Churchill: The Epic Rivalry That Destroyed an Empire and Forged Our Age* (New York: Bantam Books, 2008), 512–15 points out that the new viceroy in 1943, Field Marshal Sir Archibald Wavell, insisted on Churchill allowing more food to be sent to Bengal, particularly from other parts of India which, overall, had recorded a huge rice harvest in 1943. Jonathan Rose, *The Literary Churchill*, 378–82 presents Churchill's ambivalence, the competing pressures of war, and a reminder that Roosevelt refused a request to send 40–50,000 tons of grain to India. See also Khan, *The Raj at War*, 200–16.

her husband to do more for American blacks, the same could easily be said of the president whose Democratic party contained a powerful contingent of southern white segregationists. After lunch the group went to see silver models of the floating "Mulberry" harbours towed for landings to the Normandy beaches on D-Day that Churchill had brought as gifts for the president and Mackenzie King. Eleanor Roosevelt pushed her husband's wheelchair and King noticed that he was perspiring from what he thought must be weakness but was probably angina. She was anxious to get him to bed for his much-needed afternoon sleep.

Mackenzie King had arranged to have dinner with Sir John Dill so was not present to record Roosevelt's condition and the conversation at that meal, which was attended by the British and American chiefs of staff. Dill was also seriously failing from anemia which eventually killed him in under two months' time. He told King that he expected the European war to be over in November since the Germans did not have the reserves to last through the winter. Dill said that Churchill "enjoyed" the war (the quotation marks are King's) and King agreed that it was "the very breath of life to him." Dill dreaded the now highly probable atomic bomb, which he longed to have "buried in the centre of the earth." He was sure that the Soviets were working on one, but not the Germans since when they had been friends with the USSR they had never requested uranium. After dinner, King joined the party at the Citadelle to bid farewell to the Athlones who were going on a railway tour until the end of the conference. Sir Alan Brooke contributed to King's peace of mind by agreeing with Dill that the war was rapidly coming to an end.[25]

* * *

The next day saw the opening plenary session of the "Octagon" military conference between Churchill and Roosevelt and the joint chiefs of staff committee.[26] With the war going well everywhere, although far slower than expected in Europe, relations between officials were relatively harmonious. But heat was still generated by the American chiefs' resistance to the continued British pressure for an offensive from "the armpit" (Churchill's term) of the Adriatic to Vienna, and

25 Diary, September 12, 1944.
26 Hamilton, *War and Peace*, 333–67; Daniels, *Franklin D. Roosevelt*, 420–2; Lelyveld, *His Final Battle*, 208–12; Roberts, *Masters and Commanders*, 512–26; Hastings, *Finest Years*, 510–13; Dilks, *The Great Dominion*, 309–55; Woolner, *The Second Quebec Conference Revisited*.

their persistence in demanding a leading role, particularly for the Royal Navy, in the war against Japan and the recovery of British colonies. The Americans continued to contend that they were not fighting for the British, the Dutch, the French, or any other empire. But Roosevelt, probably realizing that the British could in any event not manage a huge contribution, overlooked his own anti-imperialism and agreed to accept help in the Pacific, leaving it to the military to work out the contentious details of co-operation.

Mackenzie King, at the same time, discussed with his war cabinet Canada's role against Japan. He had no hesitation about fighting the enemy but, equally, had no interest in helping to recapture British colonies in "what would be termed Imperial wars. Our people, I know, would never agree to paying our taxes for Canadian troops fighting whether in the air or at sea or on land for the protection of [the British position in] India, the recovery of Burma and Singapore." Nor did he intend to allow the Pacific war to raise the dread fear of overseas conscription. He proposed restricting Canada's contribution to north of the Philippines, the only British colony there being Hong Kong where Canadian troops had fallen in 1941. After some dissent from a couple of particularly pro-British ministers, who wanted a broader commitment, this decision was conveyed to the Canadian service chiefs. While the cabinet was deliberating, word arrived that the Americans and British had agreed to fight together, removing the awkwardness of Canada having to choose which one its forces would join.

That evening, Mackenzie King escorted Clementine Churchill and Eleanor Roosevelt (who left the next day, partly to prepare for the Churchills at Hyde Park) to a Canadian government supper for the military and civilian staffs at Chateau Frontenac. When they left the Citadelle, Roosevelt and Churchill were dining with the US Treasury Secretary Henry Morgenthau, Lord Cherwell, Lord Moran and others. When the King party returned from the hotel two and a half hours later, at 11:30 p.m., the others were still at table and both wives insisted that their husbands go to bed.[27] King did not know it but they had been talking about Morgenthau's plan to prevent Germany causing another war not only by disarmament but by dismantling its industry, closing its mines, and returning it to an agricultural economy. Roosevelt had been persuaded by Morgenthau before going to Quebec but Churchill was strenuously opposed until Cherwell, whom he trusted on such matters, argued that eliminating this powerful industrial

27 Diary, September 13, 1944.

competitor would help Britain's recovery from the war. Even more importantly in regard to changing Churchill's mind was Morgenthau's offer of generous aid to help Britain out of its practical bankruptcy. On the treasury secretary's recommendation, Roosevelt agreed to prolong lend-lease until the end of the war against Japan (which was expected to last into 1946), with $3.5 billion for munitions, $3 billion for other supplies, and permission for Britain to revive its export industries rather than being forced to continue concentrating on war production.

The following day, the two leaders initialled the Morgenthau plan to "pastoralize" Germany. This was strongly opposed by Anthony Eden, Cordell Hull, and Henry Simson who argued that a peaceful and prosperous Europe could not be built by imposing on the defeated country terms that were even harder than those after the First World War. The scheme was soon quietly abandoned. So was extended aid to Britain, following Roosevelt's re-election in November. Members of his administration, the armed services, and, most importantly Congress objected that this went well beyond the intent of lend-lease. Aid did continue at a reduced level after the defeat of Germany but was sudden cancelled when Japan surrendered. At Quebec, however, Churchill could tell his secretary that the American financial promises were "beyond the dreams of justice."[28]

* * *

Buoyed by Roosevelt's apparent guarantees that the United States would sustain Britain economically, Churchill was in fine form at the meeting with Canadians next day. When King explained to his war cabinet the political reasons for restricting Canada's military involvement to the northern Pacific, Churchill waved away any need for Canadians to be involved in tropical regions, which was one way of putting it. When the military chiefs joined the discussion, Churchill reiterated his comments and seemed to King to take the view that Canadian forces "would hardly be needed at all. Certainly he pressed for nothing and asked for nothing." When King suggested that Canada should conserve its strength, as in Europe, for the last phase of the war against Japan, Churchill readily concurred

---

28 John Colville, *The Fringes of Power: Downing Street Diaries 1939–1955* (London: Hodder and Stoughton, 1985), 515. (Diary entry, September 14, 1944); Clarke, *The Last Thousand Days of the British Empire*, 47–66; Lelyveld, *His Final Battle*, 210–11; Leon Martel, *Lend-Lease, Loans, and the Coming of the Cold War: A Study of the Implementation of Foreign Policy* (Boulder, CO: Westview Press, 1979), 86–8.

and pointedly asked Air Marshal Sir Charles Portal, the chief of the RAF, why he was placing such a heavy burden on Canadians. Portal said that this was what Canada's military mission in Britain wanted. This was news to King who responded that his government had never agreed to a large commitment in the far east.

King was even more pleased by Churchill saying that after the defeat of Germany, Canada's role in the transition to peace could be other than military: "all that would be expected in the light of our past contribution would be assisting in the policing of Europe for a time." The Germans themselves, said Churchill, were well suited to keeping their own order: "They were a race that loved that sort of thing." All the Allies would need was fortified bases in various cities: "If there was any difficulty, [the troublemakers] could be threatened with a local bombardment. If the difficulty kept up they could be given an effective one from the skies. He did not contemplate continued active fighting."

When King prompted Churchill to tell the group how long the European war would last, he repeated that, contrary to military opinion, his judgement was that it would last through the winter. Even then there might be no real conclusion: "it would drag on with resistance in different places. Hitler and his cronies knew that their lives were at stake and would fight to the bitter end." At some point, Churchill thought that the Allies would have to decide that the war was won except for "mopping up groups here and there." At the end of the session, Churchill delivered an eloquent tribute to King and Canada's war contribution, including air pilot training, but above all finance. King returned the compliment and Churchill shook hands across the table with "My dear old friend."

In the afternoon of this love feast, King and Churchill went across the street from the Citadelle to the legislature to meet Premier Duplessis and his ministers. Riding in Roosevelt's open car, Churchill, as usual, enjoyed greeting those who happened to be about. (No notice had been given.) In his welcome, Duplessis declared that nowhere was more loyal (presumably to Britain) than Quebec. Since the ministry had changed since his last visit, Churchill remarked that British institutions gave governments of different political shades their opportunity, but the problems remained the same. Reviewing the events of the past year, he emphasized the liberation of France and imminent victory in Europe. When Duplessis called on the prime minister of Canada to speak, King tactfully testified that throughout the war he had been able to assure Churchill that "all the provinces of Canada were united in the determination to see the Nazis destroyed, but while inevitable differences existed here and there, we were all at one in our determination to see victory." In a rare access of wit, King, who had given a rousing lunchtime speech to the party faithful at the (Liberal) Reform Club, said that he did not often get "a chance to convert the heathen. I added that perhaps I'd better not continue speaking too long lest I might succeed, and therefore impose on Mr. Duplessis by taking advantage of his hospitality."

In the car, King and Churchill talked about their respective elections after the end of the war in Europe. Churchill did not think it accorded with democratic principles to prolong the 1935 parliament any longer than necessary. He now expected that the Labour party would insist (as it did) on leaving the coalition and said he did not regret a straight party contest. He believed that he would be returned (carrying the Conservative party that he had so criticized before the war). He would then form another political coalition to deal with domestic problems, blithely ignoring that his own party might object to working with others if it had a majority. He said that he would stay in office for at least a year, until Japan was beaten and demobilization complete. King privately doubted that he would be able to remain so long, "for reasons of health if no other, but to look at him today one would think he was a boy."

King told Churchill that he should not postpone leaving for too long and should concentrate on writing his account of the war. Churchill was conscious enough of this lucrative literary opportunity and securing his reputation by being the first in the field to publish his version, but he was even more interested in directing affairs. Perhaps he thought that he could, as before, combine writing and political office in peacetime. He told King that the story of the war was practically all in his papers (from the very beginning, regular summaries of documents had been kept) and "except to give it a certain turn, there was nothing he could tell that would not be known in that way."

In Canada, Churchill flatteringly repeated that King's electoral chances were better than a year earlier. He thought that John Bracken, the Progressive Conservative leader, was finished and found it extraordinary that he was still not even a member of parliament. He then made the astonishing offer to come to Canada to make speeches on behalf of King if that would be useful. Intervening in a Canadian election on behalf of the Liberals would have been enough to turn the Conservatives into republicans. King could not possibly countenance the idea or reconcile it with his strongly held position that the dominions were independent countries voluntarily linked to Britain and each other. He deflected the proposal by telling Churchill had that he had already said things that were more helpful than speeches: "the tributes he had paid me were greater I believed than any man could have received from another." But Churchill's offer demonstrates how important he considered King personally to be, in peace as well as war, and how strong the bond between them was.

At dinner that night, King, Churchill, Roosevelt, Morgenthau, and Cherwell were joined by Sir Alexander Cadogan, who came from Washington where he was engaged in discussions to establish a permanent organization for the allied United Nations, and Anthony Eden, who arrived by an eighteen-hour flight from Britain. The conversation did not break any new ground but King, who arrived before the others, had a good chance to talk with Roosevelt, as he mixed cocktails, about Canada's part in the war against Japan. Roosevelt concurred with Churchill that it was sufficient for Canada to fight only in the northern Pacific. Wanting to keep that operation primarily in American hands, he thought that Canada need supply only token representation, although at the very end Canadian help might be useful in driving the Japanese out of northern China. This was a great relief to King, for the cost in lives, the recovery of colonies issue, and conscription.

The 1944 Quebec Conference was the only one of Roosevelt's throughout the war that Harry Hopkins did not attend. Churchill was much concerned about the absence of this reliable ally but Hopkins was recovering from an operation that someone said at dinner had removed a yard of his plumbing. That was only part of it. His unparalleled influence with the president had been waning since the end of 1943 when he and his wife and daughter had moved out of the White House. He was no longer constantly available whenever Roosevelt wanted to talk policy, or simply enjoy his company. The charge of Roosevelt's opponents that Hopkins was too pro-British was probably also an important reason to exclude him from this meeting less than two months before the presidential election.

In his place, Hopkins sent a movie that was shown after dinner. Even Mackenzie King, who had a high tolerance for mawkishness, felt sorry for the president, who sat beside him, having to endure *Hail the Conquering Hero* until midnight. The sentimental comedy depicted a US serviceman being welcomed home from the Pacific in the mistaken assumption that he was a hero; in the end, his honesty and small town virtues triumph. King again noticed Roosevelt mopping sweat from his brow, almost certainly from angina rather than mind-numbing boredom. Churchill left for part of the film, not for the remainder and not from dislike as is usually said, but to take a telephone call from the Duke of Windsor who was in New York (where the duchess was having an operation). Roosevelt told King that the duke, whom he referred to as "David," was trying to get an appointment in Washington but he had told Windsor that he could not possibly accept a former British monarch.[29]

* * *

King scarcely saw Churchill and Roosevelt the next day but unexpectedly found himself involved in a matter that concerned them. In the morning, J. W. McConnell, the owner of the (Liberal) *Montreal Star*, telephoned to say that McGill University, of which he was a governor, would like to confer honorary degrees on the president and the British prime minister. The only possible time was the following day. King went to the Citadelle to get their agreement at the end of lunch, which had lasted until 4 p.m. Beforehand, and throughout the meal, they, and some of their advisors had a discussion that was characterized by the punctilious civil servant, Sir Alexander Cadogan, as rambling "on a variety of things. It is quite impossible to do business this way." Whenever Cadogan tried to get the president and prime minister to focus on plans for the organization of the United Nations, "they always wandered away."[30] They were more prompt in response to Mackenzie King's request. Churchill thought it would be "a nice little ceremony" and the president eventually agreed to holding it at 3 p.m., just before he left. Once this was settled, the president of the Canadian Pacific Railway obligingly provided a special train for the university representatives, which King insisted be limited to fifteen. McConnell sweetened the occasion by providing a cheque for £5,000 for Clementine Churchill's war work. (At the previous year's conference, he had donated a similar £2,000 which she gave to the YMCA in Canada and elsewhere).[31]

The short university ceremony was held in warm sunshine on the terrace of the Citadelle after lunch. The academic gown provided for Churchill was so absurdly small that King (who already had an honorary degree from McGill) insisted on exchanging it for his own. Roosevelt said briefly that the honour reflected a closer bond with Canada. Churchill, in a somewhat longer speech, articulated eloquently and passionately the significance of the war and the way in which it had bought Britain and the United States together. King added to

29 Diary, September 14, 1944.
30 Dilks, *The Diaries of Sir Alexander Cadogan 1938–1945*, 665; Diary entry, September 15, 1944.
31 Diary, September 15, 1944.

the honours of the closing courtesies by providing Roosevelt and Churchill with a specially bound and inscribed copy of Emil Ludwig's biographical sketch of King.

The press conference followed immediately the degree ceremony on the terrace. Mackenzie King presided between the American and British leaders, confronting two hundred reporters who had been waiting all week for some real news. All they learned was the unsurprising determination to concentrate on Japan after the defeat of Germany. Roosevelt made a few comments on the Pacific war, the pleasantness of the meeting and thanked Canada for its hospitality. Churchill spoke at greater length and in entertaining tones, pointing to the great progress of the war since the last Quebec conference, asserting that Britain would take a major part in the defeat of Japan, testifying to Canada's eagerness to participate as well, and proclaiming the importance of personal discussions on a range of issues. There was no formal communiqué and with so little to report, one Canadian newspaper took refuge in telling its readers: "Action to Speak for Quebec."[32] King thanked the journalists for their cooperation and encouraged their goodwill by inviting them all to dinner that night at the Chateau Frontenac. At this festive event, the RCAF band played, King shook hands with everyone, and the well-oiled reporters expressed their gratitude by singing "For He's A Jolly Good Fellow."

After the press conference, King and the governor general rode with Roosevelt in his car to the train. The time had not been announced and not many people were on the streets. King again noted that Roosevelt "certainly has not the grasp that he had a year ago. He looks very tired." In the railway car, his face was flushed as he was moved from his wheelchair to a large arm chair, in which he seemed even more frail.[33] The next day, seeing the US flag gone from its pole at the Citadelle, King wondered if it was an omen that Roosevelt might be the first of the three to die, "though I might well be the first myself or Churchill." It was the last time that the three met.

* * *

32 *Globe and Mail*, September 18, 1944. Churchill's statement is reprinted in Dilks, *The Great Dominion*, 343–4.
33 Diary, September 16, 1945.

Mackenzie King must have been one of the few to attend the journalists' dinner not suffering a hangover the next (Sunday) morning. He escorted Clementine Churchill to the Anglican cathedral, where he experienced the displeasure of being greeted and overshadowed by Lord Athlone and Princess Alice. Worst of all was the governor general saying loftily, as he and his wife left after the service, that he was glad that King (a Presbyterian whose denominational church was close by) "had come along." As so often, the prime minister claimed not to be personally offended but he resented the implication that he was butting in and his position was being blotted out by those from another land: "I cannot get rid of the feeling of resentment at Englishmen coming here and holding in the eyes of any body of Canadians a place more honourable or worthy than that of those who have been born in Canada itself and are their chosen representatives." He had a sudden revelation that the Athlones wanted to be more prominent than at the 1943 conference in order to emphasize "before the Americans and people of England and others the place which privileged position and the Crown continues to hold in Canada."

In this sour mood, King extended his indictment to Roosevelt for referring to the dominions as being under Churchill and "his love for Crowned heads and the importance he attaches to crowned heads and the like and his love to make apparent his position of equality with them . . . It is a bad alloy which a man with real love of the people should not possess." The supposed cathedral snub, like many similar ones, continued to fester in King's mind. When he raised it with the governor general a month later, Athlone protested that he had been expressing pleasure at King's presence and thought that Churchill should have come as well.[34] It was some consolation at the time that, after the Athlones left the cathedral, King and Clementine Churchill were finely received by the congregation and others in the forecourt.

Even more pleasing on their return to the Citadelle was a hand written letter, "as fine a letter as I have received from anyone," from Churchill thanking King for the Ludwig biography. King was glad that he had declined the Quebec lieutenant governor's invitation to lunch, without even knowing that it was in honour of the Athlones. Instead, he joined the Churchills, whose guests included Eden, Cherwell, Prince Otto of Austria, who was lobbying for the restoration of the monarchy, and colonel F. W. Clarke, whose fishing lodge Churchill had visited

34 Diary, October 16, 1944.

the previous year. When Eden said that he was flying back to Britain that day, Churchill, addressing primarily Clementine, said that he was determined not to be prevented from flying. He spoke about the luxurious aircraft that were being built for himself and Roosevelt and, while unconvincingly claiming to dislike planes, internal combustion engines, and "all that made for the conditions that we have today," saw no reason to be denied their benefits. He was not going to give up everything from fear of dying.

Churchill's deprecation of modern times reminded King that only a few nights earlier he himself had said that he was glad that the era of Jane Austen was gone: "It was an age that put its emphasis on wealth, it was wholly wrong. He hoped nothing of the kind would ever return." Still smarting from Athlone's slight, King was happy to be invited to the Churchills' final dinner before they left for Hyde Park. Churchill, he observed, was "exceedingly thoughtful in that way," unlike some Britons King could have named, "never failing to extend an invitation."

Clementine Churchill persuaded King at dinner to have a glass of champagne in honour of the occasion. He noticed that Churchill presided like the father of a family. Seldom had King seen him "in a more placid, quiet and in a thoroughly contented mood." With Roosevelt gone, Churchill talked freely about de Gaulle, who he said he distrusted and considered at heart an enemy of Britain, although granting he had more ability than Giraud and much popular appeal. He also spoke of the recent allied advance into the Netherlands (which was soon halted until the spring) and the magnificent fighting of Canadians; he regretted their losses and touched glasses across with King's in tribute. King once more observed that the war had drawn the British Empire closer together, "owing to the fact that we all felt a special pride in having gone into the war, voluntarily from the very beginning." Churchill insisted on "our" (meaning the empire) not desiring an acre of land or additional power, "but fighting simply for the maintenance of our honour and the preservation of freedom." King recalled that it was forty-four years since they had first met. As Churchill prepared to leave, King lifted his glass and said, "God bless, guard and guide you." Churchill's eyes filled with tears. He put his arm in King's and spoke of their years together, "how faithful a friend I have been; of the little dance we had together at Chequers. I told him if spared we would have another in the days of Victory." Arm in arm, they went to the map room for the latest news about the European fronts.

Just before 10 p.m., the Churchills proceeded to the railway station in a small car, King sitting between them. Churchill spoke of the historic signifi-cance of the two Quebec conferences and hoped that there would be a plaque to commemorate them.[35] To King's surprise, probably to encourage his goodwill, Churchill said that he agreed entirely that the dominions should completely direct their own affairs: "The relationship must be one of co-operation not central-ization." They were also in harmony that an imperial war cabinet would have been a mistake, recalling Robert Menzies's desire to replace Churchill and his attempt to involve King in the scheme. King repeated his assurance that as long as the dominions were consulted and could comment on policies before they were settled, it was better for the world to leave the war leadership to the British prime minister and American president. He proudly added, giving hostages to fortune, as it soon turned out, that there had not been a single difference between the Canadian military and the civilian power.

As the train left the station, the crowd sang "Auld Lang Syne" and Churchill reached over the railing of the observation deck to shake hands with King. He was struck by the vitality of both Churchills in contrast to Roosevelt who had looked so shrunken and whose legs were so weak as he sat in the armchair in his railway car that he could not keep them together.[36]

* * *

By the time the Churchills arrived at Hyde Park the next morning, Roosevelt had had a day to recover from Quebec. Among the other guests was the Duke of Windsor who had come from New York, still pestering to be rescued from the Bahamas. Churchill was far more delighted by the presence of Harry Hopkins, apparently now well recovered from his operation. He admitted to Churchill that his standing with the president was not what it had been, although it rose again as Morgenthau's fell, in the criticism of his plan to dismantle German industry. In the Churchills' two days at Hyde Park there were picnics, leisurely meals, and much relaxation. But, as in 1943, it was also the important last act of the Quebec conference. The main topic this time was atomic research.

Scientists now predicted that a bomb would be developed within a year. Niels Bohr, the refugee Danish physicist and a key figure in the project, wanted interna-tional control of atomic weapons. He had urged the case directly to Churchill in

35 Half a century later, a memorial was erected at the entrance to the Citadelle, with busts of Churchill and Roosevelt. A sign about the meetings of the chiefs of staff had been placed much earlier on the Chateau Frontenac.
36 Diary, September 17, 1944.

May and to Roosevelt in August, saying that their Soviet ally should be told about Anglo-American progress. The president in his affable way seemed agreeable but Churchill was furious. He considered the Anglo-American nuclear monopoly a great strength, an assurance of close harmony between the two countries and a means to guarantee world peace by intimidating the USSR into curbing its own ambitions and playing its part in policing other countries. He suspected Bohr of subverting this by giving nuclear information to the Soviets. At Hyde Park, Churchill persuaded Roosevelt to initial with him a secret agreement that he had almost certainly drafted. The two leaders agreed that they would not reveal atomic research to any other country; that they might use an atomic bomb against Japan (victory over Germany was expected before one would be created); that they would continue to cooperate fully on both military and commercial atomic matters until the defeat of Japan; and that Bohr would be watched to ensure that he was not passing secrets to the Soviets. Roosevelt agreed because he thought that an atomic partnership would strengthen Britain as one of the post-war world policemen, the same reason he had promised to continue lend-lease at Quebec and was relenting in his opposition to the British Empire.[37]

Churchill did not realize it, but it was not Bohr but British and American scientists who were informing the Soviets about atomic research. There was also an important Canadian link, which Mackenzie King knew nothing about, although it was based almost next door to Laurier House. In the autumn of 1942, Canada and the USSR had established diplomatic relations, principally to help with Canadian war supplies to the Soviet Union. Canada sent as its minister the very best qualified person, the fifty-year-old Dana Wilgress, the deputy minister of trade and commerce. In the Great War, he had been a trade commissioner in Russia, learned the language, and married the daughter of a Swiss engineer and a Russian mother. In the second war, his highly regarded dispatches were circulated to Washington and London.

The Soviet Union also sent their most suitable person to Canada. This was Fedor Gusev (also translated and usually known to Mackenzie King as Gousev), a fast-rising, thirty-seven-year-old foreign ministry official and former officer of the Soviet secret police (OGPU), evidently a captain since King sometimes used that title.[38] He made scarcely any impression on sleepy Ottawa and was rarely

---

37 Ruane, *Churchill and the Bomb*, 82–6; Daniels, *Franklin D. Roosevelt*, 422–3.
38 John Hilliker, *Canada's Department of External Affairs*. Vol. I: *The Early Years 1909–1946* (Montreal: McGill–Queen's University Press, 1990), 265; Granatstein, *The Ottawa Men*, 227–32; Dilks ed., *Diaries of Sir Alexander Cadogan*, 565 n.

mentioned, then or later. This was exactly as he and his country wanted. The USSR was well aware of Anglo-American atomic bomb research and needed information from that huge enterprise, now concentrated in North America, for its own small, hard-pressed programme. Since this was not supplied, or even acknowledged, the Soviets set out to acquire it from sympathetic insiders. The quiet Canadian capital was the perfect place for a spy headquarters.

Two years before the second Quebec conference, on Thanksgiving Day 1942, Mackenzie King had welcomed Gusev, his wife and three-year-old daughter to Ottawa. He assured the new minister that "our hearts were full of thanksgiving to Russia and that the country was very much in our thoughts. I could not express too strongly the admiration we had for their people and army." King had no suspicion of Gusev's principal task and innocently described him as "typically one of the people; simple and unostentatious, quiet and resolute."[39] The last three qualities were certainly appropriate to his task. The Gusevs carefully cultivated King, who enjoyed their company and hospitality at the legation, even taking a little vodka which he enjoyed. He was also interested in the minister's account of the transformation of the Soviet economy.[40] When they left, he gave Gusev and his wife each a photograph of himself.[41] This occurred within a year, the minister being rewarded for his secret success in Ottawa by promotion to one of the top diplomatic posts, the embassy to Britain. The caustic Sir Alexander Cadogan called Gusev "Frogface." One of his first duties was to receive Stalin's unacceptable letter about winter convoys back from Churchill. By the time the Soviet espionage network was suddenly exposed by a Soviet defector in Ottawa in September 1945, Gusev had been gone so long that his connection went totally unsuspected.

* * *

On the evening of September 19, 1944, Winston and Clementine Churchill left Hyde Park by train, and the following morning they sailed from New York aboard the *Queen Mary*. Roosevelt was completely worn out. Going straight to bed after the guests departed, he announced that he intended to sleep straight through the

39 Diary, October 12, 1942.
40 Diary, February 23 and 24, 1943.
41 Diary, October 23, 1943.

next morning.[42] The next time Mackenzie King saw him, half a year later, he was failing fast. King did not see Churchill for two years after Quebec, by which time King was the only one of the three still in office. Yet at the end of the second Quebec conference, it seemed that it was his political career that might end first.

42 Goodwin, *No Ordinary Time*, 545–6; Meacham, *Franklin and Winston*, 302–3; Roll, *The Hopkins Touch*, 346.

CHAPTER TWELVE

"A brave fellow, breaking up"

MACKENZIE KING LEFT QUEBEC in September 1943 as contented as Churchill left Hyde Park. Although predictions were not
unanimous, the prevailing military view was that the European war
would soon be over. Even if Churchill was right and it lasted through the winter, it seemed that the decisive battles would be fought before long, leaving only
pockets of resistance. Both Churchill and Roosevelt had concurred that no great
Canadian contribution would be wanted in the Pacific. As King suggested in his
speech to the Quebec Reform Club during the conference, the conscription issue
was subsiding in Canada. J. L. Ralston, the minister of national defence, who
was not present at the club, refused to surrender the principle and possibility of
conscription. King placated him by insisting that his speech had not gone beyond
reiterating that conscription would be invoked only if necessary. At this late stage,
he told Ralston, this was highly unlikely. Canada, he added, would never stand
for conscription in the Pacific.[1] For King, it was the time to start reducing military
costs, to concentrate on demobilization, social benefits, maintaining employment
in the transition to peace-time society, and the impending general election. This
contented and confident mood lasted scarcely a month.

In mid-October, Ralston and general Kenneth Stuart returned from a three-
week visit to Europe to report that there was a looming shortage of frontline
troops. Eisenhower and Montgomery expected the war to go on until the spring.

---

1   Diary, September 15, 1944.

Fighting was becoming harder as German defence lines shortened, Allied supply lines lengthened, and casualties had become far higher than expected. The German government and army showed no signs of weakening and Eisenhower was determined to keep up the fighting through the winter. There was no lack of Canadian troops in Europe, particularly in ancillary units. The scarcity was in infantry, both in Italy and France. Soldiers transferred from support services to the front line were insufficiently trained, and reserves were in any event forecast to be depleted by the end of the year. For the army leaders, Ralston, and cabinet ministers who favoured overseas conscription, the clear solution was to order those infantry conscripts trained for service in Canada to Europe.

Mackenzie King was aghast. Overseas compulsion threatened to destroy the unity of the country, divide the Liberals, and open the way for the socialist CCF to win the election. French Canada was as opposed as ever to overseas conscription while most of English Canada believed just as fervently that "Zombies" – conscripts who refused to volunteer for active overseas service – should be forced into a combat role. King argued that, even if the military situation was far worse than it had appeared at the Quebec conference, victory was still close to hand. Already, Canada was reducing its air force and navy and the other dominions were doing the same with their armies. But the interpretation of the 1942 plebiscite revealed a fundamental difference: for King it meant conscription only if necessary to win the war; for Ralston it meant authorization to keep up the strength of the fighting army.[2]

Without consulting the war cabinet, King appealed to Churchill, who had said that conscription would not be necessary and even promised political help to the Canadian government.[3] King confided in Malcolm MacDonald, on the grounds that they were fellow British privy counsellors. The high commissioner pleasingly said that raising conscription at the eleventh hour was the most absurd thing he had ever heard and alerted the British government that an important message would be arriving from the Canadian prime minister. King tried to prescribe the British response in his letter by suggesting the consolidation of the Canadian armies in Italy and northern Europe as well as pointing to everything Canada had done as a reason for "having matters arranged so that the situation could be met without any conscription being raised at this time." When

2 Diary, October 18–20, 1944.
3 Diary, October 20, 1944.

MacDonald said to King that it was too bad that the matter had not come up in time to be discussed at Quebec, the prime minister replied that he been assured before the meeting that there were plenty of reinforcements.[4]

Beginning his message to Churchill with the hands of the clock auspiciously together at five to eleven, King starkly announced that he was facing "the most critical situation which had arisen since Canada's entry to the war," one that threatened dangerous consequences for "the remainder of Canada's war effort in Europe and Asia, to the future of Canada, to future relations within the Commonwealth, and to all Government war activities and policies, including those being considered with respect to organization for the maintenance of world peace . . ." Disclaiming any desire to shift responsibility to Churchill, he said that he felt an obligation to bring the repercussions of such an upheaval to his attention. He asked the British prime minister's opinion on the likely duration of the European war and of Canadian troops being involved in the next major operation, adding the helpful information that Montgomery had told Ralston that they would not be needed. Prompting Churchill's memory of the pronouncements he had made on the subject, King was sure that he would recognize that "nothing in the way of conscription becomes necessary at this end."[5]

King revealed nothing of this overture in warning the cabinet about the consequences of conscription. Whether the government accepted or rejected it, he predicted that the issue would probably throw the election to the CCF. He reminded his colleagues that the present administration and its good influence meant a great deal to Churchill and Roosevelt as they faced the complexities of preserving world peace. Much as he personally disliked any form of force, he was willing to accept a world organization that could use it against aggression. But if the CCF came to office and refused to cooperate, he predicted that the other dominions would follow and the whole enterprise might fail before it was established. Contradicting his usual defence of Canadian autonomy, he said that he was ready to leave immediately to discuss the situation with Churchill and to inform the Americans.[6]

Churchill had just returned from meeting Stalin in Moscow, where he had in effect agreed, on his own behalf, to trade eastern Europe, which was or soon would be controlled by Soviet troops, for the Soviets agreeing to the preservation

4   Diary, October 21, 1944.
5   Diary, October 22, 1944; King to Churchill, October 22, 1944. DCER, Vol. 10, Part I, 329–31.
6   Diary, October 25, 1944.

of British influence in Greece and the Mediterranean. By hand, he wrote what was ostensibly only a guide, giving the USSR ninety percent influence in Romania and seventy-five percent in Bulgaria; Britain and the United States ninety percent in Greece; and the Soviets and the West fifty percent each in Hungary and Yugoslavia. Stalin accepted by a large pencil tick what Churchill admitted was a "naughty document." This did not commit the United States. Churchill had wanted to represent Roosevelt in his discussion with Stalin but this was prevented in the nick of time. The president wrote directly to the Soviet leader that he regarded the meeting as a preliminary to a conference of the three, who alone could decide matters.[7]

On Churchill's arrival in London, he read MacDonald's cable urging him at least to give an assurance that he was considering King's request: "By this means he could hold the situation for a few days. He hopes that he can avert the storm altogether. But at present it is brewing very badly and it may still get beyond his control." King himself was by this point beginning to doubt that Churchill could help since he was under pressure from his own MPs to keep up the strength of the army by shortening the leave of soldiers with more than five years' service.[8]

In his two-paragraph reply, Churchill did not mention conscription but said that he had referred King's concerns to the chiefs of staff. Sir Alan Brooke recorded a discussion about getting sufficient reinforcements from the trained soldiers in Canada "without upsetting the equilibrium of Mr. Mackenzie King's political position" but had nothing to suggest. Churchill himself could not possibly declare against conscription in any statement that might get into the public record. He told King that the military leaders now agreed with him that the European war might well last into the summer of 1945. While the Canadian army would be engaged in the final large-scale battle, it was impossible to say if it would be part of the next major operation since the plans were not complete.

This may have been an indication that conscription was not immediately necessary. (The Canadian army was given three months' rest after the fall of Walcheren on November 8, but this did not stem the number of serious casualties as it was encamped opposite the German line.)[9] Churchill was still too

7 Roll, *The Hopkins Touch*, 347–8; Clarke, *The Last Thousand Days of the British Empire*, 69–73; Hastings, *Finest Years*, 514–20.
8 Diary, October 26, 1944; MacDonald to Cranborne, October 26, 1944. DCER, Vol. 10, Part 1, 331–2.
9 Cook, *Fight to the Finish*, 377–8.

committed to the Italian front to comment on bringing the forces there to the north and the opposite would have been impossible. He expressed his sympathy with King's political difficulty, "the seriousness of which I can fully appreciate," but maintained that "no comment is called for from me at this juncture." In a concluding rhetorical flourish, he said, without specifying King and his ministry, that however the matter was decided, "it would in no way prevent His Majesty's Government and myself from continuing to pay the warmest tributes to the brilliant and massive help which the Canadian Army has given to the whole of our war effort, for which the British nation will ever remain profoundly grateful."[10]

This non-committal message, and the prediction that the European war would last well into 1945, was a bitter disappointment to King. He composed a brief, civil acknowledgement of gratitude that Churchill was aware of the gravity of the situation but, in his diary, gave voice to his sense of betrayal by railing that the response showed what was wrong with Churchill and the British. They regarded "the war as theirs and that we were giving them help, not that it was a war which was of concern to freedom everywhere." To his colleagues, King boldly lied that he was not contacting Churchill until he heard from the Canadian overseas commanders, lest it seemed that he did not have confidence in the country's military leaders and service ministers.[11] Whether he liked it or not in this particular case, the dominion autonomy that he championed meant that the size and nature of the army was entirely Canada's responsibility. The British, and Americans for that matter, were not complaining about what was provided, or asking for more, although they would obviously welcome all that Canada supplied.

A few days later Mackenzie King thought he had found the perfect solution to the problem by accepting the resignation that J. L. Ralston had submitted at the time of the 1942 plebiscite and replacing him as minister of national defence with General Andrew McNaughton. No one else left the cabinet and Ralston loyally refused to become the focus of criticism of King.[12] McNaughton, removed from his post as commander of the Canadian army in Europe at the end of 1943 for his shortcomings as a field commander, was still a significant figure in the army and the country. King had considered him as governor general to succeed Lord Athlone and the Conservatives tried to attract him into parliament. Probably

10 Churchill to King, October 27, 1944. DCER, Vol. 10, Part I, 332–3; Danchev and Todman, *War Diaries 1939–1945: Field Marshal Lord Alanbrooke*, 614; Diary entry, October 25, 1944)
11 Diary, October 27, 1944.
12 Cook, *War Lords*, 318–35; Bercuson, *Our Finest Hour*, 211–14; Granatstein, *Canada's War*, 333–81.

informed of what was going on behind the scenes, McNaughton gave a speech at Queen's University in which he proclaimed that compulsion was contrary to Canadian practice.[13] As minister of defence, he was confident that he would be able to persuade sufficient soldiers to serve abroad. Malcolm MacDonald congratulated King on solving the difficulty at a stroke, and King rejoiced that he had been left by Churchill to handle the matter alone.[14] In fact, far worse lay ahead.

* * *

In all this agitation, King could not spare much attention for the last stage of the American presidential campaign. But on election night, November 7, he was relieved by the radio reports that there was little doubt of Roosevelt's return: "This is tremendously comforting. It is a record of public confidence and popularity unparalleled on this continent and not likely ever to be repeated." Before going to bed he sent the president a brief telegram: "My dear friend: I am delighted."[15] Roosevelt won almost eighty percent of the electoral college and the Democratic party remained in control of Congress, losing one seat in the Senate and gaining twenty in the House of Representatives. Two days after the election, King, who knew Roosevelt's true physical condition behind the bravura displays of stamina during the final part of the campaign, was "horrified and deeply saddened" by newspaper photographs showing him casting his ballot and sitting as usual on the porch of his house at Hyde Park to greet the torchlight parade of neighbours when the results were clear. "Trying as my present situation is, and triumphant as his is," wrote King, "I would not exchange places with him for anything. His victories have practically cost him his life or what there may be of further enjoyment of life for him." The same day, he listened to the broadcast of Churchill's speech at the annual Lord Mayor's banquet and thought it also halting and showing signs of weariness.[16]

King had thought of appealing to Roosevelt about conscription before the election. Even with McNaughton as minister of national defence, there was no guarantee that the threat had disappeared. Sir John Dill, whom King thought would have been a good person to consult on the matter, died three days before

13 Diary, October 21, 1944.
14 Diary, November 1 and 4, 1944.
15 Diary, November 7, 1944.
16 Diary, November 9, 1944.

the US election. Hugely admired in military and official circles in Washington, Dill was given a first-class send-off: a funeral in the National Cathedral and streets lined with troops to Arlington National Cemetery, where he is the only foreigner buried there (and has one of only two equestrian statues). Major-General Maurice Pope, the anti-conscriptionist military secretary to Mackenzie King's war cabinet, who while head of the Canadian joint staff mission had known Dill in Washington, proposed that he represent Canada at the funeral. While in Washington, he could discuss conscription with some of his British military friends, and even General Marshall. King jumped at the idea, adding that Pope should also see Roosevelt, who "would do anything that he can to help me" in appreciation for strengthening the relationship with Britain and supporting the proposed world organization. He gave Pope a letter to the president and enjoined him to impress that "if, as a friend, he could help me in this situation, I would be grateful. To emphasize it was as an ally. That I wished him to understand all that was at stake." King thought, incorrectly, that Roosevelt would be going to London after the election and wanted him and Churchill "to see if some way could not be worked out which would help me to meet the situation in the best interests of all."[17]

After a week, King still had no word from Pope. He telephoned and Pope said that Leighton McCarthy had just heard that the president had received King's letter, but no time had been set for an appointment. King thought that if this could not be arranged for the next day, Pope might as well come home and go back when it could.[18] Next morning, Pope called to say that McCarthy was hesitating to inform the White House about King's agitation to have a meeting and doubted that it would help diplomacy to press the matter. This, and the suspiciously long delay in forwarding his prime minister's letter to Roosevelt, suggests that McCarthy, a First World War Liberal conscriptionist who did not support to King's position, was trying to spare the president an awkward conversation. King did not recognize this motive but thought it "a strange sort of Ambassador who will not carry out at all costs the directions of the P.M. of the country he represents, particularly when it relates to a matter between Allies and he knows the nature of my relationship with the President." Circumventing the diplomatic obstruction, he telephoned Grace Tully who said that the president

17 Diary, November 6, 1944.
18 Diary, November 14, 1944.

would be delighted to see Pope that afternoon. King pointedly told Pope to inform McCarthy.[19]

Two days later, Pope, in Ottawa, reported to King on the conversation. Although he had found Roosevelt looking far from well, his face "ashy grey and devoid of colour," he told the exact opposite to King, who attributed the president's good health to the electoral victory. Forewarned by King's letter, and probably also by McCarthy, Roosevelt claimed to know little about events in Canada, having been absorbed in his own election campaign. Pope outlined the conscription controversy, disingenuously claiming that this was only informa-tion for an ally and that King was not asking for anything. At the same time, he warned that the matter might have important implications for the post-war peacekeeping organization. Roosevelt got the signal.

Like Churchill, Roosevelt could not speak against conscription but in his genial way he asked Pope to "tell Mackenzie that any help that I can give him in the psychological field, I shall be glad to give." He said that Eisenhower seemed to think the European war might be over by the end of the year (exactly the opposite of what the commander had told Ralston a few weeks earlier), pinning his hopes on a big advance all the way from the Netherlands to Switzerland. Roosevelt himself was less confident but the apparent word from Eisenhower was enough for King to grasp the hope that the president and Churchill were talking about a long, hard fight as a cover for what they expected to be a major break-through: "They are doing what was done in the case of the [D-Day] invasion, letting it appear that it would be later rather than it was and much more difficult than it was." Pope had also spoken to general Gordon Macready, the head of the British army mission to the United States, who asked for a memorandum on the situation for Brooke to pass to Churchill, neither he nor Pope knowing about King's exchange with Churchill.[20] A few days later Pope received a message from Macready saying that Brooke's response was that anything that was done would have to be in the political arena. King was mortified that anyone should think that he was interfering with military plans.[21]

The day after Pope returned to Ottawa, Malcolm MacDonald came from Britain. He had not seen Churchill, who had been in liberated Paris parading down the Champs Elysées with de Gaulle. But King was pleased that Lord Cranborne regarded taking McNaughton into the cabinet as a master stroke. At the same time, the general's critics told MacDonald that McNaughton was a very sick man with one foot in the grave. (He hung on only for another active twenty-two years). MacDonald said that the prevailing British impression was that the war in Europe would last until March and no longer.[22] The night before, Eisenhower had sent King a message saying that the last big effort was underway, but this had foundered in wet weather and mud. A month later came a surprise German attack through the Ardennes against the weakest part of the American front. Allied reinforcements were poured into the Battle of the Bulge but not until the end of January was the mid-December line regained. American commanders thereafter were cautious, but not the Soviets who took advantage of the German concentration in the west to launch a huge drive towards Berlin on January 12.[23]

* * *

Mackenzie King was on his own in handling Canadian overseas conscription and, in fact, the better for it. He was by now as much a master of parliamentary tactics as Churchill and any invocation of the authority of the British and American leaders would have exposed him to charges of weakness and subservience, and possibly ridicule.

Five days after Eisenhower's major offensive, the Canadian parliament met on November 22 to debate Ralston's resignation and hold a vote of confidence in the government. Scant hours before it began, McNaughton telephoned King with the dread news that the volunteers were not sufficient to fill the need in Europe. The base commander at Winnipeg had submitted his resignation. Others might do the same and without conscription the whole military organization might disintegrate. Bad as this blow was, it was far worse in the middle of the debate. King was stunned but, like Stanley Baldwin whom he so much resembled, he was always a good fighter in the last ditch. Fear mixed with excitement as he recognized that compulsion was well-nigh inevitable but could be limited. The solution was to order enough troops overseas to blunt the attack of conscriptionists but not so many as to alienate beyond recall those who were adamantly opposed. At

22 Diary, November 18, 1944.
23 Hastings, *All Hell Let Loose*, 590–5.

the cabinet meeting the night before restricted compulsion was announced, only the air minister, "Chubby" Power stood by his consistent objection and resigned; and even he accepted that King was following the right course. Other ministers wavered but stayed including, most importantly, to King's relief, the French-Canadian ones.[24] An order in council directed up to 16,000 soldiers to be sent to Europe, with more to be added if necessary. After alerting the major Liberal newspapers, the Quebec provincial Liberal leader, and Cardinal Villeneuve, who promised to insert something helpful into his message on his recent visit to Canadian troops in Europe, King revealed the directive to the Liberal caucus before parliament met. Threatening in passionate terms to resign if he was not supported, he argued that the fall of the government would not help the war; a new administration would bring in complete conscription; intended social legislation would vanish; the party would probably be destroyed; and the country would be in grave danger. On the other hand, he held out the chance that the European war might end before the reinforcements were needed.

When King read the order in council to a packed House of Commons, most Liberals applauded while the Conservatives were silent, furious that they had been pre-empted. In a characteristically long speech, King repeated what he had said to the cabinet and party, warning that if the government fell, a general election would mean at least two months without effective leadership of the country. McNaughton, who was not an MP, was permitted to appear before the Commons to present the military case and was relentlessly questioned by the Conservatives. But King knew that he had carried off a coup. He felt "in better shape than I have felt at almost any time. Quite happy in fact." Leaving the building just after 1 a.m., he was "greatly relieved in my mind; very much at rest. I felt that the day of Crucifixion had passed and that I was reaching the morning of Resurrection."[25]

A week later, Ralston announced that he would support the motion of confidence. On the final night before the vote, December 7, the CCF moved an amendment altering the wording, expecting it to be rejected but King nimbly accepted it, forcing that party to vote for the government. The margin was 143 to 70, with 19 French-Canadian MPs siding with the government. Having expected a slight majority, King was "really amazed" at the result: "It took me some little time after to realize that I had 2/3 of the House with me."[26]

---

24 Diary, November 22, 1941.
25 Diary, November 23, 1944.
26 Diary, December 7, 1944.

The divisions in the country, however, continued. There was a mutiny of English and French speaking troops at the army base in Terrace, B. C., and riots in Montreal and Quebec City. In March, the Quebec legislature passed a resolution against conscription. The Conservatives did not cease from demanding total compulsion, including for the Pacific. When McNaughton tried to get into parliament at a by-election in rural Ontario in February, he was decisively defeated by the Conservative candidate in a three-way race. Even King's domestic staff was torn. The sullenness of Robert Lay, his British driver, showed his support for conscription. To make matters even worse, King suspected that Lay was "increasingly becoming a Red." His valet, John Nicol was more sympathetic, as were the maids, although they were also from Britain.[27] But the order in council turned out to be less disruptive than had been feared. Volunteering for overseas service increased, as did enlistment from the reserve army and by civilians. A total of 13,000 soldiers were sent to Europe, of which 2,463 were assigned to fighting units. The casualty rate was lower than anticipated, partly because experienced Canadian troops from Italy joined those in the north before they returned to action in February.[28] By then, the war against Germany really was in its final stage.

Throughout this time of trial Mackenzie King was disheartened to receive no encouragement from Churchill or Roosevelt. In the middle of the parliamentary debate, he cabled brief birthday wishes to Churchill, hoping to prompt a response: "It is in a crisis that one learns how far men are prepared to go."[29] But no reply came. Four days later, both John Maynard Keynes and Leighton McCarthy reported that Roosevelt sent his love and best wishes. "I had missed not hearing from him in such terms since the present crisis," King commented wistfully.[30] Keynes had been in Ottawa seeking more financial aid for Britain. McCarthy had been with Roosevelt at Warm Springs as the president spent three weeks recovering from the election. Two days after his parliamentary triumph, King was delighted finally to receive a cable from Churchill: "Without venturing to enter in any way into Canadian politics, I feel I may now say what relief and pleasure it has given me to find you so effectively at the helm." King thought this "a fine message. Churchill has the marvelous gift of expression using the right

---

27 Diary, December 7, 1944.
28 Granatstein, *Canada's War*, 371 n. and 373; Cook, *War Lords*, 334–5.
29 Diary, November 29, 1944.
30 Diary, December 3, 1944.

word at the right place. It is a comforting message. A fine word to receive from the Prime Minister of Great Britain."[31]

King telephoned McCarthy at Warm Springs in early December, ostensibly to congratulate him on his seventy-fifth birthday, but really for the purpose of finding out about the president. Having heard on the radio that morning that Churchill was appealing to Roosevelt and Stalin to come to Britain, King feared that Roosevelt would make the same mistake as Woodrow Wilson, "being anxious at all costs to drive through the streets of London and to be loudly acclaimed in Europe." He thought it far better for the president to stay in the United States until the decisive battles were over, or for the three to meet in some undisclosed place, which was, in fact, what happened. McCarthy did not think, and certainly hoped that Roosevelt would not go to Britain before the inauguration in January. He told King that both he and the president had followed the conscription controversy closely and at the end Roosevelt declared: "I think this will make Mackenzie stronger." King thought that would be true of Canada as well. McCarthy insisted that the president was looking much better, although the weather had been dreary and only twice had he been in the hot mineral pool. McCarthy judged that another couple of weeks at Warm Springs would help but Roosevelt needed to return to Washington.[32] Daisy Suckley, the president's devoted, unmarried cousin and Hudson Valley neighbour, had dinner with McCarthy and Roosevelt the next day, describing the ambassador as "a dear person & the Pres. is devoted to him & enjoys talking to him." Roosevelt regretted McCarthy's decision to retire at the end of the month but consoled himself with the thought that they would continue to meet at Warm Springs.[33]

* * *

On New Year's Eve, Mackenzie King telephoned Roosevelt at the White House. The president said how much he would miss McCarthy, who he said had provided him with day-to-day information about the conscription crisis. Roosevelt affirmed that he had never doubted that King would prevail. He invited the prime minister

---

31 Diary, December 9, 1944.
32 Diary, December 15, 1944.
33 Geoffrey C. Ward ed., *Closest Companion: The Unknown Story of the Intimate Friendship between Franklin Roosevelt and Margaret Suckley* (Boston: Houghton Mifflin, 1995), 362 and 364–4; Diary entries, December 14–17, 1944.

to Washington, ideally for the inauguration on January 20. King, while not defi-
nitely refusing, thought it better to stay at home. The hard-fought McNaughton
by-election was on February 5 and attending a presidential ceremony two weeks
before would raise the charge that King was detaching Canada from Britain and
the Commonwealth and bringing it closer to the United States.

Roosevelt confided to King that he was going to Britain later in January. In
fact, he was going to Yalta in the Soviet Crimea for a "Big Three" conference,
meeting Churchill on the way at Malta. He observed that Churchill was having
a hard time with the uproar on both sides of the Atlantic for his heavy-handed
political and military involvement in liberated Greece to prevent the communists
taking power. Roosevelt dismissed these events, which portended the Cold War,
as not amounting to much. King had strong views of his own. He supported
Churchill (as Roosevelt did privately, but not openly owing to American anti-
colonial opinion), on the ground that democracy was not mob rule. But he made
it clear to Churchill that Canadian troops could not to be used in Greece, adding
the warning that this might be announced publicly.

Churchill stiffly responded that there was no such intention of using Canadian
troops in Greece but cautioned that such a statement would add to the difficulties.
Saying that Britain had intervened at the request of the Greek prime minister,
with the (secret) approval of the Americans and the assent (by the percentages
agreement) of the Soviets, he asserted: "We cannot abandon this task without
loss and a blow to British prestige." In tones reminiscent of Chanak, which had
divided them close to quarter of a century ago, Churchill told King: "It is on such
occasions as this that the British Commonwealth should stand together." This
time King, agreed with Churchill's aim and did not take umbrage but accepted
his assurance about Greece.[34]

When Roosevelt told King in their New Year's Eve conversation that he was
going to cross the Atlantic for the meeting by ship, which would give him a week's
rest, King expressed no concern about the president's health.[35] But a month and
a half later, in the middle of February, he decided that he had better not delay
visiting Roosevelt, who gave the appearance that he could not live much longer.[36]

34 Diary, December 17, 1944; Churchill to King, December 16, 1944. Gilbert, *Winston S. Churchill*,
    Vol. VII, 1101–2, Kimball, *The Juggler*, 164–70; Hastings, *Finest Years*, 523–45.
35 Diary, December 31, 1944.
36 Diary, February 16, 1944.

* * *

For those who knew Franklin Roosevelt as well as Mackenzie King, there was plenty of evidence that, behind the carefully controlled press photographs he was deteriorating badly. For the second year in a row, he sent a written report on the State of the Union to Congress rather than delivering the address in person. Shortly after the election, he also announced that his fourth inauguration would be an attenuated ceremony on the south portico of the White House rather than the usual pomp outside the Capitol with a parade back and forth. This was ostensibly because the country was at war but was, in reality, to reduce the physical demands on the president. The event lasted a mere fifteen minutes with a six-minute address, the shortest ever. There were a hundred dignitaries on the balcony and about 8,000 spectators below on the snow-covered lawn. Despite the cold, Roosevelt wore only a suit and stood bare-headed to take the oath and give his speech. This was the last time he ever stood. Shakily grasping the lectern, he exhorted Americans to maintain their courage to the end of the war; to reject isolationism and build a just and durable peace; to remember that it was God who had given strength to the United States; and to assure them that the course of civilization was ever upward. He suffered some kind of seizure, probably an angina attack, from which he recovered with a stiff drink in the house. He managed to greet the two thousand guests at the buffet luncheon of chicken salad, which was remarkable for the lack of chicken, but ate privately with a few intimates, including Princess Martha.[37] If King had attended, he would almost certainly have been in the group.

Two and a half weeks later, in early February, the prime minister received "a terrifying impression" of the president in a letter from Emil Ludwig. On the same day, Queen Juliana of the Netherlands told King at lunch in Ottawa that she had also been shocked by Roosevelt's appearance: "He seemed tired and worn as well as looking so changed."[38] King hastened to propose a visit and received an immediate reply that that the president was looking forward to it and suggesting the first week of March.[39]

Roosevelt had much to discuss with King. At the moment, the president was sailing home from the Big Three meeting at Yalta. He had left Washington

---

37 Lelyveld, *His Final Battle*, 261–4; *Franklin D. Roosevelt*, 465–6; Goodwin, *No Ordinary Time*, 572–3.
38 Diary, February 7, 1945.
39 Diary, February 16, 1945.

secretly two days after the inauguration, taking in the place of his disappointed wife, their daughter Anna Boettiger, who (with her mother so often absent) had moved into the White House and served as his hostess and protector. After ten days at sea, he met Churchill at Malta, who was similarly accompanied by his daughter Sarah, an aerial photograph interpreter in the Women's Auxiliary Air Force. The prime minister was also far from well, but far better than the president, even after the relaxation of the voyage. During their day together in Malta, Roosevelt, as before the Tehran conference over a year before, was careful to avoid being drawn into any policy discussion with Churchill before the talks with Stalin.

The two and their entourages – a total of seven hundred people – flew to Crimea and were transported by road for three hours through countryside recently devastated by the retreating Germans. Their destination was the former Romanov palace at the resort of Yalta. Stalin, who had good reason to fear flying, arrived the next day by armoured train. Every afternoon for eight days from February 3 to 11 there were formal sessions. There were also casual talks, consultations among diplomats and the military chiefs as well as lavish, protracted banquets.[40] This took a heavy toll on Roosevelt's frail physique, and he was not the only one. Harry Hopkins, who as usual helped to smooth relations between the Big Three, seemed in even worse health. Unable to face the voyage home, he returned by air and went straight to hospital. General Edwin "Pa" Watson, the president's appointments secretary, had a stroke in the Mediterranean on the way back and died at sea two days later at the age of sixty-one. Mackenzie King, reading the obituary, remembered that he had been a friend of Watson's wife, the concert pianist Frances Nash.[41]

Whatever Roosevelt's physical condition, he had firmly in mind what he wanted to accomplish with Stalin. The Soviet leader confirmed that he would go to war against Japan a couple of months after the defeat of Germany in return for territorial and commercial concessions from Japan and, more controversially, from allied China. Roosevelt was even more gratified that Stalin agreed to the Soviet Union joining the United Nations Organization (UNO), providing that there had to be unanimity in the Security Council for action (meaning a veto

40 Hamilton, *War and Peace*, 407–57; Clarke, *The Last Thousand Days of the British Empire*, 179–221; Daniels, *Franklin D. Roosevelt*, 468–84; Lelyveld, *His Final Battle*, 264–95; Roll, *The Hopkins Touch*, 356–78; Hastings, *Finest Years*, 546–54; Roberts, *Masters and Commanders*, 545–56.
41 Diary, February 28, 1945.

381

for any member), and the (secret) promise of additional seats in the General Assembly for the Soviet Republics of Belarus and Ukraine.

Churchill had wanted de Gaulle to be present, at least to discuss French affairs, but Roosevelt refused, as would have Stalin in all probability. The president had finally officially recognized de Gaulle as head of the provisional government in October and on New Year's Day, in a ceremony at the US State Department, France was admitted to the United Nations alliance. Roosevelt now accepted Churchill's argument for recognizing France as one of the great world powers in order to strengthen Europe against the Soviet Union, in return for Churchill ending his objection to China.[42] Stalin concurred in giving France a permanent seat on the Security Council and being one of the four occupying powers of Germany, so long as the French zone was carved out of the British and American ones. From Roosevelt's perspective, it seemed that at least four of the now Big Five would act together under US leadership, or joint British leadership, as Churchill saw it. But Stalin had no fear that any of this would threaten the Soviet Union so long as it had a veto on the UNO.

The biggest problem at Yalta was Poland, for which Britain had gone to war in 1939. Stalin was adamant about controlling Poland – which had been part of the Russian Empire until the First World War and was now occupied by Soviet troops – as a barrier against attack from the West. Roosevelt and Churchill reluctantly confirmed that the Soviet border would be that of the 1939 Nazi-Soviet pact. (Stalin pointed out that this was the "Curzon line," the ethnically defensible boundary proposed by the British foreign secretary at the end of the last war). Poland, in turn, would be compensated by territory from Germany, which would further increase Soviet protection. Far more embarrassing for the western leaders was Stalin's insistence on the core of the Polish government being the communist exiles in Moscow rather than their rivals in London. In an apparent spirit of cooperation, he agreed to include some of the London group and to hold free elections. He improved his case by pointing out that no one had elected de Gaulle. Short of alienating the Soviet Union from the proposed UNO and the preservation of peace, or the unthinkable alternative of going to war against the USSR for Poland, Roosevelt and Churchill had no choice but to put the most optimistic interpretation on Stalin's promises and hope for the best. As an expression of this optimism, the three leaders on the final day of

42 Berthon, *Allies at War*, 324–5; Daniels, *Franklin D. Roosevelt*, 461.

the conference issued The Declaration on Liberated Europe, drafted by the US State Department, promising independence and self-government for countries liberated from Germany and Italy.

When Roosevelt and Churchill returned to the Middle East, they discussed the atomic bomb, which was expected to be tested by September. Churchill was anxious about the president's health, although he still assumed that the president would come to Britain in June, which could not fail to help the prime minister as he faced a long overdue election. But it was acutely discomforting to the British leader that Roosevelt met alone with the louche young King Farouk of Egypt (which was nominally independent and neutral in the war but regarded as a client state if not a kind of colony by the British), the Emperor Haile Selassie of Ethiopia and, most important of all, Ibn Saud, the king of Saudi Arabia who flatly rejected the president's appeal for Palestine as a homeland for the Jews and for the admission of survivors from Europe.

* * *

Both Churchill and Roosevelt delivered reports on the Yalta conference to their legislatures. By far the most important section of Churchill's speech opening a two-day parliamentary debate concerned Poland. Neville Chamberlain loyalists bayed angrily about betrayal. All too conscious that he was making the same kind of optimistic case as Chamberlain about the Munich agreement, Churchill insisted that Poland in its new borders would have an independent and prosperous existence, although this claim was gravely undermined by stating that members of Polish armed services in Britain who did not want to return would be offered British citizenship.

Over a drink in the smoking room afterwards, Churchill told his great admirer Harold Nicolson that he did not see what else could possibly be done: "Not only are the Russians very powerful, but they are on the spot; even the massed majesty of the British Empire would not avail to turn them off that spot." Nicolson, who had a high reputation on foreign policy as a former diplomat and opponent of appeasement, supported the prime minister in a speech saying that Poland had been saved from a worse fate. He and Churchill took embarrassed amusement in the fact that "the warmongers of the Munich period have now become the appeasers, while the appeasers have become warmongers." The amendment deploring the transfer of Polish territory and the failure to ensure a government free of outside influence was defeated by 396 to 25 votes, and the main motion of confidence passed without opposition (although there were abstentions).[43]

That same day, Mackenzie King, who had not shown much sympathy with Poland even in 1939, and probably had little understanding of the issue in 1945, received what he described as "a very fine" report on Yalta from Churchill. He trusted what he was told and believed that the decisions were wise ones made by three harmonious leaders with a common interest in security and freedom. However, more alarming was Churchill's assessment that the military did not expect the war against Germany to end before July 1 and thought that it might even run to the end of the year. Then there would be another year and a half of fighting in the Pacific. Fearful, once again, of the implications for conscription with a Canadian election looming, King sought comfort in the belief that there must be a wide range in these estimates. He himself guessed – or hoped – that the Germans could not hold out more than another month. His was the right prediction.[44]

Roosevelt, on the morning following his return to the United States, took the unusual course of giving an address on the Yalta conference to a joint meeting of Congress. It was the first time that he had spoken there for two years and, in a way, this compensated for the annual State of the Union addresses. Politically, he had an easier time than Churchill since there was no debate, no questions, and no vote. There was also great personal sympathy for the obviously ailing president, who entered the house for the first time in his wheelchair and spoke from a desk on the floor of the chamber rather than standing at the rostrum. Publicly acknowledging his disability, he told Congress and those listening by radio that it was easier for him not to have ten pounds of steel on his legs, which to much of the public, must have been a revelation. The speech was a long way from his customary rhetorical standard. He kept wandering from the text, either in an attempt to add an informal note or because he lacked mental concentration. He claimed that Yalta was a good start to the peace; that it ended the old diplomacy of unilateral action, exclusive alliances, and spheres of influence and balances of power. Instead, it laid the base for a new order founded on the UNO. To ensure its success, he called on the support of Congress and for the rejection of isolationism. Like Churchill, he insisted that the Polish arrangement was the best

43 Clarke, *The Last Thousand Days of the British Empire*, 236–43; Nicolson, *Diaries and Letters 1939–45*, 436–38; (Diary entry, February 27 and Nicolson to Vita Sackville-West, February 28, 1945).
44 Diary, February 28, 1945.

possible for that country's freedom and prosperity, "an outstanding example of joint action by the three major Allied powers in the liberated areas."

Mackenzie King, listening by radio, was not impressed. He thought there were "bits of his speech which were more like a talk to a body of school children than to members of the Congress." He noticed that Roosevelt spoke much more rapidly than usual, quite loudly but his voice gave indication of high nervous tension. It has lost a certain melodious note. It was sharper but what was particularly noticeable was the extent to which he slurred over some of his words and seemed to encounter particular difficulty in pronouncing some words that had an "r" or "l" in them, such as "British" or "colonel", as though his speech were just a little affected. King thought the substance "very thin and protracted and in many places disconnected." He was "quite sad to notice the change that has come over him. The loss of poise, of consecutive, constructive thought, of natural emphasis and of convincing appeal. It would have been much better had he spoken for twenty minutes than nearly an hour." At the end, King told his secretary, Jack Pickersgill: "He is a brave fellow, but he is breaking up." King felt "sick at heart." The applause he considered recognition for "the heroic manner in which he continues to struggle with the great burdens he is carrying . . . rather than because of what he had said. I pray he suffers no ill effects from this particular effort."[45] Never again did Roosevelt address Congress. A week later, King was able to see the president's condition for himself. To his surprise, King found him in better form than expected.

* * *

On the evening of March 8, Mackenzie King began the familiar rail journey to Washington. Between New York and Newark, New Jersey he was joined briefly by Emil Ludwig seeking help in getting an interview with Churchill and visiting Canadian troops in Europe. The train arrived too late for the lunch that Lester Pearson, who had replaced McCarthy, had arranged at the embassy but King joined the group for coffee. In attendance were the now practically blind Julia Grant and Norman Armour, the US minister to Canada from 1935 to 1939, now ambassador to Spain and married to a Tatar princess he had met at the beginning of his career in Russia in 1917. After Churchill's gloomy prognosis about

45 Diary, March 1, 1945; Lelyveld, *His Final Battle*, 297–302; Daniels, *Franklin D. Roosevelt*, 484–6.

the duration of the war, King was heartened by the news that American troops had crossed the Rhine into Germany. The news from the Pacific was also good.

At 5 p.m., King went to the White House, where he was staying overnight. He took tea with Eleanor Roosevelt and her long-time secretary "Tommy" (Malvina) Thompson, who left when the president arrived. Probably to prepare King for her husband's condition, Eleanor said that he had been tired after his journey to Yalta and was very thin. King thought she herself looked older, more worn, and anxious about the president. She talked about the unpleasant side of politics, "how ungrateful people were, terrible pressure, etc."

When Roosevelt entered in his wheelchair, King "felt a deep compassion for him. He looked much older; face much thinner, particularly the lower part. Quite thin." When King went to shake hands, the president held up his cheek to be kissed. Roosevelt moved to the middle of the sofa, with King on one side and Eleanor on the other. King paid close attention to the president, noting that he was quite weary and his eyes very tired, but Roosevelt's flesh looked firmer than the last time they had met, the weight loss now consolidating "into a man of different size and shape, looking more like President Wilson. His front features thinner in the lower part of the face." Roosevelt said that he thought that he would be well if only he were out of office and free, suggesting an ambivalence about his fourth term. He also said he was determined to go to Britain in June. Eleanor Roosevelt thought it would be a help if he had cabinet meetings at Hyde Park in the summer.

The president talked about his trip to Yalta, particularly the meetings with the king of Saudi Arabia and the Emperor Haile Selassie of Ethiopia (Farouk evidently did not rate a mention). He said that Churchill had been in good form at the conference and did about ninety percent of the talking. Stalin he characterized as very friendly to both western leaders, more to himself than to Churchill. He had a good deal of humour and the president liked him: "Found him very direct." Later, Roosevelt added that he did not think there was anything to fear from the Soviet leader: "He had a big programme himself to deal with." He also confided that Stalin would end relations with Japan as soon as he had enough troops in Manchuria.

Dinner was a family affair. Apart from King and the two Roosevelts, the only others were their daughter Anna, and Belle Roosevelt, widow of Theodore Roosevelt's son Kermit. The president did not urge cocktails on King, who noticed that there was no wine at table and no drinks afterwards. Roosevelt said that when he had mentioned "prima donnas" in his speech to Congress, the reference was to Josip Tito, the communist leader of Yugoslavia, not de Gaulle as was generally assumed. De Gaulle had refused to meet the president in the Mediterranean and Roosevelt remarked that he had two natures: extraordinarily pleasant and the opposite. This led to talk of families being disposed to mental problems since de Gaulle's daughter had Down's syndrome. This was close to home since Kermit Roosevelt had been an alcoholic depressive who committed suicide while his uncle, Eleanor Roosevelt's father, suffered the same but failed, as he had in so many things, in taking his own life.

In the president's study afterwards, Roosevelt talked steadily from 8:30 p.m. until almost midnight. This was undoubtedly a pleasure for him but it must also have been a strain. He offered more details from Yalta, again emphasizing the friendliness and humour of Stalin. At one point, as Churchill was making a long speech, Stalin "put his hand up to the side of his face, turned to the President and winked one of his eyes as much as to say: there he is talking again." When King asked how long the war would last, Roosevelt said he had not made any public statement but thought that the fighting in Europe would be over by the end of April. This was a great relief to King after Churchill's latest estimate. So was the prediction that Japan would then soon collapse, perhaps in three months. When King inquired about "certain weapons," Roosevelt responded that they should be in shape by August but said nothing about using them against Japan. He said that the Soviets had also been experimenting towards an atomic bomb and were aware of some of what was happening in the west. He thought it was time to tell them how far developments had gone but Churchill refused. King judged that it would be unfortunate if the Soviets discovered that things had been held back from them. On the occupation of Germany and Japan, Roosevelt thought ten years would be necessary, perhaps even longer. He also said that Stalin wanted reparations from Germany in the form of machinery and equipment and 100,000 prisoners of war to work for a decade on restoration in the Soviet Union.

Discussing his great hope for the future, Roosevelt thought that it would be a mistake for the San Francisco conference to establish the UNO, approaching in April, to last more than a month. Once the main principles were in place, whatever remained could be done later. He himself would open the proceedings and then leave immediately. He did not expect Churchill to come. He regretted that Cordell Hull, who had been so responsible for the details of the scheme (for which he received the 1945 Nobel Peace Prize), had been too ill to continue as secretary of state after the election and would not be well enough to attend. Roosevelt thought that the Security Council should meet at various places, away from the press: possibly in the Azores, for European matters; Canada for North American ones; and Hawaii for the Pacific. The General Assembly should likewise convene in different countries since Geneva, after the failure of the League, did not have a good reputation; but King pointed out the practical problem of housing large staffs, entertainment and the need for hotels if there was no permanent place. The president said he would welcome an armed outbreak – presumably a small one – between a couple of countries to test the machinery for preventing war: "Let them see how it works before working out too many treaties as to military undertakings." The disquieting prospect of member countries being automatically committed to the use of force revived King's fears about the League of Nations, prompting him to ask if the matter would first be referred to national parliaments. Roosevelt assured him that this was the intention.[46]

* * *

Next morning at the White House, Mackenzie King had two visitors. The first was Joseph Grew, the under-secretary of state, who came in the place of his absent chief, Edward Stettinius Jr. Grew had been ambassador to Japan for almost a decade until Pearl Harbor and his son-in-law, Jay Pierrepont Moffatt, had been the US minister in Ottawa until his death at the beginning of 1943. Grew also thought the European war would soon be over but, unlike the president, he expected very hard fighting against the Japanese, despite their shock at the aerial devastation of Tokyo. He believed that only complete defeat would avoid a future war but said that the emperor must be kept, at least for now, as the only person with whom peace could be negotiated. The second caller was Lord Halifax who agreed with Grew about the European war. His main concern was to determine King's impression of Roosevelt's health and to learn if the president was going to San Francisco. When King said he expected that he was, the ambassador decided that he would go himself (as he did), although he was waiting for instructions from his government.

Lunch with Roosevelt was in the sun room. Anna Boettiger was the only other person present and she left at the end of the meal. King and the president lingered for over two hours. Roosevelt talked excitedly about his intended

46 Diary, March 9, 1945.

trip to Europe in June and evidently expected to be energized by it. He would go by ship, stay at Buckingham Palace, drive with the king through the streets of London, spend a weekend with Churchill at Chequers, receive the freedom of the City of London, and address the Houses of Parliament. He also intended to visit American troops, Queen Wilhelmina at The Hague, and perhaps Paris but, given the prickliness of de Gaulle, he would not say anything about that in advance. It was clear to King that Roosevelt and Churchill expected the fighting to be over before this "sort of triumphal close to the war itself," and that the president regarded this as "in some ways the most important information he has given me so far." King raised the issue of all countries that had contributed troops to the defeat of Germany being recognized in the surrender, which the president promised to raise with Churchill.

Dreaming ahead to his retirement in 1949, Roosevelt said that he hoped to publish a daily newspaper, a news digest of three or four small pages like those printed aboard ships, giving only the main items, without editorials, and priced at one cent. King was struck at the president's assurance of being able to take on new things by then. He judged Roosevelt to be in better physical form than the day before but was struck that he was still mainly concerned only with the surface of events. He repeated himself a good deal, which embarrassed his family. Another weakness, King thought, was the president's tendency to credit himself with initiating many things, particularly the UNO, which King knew owed a great deal to Cordell Hull and the state department: "That is one of the terrible dangers of a situation like the present where 2 or 3 men do so much in directing the affairs of the world." Observing Roosevelt closely, King noticed that "one eye has a clear, direct look-that is the left eye as he faces one. The right one is not quite on the square with the left one but has a little sort of stigmata appearance in the centre."

In the afternoon King accompanied Edouard Handy to the Bethesda Naval Hospital to see Cordell Hull. The seventy-three-year-old former secretary of state was suffering from diabetes and inflammation of the lungs, a consequence of tuberculosis earlier in life. To King, his skin seemed like leather and there were tears in his eyes. He was out of bed for the first time in five months, sitting in a reclining chair in his small room on the seventeenth floor with his wife beside him. He told King that he had simply not been able to hang on to office any longer. He had continued until the election, although in hospital and unable to work, only to avoid charges of resigning over a difference with the president. He doubted that he would be able to go to San Francisco but hoped to exercise some influence from Washington. King told him that the whole world was under obligation to him for his service to international goodwill. In his diary, he wrote that Hull was "perhaps the greatest of the men of the U.S., so far as its foreign policy and shaping of world affairs was concerned, and to be also with the President at this particular period." King gave him a copy of the Ludwig biography, which both he and the author had signed. As he left, "the old gentleman" (who was only four years older than King and outlived him by five) broke down.

Dinner at the White House was again a small, mainly family event. Eleanor had been in Philadelphia during the day, giving a speech, attending meetings, and writing in the train. Anna and John Boettiger and Belle Roosevelt were also present. The outside guests were Robert Murphy, the former chargé d'affaires to the Vichy government and afterwards the president's representative to the French in north Africa, and a young French lieutenant who had been training for half a year in Saskatchewan and probably knew the city of Prince Albert better than its MP, Mackenzie King. Once again, King noticed there was no wine. Afterwards there were newsreels of the Yalta conference, part of Roosevelt's speech to Congress, the German massacres in Poland and a close–range film, the most graphic of the war King had yet seen, of US Marines landing on the tiny island of Iwo Jima, 700 miles south of Japan. Two weeks later, after a month of horrific fighting, it was finally captured at a cost of 24,000 American casualties, including 7,184 dead.[47]

When the screening was over King went to his railway car, which left for Williamsburg, Virginia the next morning. He accepted Roosevelt's invitation to attend his press conference three days later, on Tuesday, March 11. Glad as he was of the company and close relationship with the president, he declined the entreaties of the Roosevelts to stay at the White House for his whole time in the United States. If only for a couple of days, he needed time to rest and work on his speech for San Francisco.

Before going to bed, King spent an hour dictating his diary. Overall he concluded that Roosevelt, while distinctly failing, "is not quite as bad or in as poor shape as he appeared from photographs." He looked older and wearier and had lost "a certain merriment." His memory was fading. He talked continuously and often repeated himself but he still retained "a certain firmness which might carry him along for some time." He listened and took things in keenly but linked

---

47 Hastings, *All Hell Let Loose*, 635–6.

everything to himself. This was a reason, King thought, that no one should have the power that Roosevelt, Churchill and Stalin possessed: "their thoughts are very largely of the world that they believe that they themselves are shaping and where they will be seen in history." For King, in the sight of God, "I think there is a profounder reality-much profounder, and that publicity tends to destroy this."[48]

* * *

After two days of spring sunshine in Williamsburg, King returned to Washington. He expected to stay the night at the White House but when Anna Boettiger said nothing about it, he arranged to go overnight to New York and enjoy a day there. Before the press conference, Roosevelt told King about surrender overtures from the German army in Italy and his intentions for San Francisco. King found the press session in the Oval Office a curious business. Reporters crowded around the president's desk, which was covered with trinkets. Roosevelt praised his friendship with King which had enabled them to settle such matters between their two countries as the Ogdensburg and Hyde Park agreements. Once again, he hailed Canada and the United States as an example to the world. He was asked questions mainly about domestic matters. King noticed that he answered some directly, most evasively, and to a few said he did not know enough to respond. After the press left, he seemed to enjoy talking to King and was in no hurry to send for work. King now revised downward his earlier assessment of the president, judging that he has "pretty well lost his spring. He is a very tired man. He is kindly, gentle and humorous, but I can see is hardly in shape to cope with problems. He wisely lets himself be guided by others and has everything carefully brought before him."

Dinner was a more intimate event than Mackenzie King realized. Eleanor Roosevelt was away for a few days and the only other person, in addition to Anna and John Boettiger, was introduced as a Mrs. Rutherfurd, a relative from South Carolina. King found her "a very lovely woman and of great charm. I should think she has an exceptionally fine character." He was so smitten that he had one of the president's cocktails. King did not know it but Lucy Page (Mercer) Rutherfurd was the great love of Roosevelt's life. She did have a winter estate in South Carolina, two hundred miles from Warm Springs, but her main mansion was in New Jersey. Her sister Violetta conveniently lived in Washington. After

48 Diary, March 10, 1945.

the death of her husband in March 1944, which coincided with Roosevelt's heart disease, she came back into the president's life in a major way. With the collusion of Anna, who appreciated Lucy's stimulating effect on her father, she became a regular guest at the White House during Eleanor's frequent absences. The day before meeting King, she had been there for dinner and the day after she was there for both lunch and dinner.[49] This may have been the reason that Anna said nothing to King about staying overnight.

The table talk was about the king and queen's visit to Hyde Park, other occasions attended by Roosevelt and King, and the recent trip to Yalta. Afterwards, while Roosevelt told stories of receiving presents from the three kings of the Orient and the Boettigers opened the cases, displaying rich garments, perfumes and gold scabbards with diamonds. King left at 9:30 p.m., the president looking forward to seeing him at San Francisco, when they both hoped the war would be over. He also invited him to come again to the White House, Hyde Park, or Warm Springs. If there was any way he could help in the Canadian election, he would. When King doubted (correctly) that he would win his own seat, the president in a flash of his old optimism said that he was sure that he would.

Anna and John Boettiger went with King to the door, leaving Roosevelt and Lucy Rutherfurd to entertain themselves as best they might. They could not believe that King was older than the president, which given Roosevelt's condition was no empty praise. Anna said that her father had told her that there was "a great friend of his coming to the White House, one of whom he was very fond. That they were to treat him as one of the family. He was a very easy person to get on with and that they need not be concerned about anything." She said that her father missed other old friends such as "Missy" LeHand and "Pa" Watson and liked King to come for conversation. "Apparently he had given more time to me than to anyone else in the last few days, and seemed to want to continue talking." This was in striking contrast to the state visit of Lord Athlone and Princess Alice a few days later. The governor general complained that they had been "left very much to themselves at the White House. They had no information in advance as to who would be at dinner, or who they would be sitting beside at dinner. Saw very few people." Like King, they found Roosevelt much older and more repetitious and forgetful than at Quebec six months earlier.[50]

49 Persico, *Franklin and Lucy*, 301–3 and 325–6; Lelyveld, *His Final Battle*, 94–5, 148–50 and 307.
50 Diary, March 25, 1945.

King recorded that his visit to the White House was "another memorable link the long chain of close associations with the President."[51] Despite Roosevelt's frailty, he was reassured that the president was in good enough form for them to meet again many times, starting with San Francisco the following month. Others who saw the president regularly also expected him to carry on, if in diminished fashion, for years to come. He had, after all, been an invalid for quarter of a century without it affecting his mental faculties. But it was also no surprise to those who knew his condition that he died suddenly, one month after King's visit.

* * *

On March 29 Roosevelt went to Warm Springs, to rest and to work above all on the speech that would set the tone at the opening of the conference to establish the UNO on April 25.[52] Among those, he took aboard his train were his devoted cousins, Daisy Suckley and Polly Delano; Basil O'Connor, his former law partner; and Leighton McCarthy, the retired Canadian ambassador. Henry Morgenthau stopped by later, on his way to Florida, where his wife had had a heart attack. As usual, the president's absence from Washington was not publicized; he kept in touch by telephone and papers were flown back and forth. He did not look well, slept a great deal, and was far too weak to swim in the hot mineral pool. But he did take drives and attend church with his fellow polio sufferers and, on what turned out to be his last day, he was scheduled to attend a barbeque in his honour followed by the dress rehearsal of a minstrel show by young patients. After a week of sun, sleep, and relaxation, his appetite and complexion began to improve. Lucy Rutherfurd came from South Carolina to stay in a guest cottage, bringing a photographer and also her friend, the noted society artist Elizabeth Shoumantoff, to paint a portrait of Roosevelt for Lucy's daughter, Barbara. Just before lunch on their third day there, Thursday, April 12, the president was signing documents at a card table while Lucy Rutherfurd sat in front of him and Elizabeth Shoumantoff sketched for the portrait. Suddenly he slumped forward, complaining of a terrible pain in his head. He had suffered a stroke and never regained consciousness. The doctors could not revive him and at 3:35 p.m. he

51 Diary, March 13, 1945; Goodwin, *No Ordinary Time*, 591–3.
52 Lelyveld, *His Final Battle*, 312–27; Persico, *Franklin and Lucy*, 328–47; Daniels, *Franklin D. Roosevelt*, 491–9; Ward, *Closest Companion*, 401–22; Lippman, *The Squire of Warm Springs*, 237–41.

died. Lucy Rutherfurd and Elizabeth Shoumantoff left as soon as he collapsed and learned of his death on their way back to South Carolina.

Mackenzie King was having a massage when he heard the news. His response was that "there are apt to be all kinds of rumours at any time." Only two days earlier, a letter from Leighton McCarthy said that the president was weak but benefitting from Warm Springs. But when a few minutes later one of King's secretaries telephoned the osteopath's office, he sensed the significance and took the call. The Canadian prime minister was the only person other than Churchill and Stalin to whom the American secretary of state cabled an announcement of the death. It was no shock to King, who was himself too exhausted for strong emotion: "It all seemed like part of the heavy day's work. Just one more in fact." Death for him was in any event no more than transition from the physical to the spiritual sphere. King grieved the loss of Roosevelt as a friend and his effect on world events but believed that his influence would continue from the Other Side and he himself would still benefit from his late friend's wisdom, as he did from that of others who had gone before.

King immediately ordered the flag on the parliament building lowered to half-mast and the same the next day for federal government buildings throughout the country. He wrote a message by hand to Eleanor Roosevelt and hastily cobbled together a brief tribute for the House of Commons when it resumed after dinner. He told the subdued members that the president was "so great and true a friend of the Canadian people, that the word, when received, was as if one of our own had passed away." But far more than that, his death was a "loss to the whole of mankind." Other party leaders echoed the sentiments and the house adjourned as a mark of respect. Many MPs expressed their personal sympathy to King. In his heart, he was grateful for the privilege of having known Roosevelt so well, "particularly for the last happy days that we had together."

McCarthy's message from Warm Springs had conveyed the president's regret that he could not invite King to share his train to San Francisco but was sure he would understand that Anthony Eden and others had to be taken. "Nothing," thought King, "could be more friendly than such a word." He also considered it fitting that Roosevelt had died at Warm Springs and would be buried at Hyde Park, "which was dearest of all places to his heart." Both Franklin and Eleanor Roosevelt disliked large funerals and lying-in-state but a president could not be buried without some ceremony. It was immediately announced that the funeral would be at the White House and King thought it fitting for Roosevelt's last journey to link the three places of his main associations. He was happy to have been to all of them as an intimate of Roosevelt, "both in the days of his great powers and when it was clear his strength was failing."

Since it would be extremely difficult for King to leave parliament at the very end of the session, in order to attend the funeral on Saturday afternoon, he divided the representation. The governor general would fly to the service in Washington while King would go by overnight train to the burial at Hyde Park on Sunday morning. First, he telephoned McCarthy to ensure that Eleanor Roosevelt approved his attendance at the relatively private family and neigh-bourhood event. When King suggested that the governor general send to Harry Truman a message of sympathy at the loss for the United States, and extend, "in a non-committal way, his wishes for the new President on his assumption of office," Athlone replied that Truman was a crook. King thought him just inexperienced and the governor general too influenced by partisan propaganda. Certainly, the new president was an unknown quantity outside the political world of Washington. He was a moderate senator from the border state of Missouri who got along with both North and South, union leaders and blacks, without offending big business interests. He lacked Roosevelt's patrician polish, flamboyant public manner, and rhetorical talent. Many of his cronies were dis-tinctly dubious, and in the customary fashion he had been kept totally in the dark by Roosevelt. But King was wrong to think that the radical Henry Wallace "would have been more fortunate for America in the end" and that he shared Roosevelt's outlook.[53]

After Truman was sworn in as president, Eleanor Roosevelt flew to Warm Springs, where Polly Suckley could not resist spitefully telling her of Lucy Rutherfurd's presence and other meetings with her husband. The next morning, Eleanor Roosevelt began the journey back to Washington in the presidential train, now the funeral one. It travelled at twenty-five miles an hour so that the millions who gathered beside the tracks and at halts could glimpse the flag-draped coffin with a serviceman at each corner in a carriage with large windows that was kept lit.[54] At 10 a.m. on Saturday morning, it arrived in Washington DC, and the coffin was taken through packed streets to the White House on a horse-drawn caisson accompanied by military bands and planes roaring overhead. The death

---

53 Diary, April 12, 1945.
54 The journey to Washington, then to Hyde Park, the funeral and burial are well covered in Robert Klara, *FDR's Funeral Train: A Betrayed Widow, A Soviet Spy, And a Presidency in the Balance* (New York: Palgrave Macmillan, 2010).

of the commander-in-chief was listed among the military casualties. At 4 p.m. in the east room, two hundred dignitaries and representatives of foreign governments attended the short, standard Episcopalian funeral service conducted by the bishop of Washington who had himself lost a leg to polio. Harry Hopkins came from the Mayo Clinic in Rochester, Minnesota, but was too weak to go to Hyde Park. At the front of the congregation was Roosevelt's wooden wheelchair. There was no music, no singing, no speeches. At Eleanor Roosevelt's request, the bishop inserted into the liturgy the words with which her husband's presidency had begun: "There is nothing to fear but fear itself."

Lord Athlone, with a well-developed royal sense of ceremony, told Mackenzie King that the service was not well ordered and too rushed. Considering that only forty-eight hours had elapsed since Roosevelt's death, it is remarkable that it went as smoothly as it did. As King said, reflecting what Leighton McCarthy told him, both Roosevelt and his widow would have preferred to have the body taken directly to Hyde Park. Athlone's dignity was also offended by there not being any recognition of his presence and not having the opportunity to speak to Eleanor Roosevelt, her daughter, or even the latter's husband. King soothingly responded that Eleanor Roosevelt probably hardly knew what was happening. The oversight may not entirely have displeased King at this moment. He got along well with the Athlones but could be annoyed by their fixation on protocol. An hour earlier, King had telephoned for an appointment and been told by the receptionist that the vice-regal couple was at lunch. When he asked to speak to an aide de camp, he was told that they were also at table. He expostulated that this was "nonsense. It was the Prime Minister speaking and I wanted to get word at once to an ADC." Eventually one was produced.[55]

* * *

Mackenzie King's experience at the interment was exactly the opposite of Athlone's at the funeral. But he was by now a family friend of ten years' standing. He set off by train on Saturday evening, taking along some of his staff, and a niece and namesake of the president's widow, Eleanor Roosevelt Elliott, who lived in Ottawa and had appealed to him since she had no other way of getting there. Looking at the early spring vegetation, King thought it a "nice time of the year

55 Diary, April 16, 1945.

for an earthly body to be placed in the ground after the day's work was done."
Every one of his wartime journeys to the United States had been to see the president, and this almost seemed the same. Roosevelt's death had moved the world
because his greatness lay in "his love of his fellow men. Love of the oppressed
classes and the gallant fight he made for them regardless of classes and the bitter-
est kind of enmity and hatreds." It was astonishing, King thought, that Roosevelt
had escaped assassination and been spared to carry on the struggle to the end.[56]

As King's train steamed south, the funeral train made its slow way north from
Washington, again with huge crowds gathered alongside the tracks. A second
train carried the new president and the cabinet. At Hyde Park, just before he got
out of bed at 8 a.m., King thought he saw Roosevelt's train pass by, although
it might have been the other. Secret servicemen urged him go to Springwood
as soon as possible, probably because there were hardly enough cars to convey all those from the trains. King, his secretary Walter Turnbull and Eleanor
Elliott were practically the first at the estate. An official suggested waiting in the
house. This brought back memories of the visit with the king and queen but King
decided that he would rather walk in the spring sunshine with Eleanor Elliott. He
noticed that he was alone in wearing a top hat, which had been insisted on by his
strong-willed valet John Nicol, "though I kept telling him I felt sure that that the
other was correct." Unable to retrieve his homburg from the train in time, King
wore Turnbull's while the secretary carried the prime minister's silk one. King
recorded this for "psychic reasons." He and Roosevelt had enjoyed many jokes
about hats and King felt that they were sharing this one, too.

The gravesite was in the rose garden beside the presidential library. While
he waited, Mackenzie King talked to secretary of state Edward Stettinius and
Bernard Baruch (who had been dining in London with Churchill just before the
news of Roosevelt's death arrived). Stettinius was glad that King was going to
the San Francisco conference and confided that Stalin was sending Vyacheslav
Molotov, his foreign minister, which seemed a good omen for a successful meeting. King thought Roosevelt's death might help to bring the organization he had
championed into being and Stettinius agreed that "we must have his spirit dominate the conference." He made a point of introducing King to various people,
many of whom he already knew. It seems odd, even in the crush of the moment,
that King was not presented to Truman. Stettinius insisted that King stand in

56 Diary, April 14, 1945.

the front row, between himself and Henry Stimson, who at seventy-seven was none too well himself. He also prompted King to place his bouquet on the massive bank of flowers and then to repeat it for filming. King was the only member of a foreign government present, but as a friend and not in any official capacity.

Roosevelt's coffin arrived on a caisson accompanied by military bands. The brief committal service was read by the seventy-eight-year-old rector of the Hyde Park Episcopal Church. King was deeply moved by the simple ritual and the lack of class distinction in dress between the notables and neighbours: "When clothes come to be a barrier rather than a bond, they have lost part of their usefulness." Eleanor Roosevelt was supported by Anna Boettiger and Elliott Roosevelt who had been brought from Britain by Baruch (the other three sons, serving in the Pacific, did not arrive in time). Eleanor was veiled but King thought her ashen grey, however self-controlled. Behind the family stood Truman whom King could not see. After the coffin was lowered into the grave, cadets from the nearby West Point Military Academy fired three rifle volleys and each time Roosevelt's Scottish terrier, Fala, barked. The crowd then quickly dispersed since the trains to Washington were leaving in an hour. Eleanor Roosevelt stood alone at the grave for a few minutes, then joined relatives in the house.

Leighton McCarthy, who had come all the way from Warm Springs in the funeral train and was going back to Canada with King, went with the prime minister and Eleanor Elliott to express their condolences to the family. Eleanor Roosevelt said how happy she was to see King: "That she knew that Franklin would be so glad that I had been there" and that bringing her niece was the sweetest thing he could have done. King told her: "you have both fought the good fight to the very end and have kept the faith to the very end," emphasising "both" so that she would feel that the battle had also been hers, "which it had been in a very true measure." He assured her: "There is no such thing as separation. Life goes on. He will be nearer than ever at your side." They then touched cheeks.

King spoke to Anna Boettiger (with no idea of the tension with her mother after the revelation of Anna's collusion in her father's meetings with Lucy Rutherfurd). He expressed his sympathy to Elliott Roosevelt, who looked tired and drawn, and to others he knew, including Frederick Delano, Roosevelt's favourite uncle, who bore a striking resemblance to his nephew and whose wife (though not genetically related) looked like Franklin's mother. As he and McCarthy, Turnbull, and Eleanor Elliott drove to the train, it seemed to King that all nature spoke not of loss but of reward and God's providence. It was as though Roosevelt himself had been in charge of the arrangements, from his death at Warm Springs, to the funeral in Washington and the burial in the garden at Hyde Park, "and sunshine all the way."

In the train, Leighton McCarthy naturally talked about his late friend. He seems tactfully not to have mentioned Lucy Rutherfurd. He and Roosevelt had had a long lunch two days before his death and the president had reproved McCarthy for not going to church with him on Easter Sunday. McCarthy also told King about Roosevelt's last hour (which is the same as Daisy Suckley's diary record) and said how much the president was looking forward to the barbeque that afternoon. When King told McCarthy what was no more than the truth, that Roosevelt loved him very much, McCarthy burst into tears, as he had during the funeral service. In Ottawa, King dropped McCarthy at the Chateau Laurier, drove Eleanor Elliott home, and at Laurier House, fell to his knees in prayer for the great friend that God had given him in Roosevelt and for strength to continue the work he had left, along with Stettinius, Stimson and others.[57]

* * *

Two days later King read a newspaper account of the memorial service in London and Winston Churchill's eulogy to Roosevelt which followed the day after the burial at Hyde Park. The president's death was a blow to Churchill, although no more a surprise than it was to Mackenzie King. Why he decided not to go to the funeral, even with a plane waiting, remains a mystery. Many ministers were away, including Eden, who was in Washington on his way to San Francisco. He sent Churchill a cable that he was not wanted and that he himself represented Britain at the funeral. Six years later, Churchill said that not going was his greatest mistake in the war: "During the next three months tremendous decisions were made, and I had a feeling that they were being made by a man I did not know."[58] Truman had no experience of foreign policy but it soon transpired that he was much closer to Churchill's outlook, particularly on the Soviet Union, than Roosevelt had ever been.

In war-ravaged London, the service in St. Paul's Cathedral was of a standard of magnificence that would have satisfied even Lord Athlone. It was attended by the British royal family, other European royals, and a vast host of the great

57 Diary, April 15, 1945.
58 Moran, *Churchill*, 370–1; (Diary entry, October 15, 1951).

and good. British and American flags decorated the crowd-lined streets. In the cathedral there was much music and singing and the reverberation of trumpets in the huge marble dome. That afternoon in the House of Commons, Churchill paid tribute to "the greatest American friend we have ever known and the greatest champion of freedom who has ever brought help and comfort from the new world to the old." Mackenzie King was not alone in thinking that this was far from Churchill's best speech. The mood of the house, and even Churchill's manner, had been spoiled by an hour-long wrangle, in which he took a prominent part, over the claim of a newly elected Scottish nationalist MP that he should be able to take his seat without sponsors. But since the speech was not broadcast, this had no effect on the published text that King and others read. If it was not one of Churchill's finest orations, it was certainly a memorable farewell to his great partner. In terms that he must have hoped would be applied to himself if he fell at the same stage, he said that Roosevelt "died in harness, and we may say in battle harness. . . What an enviable death was his. He had brought his country through the worst of its perils and the heaviest of its toils. Victory had cast its sure and steady beam upon him."[59]

As so often, even in a speech that was about Roosevelt, Mackenzie King was annoyed that Churchill did not think to mention Canada and its great contribution to the war. But he thought it was impossible to say too much about Roosevelt's part in helping to save the world: "It is only now that he is gone that the people can realize what a tremendous part he has played." On the same day as Churchill's tribute, King was heartened by Truman's affirmation in a speech to Congress that he would continue Roosevelt's policies: "Indeed one feels there is a note in what he says of a man who means to be firm, courageous and who with the strength of a younger man [only two years so to Roosevelt], may help to steady things very much at this time." [60] It was also a reassurance to King that Churchill would long endure and continue to command world events.

59 Thompson, *Canada and the End of the Imperial Dream*, 230–1.
60 Diary, April 17, 1945.

CHAPTER THIRTEEN

Churchill's Return from Elba

OR MACKENZIE KING THE MOST immediate of Roosevelt's legacies, the United Nations Organization (UNO), was closely related to the
general election he faced on June 11. Participating in the world peacekeeping body would demonstrate that he was an international statesman. Four
days after Roosevelt's burial, he set off by train for San Francisco, prudently
encouraging bipartisan support for the UNO and eliminating the issue from the
election campaign by taking representatives of the opposition parties.[1] He was
well prepared for the deliberations by his conversations over the past three and
a half years with Roosevelt and Churchill. Truman did not appear, nor did the
invalid Cordell Hull. Churchill, whose main concern was in any event regional
alliances, had never intended to go. Presiding over delegates from the fifty states
allied against Germany and Japan was the unimpressive Edward Stettinius. Apart
from Jan Smuts, a veteran of the founding of the League of Nations who also
wrote the preamble to the UN Charter, King was the most senior head of government present. He was also in familiar company, particularly among the British
contingent which included Eden, Attlee, Cranborne, Halifax, and Cadogan.

The opening session in the San Francisco opera house King considered mere
words, falling well short of the vision that should mark such an occasion and
which he must have expected would have been provided by Roosevelt. While

1   Robert Bothwell, *Alliance and Illusion: Canada and the World, 1945–1984* (Vancouver: UBC Press,
    2007), 18–24; Adam Chapnick, *The Middle Power Project: Canada and the Founding of the United Nations*
    (Vancouver: UBC Press, 2005), 141–53.

he considered Truman's address broadcast from Washington lacklustre, he was heartened by Eden saying that the president was standing four-square with Britain. King himself, as he had told Roosevelt and Churchill, was happy to have the peace enforced, at least initially, by a harmonious Big Three (plus China and France). He saw the necessity of their having a veto in the Security Council to protect their interests and agreed to the use of force against aggression, something he had not supported for the League of Nations. But as at the League, King was opposed to the automatic commitment of any member state by a mere vote. He also wanted recognition of smaller powers, particularly those like Canada which had played a major part in the war.[2]

And Canada's part was astonishing for a vast but sparsely populated country of about twelve million (an increase of a million from the beginning of the war). Over one million men and women were in uniform as the European war drew to an end. In the final tally over 47,000 had been killed, 54,000 wounded and 8,300 had been taken prisoner. The army had five divisions and two armoured brigades, all in Europe. The Royal Canadian Navy with 450 ships had escorted half the convoys across the Atlantic and at the end of the war, owing to the destruction of the German and Japanese navies, was briefly the third largest in the world. So was the Royal Canadian Airforce, which served around the world. The Commonwealth Air Training Plan for which Canada provided $1.6 billion of the $2.2 billion, had produced 131,000 aircrew, over 72,000 of them Canadian. The country had poured out ships, aircraft, munitions, food, raw material and other supplies, doubling its gross domestic product and enabling Canada to donate without obligation $4 billion dollars to the British war effort.[3]

Despite this very impressive contribution, King in his demands at the UN meeting was far more tactful than the loud and abrasive Edward Evatt, the Australian minister of external affairs, who threatened to refuse the charter if certain provisions were not included. King considered this "quasi-insolent,"[4] though his own fundamental attitude was not much different. He told a commonwealth

---

2 Diary, April 25, 1945.
3 A good summary is the article on the Second World War in J. L. Granatstein and Dean F. Oliver, *The Oxford Companion to Canadian Military History* (Toronto: Oxford University Press, 2011), 482–8. The book also has many articles on the individual armed services and many other aspects of the war. See also Dilks, *Churchill and Company: Allies and Rivals in War and Peace* (London: I. B. Taurus, 2012), 78–154, which discusses the fact that India contributed more than all the dominions and colonies combined.
4 Diary, May 7, 1945.

meeting that after the division over conscription, the Canadian parliament would never accept the commandeering of its armed forces without the country participating and voting in the Security Council. At least the dominions might be able to rely on a British veto but he did not see how other small states could accede to the charter without such a provision.[5] He told Stettinius that Canada was willing to do its share against aggression without seeking refuge in parliamentary approval for every request, but warned that if the use of force became an issue in the forthcoming election and the government was defeated, ratification of the charter by other countries would also be affected.

Stettinius accepted King's proposal of inviting any state whose armed services were requested to join the Security Council. This became Article 44 of the charter. It has never been invoked but no one in 1945 could tell exactly how the United Nations would work. King was proud of this "victory for the smaller nations in the fight that was being made for their recognition on the security council. My part has been done quietly, unobtrusively but effectively behind the scenes."[6]

The conference had been in session for two weeks when the war in Europe finally ended on May 7. This had been expected for days and there was no need to waken King with the news. The next day was declared a holiday, although the UN meetings continued. The sale of liquor, even in restaurants, was prohibited, but there were no crowds or demonstrations on the US west coast, which was more concerned about the war that was still being waged against Japan. King's valet celebrated by going to a movie. This decorum was in stark contrast to the scene back in Canada. In Halifax, Nova Scotia there were two days of drunken rioting and looting, which were mortifying for Mackenzie King.

World leaders, including King, gave broadcasts to mark V-E Day, as victory in Europe became known. Winston Churchill spoke on the radio from Downing Street, then repeated the address in the House of Commons, which still refused radio transmission. King thought that Churchill himself wanted two presentations since "he has a great sense of the dramatic and a great regard for parliamentary institutions."[7] He found the short, simple statement with little rhetorical embellishment "natural and vigorous" and was particularly pleased by Churchill's reminder that after the fall of France it was the empire and Commonwealth that

5   Diary, May 11, 1945.
6   Diary, May 14, 1945.
7   Diary, May 5, 1945.

stood with Britain.[8] Smuts told King that George VI wanted to make Churchill a knight of the Garter, but only if they did not object. The Canadian prime minister, consistent with his principles, said that this was a matter entirely for Britain. He thought that nothing Churchill wanted or the king could offer was too good but, perhaps thinking of plain Mr. Gladstone, King pronounced that he should not accept anything: "He has the highest honour that a nation could pay and the confidence they have shown in him." Again he considered that while Churchill might stay to the end of the war against Japan, which was expected to last perhaps to the end of 1946, he would be wise to leave politics altogether.[9] Churchill, at seventy, had no more intention of retiring than King at the same age, or Smuts who was four years older.

* * *

After three weeks at San Francisco, Mackenzie King left on May 14 to begin his election campaign. Other politicians were leaving for similar reasons. The UNO was now secure, as Smuts, who stayed to the very end, said it had to be before the principals departed.[10] The details were worked out by diplomats over the next month.

Eden told King that he was advising Churchill to hold an immediate election, presumably thinking that the great hero could not fail to carry the Conservatives to victory.[11] But Churchill, despite that what he had told King at Quebec, now wanted the coalition to continue until the defeat of Japan. Attlee, who did not believe that Labour could win, was amenable to the compromise of prolonging the government until the autumn; but the Labour party executive, which had great control, insisted on accepting Churchill's stark alternative of an instant end and an election.[12] When the ministry dissolved, Churchill formed an essentially Conservative interim one, wound up parliamentary business, and announced the election for July 5. After the election, as he had told King, he intended to build a new coalition including the Liberals, Ernest Bevin, and a few others he hoped to attract from the Labour party. No one paid much attention to the fairly novel public opinion polls which indicated a Labour victory.

8 Diary, May 8, 1945.
9 Diary, May 10, 1945.
10 Diary, April 24, 1945.
11 Diary, May 11, 1945.
12 Schneer, *Ministers at War*, 225–8.

As soon as Mackenzie King's train crossed the border and reached Vancouver, he began his cross-country campaign. During a rare, four-day stop in his constituency of Prince Albert, Saskatchewan, he received a telegram from Churchill thanking him for the congratulations on V-E Day: "It was a great occasion and we were all in good heart." He reiterated how much was owed to Canada and to King personally and wished the best for all that lay before them, doubtless meaning the elections as well as post-war problems.[13] Three days later, King learned from newspapers the end of the British wartime coalition government. He thought that Churchill would be as glad as he was to have the election so close to victory in Europe. But King was still unsettled by the change. With Roosevelt gone he was no longer a link between the Big Two. Churchill was no longer the national leader but merely head of the Conservative party.[14] King predicted that Churchill would have a hard time in the election but be narrowly returned.[15]

King was by now confident of a comfortable though reduced majority from the huge one of 1940. In fact, the Liberals won only 127 of the 245 seats. King himself was barely elected by the residents of Prince Albert and defeated a week later by the service vote, its hostility probably reflecting both anger at his reluctance to impose conscription and anger at being subjected to it. (The Prince Albert Volunteers were among those who at Terrace, B.C. mutinied in November 1944.) King blamed his defeat on soldiers infected with British socialism. He was easily restored to parliament as MP for Glengarry, conveniently close to Ottawa, in a by-election on August 6, the day the atomic bomb was dropped on Hiroshima.

When he had apparently won at Prince Albert, King received a cable from Churchill anticipating his own victory and appealing again for collective dominion solidarity with Britain as a great world power: "Although it is not proper for us to engage in reciprocal congratulations upon our various fortunes at the polls, I must say with what delight I learned that you had once again attained the position whence you can lead united Canada ever deeper into the union of the British Commonwealth and Empire."[16] King contrasted Churchill's warm sentiments with the unresponsiveness – which could be construed as neutrality

13 Diary, May 20, 1945.
14 Diary, May 23, 1945.
15 Diary, May 23, 1945.
16 Diary, May 17, 1945.

– of the monarch and the governor general and his wife. Not for the first time, he grumbled that "the upholding of the monarchy is a form of idolatry."[17]

Two weeks after the election, King flew back to San Francisco for the signing of the Charter of the United Nations. Smuts was enthusiastic about King's electoral success and thought it would help Churchill. Halifax and Cranborne agreed that a loss by King would have had serious consequences for Britain, where they were not optimistic about the result. Smuts, like King, thought that Churchill had made a great mistake in his first campaign broadcast on June 4, by ignoring the carefully constructed Conservative programme of social reform and instead delivering his own warning that a Labour government would suppress freedom by some form of Nazi-like Gestapo and an army of bureaucrats, "no longer servants and no longer civil." Both had clearly forgotten that a year earlier they had encouraged Churchill in this very direction. There was nevertheless no expectation in San Francisco that Churchill's party would actually lose.

The great figure continued to occupy the thoughts of King, Smuts and the British from afar in other ways, as well. They talked about his habit of working far into the night after spending much of the afternoon in bed, but neither Smuts nor Halifax thought him overburdened since he did not try to read too many papers but gathered information from his colleagues. Earlier in the day, Smuts had warned King to beware of British attempts to build the machinery for imperial unity. Halifax criticized Evatt of Australia and Fraser of New Zealand for embarrassing the British Empire by talking too much but Smuts said that it was good for others to see that the dominions were masters in their own house, although at one on big issues. King could not disagree. Smuts pointed to his own problem with a united Commonwealth policy by saying that he needed to get home to deal with the Afrikans electoral majority, which was far more hostile to the British connection than French-Canadians or any other group in Canada.[18]

The San Francisco conference was closed by Harry Truman, who impressed King by his lack of affectation, his energy and light, rapid step (itself a novelty after twelve years of an immobile American president). King looked forward to working with him but had prudently declined an invitation to the White House during the election campaign. Probably recalling what Roosevelt and Churchill had said to him about being the international mediator, he thought that the

17 Diary, June 12, 1945.
18 Diary, 24 June 1945.

establishment of the United Nations was the beginning of an era in which he would be in demand as an international, elder statesman. As he reflected, Roosevelt was dead, Smuts was seventy-five, and Churchill (unlike King, despite his complaints) would be tired from the election campaign. Apart from Stalin, King was the only significant leader who had been in office from the beginning of the war. And more than a quarter of a century ago he had, at least in his own mind, clearly established his credentials as a man of the future by articulating in *Industry and Humanity* the social changes that would be demanded, as well as the principles of the United Nations.[19]

* * *

Mackenzie King's global importance, again to himself, increased further with the British election. This was held five days after the UN Charter was signed but counting was deferred for three weeks, to July 26, to include the overseas service vote, rather than adding it afterwards as in Canada. Churchill in the meantime, went to Potsdam to discuss with Stalin and Truman the future of Europe and arrange for a peace conference. The gulf between east and west meant that the latter was never held. Instead, individual treaties with enemy countries were worked out by the foreign ministers of the major allies. Churchill correctly, and even amiably, considering the bitterness of the recent election campaign, took the leader of the opposition in the unlikely event that he became prime minister. A seemingly more practical reason was to secure bipartisan support for whatever was decided. On July 25, the meeting was suspended for Churchill and Attlee to fly to Britain for the election results. Two days later Attlee returned alone. Stalin was not the only one astonished at the mysterious ways in which democracy moved.

When Mackenzie King turned on the radio at 8 a.m. on July 26, the headline news was that Labour was sweeping Britain (where it was already afternoon). Labour won a crushing 393 seats to 213 for the Conservatives and twelve for the Liberals. King had never doubted that Churchill would remain in power, although he had expected Labour to make big gains, writing in his diary that workers would no longer tolerate the conditions in which they were forced to exist. What the British wanted, the ultra-cautious Canadian reformer boldly asserted, was "a social revolution . . . the great body of the people are going to have a larger share of their own lives." King thought that they also disliked

19 Diary, June 25–26, 1945.

the influence of Beaverbrook and Bracken, whom he was not alone in blaming for irreparable harm to Churchill. Churchill, thought King, had all too clearly revealed that he was at heart a Tory, "though he has broad Liberal sympathies in a way, but it is the old Whig [aristocratic] style of Liberalism."

King was not short of personal sympathy for Churchill, whom he had wanted to see continue as head of a national coalition until the defeat of Japan and then drop out completely. But he could not resist the opportunity to contrast the superiority of his own unassuming style with Churchill's Icarus-like fall: "His ambition has over-reached itself and he has fallen from a terrible height. It will be an awful blow to him – the kind of blow that stimulants do not help one to recover from." People, pontificated King, did not like "any man to become a god. The higher a man rises on all counts the more humble-minded he should become." Nor did Churchill's lavish lifestyle help: "the ostentatious display of cigar, drinking etc." Far too much public money, King thought, had been spent on international conferences: "too much emphasis on the 'Big Three' business." Americans, he claimed, also disliked Roosevelt's "drastic expenditures," by which he meant the New Deal, but at least the president's infirmity had kept him in touch with ordinary people. After Churchill's great blow, King predicted that he "will age very rapidly and with his nature I would not be surprised if a certain bitterness developed."

Apart from the consequences for Churchill, King considered that the British election was all for the best. A Conservative ministry would have been "arrogant in dealing with present problems. The people now have a government of their own choice. This will have a quieting influence and will develop character in those who govern-a quieting in post-war times when it is most needed." He thought Labour would be more helpful toward international peace than the Conservatives, who would have relied on power rather than human brotherhood, antagonizing the Soviet Union and other European countries. Labour would be "quicker to recognize common rights and to come to share them, in a way which will not place burdens on the people themselves to say nothing of costing their lives." King also expected, incorrectly it turned out, a different spirit towards the Commonwealth and looked forward with relief to having no longer to combat imperial centralism. In this sphere, and in much else, he thought it inevitable that great responsibilities must now fall to the still-standing Canadian leader who was heading his sixth government.[20]

20 Diary, July 26, 1945.

The world, meaning in effect Truman and Attlee, did not, in fact, clamour for Mackenzie King's services. He continued to busy himself with international concerns even after devolving the department of external affairs to Louis St. Laurent in September 1946. As with Churchill in Britain, there were many in Canada, including in the Liberal party, who thought that King was well past his expiry date. But while he complained increasingly of tiredness (which may have been an early sign of heart disease), of the burdens that were placed on him, and insisted that he would not fight another election, King stuck doggedly to the duty he owed to the country and the world. Not much more than a month after Churchill's defeat, he was providing valuable information that helped the war leader's resurrection as a global figure.

* * *

The issue was one not one that King expected or welcomed. Sharing the hope that, after two shattering wars in thirty years, peace might be preserved by the cooperation of all the great powers, he had little sense of the extent of the gulf that was opening between the United States and Britain on one side and the USSR on the other. From discussions with Churchill and Roosevelt he knew there were tensions but thought them largely owing to the old anti-Bolshevik Churchill. King lamented the loss of Roosevelt as the moderating influence between the British leader and Stalin. Truman was an unknown quantity, but King knew Attlee well enough to regard him as a distinct improvement to promote harmony among the Big Three. Then suddenly an event occurred, in Ottawa of all places, that hardened divisions between east and west, gave substance to Churchill's view of the Soviet Union, supported Truman's inclination, and effectively marked the beginning of the Cold War.

Igor Gouzenko was a twenty-six-year-old cypher clerk trained in intelligence at the Soviet embassy in Ottawa. On the summer evening of September 5, less than a month after the surrender of Japan, and just before Gouzenko was to be returned home to the USSR, he went to the police with documents revealing a spy ring in Canada and the United States that was particularly concerned with atomic research.[21] He was so agitated and had such limited English that at first no one would take him seriously. But two days later, while he and his pregnant

---

21 Amy Knight, *How The Cold War Began: The Gouzenko Affair and the Hunt for Soviet Spies* (Toronto: McClelland and Stewart, 2005); Bothwell, *Alliance and Illusion*, 44–9; Levine, *King*, 370–8.

wife and son were sheltered by a neighbour, Soviet security officers broke into his apartment hoping to seize Gouzenko and his material. The police now changed their attitude and took the family into protection. Gouzenko and his information were examined and found trustworthy. The Soviet embassy's demand that he be handed over for stealing money was refused.

In a high state of nerves about the imminent opening of parliament, the last thing Mackenzie King needed was this diplomatic embarrassment. He had made a point of cultivating good relations with the Soviet envoys both to help the war effort and the security of peace afterwards. But once convinced of Gouzenko's claims, he felt betrayed, in that this was how Canada and other western countries were repaid for their support of the USSR. He had sided with Roosevelt in thinking that the Soviets should be told about nuclear research – ignoring that if information had been shared there might have been no need for espionage – but now he believed that it was Churchill who was wiser in refusing to share the information and in trying to prevent a Soviet atomic bomb. He had "the sounder judgement; had keener perceptions of what was at stake, what was going on." A month after two atomic bombs had been dropped on Japan to devastating effect, nuclear war was "just too appalling a thought for words." But King feared that the world was exactly "at the edge of a situation of the kind at this hour." The ink was scarcely dry on the UN Charter but the organization would be worse than useless if it merely gave the illusion of peace while the great power veto allowed the USSR to refuse investigations of its preparations for sudden war. Unless the veto was abolished, he thought it far better to form groups without the Soviet Union.[22] This was what happened, much as Churchill had argued. The United Nations continued but within a few years there were also regional security pacts, notably the North Atlantic Treaty Organization.

The risk that the Gouzenko disclosures would provoke a split between the great powers, and even lead to atomic war, convinced King to keep the matter completely secret until he consulted Truman and Attlee in person. He added Winston Churchill to this select group, with significant consequences. So sensitive was the espionage matter that King kept the record of it separate from his regular diary.[23] Setting off for Washington at the end of September, he claimed

---

22 Secret Diary, September 23, 1945.
23 The "Secret and Confidential Diary Relating to Russian Espionage Activities – September 6 to October 31, 1945" follows the regular diary entry of November 9, 1945 and is referred to here as "Secret Diary".

that he was on a purely private visit to the US president. The trip to Britain, which followed immediately, was justified on the ground of needing to become acquainted with the new ministers, never mind that King knew most of them from the wartime government. An additional benefit of the overseas excursion was a holiday from parliament, which he left to his colleagues. He allowed plenty of time to see friends and sit for his official portrait by Frank Salisbury.

On Saturday, September 29, King flew to Washington and the next morning met for two hours at the White House with Truman and Dean Acheson, now the assistant secretary of state. He was struck by the changes to the house, which had already been redecorated by the Trumans, who had been appalled at the shabby state in which the indifferent Roosevelts had lived. (Thirteen truckloads of their effects had been removed from the rickety structure that would be completely rebuilt between 1948 and 1952.[24]) The gleaming exterior looked like a sepulchre King thought. He was more approving of the interior which was also improved by being less crowded with people. In the Oval Office, the last place he and the late president had met, King was given Roosevelt's customary place on the sofa. Truman was disturbed about spying in the United States and said he would investigate it but he cautiously decided that nothing should be done until he, Attlee, and King discussed the matter together.[25] King called on Cordell Hull and Lord Halifax, then sailed from New York aboard the *Queen Mary*. Among his fellow passengers was Professor Denis Brogan of the University of Cambridge, and a specialist in American history, who was working on the draft proofs of the *History of the English-Speaking Peoples*, which Churchill was now resuming. Brogan gave King some chapters to read but he made no comment on them in his diary.[26]

* * *

When the ship docked at Southampton, King went directly to see Attlee at Chequers for the Sunday night. In customary British (and Canadian) fashion, which surprised Americans, Attlee had kept Churchill's civil service staff. Two of the secretaries, John Martin and John Peck, were at the family dinner. The talk was mainly of the election. The new prime minister acknowledged that he had not expected to win but thought there would be a stalemate, while Churchill

---

24 Seale, *The White House*, 238.
25 Diary, September 30; Secret Diary dictated October 1, 1945.
26 Diary, October 1, 1945.

had predicted a Conservative majority of fifty, sixty or even ninety. Attlee said that Churchill's mistake was to appeal too much to the past and his failure to grasp "the condition of the masses of the people and what they were really feeling about their needs." Peck added that Churchill had written his own campaign speeches, then read them to Beaverbrook and Bracken, who were the worst possible advisers, so that he ended up damaging himself. King and Attlee discussed the Gouzenko affair privately. The British prime minister agreed that there should be further investigations in the United Kingdom and the United States before any arrests were made. Discussing the UN veto, he shared King's view about the danger, but though it was the price that had to be paid to include the Soviet Union and probably the other great powers.[27]

King settled into his customary suite at the Dorchester Hotel after travelling with Attlee the next morning to London. More than he had been during his two war visits, he was struck by the shabbiness and destruction to the imperial centre he had known for close to half a century. From the hotel, he watched a two-hour long march of unemployed men who had been bombed out of their homes. A couple of days later, he wrote that the city had "a gloomy and bewildering sort of look about it . . . A certain glory has passed away. One feels that the masses of people are struggling. One wonders how they manage at all. Food is at impossible prices. Clothing hardly obtainable." Austerity was increasing as a result of the abrupt cessation of lend-lease, which had included food, on the occasion of Japan's surrender a month earlier. King felt guilty about his own luxurious quarters but quieted his conscience with the reflection that they were necessary for his position.[28] The Attlees lived in a style closer to the population than Churchill and restrained themselves in requesting extra "diplomatic" provisions to entertain important visitors. At one family dinner in Downing Street, King was served a glass of sherry, vegetable soup – which he pronounced delicious – porridge (perhaps a barley stew) and dessert.[29] In the straitened aftermath of war that this reflected, the Labour government wanted to discuss imperial preferences as a means of reviving exports. King evasively said that he had not come for that purpose and could not deal with it without consulting his cabinet. Norman Robertson, whom he allowed to go to a meeting on the subject, reported that the

27 Diary, October 7
28 Diary, October 8 and 11, 1945.
29 Diary, October 21, 1945.

CHURCHILL'S RETURN FROM ELBA

British did not seem to know what they wanted.[30] The real need, of course, was the financial aid that Roosevelt had so casually but informally promised Churchill at Quebec a year earlier.

Everywhere King went in political circles, the leading topic was Churchill and his great fall. At a dinner, foreign secretary Ernest Bevin held in honour of King, he said that he was privately very fond of Churchill and had begged him not to hold an election before the defeat of Japan, and then to step aside from partisan politics "and be available to make important statements to the world, and to assume the role of a world statesman–outside Party controversy." Bevin had expected Churchill to win with a majority of about forty. (He was equally wrong, as he frankly told King, in predicting victory for the CCF in Canada.) As consolation for their party's expected loss, Bevin had promised his wife a holiday. When Labour was elected, he wanted to be chancellor of the exchequer but was appointed to the foreign office in place of the loud and abrasive Hugh Dalton, who went instead to the treasury. When he told his wife of his new office, Bevin said: "Old girl, there is no Brighton Beach for us. It is Potsdam instead."[31]

King's first sighting of Winston Churchill, who had just returned from a holiday at Lake Como, was in the House of Commons (still sitting in the House of Lords), where the Labour government was presenting its interim budget. He was much interested in the form of the mother of parliaments, where he had not been for forty years. The House was packed with MPs who were very decorous, although Attlee, Churchill, and half a dozen others slumped low on the front benches with their feet on the table. King thought the small chamber (which like the former and future Commons held only about half the members) was better suited to debate than the Canadian one in which each member had a desk. He was impressed by Dalton's performance and humorous touches as he reduced taxes for those at the bottom of the scale and raised them for those at the top. Part way through the performance, Eden nudged Churchill who looked up to the gallery, nodded, and then waved to King who thought this "quite an experience to have had in the British H. of C." He was impressed by Churchill's brief response to Dalton. Speaking slowly and using exactly the right words, he managed to commend the chancellor of the exchequer while deploring that demobilization

30 Diary, October 13 and 15, 1945.
31 Diary, October 10, 1945.

was not faster to release people for productive work. Churchill later told King that his remarks were spontaneous and that the courteous overture was customary. Soon enough, the Conservatives would be attacking the budget. The other thing that impressed King, the master of the long, sententious speeches, was the brisk efficiency of this important occasion: within a couple of hours of arriving at parliament he was back at his hotel.[32]

* * *

Three days later, Mackenzie King went to lunch with the Churchills at their new house at 28 Hyde Park Gate, close to the Royal Albert Hall. (Before the war, they had had an apartment near parliament.) Clementine had organized the move while her husband was on holiday in Italy. As King entered the street, he met Mary and Randolph Churchill, the latter staying only for sherry since there was not enough food for all. Churchill came to the door to greet his old friend and Clementine was also pleased to see him. The former prime minister and his wife were now reduced from their wartime opulence to food rations, but like other wealthy people they supplemented the meagre allotment by such means as gifts from overseas and meals in restaurants. Lunch, which featured caviar from Russia and snipe, did not fall below their customary Edwardian standard. Game was never rationed, except by price, and Clementine had personally gone to select the birds for this occasion. There was, as always, plenty to drink, of which King had only a small amount: wine, port, and Russian vodka, which Churchill declared unfit for consumption and ordered to be thrown out and replaced by brandy. King thought it had been produced as a cue to talk about the Soviet Union, about which Churchill had no idea the Canadian prime minister had his own reason for wanting to discuss.

Churchill as usual dominated the talk, in "an exceedingly nice way. He has a marvellous mind, ranges from one subject to another with perfect ease and adequate expression." He feared that Labour's policy of equalizing incomes would reduce prosperity by discouraging high earners from working. He ascribed the dogma primarily to the wealthy, austere vegetarian Sir Stafford Cripps, the president of the board of trade, and his time in the Soviet Union, as though he had not been radical enough before. King did not mention his own sympathy with the electorate but commiserated by pointing to his own defeat at the hands

32 Diary, October 23, 1945.

of socialist soldiers. Churchill grumpily responded that at least in Canada the military vote had stood by the government better than elsewhere. King suggested that Churchill might improve his prospects by changing the name of his party: the term "conservative" did not suit the present age: "Liberal had come to mean what Liberal-Conservatives really stood for. That the CCF or Socialist Party represented the other extreme." This may have been an encouragement to Churchill, although he was almost alone among Conservatives in wanting to amalgamate with the Liberals.

The two naturally talked about Roosevelt, whose death only six months ago, must have seemed like an event from another age. Churchill repeated that it was a great loss but said that at Yalta he had seen that the president was "gone, that there was not life there, that the man was exhausted." Several times, Churchill and his wife mentioned Roosevelt's affection for King.

The major topic of conversation was the Soviet Union. Churchill was eager to have King's support for his fears, and King had much to contribute. Clementine, who had led the Red Cross Aid to Russia Fund, said that the stricken country had provided the most lavish hospitality to impress her. Her husband's theme was grimmer: the Soviets were grabbing one country after another and should have been resisted more. This implied that it was Roosevelt who had failed to resist since Churchill insisted that he himself had had "some pretty stiff talks" with Stalin (presumably excluding the one on the "percentages agreement"). He thought there was "nothing to be gained by not letting them know that we were not afraid of them. That they would not thank us for lying down before them at any stage." The Soviets were "realist lizards." They would "be as pleasant with you as they could be, although prepared to destroy you. That sentiment meant nothing with them – morals meant nothing."

When the two were alone, King told Churchill in strict confidence as a fellow privy counsellor (in both countries) about Gouzenko. Churchill found the information "indeed interesting and most important," interpreting it as corroboration that the Soviets would use any method to spread communism. Anxious to have the nefarious activity made public, he claimed that the Soviets would not mind since "they had been exposed time and time again." He approved of the United States, Britain, and Canada acting together once they had a careful plan but warned against letting the issue fade away. King's comment that neither the Commonwealth nor the United States alone could deal with the Soviet Union was exactly what Churchill wanted to hear, and he urged King to do all he could to keep all the countries together.

The ideal opportunity for Churchill to put himself back on the world stage had just arrived. He told King that he had been invited by Westminster College in Fulton, Missouri (misidentified in the diary as the University of Missouri) to give a series of lectures on European conditions. Churchill was not short of invitations but this one was special because it was commended in his own hand by president Truman, who promised to attend and give the introduction, making it an international event. Churchill never gave a set of speeches but told King that he might give a single one on the state of the world and would decline the generous honorarium (he was given instead a gold watch). He would inform the British government and Truman in advance what he intended to say, making the address a stalking horse for joint policy by both countries. What he had in mind was a warning against the USSR, like those he had delivered against Nazi Germany in the late 1930s. Whatever the risk that what he said would be rejected, and however obscure the college, the presence of Truman in his native state in the heartland of American isolation provided the right setting to urge the United States to remain involved in Europe and stand with Britain against the new threat to the world. After King's confirmation of Soviet treachery, it was no wonder that Churchill was so effusive when they parted. Enviously, he told the Canadian prime minister that "other men are as children in the leadership of the Party as compared to yourself." King, not surprisingly, thought that no words could have been kinder: "It was the sweetest side of his nature throughout—a really beautiful side. One cannot help loving him when that side of his nature is to the fore."[33] A few days later, Churchill sent King a presentation set of leather-bound volumes of his wartime speeches; all were inscribed and in one he wrote: "A Long Struggle–A Still Longer Friendship."[34]

Shortly afterwards, King was invited, purposely, to lunch at the Soviet embassy. On the face of it, this was an expected courtesy since Fedor Gusev and his wife had left Ottawa only two years earlier. But the ambassador's purpose was much deeper. He wanted to keep King's friendliness towards the USSR as well as find out what Gouzenko had revealed and what was intended to be done about it. Gusev must have set up the spy network, although it does not seem to have occurred to King, and he would have been fully briefed on everything his government knew. This included King's discussions with Truman and Attlee,

33 Diary and Secret Diary, October 26, 1945.
34 Diary, October 30, 1945.

about which the Soviets learned from informers, including Kim Philby, who had a senior position in the British intelligence service.[35] If there was any Soviet citizen who could ferret out what King knew, it was Gusev. King was wary of the ambassador's intention and did not need Norman Robertson's warning to be careful. Even less than usual was he tempted to go beyond tasting the vast array of tongue-loosening drink.

The former neighbours greeted each other warmly enough but their conversation was guarded. Gouzenko was never mentioned but it was easy for King to sense that Gusev knew about the matter and knew that King did, too. When the ambassador edged into the topic by saying that Canada had had a lot to do with developing the atomic bomb (which provided some justification for spying by the excluded ally), King insisted that although much research had been done in the country, it had not been involved in producing weapons, and it had no knowledge of the process.

By the end of their agreeable discussion, Gusev must have had the strong impression that the espionage matter could be quietly smoothed over. King told the ambassador: "you and I are old friends. We must do all we possibly can to see that good-will is promoted between different countries–particularly our respective countries. Spoke of being near neighbours. Also of the great part Russia had taken in the war, etc."[36] In diplomatic circumlocution, King appealed for the Soviet Union to repent its wicked ways and become the good world citizen that Roosevelt had hoped. Only in this way, King believed, could another war be avoided, in which Canada, geographically between the United States and the Soviet Union, would be highly vulnerable.

* * *

Sailing home aboard the *Queen Mary* after a month away, King was convinced that the consultations with the new heads of the American and British governments proved that "my association with these men and the atomic bomb problem has given me a place in world recognition that even years of war themselves did not begin to give."[37] He expected this to be solidified at the conference of the three heads of government on atomic research and the spy ring in Washington as soon

---

35 Knight, *How the Cold War Began*, 47–8.
36 Secret Diary, October 31, 1945.
37 Diary, November 4, 1945.

as he landed and Attlee arrived by air. For the British prime minister, however, an even more pressing matter was the negotiations then underway for a desperately needed loan. Unfortunately, the period of the secret meetings in Washington is the only section from 1893 to 1959 of Mackenzie King's diary that is missing. [38] There is no account of the discussions. The loss emphasizes the value of King's record for many similar occasions.

Talks between the three were held from November 10 to 15. Convinced that nuclear weapons were the key to peace, and more suspicious of the Soviets than Roosevelt, Truman was determined to preserve the American lead as long as possible. He refused to share atomic knowledge with any country, including Britain, and not just because he feared that it would thereby reach the USSR. Attlee's need for a loan and other American support left him no alternative but to acquiesce but the British government soon secretly developed its own bomb. The three leaders appealed publicly for the United Nations to establish a commission to investigate nuclear power and atomic weapons and to exercise international control. This began in January 1946 but foundered after three years on the acrimonious obstruction over information and inspection of sites, principally by the Soviet Union. On the spy network, Truman, Attlee and King agreed to act simultaneously but there was not enough evidence for legal charges. Only Canada revived wartime emergency powers to hold people without trial. But King would not move against the spies by himself. For the time being, every country simply watched the situation. [39]

Three months later, they were jolted into action when the famous American journalist Drew Pearson announced on his radio show on Sunday, February 4

---

38 At some point this volume vanished. King's regular diary ends with his landing in New York on November 9 and does not resume until January 1, 1946. The secret diary on the Gouzenko spy revelations also ends abruptly on October 31. What happened to the two documents remains a mystery. The Royal Canadian Mounted Police suspected a cover up of Canadian communist spies. It is possible that Jack Pickersgill, King's secretary, a literary executor and editor of the published extracts of the 1939–1948 diaries, wanted to protect his friends, or at least fellow Liberals, from any implication. More likely, the volumes were stolen by the photographer in the Public Archives in the 1950s who was copying the diary for the executors and made one for himself which he tried to sell. But even publications that detested King refused, for reasons of legal liability, to buy it. The photographer had just finished copying the volume before the missing ones when he was accused of the attempted sale (there was not enough evidence for prosecution) and fired. He may have kept the late 1945 material, hoping to blackmail the archives or the government into paying him for it. Or he may have feared to reveal the theft by returning it. If he did not destroy the documents, there is a chance that they might someday surface. Dummitt, *Unbuttoned*, 137–42, 236–41 and 252–6.
39 Knight, *How the Cold War Began*, 85–7.

that an espionage circle had been uncovered in Canada and that King had been to Washington to inform Truman, implying that it extended to the United States. King read a transcript of the broadcast and found the account garbled but thought that it must have been inspired by the American government to push Canada into taking the lead in legal proceedings.[40] The obvious suspect was J. Edgar Hoover, the long-serving director of the Federal Bureau of Investigation, who was paranoid about left-wing subversives and considered the Truman administration to be dangerously liberal.[41]

King was not unduly distressed by this furore or the attention to Canada and himself. He believed it "may be all for the best, as it gives us a special reason for starting immediately with our investigation" of what he expected to be "one of the major sensations of the day."[42] After confiding the matter to the cabinet, he established a royal commission of two supreme court judges to hear Gouzenko's allegations in secret. Ten days later, following its first interim report, thirteen suspects, among them a secretary at the British high commission, were arrested, held in isolation and questioned by the police without any legal niceties of counsel or being allowed to contact their families. Thirty-nine people were eventually arrested and eighteen were convicted. The most prominent was Fred Rose, the sole communist (Labour-Progressive) MP, who was found guilty of passing information about a non-nuclear explosive (RDX). The only atomic scientist charged was Alan Nunn May, a member of the University of Cambridge atomic team that had moved to Montreal during the war. He was convicted in Britain of supplying uranium samples and research reports to the Soviets. The trials increased the fear of Soviet communism and espionage in the three Atlantic countries and within a few years reached hysterical levels in the United States. Canadian diplomatic relations with the USSR were reduced to the level of chargé d'affaires, with ambassadors not being restored until after the death of Stalin in 1952. The Canadian government's actions against suspects were widely endorsed, although the CCF and Conservatives criticized the violation of civil liberties, and even Mackenzie King had qualms about the end justifying the means.[43]

40 Diary, February 5, 1946.
41 Knight, *How the Cold War Began*, 105–6.
42 Diary, February 4, 1946.
43 Knight, *How the Cold War Began*, 146–50 and 172–88.

* * *

While the Gouzenko drama publicly unfolded in Ottawa in icy February, Churchill and his wife were enjoying the sun and surf of Miami Beach at the house of the Canadian, Colonel Frank W. Clarke. Churchill was pondering the state of the world and his own future but above all, his speech in Missouri on March 5. Drew Pearson's spy network revelation seemed to set the stage. Ten days after the broadcast, Churchill invited King to Florida but the Gouzenko issue prevented him from leaving Ottawa.[44]

Two weeks later, still in Florida, Churchill telephoned, again asking King to meet him in Washington to discuss the speech, which was now only a week away. King was still too preoccupied with espionage and thought that a trip to Washington would fuel speculation. Churchill reiterated what he had said in London, that the undercover activities were a serious matter for Soviet relations, and believed that King would approve of the theme of closer Anglo-American ties in his speech.[45] The next morning Churchill called once more. Having learned that there was a private telephone line from Washington to Ottawa, he wanted to read the speech for King's opinion. While claiming that he did not to want to commit King, this was clearly his hope. He added the further flattering information that he intended to propose steadying the world by means of a US-Commonwealth defence agreement like the 1940 Canadian-American Permanent Joint Board of Defence. King was ecstatic and promised to send a copy of his own parliamentary speech on the agreement, which he thought anticipated much of what Churchill intended to say.[46] It must have slipped his mind that the Ogdensburg initiative had been entirely Roosevelt's.

Since King did not consider the telephone line between the two capitals secure, he asked the Canadian ambassador to review Churchill's text. At the British embassy, Lester Pearson found Churchill in bed reading the speech King had sent. He reported to King that Churchill's address was as fine as any he had ever made. Pearson claimed that he had persuaded Churchill to strike out the mention of a US-Commonwealth military agreement. After King's umbrage over Lord Halifax's Toronto address two years earlier, Pearson also carefully protected himself by warning King that Churchill was using strong language about the division

44 Diary, February 13, 1946.
45 Diary, February 28, 1946.
46 Diary, March 1, 1946.

of Europe and united resistance against any further Soviet encroachment. But, he pointed out, Churchill was only speaking for himself, and not for any government.

How much of the caution Pearson expressed to King was then conveyed to Churchill is impossible to know. Churchill telephoned King to say that he appreciated the ambassador's help. They also discussed the Gouzenko commission's first report, which would be released the next day. Churchill and Truman would be on the train to Fulton, but Lester Pearson had already shown the document to the American secretary of state to demonstrate authoritatively that spying extended to the United States. Churchill wanted King to issue a firm statement about the Soviet activities: "the same tactics all over again" and hoped that King would come to see him in New York before he sailed home.[47] On the eve of what he knew would be a controversial declaration, Churchill was taking care to keep King on his side.

In his speech at Westminster College, Churchill made no mention of espionage but the Gouzenko revelations were the context within which he composed it and they influenced its reception in government circles on both side of the Atlantic. In the United States, what he said was reinforced by the famous 5,000-word telegram sent to the state department ten days earlier by George Kennan, the chargé d'affaires in Moscow, who was prompted by an address by Stalin declaring that it was capitalism that was responsible for two world wars and pronouncing that the peace-loving USSR must now prepare for the next conflict. Kennan's recommendation, later elaborated as the doctrine of containment, was consistent with Churchill's warning to stand firmly against Soviet expansion.[48] The less informed public was slower to adapt to this changed perspective on the recently heroic ally. Eleanor Roosevelt urged that the United Nations be used to resolve differences and, at first, both American and British politicians circumspectly dissociated themselves from Churchill.[49] Disputes about who knew what in advance remains but both Randolph and Winston Churchill as well as Lord Halifax told King that the text was read and fully approved in Washington by Secretary of State James Byrnes and on the train by Truman and Admiral William Leahy, who had remained in place to continue serving as Truman's military chief of staff.[50]

---

47 Diary, March 3, 1946.
48 John Lewis Gaddis, *George F. Kennan: An American Life* (New York: Penguin, 2011), 215–22.
49 Cook, *Eleanor Roosevelt*, 557.
50 Diary, March 25 and May 22, 1946.

King listened to the broadcast with keen interest. He gave no indication of remembering that it was his late under-secretary, O. D. Skelton, who had given the first of the annual John Finley Green lectures at the tiny Westminster College in 1937, and where the student body numbered only 350. For Churchill's speech, the gymnasium was packed and tens of thousands outside listened to the address over loudspeakers.[51] King thought Churchill "in every way at his best. He sounded fresh and vigorous and less hesitant in speaking than I have ever heard him." He also believed that this was the opportune time for "the most courageous speech I have even listened to, considering what we know of Russia's behaviour in Europe and in Asia since the war and what has been disclosed here in Ottawa, much of which of which is not yet public." In hammer-blow cadences Churchill announced: "From Stettin in the Baltic to Trieste in the Adriatic, an iron curtain has descended across the Continent. Behind that line lie all the capitals of the ancient states of Central and Eastern Europe." The Soviets, he said, in an obvious reference to the Nazis, did not want war but "the fruits of war and the indefinite expansion of their power and doctrines." Since there was "nothing they admire so much as strength, and there is nothing for which they have less respect than for weakness, especially military weakness," the "sinews of peace" (the title of the speech, on which he had just decided) were a firm, united and powerful west that would negotiate with the USSR from strength, not in appeasement or trying to ignore the problems.

Adapting what he had termed in the 1930s – "Arms and the Covenant" – Churchill appealed for the lead in supporting the ideals of the United Nations to be taken by "the fraternal association of the English-speaking peoples. This means a special relationship between the British Commonwealth and Empire and the United States." He hoped it would lead to common citizenship but what was needed immediately was a military pact like the permanent agreement between the United States and Canada, "which is so devotedly attached to the British Commonwealth and Empire. This agreement is more effective than many of those which have often been made under formal alliances. This principle should be extended to all British Commonwealths [dominions] with full reciprocity." This scarcely disguised call for imperial unity makes clear the reason for Pearson's warning to King. Reminding the audience around the globe of his credentials for making this bold recommendation, Churchill said that last time:

51 There is a detailed account of the occasion and the reaction in Patrick Wright, *Iron Curtain* (New York: Oxford University Press, 2007), 21–61. Skelton's five lectures were published as *Our Generation* (Chicago: University of Chicago Press, 1938).

I saw it all coming and cried aloud to my own fellow-countrymen and to the world, but no one paid any attention . . . There never was a war in all history easier to prevent by timely action than the one which has just desolated such great areas of the globe . . . We surely must not let that happen again.[52]

Perhaps overcome by the invocation of the Ogdensburg agreement, King agreed with Churchill's warning about the Soviet Union, accepted the analogy with Nazi Germany, and did not object to the call for integrated Commonwealth defence. He merely regretted again not making better use of own his life and voicing the same concerns, particularly since Churchill's policy was built around a Canadian-US pact. He immediately telephoned Fulton to tell Churchill that the speech was "the most courageous made by any man at any time." Churchill replied how deeply he valued King's approval and asked him to express the same to Clement Attlee, saying that he had announced that he was speaking for himself alone because he did not want to embarrass the British prime minister, whom he disingenuously claimed he had not been able to consult in advance. This was only true of details. Churchill had told Attlee that he would speak about a close Anglo-American association, which he knew the Labour government supported. King was happy to send a cable to Attlee, although it did not affect the latter's circumspect public response. Truman came to the telephone with King and did not hedge his own approval by saying: "was that not a fine speech, a great speech, delivered by Mr. Churchill?" King agreed that Churchill had said what needed saying and added his own endorsement of the United States, Britain, Canada and other countries combining for security. At the end, Churchill returned to the telephone and reiterated the hope that King would come to meet him in New York. "The truth is," King thought, "with [Roosevelt] gone, Smuts in Africa and Eden in England, I can see wherein, excepting Halifax [!], I am about the only one he has to counsel with of those who have been nearest to him at crucial times."[53] For Churchill, it was an important consideration that King stood so stood highly with both the American and British governments.

52 "The Sinews of Peace" in Winston S. Churchill, *The Sinews of Peace: Post-War Speeches*, Randolph S. Churchill ed. (London: Cassell, 1948), 93–105. A good analysis of the speech is David Reynolds, *From World War to Cold War: Churchill, Roosevelt, and the International History of the 1940s*, (Oxford: Oxford University Press, 2006), 256–64.
53 Diary, March 5, 1946.

What soon became known as the "iron curtain" (rather than "sinews of peace") speech marked, although not immediately, Winston Churchill's political revival and his new role as watchman of the west against the threat of the USSR. At first, Attlee insisted that Churchill had, as he announced, spoken entirely for himself. Truman likewise claimed that his presence and his filmed smiling approval – to say nothing of his private comment to Mackenzie King – did not mean that he accepted what Churchill had said. Brazenly, he denied having read the speech in advance. In New York protesters outside Churchill's hotel chanted: "Winnie, Winnie, go away, UNO is here to stay"[54]

With Churchill once more so divisive a figure, Mackenzie King decided not to meet him in New York. This was ostensibly because he was still immersed in the Gouzenko matter, but in reality, he did not want to appear to be working against the USSR.[55] Despite what he said on the telephone to Churchill at Fulton, King still hoped that the Soviet Union would be persuaded to become part of the comity of nations and a pillar of world order. Perhaps Churchill's intimidations would suffice; certainly he thought they would help. Before Churchill embarked on the *Queen Mary*, King telephoned to tell him that the Fulton speech and the three following, including one at a large New York civic banquet, all of which emphasized Anglo-American unity, had been useful and necessary. Churchill, smarting from criticism, was grateful. Defensively he told King that if matters did not turn out well, "it could not be said that he had not at least sounded a warning in time; spoken out at this time. If all turned out well, it could do no harm."[56]

Even before Churchill left, the American attitude was beginning to change. This was aided by Stalin, who a week after the Fulton address denounced it as a call to war. King, from what he had heard, particularly from Roosevelt, thought that this reflected a personal feud "which is bred I fear from real enmity between the two."[57] American hardliners, however, seized on Soviet communism as the main threat to their country. They began to reconsider their instinctive isolationism and suspicions of Britain. Even the empire now seemed more benevolent than it had during the war, and Churchill was on his way to apotheosis as one of the great defenders of the United States.

---

54 Reynolds, *From World War to Cold War*, 258–9.
55 Diary, March 13 and 20, 1946.
56 Diary, March 20, 1946.
57 Diary, March 13, 1946.

* * *

Churchill's Fulton speech and the shifting congressional attitude towards the USSR was a great help in his unofficial mission to the United States, which was, on behalf of the Labour government, to hasten approval of the badly needed loan. The terms were not light, including an interest rate of two percent, a requirement for Britain to lower its tariffs (in accordance with the Atlantic Charter and subsequent agreements), and allowing the pound to be freely convertible to dollars at the pre-war rate of exchange one year after the loan was enacted. This was offset by writing off most of the lend-lease debt and adding the balance to the repayment of the loan over fifty years. On this basis, the American government agreed to a credit (to be spent in the United States) of $3.75 billion, which was well short of Britain's minimum requirement but the best that was on offer. As soon as the British parliament reluctantly agreed to the conditions in December, Truman recommended the loan to Congress.[58] There it remained stuck, opposed by those who thought that Britain was still a rich country suffering no more than a temporary cash problem, those who refused to bail out the British Empire, and those who objected to funding socialism. Five days after the Fulton speech, Lord Halifax held a dinner for Churchill to lobby congressional leaders. The great Conservative must have astonished the Americans by asserting, what he never would have in Britain, that the Labour ministers, mostly veterans of his wartime coalition, were not doctrinaire socialists and their social policies were not much different from his own party's.

The American legislators were soon more concerned to keep a reliable ally, socialist or not, against the Soviet threat. Despite this, and the obvious benefit to American industry, it still took until July for the bill to pass, by no great majorities. By then, even most Republican isolationist supported the bill. So, too, did Churchill's old friend Bernard Baruch, who initially regarded the loan as a threat to free enterprise. When King telephoned Churchill in New York, he was probably trying to convince Baruch, with whom he was having dinner.[59]

To make up the balance of Britain's needs, the Canadian government agreed to provide a $1.25 billion loan, which by the terms of the American one could not be at a lower interest rate. Even this total of five billion dollars turned out

---

58 Clarke, *The Last Thousand Days of the British Empire*, 392–401.
59 Clarke, *The Last Thousand Days of the British Empire*, 421–4 and 386.

within little over a year to be insufficient for Britain. Like Canada's financial aid to London during the war, its 1946 credit was on the basis of population and size of the economy greater than the American provision. King and his cabinet were moved by attachment to Britain and gratitude for its war effort but also, as in the case of lend-lease, by a keen sense of vulnerability if Britain's dollar purchases were confined to the United States. The Gouzenko revelations and Canadian apprehensions about the Soviet Union also helped to mute criticism as King assured his party that the loan would help to strengthen Britain in the world.[60] With the executive having far more power in a parliamentary system than the congressional one, the Canadian agreement was signed well before the American one. Indeed, the very day after the Fulton speech.

A few days later, Randolph Churchill arrived in Ottawa for a brief visit. When Mackenzie King asked about his father, Randolph said that he was suffering a bit from giddiness, which King regarded as a symptom of heart trouble or an impending stroke. He also missed official business and talked of giving up the leadership of the opposition while remaining head of the Conservative party. King had his own reason for agreeing with Randolph that this would be the worse choice: "I could follow him in his leadership of the Opposition in some things but I could not follow him in his leadership of the Conservative Party." King continued to hope that Churchill would leave partisan politics altogether and concentrate on writing about government and the war.[61] But within half a year, Churchill was re-energized by the international acclaim for his leadership of the Cold War as events fulfilled his forebodings, and also by his related championship of west European union. In the theatre of parliament, he was back in form, smiting the Labour government at erratic intervals, working hard on his war memoirs, and giving highly publicized speeches.

* * *

The dominion prime ministers gathered in London in May 1946, but since there was nothing in particular to discuss, King saw no reason to be present at the beginning. He was not unhappy to be detained by a dominion-provincial conference on the distribution of tax powers. Even afterwards, he was in no hurry to reach

---

60   Diary, March 20, 1946; Wardhaugh, *Behind the Scenes*, 299–306.
61   Diary, March 25, 1946.

Britain, sailing from New York in the familiar luxury of the *Queen Mary*. Among the other passengers were Lord Halifax, now leaving his embassy, and the senior member of his staff, Sir Gerald Campbell, the former high commissioner to Canada from 1938 to1941. Halifax told King that Churchill was keen for him to be active in Conservative politics but he considered that he owed it to the Labour ministry, which had kept him in post and valued his part in the loan discussions, to be dormant for a time. Partisanship was not part of Halifax's nature and he never again took a role in the party. His attitude on the current issue of Indian independence was the same as Labour's and could only have led to a huge conflict with Churchill. Soon enough, the two were disputing Churchill's account of pre-war diplomacy in his memoirs.[62] King demonstrated his continuing hope that the Soviet Union would change its ways by urging that Halifax, Churchill, Eisenhower and others visit the country and help bring it back into the international community.[63]

By the time King arrived in Britain in late May, the dominions conference was coming to an end. It had achieved nothing. This was papered over by a final communiqué stating that it had been an informal exchange of views on the European peace settlement and military security. The prime minister of Australia had already left, with the minister of external affairs taking his place, while New Zealand was represented by the deputy prime minister. Smuts complained to King that there were too many conferences, and that this one had been badly arranged and a mere matter of form, although it had provided some interesting information. The main business had been the attempt of Labour, exactly like the Conservatives, to achieve a unified Commonwealth policy. Smuts had rejected the long-standing proposal of military missions between Britain and the dominions and King did not hesitate to agree. He feared that war was becoming an institution and "a business of all govts. to have to do with it." He agreed that the west had to be firm on eastern Europe but refused to despair of avoiding a split with the Soviets. He urged the dominions secretary to be patient, saying that it was far better to take longer to get agreement on Europe than to line up countries against the USSR.[64] When Violet Markham urged that the Commonwealth must stand with Britain, King did not agree but he did concede that the world would only be saved by a combination of the United States and the United Kingdom.[65]

62 Roberts, *The 'Holy Fox'*, 297–9.
63 Diary, May 14, 1946.
64 Diary, May 20, 1946.
65 Diary, June 5, 1946.

The inconsequence of the conference and its rapidly approaching end left King with plenty of time for socializing and observation. On a motor trip with Frank and Maude Salisbury to Canterbury Cathedral he noticed that people on the street were better dressed than they had been six months earlier. They seemed almost back to the pre-war standard, although he recognized that this was only a matter of appearance and that much was needed to repair the war damage.[66] At lunch at Buckingham Palace with the royal family on Victoria/Empire Day (May 24), the king lamented the change of ministers. He said he missed Churchill and found it difficult to find anyone to talk to in the new government. "Clem the Clam," he claimed, never spoke at all.[67]

* * *

Mackenzie King found himself with Winston Churchill on four occasions. Churchill telephoned on his second day in London to invite him to dinner at his house two night later. The only other person present was Mary Churchill. Clementine had taken to her bed (which was not unusual) but sent her love. Since King did not mention the food and drink, the meal was probably nothing like the last. It warmed King's heart to see Churchill, despite the fact he seemed to be weaker. He said that he was having trouble with his eyes and was dizzy at times, leading King to think that he might suddenly collapse. As so often, Churchill rehearsed a forthcoming speech, in this case a parliamentary one on Egypt and foreign policy, in which he intended to advertise his superior grasp of world issues in comparison to the Labour ministers.

Above all, Churchill was concerned about the Soviet Union. He insisted that his Fulton speech had been all to the good and praised King's handling of the Gouzenko business, which would make the conduct of the USSR clear to other countries. If the Soviets were allowed to expand incrementally, "there is no doubt we will pay a greater penalty than any that the world had thus paid for the dictators." The Soviet government he said was "a terrible regime–a regime of terror." Grimly he predicted war, presumably nuclear, within eight years: "the most terrible war which might mean the end of our civilization." But, as in the case of Nazi Germany, as he had said at Fulton, it might be avoided by showing no fear

66 Diary, May 25, 1946.
67 Diary, May 24, 1946.

to the Soviets. And Churchill revealed that he still trusted Stalin more than any other Soviet leader: he was the one who could be relied upon and might save the situation. As proof, Churchill cited their 1944 percentages agreement, giving Britain ninety percent control of Greece. Although many communists had been killed in the civil war, Stalin had stood by his bargain and not interfered.

Churchill was far less optimistic about the British Empire, which he was convinced the Labour government was destroying. He still opposed self-government for India, but now prepared to concede dominion status, with the right to secede entirely, but only if, what he knew was practically impossible, the various interests, including religious minorities, princely states and the lowest social castes, agreed. Most immediately, he was preparing to denounce the withdrawal of British troops from Egypt into the canal zone, which had been specified in the 1936 treaty giving the country nominal independence which was over-ridden during the war. Retreating before nationalist threats, Churchill said, was a sign of weakness: "if I had been in office, I would have dealt with the situation in a very different way." King recognized that he would have made matters far worse but consolingly told Churchill that he should be thankful that he no longer had to try to master such events. He also declined Churchill's blandishment – "A word or two from you, spoken individually or publicly, will go very far" – to tell Labour ministers that they should feel pride in preserving the empire and Commonwealth. Within Britain, Churchill, contrary to what he had told members of the US Congress, was full of gloom that Labour was going too far in regulating and nationalizing industries, destroying private enterprise and damaging the country. But despite his policy attacks, he told King that his personal relations with the prime minister and many members of the cabinet were good. Over the objection of some Conservatives, he had accepted Attlee's invitation to drive with him to the Victory Day military review on June 8, where he would, of course, be the star of the show.

Churchill also talked about his war memoirs, saying that he had in mind to publish official documents. These would otherwise have been closed for fifty years (in 1967 reduced to thirty) and therefore guaranteed to be of huge interest. He did not think they would require a great amount of additional work. He had them regularly transcribed and told King that the copies were at Chartwell, although he was not sure that the government would allow them to be made public.[68] Negotiations on the matter were in fact already underway. Within a few months,

---

68 Diary, May 22 and 23, 1946.

for reasons of its own, the ministry agreed to allow access to confidential material and the right to publish it after review by the sympathetic cabinet secretary. What the government wanted was for Churchill to produce an authoritative but not officially sanctioned British history of the war to match American versions that did not face the same archival restrictions. This would not only demonstrate the importance of the British role but, by its assured attention, increase American sympathy to help the country in its recovery from the war. It caused the Labour ministers no grief that in the early part of the work the Conservative leader would severely criticize his pre-war party. Again, as in the American loan, Churchill was acting in collusion with his political opponents. The work brought him huge financial reward, finally putting his lavish lifestyle on a secure footing.[69] It also increased his political and literary reputation and, as first in the field, enabled him to create a definitive interpretation of the war.

A week after their dinner, King met Churchill and his wife at the Royal Institute for International Affairs (Chatham House), the British counterpart of the US Council on Foreign Relations. King must have known, though he did not mention, that the building had been donated in 1923 by the imperialist Canadian engineer and mining magnate Colonel Reuben Wells Leonard. He must also have been well aware that it was the former home of two prime ministers, the elder William Pitt (Earl of Chatham) and his hero William Gladstone. The occasion was the unveiling of a bronze bust of Lord Cecil of Chelwood, an architect and a champion of the League of Nations and now of the United Nations. Before the war, Cecil had been a greater proponent of collective security than Churchill and an anti-appeaser; in 1937 he received the Nobel Peace Prize. Churchill came straight from parliament and, most unusually, gave an impromptu speech declaring the United Nations superior to the League because the United States was not only a member but a leader. He extolled the United Nations as the best place to bridge divisions that always exist among countries. King was moved by the sentiment but feared, as Churchill's eyes filled with tears, that he might have a stroke and die on the spot.[70]

The following night there was a Commonwealth conference dinner at Buckingham Palace. Churchill, in British fashion, was present as leader of the

---

69 Lough, *No More Champagne*, 317–32; Clarke, *Mr. Churchill's Profession*, 277–80; Reynolds, *In Command of History*, 58–9 and 86–7.
70 Diary, May 29; "Architect of Peace," *The Times*, May 30, 1946. King incorrectly recorded that the bust was of Cecil Rhodes.

opposition as well as a figure familiar to the dominion leaders. After the ladies left the table, he and Attlee engaged in friendly barbs on domestic and international matters. In the drawing room afterwards, Churchill was more vehement to King about the consequences of self-government for India and the destruction of empire: "He spoke with great fervour and eloquence and earnestness. His eyes protruding from their sockets, not sparing any feeling that he had." King tried to assure him that the transfer of power in India would work out well. He also tried again to persuade him to leave the daily round of politics and take a more extensive view of the world. But Churchill's blood was up. He would not abandon his duty: "He said he was going to stay in and fight to the end."[71] He was working himself up to a long parliamentary speech on foreign affairs the following week, in which he would denounce the ministry and reiterate the message, and even some of the phrases he had used at Fulton.[72] King regretted that he did not attend since Churchill called in evidence the unmasking of the spy network in Canada and praised King's handling of it.[73]

Clement Attlee held a dinner two nights later at 10 Downing Street to honour Mackenzie King, who had just surpassed Sir John A. Macdonald, the first prime minister of Canada, for time served in office, and was closing in on the British record of Sir Robert Walpole (1721–42). Churchill added his praise of King and all that Canada had done for the war.[74] The next day, King recalled that when he had again pressed Churchill to devote himself to writing, he had insisted that "he would not give up the fight with this crowd. That he intended to defeat them and would win the next election or something to that effect." He kept coming back to what he called "the loss of India. He said these people have just given India away. He said that grieves me more than anything else. . . He said that much might have been done with India but in a different way – done by degrees." King flattered himself that he had managed to reduce Churchill's belligerence, which could only lower him in public esteem.

Next morning, King and Churchill returned to Downing Street in top hats and tail coats for the official Victory Day parade. Morning was not Churchill's finest hour but the two had a companionable conversation on a sofa. When King again inquired about his writing, Churchill said that he did some dictating on

71 Diary, May 30, 1946.
72 James, *Winston S. Churchill: Complete Speeches*, 7342–54.
73 Diary, June 6, 1946.
74 Diary, June 7, 1946.

the war documents every day, when travelling by car and at other odd moments. He said that there were things that only he knew and that he was anxious to record, meaning that he was concerned to defend his policies, particularly against American criticism, which had already begun. The main issues were his resistance to a premature second front, which he told King was one of the hardest things he had had to do, and his related ambitions in the Mediterranean. King reiterated his own conviction that a precipitous D-Day would have been disastrous; what was prevented was often more important than what was achieved. When King raised the matter of Beaverbrook's second-front campaign, Churchill carefully replied that Beaverbrook had been troublesome at times, that he was a sick man (with asthma), but whenever Churchill had asked for something really important, Beaverbrook had been ready to help. Despite his literary occupation, Churchill was determined above all to make his mark on present politics. When someone mentioned a prime minister who had won an election at an advanced age (probably Lord Palmerston at eighty or William Gladstone at eighty-two), Churchill, who was a mere seventy-one, growled that "there was time yet."

The Victory Day parade on the Mall was a long procession of armaments, commanders, armed service units (including Canadian ones), auxiliaries and such civilian defenders as firefighters. Three royal horse-drawn open carriages conveyed those in Downing Street to the saluting base. Churchill and Attlee shared the first carriage. The four overseas dominion representatives were in the second. King was inordinately pleased at being seated in precedence over Smuts, in his field marshal's uniform, although this was only proper for the prime minister of the senior dominion and by far the longest serving. Behind the dais for the British royal family were stands for the royals of allied countries and other notables. The six political leaders sat (and stood from time to time) alongside the royal platform: Attlee first, then Churchill, then King, with Smuts on his other side. Churchill said to King, "we shall never witness anything like this again," which as Britain's armed forces would go on to decline, was certainly true. Leaning across King to Smuts, Churchill added, "we three are the only ones that are left, a sort of trinity. We have been through a war as leaders but are the only ones now left." He was forgetting Stalin. King was gratified by the acclamation of the crowd and the "fine pageant of Empire" but thought "looking through the iron and steel and the universe behind it all is a terrible story of the failure of our civilization." Even Churchill mentioned the number of people in London alone who had been killed. This was apparently King's last conversation with Churchill on this visit since he did not mention any talk at the luncheon in Downing Street or at the lord chancellor's reception and viewing of fireworks that night at Westminster palace to which he took the Salisburys.[75]

* * *

Two nights later Mackenzie King left for home. The Victory Day festivities would have been a fine end to his time in London. But there was another farcical denouement, again involving Canada House although not Vincent Massey, directly, on this occasion. King had already seen the high commissioner and his wife on their way to retirement in Canada after giving cabinet consent to Massey becoming a Companion of Honour, an award which was hastily conferred by George VI the night before the couple left.[76] King called at Canada House on his own last day in London. His photograph had been moved from the back to the front door, but he was not much better pleased to find it to the side rather than facing the entrance. Again, he insisted that this was not a matter of personal dignity but rather a lese majesty against the prime minister. The acting high commissioner was Frederic Hudd, the senior trade commissioner. He responded to King's anger by protesting that a committee (directed, of course, by Massey) had decided upon the best place for the portrait after the incident of 1944. Far worse than Hudd's words was what King considered his impudent manner, addressing the prime minister "as though I was an official of Canada House." Nervously fearing that he was fast falling out of favour, Hudd burbled in the train all the way to Southampton that he would do whatever King wanted, but "as though it were a special favour from him to me." Finally, King threw him out of his shipboard cabin. In his diary he railed that Hudd, a great favourite of Massey, should never have been employed at Canada House since he was no Canadian but an Englishman with "many of the most arrogant and objectionable features of certain English types."[77] Equanimity returned during the voyage, which King shared with two thousand British war brides and children, and to whom he broadcast a welcome to their new country.[78] As usual, save in the case of political opponents, King did not hold the grudge and was amicable enough to Hudd when next in London.

75 Diary, June 8, 1946.
76 Diary, May 22, 1946.
77 Diary, June 10, 1946.
78 Diary, June 13, 1946.

Just a week after his return to Ottawa, there was a postscript to King's latest contact with Churchill. Anthony Eden, arriving with a delegation to the Empire Parliamentary Association, poured out his frustrations at Churchill's refusal to give up his position. When Churchill came back from the United States, he had said that he would chuck the leadership of the opposition and told Eden that he would have to take over. But still he did not go, although younger Conservative MPs disliked his constant wrangles with the government, his old-fashioned views and his failing strength. He had been there long enough, said Eden, who was particularly exasperated by Churchill's intervention in his own sphere of foreign policy. Eden deplored the break with Stalin and agreed with King that the west needed to be patient with the Soviet Union to reach a secure peace settlement. Strangely enough for someone supposedly in Churchill's confidence, Eden thought that it must have been something as recent as Potsdam that had estranged Churchill and Stalin. He also considered that the Fulton speech had gone too far and had sent a cable urging Churchill to say nothing further. Eden thought it might be acceptable for Churchill to remain only as leader of the Conservative party but it would be best if he left politics altogether. King said that he and Smuts had given Churchill the same advice.[79] But short of a party revolt, which no one was prepared to lead against Churchill, there was no way to force him to retire.

* * *

Mackenzie King did not meet Winston Churchill again for a year and a half, despite passing briefly through London in the summer of 1946 on his way to and from the Paris peace conference. Sailing to Europe, he had a dream of Churchill being tired and losing the power of speech and thought, which he interpreted as an expression of Churchill's feelings about being excluded from the British delegation. "Politics," said King, "is indeed tyrannical and brutal in some of its twists and turns."[80] What he thought Churchill might have added to the conference, apart from style, is a good question since he and the Labour government were practically of the same view. Churchill, too, would have had to accept Soviet control of eastern Europe, which he had since the percentages agreement, in fact if not in rhetoric.

79 Diary, June 23, 1946.
80 Diary, July 20, 1946.

The twenty-one countries that had declared war against Germany and Italy (not all of which had been conspicuous in fighting) assembled to review the peace treaties that had been drafted, as directed by the Potsdam summit, by the foreign ministers of the United States, the Soviet Union, Britain, and France for the lesser enemies. (The more contentious settlements with Germany and Austria were made later in a different manner.) Those other than the Big Four were in practice mere observers. Uneasy as King was about this, he was not willing to disrupt arrangements by clamouring for a greater voice, as did the Australian foreign minister. Highly conscious that the tension between the Soviets and the west might wreck the conference, King on the opening day appealed to the dominions to take the long view, emphasizing the work that had been done and the necessity for the success of the treaties. It was essential to secure the cooperation of the Soviet Union, "not allowing her to bring forward fresh difficulties each time fresh difficulties were raised by our own people."[81] After much wrangling the treaties were accepted two and a half months later and formally signed in Paris in February 1947.

King left the disputatious gathering at the end of August. His customary, conciliatory advice was a fitting note on which to leave the world stage as minister for external affairs. When he arrived back in Ottawa, he carried out the first stage of retirement by separating the office from that of prime minister and passing it to Louis St. Laurent, his choice as the next party leader. With Canada actively involved in the United Nations and other international organizations, it was more than time for external relations to have the full attention of a cabinet minister. It was a pleasing mark of this transition that Winston Churchill sent King as a birthday present one of the bronze medallions inscribed "Salute the Great Coalition" that he presented to the 122 ministers who had served in his government and a select few others.[82] King was delighted to be included in Churchill's "inner circle that had helped to preserve the world's freedom," at least, the great man ominously added, "for a time."[83] But a couple of months later, King declined to accept Churchill's invitation to join the non-partisan United Europe Committee to encourage the combination of continental states that he had called for at Zurich in September. Churchill declared that the union would be blessed by Britain and the Commonwealth, the United States, and

---

81 Diary, July 29, 1946.
82 Gilbert, *Winston S. Churchill*, VIII: *Never Despair*, 245–6.
83 Diary, December 17, 1946.

(to deflect criticism, although he did not expect it) the Soviet Union.[84] King was not alone at the beginning of 1947 in refusing to accept that Europe was irrevocably divided. Churchill, in any event, had no official authority and King was not going to get himself and his country into a potentially embarrassing or even dangerous situation with the leader of the British opposition. His response was that it was better for Canada to work independently.[85]

By November 1947, when King went to London for the wedding of Princess Elizabeth and Prince Philip of Greece, the division between east and west had widened considerably and Churchill's reputation as a prophet and world figure had soared. He was hailed as a founding father of the association of western European states. He was far less happy about the disintegration, "the clattering down of empire," under Labour, its natural inclination reinforced by Britain's financial inability to fight uprisings for independence. India and a separate, partitioned Pakistan were hastily granted independence in August 1947, a year before the originally intended date. Churchill reluctantly acquiesced since independence was covered by the fig leaf of them becoming dominions, although this had even less substance than in the case of Ireland in 1921. In Palestine, where the Jews were in rebellion over increased immigration and the Arabs for less, the issue was passed to the United Nations when Britain returned its mandate. The government also decided that it could not afford the cost of protecting Greece from communism, which Churchill had regarded as so vital at the end of the war. The American president, agreeing with his hardline advisers, leaped into the breach, announcing the Truman Doctrine to defend Greece and Turkey and any other free state that was threatened by communism. It was a huge relief to Churchill, and not to him alone, that the United States would remain in Europe.

Conditions within Britain in 1947 were, aside from the bombing, bleaker than they had been during the war. There were shortages of fuel, food, employment and exports. Bread was rationed as it had never been during the war. The North American loans were quickly exhausted, especially when the free convertibility of the pound came into effect in July. Within a month it had to be suspended. The new US Secretary of State, General George C. Marshall, came to the rescue by proposing credits for the economic reconstruction of all the free countries of Europe (including Allied-occupied Germany) to restore international trade and

84 Churchill, *The Sinews of Peace*, 198–202.
85 Diary, February 13, 1947.

strengthen them against Soviet communism. Like similar forms of aid, it would also help American exports. As a preliminary condition, the European states had to agree to a joint scheme for the best use of their resources, which also helped towards integration. The European proposal was complete by December and the Marshall Plan, for which Churchill got some of the credit, came into effect in April 1948, somewhat brightening the future after a grim 1947.

* * *

Mackenzie King crossed the Atlantic for the royal wedding in November 1947 aboard the *Queen Elizabeth*. He stopped briefly in London before going to Paris and the Low Countries to receive thanks for Canada's part in the war. Once in London, Clement Attlee called on him at the Dorchester Hotel. King found the British prime minister looking older, harried, and shrunken than a year and a half earlier. (Attlee was suffering from a duodenal ulcer.) He talked about the troubles in Palestine, and the civil war between Hindus and Muslims in India and Pakistan, for which he said the Labour government would have been blamed if it had not granted independence. King was sympathetic to Attlee and felt that the problems might crush him. But he also thought much of the strain came from Labour trying to do too much too quickly, by which he meant not so much decolonization as nationalization of industry (which largely halted in 1947) and greatly increased social benefits.[86] King's Victorian liberalism was at least as strong as Churchill's. A year and a half earlier, he had mused that Canada was going too far and too fast with social legislation. Family allowances (which his government had introduced before the 1945 election) "ought not to have been enacted for all time, but for the next year or two, until the end of the present parliament, with mature consideration given, meanwhile, to other aspects of health and social legislation." He feared the load that was being put on the backs of people by state provision of social services: "There is much to be said for the view that our ancestors met them in larger part by personal effort or family or community obligation."[87]

After a week of festivities on the continent, King returned to Britain for the royal wedding. Lunching at Buckingham Palace, he took Canada's wedding

86 Diary, November 7, 1947.
87 Diary, May 2, 1946.

presents to Princess Elizabeth: a mink coat, which he carried over his arm, and an eighteenth-century silver cup as the token of a complete table service. Before the meal, George VI conferred on King the Order of Merit (OM), an honour in the personal gift of the sovereign confined to twenty-four members. John Colville, formerly (and again later) Churchill's favourite prime ministerial secretary, now Princess Elizabeth's secretary, told King that Churchill was getting on well with his war memoirs and had already written over a million words.[88] This was either a great exaggeration or a misremembrance on someone's part since the whole six volumes total only about a million and a half words, most of them war documents. The next morning Churchill and his wife telephoned King to congratulate him on the OM. When King asked Churchill how he was, he replied: "pretty well, all things considered." That night King met the couple at Buckingham Palace and comforted himself in his own chronic weariness by observing that his contemporary looked "very much older. In fact, beginning to be just a bit tottering or doddering."[89]

King attended a memorial service in St Paul's Cathedral the next day for John Gilbert Winant, the US ambassador from 1941 to 1946, who suffered from depression and had committed suicide with a gun. Churchill had had a close very relationship with this steadfast supporter of Britain (and his daughter Sarah's lover) but had intended to have Clementine represent him at the service. She insisted that he would be expected.[90] Seated immediately behind the Churchills, the Attlees, and members of the cabinet, King watched Churchill with customary attentiveness, noting that he had great difficulty standing up: "One could see he is getting very much older. I saw him take some kind of pill–evidently to strengthen him." From his unusual angle, King also thought that Churchill displayed "a very powerful and not too pleasant looking lower jaw and side face."[91]

The wedding the next morning in Westminster Abbey, King thought almost like a coronation. As the senior dominion prime minister, he was seated next to Attlee with Smuts on his other side and Churchill, as mere leader of the opposition, beyond Smuts. King felt embarrassed that he and Smuts should walk out before Churchill and Clementine, who was seated separately. During the service, King saw more evidence of Churchill's frailty: "I noticed his legs trembled a

88 Diary, November 17, 1947.
89 Diary, November 18, 1947.
90 Gilbert, *Winston S. Churchill*, vol. VIII: *Never Despair*, 361–2.
91 Diary, November 19, 1947.

little. He had difficulty stooping down" (for prayers). But he also recognized that Churchill was moved by the beautiful ceremony, "as everyone indeed must have been who loves pageantry and colour." King was likewise enthralled by the lovely tableaux. But his democratic instincts, and perhaps British social conditions in 1947, inspired the prediction, so far unfulfilled, that "all this pomp was a demonstration of power and ceremonial" that would "some day be swept away in a great class struggle." The only way to avoid such a conflict was to build up a strong middle-class that he feared was being destroyed in the battle between those on top and those below. The wedding breakfast at Buckingham Palace King considered more admirable than the church ceremony, and a true reflection of a lack of pretention of the royal family: "much more dignified, quiet and natural than most weddings that I have attended. There was not a boisterousness or excessive talking that I heard. One felt what a marvellous family the Royal Family is."[92]

In addition to social events connected to the wedding, there was a meeting at 10 Downing Street of Attlee, Bevin, and other British ministers with King, Smuts, and the high commissioners of the other dominions, which now included India and Pakistan. The subject was Europe, which meant mainly the Soviet Union. Bevin talked about the threat of communism, the likelihood of the USSR blocking the peace settlements with Germany and Austria and also preventing free access to Berlin in the middle of the Soviet zone. He feared that the United States might become so impatient that events could drift into war. In what was by now, largely owing to Churchill's Fulton speech, a conventional analogy accepted across a wide political spectrum, Bevin said that the Soviet threat should be checked at the beginning, as the German one should have been, with the United States, Britain, and France standing together to save western Europe. He declared that the British ministry would not engage in appeasement. It might have been Churchill speaking.

Such strong terms did Bevin use that King feared there might be war within three weeks. [93] He could hardly sleep. The next morning, his last in London, Bevin came to the Dorchester to add more information, particularly about the Middle East, but King was in too much of a hurry and not familiar enough with the issues to make good notes. Bevin added that he was careful about what he said in the presence of the Indians and Pakistanis since they might pass it to the Soviets. He told King that the United States had to remain in the background

---

92 Diary, November 20, 1947.
93 Diary, November 24, 1947.

in the Middle East since Stalin had promised not to interfere with British policy there but might feel free to intrude if the Americans became engaged. He also reported that he had warned George Marshall that if the United States was going to be the ruling country of the world, which Bevin pronounced it now was, it must put troops into Europe and not look to Britain to do the fighting. To King, who still regarded Britain as a world power, "it sounded painful [in] my ears to hear the Foreign Minister in London tell me that he had to admit that Britain had to take second place to the U.S."

King's final lunch at the house of Sir John and Lady Anderson did nothing to ease his anxieties. The other guests were the Churchills, Smuts, and Harold Macmillan (King's publisher as well as a politician). Churchill, of course, was the star and dominated the conversation. This time, showing his variability from day to day, King thought he looked "wonderfully well. Complexion as fresh as that of a child . . . He was in a very pleasant though earnest mood." This hardly began to describe pronunciations even more apocalyptic than Bevin's. He began practising his scales with a denunciation of socialism and the ruin it would bring to Britain. This must have been uncomfortable, although familiar listening for Macmillan. Always a left-wing Conservative, he had been a member of a committee that six months earlier had produced the party's "Industrial Charter" to appeal to voters for the next election. The compromise with Labour included accepting the nationalization of industry up to the present (by which the least contentious parts of the economy had been taken into public ownership) and the comprehensive National Health Service, enacted in 1946 to come into effect in July 1948. Churchill grudgingly acquiesced in the hope that it would be the means of bringing him back to office, but while he presented the charter as official policy to the annual Conservative conference, he had no sympathy with it.[94] King in his diary agreed that Britain had become what it was by "initiative, self-reliance etc." He did not acknowledge any necessity to compensate ordinary people through social benefits for their contribution to victory, although he did think that Britain was "paying the penalty today of permitting the conditions under which the masses worked in laissez-faire days."

After this domestic overture, Churchill launched into the theme of international peril. He repeated Bevin's point by saying that if Hitler's threat to the

94 John Ramsden, *The Age of Churchill and Eden, 1940–1957* (London: Longman, 1995), 148–58; Addison, *Churchill on the Home Front*, 392–6.

Rhineland in 1936 had been resisted there would have been no war. In a similar fashion, he expected the USSR to try to enlarge its occupation zone in Germany and to defeat Marshall Aid. If these steps were allowed, another world war was absolutely certain. But Churchill was confident that the Americans would not tolerate communism in the rest of western Europe or their own country. If the Soviets refused to confine themselves to reasonable boundaries, they would be plainly told that their cities would be bombed. The countries that had fought for freedom, he warned, had had enough of this war of nerves and intimidation and would not let it continue indefinitely. He was sure that the Soviets would retreat in the face of the threat of destruction but unless they were warned, there was no hope for the world. Turning sharply to King, he claimed that the Americans had had plans for over a year to destroy Moscow and other cities with atomic bombs. He reminded King that he had predicted the last war at Sir Abe Bailey's dinner in 1936, and said that he saw the next one coming just as clearly. Unless a stand was taken in the next few weeks, "there would be another world war in which we shall all be finished." He fixed King with an earnest, beseeching look, his eyes:

> "bulging out of his head-so much so that one could see the greater part of the white of his eyes as well as the pupils, which looked as though they would come out of his head altogether . . . The gleam in his eye was like fire. There was something in his whole appearance and delivery which gave me the impression of a sort of volcano at work in his brain."

During this performance, King had "a sort of vision of a welter of the world. It might be just the effect of his own words but they were strong and powerful and deeply felt." He perfectly understood why this vital issue was withheld from the Indian and Pakistani high commissioners. It was a matter for veteran statesmen like himself: "I cannot see the wisdom of entrusting matters of this kind to types of men that some of the [high commissioners] are and may be from time to time."

In light relief from this terrifying topic, Churchill said that he was working hard at his war memoirs. The first volume would be published in 1948, the rest he expected to follow within four years. He promised to send copies to King as they appeared. King, in return, told Churchill that three days earlier he had had a spiritualist communication with Roosevelt, Missy LeHand, and "Pa" Watson, in which the late president gave King a message for Churchill. King did not say what it was but at Churchill's request sent it by hand to his house. Churchill returned it to King, who was just leaving, with "a most significant note." King was impressed by Churchill's apparent familiarity with mediums and interest in the hereafter and put the most favourable construction on his equivocal comment that "we were hardly yet to the stage where we could say much about our future existence."

For King, at least, the luncheon had an elegiac tone. He thought that Churchill and Smuts must have been as aware as he that they might never see each other again, and this was, indeed, the last time that all three met. Half a year later, Smuts was surprised to be defeated in an election by the Reunited Nationalist Party. King was not wrong to think that he had fallen from power, like Menzies in Australia, from being too concerned about being a British imperialist and losing touch with his own country.[95] Smuts was more interested in the Commonwealth and international issues than domestic ones and did have a higher reputation abroad than at home, but his weakening enthusiasm for racial segregation was a bigger liability among those who wanted a more rigid system of apartheid. As King looked around the table at lunch, he was also struck again by the conviction that Churchill was "the greatest man of our times. Not by any means the greatest in any one field but rather in a combination of fields–in the aggregate." This King felt was based on his literary intellect, his vast reading and writing, and his powerful rhetoric: "I felt that his great knowledge of History which gave him a great outlook would cause him to speak with authority, causing other men to realize how little their knowledge and vision really was. The form with which he expressed his views [was] what gave him his great influence."[96]

While Mackenzie King was on the way to retirement Churchill, by 1948, was back as a world figure. Although only leader of the opposition in Britain, his reputation in western Europe and North America was as high as it had been during the war. His warnings about the Soviet Union were soon reinforced by the first volume of his war memoirs, *The Gathering Storm*, the first part of which chronicled his forebodings about Nazi Germany. His standing during the war and after, and the official documents he was allowed to reproduce in the six volumes, gave the same authority to the whole work.[97] As the end of King's political career approached, he hoped that in a modest way he would be able to contribute something of the same.

---

95 Diary, May 28, 1948.

96 Diary, November 24 and 25, 1947. Although the luncheon was on the 25th, much of what Churchill said is in the entry for the 24th, following the account of the meeting in Downing Street.

97 The work is well analyzed and assessed in Reynolds, *In Command of History: Churchill Fighting and Writing the Second World War*.

CHAPTER FOURTEEN

Twilight and Evening Bell

NEARLY A YEAR LATER, close to half a century after their first encounter, Mackenzie King and Winston Churchill met for the last time. King was no longer the leader of the Liberal party, having carefully engineered Louis St. Laurent into that position at the convention to choose a successor in August 1948. But he remained as prime minister in order to represent Canada at a Commonwealth prime ministers conference in October. St. Laurent considered that a meeting in London would be the worst way to begin his prime ministership, particularly with a general election in the offing and his need for a strong showing in Quebec. King looked forward to his farewell appearance after quarter of a century of being the crucial figure at such events. With Smuts gone, he was unquestionably the senior dominion figure. As a parting service, he expected that the British government was counting on his experience in dealing with the new dominions of India, Pakistan, and Ceylon.[1]

On his way to London, King stopped in Paris for a session of the United Nations. Eleanor Roosevelt was there as a member of the US delegation and Chair of the Commission on Human Rights which produced the Universal Declaration of Human Rights adopted by the UN in December. She was staying in the same hotel, in a room close to King's. They did not spend much time together, but they did reminisce about the past and Eleanor repeated her

---

1 Diary, August 11, 1948.

husband's affection for King and the many confidences he had shared.[2] At a dinner of dominion representatives, Ernest Bevin gave a toast to King on his retirement. Not having been forewarned, King had no reply prepared but he spontaneously pronounced a benediction on the Commonwealth. During his long years as prime minister, he said that he had tried to keep before him:

> the best traditions of British public life. That I realized what the nations of the Commonwealth had derived in that way. Real bonds between nations of the Commonwealth were love of freedom, of liberty which had been inherited from the struggles of Britain, and the example of public men.[3]

This did not mean that King was any less suspicious that the British would try again to achieve a common defence policy across the Commonwealth.[4] Since March, Britain had been part of a military agreement with France, Belgium, the Netherlands, and Luxemburg to resist Soviet aggression. This was precipitated by the USSR a month earlier suddenly imposing a communist government in Czechoslovakia, the country that in 1938 had been dismantled at the Munich conference. The Soviet action also spurred passage of the Marshall aid bill by the US Congress; by July, the first five billion dollars of what during the next four years would be over twelve billion dollars was pouring into Europe. The United States also declared that it would join the European regional defence treaty, which led to the formation of the North Atlantic Treaty Organization in 1949.

In June 1948, the Soviets stopped rail and road traffic through their occupation zone to the American, British, and French sectors of Berlin in response to those countries beginning to amalgamate their regions. For eleven months, the Americans directed a massive airlift of supplies until the Soviets allowed the surface routes to reopen. Mackenzie King observed the tension between the Soviet Union and the west at the meeting of the United Nations assembly, but was thankful to hear the judgement at the British embassy that the USSR was not thinking of war and that there were no signs of such preparation in Moscow. King's opinion was that Stalin, at the height of his power, would not start a military conflict which he might not live to see end.[5] When after two weeks in Paris

---

2 Diary, September 23, 1948.
3 Diary, September 28, 1948.
4 Diary, September 30, 1948.
5 Diary, October 4, 1948.

he went to London, he was further reassured by Clement Attlee saying that the European situation was improving, although Berlin was still a flash point. The British prime minister also insisted that his government was not aiming at military coordination with the dominions.[6]

King was shocked by the appearance of Attlee (who had recently been treated in hospital for his ulcer), and Attlee may have felt the same about King. In Paris, King had been far more tired than usual, unable to breathe or sleep easily, and perspiring freely, all of which suggests blocked arteries.[7] Shortly after his arrival in London, he felt too unwell to leave the Dorchester Hotel. Lord Moran diagnosed heart strain for which he prescribed digitalis, sleeping pills, and morphine, and arranged for a night nurse. He went with King to a heart specialist, Sir John Parkinson, who took an x-ray and a cardiograph and detected edema (swelling) in one leg owing to poor circulation. Moran banned salt and recommended bed rest for two weeks. In fact, King remained there for three. Moran came practically every day, although there was nothing further he could provide other than encouragement. He did not charge for his services but a few months later King sent him £150.[8] King was characteristically proud that his illness, indeed his whole stay in London, cost Canadian taxpayers nothing since the expense of the conference was covered by the British government.[9] Since he could not attend the sessions, St. Laurent came by air to represent Canada after all.[10]

Lord Moran's concern in attending King was not his fee but his literary ambition. He was a prominent practitioner and medical politician (as president of the Royal College of Physicians he was known to general practitioners as "Corkscrew Charlie" for concentrating on the interests of specialists in negotiations over the National Health Scheme) who knew that his real fame depended on producing an account of his association with Winston Churchill. He was reviewing and reworking his diaries to present an attention-catching account to be published after his great patient's death, which he had no reason to think would be long delayed. King's confinement was a heaven-sent opportunity to sharpen and increase his knowledge by adding the experience of someone who had been, as Moran had not, at many private meetings and informal discussions with Churchill and also Roosevelt.

6 Diary, October 6, 1948.
7 Diary, September 28, 1948.
8 Diary, March 26, 1949.
9 Diary, November 5, 1948.
10 Diary, October 7–28, 1948.

On the very first day, they talked about Churchill for over an hour and found themselves in substantial agreement. Moran observed, and King did not dissent, that Churchill had achieved great things despite his faults. He was very strong willed, thought in big terms, and his knowledge of military history was so extensive that he could dominate any situation and not leave others much chance to say anything. Churchill recognized the value of experts but did not allow them to control. King was not so indiscreet as to tell Moran that Montgomery had said that he did not want Churchill around during the fighting, and that Alexander (now governor general of Canada) had said that he had to stand up to prevent Churchill's interference. But King did confirm that Churchill did most of the talking in cabinet and was inconsiderate of others: even Attlee and the Liberal leader, Sir Archibald Sinclair, were treated almost with contempt, and most colleagues feared to say anything. To get his way, he would work himself into an emotional state.

On the other hand, King attested that Churchill was loyal to his friends, stuck to his word in getting things done, and had great courage, "no fear in the world. In that way gave a powerful example to others." King also pointed out that many were attracted by the desire to associate with such a towering figure. He claimed not to have liked what Churchill told him about the effectiveness of flattery, although King was both susceptible and not sparing in his own use of it. While no one could say if the war would have been won if anything had happened to Churchill and Roosevelt, King considered that a change of leadership might have shortened the European conflict since the Germans were terrified of Churchill. Both he and Moran considered that unconditional surrender (which was Roosevelt's and not Churchill's insistence) had been a mistake since it had closed every door and made the fighting more intense.

Moran also wanted to discuss relations between Churchill and Roosevelt, about which King knew a great deal. He said that Churchill had repeatedly insisted that they must meet the president in every way possible and never forget that he was Britain's greatest friend. On the difference between them over sharing research on the atomic bomb with the Soviets, King, whose opinion had changed with the Cold War, now thought Churchill had been right that it should be withheld.[11] A couple of days later, Moran told King that he had noticed that Roosevelt

11   Diary, October 7, 1948.

was failing at the 1944 Quebec conference and by Yalta was completely used up.[12] This was not surprising for a detached physician and was no revelation to King, but it would have been to the public if it had been publicized on such authority, just three and a half years after Roosevelt's death.

In addition to Moran, Mackenzie King received a stream of other visitors at his bedside: St. Laurent, of course, Attlee, Jawaharlal Nehru, the prime minister of India, Ernest Bevin and Harold Macmillan, who wanted to inquire about King's memoirs which it was assumed the Macmillan company would publish. It must have been a great encouragement that Bevin, who managed to carry on in one of the most demanding jobs in the government, said that his symptoms were exactly like King's; and more people that Moran implied Bevin's condition was the result of excessive drinking.[13] This held out the expectation that King's abstemious lifestyle would speed his recovery. George VI paid his Canadian prime minister the great compliment of going to see him at the hotel. So did his uncle, Lord Athlone, who came as chancellor of the University of London with an academic delegation and an honorary degree, for which King got out of bed and dressed.[14] There were also personal friends, notably Violet Markham and the Salisburys, and three sessions with spiritualists, one of whom contacted Franklin Roosevelt as well as Lord Tweedsmuir.[15] But the highlight, on the second to last day, was Winston Churchill, whom King would have been sorry to miss.[16]

* * *

Churchill arrived with a copy of the British edition of *The Gathering Storm* (amended from the original US publication which he had already sent to King). He was sorry to find his old friend in such poor condition but not greatly concerned since he had recovered from worse himself (the next summer he would quickly recuperate from a stroke). King was amazed at how well his contemporary looked – "quite young and strong" – and the quantity of work he was able to do. Churchill said that he relaxed a lot, sometimes painting for three hours a day. He was also buoyed by having just denounced the Labour ministry's handling

---

12 Diary, October 9, 1948.
13 Diary, October 28, 1948.
14 Diary. October 25, 1948.
15 Diary, October 22, 1948.
16 Diary, October 28, 1948.

of world affairs in parliament in the same hard terms that he had used at the Conservative annual conference a couple of weeks earlier. (Attlee, who arrived later, told King that he had been hurt by the accusations of timidity towards the Soviet Union, responsibility for the slaughter following Indian independence, the chaos in Palestine, and the charge that his government would force Northern Ireland into joining Eire which was becoming an independent republic with no ties to the United Kingdom.)[17] King agreed with Attlee that Churchill's speech was extreme, even alarming in his claim that Conservative governments would come to power in Britain and all the old dominions and take proper command of the Commonwealth. Many British Conservatives were offended by Churchill's belligerence but kept their heads down and deferred to the international hero who they hoped would carry them back to office in the election that was scheduled for 1950. This mutinous feeling was expressed to King three months later by the still exasperated Anthony Eden, who told him in Ottawa that although Churchill was mellowing, he still refused to surrender the party leadership.[18]

In their bedside conversation at the Dorchester, King and Churchill did not touch on contemporary controversies but stuck to the tranquilizing triumphs of the past. Churchill declared – although it is not clear how he could have known – that King had been much missed at the Commonwealth conference. He also cheered the invalid by assuring him again of his great services during the war: "You have never failed. You were helpful always. There was nothing that you did not do, that could be done." He mentioned, in particular, the Commonwealth air training plan and King's refusal to support Robert Menzies' desire for the dominions to play a larger part in the direction of the war in order to undermine Churchill. He reiterated that King had been a bridge between Britain and the United States, specifying his help in the possible move of the Royal Navy to the United States. He recalled King's encouraging telephone call after the Fulton speech, and could not resist adding that every point in the address had since been borne out. The two parted with emotion, Churchill's eyes filling with tears yet King was annoyed that on his way out he asked the high commissioner (Norman Robertson) to ensure that the press was informed of his visit.

There was no sense that this was their last meeting. Once he recovered his health, King expected to continue visiting Britain, as he had when out of office

17 Diary, September 7, 8 and 9, 1948.
18 Diary, January 23, 1949.

in the early 1930s. Churchill hoped to go to Toronto in the spring to receive an honorary degree and wanted King to attend. King in turn invited Churchill to Ottawa.[19] In the end, Churchill did not go to Canada in 1949, but he did, however, visit the United States, and King listened with his usual awe to the broadcast speech at the Massachusetts Institute of Technology in which Churchill urged the employment of science for the benefit of the world. At the moment that the North Atlantic Treaty was about to be signed, he praised the United States for continuing to be involved in the cause of freedom against the Soviet Union. King, as so often before, sent a telegram of congratulations and received the warm thanks of Churchill and his wife.[20] If he had lived another few years he would have seen Churchill in Ottawa, as the British prime minister, in 1952 and again in 1954.

* * *

From the Dorchester Hotel, Mackenzie King made his way to the *Queen Elizabeth* by car. He spent most of the voyage in bed. In New York, he felt well enough to be on his feet and do some shopping. He travelled to Ottawa by train and was examined by his own doctor, himself old and not too well, who found King's blood pressure to be 200/100,[21] not as high as Roosevelt's in his last year but still dangerous by later standards. A week later, King formally resigned as prime minister. Immediately he telephoned Joan Patteson to say that they must get busy on his memoirs: "She will be a great help in this. I told her how really delighted I felt that this day had arrived at last."[22]

This euphoria did not last. After thirty years at the centre of politics, domestic and international, King was totally bereft and disoriented. Within half a year, he thought that he had left not too late but too soon. He should have remained as prime minister and managed by taking more holidays.[23] Almost inevitably, he felt neglected by prime minister Louis St. Laurent. Just three months after leaving office he wrote: "I just seem to be out of sorts completely, nervous tension–too much strain and uncertainty–when I ought to be the happiest man in the city, as in most ways I am the most fortunate."[24]

19 Diary, October 29, 1948.
20 Diary, April 1 and 4, 1949.
21 Diary, November 8, 1948.
22 Diary, November 15, 1948.
23 Diary, July 13, 1949.
24 Diary, March 3, 1949.

After more than a year of retirement, he was more reconciled to it by the narrow defeat in a general election of the British Conservatives and Winston Churchill's refusal to go. He himself had been far wiser: "In fact I think my action taken at the time and in the manner it was, was one of the finest examples that has been given history in the right method of proceeding where one has had a long lease of power."[25]

Lacking business of state, King filled his attention by fretting about his servants, the management of his households, improving his Kingsmere estate, and his finances, for which there was not the slightest reason for concern. Indeed, he was surprised to realize how wealthy he was. He agonized over his will and feared that, although he was leaving most of his estate to the country, the public would misunderstand the large fortune he had accumulated by carefully preserving and compounding the benefactions of Peter Larkin, Sir William Mulock, the Rockefellers, and others.[26] He depended more heavily than ever on the companionship of Joan Patteson, imagining that he was rescuing her from her difficult, retired husband and never suspecting for a moment that Godfroy's irascibility had anything to do with King's demands on his wife. Even Joan was not an unalloyed source of calm and comfort, resenting as she did the other people in King's life, including his sister Jennie, the Governor General Lord Alexander and, above all, the widowed Lily Hendrie, of Hamilton, Ontario, an old love from half a century ago, who now resurfaced with suspicious frequency. She had been aboard ship on King's last voyage to Britain and all too often came to Ottawa.[27]

King's health did improve from what it had been in London but he was never again really well. He constantly lacked energy and found it difficult even to concentrate on his voluminous correspondence with friends. He had to rest more than ever and sweated at any exertion and at night.[28] He focused, without success, on recovering his health before he could tackle his memoirs or properly reviewed his papers and diary, which records daily discouragement over hope. The relaxing summer of 1949 at Kingsmere did not rebuild his strength, and a holiday on the coast of Maine with John D. Rockefeller, Jr. was less curative and more tiring than he expected.

25 Diary, February 23, 1950.
26 Diary, March 8, 1949.
27 Diary, July 12, 1949.
28 Diary, April 30, 1949.

After a whole winter in which he was immured in Laurier House and needed a night nurse, he was convinced that spring would bring a return of strength. He planned to lighten his labour on the diary by the assistance of Fred McGregor, earlier one of his secretaries, who had been hired to superintend work on the archive. Efficient and discreet, McGregor was also one of the few who could easily read King's difficult handwriting. (It was he who dictated the handwritten diary for the typescript.) A month later, still not having begun the task, King's confidence about the whole enterprise was badly shaken when he received *The Hinge of Fate*, the third volume of Churchill's war memoirs, which covered 1941 in close to nine hundred pages of documents and narrative. King blenched at the scale and realized "how next to impossible it is going to be to ever complete my Memoirs in a way I should like to have been able to manage them."[29] But as he began to read the book, his assurance grew that it would be easy to write an even better account for Canada. He was not alone in considering that Churchill's great fault was that he did "not go out of his way to bring anyone else to the fore but himself. . . [N]o one else had a real hand in the main features of the war but himself." Even King himself had only a walk-on part. It was appalling that human society should be "so organized that the influence of any one man and his direction should be so great."[30] This should not be construed as a guarantee that King's book would have been any the less self-centred.

Two weeks later, Lord Moran passed through Ottawa (staying at Government House with Lord Alexander) and was shocked at the weight King had lost since he had last seen him a year and a half ago. He must have recognized that the end was probably nigh but he was tactfully non-committal to King about his condition and encouragingly promised to return and go on a trip with him when he was better. While he could, Moran wanted to get as much information as possible from King for his account of Churchill, on which he admitted he was not making much progress. He had been surprised at the bitterness he encountered towards Roosevelt among many Americans. King, who heard plenty of the same from his own wealthy US friends and was sympathetic to the criticism of Roosevelt's domestic policies, said that it was a matter of the purse and resentment at the redistribution of wealth in the New Deal. There was no doubt about Roosevelt's sincerity for the people but he was (unlike himself) no economist and indifferent

29 Diary, April 8, 1950.
30 Diary, April 9, 1950.

to repaying the national debt. King also considered Roosevelt's advisers, with the sole exception of Cordell Hull, to have been of no great calibre. Overall he judged Roosevelt to be not profound, vain, and liking to appear to know a great deal about everything than he did, but essentially modest and not regarding himself as a man of destiny and not setting himself up in that way.[31] The implicit contrast to Churchill was obvious.

* * *

As he prepared to move to Kingsmere for the summer of 1950, King, now seventy-five, was forced to admit that he was becoming "very mixed and confused these days as to dates, places, names etc. Indeed, I am becoming quite worried about making no headway worth speaking of with anything."[32] Sleep provided no real rest. He generally stayed in bed until late morning. He focused only fitfully on current events but the outbreak of the Korean war in June triggered old fears. What was technically an international "police" action by the United Nations to stop North Korea seizing the South was, in reality, a United States operation supported by other countries, including Canada. King was full of anxiety that the Americans were trying to draw Canada into as many such situations as possible by flattering young diplomats, who preferred the United States to the British association. The aim, King feared, as he had on so many occasions, was the annexation of Canada. For the same reason of increasing its dominance, he thought the United States sought to involve Britain and other dominions in Korea.[33] Though it was he who had been responsible for creating a distinct Canadian citizenship within British subjects at the beginning of 1947, King, like Canada's first prime minister, Sir John A. Macdonald, might well have declared that a British subject he was born and a British subject he would die.

By the summer of 1950, King realized that his remaining time might be quite short. He accepted it but in a customary bargain with death, hoped to be spared long enough to sort out and destroy some of his papers and parts of his diary.[34] There was no prospect of writing or even supervising his memoirs in his lifetime, but he still wanted at leave the material in what he considered the

31 Diary, April 22, 1950.
32 Diary, June 21, 1950.
33 Diary, June 30, 1950.
34 Diary, June 24 and July 7, 1950.

right form for an official biography. Thinking that it would provide inspiration, he had Joan Patteson read to him at Kingsmere John Gunther's new biography, *Roosevelt in Retrospect: A Profile in History*. When she got to Roosevelt's polio, King in the midst of his own suffering, marvelled: "How he ever went through what he did amazes me beyond words! Surely a miraculous life. More and more I wonder at the circumstances which brought United States so close to each other, and to have same experiences (mine not at all comparable to his)."[35] The dream that someone would produce a similar account of himself was what now sustained King. But he did not have the mental energy and concentration, the physical strength, even to start looking at his vast diary.

When a medical specialist recommended going into hospital for a week or ten days for observation, King declined: "if my condition was such that the summer at Kingsmere would not improve matters, I would rather end my days in the country in the Summer-time."[36] This last wish was granted. On July 20, his doctor arrived in the morning and the two drove around the beloved estate for an hour. After lunch, King sat in the sun until 3 p.m. until, not feeling well, he went for his customary sleep. Twenty minutes later, he had a severe heart attack. By the time the doctor returned in the evening, King was in a coma. He was given morphine and at 10:30 p.m. that night briefly regained consciousness for the last time. Seeming to recognize those in the room, he smiled and said "Fine, thank you!"[37] Two days later, at 9:42 p.m. on Saturday, July 22, with members of his family and his staff gathered around, Mackenzie King breathed his last in the middle of a great thunderstorm. The faithful Edouard Handy, who had been recalled from holiday at a nearby lake, wrote the final entries and closed the diary.[38] It lives on as the memorial to an individual at the centre of Canadian and international events for thirty years.

Winston Churchill, who outlived his contemporary by fifteen years, said to Mackenzie King in their last conversation: "you have been the great bridge between the United States and the United Kingdom. You have helped in difficult times."[39] He might have added that King had been a vital link between himself and Roosevelt, although at the time of writing his war memoirs it

35 Diary, July 16, 1950.
36 Diary, July 7, 1950.
37 Diary, July 21, 1950.
38 Diary, July 22, 1950.
39 Diary, October 29, 1948.

was not in Churchill's nature to admit that he had needed anyone to pave the path to the American leader. He assumed that all the confidences that had passed orally between the three would go with King to the grave. Only after the end of Churchill's long life in 1965 was there the intimation that King had left a detailed record of Churchill and Roosevelt, and the hope that it might eventually be revealed.

APPENDIX

The Preservation of
Mackenzie King's Diary

T HE STORY OF HOW MACKENZIE KING'S diary was saved from
destruction and the archival dance of the seven veils by which it was
revealed over the three following his death has been well told by
Christopher Dummitt and needs only be recounted briefly here.[1]

When in October 1948 King finally retired as prime minister, his main purpose in whatever remained of life was to write his memoirs, or at least supervise
an official biography. Among those who encouraged him was the British cabinet
secretary, Sir Norman Brook, who confided that he was helping Churchill with
his war memoirs and hoped that King would similarly tell the related Canadian
story.[2] The first step in the enterprise was to organize King's massive archive,
which included practically every scrap of paper that had passed through his
hands. To finance this, he received $100,000 (ultimately $300,000, about ten times
that amount in today's values) from the Rockefeller Foundation, his employer during the first world war.[3] Why a wealthy bachelor should have needed a subsidy
for his autobiography is a good question. But promising startling disclosures for
large publishing advances was the very opposite of King's style and his intentions.

---

1 Christopher Dummitt, *Unbuttoned: A History of Mackenzie King's Secret Life* (Montreal: McGill-
Queen's University Press, 2017).
2 Diary, March 17, 1949.
3 Among the helpers suggested by the principal of McGill University were the totally unsympathetic
historians Donald Creighton and Donald Masters. Diary, May 18, 1949.

By far the most important part of his papers was his diary. Transcription of the hand-written part to 1935 was begun; but the document as a whole was so personal and sensitive that King considered that only he could review it and decide what to keep. The rest he intended to be destroyed. If he was prevented by ill health from the task, the entire diary would be obliterated. His friend and benefactor, John D. Rockefeller Jr. appealed to him to keep it for publication at some time in the future. But King was adamant. Publicizing his candid account of cabinet meetings would violate his privy council oath of secrecy. There were also international matters of great consequence that should not be disclosed:

> Things for example that Roosevelt had spoken to me of to speak to Churchill about. Things that Churchill had spoken to me to speak to Roosevelt about. I had written in my own way to remind myself later on to have available as to being accurate etc. Another person might not read the language as I knew it. Also that I would wish it to die in my own breast. There were many secret confidences that I could not afford to allow others to see.[4]

In the year and a half that remained after his retirement, King never managed to summon the energy even to start examining the diary. Even if he had been in good health, it would have been a massive undertaking, with him hesitating over almost every passage and going back time and again to decide what to keep. If he had been able to persist long enough probably very little of real significance would have survived since he would have erred on the side of caution and destruction. In that case it was not just the confidences of Roosevelt and Churchill and others that would have disappeared from the record; so would most of his blunt judgments, evidence of his inconsistency and wrong predictions, the accounts of visions, spiritualist experiences, hands of the clock being auspiciously aligned at significant moments, details about the hours and quality of his sleep, the state of his bowels, and trouble with his dentures – anything that might detract from the image he wanted to preserve of a wise, high-minded statesman of the finest moral and religious principles. It might even have occurred to him that some passages were uncomfortably reminiscent of the footling concerns of Mr. Pooter in George and Weedon Goldsmith's comic masterpiece, *Diary of a Nobody*, published the year before King's own began. Fortunately, since he did not re-read a single

---

4 Diary, March 7, 1950.

page or leave more explicit formal instructions about destruction, the measure of ambiguity permitted the survival of the diary exactly as it was written, with no alterations or editing.

After King's died in July 1950 the problem of what to do with the diary passed to his literary executors. All four were close advisers, Liberals at least by inclination and highly conscious that they were the guardians of King's reputation. They evidently did not read his strong feelings about destroying the diary in the last entries; and Eduard Handy, to whom they had been dictated, was not inclined to draw the attention of the trustees to them. When they sought legal guidance from the department of justice, they were told to use their own judgment in interpreting King's will.[5]

Their debate continued for decades. In the meantime the executors hired a reliable academic (at twice his university salary) to write the official biography and allowed him to use the diary. Just before the first volume appeared in 1958,[6] he died and was succeeded by his assistant, a similar trustworthy though more probing academic. By 1976 the biography had been extended in a total of three volumes to 1939.[7] During the process J. W. "Jack" Pickersgill, a literary executors and former principal secretary to King who had seamlessly transferred to the cabinet, found himself short of occupation and income when the Liberals lost office in 1957 and remedied both deficiencies by being employed to make selections from the diary for the final decade of the biography. This was never written. Instead, Pickersgill's extracts and commentary were published between 1960 and 1970 as a supposed full and sufficient substitute.[8] Even four stout volumes required a great deal of selection; but Pickersgill's partisanship and his presence in the diaries raised much speculation about what was omitted.

None of this settled the fate of the diary once these publications were complete. In the early nineteen-seventies the executors deciding to deposit it in the national archives. They stipulated opening, once the biography to 1939 was

5   Dummitt, *Unbuttoned*, 53-4.
6   R. MacGregor Dawson, *William Lyon Mackenzie King: A Political Biography*, Volume I: 1874-1923 (Toronto: University of Toronto Press, 1958).
7   H. Blair Neatby, *The Lonely Heights, William Lyon Mackenzie King*, Volume II: *1924-1932* (Toronto: University of Toronto Press, 1963); *The Prism of Unity, William Lyon Mackenzie King*, Volume III: *1932-1939* (Toronto: University of Toronto Press, 1976).
8   Pickersgill returned to office in 1963 and was joined as editor after the first volume by the academic Donald F. Forster. J. W. Pickersgill and D. F. Forster, *The Mackenzie King Record*. 4 Volumes. (Toronto: University of Toronto Press, 1960, 1968 and 1970).

complete, in annual instalments thirty years after composition, which had been the general rule for government documents in Britain since 1967. The entire diary would thus be available by 1981. In 1977, the trustees salved their consciences about not destroying anything by burning the separate séance records,[9] which probably included the 1947 from Roosevelt to Churchill. The conflagration was not by chance. The year before high curiosity and low amusement had been stimulated about King's spiritualism, his supposed involvement with prostitutes (the evidence is ambiguous, to say the least) and other romantic relationships by a best-selling book, *A Very Double Life: The Private World of Mackenzie King*. [10] The author was colonel Charles Stacey, the official historian of the Canadian army in the second world war who had been permitted early access to the diary. Although he had not seen the spiritualist binders, there was plenty of material in the main diary and elsewhere.

The typescript of the diary was published first in microform. Now it is available online at the Library and Archives Canada website. The only missing section is for late 1945, following the disclosure of a Soviet spy ring centred on Ottawa, which is discussed in its place in this book. The accounts of King's journey around the world in 1908-9 and for the 1923 imperial conference are also not online but they are in the microform edition and are so noted in this account. The transcription admits to omitting some supposedly "inconsequential" passages. There are undoubtedly other errors, omissions and slight variations from the original manuscript; but no textual critic has volunteered to compare the several versions.[11] Some of the print is very indistinct. But none of these imperfections detract from the huge advantage of having this valuable Canadian and international resource so readily available.

---

9 Dummitt, *Unbuttoned*, 256-7.
10 C. P. Stacey, *A Very Double Life*.
11 Dummitt, *Unbuttoned*, 55.

Bibliography

Abella, Irving and Harold Troper. *None is Too Many: Canada and the Jews in Europe 1933–1948*. Toronto: University of Toronto Press, [1983] 2012.

Addison, Paul. *Churchill: The Unexpected Hero*. Oxford: Oxford University Press, [2005] 2006.

———. *Churchill on the Home Front 1900–1955*. London: Pimlico, [1992] 1993.

Alanbrooke, Field Marshal, Lord. *War Diaries 1939–1945*. Edited by Alex Danchev and Daniel Todman. Berkeley: University of California Press, 2001.

Bagehot, Walter. *Biographical Studies*. Edited by Richard Holt Hutton. London: Longmans, Green, 1881.

Baker, Elizabeth Balmer and P. J. Baker. *J. Allen Baker, M.P.: A Memoir*. London: Swarthmore Press, 1927.

Baldwin, Earl, *The Falconer Lectures*. Toronto: University of Toronto Press, 1939.

Barnes, John and David Nicholson, eds. *The Leo Amery Diaries*. Vol. I: 1896–1929, Vol. II: *The Empire at Bay: The Leo Amery Diaries 1929–1945*. London: Hutchinson, 1980 & 1988.

Bayly, Christopher and Tim Harper. *Forgotten Armies: The Fall of British Asia*. Cambridge: Harvard University Press, 2005.

Bell, Christopher M. *Churchill and Sea Power*. Oxford: Oxford University Press, 2013.

Bercuson, David J. and Holger H. Herwig. *One Christmas in Washington: The Secret Meeting between Roosevelt and Churchill that Changed the World*. Toronto: McArthur and Company, 2005.

Bercuson, David J. *Our Finest Hour: Canada Fights the Second World War*. Toronto: HarperCollins, 2015.

Berthon, Simon. *Allies at War: The Bitter Rivalry Among Churchill, Roosevelt and De Gaulle*. New York: Carroll & Graf, 2001.

Beschloss, Michael R. *Kennedy and Roosevelt: The Uneasy Alliance*. New York: W. W. Norton, 1980.

Betcherman, Lita-Rose. *Ernest Lapointe: Mackenzie King's Great Quebec Lieutenant*. Toronto: University of Toronto Press, 2002.

Black, Conrad. *Franklin Delano Roosevelt: Champion of Freedom*. New York: Public Affairs, 2003.

Boswell, James. *The Life of Samuel Johnson*. London: Oxford University Press, [1791], 1953.

Bothwell, Robert. *Alliance and Illusion: Canada and the World, 1945–1984*. Vancouver: UBC Press, 2007.

Bothwell, Robert and William Kilbourn. *C. D. Howe: A Biography*. Toronto: McClelland and Stewart, 1979.

Boyd, Douglas. *De Gaulle: The Man Who Defied Six Presidents*. Stroud: The History Press, 2013.

Bradford, Sarah. *King George VI*. London: Weidenfeld & Nicolson, 1989.

Brandon, Ruth. *The Spiritualists: The Passion for the Occult in the Nineteenth and Twentieth Centuries*. New York: Alfred A. Knopf, 1983.

Cannadine, David. *In Churchill's Shadow: Confronting the Past in Modern Britain*. London: Allen Lane/The Penguin Press, 2002.

Caquet, P. E. *The Bell of Treason: The 1938 Munich Agreement in Czechoslovakia*. New York: Other Press, 2019.

Chalmers, Floyd. *A Gentleman of the Press*. Toronto: Doubleday Canada, 1969.

Chapnick, Adam. "Testing the Bonds of Commonwealth with Viscount Halifax: Canada in the Post-War International System, 1942–44." *International History Review* 31, no. 1 (March 2009): 24–44.

———. *The Middle Power Project: Canada and the Founding of the United Nations*. Vancouver: UBC Press, 2005.

Chisholm, Anne and Michael Davie. *Lord Beaverbrook: A Life*. New York: Alfred A. Knopf, 1993.

Churchill, Randolph S. *Winston S. Churchill*, vols. 1–2. London: Heinemann, 1966 & 1967. (see also Martin Gilbert)

Churchill, Winston S. *The Aftermath*. New York: Scribner's 1929.

———. *Great Contemporaries*. London: Thornton Butterworth, revised ed., [1937], 1938.

———. *My Early Life: A Roving Commission*. London: Macmillan, [1930] 1942.

———. *The Second World War*, 6 vols. Boston: Houghton Mifflin, 1948–53.

———. *The Sinews of Peace: Post-War Speeches*. Edited by Randolph S. Churchill. London: Cassell, 1948.

———. *Thoughts and Adventures*. London: Thornton Butterworth, 1932.

Clarke, Peter. *Mr. Churchill's Profession: The Statesman as Author and the Book that Defined the "Special Relationship"*. London: Bloomsbury, 2012.

———. *The Cripps Version: The Life of Sir Stafford Cripps 1889–1952*. London: Penguin, [2002] 2003.

———. *The Last Thousand Days of the British Empire*. London: Allen Lane/Penguin, 2007.

Colville, John. *The Fringes of Power: Downing Street Diaries 1939–1955*. London: Hodder and Stoughton, 1985.

Cook, Blanche Wiesen. *Eleanor Roosevelt*. 3 vols. New York: Viking, 1993, 2000 and 2016.

Cook, Tim. *Fight to the Finish: Canadians in the Second World War*. Toronto: Allen Lane, 2015.

———. *The Necessary War: Canadians Fighting the Second World War 1939–1943*. Toronto: Allen Lane, 2014.

Conradi, Peter. *Hot Dogs and Cocktails: When FDR Met King George VI at Hyde Park on Hudson.* London: Alma Books, 2013.

Courteaux, Olivier. *Canada between Vichy and Free France 1940–1945.* Toronto: University of Toronto Press, 2013.

Cuff, R. D. and J. L. Granatstein. *Canadian-American Relations in Wartime: From the Great War to the Cold War.* Toronto: Hakkert, 1975.

Danchev, Alex. *Very Special Relationship: Field-Marshal Sir John Dill and the Anglo-American Alliance 1941–44.* London: Brassey's Defence Publishers, 1986.

Daniels, Roger. *Franklin D. Roosevelt: The War Years, 1939–1945.* Urbana: University of Illinois Press, 2016.

Darwin, John. *The Empire Project: The Rise and Fall of the British World-System, 1830–1970.* Cambridge: Cambridge University Press, 2009.

Dawson, R. MacGregor. *William Lyon Mackenzie King: A Political Biography, 1874–1923.* Toronto: University of Toronto Press, 1958.

Day, David. *Menzies & Churchill at War.* North Ryde, NSW: Angus & Robertson, 1986.

———. *The Great Betrayal: Britain, Australia & the Onset of the Pacific War 1939–1942.* North Ryde, NSW: Angus & Robertson, 1988.

Dilks, David. *Churchill and Company: Allies and Rivals in War and Peace.* London: I. B. Tauris, 2012.

——— ed. *The Diaries of Sir Alexander Cadogan 1938–1945.* New York: Putnam, 1972.

———. *"The Great Dominion": Winston Churchill in Canada 1900–1954.* Toronto: Thomas Allen, 2005.

Dimbleby, Jonathan. *The Battle of the Atlantic: How the Allies Won the War.* London: Viking, 2015.

Documents on Canadian External Relations. Ottawa: Department of External Affairs, 1976– .

Dummitt, Christopher. *Unbuttoned: The History of Mackenzie King's Secret Life.* Montreal and Kingston: McGill-Queen's University Press, 2017.

Eade, Charles, ed. *Churchill by his Contemporaries.* London: Hutchinson, 1953.

Eayrs, James. *In Defence of Canada,* Vol. II: *Appeasement and Rearmament.* Toronto: University of Toronto Press, 1965.

English, John. *The Shadow of Heaven: The Life of Lester Pearson.* Vol. I. Toronto: Lester & Orpen Dennys, 1989.

———, Kenneth McLaughlin and P. Whitney Lackenbauer, eds. *Mackenzie King: Citizenship and Community.* Toronto: Robin Brass Studio, 2002.

——— and J. O. Stubbs. *Mackenzie King: Widening the Debate.* Toronto: Macmillan, 1978.

Ferns, H. S. *Reading from Left to Right: One Man's Political History.* Toronto: University of Toronto Press, 1983.

Fisher, David E. *A Summer Bright and Terrible: Winston Churchill, Lord Dowding, Radar and the Impossible Triumph of the Battle of Britain.* Washington DC: Shoemaker & Hoard, 2005.

Freidel, Frank. *Franklin D. Roosevelt: A Rendezvous with Destiny.* Boston: Little Brown, 1990.

Fullilove, Michael. *Rendezvous with Destiny: How Franklin D. Roosevelt and Five Extraordinary Men Took America into the War and into the World.* New York: Penguin, 2013.

Gaddis, John Lewis. *George F. Kennan: An American Life.* New York: Penguin, 2011.

Gilbert, Martin, ed. *The Churchill War Papers*. 3 vols. London: Heinemann, 1993–2000.

———. *Winston S. Churchill*. vols. 3–8. London: Heinemann, 1971–88. (see also Randolph Churchill)

———. *Winston S. Churchill*. vol. 5, *Companion*. 3 parts. London: Heinemann, 1982.

Gilmour, Julie F. *Trouble on Main Street: Mackenzie King, Reason, Race and the 1907 Vancouver Riots*. Toronto: Allen Lane, 2014.

Goodwin, Doris Kearns. *No Ordinary Time: Franklin and Eleanor Roosevelt: The Home Front in World War II*. New York: Touchstone, [1994] 1995.

Gorodetsky, Gabriel, ed. *The Maisky Diaries: Red Ambassador to the Court of St. James's 1932–1943*. New Haven, CT: Yale University Press, 2015.

Graham, Roger. *Arthur Meighen: A Biography*. 3 vols. Toronto: Clarke Irwin, 1960–65.

Granatstein, J. L. *A Man of Influence: Norman A. Robertson and Canadian Statecraft 1929–68*. Ottawa: Deneau Publishers, 1981.

———. Canada's War: *The Politics of the Mackenzie King Government 1939–45*. Toronto: Oxford University Press, 1975.

———. "Dieppe: A Colossal Blunder." *The Beaver* (August/September 2009): 16–24.

———. *The Ottawa Men: The Civil Service Mandarins 1935–1957*. Toronto: Oxford University Press, 1982.

——— and Dean F. Oliver. *The Oxford Companion to Canadian Military History*. Toronto: Oxford University Press, 2011.

Greenfield, Nathan M. *The Damned: The Canadians at the Battle of Hong Kong and the POW Experience, 1941–1945*. Toronto: HarperCollins, 2010.

Guest, Dennis. *The Emergence of Social Security in Canada*. Second edition. Vancouver: UBC Press, [1980] 1985. Hallowell, Gerald, ed. *The Oxford Companion to Canadian History*. Toronto: Oxford University Press, 2004.

Hamilton, Nigel. *Commander in Chief: FDR's Battle with Churchill, 1943*. Boston: Houghton Mifflin Harcourt, 2016.

———. *The Mantle of Command: FDR at War, 1941–1942*. Boston: Houghton Mifflin Harcourt, 2014.

Harvey, John, ed. *The War Diaries of Oliver Harvey*. London: Collins, 1978.

Hassett, William D. *Off the Record with F.D.R. 1942–1945*. New Brunswick, NJ: Rutgers University Press, 1958.

Hastings, Max. *All Hell Let Loose: The World at War 1939–1945*. London: HarperPress, 2011.

———. *Finest Years: Churchill as Warlord 1940–45*. London: HarperPress, 2009.

Herman, Arthur. *Gandhi and Churchill: The Epic Rivalry That Destroyed an Empire and Forged Our Age*. New York: Bantam Books, 2008.

Hill, Christopher. *Cabinet Decisions on Foreign Policy: The British experience October 1938–June 1941*. Cambridge: Cambridge University Press, 1991.

Hilliker, John. *Canada's Department of External Affairs*. Vol. 1: *The Early Years 1909–1946*. Montreal and Kingston: McGill-Queen's University Press, 1990.

Hillmer, Norman. *O. D. Skelton: A Portrait of Canadian Ambition*. Toronto: University of Toronto Press, 2015.

Hough, Richard and Denis Richards. *The Battle of Britain: The Greatest Air Battle of World War II.* New York: W. W. Norton, [1989] 1990.Hyam, Ronald. *Elgin and Churchill at the Colonial Office 1905–1908: The Watershed of the Empire-Commonwealth.* London: Macmillan, 1968.

James, Robert Rhodes ed. *Winston S. Churchill: His Complete Speeches 1897–1963.* 8 vols. New York: Chelsea House, 1974.

Khan, Yasmin. *The Raj at War: A People's History of India's Second World War.* London: The Bodley Head, 2015.

Kimball, Warren F. ed. *Churchill and Roosevelt: The Complete Correspondence.* 3 vols. Princeton, NJ: Princeton University Press, 1984.

———. *Forged in War: Roosevelt, Churchill, and the Second World War.* New York: William Morrow, 1997.

———. *The Juggler: Franklin Roosevelt as Wartime Statesman.* Princeton, NJ: Princeton University Press, 1991.

King, W. L. Mackenzie. *Canada and the Fight for Freedom.* Toronto: Macmillan, 1944.

——— *The Message of the Carillon and Other Addresses.* Toronto: Macmillan, 1927.

Kiszely, John. *Anatomy of a Campaign: The British Fiasco in Norway, 1940.* Cambridge: Cambridge University Press, 2017.

Klara, Robert. *FDR's Funeral Train: A Betrayed Widow, A Soviet Spy, And a Presidency in the Balance.* New York: Palgrave Macmillan, 2010.

Knight, Amy. *How The Cold War Began: The Gouzenko Affair and the Hunt for Soviet Spies.* Toronto: McClelland and Stewart, 2005.

Kottman, Richard N. *Reciprocity and the North American Triangle 1932–1938.* Ithaca, NY: Cornell University Press, 1968.

Lelyveld, Joseph. *His Final Battle: The Last Months of Franklin Roosevelt.* New York: Alfred A. Knopf, 2016.

Levine, Allan. *King: William Lyon Mackenzie King: A Life Guided by the Hand of Destiny.* Vancouver: Douglas & McIntyre, 2011.

Lewis, David Levering. *The Improbable Wendell Willkie: The Businessman Who Saved the Republican Party and His Country, and Conceived a New World Order.* New York: Liveright, 2018.

Lippman, Theo Jr. *The Squire of Warm Springs: F.D.R. in Georgia 1924–1945.* Chicago: Playboy Press, 1977.

Lough, David. *No More Champagne: Churchill and His Money.* New York: Picador, 2015.

Louis, William Roger. *Imperialism at Bay: The United States and the Decolonization of the British Empire, 1941–1945.* New York: Oxford University Press, 1978.

Lovell, Richard. *Churchill's Doctor: A Biography of Lord Moran.* London: Royal Society of Medical Services Ltd, 1992.

Lownie, Andrew. *The Mountbattens: Their Lives and Loves.* London: Blink, 2019.

Ludwig, Emil. *Mackenzie King: A Portrait Sketch.* Toronto: Macmillan, 1944.

Lukacs, John. *Five Days in London: May 1940.* New Haven, CT: Yale University Press, 1999.

MacFarlane, John. *Ernest Lapointe and Quebec's Influence on Foreign Policy.* Toronto: University of Toronto Press, 1999.

MacLaren, Roy. *Commissions High: Canada in London, 1870–1971*. Montreal and Kingston: McGill-Queen's University Press, 2006.

———. Empire and Ireland: *The Transatlantic Career of the Canadian Imperialist Hamar Greenwood, 1870–1948*. Montreal and Kingston: McGill-Queen's University Press, 2015.

———. *Mackenzie King in the Age of the Dictators: Canada's Imperial Foreign Policies*. Montreal and Kingston: McGill-Queen's University Press, 2019.

McIntyre, W. David. *The Britannic Vision: Historians and the Making of the British Commonwealth of Nations, 1907–48*. Basingstoke: Palgrave Macmillan, 2009.

Markham, Violet. *Friendship's Harvest*. London: Max Reinhardt, 1956.

Martel, Leon. *Lend-Lease, Loans, and the Coming of the Cold War: A Study of the Implementation of Foreign Policy*. Boulder, Colorado: Westview Press, 1979.

Mazower, Mark. *Governing the World: The History of an Idea*. New York: Penguin, 2013.

———. *No Enchanted Palace: The End of Empire and the Ideological Origins of the United Nations*. Princeton: Princeton University Press, 2009.

Meacham, Jon. *Franklin and Winston: An Intimate Portrait of an Epic Friendship*. New York: Random House, [2003] 2004.

Middlemas, Keith and John Barnes. *Baldwin: A Biography*. London: Weidenfeld and Nicolson, 1969.

Miller, Carman. *The Canadian Career of the Fourth Earl of Minto: The Education of a Viceroy*. Waterloo, ON: Wilfrid Laurier Press, 1980.

Millman, Brock. *Polarity, Patriotism, and Dissent in Great War Canada, 1914–1919*. Toronto: University of Toronto Press, 2016.

Moran, Lord. *Churchill: Taken from the Diaries of Lord Moran: The Struggle for Survival 1940–1965*. Boston: Houghton Mifflin, 1966.

Morgan, Kenneth O. *Labour in Power 1945–1951*. Oxford: Clarendon Press, 1984.

Morton, Andrew. *13 Carnations: The Royals, the Nazis, and the Biggest Cover-Up in History*. New York: Grand Central Publishing, [2015] 2016.

Mukerjee, Madhusree. *Churchill's Secret War: The British Empire and the Ravaging of India During World War II*. New York: Basic Books, 2010.

Neatby, H. Blair. *William Lyon Mackenzie King*, vol. II: *1924–1932: The Lonely Heights*, Toronto: University of Toronto Press, 1963.

———. *William Lyon Mackenzie King*, vol. III: *1932–1939: The Prism of Unity*, Toronto: University of Toronto Press, 1976.Nicolson, Harold. *Diaries and Letters 1939–45*. Edited by Nigel Nicolson. London: Collins, 1967.

Offer, Avner, *The First World War: An Agrarian Interpretation*. Oxford: Clarendon Press, [1989] 1991.

O'Keefe, David. *One Day in August: The Untold Story Behind Canada's Tragedy at Dieppe*. Toronto: Alfred A. Knopf Canada, 2013.

Oxford Dictionary of National Biography. Edited by Colin Matthew and Brian Harrison. 60 vols.

Oxford: Oxford University Press, 2004. (Also available online at: https://www.oxforddnb.com)

Perras, Galen Roger. *Stepping Stones to Nowhere: The Aleutian Islands, Alaska and American Military Strategy, 1867–1945*. Vancouver: UBC Press, 2003.

Persico, Joseph E. *Franklin and Lucy: President Roosevelt, Mrs. Rutherford, and the Other Remarkable Women in his Life*. New York: Random House, 2008.

Pickersgill, J. W. *The Mackenzie King Record*, vol. I: 1939–1944, Toronto: University of Toronto Press, 1960.

——— and D. F. Forster. *The Mackenzie King Record*. vol. II: 1944–1945.; vol. III: 1945–1946; vol. IV: 1947–1948. Toronto: University of Toronto Press, 1968 and 1970.

Pope, Maurice A. *Soldiers and Politicians: The Memoirs of Lt.-Gen. Maurice A. Pope, C.B., M.C.* Toronto: University of Toronto Press, 1962.

Purnell, Sonia. *Clementine: The Life of Mrs. Winston Churchill*. New York: Viking, 2015.

Ramsden, John. *Man of the Century: Winston Churchill and His Legend Since 1945*. London: HarperCollins, 2002.

———. *The Age of Churchill and Eden, 1940–1957*. London: Longman, 1995.

Reardon, Terry. *Winston Churchill and Mackenzie King: So Similar, So Different*. Toronto: Dundurn, 2012.

Reynolds, David. *From World War to Cold War: Churchill, Roosevelt, and the International History of the 1940s*. Oxford: Oxford University Press, 2006.

———. *In Command of History: Churchill Fighting and Writing the Second World War*. London: Allen Lane, 2004.

———. *The Creation of the Anglo-American Alliance, 1937–41: A Study in Competitive Co-Operation*. London: Europa Publications, 1981.

Roazen, Paul. *Canada's King: An Essay in Political Psychology*. Oakville, ON: Mosaic Press, 1998.

Roberts, Andrew. *Masters and Commanders: How Roosevelt, Churchill, Marshall and Alanbrooke Won the War in the West*. London: Allen Lane, 2008.

———. *'The Holy Fox': The Life of Lord Halifax*. London: Phoenix Giant, [1991] 1997.

Rock, William R. *Chamberlain and Roosevelt: British Foreign Policy and the United States, 1937–1940*. Columbus: Ohio State University Press, 1988.

Roll, David L. *The Hopkins Touch: Harry Hopkins and the Forging of the Alliance to Defeat Hitler*. New York: Oxford University Press, 2013.

Rose, Jonathan. *The Literary Churchill: Author, Reader, Actor*. New Haven, CT: Yale University Press, 2014.

Ruane, Kevin. *Churchill and the Bomb in War and Cold War*. London: Bloomsbury Academic, 2016.

Sanger, Clive. *Malcolm MacDonald: Bringing an End to Empire*. Montreal and Kingston: McGill-Queen's University Press, 1995.

Schake, Kori. *Safe Passage: The Transition from British to American Hegemony*. Cambridge: Harvard University Press, 2017.

Schneer, Jonathan. *Ministers at War: Winston Churchill and His War Cabinet*. New York: Basic Books, 2014.

Seale, William. *The White House: The History of an American Idea*. Washington: The American Institute of Architects, 1992.

Shakespeare, Nicholas. *Six Minutes in May: How Churchill Unexpectedly Became Prime Minister.* London: Harvill Secker, 2017.

Skelton, O. D. *Our Generation.* Chicago: University of Chicago Press, 1938.

Smith, Janet Adam. *John Buchan: A Biography.* London: Rupert Hart-Davis, 1965.

Smith, Kathryn. *The Gatekeeper: Miss LeHand, FDR, and the Untold Story of the Partnership That Defined a Presidency.* New York: Touchstone, 2016.

Soames, Mary. *A Daughter's Tale: The Memoirs of Winston Churchill's Youngest Child.* New York: Random House, 2011.

———, ed. *Speaking for Themselves: The Personal Letters of Letters of Winston and Clementine Churchill.* Toronto: Stoddart, 1998.

Stacey, C. P. *Arms, Men and Governments: The War Policies of Canada 1939–1945.* Ottawa: Queen's Printer, 1970.

———. *A Very Double Life: The Private Life of Mackenzie King.* Toronto: Macmillan, 1976.

———. *Canada and the Age of Conflict: A History of Canadian External Policies,* Vol. 2: *1921–1948: The Mackenzie King Era.* Toronto: University of Toronto Press, 1981.

———. *Mackenzie King and the Atlantic Triangle.* Toronto: Macmillan, 1976.

Strang, G. Bruce. "John Bull in Search of a Suitable Russia: British Foreign Policy and the Failure of the Anglo-French-Soviet Alliance Negotiations, 1939". *Canadian Journal of History,* 41, no. 1 (2006): 47–84.

Taylor, A. J. P. *English History 1914–1945.* Oxford: Clarendon Press, 1965.

Thompson, John Herd with Allen Seager. *Canada 1922–1939: Decades of Discontent.* Toronto: McClelland and Stewart, 1985.

Thompson, John Herd and Stephen J. Randall, *Canada and the United States: Ambivalent Allies.* Fourth edition. Montreal: McGill-Queen's University Press, [1994] 2008.

Thompson, Neville. *Canada and the End of the Imperial Dream: Beverley Baxter's Reports from London through War and Peace, 1936–1960.* Toronto: Oxford University Press, 2013.

———. *The Anti-Appeasers: Conservative Opposition to Appeasement in the 1930s.* Oxford: Clarendon Press, 1971.

Tiegrob, Robert. *Four Days in Hitler's Germany: Mackenzie King's Mission to Avert a Second World War.* Toronto: University of Toronto Press, 2019.

Tippet, Maria. *Portrait in Light and Shadow: The Life of Yousuf Karsh.* Toronto: Anansi, 2007.

Toye, Richard. *Churchill's Empire: The World that Made Him and the World He Made.* London: Macmillan, 2010.

———. *Lloyd George & Churchill: Rivals for Greatness.* London: Macmillan, 2007.

Vance, Jonathan F. *Maple Leaf Empire: Canada, Britain and Two World Wars.* Toronto: Oxford University Press, 2012.

———. "Men in Manacles: The Shackling of Prisoners of War, 1942–1943." *Journal of Military History* 59, no. 3 (July 1995): 483–504.

———. *Objects of Concern: Canadian Prisoners of War Through the Twentieth Century.* Vancouver: UBC Press, 1994.

Walder, David. *The Chanak Affair.* London: Hutchinson, 1969.

Wapshott, Nicholas. *The Sphinx: Franklin Roosevelt, the Isolationists, and the Road to World War II.* New York: W. W. Norton, 2015.

Ward, Geoffrey C., ed. *Closest Companion: The Unknown Story of the Intimate Friendship between Franklin Roosevelt and Margaret Suckly.* Boston: Houghton Mifflin, 1995.

Wardhaugh, Robert A. *Behind the Scenes: The Life and Work of William Clifford Clark.* Toronto: University of Toronto Press, 2010.

Wheeler-Bennett, John W., ed. *Action This Day: Working with Churchill.* London: Macmillan, 1968.

Wilson, Theodore A. *The First Summit: Roosevelt and Churchill at Placentia Bay 1941.* Boston: Houghton Mifflin, 1969.

Winks, Robin W. *The Relevance of Canadian History: U.S. and Imperial Perspectives.* Toronto: Macmillan, 1979.

Wright, Patrick. *Iron Curtain.* New York: Oxford University Press, 2007.

Woolner, David B., ed. *The Second Quebec Conference Revisited: Waging War, Formulating Peace: Canada, Great Britain, and the United States in 1944–1945.* New York: St. Martin's Press, 1998.

———, Warren F. Kimball and David Reynolds, eds. *FDR's World: War, Peace, and Legacies.* New York: Palgrave Macmillan, 2008.

Index

186–7, dances with, 183, offers to give election speeches for, 357–8, gives wartime medallion to, 435; meetings with: see Mackenzie King, meetings with WSC, and meetings with WSC and FDR; and MacDonald, Ramsay, 43; and Mediterranean strategy, persists in, 255–6, 259, 267–8, 276–7, 299, 307, 318–19; and Menzies, Robert, attempt of to topple, 161–5, 448; and Morganthau Plan, 354–5; and Munich agreement, 81; and Ogdensburg agreement, 139–40; and Ottawa Imperial Economic Conference, 1932, 43, 44; and Poland, post-war settlement of, 3782–4; and prisoners of war, shackling of, 237–8; and National Government, 41–2, 45; and New Deal, criticizes, 50–1; and Norway strategy, 181–2; as Prime Minister, 1940, becomes, 115–17, challenged in parliament, 1942, January, 216–17, July, 232–3; and Quebec 1943 broadcast from, 298–9; and religion, 6–7; and FDR, 1, 2, 5, 46; and proposed 1938 peace conference, 74, secret correspondence with,103–4, massive aid from denied, 1940, 117–8, and 1940 plan to save Royal Navy, 120–8, and post-war aid to Britain, 351, 355, and death of and eulogy for, 399–400; and meetings with (see also Mackenzie King, meetings with WSC and FDR): Atlantic conference 1941, 170–3, Casablanca 1943, 250–2, Hyde Park, 1942, 228–9 1943, August, 285–6, September, 303–4, 1944, 363–5, Tehran, 306–7, Washington, 1941–2, 193–204, 213–15, 1942, 227–32, 1943, 302–3, Yalta, 1945, 376–9; and religion, 6–7; and Second Front, resists, 225, 228–9, 231, 256, 276, 282, 285, 298–9; and Sicily,

dispute over invasion announcement, 271–2; and Singapore, fall of,217–18; and Spanish civil war, 64; and Stalin, Marshall Joseph, opinions of, 179, 277, 299, 350, still trusts after WW II, 429; and UNO, better than League of Nations, 430; and US congress, addresses, 1941, 199, 1943, 258–9; and USSR, potential danger from, 281, 322, 326, after WW II, 415, 421–4, 441, hails as ally on German invasion, 166–7, Canadian spy network revealed to, 415; and Willkie, Wendall, in Britain 1941, 152, and anti-colonialism, 238–9, 241;and WWI, 27; and World War II memoirs, 357, 425–6, 429–30, 441, gives copies to MK, 447, 451; and work habits, 11–12, 35–6, 406

Citrine, Sir Walter, 147, 154
Clarke, Colonel Frank, 298, 361, 420
Claxton, Brooke, 14
Coney Island, MK visits, 1943, 267
"Commonwealth and Empire," WSC defines, 314, 322; Lord Cranborne defines, 312; MK on, 327–8
Commonwealth, meetings, Washington, MK attends, 1941, 201, 1942, 230–1, 1943, 265 (see also imperial conferences)
Conservative party, Canada, 4–3, 47, 58, 62, 68, 84, 138, 140, 154, 161, 219, 233, 309, 315, 338, 357, 371, 376–7, 419; and WSC, praises MK to, 186–7, 204, tries to get into coalition MK, 207, 209, 212
Conscription, Britain, 88, and other dominions, 205
Conscription, Canada, army mutiny and riots against 1944, 377, 405; Beaverbrook says unnecessity,1941, 170; WSC says unnecessary, 1941, 177, 181, 186–7, hedges on, 201, 204–5, 207, 212; Crerar says unnecessary,

Winant, John Gilbert (Gil), US
ambassador to Britain 1941–6, 53,
143–4, 191–2, 283, 329; and British
memorial service, 1947, MK attends,
438; and Churchill, Sarah, lover, 144;
and Harriman, Averell, 153

Windsor, Duke (see also Edward VIII) and
Duchess of (Wallis Simpson), 67,211,
258, 317, 358–9, 363

Yalta conference 1945, 379–83

n Reich has e...
ember tenth.

The Prime Minister of Canada,
...mbly submits to His Majesty the petition of
...he King's Privy Council for Canada that His Majesty
...may approve the issuing of such a Proclamation in
His name.

The Prime Minister of Canada remains
His Majesty's most faithful and obedient servant.

W.L. Mackenzie King.

Prime Minister of Canada.

Ottawa, September 10th, 1939.

it quite impossible
...ed, from beyond the
...and generosity.
...s if this gift had
...Mr. A. H.
...tal ball in
...on opening
...h. I had
...nd Mr.
...rt determined
...n-
...the
...been
...ber last, but

at once to reach you but
...I shall watch for the first
...I feel I cannot accept
...our heart as well as
...from you, yourself, that
...at who it is. I cannot
...ment of a vision, that
...for that to express something
...ear, never be able to let you
...ed, however, please believe that
...shed by any expression of friendship
...generous heart, and which carries
...to call upon you. I have felt,

Monday, July 10, 1933.

(Handwritten – P.19...

Before going t...
James' "The Will t...
my mind not a littl...
undoubtedly was hi...
comfort me in be E...
influences tha'...
character, f...ed...
...rd Arthur...
...ritual?Our le...
te t...

Caen which...
were muc...
little...
sights...
I met...

hu...

Caspary:

As I was leaving the Hotel shortly after five o'clock,
...from "Frank Partridge & Sons, Ltd." a box that greatly
...uriosity. I could not refrain from delaying my en-
...en it. I was amazed when I saw it contained the
...crystal I have ever beheld, something that has be...
...lmost continuously since I saw it in November
...inued to regard as wholly beyond my reach
...y I had the pleasure to put it away, and
...Mr. Lipscomb to put it away, and
...again.

...was to see this pe...
...was even more...
...t, I read

Ritz Hotel,
London, W.1.

May 13th, 1937